D1481391

RELIGION IN VICTORIAN BRITAIN

VOLUME III
SOURCES

ERRATUM
RELIGION IN VICTORIAN BRITAIN: VOLUME III: SOURCES
Please use this page to replace the original title-page

RELIGION IN VICTORIAN BRITAIN

VOLUME III
SOURCES

EDITED BY

JAMES R. MOORE

AT THE

OPEN UNIVERSITY

MANCHESTER UNIVERSITY PRESS

MANCHESTER AND NEW YORK

IN ASSOCIATION WITH THE
OPEN UNIVERSITY

DISTRIBUTED EXCLUSIVELY IN THE USA AND CANADA
BY ST. MARTIN'S PRESS

Published by Manchester University Press
Oxford Road, Manchester M13 9PL, UK
and Room 400, 175 Fifth Avenue, New York, NY 10010, USA

Distributed exclusively in the USA and Canada by St. Martin's Press, Inc.,
175 Fifth Avenue, New York, NY 10010, USA

British Library cataloguing in publication data
Religion in Victorian Britain.
   Vol. 3: Sources
   1. Great Britain. Christian church, 1837–
   1901
   I. Moore, James R.   II. Open University
   274.1′081

Library of Congress cataloging in publication data
Religion in Victorian Britain.
   Includes bibliographies and index.
   Contents: v. 1. Traditions — 2. Controversies —
v. 3. Sources — (etc.)
   1. Great Britain — Church history — 19th century.
2. Great Britain — Religion.   3. Great Britain —
Religious life and customs. I. Moore, James.
BR759.R43 1988   274.1′081   88–12359
ISBN 0–7190–2943–0 *hardback*
ISBN 0–7190–2944–9 *paperback*

This book forms part of an Open University course A331 *Religion in Victorian Britain*. For information about this course please write to the Student Enquiries Office, The Open University, PO Box 71, Walton Hall, Milton Keynes, MK7 6AG, UK

This book is set in 10pt. Baskerville
by Northern Phototypesetting Co., Bolton
Printed in Great Britain by
Richard Clay Ltd., Bungay, Suffolk

CONTENTS

PREFACE

THIS book is one of a four-volume series entitled *Religion in Victorian Britain*, published by Manchester University Press in association with the Open University. The four volumes form the nucleus of an Open University Course. Volumes I and II, *Traditions* and *Controversies* (edited by Gerald Parsons, 1988), consist of sets of specially written essays covering the major religious denominations and groups of the period and the issues and controversies between and within them. Volume III, *Sources* (edited by James R. Moore, 1988), is a collection of primary source material from the period, while Volume IV, *Interpretations* (edited by Gerald Parsons, 1988), is a collection of recent essays and articles in the field by other writers.

The authors wish to acknowledge the essential contribution made to the production of these volumes by a number of other members of Open University staff: Gillian Kay, Staff Tutor in History, for her comment and criticism, Barbara Humphrey and Wendy Clarke (secretaries), Jenny Cook (course manager), Tony Coulson (Library), Pam Higgins (Design Studio), and Jonathan Hunt (Publishing).

The authors also wish to thank Professor John Kent of the University of Bristol for his careful and constructive comments on first drafts of their essays. Each of the authors has benefited from Professor Kent's criticism and observations: needless to say, any questionable judgments which remain are the responsibility of the authors alone.

The authors of the series are all members of staff of the Faculty of Arts at the Open University:

Michael Bartholomew, Staff Tutor in History of Science and Technology
David Englander, Lecturer in European Humanities
Anthony Lentin, Reader in History
James R. Moore, Lecturer in History of Science and Technology
Gerald Parsons, Lecturer in Religious Studies
Rosemary O'Day, Senior Lecturer in History
Terence Thomas, Staff Tutor in Religious Studies

ACKNOWLEDGEMENTS

THE editor and the publisher gratefully acknowledge permission from the British Library Department of Manuscripts and the Huxley papers, Imperial College of Science and Technology, to reprint the letter 'To the Rev. Temple' (7.3.3), and from the following sources to reproduce as illustrations materials in their possession: Cambridge University Library (ill. 3); The Evangelical Library (ill. 5); Holyoake Collection, Bishopsgate Institute (ill. 9); British Library Department of Printed Books (ill. 12). Source references for all illustrations are as follows:

1: *Punch*, 1 April 1865. **2:** *Punch*, 13 February 1869. **3:** Mary Potter, *The Path of Mary*, 1878; 2nd ed. (London: Thomas Richardson and Sons), frontispiece (by permission of the Syndics of Cambridge University Press). **4:** T. Brown, *Annals of the Disruption* . . ., new ed. (Edinburgh: MacNiven & Wallace, 1892), facing p. 92. **5:** H. Grattan Guinness, *The Approaching End of the Age* . . ., 1878; 10th ed. (London: Hodder and Stoughton, 1886), facing p. 459. **6:** I. D. Sankey, comp., *Sacred Songs and Solos, with Standard Hymns, combined* (London: Morgan & Scott, n.d.). **7:** I. D. Sankey, comp., *Sacred Songs and Solos* . . . (as above). **8:** W. Booth, *In Darkest England and the Way Out* (London: Salvation Army [1890]), frontispiece. **9:** Holyoake Collection, Bishopsgate Institute, London. **10:** *The Freethinker*, 2 (5 March 1882), 1. **11:** *Punch*, 3 July 1880. **12:** British Library Department of Printed Books, 4355.df.17. **13:** *The Graphic*, 16 November 1889. **14:** *Illustrated London News*, 27 January 1872.

INTRODUCTION

THIS volume contains a comprehensive selection of primary sources illustrating the beliefs, values, and practices of the major religious traditions in Victorian Britain. Like its three companion volumes, published under the same general title, it is intended as a set book for the honours-level undergraduate course, 'Religion in Victorian Britain', taught by the Open University. Approximately half the documents have been selected by course team members for use as teaching aids in conjunction with the essays in the accompanying volumes. The editor, however, bears final responsibility for the presentation of the texts, as well as for the choice of the remaining sources. These have been selected to enrich and diversify the collection, so that as a whole the volume should be of general interest to academics in the field, particularly those who teach Victorian Studies, and to students and other historically minded individuals for whom 'Victorian values' may have acquired a special interest in the light of recent British politics.

Until lately the most ample collections of Victorian religious documents have been drawn exclusively from the literature of Dissent. But David Thompson's *Nonconformity in the Nineteenth Century* (1972) and John Briggs's and Ian Sellers's *Victorian Nonconformity* (1973) have now been augmented by volumes that range across religious traditions and deal broadly with the role of religion in Victorian culture. Tess Coslett's *Science and Religion in the Nineteenth Century* (1984) and Elizabeth Jay's *Faith and Doubt in Victorian Britain* (1986) are modest textbooks. Neither achieves, or was intended to achieve, the rich and representative sampling needed to complement the existing collections of Nonconformist sources. Richard Helmstadter and Paul T. Phillips's *Religion in Victorian Society* (1985) is more adequate in this respect. Conceived on an ecumenical scale, it reproduces important texts dealing with a wide range of nineteenth-century social issues – reform, disestablishment, political economy, urbanization, education, charity, and the like – that were debated by the churches. For this reason it remains an invaluable collection. Like Coslett and Jay, however, Helmstadter and Phillips are Anglocentric, focusing on Christianity in England. None of these editors in fact adequately represents the religious traditions of the United Kingdom as a whole, nor do any of them canvass non-Christian traditions within the period.

What these three recent collections of primary sources lack is precisely what the present volume aims to provide: namely, a comprehensive selection of materials that represent both the intellectual and the social dimensions of Victorian religion, both the Church of England and other communions (including Roman Catholics and Unitarians), both the traditions of Christianity and those of other religious faiths. That is to say, this third volume of *Religion in Victorian Britain* purports to live up to its name.

Among the notable features of the collection is the diversity of themes of which it touches. There are, for example, sources concerned with the vicissitudes of belief within a single university, Oxford (1.1, 1.5, 3.1.2, 5.4.3, 6.2, 7.4.1), the problem of gender and sex in religion (2.1, 2.2, 4.2.2, 5.2.1), the Irish question (1.4.1, 2.4), heresy litigations (3.2), millenarianism (4.1.3, 4.3), revivalism (5.2.3, 5.3.4), Christian socialism (2.2.3), Secularism as a persecuted faith (6.3, 6.4), scientific naturalism as a reforming creed (7.1, 7.2) and an expression of religious dissent (3.3.2, 7.3, 7.4), religion in ethnographic and anthropological perspective (7.2.3, 8.1.3, 8.3), Judaism in England (8.2), and the sociological interpretation of religion (8.4).

It is also noteworthy that by far the greater portion of the sources selected for inclusion in this volume have not been reprinted since Victorian times. Many of these are little known or difficult to obtain: namely, a number of legal submissions, defences, and judgments (1.2.1, 6.3), the transcripts of parliamentary debates (1.5.1, 8.2.3) and conference proceedings (3.1.3, 3.2.2, 5.1.2), trenchant newspaper reports (4.3.1, 5.3.3, 7.4.2, 8.2.2), famous sermons, letters, lectures, decrees, and pronouncements (1.4.1, 2.1.3, 2.3.2, 3.1.1, 5.5.1), and one item hitherto incompletely published (7.3.3). The most elusive source in the collection, now reprinted for the first time, is the anonymous 'Prospectus' for the new series of the *Westminster Review*, which began in January 1852 (7.3.2). This was written by Marian Evans – the novelist George Eliot – but, although its existence has long been known to scholars, the full text has proved almost unobtainable.

For advice on tracking down the Eliot item I am grateful to Gillian Beer, Sally Shuttleworth, Nick Furbank, Bob Owens, Jean Slingerland, Mary N. Haight, Rosemary T. Van Arsdel, and – not least – the staff of the Open University Library, who on this occasion, as on so many others, actually produced the goods. I have also been assisted regularly by the staffs of Dr Williams's Library, Cambridge University Library, the British Library, the University of London Library at Senate House, and the Library of the Wellcome Institute for the History of Medicine. Most of all, I am indebted to my Open University colleagues: to Gillian Kay, Tony Lentin, and Gerald Parsons especially for timely selections of documents; to Jenny Cook and John Fauvel for supportive comments and helping me finish the job; to Gaynor Arrowsmith, who cared. Two others also deserve special mention. David Kohn of Drew University and Art Wheeler, formerly of the University of Notre Dame, responded enthusiastically to my early plans for this collection and made numerous constructive proposals.

It is a better book by far for their involvement.

Finally, a note on editorial policy. The sources are reproduced verbatim except for (1) punctuation changes to bring the various texts into conformity with a single style; (2) omissions, which are indicated by the ellipsis; (3) editorial interpolations, which, except for ellipses, always appear in square brackets; (4) transliteration of Greek words; and (5) the removal of author's footnotes, except where these have been judged to affect the meaning of the text or otherwise to be of historical importance. In a very few instances the paragraph structure of a text has been altered for the sake of comprehension or to allow insertion of apposite material. This is usually indicated in the editorial introduction to the section in which the text appears or in the 'Sources' list at the end of the volume, which gives the full and precise reference for every item in the collection.

J.R.M.

1

THE CHURCH AND
ITS CREEDS

1.1 THE HIGH CHURCH: A COUNTER-REFORM AT OXFORD

IN 1833 a movement emerged at Oxford among young High
Churchmen and disillusioned Evangelicals to defend the Church
of England against the depredations, or threatened depredations, of
a reformed Parliament. Richard Hurrell Froude (1803–1836) and John
Henry Newman (1801–1890), who were then intimate friends, became
leading lights of the early 'Oxford Movement'. Froude supplied much of
the conviction and animus for the initial attack on reform. After his
untimely death, Newman oversaw the publication of his *Remains*
(1838–39), which include a characteristic view of state interference dating
from 1833 (**1.1.1**). Newman, in the same year, opened the Movement's
series of ninety *Tracts for the Times* with a call for fellow-clergymen to
realize the transcendent spirituality of their profession (**1.1.2**). Echoing
Froude's warning, 'By standing still you become a party to revolution', he
quoted Jesus's words, 'He that is not with me is against me.' By 1841,
however, in the last of the *Tracts*, Newman could argue that so Protestant a
document as the Thirty-nine Articles nevertheless made it possible for
English clergy to accept their calling and their beliefs on the authority of
the Church of Rome (**1.1.3**). Reaction to his anonymous tract caused
Newman to own up to his convictions. In 1843 he resigned his benefice
and two years later he became a Roman Catholic. The Oxford Movement,
having lost its greatest intellect, carried on under lesser leaders, increasingly preoccupied with questions of ritual.

1.1.1 R. H. FROUDE ON STATE INTERFERENCE IN
MATTERS SPIRITUAL, 1833

The joint effect of three recent and important Acts, (1.) the Repeal of the
Test and Corporation Acts, (2.) the Concessions to the Roman Catholics,
(3.) the late Act for Parliamentary Reform, has most certainly been to
efface in at least one branch of our Civil Legislature, that character which,
according to our great Authorities, qualified it to be at the same time our
Ecclesiastical Legislature, and thus to cancel the conditions on which it has
been allowed to interfere in matters spiritual. . . .

. . . It seems at first sight something short of reasonable, that persons, not necessarily interested in the welfare of the Church, should deliberate for its good; and still less so, that they should be allowed to dictate laws to it, without the consent of those who are necessarily interested; and least reasonable of all, when we add the consideration, that many of the persons so dictating, are, as a fact, its avowed enemies, and that their dictates are deeply reprobated by the great body of its attached members. And yet that the Parliament of Great Britain and Ireland are not necessarily interested in the welfare of the Church, indeed that many of its members are our avowed enemies, and that the Church, as a body, deeply deplores this interference in its concerns, are, it is supposed, admitted facts. So that persons, who have been led to canvass the question on its own merits, have felt in some degree perplexed at the recognition of a claim apparently so ill according with common sense. . . .

It is with a view of this perplexity that the following considerations are put together. They are addressed to persons who fear to trust their common sense in a matter of such importance, and who, though they cannot justify the system of government under which they live, still feel inclined to acquiesce in it, out of deference to their wiser predecessors. . . .

'A *union* between *excellent* men of *all parties* for the maintenance of peace and order!' *excellent* truly, and of *all parties!* parties who agree in nothing but a wish to maintain peace and good order! who differ in opinion respecting all man's higher interests and duties, respecting all those points about which to differ is to disapprove; who will unite on no other basis than that of selfish worldly convenience; and yet who are to recognise each other as *excellent men!* How can one protest too earnestly against such mawkishness as this?

Excellent Independents forsooth; and excellent Socinians; and excellent Jews; excellent aliens from the Church of Christ; excellent unbelievers in the faith, in the which 'he that believeth not shall be damned;' and, to amalgamate the strange mass, excellent latitudinarians, who, like Gallio, 'care for none of these things!' These *excellent persons* are to come together, and, waving those *minor points* on which they differ, to unite on those of which all acknowledge the importance,—*the maintenance of peace and good order.*

And yet, say many considerate persons, it is much easier to declaim against the absurdity of such an arrangement than to suggest a substitute for it, which is at once better and practicable. It may be very true that peace and good order are but of secondary importance to the well-being of society; it may be very sad and grievous to abandon the nobler parts of our political system; it may be a revolting task to co-operate with those for whom we entertain a just and deep-rooted antipathy: all this may be, and yet it may become a wise and good man to lay a strong restraint upon his feelings, and to accept, as an alternative, what in itself he considers ever so objectionable.

Such is the tone of many considerate and right-minded persons, who, looking to the present dispositions of Parliament, and to the probable current of what is called public opinion, have judged it, humanly speaking, impossible for the Church of England to recover her lost ascendancy in the councils of this nation. They believe, and perhaps justly, that the changes lately introduced into the British constitution have enabled the dissenting and latitudinarian parties to otherthrow any government formed on exclusive principles; and that no set of men will ever again share a preponderating influence except on the basis of concession; in short, that an effort to secure to ourselves any thing more than peace and good order, can end in nothing less than anarchy and confusion.

Now is this the real state of the case? Is our position indeed so altered in the course of the last few years? This is no unimportant question, no dreamy unpractical speculation, no subject for profitless inquiry or otiose acquiescence. If we must indeed make up our minds to the course which is here prescribed; if we must abandon all hopes of recovering our lost position; if we are no longer to contend for the exclusive supremacy that was formerly deemed the right of the Church of England; – if so, then it is high time for us to look the truth in the face, to examine it in all its bearings, and follow it out into all its consequences. It is not for us to hope and to wait, and to praise caution, and to deprecate gloomy views, and to trust things may turn out better than we expect, and to lull our apprehensions by dreaming about 'excellent men,' and 'minor points,' and 'peace and good order,'

Non hoc ista sibi tempus spectacula poscit.

If Churchmen must submit to a union with dissenters and latitudinarians, they should at least do so with their eyes open. If they must make up their minds to concession, they should at least see clearly what they can concede legally and without impiety; what parts of their system they *may* relinqish, and what they *must* maintain at all costs. For whatever sacrifices we may be prepared to make for peace and good order, we must sacrifice even these for the Church of Christ.

The practical question, then, on which we have to decide, is this: – Is it possible so to remodify our Church system as to propitiate the dissenting and latitudinarian parties? and if so, have we a right to do this? Nor do I doubt that most persons will feel themselves prepared with a ready answer to both these questions. It seems to be generally assumed that such a reconciliation would be no hard matter; that the worst we have to fear is such a rearrangement of Church property as should render the higher clergy less obnoxious to envy, and perhaps lower the body generally as a caste of society. This seems to be the very worst fear of the most apprehensive persons; and to all this it seems to be admitted that we might consent without a compromise of principle.

But let the good persons, who satisfy themselves so easily, but open their eyes a little wider. Let them not look forward so many moves; but observe more closely how things stand at present. Let them not flatter themselves that the changes about which they deliberate are future and distant. They are present, – nay, past. A great change has taken place already in the constitution of the Church of England, – a change which affects her welfare not remotely or virtually, but actually and at once. Whenever it was that the Church of England lost her exclusive supremacy in the councils of this nation, then, at that very instant, a change took place in her internal constitution – a change, too, of no ordinary magnitude or importance, but a *down-right Revolution*. A trust, which had been reposed by our Apostolical predecessors on a power internal to the Church, was then allowed to devolve upon aliens; and that, too, in a matter of the very highest consequence, virtually affecting her well-being, perhaps even her existence as a visible society.

As long as the governing power was restricted, either by law or in fact, to persons in communion with the Church, so long it was safe and proper to confide to that power the nomination of our ecclesiastical superiors. But now, that neither law secures to us such a government, nor does the existing state of things permit us ever again to hope for it, the question assumes a very altered aspect. 'Quel sera la garantie de leur choix?' says one of the able writers of the 'Avenir,' under circumstances very similar to our own. 'Quel sera en effet pour nous la garantie de leur choix? Depuis que la religion Catholique n'est plus la religion de la Patrie, les Ministres d'état sont et *doivent être* dans une *indifférence légale* à notre egard: est-ce leur indifférence qui sera notre garantie? Ils sont laïcs, ils *peuvent être Protestants, Juïfs, Athées:* est-ce leur conscience qui sera notre garantie? Ils sont choisis dans les rangs d'une société imbue d'un préjugé opiniatré contre nous: est-ce leur préjugé qui sera notre garantie? Ils régnent enfin depuis quatre mois: est-ce leur passé qui sera notre garantie?'

So too with us, according to the wretched principles which it is supposed impossible any longer to withstand. His Majesty's Ministers, in future must be, and ought to be, at least in their public capacity, *detached from religious parties*, – dans une *indifférence légale* à notre égard: with us, then, as with the Catholics of France, – est-ce leur indifférence qui sera notre garantie? Nor is *indifference* the worst we have to fear; they *ought* to be indifferent; they *may be*, on conscientious principles doubtless, *our enemies*; they may be conscientious dissenters, or conscientious Jews, or conscientious Atheists; est-ce leur conscience qui sera notre garantie? Finally, and with sorrow be it spoken, we have ground for alarm not merely in what they *ought to be* or what they *may be*; melancholy indeed is the truth, but nevertheless it is a truth, that we can look with no greater confidence to what they *have been*. 'Est-ce leur passé qui sera notre garantie? Ils n'ont ouvert la bouche que pour nous ménacer; ils n'ont étendu la main que pour abattre nos croix; ils n'ont signé les ordonnances ecclésiastiques que pour sanctionner les actes arbitraires dont nous étions victimes; . . . ils ne nous ont pas protégés une seule fois sur un seul point de France; ils nous ont offert un holocauste prémature à toutes les passions.' And here too the painful parallel of our situations will suggest itself but too vividly. "Voila les motifs de securite q'ils nous presentent! Voila les hommes de qui vous consentiriez a recevoir vos collegues dans la charge de Premiers Pasteurs.'

Nor need we fear, continues this able writer, to reassert our privileges; the power as well as the right is ours; let us know our strength and use it. Que craignez vous! N'etes vous pas Eveques? Bishops of Christ's holy everlasting Church, who shall interfere with the free exercise of your indelible prerogative? Consecrate or refuse to consecrate: who shall reverse your decree? You can bind, and who shall loose? Une seule chose leur est possible; le retranchment de notre budget. Evêques de France! nous de vous en disons pas d'avantage: c'est à vous de voir lequel vous préférez laisser sur vos sièges, en mourant, ou d'un Episcopat riche et corrupteur, ou d'un Episcopat pauvre et digne de vous succéder.'

Such are the sentiments of a true conservative: a conservative, not of names, but of things; not of appearances, but of realities: a conservative that would conserve, not to a latitudinarian government trusts that had been reposed in an exclusive government, merely because it was a government, and is a government, but to the representatives of the Church, rights which have always belonged to the Church, though they were once a ruling party, and are now a persecuted party.

And now, good cautious people, you that praise peace and order, and thank Heaven you are not ultras, be at the pains to give these suggestions just so much thought as to see that they cannot be set aside by a shake of the head, or a shrug of the shoulders, or a declaration that 'you cannot go these lengths.' Look fairly at the question before you; make up your mind, not whether you will 'go these lengths' or remain where you are, but whether you will go *these* lengths or *other* lengths. Lengths you must go, whether you will or no; lengths you have already gone, and intolerable lengths. Open your eyes to the fearful change which has been so noiselessly effected; and acknowledge that by standing still you become a party to revolution.

1.1.2   J. H. NEWMAN ON THE MINISTERIAL COMMISSION, 1833

I am but one of yourselves, – a Presbyter; and therefore I conceal my name, lest I should take too much on myself by speaking in my own person. Yet speak I must; for the times are very evil, yet no one speaks against them. . . .

. . . Should the Government and Country so far forget their God as to cast off the Church, to deprive it of its temporal honors and substance, *on what* will you rest the claim of respect and attention which you make upon your flocks? Hitherto you have been upheld by your birth, your education, your wealth, your connexions; should these secular advantages cease, on what must CHRIST'S Ministers depend? Is not this a serious practical question? We know how miserable is the state of religious bodies not supported by the State. Look at the Dissenters on all sides of you, and you will see at once that their Ministers, depending simply upon the people, become the *creatures* of the people. Are you content that this should be your case? Alas! can a greater evil befall Christians, than for their teachers to be guided by them, instead of guiding? How can we 'hold fast the form of sound words,' and 'keep that which is committed to our trust,' if our influence is to depend simply on our popularity? Is it not our very office to *oppose* the world, can we then allow ourselves to *court* it? to preach smooth things and prophesy deceits? to make the way of life easy to the rich and indolent, and to bribe the humbler classes by excitements and strong intoxicating doctrine? Surely it must not be so; – and the question recurs, on *what* are we to rest our authority, when the State deserts us?

CHRIST has not left His Church without claim of its own upon the attention of men. Surely not. Hard Master He cannot be, to bid us oppose the world, yet give us no credentials for so doing. There are some who rest their divine mission on their own unsupported assertion; others, who rest it upon their popularity; others, on their success; and others, who rest it upon their temporal distinctions. This last case has, perhaps, been too much our own; I fear we have neglected the real ground on which our authority is built, – OUR APOSTOLICAL DESCENT.

We have been born, not of blood, nor of the will of the flesh, nor of the will of man, but of GOD. The Lord JESUS CHRIST gave His Spirit to His Apostles; they in turn laid their hands on those who should succeed them; and these again on others; and so the sacred gift has been handed down to our present Bishops, who have appointed us as their assistants, and in some sense representatives. . . .

Therefore, my dear Brethren, act up to your professions. Let it not be said that you have neglected a gift; for if you have the Spirit of the Apostles on you, surely this *is* a great gift. 'Stir up the gift of GOD which is in you.' Make much of it. Show your value of it. Keep it before your minds as an honorable badge, far higher than that secular respectability, or cultivation, or polish, or learning, or rank, which gives you a hearing with the many. Tell *them* of your gift. The times will soon drive you to do this, if you mean to be still any thing. But wait not for the times. Do not be compelled, by the world's forsaking you, to recur as if unwillingly to the high source of your authority. Speak out now, before you are forced, both as glorying in your privilege, and to ensure your rightful honor from your people. A notion has gone abroad, that they can take away your power. They think they have given and can take it away. They think it lies in the Church property, and they know that they have politically the power to confiscate that property. They have been deluded into a notion that present palpable usefulness, produceable results, acceptableness to your flocks, that these and such like are the tests of your Divine commission. Enlighten them in this matter. Exalt our Holy Fathers the Bishops, as the Representatives of the Apostles, and the Angels of the Churches; and magnify your office, as being ordained by them to take part in their Ministry.

But, if you will not adopt my view of the subject, which I offer to you, not doubtingly, yet (I hope) respectfully, at all events, CHOOSE YOUR SIDE. To remain neuter much longer will be itself to take a part. *Choose* your side; since side you shortly must, with one or other party, even though you do nothing. Fear to be of those, whose line is decided for them by chance circumstances, and who may perchance find themselves with the enemies of CHRIST, while they think but to remove themselves from worldly politics. Such abstinence is impossible in troublous times. HE THAT IS NOT WITH ME, IS AGAINST ME, AND HE THAT GATHERETH NOT WITH ME SCATTERETH ABROAD.

1.1.3   J. H. NEWMAN ON THE THIRTY-NINE ARTICLES, 1841

One remark may be made in conclusion. It may be objected that the tenor of the above explanations is anti-Protestant, whereas it is notorious that the Articles were drawn up by Protestants, and intended for the establishment of Protestantism; accordingly, that it is an evasion of their meaning to give them any other than a Protestant drift, possible as it may be to do so grammatically, or in each separate part.

But the answer is simple:

1. In the first place, it is a *duty* which we owe both to the Catholic Church and to our own, to take our reformed confessions in the most Catholic sense they will admit; we have no duties toward their framers. Nor do we receive the Articles from their original framers, but from several successive convocations after their time; in the last instance, from that of 1662.

2. In giving the Articles a Catholic interpretation, we bring them into harmony with the Book of Common Prayer, an object of the most serious moment in those who have given their assent to both formularies.

3. Whatever be the authority of the Declaration prefixed to the Articles, so far as it has any weight at all, it sanctions the mode of interpreting them above given. For its injoining the 'literal and grammatical sense,' relieves us from the necessity of making the known opinions of their framers a comment upon their text; and its forbidding any person to 'affix any *new* sense to any Article,' was promulgated at a time when the leading men of our Church were especially noted for those Catholic views which have been here advocated.

4. It may be remarked, moreover, that such an interpretation is in accordance with the well-known general leaning of Melanchthon, from whose writings our Articles are principally drawn, and whose Catholic tendencies gained for him that same reproach of popery, which has ever been so freely bestowed upon members of our own reformed Church. . . .

5. Further: the Articles are evidently framed on the principle of leaving open large questions, on which the controversy hinges. They state broadly extreme truths, and are silent about their adjustment. For instance, they say that all necessary faith must be proved from Scripture, but do not say *who* is to prove it. They say that the Church has authority in controversies, they do not say *what* authority. They say that it may enforce nothing beyond Scripture, but do not say *where* the remedy lies when it does. They say that works *before* grace *and* justification are worthless and worse, and that works *after* grace *and* justification are acceptable, but they do not speak at all of works *with* GOD'S aid, *before* justification. They say that men are lawfully called and sent to minister and preach, who are chosen and called by men who have public authority *given* them in the congregation to call and send; but they do not add *by whom* the authority is to be given. They say that councils called *by princes* may err; they do not determine whether councils called *in the name of* CHRIST will err.

6. The variety of doctrinal views contained in the Homilies, as above shown, views which cannot be brought under Protestantism itself, in its widest comprehension of opinions, is an additional proof, considering the connexion of the Articles with the Homilies, that the Articles are not framed on the principle of excluding those who prefer the theology of the early ages to that of the Reformation; or rather since both Homilies and Articles appeal to the Fathers and Catholic antiquity, let it be considered whether, in interpreting them by these, we are not going to the very authority to which they profess to submit themselves.

7. Lastly, their framers constructed them in such a way as best to comprehend those who did not go so far in Protestantism as themselves. Anglo-Catholics then are but the successors and representatives of those

moderate reformers; and their case has been directly anticipated in the wording of the Articles. It follows that they are not perverting, they are using them, for an express purpose for which among others their authors framed them. The interpretation they take was intended to be admissible; though not that which their authors took themselves. Had it not been provided for, possibly the Articles never would have been accepted by our Church at all. If, then, their framers have gained their side of the compact in effecting the reception of the Articles, let Catholics have theirs too in retaining their own Catholic interpretation of them.

An illustration of this occurs in the history of the 28th Article. In the beginning of Elizabeth's reign a paragraph formed part of it, much like that which is now appended to the Communion Service, but in which the Real Presence was *denied in words.* It was adopted by the clergy at the first convocation, but not published. Burnet observes on it thus:—

> When these Articles were at first prepared by the convocation in Queen Elizabeth's reign, this paragraph was made a part of them; for the original subscription by both houses of convocation, yet extant, shows this. But the *design of the government* was at that time much turned *to the drawing over the body of the nation to the Reformation,* in whom the old leaven had gone deep; and no part of it deeper than the belief of the corporeal presence of CHRIST in the Sacrament; therefore it was *thought not expedient* to *offend* them by so particular a definition in this matter; in which the very word Real Presence was rejected. It might, perhaps, be also suggested, that here a definition was made that went too much upon the principles of natural philosophy; which, how true soever, they might not be the proper subject of an article of religion. Therefore it was thought fit to suppress this paragraph; though it was a part of the Article that was subscribed, yet it was not published, but the paragraph that follows, 'The Body of CHRIST,' &c. was put in its stead, and was received and published by the next convocation; which upon the matter was a full explanation of the way of CHRIST'S presence in this Sacrament; that 'He is present in a heavenly and spiritual manner, and that faith is the means by which He is received.' This seemed to be more theological; and it does indeed amount to the same thing. But howsoever we see what was the sense of the first convocation in Queen Elizabeth's reign; it differed in nothing from that in King Edward's time; and therefore though this paragraph is now no part of our Articles, yet we are certain that the clergy at that time did not at all doubt of the truth of it; we are sure it was their opinion; since they subscribed it, though *they did not think fit* to publish it at first; and

though it was afterwards changed for another, that was the same in sense. – *Burnet on Article* XXVIII. p. 416.

What has lately taken place in the political world will afford an illustration in point. A French minister, desirous of war, nevertheless, as a matter of policy, draws up his state papers in such moderate language, that his successor, who is for peace, can act up to them, without compromising his own principles. The world, observing this, has considered it a circumstance for congratulation; as if the former minister, who acted a double part, had been caught in his own snare. It is neither decorous, nor necessary, nor altogether fair, to urge the parallel rigidly; but it will explain what it is here meant to convey. The Protestant Confession was drawn up with the purpose of including Catholics; and Catholics now will not be excluded. What was an economy in the reformers, is a protection to us. What would have been a perplexity to us then, is a perplexity to Protestants now. We could not then have found fault with their words; they cannot now repudiate our meaning.

1.2 BAPTISM AND ETERNAL DAMNATION

If the Articles and formularies of the Church of England indeed permitted such latitude of interpretation as to be found compatible with the teachings of the Church of Rome (as Newman argued in Tract 90), this liberty would prove useful to more than one ecclesiastical party. In the winter of 1847–48 an Evangelical clergyman named George Gorham was subjected by his bishop, the crusty conservative Henry Phillpotts of Exeter, to over fifty hours of interrogation on the subject of baptismal regeneration. Phillpotts judged Gorham's views to be heretical and declined to institute him to a living. Evangelicals, who generally believed baptism to be a sign of regenerating grace rather than its vehicle, feared for Church unity when in 1849 the Court of Arches dismissed Gorham's appeal with costs to the bishop. Tractarians in turn, became fearful when Gorham proceeded to take his case to the Judicial Committee of the Privy Council. The constitutional issues were grave. In March 1850, the 'Gorham Judgment', as it became known, declared quite simply that the Articles and formularies of the Church were not worded with sufficient precision to serve as the standard by which to condemn Gorham as a heretic (**1.2.1**). The correctness of his views, or otherwise, was ignored. There were eminent dissenters, of course. A respected lawyer and distinguished High Churchman, Roundell Palmer (1812–1895, later Lord and Lord Chancellor Selborne, wrote to Lady Brodie that the Privy Council had, in his view, not only got it wrong as a matter of law, but had misrepresented Anglican doctrine as well (**1.2.2**) His concern, shared by

Evangelicals, that the judgment would result in a general erosion of the distinction 'between truth and error' in the Church was not entirely misplaced. Heretics were turning up in high places. In 1853 the Revd Frederick Denison Maurice (1805–1872), a Christian Socialist, preached a sermon in Lincoln's Inn chapel, which he incorporated later that year into the concluding chapter of his *Theological Essays*. In it he denied the doctrine of eternal punishment as commonly received, arguing tortuously on biblical, historical, philosophical, and moral grounds that 'eternal' was to be interpreted as qualitative rather than quantitative and durational (**1.2.3**). Although Maurice had the advantage of standing for God's love among the unchurched masses, the clergy of King's College, London, where he was entrusted with teaching ordinands, retained the power to punish. In November 1853 they relieved him of his duties.

1.2.1   THE GORHAM JUDGMENT, 1850

ON FRIDAY, March 8, 1850, the JUDICIAL COMMITTEE of HER MAJESTY'S PRIVY COUNCIL met at the Privy Council Office, in Downing-street; – Present: the Right Hon. Lord Campbell, the Right Hon. Lord Langdale, the Right Hon. Sir Stephen Lushington, the Right Hon. T. Pemberton Leigh; together with Lords Monteagle, Brougham, and many other distinguished persons; when JUDGMENT in this important Case was given by Lord Langdale in the following terms:— . . .

. . . The doctrine held by Mr. Gorham appears to us to be this – that Baptism is a Sacrament generally necessary to salvation, but that the grace of regeneration does not so necessarily accompany the act of Baptism that regeneration invariably takes place in Baptism; that the grace may be granted before, in, or after Baptism; that Baptism is an effectual sign of grace, by which God works invisibly in us, but only in such as worthily receive it, – in them alone it has a wholesome effect; and that without reference to the qualification of the recipient, it is not in itself an effectual sign of grace. That infants baptized, and dying before actual sin, are certainly saved; but that in no case is regeneration in Baptism unconditional.

These being, as we collect them, the opinions of Mr. Gorham, the question which we have to decide is, not whether they are theologically sound or unsound – not whether, upon some of the doctrines comprised in the opinions, other opinions opposite to them may or may not be held with equal or even greater reason by other learned and pious ministers of the Church, but whether these opinions now under our consideration are contrary or repugnant to the doctrines which the Church of England, by its

Articles, Formularies, and Rubrics requires to be held by its ministers, so that, upon the ground of those opinions, the appellant can lawfully be excluded from the benefice to which he has been presented. . . .

It appears from the resolutions and discussions of the Church itself, and from the history of the time, that, from the first dawn of the Reformation until the final settlement of the Articles and Formularies, the Church was harassed by a great variety of opinions respecting Baptism and its efficacy, as well as upon other matters of doctrine.

The Church having resolved to frame Articles of faith, as a means of avoiding diversities of opinion and establishing consent touching true religion, must be presumed to have desired to accomplish that object as far as it could, and to have decided such of the questions then under discussion as it was thought proper, prudent, and practicable to decide; but it could not have intended to attempt the determination of all the questions which had arisen or might arise, or to include in the Articles an authoritative statement of all Christian doctrine; and in making the necessary selection of those points which it was intended to decide, regard was had to the points which were deemed to be most important to be made known to, and to be accepted by, the members of the Church, and to those questions upon which the members of the Church could agree; and that other points and other questions were left for future decision by competent authority; and in the meantime to the private judgment of pious and conscientious persons.

Under such circumstances it would perhaps have been impossible, even if it had been thought desirable, to employ language which did not admit of some latitude of interpretation; if the latitude were confined within such limits as might be allowed without danger to any doctrine necessary to salvation, the possible or probable difference of interpretation may have been designedly intended even by the framers of the Articles themselves; and in all cases in which the Articles, considered as a test, admit of different interpretations, it must be held that any sense of which the words fairly admit may be allowed, if that sense be not contradictory to something which the Church has elsewhere allowed or required – and in such a case it seems perfectly right to conclude that those who impose the test command no more than the form of the words employed in their literal and grammatical sense conveys or implies; and that those who agree to them are entitled to such latitude or diversity of interpretation as the same form admits.

If it were supposed that all points of doctrine were decided by the Church of England, the law could not consider any point as left doubtful. The application of the law, or of the doctrine of the Church of England, to any theological question which arose, must be the subject of decision; and the decision would be governed by the construction of the terms in which the doctrine of the Church is expressed, viz, the construction which on the whole would seem most likely to be right.

But if the case be, as undoubtedly it is, that in the Church of England many points of theological doctrine have not been decided, then the first and great question which arises in such cases as the present is, whether the disputed point is or was meant to be settled at all, or whether it is left open for each member of the Church to decide for himself according to his own conscientious opinion. If there be any doctrine on which the Articles are silent or ambiguously expressed, so as to be capable of two meanings, we must suppose that it was intended to leave that doctrine to private judgment, unless the Rubrics and Formularies clearly and distinctly decide it. If they do, we must conclude that the doctrine so decided is the doctrine of the Church. But, on the other hand, if the expressions used in the Rubrics and Formularies are ambiguous, it is not to be concluded that the Church meant to establish indirectly as a doctrine that which it did not establish directly as such by the Articles of faith – the code avowedly made for the avoiding of diversities of opinions, and for the establishing of consent touching true religion. . . .

Upright and conscientious men cannot in all respects agree upon subjects so difficult; and it must be carefully borne in mind that the question, and the only question for us to decide, is, whether Mr. Gorham's doctrine is contrary or repugnant to the doctrine of the Church of England as by law established. Mr. Gorham's doctrine may be contrary to the opinions entertained by many learned and pious persons, contrary to the opinion which such persons have, by their own particular studies, deduced from Holy Scripture – contrary to the opinion which they have deduced from the usages and doctrines of the primitive Church – or contrary to the opinion which they have deduced from uncertain and ambiguous expressions in the Formularies; still, if the doctrine of Mr. Gorham is not contrary or repugnant to the doctrine of the Church of England as by law established, it cannot afford a legal ground for refusing him institution to the living to which he has been lawfully presented.

This Court, constituted for the purpose of advising Her Majesty in matters which come within its competency, has no jurisdiction or authority to settle matters of faith, or to determine what ought in any particular to be the doctrine of the Church of England. Its duty extends only to the consideration of that which is by law established to be the doctrine of the Church of England, upon the true and legal construction of her Articles and Formularies; and we consider that it is not the duty of any Court to be minute and rigid in cases of this sort. We agree with Sir Wm. Scott in the opinion which he expressed in *Stone's Case,* in the Consistory Court of London:— 'That if any article is really a subject of dubious interpretation it would be highly improper that this Court should fix on one meaning, and prosecute all those who hold a contrary opinion regarding its interpretation.'

In the examination of this case we have not relied upon the doctrinal opinions of any of the eminent writers by whose piety, learning, and ability the Church of England has been distinguished; but it appears that opinions which we cannot in any important particular distinguish from those entertained by Mr. Gorham, have been propounded and maintained by many eminent and illustrious prelates and divines who have adorned the Church from the time when the Articles were first, without censure or reproach, established. . . .

We express no opinion upon the theological accuracy of these opinions, or any of them. The writers whom we have cited are not always consistent with themselves, and other writers of great eminence and worthy of great respect have held and published very different opinions. But the mere fact that such opinions have been propounded and maintained by persons so eminent and so much respected, as well as by very many others, appears to us sufficiently to prove that the liberty which was left by the Articles and Formularies has been actually enjoyed and exercised by the members and ministers of the Church of England.

The case not requiring it, we have abstained from expressing any opinion of our own upon the theological correctness or error of the doctrine of Mr. Gorham, which was discussed before us at such great length, and with so much learning. His Honour the Vice-Chancellor Knight Bruce dissents from the opinion we have formed, but all the other members of the Judicial Committee who were present are unanimously agreed in opinion that the doctrine held by Mr. Gorham is not contrary or repugnant to the declared doctrine of the Church of England as by law established, and that Mr. Gorham ought not, by reason of the doctrine held by him, to have been refused admission to the vicarage of Brampford Speke.

And we shall, therefore, humbly report to Her Majesty that the sentence pronounced by the Learned Judge in the Arches Court of Canterbury ought to be reversed, and that it ought to be declared that the Lord Bishop of Exeter has not shown sufficient cause why he did not institute Mr. Gorham in the said vicarage. . . .

1.2.2 ROUNDELL PALMER ON THE GORHAM JUDGMENT, 1850

In the view I take of it, the judgment is not only wrong; but (taking the effect of it from the reasons given by the Court itself, and not from anything else . . .) it is of such a nature as to place the Church of England in a false and inconsistent position, with respect to the whole practice of Infant Baptism. I look upon the question as much more one of infant baptism than of baptismal regeneration. The Court appears to me to have treated it as the clear doctrine of the Church of England, that *all who receive baptism rightly are spiritually regenerated,* either in baptism or by a prevenient act of grace, of which baptism is the seal; and, so far, I see nothing to complain of in the judgment. But then the question arises, whether the Church of England does or does not hold that all infants brought to baptism according to her order and appointment receive baptism rightly? And it was certainly decided (as I understand the judgment) that the Church of England does *not* affirm this, so as to make it repugnant to her doctrine for a clergyman to hold and teach the contrary. How this can be reconciled with the practice of infant baptism, – with the Article affirming that 'the baptism of young children is in any wise to be retained, as most agreeable with the institution of Christ,' – with the use of an office so worded as ours of Infant Baptism, – or with the declarations of our Church as to the danger of profaning sacraments by unworthily receiving them, – I cannot understand. For it comes to this, that the Church requires this sacrament to be administered to the generality of mankind, at a time and under circumstances which make it impossible to distinguish, by any evidence whatever, even of a probable kind, whether any person so baptized is capable of receiving baptism rightly or not. Nothing like this takes place in adult baptism, from which an argument has been drawn. In adult baptism, the service (no doubt) proceeds upon the supposition that the adult has the qualifications necessary for a right reception. But that supposition is only made in reliance upon the positive (though not infallible) evidence of fitness, afforded by his apparently sincere profession of repentance and faith. How can a Church be justified, upon any pretence of charity, in making that supposition in a case in which there is neither this evidence of fitness nor any other? For, if the fact of infancy itself be not evidence, scripturally and reasonably sufficient to induce the belief that every infant baptized according to the order of the Church receives baptism rightly, there is plainly no other evidence on which such a belief can be rested in any particular case; and the very generality of the practice shows most clearly that the Church *does* assume the fitness of all. If I did not believe that when the Lord says, 'Suffer the little children to come unto me,' He means *all* the little children whom in His Providence He causes to be brought, I should be at a loss for any scriptural warrant for bringing my own child, before she had at least grown to an age at which the signs of grace might be capable of appearing.

It is on these grounds that I think our Church dishonoured by this judgment. And when I bear in mind that in placing a construction upon the formularies *against* the literal meaning of plain words, the Court did not profess to derive aid from Scripture, or from the doctrine with which infant baptism was accompanied and explained in the Church from the beginning – nor, indeed, from any theological principle whatever – I can place no limits to the influence which this judgment may hereafter have, in breaking down the landmarks between truth and error in the Church of England, not on this subject only, but on others of even greater moment, on which the whole body of the Evangelical clergy will be as anxious to maintain them as myself. . . .

1.2.3   F. D. MAURICE ON ETERNAL LIFE AND ETERNAL DEATH, 1853

. . . The Trinity is, as I believe, the ground on which the Church stands, and on which Humanity stands. . . . But . . . Unitarians, and multitudes who are not Unitarians, declare that . . . there is another doctrine which . . . is as much an article of my faith as the Trinity itself. 'Your Church,' they say, 'maintains the notion of everlasting punishment after death. Consider what is included in that notion. You cannot thrust it into a corner, as you might naturally wish to do. You cannot mention it as something by the way. If it is anything, it is fundamental. Theologians and popular preachers treat it as such. They start from it; they put it forth as the ground of their exhortations. The world, according to them, lies under a sentence of condemnation. An immense – an incalculable – majority of all that have been born into it, must, if their statements mean anything, if they are not merely idle, frivolous rhetoric, be hopelessly doomed. Their object is to point out how a few, a very few, may be saved from the sentence.' . . .

'. . . Experience, which is said to teach individuals a little – nations almost nothing – has taught theologians, it seems, to be *more* outrageous, *more* contemptuous to human sympathies and conscience, than they used to be when all men bowed the neck to their yoke. This tenet must be accepted with *greater* precision now than in the days gone by. The Evangelical Alliance, longing to embrace all Protestant schools and parties, makes it one of its nine articles of faith, one of those first principles which are involved in the very nature of a comprehensive Christianity. It is clear that they are not solitary in their wish to give the doctrine of everlasting punishment this character. Your orthodox English Churchmen, though they may dissent from some of their opinions as too wide, will join heart and soul with them whenever they are narrow and exclusive. They may suffer doubts and modifications in some points; on this, be sure, they will demand simple, unqualified acquiescence.'

These statements may be heard in all circles, from young and old, from men and women, from persons longing to believe, from those who are settled down into indifference. Those who know say that they are producing infidelity in the highest classes; hard-working clergymen in the Metropolis can bear witness that they supply the most staple arguments to those who are preaching infidelity among the lowest. How impossible it is that I can pass them by, every one must perceive. . . . I am bound to admit that the evidence for them is very strong. Perhaps I may be permitted to trace some of the causes which have led to this state of feeling. They will account, I think, for the existence of it, at least under certain modifications, in very good men. They will explain what are likely to be the issues of it if it is not counteracted. They may help to show English Churchmen, and especially English Clergymen, what their standing-ground is, and what their obligations are, if they are really stewards of the everlasting Gospel.

1. Every one must be aware how much the philosophical teaching under which we have grown up unconsciously modifies our thoughts and opinions on a multitude of subjects which we suppose to be beyond its range. Luther's first battles, as his letters show us, were with Aristotle: he found how much the habits of thought learnt from him, and consecrated in the schools, interfered with the understanding of St. Paul. He wanted his pupils to look directly at the sense of Scripture; they came with certain preconceived notions which they imputed to the sacred writers; any one who construed them without reference to these notions was supposed to depart from their natural, simple meaning. . . .

What Aristotle was to the German in the sixteenth century, John Locke is to an Englishman in the nineteenth. His dogmas have become part of our habitual faith; they are accepted, without study, as a tradition. In this respect he resembles his predecessor. Proscribed at first by divines for the Essay on the Understanding more than for his politics or his interpretations of Scripture, just as Aristotle was proscribed by popes in the twelfth century, – divines now assume that Essay to be the rule and measure of thought and language, even as in the thirteenth century the Stagirite

Metaphysics became the rule and measure of thought and language to all orthodox schoolmen. But there is this difference: Aristotle belongs merely to the schools; Locke connects the schools with the world. He found a number of mystifications which doctors were canonising. He courageously applied himself to the removal of them. The conscience of ordinary men recognised him as their champion. He spoke to the love of the simple and practical, in which lies the strength of the English character. He asked men who were using phrases which they had inherited, and to which they attached no meaning, to give an account of them, and if they could not, to surrender them. It was evident that he had an immense advantage over his opponents, because he understood himself, and because he had determined to be faithful to his own convictions. He succeeded in persuading those who believed very little, not to pretend to believe more than they did. Who can doubt that this was a good and great service to mankind? But it involved this consequence. If men should chance hereafter to discover that some of the principles held by their ancestors had a substance and meaning in them, however little that substance and meaning might be represented in the dialect of the day, there would be considerable difficulty in recovering the possession. It would be supposed that the good sense of a great man had settled the question for ever, and those who knew little how it had been settled, or what there was to settle, would be just as zealous in discountenancing and ridiculing any further investigation, as if they were bowing to a dictator, not accepting help from one who had protested against dictation.

When any one ventures to say to an English audience that Eternity is not a mere negation of time, that it denotes something real, substantial, before all time, he is told at once that he is departing from the simple intelligible meaning of words; that he is introducing novelties; that he is talking abstractions. This language is perfectly honest in the mouths of those who use it. But they do not know where they learnt it. They did not get it from peasants or women or children. They did not get it from the Bible. They got it from Locke. And if I find that I cannot interpret the language and thoughts of peasants and women and children, and that I cannot interpret the plainest passages of the Bible or the whole context of it, while I look through the Locke spectacles, – I must cast them aside. I am sure Locke would wish me to do so, for I believe he was a thoroughly honest man, and one who desired nothing less in the world than that he should become an oppressor to the spirits which he supposed he was setting free.

Here, then, is one cause of our present state of feeling respecting the question which I am now considering; here is a proof how much that state of feeling must affect a multitude of subjects, besides that of everlasting punishment. 'When the Scriptures speak of Eternity they *must* mean endlessness; they *can* mean nothing else. To be sure they *do* mean something else, when they speak of God's eternity; but we have only to put in also "without beginning" to that, and all is right.' The divines who use such language are supported by those who most object to the conclusion which they deduce from it. The old Unitarian cannot give up Locke. The orthodox Dissenters have always supposed that he must be right, because Churchmen disliked him for his notions of government and toleration. Practical men suspect that some German mysticism must be near, when his decrees are disputed. . . . Nearly all people, therefore, in this country, who speak on such matters, are agreed that the words of the Gospel, if they were taken strictly and fairly, must have the hardest (I do not say the most awful, for I believe the sense I contend for is much more awful) meaning which has ever been given them. Only the tens and hundreds of thousands who cannot speak dissent from that decision.

2. However hard and exclusive the Romish Church may have been, – though the great complaint we make of her is, that she excommunicates those who are members of the body of Christ as much as she is, – it is impossible not to see that she takes up a position which looks, at least, much more comprehensive than that of the Protestant bodies. She assumes the Church to represent mankind. The day before Good Friday the Pope blesses the universe. The sacrifice which she presents day by day is declared to be that sacrifice which was made for the sins of the whole world. We believe that the strongest witness we have to bear is, that the sacrifice was made once for all; that our acts do not complete it, but are only possible because it is complete; that they are grounded upon our right to present that continually to the Father, with which He has declared Himself well pleased. We *ought,* therefore, to assert the redemption of mankind more distinctly than they do. But it is clear that in practice we do not seem to the world to do so, nor seem to ourselves to do so. The distinctiveness, the individuality, of Protestantism is its strength. But close to that strength is its greatest weakness, that which we all feel, which all in some sort confess, which is the root of our sectarianism, which is continually kept alive by it, and yet which is destroying the very bodies that it has created. What is the consequence to theology? The religious men, the saved men, are looked upon as the exceptions to a rule; the world is fallen, outcast, ruined; a few Christians, about the signs and tokens of whose Christianity each sect differs, have been rescued from the ruin. . . .

Damnation does not mean what its etymology would lead us to suppose that it means, what it certainly did mean to the Church in former days, amidst all its perplexities and confusions. It is not the loss of a mighty gift which has been bestowed upon the race. Men are not regarded as *rejecting the counsel of God against themselves.* God is represented as the destroyer. Nay, divines go the length of asserting – even of taking it for granted, – that our Lord Himself taught this lesson to His disciples when He said, *And*

I say unto you my friends, Be not afraid of them which kill the body, and after that
have no more that they can do; but I will forewarn you whom ye shall fear: Fear him,
which, after he hath killed, hath power to cast into hell, yea, I say unto you, Fear him.
Are not five sparrows sold for two farthings, and not one of them is forgotten before
God? But even the very hairs of your head are all numbered. Fear not, therefore; ye
are of more value than many sparrows. We are come to such a pass as actually to
suppose that Christ tells those whom He calls His *friends* not to be afraid of
the poor and feeble enemies who can only kill the body, but of that greater
enemy who can destroy their very selves, and that this enemy is – not the
devil, not the spirit who is going about seeking whom he may devour, not
him who was a murderer from the beginning, – but that God who cares for
the sparrows! They are to be afraid lest He who numbers the hairs of their
heads should be plotting their ruin! Does not this interpretation, which
has become so familiar that one hears it without even a hint that there is
another, show us on the edge of what an abyss we are standing, how likely
we are to confound the Father of lights with the Spirit of darkness?

While this temper of mind continues, it is absolutely inevitable that we
should not merely look upon the immense majority of our fellow-creatures as doomed to perdition, but that we should regard the Gospel as
itself pronouncing their doom. The message which, according to this view
of the case, Christ brings from Heaven to earth is, 'Your Father has
created multitudes whom He means to perish for ever and ever. By my
agony and bloody sweat, by my cross and passion, I have induced Him in
the case of an inconceivably small majority to forego that design.' Dare we
state that proposition to ourselves, – dare we get up into a pulpit and
preach it? But if we dare not, seeing it is a matter of life and death, and
there must be no trifling or equivocation about it, let us distinctly tell
ourselves what we do mean; and if we find that a blasphemous thought has
mingled with our belief hitherto, let us confess that thought to God, and
ask Him to deliver us from it.

3. I cannot wonder that Divines, – even those who would shrink with
horror from such a view of God's character and His Gospel as this, –
should crave for some more distinct apprehensions, nay, even statements
respecting eternal punishment, than might perhaps be needful in former
days. . . . If we believe that the words Eternal Damnation or Death have a
very terrible significance, such as the Bible tells us they have, is it nothing
that they should be losing all their significance for our countrymen? Is it
nothing that they should seem to them mere idle nursery-words that
frighten children, but with which men have nothing to do? Is it nothing,
that a vague dream of bliss hereafter, into which righteousness and
goodness do not enter, which has no relation to God, should float before
the minds of numbers; but that it should have just as little power to awaken
them to any higher or better life, as the dread of the future has to keep

them from any evil? . . .

. . . We do, it seems to me, need to have a more distinct and awful idea of eternal death and eternal punishment than we have. I use both words, *Death* and *Punishment,* that I may not appear to shrink from the sense which is contained in either. Punishment, I believe, seems to most men less dreadful than death, because they cannot separate it from a punisher, because they believe, however faintly, that He who is punishing them is a Father. The thought of His ceasing to punish them, of His letting them alone, of His leaving them to themselves, is the real, the unutterable horror. A man may be living without God in the world; he may be trembling at His Name, sometimes wishing that He did not exist; and yet, if you told him that he was going where there would be no God, no one to watch over him, no one to care for him, the news would be almost intolerable. We do shrink from this; all men, whatever they may fancy, are more appalled at the thoughts of being friendless, homeless, fatherless, than at any outward terrors you can threaten them with. I know well how the conscience confuses this anticipation with that of meeting God, with being brought face to face with Him. The mixture of feelings adds infinitely to the horror of them. There is a sense of wrath abiding on the spirit which has refused the yoke of love. This is one part of the misery. There is a sense of loneliness and atheism. This is another. And surely this, this is the bottomless pit which men see before them, and to which they feel that they are hurrying, when they have led selfish lives, and are growing harder and colder and darker every hour. Can we not tell them that it is even so; that this is the abyss of death, that second death, of which all material images offer only the faintest picture? Will not that show them more clearly what life is, – the risen life, the eternal life, that which was with the Father, and has been manifested to us? Will it not enable us to say, 'This life is that for which God has created man, for which He has redeemed man in His Son, which He is sending His Spirit to work out in man?' Will it not enable us to say, 'This eternal death is that from which God sent His Son to deliver men, from which He has delivered them? If they fall into it, it is because they choose it, because they embrace it, because they resist a power which is always at work to save them from it.' By delivering such a message as this to men, should we not be doing more to make them aware how the revelation of God's righteousness for the redemption of sinners is at the same time the revelation of the wrath of God against all unrighteousness and ungodliness? Would not such a message show that a Gospel of eternal love must bring out more clearly than any mere law can that state which is the resistance to it and the contradiction of it? But would not such a message at the same time present itself to the conscience of men, not as an outrage on their experience, but as the faithful interpreter of it, not as disproving everything that they have dreamed of the willingness of God to save them, but as proving that He is willing and able to save them to the very uttermost?

Suppose, instead of taking this method of asserting the truth of all God's words, the most blessed and the most tremendous, we . . . enact an article declaring that all are heretics and deniers of the truth who do not hold that Eternal means endless, and that there cannot be a deliverance from eternal punishment. What is the consequence? Simply this, I believe: the whole Gospel of God is set aside. The state of eternal life and eternal death is not one we can refer only to the future, or that we can in anywise identify with the future. Every man who knows what it is to have been in a state of sin, knows what it is to have been in a state of death. He cannot connect that death with time; he must say that Christ has brought him out of the bonds of *eternal* death. Throw that idea into the future, and you deprive it of all its reality, of all its power. I know what it means all too well while you let me connect it with my present and personal being, with the pangs of conscience which I suffer now. It become a mere vague dream and shadow to me, when you project it into a distant world. And if you take from me the belief that God is always righteous, always maintaining a fight with evil, always seeking to bring His creatures out of it, you take everything from me, all hope now, all hope in the world to come. Atonement, Redemption, Satisfaction, Regeneration, become mere words to which there is no counterpart in reality.

I ask no one to pronounce, for I dare not pronounce myself, what are the possibilities of resistance in a human will to the loving will of God. There are times when they seem to me – thinking of myself more than of others – almost infinite. But I know that there is something which must be infinite. I am obliged to believe in an abyss of love which is deeper than the abyss of death: I dare not lose faith in that love. I sink into death, eternal death, if I do. I must feel that this love is compassing the universe. More about it I cannot know. But God knows. I leave myself and all to Him. . . .

1.3   THE BROAD CHURCH: A REFORMED BIBLE

By the mid-1850s the term 'broad church' had come to designate a group of liberal Anglicans, represented then chiefly by Maurice, who sought to restate traditional doctrines in line with developing moral sensibilities and German critical scholarship. Their apotheosis came in early 1860 with the publication of *Essays and Reviews*. Of the seven contributors to the volume, Benjamin Jowett (1817–1893), professor of Greek at Oxford, was the boldest in disclosing that the Broad Church idea of Christianity was not conceived on the basis of an infallibly inspired Bible (**1.3.1**). His insistence that the Bible should be interpreted 'like any other book' offended just about everyone who was not a Broad Churchman or an unbeliever. Still more disturbing, however, were the instalments of *The Pentateuch and Book of Joshua Critically Examined*, which began appearing in the same year. The author, John William Colenso (1814–1883), the missionary bishop of Natal, had studied mathematics at Cambridge. Inspired by German critics, he used the numerical data in the first six books of the Old Testament to compute their fantastic unreliability (**1.3.2**). For his efforts he was deposed from his see in 1863. The Judicial Committee of the Privy Council declared the proceedings null and void, but Colenso was not allowed to return to his post – indeed, was eventually excommunicated – and his case became a *cause célèbre* among British liberals for many years. But some Broad Churchmen, while sympathetic with the bishop's plight, found his approach to biblical history frankly crude. In a masterful statement of the Bible's role in Broad Church theology, Arthur Penrhyn Stanley (1815–1881), dean of Westminster and perhaps the broadest of Broad Churchmen, signally omitted to connect Colenso's name with the 'new reformation' he saw emerging within the Church through the agency of German critical scholarship (**1.3.3**).

1.3.1   B. JOWETT ON THE INTERPRETATION OF SCRIPTURE, 1860

. . . That there has been no rude, or improper unveiling of the difficulties of Scripture in the preceding pages, is thought to be shown by the following considerations:

First, that the difficulties referred to are very well known; they force themselves on the attention, not only of the student, but of every intelligent reader of the New Testament, whether in Greek or English. The treatment of such difficulties in theological works is no measure of public opinion respecting them. Thoughtful persons, whose minds have turned towards theology, are continually discovering that the critical observations which they make themselves have been made also by others apparently without concert. The truth is that they have been led to them by the same causes, and these again lie deep in the tendencies of education and literature in the present age. But no one is willing to break through the reticence which is observed on these subjects; hence a sort of smouldering scepticism. It is probable that the distrust is greatest at the time when the greatest efforts are made to conceal it. Doubt comes in at the window, when Inquiry is denied at the door. The thoughts of able and highly educated young men almost always stray towards the first principles of things; it is a great injury to them, and tends to raise in their minds a sort of incurable suspicion, to find that there is one book of the fruit of the knowledge of which they are forbidden freely to taste, that is, the Bible. The same spirit renders the Christian Minister almost powerless in the hands of his opponents. He can give no true answer to the mechanic or artisan who has either discovered by his mother-wit or who retails at second-hand the objections of critics; for he is unable to look at things as they truly are.

Secondly, as the time has come when it is no longer possible to ignore the results of criticism, it is of importance that Christianity should be seen to be in harmony with them. That objections to some received views should be valid, and yet that they should be always held up as the objections of infidels, is a mischief to the Christian cause. It is a mischief that critical observations which any intelligent man can make for himself, should be ascribed to atheism or unbelief. It would be a strange and almost incredible thing that the Gospel, which at first made war only on the vices of mankind, should now be opposed to one of the highest and rarest of human virtues – the love of truth. And that in the present day the great object of Christianity should be, not to change the lives of men, but to prevent them from changing their opinions; that would be a singular inversion of the purposes for which Christ came into the world. The Christian religion is in a false position when all the tendencies of knowledge are opposed to it. Such a position cannot be long maintained, or can only end in the withdrawal of the educated classes from the influences of religion. It is a grave consideration whether we ourselves may not be in an earlier stage of the same religious dissolution, which seems to have gone further in Italy and France. The reason for thinking so is not to be sought in the external circumstances of our own or any other religious communion, but in the progress of ideas with which Christian teachers seem to be ill at ease. Time was when the Gospel was before the age; when it breathed a new life into a decaying world – when the difficulties of Christianity were difficulties of the heart only, and the highest minds found in its truths not only the rule of their lives, but a well-spring of intellectual delight. Is it to be held a thing impossible that the Christian religion, instead of shrinking into itself, may again embrace the thoughts of men upon the earth? Or is it true that since the Reformation 'all intellect has gone the other way'? and that in Protestant countries reconciliation is as hopeless as Protestants commonly believe to be the case in Catholic?

Those who hold the possibility of such a reconcilement or restoration of belief, are anxious to disengage Christianity from all suspicion of disguise or unfairness. They wish to preserve the historical use of Scripture as the continuous witness in all ages of the higher things in the heart of man, as the inspired source of truth and the way to the better life. They are willing to take away some of the external supports, because they are not needed and do harm; also, because they interfere with the meaning. They have a faith, not that after a period of transition all things will remain just as they were before, but that they will all come round again to the use of man and to the glory of God. When interpreted like any other book, by the same rules of evidence and the same canons of criticism, the Bible will still remain unlike any other book; its beauty will be freshly seen, as of a picture which is restored after many ages to its original state; it will create a new interest and make for itself a new kind of authority by the life which is in it. It will be a spirit and not a letter; as it was in the beginning, having an influence like that of the spoken word, or the book newly found. The purer the light in the human heart, the more it will have an expression of itself in the mind of Christ; the greater the knowledge of the development of man, the truer will be the insight gained into the 'increasing purpose' of revelation. In which also the individual soul has a practical part, finding a sympathy with its own imperfect feelings, in the broken utterance of the Psalmist or the Prophet as well as in the fulness of Christ. The harmony between Scripture and the life of man, in all its stages, may be far greater than appears at present. No one can form any notion from what we see around us, of the power which Christianity might have if it were at one with the conscience of man, and not at variance with his intellectual convictions. There, a world weary of the heat and dust of controversy – of speculations about God and man – weary too of the rapidity of its own motion, would return home and find rest.

But for the faith that the Gospel might win again the minds of intellectual men, it would be better to leave religion to itself, instead of attempting to draw them together. Other walks in literature have peace and pleasure and profit; the path of the critical Interpreter of Scripture is almost always a thorny one in England. It is not worth while for any one to enter upon it who is not supported by a sense that he has a Christian and moral object. For although an Interpreter of Scripture in modern times will hardly say with the emphasis of the Apostle, 'Woe is me, if I speak not the truth without regard to consequences,' yet he too may feel it a matter of duty not to conceal the things which he knows. He does not hide the discrepancies of Scripture, because the acknowledgment of them is the first step towards agreement among interpreters. He would restore the original meaning because 'seven other' meanings take the place of it; the book is made the sport of opinion and the instrument of perversion of life. He would take the excuses of the head out of the way of the heart; there is hope too that by drawing Christians together on the ground of Scripture, he may also draw them nearer to one another. He is not afraid that inquiries, which have for their object the truth, can ever be displeasing to the God of truth; or that the Word of God is in any such sense a word as to be hurt by investigations into its human origin and conception. . . .

What remains may be comprised in a few precepts, or rather is the expansion of a single one. *Interpret the Scripture like any other book.* There are many respects in which Scripture is unlike any other book; these will appear in the results of such an interpretation. The first step is to know the meaning, and this can only be done in the same careful and impartial way that we ascertain the meaning of Sophocles or of Plato. The subordinate principles which flow out of this general one will also be gathered from the observation of Scripture. No other science of Hermeneutics is possible but an inductive one, that is to say, one based on the language and thoughts and narrations of the sacred writers. And it would be well to carry the theory of interpretation no further than in the case of other works. Excessive system tends to create an impression that the meaning of Scripture is out of our reach, or is to be attained in some other way than by the exercise of manly sense and industry. Who would write a bulky treatise about the method to be pursued in interpreting Plato or Sophocles? Let us not set out on our journey so heavily equipped that there is little chance of our arriving at the end of it. The method creates itself as we go on, beginning only with a few reflections directed against plain errors. Such reflections are the rules of common sense, which we acknowledge with respect to other works written in dead languages; without pretending to novelty they may help us to 'return to nature' in the study of the sacred writings.

First, it may be laid down, that Scripture has one meaning – the meaning which it had to the mind of the Prophet or Evangelist who first uttered or wrote, to the hearers or readers who first received it. Another view may be easier or more familiar to us, seeming to receive a light and interest from the circumstances of our own age. But such accommodation of the text must be laid aside by the interpreter, whose business is, to place himself as nearly as possible in the position of the sacred writer. . . . One consideration should be borne in mind, that the Bible is the only book in the world written in different styles and at many different times, which is in the hands of persons of all degrees of knowledge and education. The benefit of this outweighs the evil, yet the evil should be admitted – namely, that it leads to a hasty and partial interpretation of Scripture, which often obscures the true one. A sort of conflict arises between scientific criticism and popular opinion. The indiscriminate use of Scripture has a further tendency to maintain erroneous readings or translations; some which are allowed to be such by scholars have been stereotyped in the mind of the English reader; and it becomes almost a political question how far we can venture to disturb them.

There are difficulties of another kind in many parts of Scripture, the depth and inwardness of which require a measure of the same qualities in the interpreter himself. There are notes struck in places, which like some discoveries of science have sounded before their time; and only after many days have been caught up and found a response on the earth. There are germs of truth which after thousands of years have never yet taken root in the world. There are lessons in the Prophets which, however simple, mankind have not yet learned even in theory; and which the complexity of society rather tends to hide; aspects of human life in Job and Ecclesiastes which have a truth of desolation about them which we faintly realize in ordinary circumstances. It is, perhaps, the greatest difficulty of all to enter into the meaning of the words of Christ – so gentle, so human, so divine, neither adding to them nor marring their simplicity. The attempt to illustrate or draw them out in detail, even to guard against their abuse, is apt to disturb the balance of truth. The interpreter needs nothing short of 'fashioning' in himself the image of the mind of Christ. He has to be born again into a new spiritual or intellectual world, from which the thoughts of this world are shut out. It is one of the highest tasks on which the labour of a life can be spent, to bring the words of Christ a little nearer the heart of man.

But while acknowledging this inexhaustible or infinite character of the sacred writings, it does not, therefore, follow that we are willing to admit of hidden or mysterious meanings in them: in the same way we recognise the wonders and complexity of the laws of nature to be far beyond what eye has seen or knowledge reached, yet it is not therefore to be supposed, that we acknowledge the existence of some other laws different in kind from those we know which are incapable of philosophical analysis. In like manner we have no reason to attribute to the Prophet or Evangelist any second or hidden sense different from that which appears on the surface. All that the Prophet meant may not have been consciously present to his mind; there were depths which to himself also were but half revealed. . . . Prophetic symbols, again, have often the same meaning in different places (*e.g.*, the four beasts or living creatures, the colours white or red); the reason is that this meaning is derived from some natural association (as of fruitlessness, purity, or the like); or again, they are borrowed in some of the later prophecies from earlier ones; we are not, therefore, justified in supposing any hidden connexion in the prophecies where they occur. Neither is there any ground for assuming design of any other kind in Scripture any more than in Plato or Homer. Wherever there is beauty and order, there is design; but there is no proof of any artificial design, such as is often traced by the Fathers, in the relation of the several parts of a book, or of the several books to each other. That is one of those mischievous notions which enables us, under the disguise of reverence, to make Scripture mean what we please. Nothing that can be said of the greatness or sublimity, or truth, or depth, or tenderness, of many passages, is too much. But that greatness is of a simple kind; it is not increased by double senses, or systems of types, or elaborate structure, or design. If every sentence was a mystery, every word a riddle, every letter a symbol, that would not make the Scriptures more worthy of a Divine author; it is a heathenish or Rabbinical fancy which reads them in this way. Such complexity would not place them above but below human compositions in general; for it would deprive them of the ordinary intelligibleness of human language. It is not for a Christian theologian to say that words were given to mankind to conceal their thoughts, neither was revelation given them to conceal the Divine.

The second rule is an application of the general principle; 'interpret Scripture from itself' as in other respects, like any other book written in an age and country of which little or no other literature survives, and about which we know almost nothing except what is derived from its pages. Not that all the parts of Scripture are to be regarded as an indistinguishable mass. The Old Testament is not to be identified with the New, nor the Law with the Prophets, nor the Gospels with the Epistles, nor the Epistles of St. Paul to be violently harmonized with the Epistle of St. James. Each writer, each successive age, has characteristics of its own, as strongly marked, or more strongly than those which are found in the authors or periods of classical literature. These differences are not to be lost in the idea of a Spirit from whom they proceed or by which they were overruled. And therefore, illustration of one part of Scripture by another should be confined to writings of the same age and the same authors, except where the writings of different ages or persons offer obvious similarities. It may be said further that illustration should be chiefly derived, not only from the same author, but from the same writing, or from one of the same period of his life. . . .

But supposing all this to be understood, and that by the interpretation of Scripture from itself is meant a real interpretation of like by like, it may be asked, what is it that we gain from a minute comparison of a particular author or writing? The indiscriminate use of parallel passages taken from one end of Scripture and applied to the other (except so far as earlier compositions may have afforded the material or the form of later ones) is useless and uncritical. The uneducated, or imperfectly educated person who looks out the marginal references of the English Bible, imagining himself in this way to gain a clearer insight into the Divine meaning, is really following the religious associations of his own mind. Even the critical use of parallel passages is not without danger. For are we to conclude that an author meant in one place what he says in another? Shall we venture to mend a corrupt phrase on the model of some other phrase, which memory, prevailing over judgment, calls up and thrusts into the text? It is this fallacy which has filled the pages of classical writers with useless and unfounded emendations.

The meaning of the Canon 'Non nisi ex Scripturâ Scripturam potes interpretari,' is only this, 'That we cannot understand Scripture without becoming familiar with it.' Scripture is a world by itself, from which we must exclude foreign influences, whether theological or classical. To get inside that world is an effort of thought and imagination, requiring the sense of a poet as well as a critic – demanding, much more than learning, a degree of original power and intensity of mind. Any one who, instead of burying himself in the pages of the commentators, would learn the sacred writings by heart, and paraphrase them in English, will probably make a nearer approach to their true meaning than he would gather from any commentary. The intelligent mind will ask its own questions, and find for the most part its own answers. The true use of interpretation is to get rid of interpretation, and leave us alone in company with the author. . . .

Yet in this consideration of the separate books of Scripture it is not to be forgotten that they have also a sort of continuity. We make a separate study of the subject, of the mode of thought, in some degree also, of the language of each book. And at length the idea arises in our minds of a common literature, a pervading life, an overruling law. It may be compared to the effect of some natural scene in which we suddenly perceive a harmony or picture, or to the imperfect appearance of design which suggests itself in looking at the surface of the globe. That is to say, there is nothing miraculous or artificial in the arrangement of the books of Scripture; it is the result, not the design, which appears in them when bound in the same volume. Or if we like so to say, there is design, but a natural design which is revealed to after ages. Such continuity or design is best expressed under some notion of progress or growth, not regular, however, but with broken and imperfect stages which the want of knowledge prevents our minutely defining. . . .

Such a growth or development may be regarded as a kind of progress from childhood to manhood. In the child there is an anticipation of truth; his reason is latent in the form of feeling; many words are used by him which he imperfectly understands; he is led by temporal promises, believing, that to be good is to be happy always; he is pleased by marvels and has vague terrors. He is confined to a spot of earth, and lives in a sort of prison of sense, yet is bursting also with a fulness of childish life: he imagines God to be like a human father, only greater and more awful; he is easily impressed with solemn thoughts, but soon 'rises up to play' with other children. It is observable that his ideas of right and wrong are very simple, hardly extending to another life; they consist chiefly in obedience to his parents, whose word is his law. As he grows older he mixes more and more with others; first with one or two who have a great influence in the direction of his mind. At length the world opens upon him; another work of education begins; and he learns to discern more truly the meaning of things and his relation to men in general. You may complete the image, by supposing that there was a time in his early days when he was a helpless outcast 'in the land of Egypt and the house of bondage.' And as he arrives at manhood he reflects on his former years, the progress of his education, the hardships of his infancy, the home of his youth (the thought of which is ineffaceable in after life), and he now understands that all this was but a preparation for another state of being, in which he is to play a part for himself. And once more in age you may imagine him like the patriarch looking back on the entire past, which he reads anew, perceiving that the events of life had a purpose or result which was not seen at the time; they seem to him bound 'each to each by natural piety.'

'Which things are an allegory,' the particulars of which any one may interpret for himself. For the child born after the flesh is the symbol of the child born after the Spirit. 'The law was a schoolmaster to bring men to Christ,' and now 'we are under a schoolmaster' no longer. The anticipation of truth which came from without to the childhood or youth of the human race is witnessed to within; the revelation of God is not lost but renewed in the heart and understanding of the man. Experience has taught us the application of the lesson in a wider sphere. And many influences have combined to form the 'after life' of the world. When at the close (shall we say) of a great period in the history of man, we cast our eyes back on the course of events, from the 'angel of his presence in the wilderness' to the multitude of peoples, nations, languages, who are being drawn together by His Providence – from the simplicity of the pastoral state in the dawn of the world's day, to all the elements of civilization and knowledge which are beginning to meet and mingle in a common life, we also understand that we are no longer in our early home, to which, nevertheless, we fondly look; and that the end is yet unseen, and the purposes of God towards the human race only half revealed. And to turn once more to the Interpreter of Scripture, he too feels that the continuous growth of revelation which he traces in the Old and New Testament, is a part of a larger whole extending over the earth and reaching to another world. . . .

1.3.2　J. W. COLENSO ON THE PENTATEUCH, 1865

ADVERTISEMENT TO THE PEOPLE'S EDITION

In this edition of my work on the Pentateuch, I have desired to place, in a clear and intelligible form, before the eyes of the general reader, the main arguments which have been advanced in my first four Parts, as proving the *unhistorical character*, the *later origin*, and the *compound authorship*, of the five books usually attributed to Moses.

Hitherto I have addressed myself only to the Clergy and to the more highly-educated among the Laity; and the difficulties, connected with the strict scientific treatment of the subject, have confined, of course, the study of my work to a comparatively limited, though still in itself extensive, circle. But now I address the general public. I should feel, indeed, that, unless I had first stated at length, for the consideration and examination of the learned, the grounds on which my conclusions are based, I should not be justified in bringing the discussion of these questions in this form within the reach of the People at large. But a long interval has now elapsed, since my First Part was published; and I have sufficiently tested the validity of my arguments by the character of the answers, which have been given to some of them. Being thus satisfied of the soundness of my position, and the general truth of the main results of my critical labours, I here lay my work before the many, corrected and condensed, without any loss of real substance, but stripped of the Hebrew quotations and some more difficult details, for which reference may be made to the larger volumes. And I have the less hesitation in doing this, inasmuch as the subjects here treated of have been of late, and are still, discussed freely in the public journals; so that no thoughtful person can fail to see that we have here before us one of the great questions of the time, of which *this* generation must give account to future ages.

Further, the violent denunciations which in so many instances have taken the place of argument, and the course adopted by the Society for Promoting Christian Knowledge, in circulating a 'People's Edition' of the late Dr M'CAUL'S 'Reply,' which has been commended by the Bishop (BICKERSTETH) of RIPON in his recent Charge as having given to my work 'a

---

1　Lord Westbury's judgment on the Colenso case in the Judicial Committee of the Privy Council, 20th March 1865, according to *Punch*. The theological issue was never even considered: Colenso's allegiance to Bishop Robert Gray as his 'metropolitan' and Gray's dismissal of Colenso were ruled, on purely technical grounds, null and void.

BISHOP OF CAPE TOWN.   LORD CHANCELLOR.   BISHOP OF NATAL.

THE COLENSO JUDGMENT.

"COLENSO HAD NO RIGHT TO SWEAR   AND GRAY NO TITLE TO EXACT
OBEDIENCE TO AN EMPTY CHAIR,   A COMPACT THAT WAS BOSH, IN FACT."

decisive and complete refutation,' have made it the more desirable that the 'People' themselves, – that is, all persons of common sense, whether learned or otherwise, – should have the opportunity of seeing with their own eyes what is the real state of the case. And especially I must desire that the inhabitants of Natal and of South Africa, generally, who have heard me condemned in very violent terms by the Metropolitan Bishop of CAPETOWN, and who cannot be expected to have made much acquaintance with my books in their larger form, should be able to judge for themselves as to the contents, and as to the whole tone and spirit, of my work. . . .

THE NUMBER OF PRIESTS AT THE EXODUS

The book of Leviticus [*L*] is chiefly occupied in giving directions to the Priests for the proper discharge of the different duties of their office, and further directions are given in the book of Numbers [*N*]. . . . Let us ask, for all these multifarious duties, during the forty years' sojourn in the wilderness, – for all the burnt-offerings, meat-offerings, peace-offerings, sin-offerings, trespass-offerings, thank-offerings, &c., of a population like that of the city of LONDON, besides the daily and extra-ordinary sacrifices, – how many Priests were there?

The answer is very simple. There were only *three*, – Aaron, (till his death,) and his two sons, Eleazer and Ithamar. And it is laid down very solemnly in *N*.iii.10,—

> Thou shalt appoint Aaron and his sons, and they shall wait in the Priest's office; and *the stranger, that cometh nigh, shall be put to death.*

Yet how was it possible that these two or three men should have discharged all these duties for such a vast multitude? The single work, of offering the double sacrifice for women after child-birth, must have utterly overpowered three Priests, though engaged without cessation from morning to night. As we have seen, . . . the births among two millions of people may be reckoned as, at least, 250 a day, for which, consequently, 500 sacrifices (250 burnt-offerings and 250 sin-offerings) would have had to be offered daily. Looking at the directions in *L*.i,ix, we can scarcely allow less than *five minutes* for each sacrifice; so that these sacrifices alone, if offered separately, would have taken 2,500 minutes or nearly 42 hours, and could not have been offered in a single day of twelve hours, though each of the three Priests had been employed in the one sole incessant labour of offering them, without a moment's rest or inter-mission.

It may, perhaps, be said that *many* such sacrifices might have been offered at the same time. This is, surely, somewhat contrary to the notion of a sacrifice, as derived from the book of Leviticus; nor is there the slightest intimation, in the whole Pentateuch, of any such heaping together of sacrifices; and it must be borne in mind that there was but *one* altar, five cubits (about 9 feet) square, *E*[xodus].xxvii.1, at which we have already supposed all the three Priests to be officiating at the same moment, actually offering, therefore, upon the altar *three* sacrifices *at once*, of which the *burnt*-offerings would, except in the case of poor women, *L.*xii.8, be *lambs*, and not pigeons. . . .

Again we have in *N.*xviii . . . commands, addressed to Aaron by Jehovah Himself. . . . Similar directions are also laid down in *L.*vii:—

> As the *sin*- offering is, so is the *trespass*-offering; there is one law for them: the Priest, that maketh atonement therewith, shall have it. And the Priest, which offereth any man's *burnt*-offering, even the Priest shall have to himself the skin of the *burnt*-offering which he hath offered. And all the *meat*-offering that is baked in the oven, and all that is dressed in the frying-pan and in the pan, shall be the Priest's that offereth it. And every *meat*-offering, mingled with oil, and dry, shall all the sons of Aaron have, one as much as another.' *v.*7–10.
>
> 'For the wave-breast and the heave-shoulder have I taken of the children of Israel from off the sacrifices of their *peace*-offerings, and have given them unto Aaron the Priest and unto his sons, by a statute for ever, from among the children of Israel.' *v.*34.

These last directions are given in the story before Aaron and his sons were consecrated. Hence they must be considered as intended to apply to them, while the Camp was in the wilderness, as well as to the 'sons of Aaron' in future generations. But what an enormous provision was this for Aaron and his four, afterwards two, sons and their families! They were to have the skins of the *burnt*-offerings, and the shoulder and breast (that is, double-breast) of the *peace*-offerings, of a congregation of two millions of people, for the general use of their three families! But, besides these, they were to have the whole of the *sin*-offerings, and *trespass*-offerings, except the suet, which was to be burnt upon the Altar, *L.*iv.31,35,v.6; and the whole of the *meat*-offerings, except a handful, to be burnt as a memorial, *L.*ii.2; and all this was to be eaten *only by the three males, in the most holy place, N.*xviii.10!

And it would seem that they were not at liberty to *burn* the sin-offerings, or consume them in some other way than by eating: they must be 'eaten in the holy place.'. . . The very pigeons, to be brought as *sin*-offerings for the birth of children, would have averaged, according to the story, more than 250 a day; and each Priest would have had to eat daily more than 80, for his own portion. . . .

Once more, how did these three Priests manage at the celebration of the Passover?

We are told, 2Ch[ronicles].xxx.16, xxxv.11, that the people killed the Passover, but,—

The Priests sprinkled the blood from their hands, and the Levites flayed them.

Hence, when they kept the second passover under Sinai, *N*.ix.5, where we must suppose that 150,000 lambs . . . were killed at one time 'between the two evenings.' *E*.xii.6, for the two millions of people, – at which time, certainly, there were only *three* Priests, Aaron, Eleazar, and Ithamar, *L*.viii.2, *N*.iii.4, each Priest must have had to sprinkle the blood of 50,000 lambs in about two hours, that is, at the rate of about *four hundred lambs every minute for two hours together!*

Further, in the time of Hezekiah and Josiah, when it was desired to keep the Passover very strictly, 'in such sort as it was written,' 2*Ch*.xxx.5, the lambs were manifestly killed *in the Court of the Temple.* We must suppose, then, that the Paschal lambs in the wilderness were killed *in the Court of the Tabernacle,* – in accordance, in fact, with the strict injunctions of the Levitical Law, that all burnt-offerings, peace-offerings, sin-offerings, and trespass-offerings, should be killed 'before Jehovah,' at the door of the Tabernacle of the Congregation. . . . How, in fact, could the Priests have sprinkled the blood at all, if this were not the case, that the animals were killed in the Court of the Tabernacle?

But the area of the Court contained, as we have seen, . . . only 1,692 square yards, and could only have held, when thronged to the uttermost, about 5,000 people. How then are we to conceive of 150,000 lambs being killed within it, by, at least, 150,000 people, in the space of two hours, – that is, *at the rate of* 1,250 *lambs a minute?* . . .

From the above considerations it seems to follow, that the account of the Exodus of the Israelites, as given in the Pentateuch, whatever real foundation it may have had in the ancient history of the people, is mixed up, at all events, with so great an amount of contradictory matter, that it cannot be regarded as historically true, so as to be appealed to, as absolute, incontestable matter of fact. For the objections, which have been produced, are not such as touch only one or two points of the story. They affect the entire substance of it; and, until they are removed, they make it impossible for a thoughtful person to receive, without further enquiry, any considerable portion of it, *as certainly true* in an historical point of view.

We cannot here have recourse to the ordinary supposition, that there may be something wrong in the *Hebrew numerals.* First, the number '600,000 on foot, that were male beside children,' is given distinctly in *E*.xii.37, at the time of their leaving Egypt; then we have it recorded again, as we have said, *thrice over, in different forms,* in *E*.xxxviii.25–28, at the beginning of the forty years' wanderings, when the number of all that 'went to be numbered, from twenty years old and upward,' is reckoned at 603,550; and this is repeated again in *N*.i.46; and it is modified once more, at the end of the wanderings, to 601,730, *N*.xxvi.51. Besides which, on each occasion of numbering, each separate tribe is numbered, and the sum of the separate results makes up the whole.

Thus this number is woven, as a kind of thread, into the whole story of the Exodus, and cannot be taken out, without tearing the whole fabric to pieces. It affects, directly, the account of the construction of the Tabernacle, *E*.xxxviii.25–28, and, therefore, also the account of the institutions, whether of the Priesthood or of Sacrifice, connected with it. And the multiplied impossibilities introduced by this number alone, independently of all other considerations, are enough to throw discredit upon the historical character of the general narrative. . . .

But how thankful we must be, that we are no longer obliged to believe, as a matter of fact, of vital consequence to our eternal hope, each separate statement contained in the Pentateuch, such, for instance, as the story related in *N*.xxxi! – where we are told that a force of 12,000 Israelites slew *all* the males of the Midianites, took captive *all* the females and children, seized *all* their cattle and flocks, (72,000 oxen, 61,000 asses, 675,000 sheep), and *all* their goods, and 'burnt *all* their cities, and *all* their goodly castles,' without the loss of a single man, – and then, by command of Moses, butchered in cold blood all the women and children, except—

> All the women-children, who have not known a man by lying with him, *v*.18.

These last they were to 'keep alive for themselves.' They amounted, to 32,000, *v*.35, mostly, we must suppose, under the age of sixteen or eighteen. We may fairly reckon that there were as many more under the age of forty, and half as many more above forty, making altogether 80,000 females, of whom, according to the story, Moses ordered 48,000 to be killed, besides (say) 20,000 young boys. . . . And these 48,000 females must have represented 48,000 men, all of whom, in that case, we must also believe to have been killed, their property pillaged, their castles demolished, and towns destroyed, by 12,000 Israelites, who, in addition, must have carried off 100,000 captives, (more than eight persons to each man,) and driven before them 808,000 head of cattle, (more than sixty-seven for each man,) and all without the loss of a single man! How is it possible to quote the Bible as in any way condemning slavery, when we read here, *v*.40, of 'Jehovah's tribute' of slaves, thirty-two persons, who were given to Eleazar the Priest, while three-hundred-and-twenty were given to the Levites, *v*.46,47?

Who is it that really dishonours the Word, and blasphemes the Name, of God Most High? – he who believes, and teaches others to believe, that such acts, as those above recorded, were really perpetrated by Moses under express Divine sanction and command, or he who declares that such commands as these could never have emanated from the Holy and Blessed One, the All-Just and All-Loving, the Father of the spirits of all flesh, – that we must not, dare not, believe this, – that we are bound not to do so by the express authority of that Divine Law, which we hear in our hearts, which is written in our consciences, and answers there to the voice which speaks to us from without, *D*[euteronomy]xiii.1–3, – that we *must not* 'hear' such doctrine as this, no, not though all the Doctors and Divines in the world should assert it, and appeal to any number of prophecies or miracles to prove it, – nay, not though 'the signs or wonders, whereof they spake to us,' should 'come to pass' before our very eyes. For, when we hear these things from our fellow-men, however great in learning or high in authority, however near and dear to us, even the 'friend which is as our own soul,' we must consider in our hearts that at such times 'the Living God, our God, is proving us, to know whether we love the Living God, our God,' – His Truth, His Righteousness, and the honour of His Holy Name, – more than all the precepts and teachings of men, 'with all our heart and with all our soul.' . . .

1.3.3 A. P. STANLEY ON THE THEOLOGY OF THE NINETEENTH CENTURY, 1865

. . . The religious feeling itself, no doubt, varies from age to age; but still it is much more nearly the same than is the case with the theories of thinking men, who, by their reasonings upon it, produce what is called Theology. Sometimes the Religion is behind the Theology of an age – sometimes before it – always more or less independent of it. . . .

. . . As regards Religion, properly so called, the Bible has done its blessed work in all ages – even when in the hands of but a few – by keeping alive directly and indirectly the substantial truths of the Jewish and Christian dispensations. There have, of course, been always some who have studied it as faithfully as their knowledge permitted; but these, as far as Theology was concerned, are the exceptions. . . . It was, speaking generally, from the time when the Germans began to interpret the Bible with the same freedom from party feeling, the same single-minded love of truth, the same fearlessness of consequences – it must be unfortunately added, in some instances, with the same arbitrary and supercilious dogmatism, as that which they employed on other books; it was from that moment that the Bible attracted theologians towards itself, not for the sake of making systems out of it, but for the sake of discovering what it actually contained. . . .

These are but a few instances of the nearer approach to the sacred writers which may fairly be expected, and which has to a certain degree been won, from the theology of our age. Its extreme difficulty is obvious. In order to enter even into this outer court of the Kingdom of Heaven we must, indeed, become again 'as little children.' We must get rid of our preconceived theories of what the Bible ought to be, in order to make out what it really is. The immense layers of Puritanic, Scholastic, Papal, Patristic systems which intervene between us and the Apostolic or Prophetic ages – the elevation of the point of view on which those ages stand above our own – aggravate the intensity of the effort to the natural sluggishness of the human heart and intellect. Thanks to Herder and to Coleridge, thanks to the *Christian Year* and to Arnold, thanks to Bishop Thirlwall and Archdeacon Hare, thanks to Archbishop Trench and Dean Milman, thanks to the *Essays and Reviews* and the *Aids to Faith*, thanks to the *Biblical Dictionary* and to Ewald, who have achieved, or helped to achieve, this work for us. So to discern the sacred past by the telescopic power of genius, and by the microscopic power of scholarship, is one of the chief ends for which universities and cathedrals are endowed, and for which Theology exists.

The general results are as great as the particular gains. This is the only solution of (what we sometimes erroneously call the great question of the day) the question of Inspiration. It is, properly speaking, no real theological doctrine which is at stake. What is or ought to be asked is a simple question of fact. These conflicts are the mere scintillations or filings thrown off by the friction between fact and theory. All that we have to ascertain is not what theories this or that man holds, or may claim to hold about the Bible, but what are the actual characteristics of the Bible itself. Find out what the sacred writers really said – what they really intended – and then, whatever it be, whether it be prose or poetry, poetry or history, exact accuracy, – scientific, historical, linguistic, – or manifold inaccuracies, contradictions, imperfections of language, science, and history, – that is part of the Bible, that is what must be included within the range of Biblical Inspiration. Every fact we thus ascertain from astronomer, geologist, ethnologist, scholar, or divine, is the best approach to the true solution of the only question at issue.

Again, it cannot be gainsayed that the paramount glory and power of the Bible has become far more evident to us by this nearer, closer investigation. I speak not here of that Divine Faith and supernatural spiritual excellence, which is wholly independent of all such lesser details, but of the increased profit, delight, veneration, derived from a knowledge even of these. Can any one, for example, doubt that the enjoyment which a merely ordinary student possesses of the Song of Deborah, or the Book of Job, far exceeds that of the Fathers and the Schoolmen, in whom those magnificent poems inspired hardly a spark of poetic recognition, who saw in them chiefly the repetition of allegories, which might equally well have been drawn from any other book whatever? Can any one doubt that the characters of David and St. Paul are better appreciated, more dearly loved, by a man like Ewald, who approaches them with a profound insight into their language, their thoughts, their customs, their history, than by a Scholastic or Puritanical divine from whom the atmosphere in which the King and the Apostle moved was almost entirely shut out?

And, further, if the original sources of the written Revelation be thus known to us in a manner in which they were not, and could not be, known before, is not this of itself almost equivalent to a new Reformation? Does not the very magnitude of the subject thus brought home to us throw our former systems of theology into new proportions? Is it possible that we can now return from this higher knowledge of the Bible to the grooves of the *Summa Theologiæ* or of the Westminster Confession? Most useful are these and like works in their place and for their own purposes. But wherever the Theology of the nineteenth century has spread, they are no longer in the first rank. The celebrated Benedictine monk, Padre Tosti, was speaking not long ago of the effects of modern criticism – partly with praise, partly with blame – 'At least,' he said, 'it has had this advantage, that it has caused you to shut up all your Symbolical Books [referring, of course, to the well-known collections of Reformed and Lutheran Confessions of Faith].' I do not say that it has done this; but it has placed them for the first time in entire subordination to the higher theology of the Scriptures, to which they have always before professed an obedience, never till now completely paid. And it is this which produces a kind of unity of religious thought unknown before since the sixteenth century. When French Catholics and French Protestants, and German Catholics and German Protestants, and English Churchmen and English Nonconformists, are for the first time employed in studying the same Book on the same general principles, it is impossible but that greater unity will emerge – greater unity of interest, if not of sentiment. Christian Theology ceases to be a collection of statements, hung on strings of texts often misapplied, and becomes a coherent attempt to ascertain the real design and scope of each book, each prophet, each apostle, in the different parts of the Bible – to know what we should lose were any of the sacred books struck out – what we gain by their recognition. Most applicable to this are the words of Lord Bacon – 'No perfect discovery can be made upon a flat or a level; neither is it possible to discover the more remote and deeper parts of any science, if you stand but upon the level of the same science and ascend not to a higher science.' That higher science has been given us by mounting into the higher region of the theologians of the Bible itself. . . .

1.4   THE 'REVOLUTION OF 1869'

The travails of the Church reached their consummation in a single year. Or so it seemed to George Anthony Denison (1805–1896), archdeacon of Taunton, and to other High Church critics of everything called progress in the history of England. With the passage by a Liberal parliamentary majority of an act to disestablish the Church of Ireland, followed by the nomination of Frederick Temple (1821–1902), the lead author of *Essays and Reviews*, to the see of Exeter by the Liberal prime minister, Gladstone, the will of the Church had been rudely cast aside. The extension of civil and religious liberties had brought about the revolution foreseen by the early Tractarians, Denison's old associates at Oxford, and schism was now inevitable (**1.4.1**). From the eye of the storm at Rugby School, where he was as yet the headmaster, Temple responded to his opponents in private letters. To a supporter in the Exeter diocese, where twenty per cent of the clergy, including Archdeacon Philip Freeman, signed a memorial against his nomination, he explained that, officially, conscience had sealed his lips. Nothing would induce him to narrow the limits of belief in the Church of England by acting as if people had a right to impose a test of orthodoxy beyond that of submission to the Thirty-nine Articles. The perils of doing so he set out in a letter to Archdeacon Freeman himself (**1.4.2**).

1.4.1   G. A. DENISON ON THE STATE OF THE CHURCH OF ENGLAND, 1869

I believe that English Churchmen are fast coming to see – what others, not being English Churchmen, have seen long ago, that, in the natural course of 'Civil and Religious Liberty,' the Church of England *cannot*, and *may not*, continue to be 'Established by Law' as 'the National Church.' *Cannot*, socially and politically: *may not*, religiously.

Men will of course differ widely as to the time and the circumstances under which this is, no longer a prospect but, a fact. They will also differ widely as to the exigency which not only justifies the ceasing to contend for 'Church and State,' but makes imperative, as matter of faithfulness to CHRIST, the active and steady endeavour to relieve the Church from all control of, or interference with her spiritual life on the part of the Civil Power.

For myself, having publicly contended for some thirty years for 'Church and State,' I have come to see that the contention is no longer admissible. I see not only that *theoretically*, the Church of England has ceased to be 'the National Church' by the Act of 1869, which has formally set aside, by the hand of the Crown and of the three Estates of the Realm in Parliament assembled, the only principle upon which a 'National Church' depends; but that, *practically,* the time and the exigency are come. The designation on the part of the Crown, of Dr Temple for the See of Exeter, has brought the matter to an issue from which there is no escape. It has filled up the measure nearly filled before with many offences against the Church.

But, great as is the sin of the Minister, there is a 'greater sin.' The Dean and Chapter who elect, and the Archbishop and Bishops who consecrate, will sin 'the greater sin.'

We know Who has said, 'Woe unto the world because of offences! for it must needs be that offences come, but woe to that man by whom the offence cometh.' What then of him who delights to honour the offender? What of those, who having proclaimed the 'offence,' and denounced it by their own Judgment, advance the offender with their own hands to the Bishop's throne?

In February, 1861, the two English Archbishops and twenty-four Bishops attached their signatures to a Declaration against the book called 'Essays and Reviews' as being 'essentially at variance with many fundamental Doctrines of the Church.'

On June 21, 1861, the Lower House of Convocation of Canterbury, upon the Report of its Committee, appointed by direction of the Upper House, March 14, 1861, resolved:

> That in the opinion of this House there are sufficient grounds for proceedings to a Synodical Judgment upon the book entitled 'Essays and Reviews.'

This Resolution, with a copy of the Report of the Committee, having been communicated to the Upper House, the Upper House resolved, July 9, 1861:—

> That His Grace the President be requested to communicate to the Lower House that this house, having taken into their consideration the communication of the Lower House, touching a book entitled 'Essays and Reviews,' have resolved:— 'That, whereas since this house formerly considered this question, a suit has been commenced against one of the writers of the said book for his contribution thereto; and whereas his Grace the President of this Synod, and the other Bishops, Privy Councillors, may, in the course of appeal, have to decide in the said suit judicially; and whereas it appears to this house inexpedient, either to proceed with the consideration of this subject in the absence of the President and such members of this house, or to embarrass them as to

hereafter sitting as Judges in the pending suit, by their having joined in a Synodical condemnation of the book, it is expedient to adjourn the further consideration of this subject pending the course of such suit.

On April 20, 1864, the Upper House received the Gravamen following, signed by forty members of the Lower House:—

That a remarkable instance of the injury which is caused to the Church by the confusion of jurisdictions now involved in the constitution of the Appeal Court, in respect of questions of alleged false doctrine, is found in the present position of the endeavour made by this house, June 21, 1861, to procure a Synodical condemnation of the book entitled 'Essays and Reviews:' inasmuch as the Upper House (which had directed the appointment of the Committee of this house), in acknowledging, July 9, 1861, the communication of the resolution of this house, founded upon the report of the Committee, declared it 'expedient to adjourn the further consideration of the subject pending the course of a suit instituted against one of the writers in the said book,' on the specific ground that 'the President of this Synod and other Bishops, Privy Councillors, might, in the course of appeal, have to decide the said suit judicially.'

That the suit having now been brought to a close, the injury done to the Church by the delay of Synodical judgment may be in part repaired by proceeding to such judgment.

The same day it was moved by the Bishop of Oxford, and carried—

That this house having received, on the 21st of June, 1861, from the Lower House, their resolution of June the 2nd, 1861, that in its opinion there are sufficient grounds for proceeding to a Synodical judgment on the 'Essays and Reviews;' and having on the 9th of July, 1861, adjourned the consideration of the subject pending the course of the then existing suit; and that suit being now concluded, – Resolved, that this house resume the consideration of the subject, and that a Committee of this house be appointed, first, to consider the communications made on this subject by the Lower House; secondly, to consider the book referred to in such communications; and thirdly, to report thereon to the house.

The Committee consisted of the Archbishop and Bishops of the Province of Canterbury. It was a Committee of the whole house. It reported, June 21, 1864, and the report was received and adopted.

The Bishop of Oxford then moved and carried the Resolution following:—

That the Upper House of Convocation, having received and adopted the report of the Committee of the whole house appointed by them to examine the volume entitled 'Essays and Reviews,' invite the Lower House to concur with them in the following Judgment:—

That this Synod, having appointed Committees of the Upper and Lower Houses to examine and report upon the volume entitled 'Essays and Reviews,' and the said Committees having, severally, reported thereon, doth hereby Synodically condemn the said volume, as containing teaching contrary to the Doctrine received by the United Church of England and Ireland, in common with the whole Catholic Church of CHRIST.

The above Resolution having been communicated to the Lower House, on June 21, 1864 I moved the Resolution following, which was carried June 24:—

That the house respectfully and heartily tenders its thanks to His Grace the President and the Bishops of the Upper House for their care in Defence of The Faith; and that this house does thankfully accept and concur in the condemnation of the book by the Upper House, to which their concurrence has been invited by the Upper House.

The Report of the Committee of the Upper House, referring to Essay I. – that of Dr Temple – has these words;—

The Committee regret to add that the argument of the first Essay (pp. 24–25) by denying the probability of the recognition of the Divinity of our LORD in the more matured age of the world, appears to them to involve a similar denial of all miracles as historical facts: for it is asserted that 'the faculty of Faith has turned inwards, and cannot now accept any outer manifestations of the Truth of GOD' (p. 24.)

Dr Temple has retracted nothing; and has disavowed nothing.

It is said that it will take many such blows as that which is falling now to make the Church of England learn the lesson of repentance and faithfulness to CHRIST. I believe it. I believe more – I believe that nothing but some terrible scourge from GOD will prevail to do this. Meantime we have blow after blow, each one in succession falling upon a more self-sufficient, self-righteous, and therefore upon a colder and a harder heart. . . .

Scepticism, Free-handling of the Scriptures, Infidelity are terrible things. What is to be said of the Church which denounces and condemns a book, the exponent of all these, in the only way in which it is in her power to do it; and a very few years after submits to receive at the hands of the Civil Power, and proceeds to consecrate as Bishop, by the hands of her Archbishop and Bishops, one of the writers of that book? Is there no fear among us of a jealous GOD? . . .

In the year of Grace, then, 1869, the British people – to use the name which describes the people collectively – have, for the first time in their history, formally declared by the act of an united Legislature that forms of faith are, from a national point of view, indifferent things. They have done more. They have dispossessed that particular form of faith, which three hundred years ago they established as 'The National Faith' – an Establishment witnessed to in many deaths by fire and sword. I use the words 'Established' and a 'Establishment' in their received acceptation, as expressing the relation of the State to the Church, settled, for England and for Ireland, by the concurrent operation of common and statute law in the 16th century. They have dispossessed it of place, and privilege, and power; and of means of doing its Master's work; of the remnants of its own rightful and legal inheritance. They have done more. They have done all this, not avowedly, indeed, but really, in favour of that particular form of faith which then and since they protested against, condemned, and excluded. They have done this in the year of Grace 1869; and this is what I call the Revolution of 1869, which, and none other, is the true name for it. There have been other revolutions, many of them full of blood; but there has never been one greater, more unprincipled, or more full of evil issues, than the Revolution of 1869. . . .

. . . Let me pray, my brother Churchmen in England, not to delude themselves, which I imagine not a few are still disposed to do, even with the case of Ireland staring them in the face. The freedom they so earnestly desire will only be freedom coupled with the spoiling of their goods – *i.e.,* of their trust property – liberty bought at the price of the greater part of the endowments remaining. For our present freedom, we all know what that is. The case of the Church is certainly a hard case. All else in England is free to do its own proper work. The one thing that is not free in England, to do its own proper work, is the Church of England. A Legislature of all religions and of no religion not only circumscribes and controls, but hinders and damages her actions at every step. All causes of her doctrine and discipline are subject to the final decision of a Court, which is, not only incompetent, but, morally and religiously unfit to decide. For the assertion that the Judicial Committee of Privy Council does not rule doctrine is untenable. The Court of Final Appeal, inter-preting the documents of the Church established by law, affixing or

OUR SIAMESE TWINS.

MR. BULL. "YOU DON'T THINK THE OPERATION WILL BE FATAL TO EITHER?"
DR. GLADSTONE. "OH, NO!"
DR. BRIGHT. "NOT A BIT!—DO 'EM BOTH ALL THE GOOD IN THE WORLD."

withholding penalties, and, in the last resort, regulating the keeping or the losing of a benefice with cure of souls, does rule what is and what is not the doctrine of the Church established by law; and no amount of special pleading can make its decision to be anything else. It is true that the whole force of the ruling turns upon the legal position; and it may be that the choice will soon have to be made between the legal position and Primitive and Catholic truth; but so long as the legal position subsists, the case is, I apprehend, as I have stated it. The conclusion is heavily weighted already with the anti-Catholic character of the judgment in the Gorham case; and of other judgments connected with the administration of the Holy Eucharist. The Gorham judgment has allowed heresy in the matter of the Sacrament of Holy Baptism. Other judgments have disallowed Primitive and Catholic symbols, and exponents of the doctrine of the Holy Eucharist. When there shall be a judgment *disallowing* the doctrine of either Sacrament as held and taught by the Church Primitive and Catholic, and, *therefore,* as held and taught by the Church of England, the measure will have been filled up.

The Act of 1828, commonly called the Test and Corporation Act, admitting Nonconformists to the Municipalities, was . . . a great step, therefore, *de facto* towards the overthrow of 'Church and State.' But this Act would of itself have availed little towards producing the present position, if it had not been for the Roman Catholic Emancipation Act of 1829. That Act brought an accession of Parliamentary strength to the adversaries of the United Church of England and Ireland, which, over-riding all the feeble and senseless securities comprised in the Act, has now prevailed to destroy the principle of a National Church for all this people. Nonconformists, for 300 years bent upon the overthrow of 'Church and State;' Roman Catholics, for 300 years bent upon the overthrow of the Church; men of no particular religion, and others – Churchmen themselves, but with anti-Church constituents and party exigencies to satisfy – have all combined, upon divers and conflicting principles, to make a huge majority in the House of Commons for the devastation of the National Church. To this majority of the Commons the majority of the Lords has made, to say the least of it, one of the poorest, weakest, and most abortive attempts at resistance upon record. Some Lords and other 'Conservatives' call it a battle; some go the length of calling it a drawn battle. I call it a defeat; from first to last a crushing, ignominious, and pitiable defeat. . . . It is true that very general applause has been heaped

2 Archdeacon Denison's complaint about Irish disestablishment personified in *Punch.* It was the thin end of the wedge, fatal to Irish and Anglican churches alike.

upon the Lords for their ability and eloquence, as shown in the debate which has had so miserable an issue. But I know of nothing more full of evil omen than applause like this. It is said, with much 'Liberal' condescension, that this exhibition of intellectual power has secured the House of Lords a fresh lease for some years. So much for the primary 'Liberal' test of worth and excellence in the nineteenth century. It is not the wisdom of the legislator which maintains at all costs a Divine trust, but the wisdom which invents excuses for not maintaining it, and clothes them in language able and eloquent, which has called forth the applause. Mr Gladstone has carried his bill for Nonconformity, and against 'Church and State;' but only by the help of the 'Conservative' Peers and of Rome. Rome has helped Nonconformity to win the battle against 'Church and State.' Nonconformity, in return, blind to its own certain fate, is helping Rome to win the battle against the Church. Non-religious men and political churchmen have tied themselves to the chariot wheels of the Church of Rome. The chariot rolls on steadily and surely, bearing within it the balance of Parliamentary power. The tree planted in 1829 has come to its full vigour in forty years. . . .

1.4.2   F. TEMPLE ON THE CONSCIENCE OF A BISHOP, 1869

RUGBY, *October* 16, 1869.

MY DEAR COOK

. . . To make any public statement or to answer any question appears to me to be quite inconsistent with my position. It would sanction a most dangerous precedent, sure to be imitated, and sure to have dangerous consequences.

Whatever you may think of it now, you may depend upon it, it would distinctly weaken me for my work. I should become a bishop more easily, but a damaged bishop.

But further, no statement that I could rightly make would disarm the opposition. If I say anything I must be full and open. A full and open statement would satisfy you. But it would be received with shrieks by —— and his followers. I preached a sermon in Whitehall some little time ago (which Gladstone at the time sent for and read) to express my belief, *inter alia,* that the beginning of Genesis was a poem, to be interpreted as we interpret the Apocalypse or the last part of Ezekiel. You very likely would disagree with such a view. But you would not say that a man who held it was no Christian. Yet the chief leaders of all this agitation would say that this was as bad as anything.

Lastly, though I am unwilling to bring in personal considerations in such a case, yet it is inevitable. What can a bishop be worth who has no regard for personal character? It would seem to me so inconsistent with all personal self-respect to say one word about the other writers of *Essays and Reviews,* that I cannot imagine anything that would induce me to do it directly or indirectly: certainly not a bishopric. A right-minded man *cannot* enter on such an office by beginning with what lowers him before his own conscience. . . .

One report I have heard that you may perhaps come across and wish to meet, viz., that I was the editor of the Book. I was not the editor, as I think you know; and I never saw any Essay but my own till the Book was published. I should not like to be quoted as saying this just now. But still it is a bare fact which you may as well know.

[Undated.]

MY DEAR ARCHDEACON

. . . It must be a matter of regret whenever pain or doubt or want of cordiality affects the relations between the clergy and the bishop. No diocese can fail to suffer if there be any degree of disagreement between those who ought to co-operate so entirely. But any man who reflects must see that this is the price we pay for the liberty that our Church, beyond all others, allows to its members and its officers. That liberty has repeatedly proved of the highest value. It has saved from extinction most valuable schools of thought which the Church could ill have spared. It has given the Church a more truly Catholic character than any other body of Christians now possesses. It has allowed a freer and truer study of God's works. It and it alone has made the Church national, and enabled it to satisfy those needs which only a National Church can satisfy.

Nothing would more seriously imperil this liberty than to commence a course of extorting declarations of opinion from those who happened to hold, or to be suspected of holding, whatever might be at the moment least popular. If this practice once began it would be easy to continue it, and to press it with perpetually increasing force. Those who now ask for it might live to find their own weapons turned against themselves with fatal effect. The pretext for such demands can be easily varied. Sometimes the plea is duty; sometimes charity and tenderness; sometimes the good of the Church. Sometimes the demand is enforced by a threat, and the declaration is made a condition of holding office. But the result is in every case the same; the first who yields may yield to persuasion; those who follow have to yield to compulsion. I have always refused to satisfy such demands, and must always continue to refuse. They seem to me inconsistent with the plainest duty to the Church and to our Lord. . . .

1.5   TESTS AND THE TESTAMENTS: OXFORD REVISITED

Anglican conservatism was dealt a further blow in 1871 when Gladstone's government passed an act opening all degrees and offices, except those tied to holy orders, to individuals of any religion and none at the universities of Oxford, Cambridge, and Durham. The bill did not proceed unopposed. On 8 May 1871, Lord Salisbury (1830–1903), chancellor of Oxford and later a Conservative prime minister, moved an amendment designed to protect the interests of Christian parents and to stem the 'moral infection' spread by the study of 'infidelity'. University tutors, he proposed, should be required to declare that in exercising their office, 'they will teach nothing contrary to the Divine authority and teaching of the Holy Scriptures of the Old and New Testament'. For the Liberal government, Lord Westbury (1800–1873), who as Lord Chancellor had given judgment on Colenso and the authors of *Essays and Reviews* in the Judicial Committee of the Privy Council, replied with inimitable scorn, and the amendment was eventually defeated (**1.5.1**). Thirty years later, the liberalizing effects of the Tests Act could be seen in the essays of *Lux Mundi* (1889) and in the reply to critics of the volume by the editor, Charles Gore (1853–1932), in his preface to the tenth edition (**1.5.2**). So far had the High Church party progressed that the main results of Old Testament criticism could now be reconciled with ecclesiastical authority; the Bible could be described as 'the record of the proclamation of the revelation, not the revelation itself'. All the authors of *Lux Mundi*, including Gore, had been students or tutors at Oxford.

1.5.1   LORDS SALISBURY AND WESTBURY ON THE UNIVERSITY TESTS BILL, 1871

THE MARQUESS OF SALISBURY: My Lords, . . . the most numerous of those who have urged the relaxation or abolition of the Tests are what are commonly called the orthodox Dissenters. To them the question at issue was not strongly a religious one, but rather one of political equality, of social standing, and of conflicting claims to certain endowments, some of which have descended from very ancient times. We think they are wrong; but they hold firmly and strongly that they have an equal claim with all Churchmen not only to these colleges, which had been dealt with summarily at the Reformation, but they hold also that as to the Universities, which possess national privileges, they have claims not only for equal education but also for an equal enjoyment of all their emoluments. These persons form the mass and strength of the agitation for this Bill; but they do not take the direction of it – its leadership and guidance are in the hands of men of very different aims and temperaments. Those who now direct the movement and the forces by which it is carried on desire something very different from an equal share of education and emolument between Church and Dissent. They desire that the dogmatic theology which has hitherto been considered identical with Christianity shall not be taught as of necessity in these national places of education, and that secular objects of study shall be put in a far superior position, and be treated as of more account than any religious instruction with reference to dogmatic belief. . . . Whatever jusification there may be for the claims which the Church has set up and in past years maintained for the exclusive enjoyment of the emoluments of the Universities, we are ready to concede two things – first, that in the existing political constitution those claims are hardly maintainable; and, secondly, that they are of infinitely smaller importance than the other matters involved in the issue before us. We value, of course, the secular rights of the Church, but we treat them as mere dirt compared to the paramount object of securing the supremacy of religion in the education of the young. That is the feeling that has guided us in making the recommendations that have been laid before you. Our recommendations are briefly these. We desire that all honours and emoluments, all fellowships and scholarships, shall be thrown open without distinction to all subjects of the Queen. We are further willing that all offices involving teaching shall be thrown open to all those who agree upon the essential points of Christianity – that is to say, to 99 out of every 100, and, indeed, a much larger proportion – of the population of these islands. We say, however, that the office of teaching rests upon a very different footing from the enjoyment of emoluments. . . . We propose that the tutors should be required to make a declaration – that is, a promise, that in the exercise of their office they will teach nothing contrary to the Divine authority and teaching of the Holy Scriptures of the Old and New Testament. That is the Motion which I shall place in the hands of the noble and learned Lord in the chair (Lord Redesdale) when I sit down. We also propose that the chapel services shall be obligatory; that sufficient religious instruction shall be given to those members of the Church of England in each college who desire it; that no one shall be forced against his conscience to attend any kind of lecture; and that the head of the college shall be excluded from the operation of the Bill. . . . Of course, the main point is the question whether tutors are by promise to be prevented from teaching doctrines contrary to the Divine authority and teaching of the Holy Scriptures. . . . The value of the test . . . is not a legal security, but it is a security in the court of honour or the court of conscience. We have not arrived at such a point that we are to suspect the generality of those who reach high academical position of a deliberate attempt to deceive or evade by subterfuge. I feel certain that there is no such danger. All the evidence we have received leads us rather to believe that any indication of the will of Parliament is received by those in the Universities with a devotion and an obsequiousness which to us of the outside world appear rather superstitious. I feel sure that when Parliament has indicated its intention, and when these men have pledged their personal honour to the promise that they will not teach anything contrary to the Scriptures, you are in the vast majority of instances absolutely secure against any breach of your confidence. It is not merely their personal feelings that you have to appeal to – and I believe in the majority of cases that would be quite enough. But all their teaching is carried on in public, in the presence of those who are sufficiently prone to criticism as it is, and they would certainly be looked on with little respect in their college or by their pupils if they deliberately, for the sake of proselytism, broke a solemn declaration deliberately made. In these days, when feelings of honour are very much stronger than, I regret to say, feelings of conscience are, I am sure that a declaration of this kind will not err upon the side of weakness, and that when you have obtained this promise from the tutors you may be quite certain that in the vast majority of cases it will not be broken. . . . Well, supposing it to be admitted that this test is efficacious, you will ask – 'Have we a right to enforce it?' It will be said – 'You are interfering with liberty of conscience.'. . . . The responsibility ought to be left to the colleges if you had left to the colleges the correlative of responsibility – namely, unrestricted liberty; but you have tied them up in every way. You have told them that they are no longer, as they did 20 years ago, to select fellows at their will, but are to be tied by the result of a competitive examination; and now you are about to tell them that they shall apply no test whatever to ascertain the religious or doctrinal fitness of those whom they select. If you thus set the Universities aside you put yourselves in their place; you accept their responsibility, and are bound to do that which they would have been bound to do – namely, to satisfy the parents who send their children there that you will fulfil the duties which the colleges formerly undertook. You have forcibly brought the colleges under control, and you stand as their representative and share their responsibility before the nation – or, rather, before the parents whose children you receive. I am conscious that in mentioning parents I am introducing what is deemed rather an ungenial element in the question of University education. Among University Liberals the popular view is that a parent is nothing but an inconvenient appendage to an undergraduate. I do not share their view. They repel with extreme irritation the idea that their magnificent philosophies and splendid researches are to be subjected to anything so prosaic as the wishes of the parents whose children they educate. I take a different view, and look at all this grand machinery as merely representing the relations of employer and employed. Parents employ the University to educate their children. If you left it free, I have no doubt it would consult their wishes; but if you deprive the colleges of their liberty and force them to educate as you like, you then assume the same responsibility towards the parents. You are the employed, and it is your business to bring up the children in the manner desired by the parents. The question narrows itself to this – Is there any danger in the present state of the Universities that young men, if the Bill passes, will be brought up in a manner to which the parents will object? If there is any moral infection that taints the air – if there is any spiritual evil creeping over the Universities or threatening to do so – it is your duty, having accepted the responsibilities of the colleges and Universities, to take sufficient measures of precaution that this infection shall not spread, and that this poison shall not infect those committed to your care. Is there any such poison? Nobody who watches the literature of the day can be unaware that in a very narrow, though influential, class of society there exists a strong tendency to extreme speculation – that there is a bitter hostility to Christianity itself, and that that hostility has reached such a point that they will rather advocate the most *bizarre* and extravagant propositions than accept Christian belief. That is the state of things to a terrible extent on the Continent. I am happy to say that it prevails to a much smaller extent in this country; but still we all know that we can lay our hands on half a dozen influential publications of recent times which have for their principal objects to destroy the beliefs on which the hopes of Christians rest. . . . One of the most striking facts brought out by the investigation of the Committee has been that in one of the Universities, at least, not only is there a full response to whatever infidel invitations modern literature may hold out, but that the studies of the University itself are affected in a manner which, if it had the free course given to it by this Bill, would lead to the most terrible and dangerous results. The most important evidence on this point is that of a gentleman who is in favour of the Bill, and whose evidence, therefore, is all the more entitled to weight. Mr. Charles Appleton, a fellow of St. John's College, Oxford, and a gentleman of distinguished literary reputation, gives this evidence— . . .

> So far as I know, the strictest and most delicate reticence is always observed in approaching the mind of a young man, so as not to upset his beliefs; but I believe the upsetting of his beliefs, and the entire loosening of them from all their moorings, is an inevitable consequence of the system of education which now exists in Oxford.

[*Ministerial cheers.*] I think I can interpret that cheer. It means that even under a system of tests these things will happen. This, however, is not the deliberate action of the fellows of colleges, or tutors, or examiners. This is, so to speak, the automatic and mechanical result of the mode of study, the subjects of study, and the time allowed to study. Within three years it is expected that a man is to master most difficult subjects of metaphysical study. He is expected, according to the same witness, to—

> Read Spinoza, Hobbes – I do not say all, of course, but portions of their writings – portions of Locke, of Berkeley, and of Hume are also read, and the *First Principles* and *Psychology* of Mr. Herbert Spencer are beginning to be very widely studied.

Kant and Hegel are also among the authors studied. The natural result is that, having to master these things within a limited time, and being forced to complete his line of study before the examination comes on, he has no time to enter into the opposite arguments. Negative philosophy is the easiest to master, and will carry most honours in the schools, and that is all which the young man, or those who press him forward, care for. Whatever the cause, here, at all events, is the result, as stated by a liberal witness favourable to the Bill – that the present system of education tends to unloosen all belief. . . . Canon Liddon, also, with whose name, and probably with whose words, many of your Lordships are well acquainted, says—

> Cases have come within my own experience of men who have come up from school as Christians, and have been earnest Christians up to the time of beginning to read philosophy for the final school, but who, during the year and a-half or two years employed in this study, have surrendered, first their Christianity and next their belief in God, and have left the University not believing in a Supreme Being.

With that knowledge and that testimony I think I may well say that the question raised by this Bill is not a question between Church and Dissent, but between Christianity and infidelity. Now, I think none of your Lordships will doubt that the parents of England, if their opinions could be collected, would strongly object to submit their sons to teaching of persons of this kind. Some persons, I know, entertain a notion that the proper way to educate a young man of 18 is to put before him all the arguments and systems of belief which ever have been or can be devised, and let him take his choice; but I am quite convinced that no such notion will ever commend itself to the general mass of parents in this country. They are well aware that thorny questions of controversy are not fit for men of unripe and unpractised minds, and that the only effect of asking them to choose impartially between all beliefs is to make them think that no belief is of much importance, and that at an age when temptations are strongest they may come to the conclusion that the moral maxims which rest on belief and belief alone are mere ancient and valueless superstitions. I am sure that no more certain method, not only of dechristianizing, but demoralizing the youth of the classes who send their children to the Universities could be found than subjecting them to the influence of tutors who would start with the idea that all beliefs should be submitted for free selection to the consciences and intelligences of their pupils. The only argument that remains in support of this Bill is the common phrase that public opinion has decided in its favour. I utterly deny it. Public opinion has never decided the issue as we have put it, and has never had that issue before it. . . . Will the constituencies of the country . . . or will they not sustain the doctrine that the first and most important point of education is religion, and that education which is not Scriptural is worse than no education at all? That is the issue we have to lay before them. . . .

LORD WESTBURY: My Lords, I have listened with sincere regret, and with some alarm, to the dreadful picture which has been drawn of the moral and religious condition of the University. If that picture be true, I regret there is no warning voice to dispel the notion that the University is a temple of religion, and to proclaim instead that it is a den of infidelity and hypocrisy. Now, how has this result been produced? Has it been produced by the want of tests? Has it been produced by the want of bigotry? I tell you how it has been produced. You have for centuries insisted that the University of Oxford should be deemed the special inheritance of the Church of England. You have insisted that nothing but dogmatic theology should be taught there. And now the human mind, rising up against that system, takes its revenge by inculcating a greater amount of liberality in proportion to the fetters you have imposed upon it. What the noble Marquess (the Marquess of Salisbury) proposes is a sheer mockery, and worse than a mockery. Just consider for a moment what will be the operation of this test. By whom is a tutor appointed now? Either by the heads of colleges or the Governing Body. If he takes from the men who appoint him this obligation, who is to determine when the obligation is fulfilled? Primarily the persons who appoint. But then the person who is appointed, appealing from the judgment of those who appoint, goes to the Visitor of his college. Now, instead of furnishing any real security, the words which the noble Marquess has selected will, in my opinion, serve no other end but to raise a difficult question, on which hardly two of those to whom the appeal may be made will ultimately be found to agree. The law, therefore, to which the tutors are to be subjected will be uncertain and unknown. But *misera est servitus, ubi jus vagum aut incognitum.* Again, consider for a moment who it is whom you will drive from the office of tutor by requiring that this test should be taken. You will drive from it the conscientious man, because he will say – 'I am called upon to take on myself a solemn obligation, and I know not by what standard the fulfilment of that obligation is to be measured.' The independent man also will say – 'I am called upon to fulfil a solemn duty; but whether I fulfil it or not is to be determined first by the judgment of one and then by the judgment of another.' The tutor of College A will be subjected to a different judgment from the tutor of College B. What, then, will be the result of the noble Marquess's provision? To drive men from the office of tutor who are worthy of it, and to place in it those who care nothing about it or the mode in which it is administered. Is this the sort of provision with the view to the security of religion which comes from the noble Marquess the Chancellor of the University of Oxford? Will it not be a mockery, and will it not end in introducing a miserable hypocrisy into our Universities? What is its object unless it is to secure religious teaching? But in order to have religious teaching you must have religious teachers, and you cannot bind men by this form of words; nor by a standard which in truth is no standard at all, and which allows it to be decided by every feeble man's judgment, whether the obligation has or has not been complied with. I quite concur with the noble Marquess in the opinion that the foundation of all teaching should be the sanctions of religion; I entirely agree with him in his desire that religious teaching should be carried into effect in our Universities: – and I am happy to say that having spent yesterday and the antecedent day at the University of Oxford, and having visited St. Mary's and some chapels in Oxford, I observed there nothing to justify the strictures which the noble Marquess has passed on the state of religion in that University – strictures which, were it not for the source from which they have proceeded, I might almost be tempted to designate as a slander. Let us trust the Universities freely. For my part I am not afraid of the tutors of our Universities, either in point of religion, morality, or acquisition; but if you rely upon this miserable substitute for better things, you may depend upon it that while you get men in whose case it will be no security, you will shut the door against men animated by the highest motives, but which highest motives can be found only in company with great liberty of thought and great liberty of conscience. I trust the noble Marquess will have more confidence in the University over which he so worthily presides than to insist upon this test, which is unnecessary, unworthy, and incomplete – which will serve only to generate endless controversies, instead of producing that harmony which it is so desirable should exist. . . .

1.5.2   C. GORE ON THE RESULTS OF BIBLICAL CRITICISM, 1890

. . . I do not think that we can conceal from ourselves that if we are to defend a purely conservative attitude in regard to Old Testament litera-ture, we shall require quite different canons of evidence from those which we are able so successfully to use in vindicating the historical character of the New Testament: or again, in vindicating the claims of the apostolic ministry and the sacramental system to be part of the original fabric of the Christian Church. In other words, the critical principles of historical enquiry which *do* so amply justify us in retaining substantially the traditional position in regard as well to the New Testament documents as to our Church principles, *do not* carry us to the same point in the field of the Old Testament. No doubt there the vastness of the field is a permanent obstacle to uniformly certain results. A great deal must remain, and probably for ever, more or less an open question. But this necessary uncertainty, if it imposes on critics an obligation of caution, imposes also on us churchmen an obligation of reserve in dogmatic requirement. We do not wish to run the risk of making a claim on men's minds for the acceptance of positions for which we have only this to urge, that they cannot be absolutely disproved. . . .

No serious attempt has, I think, been made to show that the view of the development of the Old Testament literature which the modern critical schools, with great unanimity, demand of us, is contrary to any determination of Church authority. By this it is not meant that the theology of the Church suggests this view: it is not the function of the Church to advance literary knowledge, except indirectly; and thus the Church has not had the power to anticipate the critical, any more than it had to anticipate the scientific movement. The advance of knowledge comes in all departments through the natural processes of intellectual enquiry. It is only now, in fact, that the critical problem is before the Church; but now that it is before the Church it does not seem that the Church ought to have any *more* difficulty in welcoming it and assimilating it, than it has had in welcoming and assimilating the legitimate claims of science. . . .

But does the authority of our Lord bind us to repudiate, in loyalty to Him, the modern views of the origin of the Old Testament books? On this subject I wish to express my sincere regret that I should have written so briefly in my essay as to lay myself open to be misunderstood to suggest our Lord's fallibility as a teacher. I trust that the passage, as it has stood since the fourth edition, will be at least recognised as plain in its meaning and theologically innocent. I must ask leave to defer to another occasion the fuller discussion of this important subject in connection with the doctrine of the Person of Christ. Meanwhile I would suggest that the longer one thinks of it the more apparent it will become that *any hypothesis as to the origin of any one book of the Old Testament, which is consistent with a belief in its inspiration, must be consistent also with our Lord having given it His authorisation.* If His Spirit could inspire it, He, in that Spirit, could give it His recognition – His recognition, that is to say, in regard to its spiritual function and character. Thus as we scan carefully our Lord's use of the Old Testament books, we are surely struck with the fact that nothing in

His use of them depends on questions of authorship or date; He appeals to them in that spiritual aspect which abides through all changes of literary theory – their testimony to the Christ: 'Search the Scriptures . . . they are they which testify of Me.' He would thus lead men to ask about each book of the Old Testament simply the question, – What is the element of teaching preparatory to the Incarnation, what is the testimony to Christ, which it supplies? I do not see how with due regard to the self-limitation which all use of human forms of thought and speech must on all showing have involved to the Eternal Son, it can be a difficulty in the way of accepting the modern hypothesis, that our Lord referred to the inspired books under the only name by which His reference would have been intelligible to His hearers. Unless He had violated the whole principle of the Incarnation, by anticipating the slow development of natural knowledge, He must have spoken of the Deuteronomist as 'Moses,' as naturally as He spoke of the sun 'rising.' Nor does there seem in fact any greater difficulty in His speaking of one who wrote 'in the spirit and power' of Moses as Moses, than in His speaking of one who, according to the prophecy, came 'in the spirit and power of Elias' as himself, Elias. 'If ye will receive it, this is Elias.' 'Elias is already come.'

Once more: if the Holy Spirit could use the tradition of the flood to teach men about divine judgments, then our Lord in the same Spirit can refer to the flood, for the same purpose. It has however been recently denied that this can be so, unless the tradition accurately represents history. 'I venture to ask,' Professor Huxley writes, 'what sort of value as an illustration of God's method of dealing with sin has an account of an event that never happened?' I should like to meet this question by asking another. Has the story of the rich man and Lazarus any value as an illustration of God's method of dealing with men? Undoubtedly it has. Now what sort of narrative is this? Not a narrative of events that actually happened, in the sense that there was a particular beggar to whom our Lord was referring. The narrative is a *representative* narrative, a narrative of what is constantly occurring under the form of a particular typical incident. Now the narrative of the flood belongs to a quite different class of literature, inasmuch as it is not due to any *deliberate* action of imagination; but it resembles our Lord's story *at least* in being representative. It is no doubt based on fact. The traditions of the flood in all races must run back to a real occurrence. But the actual occurrence cannot be exactly estimated. What we have in Genesis is a tradition used as a vehicle for spiritual teaching. As the story is told it becomes, like that of Dives and Lazarus, a typical narrative of what is again and again happening. Again and again, as in the destruction of Jerusalem, or in the French Revolution, God's judgments come on men for their sin: again and again teachers of righteousness are sent to warn of coming judgment and are ridiculed by a world which goes on buying and selling, marrying and giving in marriage, till the flood of God's judgment breaks out and overwhelms them. Again and again, through these great judgments there emerges a remnant, a faithful stock, to be the fountain head of a new and fresh development. The narrative of the flood is a representative narrative, and our Lord, who used the story of Dives and Lazarus, can use this too.

Professor Huxley's article alluded to just now is a somewhat melancholy example of a mode of reasoning which one had hoped had vanished from 'educated circles' for ever – that namely which regards Christianity as a 'religion of a book' in such sense that it is supposed to propose for men's acceptance a volume to be received in all its parts as on the same level, and in the same sense, Divine. On the contrary, Christianity is a religion of a Person. It propounds for our acceptance Jesus Christ, as the revealer of the Father. The test question of the Church to her catechumens has never been: 'Dost thou believe the Bible?' but 'Dost thou believe that Jesus Christ is the Son of God?' If we do believe that, then we shall further believe in the Bible: in the Old Testament as recording how God prepared the way for Christ: in the New Testament as recording how Christ lived and taught, and containing the witness borne to Him by His earthly friends and ministers. The Bible thus 'ought to be viewed as not a revelation itself, but a record of the proclaiming and receiving of a revelation, by a body which is still existent, and which propounds the revelation to us, namely the body of Christians commonly called the Church.' The Bible is the record of the proclamation of the revelation, not the revelation itself. The revelation is in the Person of Christ, and the whole stress therefore of *evidential* enquiry should be laid upon the central question whether the Divine claim made for Jesus Christ by the Church is historically justified. The whole evidential battle of Christianity must thus be fought out on the field of the New Testament, not of the Old. If Christ be God, the Son of God, incarnate, as the Creeds assert, Christianity is true. No one in that case will find any permanent difficulty in seeing that in a most real sense the Bible, containing both Old and New Testaments, is an 'inspired volume.'

Now faith in the Godhead of our Lord is very far from being a mere matter of 'evidences.' On this enough is said by more than one writer in this volume. But so far as 'historical evidences' go, we have them in our generation in quite fresh force and power. For our New Testament documents have passed through a critical sifting and analysis of the most trenchant and thorough sort in the fifty years that lie behind us. From such sifting we are learning much about the process through which they took their present shape. But in all that is material we feel that this critical investigation has only reassured us in asserting the historical truth of the records on which our Christian faith rests. This reassurance has been both as to the substance, and as to the quality of the original apostolic testimony to Christ. As to its substance, because the critical investigation justifies us in the confident assertion – more confident as the investigation has been more thorough than ever before – that the Christ of our four Gospels, the Christ with His Divine claim and miraculous life-giving power, the Christ raised from the dead the third day and glorified at God's right hand, the Christ who is the Son of God incarnate, is the original Jesus of Nazareth, as they beheld Him and bore witness who had been educated in closest intercourse with Him. We are reassured also as to the quality of the apostolic testimony. In some ages testimony has been careless – so careless, so clouded with superstition and credulity, as to be practically valueless. But in the apostles we have men who knew thoroughly the value of testimony and what depended upon it, who bore witness to what they had seen, and in all cases, save in the exceptional case of S. Paul, to what they had seen over a prolonged period of years; whose conviction about Christ had been gradually formed in spite of much 'slowness of heart,' and even persistent 'unbelief'; formed also in the face of Sadducean scepticism and in the consciousness of what would be said against them; formed into such irresistible strength and unanimity by the solid impress of facts that nothing could shake it, either in the individual or in the body. Such testimony does all for us that testimony can do in such a case. It supports externally and justifies a traditional faith, which is commended to us at the same time internally by its self-evidencing power. And with that faith as the strength of our life we can await with confidence the issue of minor controversies.

It may be hoped that the discussion which this book has raised may do good in two ways.

It may enable people to put the Bible into its right place in the fabric of their Christian belief. It may help to make it plain that in the full sense the Christian's faith is faith only in a Person, and that Person Jesus Christ: that to justify this faith he needs from the Scriptures only the witness of some New Testament documents, considered as containing history: while his belief in the Bible as inspired is, speaking logically, subsequent to his belief in Christ, and even, when we include the New Testament, subsequent to his belief in the Church, as the Body of Christ, rather than prior to it.

There is also another good result to which we may hope to see the present controversy minister – the drawing of a clear line in regard to development between the Old Testament and the New. For all modern criticism goes to emphasize the gradualness of the process through which, under the Old Covenant, God prepared the way for Christ. Now all that can be brought to light in this sense, the Church can await with indifference from a theological point of view, because it is of the essence of the Old Testament to be the record of a gradual self-disclosure of God continuous and progressive till the incarnation of Jesus Christ. It is, on the other hand, of the essence of the New Testament revelation that, as given in Christ and proclaimed by His apostles, it is, as far as this world is concerned, in its substance, final and adequate for all ages. It is this, because of its essential nature. If Christ is 'the Word made flesh,' the 'Son of God made Son of Man,' then finality essentially belongs to this disclosure of Godhead and this exhibition of manhood. 'He that hath seen Him hath seen the Father,' and he that hath seen Him hath seen perfect man, hath seen our manhood in its closest conceivable relation to God, at the goal of all possible spiritual and moral development. All our growth henceforth can only be growth into 'the measure of the stature of His fulness' – a growth into the understanding and possession of Him who was once manifested. Finality is of the essence of the New Covenant, as gradual communication of truth was of the Old.

If these two results are obtained, we shall not be liable any more to be asked 'where we are going to stop' in admitting historical uncertainty. 'If you admit so much uncertainty in the Old Testament, why do you not admit the same in the New?' We shall not be liable to be asked this question, because it will be apparent that the starting-point as of enquiry, so of security, lies in the New Testament and then proceeds to extend itself to the Old. For us, at least, the Old Testament depends upon the New, not the New upon the Old.

Nor shall we be liable any more to be asked, 'Why, if you admit so much development in actual substance in the truth revealed under the Old Covenant, cannot you admit a similar augmentation under the New?' This question will be prevented, because it will be apparent that the essential conditions are different in the two cases. Progress in Christianity is always reversion to an original and perfect type, not addition to it: it is progress only in the understanding of the Christ. 'Regnum tuum, Domine, regnum omnium saeculorum; et dominatio tua in omni generatione et generationem.'

1.6   A PARTING VIEW: LESLIE STEPHEN

By the end of Victoria's reign the Broad Church spirit of critical enquiry and moral synthesis had penetrated to some extent almost everywhere within the Church of England. But this apparent triumph for the ideals of Maurice, Jowett, and Stanley was not achieved bloodlessly. While Colenso and others were hunted down as heretics and excommunicated, many sensitive Anglicans immolated themselves. In the middle decades of the century there was a notable haemorrhage of talent to the ranks of 'unbelief'. Leslie Stephen (1832–1904), of impeccable evangelical ancestry, was ordained a priest in 1859. He left the Church under pressure of the controversies of the ensuing decade and became the nation's leading literary agnostic, the editor of the *Dictionary of National Biography,* and the father of Virginia Woolf. In 1870 he explained why even the Broad Church enclave, the last outpost of 'thinking men' within the Church of England, could not sustain his faith. He used with telling effect the case of Charles Voysey, the Yorkshire vicar subsequently ejected from the Church on appeal to the Judicial Committee of the Privy Council. His basic charge, suitably hedged to avoid recriminations, was one of intellectual dishonesty. By subtle manipulation of meanings, Broad Churchmen deceived both themselves and their parishioners into thinking that ancient creeds and formularies could still serve as the basis of a vital and united Church. Stephen – still an evangelical at heart – loftily deplored the moral influence of their failure to speak truthfully and sincerely, but his essay none the less remains the most memorable analysis of a dominant tendency in contemporary Anglican thought.

ON THE INFLUENCE OF THE BROAD CHURCH PARTY, 1870

. . . Is it desirable that men who believe that many of the popular views of Christianity are erroneous and immoral, but who believe nevertheless that Christianity in some sense will be the ultimate religion of the world, should hold on to the Established Church, should use the old formulæ and trust they will gradually purify themselves from that 'crust of human error,' or that they should break with the old state of things and try a fresh start? Is it time for adaptation or for entire reconstruction? Shall we have the best standing-ground by demanding reform from within or from without? Is there vitality enough in the existing organisation to give promise of a renewed vigour when it is freed from the dead excrescences which hamper and impede its growth; or must we decide that the constraints which it imposes more than counter-balance the advantages which it offers? There is always fair ground for hesitation at such a period as the present. It is difficult to decide the precise point of time at which wise conservatism passes into obstructiveness. Many of the best men amongst us will have the tenderest attachment to the old beliefs and be most reluctant to give up even the old phraseology. Whatever claims are still possessed by the Church of England to the allegiance of thinking men are due to the Broad Church element amongst the clergy. Evangelicals may still appeal to the large class of partial cultivation which finds all religion insipid without plenty of damnation; and the High Church may gather round it the increasing numbers who hate and dread the progress of intellectual freedom. Both of them may have great merits in point of practical zeal. But were it not that a party of equal sincerity and greater breadth of opinion still remains within the Church, it would be hard for any male person of liberal views to have anything to do with it. Such a man would stand aside and let the dead bury their dead. He would be curious to know how long a creed can retain its vitality after the brains had been taken out, but would take little interest in the precise details of the decay which must inevitably ensue. . . .

. . . The greatest danger to which we are exposed at the present moment is not that people find the old faiths failing them, but that they begin to doubt that there is anywhere such a thing to be found as faith in anything. A father naturally shrinks from telling his children that the biblical stories which they hear at school or from their mother are not undoubted truths. A clever child probably strikes out some little fragment of scepticism; he doubts whether all the animals in the Zoological Gardens could have been got into the ark; or whether Samson could have found the jaw-bone of an ass so effective a weapon as is represented in the Bible. His parent probably tells him that good little boys believe all that their masters say. Presently the boy grows towards manhood and learns without much trouble that Samson's jawbone and Noah's ark are reckoned amongst childish fables by his own father and by most sensible men. The discovery gives a much greater shock to his faith than he would have received from an originally frank explanation, and had he always believed that the adventures of Samson were as little to be relied upon and had as little to do with rational religion as the adventures of Hercules. He begins to discover, or to think he discovers, that religions are preached, not because they are true, but because they are a highly convenient substitute for police regulations. There may be no such place as hell, but we can't afford to let the criminal classes into the secret. We all make-believe as hard as we possibly can; we go to church with the most praiseworthy punctuality; we shake our heads at the preacher's lamentations over the progress of rationalism; and some of us go home to lunch and treat the whole history as Socrates treated the polytheism of his time. It was highly useful, but not worth arguing seriously with intelligent people. . . .

. . . The argument of Christian apologists has undergone a singular change. The old advocates of orthodox opinions said, in substance, Believe this because it is true. The sum and substance of most modern advocacy is, Believe this, true or not true, because it is convenient. It is hard indeed to find what is the ultimate foundation upon which most modern controversialists would rest their arguments in the last resort. They play so many tricks with faith and reason that we are puzzled to say precisely in what name they speak. But the whole tendency of a large and zealous school is to deny the competence of reason, which when put into plain English and stripped of all the ingenious logical devices by which we may be perplexed and thrown off the scent, amounts pretty much to denying that the question whether a doctrine is or is not true, is a relevant argument in deciding whether we are to believe it. . . . The apologists do not attempt to prove that the events recorded in the Bible really happened, or possess such evidence as would convince a reasonable man; but confine themselves to showing that it is not proved that they did not happen. We can believe them without encountering any invincible shock to our credulity, if we try very hard to believe them; and that is quite enough for our imaginations, if we are not wicked enough to be troublesome with our critical faculties. Religion, in short, is so beautiful a thing; it gives such fine scope for our best emotions; it affords such healthy exercise for the soul, that we ought to believe all the dogmas upon which it is founded without looking closely upon the evidence. Nobody wants to know whether Homer is an accurate historian before enjoying his poetry; it is enough that we can grant to him, so long as we are reading him, a sufficient degree of belief to be delighted with the pictures set before us. In the same way, we may derive as much pleasure from St. John or St. Paul, whether all the anecdotes of their lives are founded on fact or merely poetical images.

When language approaching to this, though neither so frank nor so extravagant, is openly talked, it is in fact a concession to the covert scepticism of which I have spoken. Christianity, says the freethinker, is very good for women and children and clergymen; but it is not worth the serious discussion of educated men. Putting this sentiment into a decent theological dress, it is the equivalent of the theological assertion, that religion is a matter of faith and not of reason. The two parties may be perfectly harmonious; and a kind of tacit compact may be arranged in virtue of which we may talk as we please in private, but allow the clergy to have their say in public, and affect to shrug our shoulders at Voltaire and his more scientific successors.

Such an arrangement is common enough amongst educated Roman Catholics; and is commoner than is generally admitted in England. I need not argue that it is essentially immoral and must ultimately be ruinous to the creed which accepts so treacherous a support. The Broad Church, however, distinguish themselves by repudiating any such compromise in theory. They tell us with a frankness which does them honour, that the Bible records must be tested by every method which the ingenuity of critics has discovered, and that they do not ask us to accept it unless it will stand an examination as searching as we should demand in the case of profane history: or as Mr. Jowett forcibly put it that the Bible must be criticised 'like any other book.' They assert further that Christianity must be divine because its moral teaching is incomparably purer than that of any other creed, and includes and reconciles all the half-thoughts of merely human creatures; they admit that if these propositions could not be established, if it could be proved that the Christian morality were imperfect or positively erroneous we should be bound to reject it. They confess that the ultimate test of religious truth must lie in its conformity to our moral sense and the historical accuracy of the assertions upon which it is founded. They therefore ask for our belief on straight-forward grounds and do not seek to perplex the question by irrelevant appeals to considerations which could have no weight in the court of pure reason. Every fair reasoner is therefore bound to respect them even if (as I confess is the case with me) he is compelled to reject their conclusions. . . . The great merit of Broad Churchmen, in my eyes, is that they meet argument fairly, and admit in theory the importance of searching, fair, and unfettered inquiry. If they admitted it in practice as well as in theory, there would be no more to be said.

Is there then anything about them which may lead us to believe not that they are consciously insincere but that they do not in practice allow free play to the convictions thus stated?

To this it must be answered that there is one cause of bewilderment to everybody who has studied the writings of the school. . . . Our creed still contains a vast number of obsolete dogmas which are kept for show instead of for use. . . . The Articles are an expression of the views about theology current in this part of the British islands in the sixteenth century; they embody all sorts of dogmas which have floated down from distant ages, the sense of many of them entirely evaporating on the road; they represent the best available compromise which could be struck out under the circumstances of the time; and it need not be said that the whole current of modern thought has ebbed away from many of the questions discussed and left nothing but the bare husks of extinct opinions which for ordinary Englishmen have next to no significance. Next comes a gentleman of great candour and abilities, thoroughly versed in all modern philosophy, who professes to have started from first principles, to have worked out his conclusions without fear or favour; to have followed the united teaching of reason and revelation wherever it led him; and behold! he discovers that these Articles exactly express his very deepest convictions in the most unequivocal language. When such a phenomenon occurs, as it sometimes does, I must confess it gives me a very unpleasant sensation. One of two conclusions is inevitable. Either there is a coincidence which may almost be called miraculous; if Lord Bacon or the wisest man of his time, whoever he was, had drawn up a scheme of politics, we should now have pronounced it defective and erroneous, and altogether beside the modern modes of thought; theology has undergone a change not less profound and extensive; yet this formula, drawn up by men ignorant of our modern doubts and convictions, turns out to be so flexible or to have such vitality that it exactly expresses the ripest conclusions of an eminent modern thinker, – a result which is to me as singular as if the strategies of days before gunpowder were precisely suitable for the era of ironclads and Henry rifles. Or else – and I confess this is the only conclusions at which I could arrive – the eminent modern thinker, like many other eminent men, has been unconsciously biassed in his reasonings by the desire to reach certain foregone conclusions.

It is this constantly recurring difficulty which, as it seems to me, damages very seriously the influence of the Broad Church party. They protest, and I doubt not with perfect sincerity, that they throw aside all considerations except the simple desire of discovering the truth. And yet their investigations always end in opinions which are at least capable of expression in the words of the most antiquated formulæ. It is as if a man should say that he always steered due north and yet his course should invariably take him safely through all the shoals and tortuosities of the Thames and land him conveniently at Lambeth stairs. I should think that there must be something very odd about his compasses. We talk of the dishonesty of the men who sidle up to the Roman Catholic Church in spite of every obstacle raised by rubrics and Privy Council decisions. I do not believe that many, if any, such men are consciously dishonest; but I do believe that precisely the same argument may be urged with precisely the same force against those who are trying to accommodate the Church of England doctrines to semi-rationalist views.

I can, of course, anticipate the answer which may be made with some plausibility, and it deserves its due weight. By good fortune, it is said, the tests were originally so lax and they have since been so much strained and loosened that the articles and other formularies of the Church of England are compatible with the widest divergence of sentiment. This statement, however, requires a little examination. Every one will of course admit that a man is not bound legally or morally by the popular glosses (to use an expression from a remarkable paper, to which I must directly recur) which have been put upon the Articles. He is not bound to hold, as some people appear to hold, that every word of the authorised version is strictly true. Dr. Temple, for example, said in his first sermon at Exeter (if he was correctly reported and if I understood the report correctly) that, whilst every part of the Bible which concerned our spiritual welfare was strictly true, it was not made out that the same accuracy could be predicated of the historical records of unimportant circumstances. In other words, statements may possibly be false, whose truth or falsehood is not of the slightest importance to any human being; we must accept all about the delivery of the Law or the massacre of the Canaanites, but we may dispute as to the name of Abraham's father, or doubt whether a day in the first chapter of Genesis means a day. So modified a degree of freethinking could shock nobody's faith; and it is not inconsistent with the most impartial interpretation of the Articles. But between Dr. Temple and such men as Bishop Colenso or Mr. Voysey there is a wide interval. Dr. Temple might naturally feel not merely that he could conscientiously sign the tests but that the formularies of the Church provided the most natural expression for his religious convictions. I am only speaking of those members of the Broad Church whose sentiments seem to fit with a certain awkwardness into the phraseology officially provided for them; and who substantially argue that they are justified in using rather strained versions of ordinary language, because the law has sanctioned very wide methods of interpretation. As there are so many shades of opinion, it is impossible to speak in terms applicable to the whole party; nor do I in fact argue that the same course would be appropriate for all. I will therefore take one, and it must be admitted, an extreme case, by way of illustrating the point. Mr. Voysey exemplifies the most advanced stage of opinion at which a man can very well claim to remain within the Church. Whether his position is legal or not is still an open question; but I have the less scruple in quoting from his very powerful defence because, as he himself remarks, his desire to remain within the Church cannot possibly be imputed to interested motives. . . .

Mr. Voysey was accused of heretical teaching in regard to the doctrines of the Atonement, of Justification by Faith, of the Incarnation, and of the Inspiration of the Bible. He admits, or rather proclaims, that he disputes the popular interpretation of all those doctrines. But he asserts that his view is within the liberty allowed by law to the clergy. Supposing these statements to be justified, let us see what his position would be. I will take one or two specimens of his general line of argument. The 2nd Article, he says, tells us that 'the Son was crucified, dead and buried, to reconcile his Father to us, and to be a sacrifice, not only for original guilt, but also for all actual sins of men.' The 31st Article adds that 'the offering of Christ once made is that perfect redemption, propitiation, and satisfaction for all the sins of the whole world, both original and actual: and there is none other satisfaction for sin but that alone.' The assertion contained in these words, says Mr. Voysey, is a mystery. It is an assertion as to a matter upon which the human mind can form absolutely no conception at all. It is as unmeaning as a statement made in an unknown tongue or a cipher. We know it to be true, but we are no more enlightened by it (to take an illustration from Toland, the deist) than if we knew by infallible authority that 'something called a Blictri had a being in nature, and were not told what a Blictri was.' The only way of contradicting this assertion would be the assertion that nothing called a Blictri had a being in nature. Similarly, unless we insert a negative between the predicate and the subject in the proposition put before us, we do not and cannot contradict the Article. Foolish men, however, have chosen to interpret this inconceivable assertion into certain very plain and very erroneous teaching. Mr. Voysey therefore declares, that it is blasphemous and false to say that 'the Father and the Son are to be regarded as two distinct beings driving a bargain, the nature of which bargain is that the Father, in consideration of the pain suffered by the Son, will abstain from torturing after death people whom he otherwise would have tortured.' Further, he utterly denies the absurd theory that Adam was 'morally perfect, whereas he fell into sin at the very first temptation, as most of his posterity do now.' Moreover, it is an odious mixture of falsehood and absurdity to say that 'when he ate the apple, God the Father cursed the whole human race, and determined that they should all be perpetually tortured in hell-fire after death, and that either before, or at the time, or afterwards, he made a covenant with God the Son, that if God the Son would be crucified (which the contracting parties regarded as being equivalent to being cursed) God the Father would relieve all or some of the human race from the curse which he had set upon them, upon some condition as to their believing something or other of which most of them had never heard.' In the same way, he denies that view of the Incarnation which regards it as Deity coming from heaven and dwelling in an individual man for some years and then going away again; and he would, of course, deal with equal freedom with other mysterious doctrines.

Upon this, and more to the same purpose, I must make one observation. The doctrine which Mr. Voysey denounces is, I doubt not, as false and blasphemous as he asserts. But if the fact that a doctrine deals with matters altogether above our apprehension is enough to save it from being blasphemous by depriving it of all intelligible meaning, why are not the plain statements denounced by Mr. Voysey just as meaningless as the technical terms of the article? If, on the other hand, we can make intelligible propositions about these ineffable mysteries, why is not the Article as revolting as the statements denounced by Mr. Voysey? How can he save the authors of the Article from the charge of being blasphemous without extending the same favourable construction to its popular interpreters? At any rate, how can Mr. Voysey use language under the excuse that it has no meaning when he asserts that it is so easy to invest it with a meaning, which he declares to be horribly blasphemous? The whole may be meaningless because referring to ineffable mysteries; but that which shocks ordinary minds is precisely the assumption implied in the Article that definite statements can be made about such mysteries.

Mr. Voysey's language about the Bible is perhaps less startling; but it raises a similar difficulty. He quotes from Mr. Fitzjames Stephen's defence of Dr. Rowland Williams a passage summing up the views taken by various eminent divines of the English Church. . . . Other authorities are quoted, and it is said that we may put all this together, and consequently enjoy almost any amount of liberty. It was decided, as we have seen, that Mr. Wilson was justified in saying that there was a dark crust of human error and passion over parts of the Bible; and that Dr. Williams might lawfully deny that Moses wrote the Pentateuch, Peter the Second Epistle of Peter, and Daniel the book of Daniel. Mr. Voysey apparently used the liberty thus conferred, by arguing that St. John did not write the gospel bearing his name, and that parts of it contained immoral doctrine. He had, he says, a legal right to make these assertions, and, holding the views he did, it became his moral duty to make use of that legal right.

I have no wish to dispute Mr. Voysey's conception of his moral duty. I only urge that an equally honest man might take a very different view of his moral duty. The ordinary view of the doctrine of the Atonement is in his opinion inexpressibly repulsive. The language of the Articles and of the Liturgy is generally used to confirm that view. Were it not for the supposed need of maintaining liberal sentiment within the Church, a plain man would naturally use language as remote as possible from that which has been applied to so degrading a purpose; and scrupulously avoid even the appearance of treading in the old tracks. The policy recommended in the name of true liberalism is to use the old language in a different sense or to try to deprive it of all sense whatever. If we wished to dissipate the superstition about witchcraft, we should naturally say that there were no such things as witches, and that a bargain with the devil was a simple impossibility. According to this plan, we should still talk about witches, but explain that witchcraft was merely a roundabout term for a special variety of disease, and that talk about the devil was necessarily a metaphorical use of language. Which course of conduct would be most likely to put down the superstition, and to convince those who believed in it of the sincerity of its opponents? But for the supposed necessity of leavening the clergy with some liberal spirit, there can be no doubt that men like Mr. Voysey would repudiate the whole doctrine of the Atonement, and be at least as willing to sign the contradictory of the Article as the words to which they now subscribe. How far they benefit the Church may be a matter of discussion, but it seems probable that this covert mode of attack is quite as profitable to their antagonists as to themselves.

Take again the doctrine about the Bible. Mr. Voysey would apparently say that the gospel of St. John is not authentic; that parts of it are immoral; he would, I should imagine, declare that many parts of the Old Testament contain mere legend or even childish fables; he would say that the massacres of the Canaanites approved by the Hebrew God, were hideous atrocities, which we should describe as they deserved if committed by Mahommedans or Mormons, but to which we have become familiarised by long association. All this and more than this might perhaps be said without any breach of faith, so far as the tests imposed upon the clergy are concerned. But then would any sensible man holding such opinions get up and read these fables and demoralising stories in church with a solemnity calculated to impress their sacred character upon the minds of his congregation? Much of the Bible is, on this showing, no better than Livy, or Hume's History of England. Would it be an improving practice to read fragments of Hume and Livy in church to people already too much disposed to receive them as infallible guides? One of the superstitions against which we have specially to contend in England is the excessive idolatry of the Bible. Does it confirm or weaken that superstition when the clergyman reads a passage from the Old Testament with the solemn preface, 'God spake these words'? The law may say that these words do not imply what they seem to imply; but the legal interpretation is not present to the minds of the hearers, and has no effect upon them. If the reader afterwards gets up in the pulpit and explains that he has merely been reading some very questionable legends, the hearers are far more likely to be confused than edified. I may say from experience . . . that the necessity of going through this mockery, as it must appear to any one holding opinions resembling those of Mr. Voysey, is a far greater strain upon the conscience than the necessity of signing any tests before men who are personally qualified to judge of their true interpretation. Or with what satisfaction can such a man repeat the creeds as the expression of his devout belief? I say nothing of the revolting damnatory clauses of the Athanasian creed, through which perhaps a sufficient number of loopholes have been made by assiduous labourers of infinite skill in that branch of industry. But it is hard enough to repeat the clauses which define the doctrine of the Trinity; when one's real meaning is, Here are a number of obscure statements about matters altogether above our understanding, which were thought to have some meaning by believers in an utterly exploded school of philosophy, which now remain like the rudimentary organs in animals as marks of extinct controversies, and which I do not repudiate because they have no particular significance whatever. This is bad enough, without adding that people who won't say as much will be damned. Or, again, it is not pleasant to repeat even the Apostles' creed by way of expressing the opinion that there is, on the whole, sufficient evidence to make me think it more probable than not that Christ was crucified under Pontius Pilate, and rose again on the third day.

Most Broad Churchmen do not of course go so far as this. Many of them, as I have said, declare – and strange as it appears to me, I give them full credit for believing sincerely – that the formularies of the Church are the natural expression of their deepest convictions. If they all sincerely believe this, of course my argument falls to the ground. I assume, however, that many of them feel a great difficulty in adjusting their beliefs to the expressions provided for them by authority. If it were not so there would be no need of the advice so liberally administered to them, to take advantage of the legal interpretations of apparently disagreeable dogmas. Indeed, the doctrines which Mr. Voysey is accused of contradicting do notoriously cause much trouble amongst Broad Churchmen. They tend to melt away under their hands. The Atonement is spiritualised till it becomes difficult to attach any definite meaning to it whatever. The authority of the Bible becomes more difficult to define and to distinguish from the authority of any other good book. Everlasting punishment is put out of the way by the aid of judicious metaphysical distinctions. The sharp edges of old-fashioned doctrine are rounded off till the whole outline of the creed is materially altered. Phrases that once seemed perfectly definite turn out to have no meaning, and to become mere surplusage. And the gap between the ordinary interpretation and that which our new teachers put upon their tests imperceptibly widens, until in some places the directions of the old and new teaching seem to be diametrically opposite. The test which might be applied in such cases would be simple. Let a man put out of his mind, as far as possible, all the old phrases with which he has become familiar, and simply express his thoughts in the clearest language he can find. If this new expression falls in naturally with the old, there is no more to be said. If there is a palpable difficulty in reconciling them, the problem occurs whether he shall use the old in a new sense, or simply abandon language with so many misleading associations? The answer must be given by deciding which duty is just now the most important: to speak out with the utmost clearness, or to keep the Church of England together a little longer.

I do not quarrel with those who decide for the last. There is much to be said for the Church of England, and though I am not precisely one of its devoted sons, I can sympathise with men who see in it a great instrument for the education of the nation, in whose cause it is worth making some sacrifice, even of clear expression of a man's convictions. Even so, it would be an equally honest, though it may be a hopeless, course to demand an alteration of obsolete Articles, instead of systematically evading them. The system advocated gives to the opponents of any change the argument that tests which are so little burdensome need not be relaxed. But admitting that men are morally justified in taking this view, I deny their right to complain of those who take the opposite view. The one duty which at the present moment seems to me to be of paramount importance, is the duty of perfect intellectual sincerity. We are specially bound not only to avoid deceiving others, but to avoid deceiving ourselves. . . . Now I cannot conceive any doctrine more fatal to genuine veracity of mind than one which exalts into a duty, what seems to me the most dangerous habit of forcing our genuine convictions into the moulds of ancient thought. We are only too much inclined to do so in all cases, and to put off a spirit of inquiry by mere phrases, instead of sincere principles. The process is at once attractive and easy. It is much pleasanter to say that we believe in everlasting punishment, but that everlasting punishment means nothing that can shock the most humane mind, than to denounce the doctrine as untrue and immoral. The habit grows upon us till creeds grow to be mere screens under cover of which we may slink out of the orthodox intrenchments into the opposite camp. Possibly we may do something towards facilitating the admission of timid tendencies towards liberalism; but by using the language of our opponents we lose the one great advantage of appealing boldly and clearly to the sympathies of mankind. . . .

Hence follows the only other remark to be made at present. Why, it is said, should Broad Churchmen be assailed by those who have many points of sympathy with them? If we regard them as traitors in the hostile camp, should we not leave the commanders of that camp to deal with them? No sensible general would discourage desertion from the opposite side even if he despised the deserters. My answer is very simple. I object to the policy advocated, because, with the highest respect for its advocates, I think they do serious injury, not to the Church of England or to Christianity, but to the highest interests of truth and sincerity. Their motives are excellent; and many of them speak with as little mental reservation as any party whatever. But I think that their practical influence is in this respect most unfortunate. I believe they do as much harm to the one necessary element of satisfactory discussion – a perfect confidence in the mental sincerity of the disputants – as can well be done by thoroughly honest and able men. I do not know how much truth there may be in their opinions; but whatever there is – and no doubt they might contribute much to the general stock – is obscured by the general atmosphere of doubt and uncertainty, which is owing to our never being able to tell whether a given doctrine is supported because it is true and the most natural expression of truth, or because it is language used in an unnatural sense by way of concession to the interests of the Church of England. . . . It is incomparably more important that men should speak the plain unsophisticated truth and have it spoken to them, than that they should support the Articles, or the Church of England, or any other Church whatever.

2

GENDER, POLITICS, AND ROME

2.1 CONVERSION AND MASCULINITY

CHURCH, creed, or canon – the source of authority in religion was a central issue of Victorian ecclesiastical debates. But whence the impulse to *submit* to authority as its legitimate claims were recognized? Here personality and temperament entered the issue, and, quite naturally in Victorian culture, the response to authority was differentiated according to sex. Women, regarded as emotional creatures, were thought especially vulnerable to authoritarian appeals. Men, considered to be essentially rational, were thought less likely to sacrifice intellect on the altar of feeling. It followed from this confusion of sex and gender that men whose reason yielded to religious authority, particularly those who saw virtue in celibacy and became Roman Catholic priests, could be suspected of being in some sense effeminate. The insinuation was made not infrequently after the secession of Oxford High Churchmen to Rome. By 1867, when Henry Edward, Cardinal Manning (1808–1892), published *England and Christendom*, the Catholic Church was on the defensive. Manning, an ultramontane controversialist, had converted in 1851. He characterized the secessionists conspicuously as a 'vigorous and masculine movement' (**2.1.1**). His motive, apart from personal distaste, is not hard to find. Three years earlier, the Revd Charles Kingsley (1819–1875), professor of modern history at Cambridge but better known as a novelist, had assailed Manning's fellow-convert, Newman, for holding that 'cunning is the weapon which heaven has given to the saints to withstand the brute male force of the wicked world, which marries and is given in marriage'. This personal attack elicited Newman's conclusive *Apologia pro Vita sua*, but still Kingsley maintained the essential effeminacy of the Church of Rome. In his sermons on David, preached before the young men of Cambridge in 1865, he upheld the monogamous heterosexual couple and their family as the one true scriptural and historical ideal for humanity (**2.1.3**). Lest, however, it be thought that Kingsley had nothing within contemporary experience against which, rightly or wrongly, to react, the reminiscences of St George Jackson Mivart (1827–1900), written between 1881 and 1885, may appear relevant (**2.1.2**). Mivart, who became an accomplished zoologist and Charles Darwin's leading British critic before his excommunication by Cardinal Vaughan, described the adolescent experiences that led him, at the age of seventeen, to become a Roman Catholic. His aesthetic preferences – architectural, theatrical, sartorial – his perceptions of older men, and the single-sex camaraderie of his education will not go unnoticed by twentieth-century readers. These suggest rather different explanations than Manning offered for the penetration of the Catholic Church in England.

2.1.1   H. E. MANNING ON THE PENETRATION OF THE CATHOLIC CHURCH IN ENGLAND, 1867

In the last thirty years a vigorous and masculine movement took possession of the intellects and the wills of great numbers in the Anglican Church. New truths arose upon them – the Succession of the Apostles, the Divine foundation, order, and perpetuity of the Church, the unwritten Word of God, the authority of universal Tradition, the character of Priesthood, the power of Sacrifice and of the Keys, the Church Militant, Purifying and Triumphant, the law of unity, the claim of authority, – all these began, one by one, to dawn upon the clergy and the laity of the Church of England. They then moved onwards and upwards towards a higher system, and nearer towards the Catholic Church, without so much as a desire or thought of entering it. In others these truths suddenly, and with an intensity of light, culminated in the indissoluble Unity and perpetual Infallibility of the one only Church, or rather in the presence and office of the Holy Ghost – the author of all Unity and Truth. One by one, such minds submitted to the only Church from which their forefathers had rent them, as Adam separated us all from God. And yet, it was not the preaching, nor direct action of the Catholic Church, which produced these convictions. They never set foot in a Catholic Church, or saw the face of a Catholic priest. It seemed to come upon them in their thoughts and prayers, – like as the ear anticipates the next chords in a melody from the notes which already fill the sense. Be it as it may, they found their way, one by one, into the noontide – up into the Guest Chamber, where the lights of Pentecost are still luminous and changeless. What was before an act of Reason, became a habit of Faith; what was an argument of the intellect, became a consciousness of the soul. When men asked them, 'How was it?' all they could say was, 'Whereas I was blind, now I see.' And when friends reproached them and ascribed their Faith to unknown agencies of evil, all they could say was, 'Herein is a wonderful thing, that you know not from whence He is, and He hath opened my eyes' [St. John, ix. 25–30]. The consciousness that what they believed is the Faith of all the world, supported them in their isolation. The unity and universality of Christendom were the countersign and the counterpart of their lonely faith.

In this way, from 1830–1860, the Catholic Church in England spread and penetrated. . . .

2.1.2 ST GEORGE MIVART ON A YOUNG MAN'S INITIATION, 1842–45

. . . I gradually became dissatisfied with Low Church Protestantism, partly owing to my increasing taste for the study of church architecture and archæology, partly through the influence of one or two friends, one, a man, and one a boy bigger than myself, named Wrench, who afterwards became a parson. I recollect being much impressed on hearing the latter say, 'If I had been born a Roman Catholic nothing would have made me turn Protestant.' He was my principal guide in my study of architecture, and we made excursions together to see sundry new churches. . . .

My process of evolution was naturally aided by my older brothers. My own brother Charles was rather a dandy, with elaborate embroidered waistcoats of satin and velvet (then fashionable), lace shirts and a certain amount of jewellery. He was devoted to the theatre and opera, a taste innate in him, as when a boy he used to have elaborate performances with a toy theatre and figures on cardboard, to see which audiences were invited – our cousin John being his fellow-manager, and my cousin Maria, at the piano, being the orchestra. Charles was a fair horseman and a very good climber and in his travels always climbed whenever he could, whether church towers or mountains.

My half-brother James was shorter than we were and a very neat figure. He was a thorough sporting man and down to the last dressed in horsey style, though very neatly. He was a good dancer, good shot, and could drive a four-in-hand. . . . Poor Jim had the unlucky good fortune to be much liked by men in an altogether different social position to his own. Thus he was led into expensive habits, from the effects of which he suffered to his latest days. In his youth cock-fighting was still in vogue and prize-fighting very popular, James being a good boxer himself. Cambridge was a very fast place when James was there and the morals of the town, as also of London, were ostensibly very different from what they appear now. . . .

I was present, I do not remember under what circumstance, at the trial of Gregory, the editor of the *Satirist* newspaper. It was a scurrilous paper which came out weekly and contained a number of short paragraphs (like our present society papers) with more or less shameful accusations and jokes about people indicated only by initials, innuendoes, or nicknames. At the trial I heard Sergeant Talfourd's powerful attack which brought about the suppression of the paper. The late much disesteemed Duke of

Brunswick was present on the Bench, and when he came in other noblemen immediately quitted it, or at least, his vicinity. He was a strange man. He used sometimes to wear pink silk trousers. He painted his face, and was considered altogether objectionable. Thus along with inclinations fostered in me by architectural studies and the controversial exhortations of friends, and the pious influence of my mother, together with my rapidly increasing interest in religious questions, other very conflicting influences were already at work. With waning tendencies towards Geneva came allurements to Babylon no less than to Rome.

The church we attended was St. Mark's, North Audley Street, in the vaults of which lie my brother Edward, my grandmother, and one of my aunts. Of this church Mr. Cooper was incumbent and Mr. Wingfield was his curate. Mr. Cooper was a moderate High Church man. He had not adopted the recently introduced startling novelty of preaching in a surplice, neither were there candles lighted on the Communion table, neither was there weekly Communion. Mr. Wingfield was a Tractarian, severe and austere-looking, and as I was told, very rigorous in his fasting. I forget how I made his acquaintance, but it soon ripened. He used to take me out walking with him and frequently asked me to breakfast at his lodgings in Green Street. I there met his sister, whom I had known by sight in church, and the celebrated man she afterwards married, Dr. (then Mr.) Ward. The point which I recollect that Mr. Wingfield urged on me most convincingly was the necessary absurdity of a merely national religion, and the essentially 'Catholic' nature of the Christian Church. I recollect one day going with Ward and Wingfield to afternoon service at Margaret Street Chapel, of which Oakley was then incumbent. It occupied part of the site of the now magnificent 'All Saints.' This was considered one of the most extremely High Church places of worship. I recollect Oakley hobbling up the pulpit steps in his surplice for the sermon. There were two lighted candles on the Communion table and a small bag attached to a stick was handed about for collecting. From this it is plain how very slight in 1842 was the ritualistic development when compared with what it has since attained.

I now left Clapham Grammar School finally, and for a short time had a private tutor who used to come to me daily at Addison Road. He was the Rev. Davies; a very Low Church, and decidedly vulgar man, who dressed shabbily and bit his nails to the quick. He was, I believe, purposely given to me to counteract the too High-Church tendencies impressed on me by Wingfield, but these very tendencies he confirmed and much developed by the repulsion with which he inspired me for himself and his own views, and by the intellectual feebleness of his arguments against the Catholic doctrine. I had no Roman Catholic friends except certain musical and theatrical friends of my father's, and these were worthless social parasites without any religious sympathies as far as could be perceived. One of them, a rather well-known opera singer, used to sing at the High Mass at Warwick Street, then sometimes called the 'shilling opera.' He once took me there with him, but the whole thing by no means helped me along Romewards, and was, as a service, quite incomprehensible to me.

My next move was to King's College, and while there I resided with Dr. Brewer (then one of the masters) in a house on the north side of Euston Road near Euston Square. Dr. Brewer professed to hold all Roman doctrines except that of Papal Supremacy. He was closely shaved and wore a cassock buttoned down to his ankles. The whole atmosphere of the establishment was very High Church, Mr. Cullington, a frequent visitor, fully participating in the family feeling. At this time I had gone so far as to have a *Garden of the Soul* and I habitually said the 'Memorare,' though I duly attended Anglican worship. I recollect receiving Communion with great devotion at St. Paul's, Knightsbridge, indeed, I have rarely felt greater devotion since. Even while at Clapham I had gone far towards accepting the doctrine of the Real Presence and had a High Church Manual of Devotion with a translation of the *Lauda Sion*. While at Addison Road under Davies' tuition I had read a variety of Catholic controversial tracts and was studying carefully Milner's *End of Religious Controversy*. No book was ever written, I believe, more fully convincing in the special dispute between Catholic and orthodox Protestant, and it was little wonder that poor Davies was powerless in arguing with me, armed as I then was. . . .

I was much charmed with A. W. Pugin's books, his *A Plea for the Revival of Christian Architecture*, his *Present State of Christian Architecture in England*, his *Contrasts*, and a smaller work reprinted from the *Dublin Review* in which was much anti-reformation matter, and many attractive plates of Catholic churches recently built. I quite hungered and thirsted to see these, and at last in the spring of 1844, I got permission to make a tour and see as many as I could of them, being accompanied by an Italian manservant named Luigi.

I began, on Easter Monday, 1844, by going by rail from Euston Square to Birmingham. I put up at the 'Hen and Chickens,' thenceforth my constant resort when at Birmingham. I had a great desire not only to see Pugin's buildings but also to obtain some practical knowledge of the Catholic Church, to understand its working, and to make acquaintance with some members of its clergy.

My first visit, therefore, was to St. Chad's Cathedral. . . . After seeing the church I expressed a wish to visit the bishop's house, which I already knew by the illustrations in Pugin's article republished from the *Dublin Review*. Whilst I was seeing the dining hall (a very successful room) the Reverend John Moore, Head Priest of the Mission, came in and we introduced ourselves to each other. 'Are you a Catholic?' 'No.' 'Why not?' 'I hardly know,' were among the first sentences we exchanged, for I had already almost convinced myself of the truth of Catholicism, and but few difficulties remained. In the afternoon Mr. Moore took me to see the Convent of the Sisters of Mercy at Handsworth. I was greatly delighted with the Convent, and while returning, my guide put an end to the difficulty I had until then felt as to Communion in one kind. We then returned to the Cathedral, in the evening service of which I heartily joined and certainly prayed earnestly for guidance and direction.

On Easter Tuesday I was up early and heard a 'Missa Cantata' at St. Chad's, but was quite unable to follow the Mass with my Missal.

I then started to see Pugin's church of St. Giles at Cheadle. . . . I then visited Alton Towers, but I was much less pleased with that house than with the partially built 'Hospital of St. John,' which seemed to me a gem of Gothic architecture. I had come to Alton in a post-chaise and in that I returned to Lichfield, which I reached at 2 o'clock in the morning of April 10th.

In spite of my late hour of going to bed I was in Lichfield Cathedral at 8 o'clock next morning, being impatient to return to Birmingham, which I reached at an early hour, only to leave it again for Nottingham after having settled with Mr. Moore a course of proceeding for the next two days.

On my arrival at Nottingham I went to the priest's house, where I accepted an invitation to early dinner, and dined with the Right Reverend Drs. Walsh and Wiseman, both then seen for the first time. The benign kindness of old Dr. Walsh pleased me greatly. After dinner we walked to see the Church of St. Barnabas (then in course of construction) and later I went by rail with the two Bishops to Derby. The Rev. Mr. Faber, then a High Church parson, was in the carriage with us and I was greatly impressed by the refined courtesy of his manner. After calling to see the church and making acquaintance with the Rev. Mr. Sing, I returned to Birmingham that night.

On Thursday, April 11th, I paid my first visit to Oscott, driving over with Mr. Moore after hearing Mass at St. Chad's. At Oscott I then first made the acquaintance of the Rev. George Spencer (afterwards Father Ignatius), the Rev. Dr. Errington (afterwards Archbishop), the Rev. F. Searle, the Rev. [*sic* F.] Amherst (afterwards Bishop), P. L. P. Renouf and George Mann.

On the 13th I returned to London and there remained until the 23rd. During this interval I resided at Mr. Brewer's and went to King's College, occasionally attending Vespers at Warwick Street, or hearing an 8 o'clock Mass there.

On Ascension Day, May 16th, I attended a Protestant service at King's

College Chapel and immediately afterwards High Mass at Warwick Street.

Sunday, May 19th, was the last time I attended the Protestant service. Having obtained leave of absence from Dr. Jelf, Head of King's College, I started for Nottingham on May 23rd with Luigi, as before, for my servant. My father and mother had now much fear that I should become a Catholic, and if I did this my father told me he should no longer consider me as his son. But I felt he was much too kind and indulgent to carry out any such threat, however much he might mean it when he said it.

On May 24th I went to St. Bernard's Cistercian Monastery, the new building (designed by Pugin) which was then being erected. A lay brother, Brother Xavier, showed me round and I saw Father Bernard Palmer, the prior. I was much impressed with the air of reality about the whole thing. After my visit I went on to Birmingham where, on the morning of the 25th, Mr. Moore all but persuaded me to become a Catholic there and then, putting before me the example of the Apostle and the Eunuch, etc. Luigi was terribly dismayed at this, fearing the unpleasant consequences which might ensue to him should I consent, so I sent him home with a letter to my parents while I took up my abode at the Bishop's house.

On the 27th, while sitting at dinner in the refectory, I was called to my mother who had come down by the first available train full of distress and anxiety. So great was her trouble that I could not refuse to return home with her and wait a little. Delighted at my consent, she very willingly went with me to see the church which I was very anxious should, as well as the clergy, impress her favourably. The church did please her, as also did the Rev. Mr. Leith, whom we found at prayer within it. She also accompanied me to the convent and heard Benediction, and she seemed to like all except Mr. Moore, whom she very naturally distrusted, saying he looked 'a regular Jesuit.'

On the 28th we returned to Brook Street where I endeavoured to please my father and mother as much as possible, and at their request went to call on our parish minister, the Rev. Mr. Cooper, at his house, to listen to all his arguments against the Church of Rome. I was amazed, and am so still, at my own success with him. He seemed unable to reply to my arguments, and gave my father to understand that his opinion was that my father had better let me go as it seemed to be God's Will.

On June 1st my father received a letter from Dr. Wiseman which, coming as it did upon Mr. Cooper's expression of opinion, decided him to let me go. Accordingly I set off as quickly as possible for the third time under the care of Luigi. My father having been called away to the City on some important business, I could not see him before I left home. To my great joy, however, he came to Euston Square Station and saw me. I was in the train about to start when he appeared and said very kindly, 'I felt I must come and say, God bless you, before you left London.'

On my arrival at Birmingham I was welcomed at the Bishop's house and there remained, and that evening made the acquaintance of Charles Delabarre Bodenham, a very amiable young man.

June 2nd, Trinity Sunday. – On this day I was received into the Church. At Mr. Moore's particular request the ceremony took place immediately after High Mass. The priest and assistants came to the front of the sanctuary, Mr. Moore (celebrant) being seated, while I, standing under the arch of St. Chad's rood-screen, read out the Creed of Pius IV. It was for me a nervous business, and the congregation crowded round to have a nearer view of me, but Mr. Moore came to the rescue and took me away over to the Bishop's house. . . .

Sunday, June 9th. – On this day I made my first Communion. . . .

June 21st. – On this day I went to Confession at Spanish Place Chapel. . . .

It was now high time that my education, which had been interrupted by my conversion and consequent separation from King's College, should be resumed. Mr. Moore had persuaded my parents and me that this should be done at Oscott, and on this day my mother and I started for Birmingham to settle all the arrangements. . . . It was finally arranged that I should take a trip to France in company with Mr. Moore, and should thereafter enter at Oscott. . . . I had a room in St. Joseph's corridor, its windows looking out on to the chapel. The Hon. and Rev. George Spencer acted as parish priest. He was a popular confessor, and mine; a man of singular sweetness. John Wheble (who died as military chaplain in the Crimea), of Reading, was sacristan. All the chapel functions, and its furniture, vestments, etc., were in excellent taste and the authorities were generally under the full influence of the Pugin movement. . . .

On November 1st Bishop Wiseman drove me into Birmingham with him for the function at St. Chad's. From this to Christmas I did not learn much. Renouf was not a good teacher, not seeming able to explain sufficiently. One day he set me a paper on which I found 'Analyse your ideas of Space and Time.' This was to me a poser. Later he explained to me Idealism, and something of Fichte and Kant. Also he gave me Guizot's *History of Civilization* to read, and some of Ida von Hahn-Hahn's novels translated, of which I only now recollect *Ulrich*.' . . .

[April 24th, 1845]: This evening, having received a hamper of wine and various things from home, I had a few friends to visit my room, amongst them Frank Amherst, Eyre, and other divines. Under the cheering influence of the contents of my hamper they became rather boisterous, dressing up in some of my things, including my cap and cassock, and I think some eccentric dance steps were being executed when suddenly the door opened and Bishop Wiseman's head appeared, whereat one jumped on to the bed, another dived under it, another under the table, and so on. 'Come! come! Go to bed! Go to bed!' was all the Bishop said, but next day I called upon him to make a formal apology.

Frank Amherst (afterwards Bishop) was a delightful companion, full of interesting anecdotes of matters observed by him abroad, and of sympathy and good taste in matters ecclesiastical. He was a fine manly fellow, a passionate lover of hunting. I have hitherto omitted to say that my position at Oscott was that of parlour-boarder, so that I belonged to a category of my own, there being no other such boarder, and I seemed to rank between a 'Divine' and a 'Philosopher,' the highest class of lay student being so-called. As, however, I had some leanings towards the ecclesiastical state, I was allowed to wear a cassock and a square-topped Oxford cap. At this time Oscott was at its best, Dr. Wiseman having so great a reputation. . . .

On May 11th, 1845, I was confirmed by Dr. Wiseman and for my confirmation name took that of Francis, having had a special attraction to St. Francis of Assisi before I joined the Catholic Church. . . .

2.1.3   C. KINGSLEY ON 'MUSCULAR CHRISTIANITY' AND MARRIAGE, 1865

We have heard much of late about 'Muscular Christianity.' A clever expression, spoken in jest by I know not whom, has been bandied about the world, and supposed by many to represent some new ideal of the Christian character.

For myself, I do not understand what it means. It may mean . . . simply a healthy and manful Christianity, one which does not exalt the feminine virtues to the exclusion of the masculine.

That certain forms of Christianity have committed this last fault cannot be doubted. The tendency of Christianity, during the patristic and the middle ages, was certainly in that direction. Christians were persecuted and defenceless, and they betook themselves to the only virtues which they had the opportunity of practising, – gentleness, patience, resignation, self-sacrifice, and self-devotion, – all that is loveliest in the ideal female character. And God forbid that that side of the Christian life should ever be undervalued. It has its own beauty, its own strength too, made perfect in weakness; in prison, in torture, at the fiery stake, on the lonely sick bed, in long years of self-devotion and resignation, and in a thousand womanly sacrifices, unknown to man, but written for ever in God's book of life.

But as time went on, and the monastic life, which, whether practised by man or by woman, is essentially a feminine life, became more and more exclusively the religious ideal, grave defects began to appear in what was really too narrow a conception of the human character.

The monks of the middle ages, in aiming exclusively at the virtues of women, generally copied little but their vices. Their unnatural attempt to be wiser than God, and to unsex themselves, had done little but disease their mind and heart. They resorted more and more to those arts which are the weapons of crafty, ambitious, and unprincipled women. They were too apt to be cunning, false, intriguing. They were personally cowardly, as their own chronicles declare; querulous, passionate, prone to unmanly tears; prone, as their writings abundantly testify, to scold, to use the most virulent language against all who differed from them; they were, at times, fearfully cruel, as evil women will be; cruel with that worst cruelty which springs from cowardice. If I seem to have drawn a harsh picture of them, I can only answer, that their own documents justify abundantly all that I have said.

Gradually, to supply their defects, another ideal arose. The warriors of the middle ages hoped that they might be able to serve God in the world, even in the battle-field. At least, the world and the battle-field they would not relinquish, but make the best of them. And among them arose a new and a very fair ideal of manhood; that of the 'gentle very perfect knight,' loyal to his king and to his God, bound to defend the weak, succour the oppressed, and put down the wrong-doer; with his lady, or bread-giver, dealing forth bounteously the goods of this life to all who needed; occupied in the seven works of mercy, yet living in the world, and in the perfect enjoyment of wedded and family life. This was the ideal. Of course sinful human nature fell short of it; and defaced it by absurdities: but I do not hesitate to say that it was a higher ideal of Christian excellence than had appeared since the time of the Apostles, putting aside the quite exceptional ideal of the blessed martyrs. . . .

. . . That exalting and purifying ideal of the relations between man and woman . . . is enunciated, remember always, in the oldest Hebrew document. On the very threshold of the Bible, in the very first chapters of Genesis, it is enunciated in its most ideal purity and perfection. But in practice it was never fulfilled. No man seems to have attempted to fulfil it. Man becomes a polygamist, lower than the very birds of the air. Abraham, the father of the faithful, has his Sarah, his princess-wife: but he has others beside, as many as he will. And so has David in like wise, to the grief and harm of both him and Abraham.

So, it would seem, had the majority of the Jews till after the Captivity; and even then the law of divorce seems to have been as indulgent toward the man, as it was unjust and cruel toward the woman. Then our blessed Lord reasserted the ideal and primæval law. He testified in behalf of woman, the puppet of a tyrant who repudiated her upon the most frivolous pretext, and declared that in the beginning God made them male and female; the one husband for the one wife. But His words fell on unwilling ears. His disciples answered, that if the case of a man with his wife be such, it is not good for a man to marry. And such, as a fact, was the general opinion of Christendom for many centuries.

But of that, as of other sayings of our Lord's, were His own words fulfilled, that the kingdom of God is as if a man should put seed into the ground, and sleep and wake, and the seed should spring up, and bear fruit, he knew not how.

In due course of time, when the Teutonic nations were Christianized, there sprang up among them an idea of married love, which shewed that our Lord's words had at last fallen on good ground, and were destined to bear fruit an hundredfold.

Gradually, with many confusions, and sometimes sinful mistakes, there arose, not in the cloister; not in the study; not even, alas! in the churches of God, as they were then: but in the flowery meads of May; under the forest boughs, where birds sang to their mates; by the side of the winter hearth; from the lips of wandering minstrels; in the hearts of young creatures, whom neither the profligacy of worldlings, nor the prudery of monks, had yet defiled; from them arose a voice, most human and yet most divine, reasserting once more the lost law of Eden, and finding in its fulfilment strength and purity, self-sacrifice and self-restraint. . . .

. . . A higher ideal, I say, was chivalry, with all its shortcomings. And for this reason; that it asserted the possibility of consecrating the whole manhood, and not merely a few faculties thereof, to God; and it thus contained the first germ of that Protestantism which conquered at the Reformation.

Then was asserted, once for all, on the grounds of nature and reason, as well as of Holy Scripture, the absolute sanctity of family and national life, and the correlative idea, namely, the consecration of the whole of human nature to the service of God, in that station to which God had called each man. Then the Old Testament, with the honour which it puts upon family and national life, became precious to man, as it had never been before; and such a history as David's became, not as it was with the mediæval monks, a mere repertory of fanciful metaphors and allegories: but the solemn example, for good and for evil, of a man of like passions and like duties, with the men of the modern world.

These great truths, once asserted, could not but conquer; and they will conquer to the end. All attempts to restore the monastic and feminine ideal, like that of good Nicholas Ferrar at Little Gidding, failed. They withered like hot-house exotics in the free keen bracing English air; and in our civil wars, Cavalier and Puritan, in whatever they differed, never differed in their sound and healthy conviction that true religion did not crush, but strengthened and consecrated a valiant and noble manhood.

. . . The highest ideal of family life became possible to the family and to the nation, in proportion as they accepted the teaching of the Reformation: and impossible alas! in proportion as they still allowed themselves to be ruled by a priesthood who asserted the truly monstrous dogma, that the sexes reach each their highest excellence, only when parted from each other. . . .

Now if all that Muscular Christianity means is that, then the expression is altogether unnecessary; for we have had the thing for three centuries – and defective likewise, for it is not a merely muscular but a human Christianity, which the Bible taught our forefathers, and which our forefathers have handed down to us. . . .

2.2 MARY AND WOMANKIND

Although Catholic religion, both Roman and Anglican, was dominated by men, it reserved a prominent place in its devotional life for women. The motives and consequences of this were profoundly ambiguous, as may be seen in Victorian writings on the Virgin Mary. Frederick William Faber (1814–1863), who followed Newman into the Church of Rome and founded the London Oratory in 1849, became a specialist in Catholic devotion after the Italian rite. In *The Foot of the Cross* he waxed lyrical about the bloody tortures and perpetual virgin agony of the divine Mother, whose Immaculate Conception had been decreed from Rome in 1854 (**2.2.1**). But Mary's suffering was only one lesson extractable from tradition and Scripture. In *Womankind* Charlotte Yonge (1823–1901), the Anglican novelist, interpreted the Marian life and mission as the source of woman's elevation 'to her rightful position as the help-meet'. Not only was motherhood ennobled by the Virgin Birth; maidenhood, too, found its true glory in consecrated service to the Church, yielding to 'the whole Body whom Christ the Lord has left to be waited on as Himself' (**2.2.2**). In her novels, however, Yonge wrote of a staid rural and sacramental order that, like her readership, had grown old and unrepresentative of the mainstream of ecclesiastical life by the late 1880s. It was then that a remarkable High Churchman, Thomas Hancock (1832–1903) of St Nicholas Cole Abbey in the City of London, could portray the Magnificat, sung by Mary at the Annunciation, as 'the hymn of the social revolution' (**2.2.3**). Preaching amid growing labour unrest in the capital, Hancock stood the papal Virgin on her head, or rather right side-up. To him, her 'disguised socialist war-song' proclaimed God's victory to the suffering poor.

2.2.1   F. W. FABER ON THE SORROWS OF MARY, 1858

THE CHARACTERISTICS OF OUR LADY'S DOLOURS

The characteristics of our Lady's dolours are, as might be expected, closely connected with the fountains out of which they spring, and these must now be the subject of inquiry. . . . The first characteristic of her sorrows was that they were lifelong, or nearly so. It is generally agreed that our Blessed Lady did not know she was to be the Mother of God before the moment of the Incarnation. . . . When she actually bore within herself the Eternal Word made flesh, a great change must have come over her. . . . She was in such unutterable union with God, and understood so deeply and truly the mystery of the Incarnation, and such a light was shed for her upon the depths of Hebrew prophecy, that it is impossible not to believe that the Passion of Jesus lay clearly before her, with all the Thirty-Three Years of poverty, hardship, and abasement, and consequently with it, at least in its main outlines, her own Compassion. . . . Mary's subjection to sorrow was riveted upon her as if with iron. It never relaxed. It never grew milder. It gave her no respite. It was in her life, and only by laying down her life could she extricate herself from its inseparable companionship. The Passion was not a dark end to a bright life, or an obscure sunset after a checkered day of light and gloom, or an isolated tragedy in sixty-three years of common human vicissitudes. It was part of a whole, with consistent antecedents, a deepening certainly of the darkness, but a portion of the lifelong darkness which for years had known, in this respect at least, no light. . . .

But her sorrows were not only lifelong; they were continually increasing. The more she became familiarised with the vision of them, the more also she realised them, and the more terrible they seemed. This growth of them does not appear incompatible with the immensity of her science, or do any dishonour to it. They gave up new features, new pains, new depths, new possibilities to her continual meditation. . . . Jesus waxed more beautiful day by day. The first twelve years ran out, leaving results of heavenly loveliness and love beyond our power of summing. Then the next eighteen, when every word, and every look, and every meek subjection were thick with mysteries of heaven. Her life had almost passed out of her into Him, so exceedingly had He become her light, and life, and love, and all. Then came the three years' ministry, and it seemed as if the Babe of Bethlehem, or the Boy of Nazareth, had been nothing to the Preacher of love, whose words and works and miracles appeared to charge the world with more of supernatural beauty than it could bear, so that men rose up madly to put out the light which hurt them by its strong shining. As this loveliness increased, her love increased, and with her love her agony. . . . Jesus had become a habit to her: could He be torn from her, and she survive? And so one motive grew to another, and one thought quickened another, and one affection intensified another, and thus her dolours grew, quicker than the gourds in summer, and all the quicker as the time drew near.

It was also a characteristic of her sorrows that they were in her soul, rather than in her body. . . . The more refined and delicate the soul, the more excruciating is its agony. What then must have been the pains of a soul which was such an immaculate vessel of grace as hers was? We have no standards by which to measure what she felt. Her powers of suffering are beyond our comprehension. All we know is that they transcended all human experience, and that the two Hearts of Jesus and Mary were raised into a world of suffering of their own, where no other hearts of flesh can follow them. Her pains were martyrdom reversed; for the seat of the anguish was in the soul and flowed over, blistering and burning, on the sympathetic flesh, while with the martyrs the soul poured sweet balm into the wounded flesh, and the heaven within burned more brightly than the lighted fire or the wild beast's eye without. . . .

Another characteristic of our Lady's sorrows is the union of their great variety with the fact of their being interior, that is, of their being unitedly felt in one place, her heart. . . . The bodily pains of the Passion, the mental sufferings, the deep abasements, the cries, the faces, the very visible thoughts of the multitudes around, were so many different kinds of pain to her. And then the complete unity of her undivided affections added immensely to them all. She loved only One. The causes of her martyrdom were all centered in one. There was . . . no diversion to her woes. Innumerable as they were, they ran up into one supernatural, many-headed point, and pierced with all their might the very centre of her life, the beautiful sanctuary of her loving heart. . . .

These were the characteristics of her sorrows; and what is every word that has been said but a deepening shade to the dark, dark picture? What then shall we think of that last characteristic of her dolours, . . . the moderation with which she bore them? Who is ever able to forget, when they meditate upon our Blessed Mother, the heavenly tranquillity of her 'Behold the handmaid of the Lord,' at the Annunciation? The same tranquillity is unbroken even when her heart is breaking beneath the Cross. . . . Nevertheless, this tranquillity was no protection to her against the intensity of suffering. It rather enabled her to suffer more. It allowed the grief to penetrate more unresistedly into every part of her. Yet there was no wildness, no loud sighs, no broken sobs, no outspoken words of complaint. Still less – the thought is one which would never have crossed the mind of an intelligent lover of Mary, if careless untheological pictures had not indecorously brought it before so many of us – still less were there any vehement attitudes of grief, any contortions of the venerable beauty of her face, any womanish wringing of the hands, any negligence of dishevelled hair, any prostrations on the ground as of one overcome with mortal anguish, least of all any fainting away, any need of a supporting arm around her, whether it were that of John or Magdalen, any suspension of that glorious reason which sleep even had not interrupted in its magnificent exercises since the very first moment of the Immaculate Conception. Let us in indignant love give to the flames these ignorant dishonourable representation, and drive out of ourselves the odious images which their skill and beauty may have left upon our minds. Mary '*stood*' beneath the Cross; . . . she stood in calmest queenliest dignity, quiet, not as a sweet evening landscape, or a noontide summer sea, or a green wood at dawn, or a moonlit mountain-top, or as any other image in the poetry of nature, but quiet, in her measure and degree, as the Divine Nature of our Lord while the tumult of the Passion was trampling His Human Nature to death. Her tranquillity was the image of that tranquillity. It was one of many participations in Himself which Jesus gave to her in those dark hours.

HOW OUR LADY COULD REJOICE IN HER DOLOURS

Having thus considered the characteristics of our Lady's dolours, we must now pass to a peculiarity of them, which it is necessary always to bear in mind, namely, their union with the intensest joy. . . . If our Lady's dolours had not risen out of her love and been animated by it, they would not have been meritorious. But in truth love was the very cause of them. Out of the excess of love came the excess of sorrow. Now it is undeniable that love cannot exist without delectation. Love is of itself essentially a joy; and in proportion to the eminence of our Mother's love must also be the eminence of her celestial joy. . . . Her joy, so far from alleviating her sufferings, probably made her suffer more. . . . O Mother! we cannot tell how it was, only that so it was! Thou wert all joy, and being so near God, how couldst thou help but be so? Thou wert all sorrow, and what else couldst thou be in those dark abysses of the Passion? And thy sorrow had no power over thy joy; but thy joy had power over thy sorrow, and gave it a brisker acid, a more volatile and pervasive bitterness! Glad creature! sorrow crushed thee, and then a joy, like that of heaven, sat upon thy burden, and made it tenfold more hard to bear!

Yet we are hardly doing justice to her sorrows when we say that they had no influence upon her joys. Doubtless they increased them, and were to her the fountains of new joys which she had never had before, or of new degrees of old accustomed joys. . . . She, who had been allowed to fathom sin so deeply, and who in the spirit of Gethsemane had tasted somewhat of the Father's anger, could exult in the satisfaction of His justice, as neither angel nor saint could do. She, who had lived thirty-three years with Jesus, and had caught from Him His passionate yearning for His Father's honour, could find depths of blissful congratulation in the restoring of that honour, which not all creatures together could discover. . . .

There was joy also in her foresight of the exaltation of Jesus. She saw Him already at the Right Hand of the Father, His Sacred Humanity, enthroned there as an object of highest worship for ever. To her eyes the bright clouds of Ascension Day were strangely interlaced with the darkness of the dun eclipse on Calvary. She saw the feet that were dropping blood, as if they were rising up in the sunny air, each with its glorified stigma gleaming like a roseate sun. She almost saw the angels in their glistening white, moving about amid the horses of those ruthless foreign centurions. The darkness of the depth set off the brightness of the exaltation, as if it were a background of storm throwing forward the bright things in front of it with vivid, lifelike light. There was joy also in her participation at the time in the interior joy of Jesus. For that failing Heart upon the Cross had a very ocean of gladness within itself, a gladness none on earth but His Mother knew, a gladness none else could share, because none else could understand it. If her share of it were parted among the numberless elect, we should each have more than we could bear. It was a joy also, of a peculiar kind, to see Him paying then and there for the glorious prerogatives He had given her. When the blood moistened her hand and stained its whiteness, she recognised and worshipped it as the price of her Immaculate Conception. Could she see that, and then not love Him ten thousand times more than she had loved Him hitherto? And with the rush of love must needs come a rush of joy as well. . . .

THE SPIRIT OF DEVOTION TO OUR LADY'S DOLOURS

Such is a general description of the dolours of Mary. The Church puts them before us as part of the Gospel, as one of the facts of the Gospel, and as an object of special devotion. . . . Before concluding, . . . however, it seems necessary to say something on the spirit of this beautiful and popular devotion. It produces in our minds an extreme tenderness towards our Blessed Lord, united with the profoundest reverence. . . . The way in which our Lady's dolours keep His Passion continually before us has a special virtue to produce this tenderness in us. We love Him, who is infinitely to be loved in all ways, in a peculiar manner when He is reflected in His Mother's heart; and although it is absolutely necessary for us perpetually to contemplate His Passion in all the nakedness of its harrowing circumstances and revolting shame, for else we shall never have a true idea of the sinfulness of sin, yet there is something in the Passion, seen through Mary, which makes us forget ourselves, and tranquilly engrosses us in the most melting tenderness and endearing sympathy towards our Blessed Lord. The emotions which are awakened by the Passion in itself are manifold and exciting, whereas the spirit of tenderness presides over Mary's sorrows with one exclusive, constraining presence.

But out of this tenderness comes also a great hatred of sin. . . . Devotion to our Lady's dolours is a great help both to acquiring the hatred of sin as a habit, and to meriting it as a grace. The desolation wrought by sin in the heart of the sinless Mother, and the reflection that her sorrows were not, like those of Jesus, the redemption of the world, fill us with horror, with pity, with indignation, with self-reproach. There is nothing to distract us from this thought, as there is in the sacrifice of our Lord, who was thus accomplishing His own great work, satisfying the justice of His Father, earning the exaltation of His Sacred Humanity, and becoming the Father Himself of a countless multitude of the elect. The Mother's heart bleeds, simply because she is His Mother, and it is our sins which are making it bleed so cruelly. We are ourselves part of the shadow of that eclipse which is passing so darkly over her spotless life. . . .

He, who is growing in devotion to the Mother of God, is growing in all good things. His time cannot be better spent; his eternity cannot be more infallibly secured. But devotion is, on the whole, more a growth of love than of reverence, though never detached from reverence. And there is nothing about our Lady which stimulates our love more effectually than her dolours. In delight and fear we shade our eyes when the bright light of her Immaculate Conception bursts upon us in its heavenly effulgence. We fathom with awe and wonder the depths of her Divine Maternity. The vastness of her science, the sublimities of her holiness, the singularity of her prerogatives, fill us with joyful admiration united with reverential fear. It is a jubilee to us that all these things belong to our own Mother, whose fondness for us knows no bounds. But somehow we get tired of always looking up into the bright face of heaven. The very silver linings of the clouds make our eyes ache, and they look down for rest and find it in the green grass of the earth. The moon is beautiful, gilding with rosy gold her own purple region of the sky, but her light is more beautiful to our homesick hearts when it is raining over field, and tree, and lapsing stream, and the great undulating ocean. For earth after all is a home, for which one may be sick. So, when theology has been teaching us our Mother's grandeurs in those lofty, unshared mysteries, our devotion, because of its very infirmity, is conscious to itself of a kind of strain. O how, after long meditation on the Immaculate Conception, love gushes out of every pore of our hearts when we think of that almost more than mortal queen, heartbroken, and with blood-stains on her hand, beneath the Cross! O Mother! we have been craving for more human thoughts of thee; we have

"Come all to me, I am your Mother."

3 'The dear mother you have in heaven, loving you with the real human heart that on earth suffered so much for you.' Popular devotion to 'the Immaculate Virgin Heart of Mary' was, as Mary Potter's booklet *The Path of Mary* (1878) illustrates, directly inspired by no one more than 'the true holy man', Father Faber.

wanted to feel thee nearer to us; we can weep for joy at the greatness of thy throne, but they are not such tears as we can shed with thee on Calvary: they do not rest us so. But when once more we see thy sweet sad face of maternal sorrow, the tears streaming down thy cheeks, the quietness of thy great woe, and the blue mantle we have known so long, it seems as if we had found thee after losing thee, and that thou wert another Mary from that glorious portent in the heavens, or at least a fitter mother for us on the low summit of Calvary than scaling those unapproachable mountain-heights of heaven! See how the children's affections break out with new love from undiscovered recesses in their hearts, and run round their newly widowed mother like a river, as if to supply her inexhaustibly with tears, and divide her off with a great broad frontier of love from the assault of any fresh calamity. The house of sorrow is always a house of love. This is what takes place in us regarding Mary's dolours. One of the thousand ends of the Incarnation was God's condescending to meet and gratify the weakness of humanity, for ever falling into idolatry because it was so hard to be always looking upwards, always gazing fixedly into inaccessible furnaces of light. So are Mary's dolours to her grandeurs. The new strength of faith and devotion, which we have gained in contemplating her celestial splendours, furnishes us with new capabilities of loving; and all our loves, the new and the old as well, rally round her in her agony at the foot of the Cross of Jesus. Love for her grows quickest there. It is our birthplace. We became her children there. She suffered all that because of us. Sinlessness is not common to our Mother and to us. But sorrow is. It is the one thing we share, the one common thing betwixt us. We will sit with her therefore and sorrow with her, and grow more full of love, not forgetting her grandeurs, – O surely never! – but pressing to our hearts with fondest predilection the memory of her exceeding martyrdom. . . .

But, when we speak of the spirit of this devotion, we must not omit to speak also of its power. We must not dwell exclusively on the spiritual effects it produces on ourselves, without reminding ourselves of its real power with God. . . . When we think of the Sacred Heart of Jesus, of the immensity of His love for Mary, and of the great part of the Passion which it was to Him to see her suffer, we cannot for a moment doubt, without thinking of obligation, the extreme persuasiveness to Him of devotion to her dolours, a devotion which He Himself began, a devotion which was actually a solid part of His ever-blessed Passion. We draw Him towards us the moment we begin to think of His Mother's sorrows. He is beforehand, says St. Anselm, with those who meditate His Mother's woes. And do we not stand in need of power in Heaven? What a great work we have to do in our souls, and how little of it is already done! How slight is the impression we have made yet on our ruling passion, on our besetting sin! How superficial is our spirit of prayer, how childishly timid our spirit of penance, how transitory our moments of union with God! We want vigour, determination, consistency, solidity, and a more venturous aspiration. In short, our spiritual life wants power. And here is a devotion, so solid and efficacious, that it is eminently calculated to give us this power, as well by its masculine products in the soul, as by its actual influence over the Heart of our Blessed Lord. Who, that looks well at the saints, and sees what it has done for them, but will do his best to cultivate this devotion in himself? . . .

2.2.2   C. M. YONGE ON WOMAN AND THE CHURCH, 1876

. . . I have no hesitation in declaring my full belief in the inferiority of woman, nor that she brought it upon herself. I believe – as entirely as any other truth which has been from the beginning – that woman was created as a help-meet to man. How far she was then on an equality with him, no one can pretend to guess; but when the test came, whether the two human beings would pay allegiance to God or to the Tempter, it was the woman who was the first to fail, and to draw her husband into the same transgression. Thence her punishment of physical weakness and subordination, mitigated by the promise that she should be the means of bringing the Redeemer to renovate the world, and break the dominion of Satan. . . . The Blessing conferred upon the holy Mother of our Lord became the antidote to the punishment of Eve's transgression; and in proportion to the full reception of the spirit of Christianity has woman thenceforth been elevated to her rightful position as the help-meet.

There, however, comes in the woman's question of the day – Is she meant to be nothing but the help-meet? If by this is meant the wife, or even the sister or daughter, attached to the aid of some particular man, I do not think she is. It is her most natural, most obvious, most easy destiny; but one of the greatest incidental benefits that Christianity brought the whole sex was that of rendering marriage no longer the only lot of all, and thus making both the wife and the maiden stand on higher ground.

'Thy desire shall be to thy husband, and he shall rule over thee,' had been said to Eve. Without a husband the woman had hitherto been absolutely nothing. Wife, mother, or slave, were her sole vocations; and if her numbers became superfluous, polygamy and female infanticide were the alternatives.

But the Church did away with this state of things. Wifehood was dignified by becoming a faint type or shadow of the Union of the Church with her Lord. Motherhood was ennobled by the Birth that saves the world; and Maidenhood acquired a glory it had never had before, and which taught the unmarried to regard themselves, not as beings who had failed in the purpose of their existence, but as pure creatures, free to devote themselves to the service of their Lord; for if His Birth had consecrated maternity, it had also consecrated virginity.

The dim idea of pure dedicated creatures had, in the ancient days of Rome, suggested the order of Vestal Virgins. Rome had grown so corrupt, that it was almost impossible to keep up even the small number of these priestesses; but there was enough of the idea latent in the minds of the nation to make the consecration of Christian purity congenial; and the high Roman courage, now refined, soon produced its whole army of brave Virgin Martyrs. Then it became understood that woman might look to no earthly lord, but might turn all her yearnings for love and protection to Him who has become the Son of Man, 'her celestial Spouse and King,' and that her freedom from other ties enabled her to devote herself wholly to Him. And how? Not only by direct contemplation and devotion, but 'Inasmuch as ye have done it to one of the least of these, ye have done it unto Me.'

So began the vocation of the dedicated Virgin, the Deaconess, the Nun. The life in community became needful when no security could be had save in a fortress; and this, together with the absolute need of the feminine nature for discipline and obedience, led to the monastic life being, with rare exceptions, the only choice of the unwedded throughout the middle ages; but this safe and honourable refuge for the single daughters of families did, to take it on the very lowest grounds, much to enhance the estimation in which their secular sisters were held.

It is not, however, my purpose here to dwell on monasticism. All I want to do is to define what I believe to be the safe and true aspect in which woman ought to regard herself – namely, as the help-meet of man; not necessarily of any individual man, but of the whole Body whom Christ our Lord has left to be waited on as Himself. He is her Lord. He will find her work to do for Him. It may be that it will lie in the ordinary course of nature. It is almost certain that she will begin as help-meet to her father or brothers; and to many, there comes the Divinely-ordained estate of marriage, and the duties and blessings it entails, all sanctified through Him. It may be, again, that her lot is attendance on a parent – still a work of ministry especially blest by Him; and so with all those obvious family claims that Providence marks out by the mere fact of there being no one else to undertake them. And for those who are without such calls, or from whom their tasks have fallen away, what is there left? Nay, not left as a remnant, for He has been there through all. Their Lord is ready for their direct, complete, uneclipsed service in whatever branch seems their vocation. His Church is the visibly present Mother to guide them; and as daughters of the Church their place and occupation is found.

Previously they had no status, except as appendages to some individual man. Now, as members of one great Body, each has her place and office, whether domestic or in some special outer field. And in proportion as this is recognised, the single woman ceases to be *manquée*, and enjoys honour and happiness.

The change makes less visible difference to the married woman; because, by the original Divine ordinance, her husband has always been so much her lord that her duty to him becomes a sort of religion, and her cares as wife and mother occupy her mind and affections. Thus there is no state of society or religion – at least, where the sacredness of the tie of marriage is understood – that does not present instances of the exemplary woman, whose affections have been a law to her, and have trained her in self-denial, patience, meekness, pity, and modesty. History, and the experience of travellers and of missionaries, alike prove this fact.

But the woman destitute of such a direct object for her obedience, cares, interests and affections, is apt, when her first youth is over, to crave for something further, unless she have recognised her relation to the universal Body and to its Head. As long as girlhood lasts – and this often is a good way on into life – she has sufficient food for her interests, at home or abroad, in studies or amusements; but let her home break up, or let her not feel herself a necessary wheel in its machinery, she becomes at a loss. The *cui bono* feeling comes over her studies; amusements become weary, or she finds herself looked at by the younger generation as *de trop:* and she either sinks into dull routine in a narrow home, or is an aimless guest at country houses; or, on the other hand, she takes to being one of the equally purposeless travellers and sight-seers – ever roving, ever gazing; or lastly, she struggles for the position and privileges of man. His independence she has, and a very doleful thing she finds it – vanity and vexation of spirit to herself; and while she strips herself of all grace and softness, she becomes ridiculous and absurd in his sight, and renders him averse to the culture to which he erroneously ascribes her unfemininineness.

But let her feel herself responsible to the one great Society of which she is a part, and let her look for the services that she can fulfil by head or by hands, by superintendence or by labour, by pen or pencil, by needle or by activity, by voice or by music, by teaching or by nursing – nay, by the gentle sympathy and earnest prayers of an invalid; and the vague discontent is appeased. . . . She has found a vocation, or it has been found for her. It may be an outwardly secular life that she lives, and there is no visible difference between her pursuits and those of others; but they are dedicated, they have their object; and if her heart rests in Him, she is content. . . .

It is only as a daughter of the Church that woman can have her place, or be satisfied as to her vocation. . . .

2.2.3 T. HANCOCK ON THE MAGNIFICAT, 1886

He hath shewed strength with His arm; He hath scattered the proud in the imagination of their hearts; He hath put down the mighty from their seat, and hath exalted the humble and meek. He hath filled the hungry with good things; and the rich He hath sent empty away. – ST. LUKE i. 51–53.

. . . Every nation has what is called its national hymn, but the *Magnificat* is the hymn of all peoples. It is the hymn of humanity, the hymn of all parishes. In every local commune of the Western nations, where the wholesome customs of the Church are kept, this hymn is said or sung every afternoon. For at least twelve hundred years this has been the practice of the Churches. The parishes or communes of Christendom – those old local, secular societies which become by baptism the congregations of the Church – are far older societies than the national Kingdoms and Republics; so this local parish hymn, the *Magnificat,* is much more ancient in its use than any of the so-called national hymns, such as 'God save the Queen,' or *'Rufst du mein Vaterland!'* or the *'Marseillaise.'* It will outlive them all. For every so-called national hymn has war, competition, the murderous destruction or crippling of sister nations, as its actual or implied motive; while the *Magnificat* has as its motive the scattering, disappointment, and depression by God's Son of those classes in every nation which make wars, which thrive by them, which stir up unbrotherly hatred and competition between people and people – those three castes whom Mary calls 'the proud,' 'the mighty,' and 'the rich,' against whom the Everlasting Father, as He says by the incarnation of His Son, has declared war.

When the Church, evening after evening, in all her parishes, is saying this hymn, she is unconsciously foretelling – the most ignorant and prejudiced of her priests and people are foretelling – that greatest of all revolutions, which the Blessed Virgin saw to be involved in the birth and work of Him whom she carried in her womb. To Mary, at that awful moment of inspiration in which her lips poured forth this song of humanity, this *Marseillaise* of all the nations, was revealed the stupendous social and political reversal which the birth of the Son of God as the Son of Man, as the son of a poor carpenter's wife, was bound sooner or later to produce in all the world. She stood at that moment upon the eternal ground where past and present and future are unknown, where our distinction called 'time' has no place: and therefore she spoke as if the far-off end of the Father for mankind were near and present, and already reached. She sings of the social revolution not as about to come down from heaven, and to occupy ages in the coming, but as having actually come. The *Magnificat* is the inspired summary of the tendency and direction of the future social history of the humankind. We are so used to this daily hymn – as we are to the air by which we live – that it is not easy for us without a special act of thought to realise the tremendous character of its contents, and its awful importance to all sorts and conditions of men and women in the daily ordering of their lives. In this afternoon hymn of the universal Church every parish is declaring, and professes to be joyfully proclaiming, what is the real end of God in His government of the nations; how the Son of God is now actually using that supreme power which has been given to Him in heaven and in earth; to what issue He that sitteth in the heavens is slowly but most surely developing all 'the imagination of the hearts' of the Herods and the Pilates, the Pharisees and the Sadducees, the Cæsars and the mobs of every age and every place. 'We see not yet,' as the Apostle says, 'all things put under Him.' But we know by faith that 'He is showing strength with His arm, that He is scattering the proud in the imagination of their hearts; that He is putting down the mighty from their seat; that He is exalting the humble and meek; that He is filling the hungry with good things, and that He is sending the rich empty away.'

The sword which went through Mary's bosom, as she saw the apparent defeat of the Son of God upon the Cross, must in its degree go through ours also as 'we see not yet all things put under Him.' But all these things the arm of the Lord had already rehearsed in the Egyptian revolution, with which the history of Mary's nation began, and wherein and whereby God revealed the law and the process of the social future. The rudimentary materials of Mary's song are historical and political; they are all to be found in outline in the song of Hannah at the birth of the last great prophet of the republican period of Israel, and in the national Psalter. God is the same in all generations. If He looked upon the children of Israel enslaved and cheated out of the fruits of their labour in the brickfields of 'the proud,' 'the mighty,' and 'the rich' Egyptians, so He must have been regarding the homeless, the workless, and the hungry everywhere in Mary's day; so must He be regarding them in our day in London. Although they think that He has forgotten them, although it often seems to the lowly and the hungry as if God Himself were neglecting them, they are everywhere more the objects of His regard, more important to Him, than all 'the proud,' 'the mighty,' and 'the rich.' God is always and everywhere at war against these three classes – as the Church declares with joy every afternoon in this hymn – on behalf of the humble, the meek, and the hungry.

The poor think that no one is on their side, but if they have the faith of the carpenter's wife they will see that their cause is moving 'the arm of the Lord.' The object of the counsels of the Most High is the 'scattering' of the clever plots and arrangements made by the proud statesmen and diplomatists of this world in the conceit of their hearts; the hurling down of dynasties, as St. Luke has it in the Greek, 'from thrones,' the confusion of imperialist schemes. The invisible armies of the incarnate Word of God are fighting on the side of those who are conquered and beaten on earth; the angelic almsgivers of the Father are giving joys and pleasures to ragged children in narrow streets, and even a possession of the world which the idle rich and the fine lady would be glad to buy with thousands of pounds. A great lord 'owns' a park; but he complains that he can never enjoy it, as some poor landscape painter does who perhaps has only a few pence in his pocket.

In the *Magnificat* we thank God for giving such alleviations to the humble, the meek, and the hungry. But the Song predicts, and it demands, for the millions of our kind, much more than alleviations. The proud, the mighty, and the rich – in Jewry, Heathendom, or in Christendom – have never yet realised the actual contents of the *Magnificat*. Have the faithful, the humble, the hungry ever yet realised them? No such revolutionary hymn, no such socialist song, has ever been sung by angry crowds, as that which is so quietly and unsuspectedly said or sung every afternoon in the thousands of Christian parishes. What is more wonderful is that it is said or sung daily by the proud, the mighty, and the rich themselves to their own condemnation. If there had not been a tacit assumption amongst us all that its words are not to be taken in their plain meaning, that it is the business of the clergy to spiritualise away its three terrible contrasts – the moral contrast, the political-social contrast, and the economical contrast – into meaning something distant and unreal, would not the police, in some lands at least, have prohibited such words from being publicly said or sung? 'This carpenter's wife,' they would say, 'is exciting the parishes to revolution. Her so-called hymn is nothing less than a disguised socialist war-song; it is setting class against class; it implies that the three classes, whom she describes as the proud, the mighty, and the rich, are opposing themselves to God and goodness, to the coming of the Father's Kingdom and the doing of His Will on earth. She does not utter one word in condemnation of the evident vices of the poor and the hungry. She speaks of the proud being scattered, the mighty put down from their seats, and the rich sent empty away; she actually rejoices in the vision of this catastrophe of wholesale confiscation. She has not a word to say on behalf of the rights of property and class, or of a fair compensation. The bishops and clergy, if they would earn their pay and justify their social position, ought to point out the dangerous tendencies of these revolutionary stanzas. It would be a very fortunate thing for respectable society if some eminent critic could prove that it was spurious, or if some very early manuscript of the third Gospel could be discovered in which the *Magnificat* is wanting.' Indeed, it is impossible to imagine anything more contrary to the sort of hymn which would proceed from the Virgin of Lourdes, or the Virgin of La Salette, or the Virgin of Marpingen, or the Virgin of Einsiedeln, or any other of those local Virgins to whose statues sound Conservatives and Reactionists all over Europe are now going on pilgrimage. A Pope has declared that the Blessed Virgin is the great foe of Socialism. If the *Magnificat* be her song, it would be far more reasonable to call her the Mother of it. . . .

2.3   THE POPE: A THREAT TO ENGLAND?

The authority claimed by the Church of Rome over Victorian women and men extended quite beyond their individual spiritual lives. As Father Faber (2.2.1) made clear in his 1860 New Year's sermon *Devotion to the Pope,* allegiance to Christ's appointed head of the Church, must be absolute and unswerving in all things. 'The Pope . . . enjoys among the monarchs of the world all the rights and sovereignty of the Sacred Humanity of Jesus. No crown can be above his crown.' 'Even his temporal Kingship is part of our religion' (**2.3.1**). Between the lines of Faber's sermon may be discerned the late affairs of the Italian peninsula: the retreat of temporal power before the armies of Victor Emmanuel II and the corrosive influence of liberalism on respect for Catholic dogma. These affairs also formed the immediate backdrop for the harsh judgments contained in the Syllabus of Errors, which appeared in 1864 as an appendix to the papal encyclical *Quanta cura.* Critics of the Syllabus, including some English Catholics, did not always appreciate the extent to which its eighty propositions, including many concerned with the Church's temporal prerogatives, were intended as a classified index to past papal condemnations of errors that had arisen under particular circumstances. After the Vatican Council of 1870, however, it became more difficult to localize papal claims to spiritual and temporal supremacy. The First Dogmatic Constitution on the Church of Christ, with its conspicuous anathemas, proclaimed the infallibility of the Pope in all matters of which he elects to speak '*ex cathedra*' (**2.3.2**). In 1874 William Ewart Gladstone (1809–1898), with time to spare after retiring temporarily from the leadership of the Liberal Party, thought he saw the handwriting on the wall. He wrote a 'political expostulation' on the Vatican decrees that sold 150,000 copies within the year. It challenged Catholics in general, and their spiritual leader Cardinal Manning (2.1.1) in particular, to declare ultimate allegiance to the Crown (**2.3.3**). Manning replied promptly in *The Times,* later at length. The limitation of civil allegiance 'by conscience and the law of God', as he put it, was not thoroughly defined (**2.3.4**).

2.3.1   F. W. FABER ON DEVOTION TO THE POPE, 1860

... When we serve our dearest Lord in the persons of the Poor and of the Children, we are, as it were, His superiors. We are ministering to Him of our superfluities. He comes before us in pitiable plight, and we are full of pity, and we run to His rescue, and succour Him. Sweet task indeed, and a most wonderful relief to our swelling love, which is ever growing so great as to be a burden to itself! Yet there are other kinds of love, to which we reach as we grow in grace, higher kinds bespeaking higher graces, more robust as being more proper to the fulness of our manhood in Christ. We want to obey. We want to receive commands, to hearken to teaching, to practice submission.... We want more immolation of self in our service of Jesus, than the tending of the Poor and the Children can supply. Besides, we want Jesus in all ways. We want Him as our Master, ... our real living Master, at whose feet we can lay down our frowardness, and at the sound of whose voice we can be out of love with our own judgments and conceits. Jesus left Mary to the infant Church, as well as Peter. Was it not perhaps to supply this very craving of primitive fervour, a craving which had fed itself so recently on His own dear presence in the flesh? Even the sublimities of apostolic holiness could not bear that both Jesus and Mary should be withdrawn at once. So in like manner now He has left us the Pope. The Sovereign Pontiff is a third visible presence of Jesus amongst us, of a higher order, of a deeper significance, of a more immediate importance, of a more exacting nature, than His presence in the Poor and in the Children. The Pope is the Vicar of Jesus on earth, and enjoys among the monarchs of the world all the rights and sovereignties of the Sacred Humanity of Jesus. No crown can be above his crown. By divine right he can be subject to none. All subjection is a violence, and a persecution. He is a monarch by the very force of his office; for of all kings he is the nighest to the King of kings. He is the visible shadow cast by the Invisible Head of the Church in the Blessed Sacrament. His office is an institution emanating from the same depth of the Sacred Heart, out of which ... the Blessed Sacrament, and the elevation of the Poor and of Children, take their rise. It is a manifestation of the same love, an exposition of the same principle. With what carefulness then, with what reverence, with what exceeding loyalty, ought we not to correspond to so magnificent a grace, to so marvellous a love, as this which our dearest Saviour has shown us in His choice and institution of His earthly Vicar! Peter lives always, because the Three-and-Thirty Years are always going on. The two truths belong to each other. The Pope is to us in all our conduct what the Blessed Sacrament is to us in all our adoration. The mystery of His Vicariate is akin to the mystery of the Blessed Sacrament. The two mysteries are inter-twined.

The conclusion to be drawn from all this is of the most momentous importance. It is no less than this: – that devotion to the Pope is an essential part of all Christian piety. It is not a matter which stands apart from the spiritual life, as if the Papacy were only the politics of the Church, an institution belonging to her external life, a divinely appointed convenience of ecclesiastical government. It is a doctrine and a devotion. It is an integral part of our Blessed Lord's own plan. He is in the Pope in a still higher way than He is in the Poor or in Children. What is done to the Pope, for him or against him, is done to Jesus Himself. All that is kingly, all that is priestly, in our dearest Lord is gathered up in the person of His Vicar, to receive our homage and our veneration. A man might as well try to be a good Christian without devotion to our Lady, as without devotion to the Pope; and for the same reason in both cases. Both His Mother and His Vicar are parts of our Lord's Gospel. . . .

If the Pope is the visible presence of Jesus, uniting in himself all such spiritual and temporal jurisdiction as belongs to the Sacred Humanity, and if devotion to the Pope is an indispensable element in all Christian holiness, so that without it no piety is solid, it very much concerns us to see how we feel towards the Vicar of Christ, and whether our habitual sentiments regarding him are adequate to what our Blessed Lord requires. I wish to speak of the matter from a devotional point of view; because I consider this a very important point of view. It belongs to my office and position, as well as to my tastes and instincts, to look at it in this way. In times of peace it is quite conceivable that catholics may hardly realize as they ought to do the necessity of devotion to the Pope as an essential Christian piety. They may practically come to think that their affair is to go to Church, and to frequent the Sacraments, and to perform their private spiritual exercises. It may appear to them that they are not concerned with what they may call ecclesiastical politics. This is of course a sad mistake at all times, and one from which at all times the soul must suffer, so far as regards higher graces and the advances towards perfection. In every age it has been an invariable feature of the saints that they have had a keen and sensitive devotion towards the Holy See. But, if our lot is cast in times of trouble for the Sovereign Pontiff, we shall speedily find that a decay of practical piety follows rapidly and infallibly upon any wrong views of the Papacy, or any cowardly conduct concerning the Pope. We shall be astonished at discovering how close a connection there is between highminded allegiance towards him and all our generosity towards God, as well as God's liberality towards ourselves. We must enter, it must be part of our private devotion to enter, warmly into the sympathies of the Church for her visible Head, or God will not enter into sympathy with us. In all ages, as well as in all vocations, grace is given on certain tacit conditions. In times, when God allows the Church to be assailed in the person of her visible Head, sensitiveness about the Holy See will be found to be an implied condition of all growth in grace.

What are the motives, then, upon which our devotion to the Pope should be based? First and foremost on the fact of his being the Vicar of our dearest Lord. His office is the chief way in which Jesus has made Himself visible on earth. In his jurisdiction he is to us as if he were our Blessed Lord Himself. Then, again, the fearfulness of the Pope's office is another source of our devotion to him. Can any one look over so vast a region of responsibility, and not tremble? Millions of consciences are dependent upon him. Multitudes of appeals are awaiting his decision. The interests with which he has to deal are of surpassing importance, because they bear upon the eternal interests of souls. One day's government of the Church is pregnant with more consequences than a year's government of the mightiest earthly empire. With what a weight the Sovereign Pontiff must have to lean upon God all day long! What endless inspirations of the Holy Ghost must he not anxiously expect in order to distingish truth in the clamour of contradictions or in the obscurity of distance! The Dove whispering at St. Gregory's ear, – what is it but a symbol of the Papacy? Amidst these gigantic toils, of all earthly labours perhaps the most thankless and the least appreciated, how touching is the helplessness of the Sovereign Pontiff, so like the helplessness of his beloved Master. His power is patience. His majesty is endurance. He is the victim of all the petulance and gracelessness of earth in high places. He is verily the servant of the servants of God. Men may load him with indignities, as they spat into his Master's Face. They may set him at nought with their men of war, as Herod with his men of war set at nought the Saviour of the world. They may sacrifice his rights to the momentary exigences of their own meanness, as Pontius Pilate sacrificed our Lord of old. There can be a meanness in governments, to the depths of which no individual meanness can come near; and it is especially from this meanness that the Vicar of Christ is made to suffer. Men with the gold crowns envy him with the crown of thorns. They grudge him the painful sovereignty, for which he must lay down his life, because it is his Master's trust, and not his own inheritance. In every successive generation Jesus, in the person of His Vicar, is before fresh Pilates and new Herods. The Vatican is for the most part a Calvary. Who can behold all the pathetic grandeur of this helplessness, and understand it as a Christian understands it, and not be moved to tears? . . .

But, to the unbelieving eye, the Papacy, like most divine things, is a pitiable and abject sight, provoking only an irritated scorn. For this scorn it is the object of our devotion to make constant reparation. We must honour the Vicar of Jesus with a loving faith, and with a trustful uncriticising reverence. We should not allow ourselves in one dishonouring thought, in one cowardly suspicion, in one fainthearted uncertainty, about anything which concerns either his spiritual or his temporal sovereignty; for even his temporal Kingship is part of our religion. We must not permit to ourselves the irreverent disloyalty of distinguishing in him and in his office what we may consider human from what we may acknowledge as divine. We must defend him with all the pertinacity, with all the vehemence, with all the completeness, with all the comprehensiveness, with which only love knows how to defend her holy things. We must minister to him in self-denying prayer, with a thorough, inward, heartfelt, delighted subjection, and, above all, in these abominable days of rebuke and blasphemy, with a most open, chivalrous, and unashamed allegiance. The interests of Jesus are at stake. We must neither be backward in time, nor mistaken in our side. . . .

2.3.2   THE VATICAN DECREES ON THE PRIMACY AND INFALLIBLE TEACHING OF THE ROMAN PONTIFF, 1870

CHAPTER III

On the Power and Nature of the Primacy of the Roman Pontiff

Wherefore, resting on plain testimonies of the Sacred Writings, and adhering to the plain and express decrees both of our predecessors, the Roman Pontiffs, and of the General Councils, we renew the definition of the œcumenical Council of Florence, in virtue of which all the faithful of Christ must believe that the holy Apostolic See and the Roman Pontiff possess the primacy over the whole world, and that the Roman Pontiff is the successor of blessed Peter, Prince of the Apostles, and is true vicar of Christ, and head of the whole Church, and father and teacher of all Christians; and that full power was given to him in blessed Peter to rule, feed, and govern the universal Church by Jesus Christ our Lord; as is also contained in the acts of the General Councils and in the sacred Canons.

Hence we teach and declare that by the appointment of our Lord the Roman Church possesses a superiority of ordinary power over all other churches, and that this power of jurisdiction of the Roman Pontiff, which is truly episcopal, is immediate; to which all, of whatever rite and dignity, both pastors and faithful, both individually and collectively, are bound, by their duty of hierarchical subordination and true obedience, to submit not only in matters which belong to faith and morals, but also in those that appertain to the discipline and government of the Church throughout the world, so that the Church of Christ may be one flock under one supreme pastor through the preservation of unity both of communion and of profession of the same faith with the Roman Pontiff. This is the teaching of Catholic truth, from which no one can deviate without loss of faith and of salvation.

But so far is this power of the Supreme Pontiff from being any prejudice to the ordinary and immediate power of episcopal jurisdiction, by which Bishops, who have been set by the Holy Ghost to succeed and hold the place of the Apostles, feed and govern, each his own flock, as true pastors, that this their episcopal authority is really asserted, strengthened, and protected by the supreme and universal Pastor; in accordance with the words of St. Gregory the Great: 'My honor is the honor of the whole Church. My honor is the firm strength of my brethren. I am truly honored when the honor due to each and all is not withheld.

Further, from this supreme power possessed by the Roman Pontiff of governing the universal Church, it follows that he has the right of free communication with the pastors of the whole Church, and with their flocks, that these may be taught and ruled by him in the way of salvation. Wherefore we condemn and reject the opinions of those who hold that the communication between this supreme head and the pastors and their flocks can lawfully be impeded; or who make this communication subject to the will of the secular power, so as to maintain that whatever is done by the Apostolic See, or by its authority, for the government of the Church, can not have force or value unless it be confirmed by the assent of the secular power.

And since by the divine right of Apostolic primacy the Roman Pontiff is placed over the universal Church, we further teach and declare that he is the supreme judge of the faithful, and that in all causes, the decision of which belongs to the Church, recourse may be had to his tribunal, and that none may re-open the judgment of the Apostolic See, than whose authority there is no greater, nor can any lawfully review its judgment. Wherefore they err from the right course who assert that it is lawful to appeal from the judgments of the Roman Pontiffs to an œcumenical Council, as to an authority higher than that of the Roman Pontiff.

If, then, any shall say that the Roman Pontiff has the office merely of inspection or direction, and not full and supreme power of jurisdiction over the universal Church, not only in things which belong to faith and morals, but also in those which relate to the discipline and government of the Church spread throughout the world; or assert that he possesses merely the principal part, and not all the fullness of this supreme power; or that this power which he enjoys is not ordinary and immediate, both over each and all the churches, and over each and all the pastors and the faithful: let him be anathema.

CHAPTER IV

Concerning the Infallible Teaching of the Roman Pontiff

Moreover, that the supreme power of teaching is also included in the Apostolic primacy, which the Roman Pontiff, as the successor of Peter, Prince of the Apostles, possesses over the whole Church, this Holy See has always held, the perpetual practice of the Church confirms, and œcumenical Councils also have declared, especially those in which the East with the West met in the union of faith and charity. For the Fathers of the Fourth Council of Constantinople, following in the footsteps of their predecessors, gave forth this solemn profession: The first condition of salvation is to keep the rule of the true faith. And because the sentence of our Lord Jesus Christ can not be passed by, who said: 'Thou art Peter, and upon this rock I will build my Church,' these things which have been said are approved by events, because in the Apostolic See the Catholic religion and her holy and well-known doctrine has always been kept undefiled. Desiring, therefore, not to be in the least degree separated from the faith and doctrine of that See, we hope that we may deserve to be in the one communion, which the Apostolic See preaches, in which is the entire and true solidity of the Christian religion. And, with the approval of the Second Council of Lyons, the Greeks professed that the holy Roman Church enjoys supreme and full primacy and pre-eminence over the whole Catholic Church, which it truly and humbly acknowledges that it has received with the plenitude of power from our Lord himself in the person of blessed Peter, Prince or Head of the Apostles, whose successor the Roman Pontiff is; and as the Apostolic See is bound before all others to defend the truth of faith, so also, if any questions regarding faith shall arise, they must be defined by its judgment. Finally, the Council of Florence defined: That the Roman Pontiff is the true vicar of Christ, and the head of the whole Church, and the father and teacher of all Christians; and that to him in blessed Peter was delivered by our Lord Jesus Christ the full power of feeding, ruling, and governing the whole Church.

To satisfy this pastoral duty, our predecessors ever made unwearied efforts that the salutary doctrine of Christ might be propagated among all the nations of the earth, and with equal care watched that it might be preserved genuine and pure where it had been received. Therefore the Bishops of the whole world, now singly, now assembled in Synod, following the long-established custom of churches, and the form of the ancient rule, sent word to this Apostolic See of those dangers especially which sprang up in matters of faith, that there the losses of faith might be most effectually repaired where the faith can not fail. And the Roman Pontiffs, according to the exigencies of times and circumstances, sometimes assembling œcumenical Councils, or asking for the mind of the Church scattered throughout the world, sometimes by particular Synods, sometimes using other helps which Divine Providence supplied, defined as to be held those things which with the help of God they had recognized as conformable with the sacred Scriptures and Apostolic traditions. For the Holy Spirit was not promised to the successors of Peter, that by his revelation they might make known new doctrine; but that by his assistance they might inviolably keep and faithfully expound the revelation or deposit of faith delivered through the Apostles. And, indeed, all the venerable Fathers have embraced, and the holy orthodox doctors have venerated and followed, their Apostolic doctrine; knowing most fully that this See of holy Peter remains ever free from all blemish of error according to the divine promise of the Lord our Saviour made to the Prince of his disciples: 'I have prayed for thee that thy faith fail not, and, when thou art converted, confirm thy brethren.'

This gift, then, of truth and never-failing faith was conferred by heaven upon Peter and his successors in this chair, that they might perform their high office for the salvation of all; that the whole flock of Christ, kept away by them from the poisonous food of error, might be nourished with the pasture of heavenly doctrine; that the occasion of schism being removed, the whole Church might be kept one, and, resting on its foundation, might stand firm against the gates of hell.

But since in this very age, in which the salutary efficacy of the Apostolic office is most of all required, not a few are found who take away from its authority, we judge it altogether necessary solemnly to assert the prerogative which the only-begotten Son of God vouchsafed to join with the supreme pastoral office.

Therefore faithfully adhering to the tradition received from the beginning of the Christian faith, for the glory of God our Saviour, the exaltation of the Catholic religion, and the salvation of Christian people, the sacred Council approving, we teach and define that it is a dogma divinely revealed: that the Roman Pontiff, when he speaks *ex cathedra*, that is, when in discharge of the office of pastor and doctor of all Christians, by virtue of his supreme Apostolic authority, he defines a doctrine regarding faith or morals to be held by the universal Church, by the divine assistance promised to him in blessed Peter, is possessed of that infallibility with which the divine Redeemer willed that his Church should be endowed for defining doctrine regarding faith or morals; and that therefore such definitions of the Roman Pontiff are irreformable of themselves, and not from the consent of the Church.

But if any one – which may God avert – presume to contradict this our definition: let him be anathema.

Given at Rome in public Session solemnly held in the Vatican Basilica in the year of our Lord one thousand eight hundred and seventy, on the eighteenth day of July, in the twenty-fifth year of our Pontificate.

2.3.3   W. E. GLADSTONE ON THE VATICAN DECREES, 1874

Will it . . . be said that the infallibility of the Pope accrues only when he speaks *ex cathedrâ*? No doubt this is a very material consideration for those who have been told that the private conscience is to derive comfort and assurance from the emanations of the Papal Chair: for there is no established or accepted definition of the phrase *ex cathedrâ*, and he has no power to obtain one, and no guide to direct him in his choice among some twelve theories on the subject, which, it is said, are bandied to and fro among Roman theologians, except the despised and discarded agency of his private judgment. But while thus sorely tantalised, he is not one whit protected. For there is still one person, and one only who can unquestionably declare *ex cathedrâ* what is *ex cathedrâ* and what is not, and who can declare it when and as he pleases. That person is the Pope himself. The provision is, that no document he issues shall be valid without a seal: but the seal remains under his own sole lock and key.

Again, it may be sought to plead, that the Pope is, after all, only operating by sanctions which unquestionably belong to the religious domain. He does not propose to invade the country, to seize Woolwich, or burn Portsmouth. He will only, at the worst, excommunicate opponents, as he has excommunicated Dr. von Döllinger and others. Is this a good answer? After all, even in the Middle Ages, it was not by the direct action of fleets and armies of their own that the Popes contended with kings who were refractory; it was mainly by interdicts, and by the refusal, which they entailed when the Bishops were not brave enough to refuse their publication, of religious offices to the people. It was thus that England suffered under John, France under Philip Augustus, Leon under Alphonso the Noble, and every country in its turn. But the inference may be drawn that they who, while using spiritual weapons for such an end, do not employ temporal means, only fail to employ them because they have them not. A religious society, which delivers volleys of spiritual censures in order to impede the performance of civil duties, does all the mischief that is in its power to do, and brings into question, in the face of the State, its title to civil protection.

Will it be said, finally, that the Infallibility touches only matter of faith and morals? Only matter of morals! Will any of the Roman casuists kindly acquaint us what are the departments and functions of human life which do not and cannot fall within the domain of morals? . . . I submit that Duty is a power which rises with us in the morning, and goes to rest with us at night. It is co-extensive with the action of our intelligence. It is the shadow which cleaves to us go where we will, and which only leaves us when we leave the light of life. So then it is the supreme direction of us in respect to all Duty, which the Pontiff declares to belong to him, *sacro approbante concilio:* and this declaration he makes, not as an otiose opinion of the schools, but *cunctis fidelibus credendam et tenendam.*

But we shall now see that, even if a loophole had at this point been left unclosed, the void is supplied by another provision of the Decrees. While the reach of the Infallibility is as wide as it may please the Pope, or those who may prompt the Pope, to make it, there is something wider still, and that is the claim to an absolute and entire Obedience. This Obedience is to be rendered to his orders in the cases I shall proceed to point out, without any qualifying condition, such as the *ex cathedrâ*. The sounding name of Infallibility has so fascinated the public mind, and riveted it on the Fourth Chapter of the Constitution *de Ecclesiâ,* that its near neighbour, the Third Chapter, has, at least in my opinion, received very much less than justice. . . . The Third Chapter is the Merovingian Monarch; the fourth is the Carlovingian Mayor of the Palace. The third has an overawing splendour; the fourth, an iron grip. Little does it matter to me whether my superior claims infallibility, so long as he is entitled to demand and exact conformity. This, it will be observed, he demands even in cases not covered by his infallibility; cases, therefore, in which he admits it to be possible that he may be wrong, but finds it intolerable to be told so. As he must be obeyed in all his judgments though not *ex cathedrâ*, it seems a pity he could not likewise give the comforting assurance that, they are all certain to be right.

But why this ostensible reduplication, this apparent surplusage? Why did the astute contrivers of this tangled scheme conclude that they could not afford to rest content with pledging the Council to Infallibility in terms which are not only wide to a high degree, but elastic beyond all measure?

Though they must have known perfectly well that 'faith and morals' carried everything, or everything worth having, in the purely individual sphere, they also knew just as well that, even where the individual was subjugated, they might and would still have to deal with the State. . . .

Our Saviour had recognised as distinct the two provinces of the civil rule and the Church: had nowhere intimated that the spiritual authority was to claim the disposal of physical force, and to control in its own domain the authority which is alone responsible for external peace, order, and safety among civilised communities of men. It has been alike the peculiarity, the pride, and the misfortune of the Roman Church, among Christian communities, to allow to itself an unbounded use, as far as its power would go, of earthly instruments for spiritual ends. . . . With what ample assurances this nation and Parliament were fed in 1826; how well and roundly the full and undivided rights of the civil power, and the separation of the two jurisdictions, were affirmed. All this had at length been undone, as far as Popes could undo it, in the Syllabus and the Encyclical. It remained to complete the undoing, through the sub-serviency or pliability of the Council.

And the work is now truly complete. Lest it should be said that supremacy in faith and morals, full dominion over personal belief and conduct, did not cover the collective action of men in States, a third province was opened, not indeed to the abstract assertion of Infallibility, but to the far more practical and decisive demand of absolute Obedience. And this is the proper work of the Third Chapter, to which I am endeavouring to do a tardy justice. . . .

Absolute obedience, it is boldly declared, is due to the Pope, at the peril of salvation, not alone in faith, in morals, but in all things which concern the discipline and government of the Church. Thus are swept into the Papal net whole multitudes of facts, whole systems of government, prevailing, though in different degrees, in every country of the world. Even in the United States, where the severance between Church and State is supposed to be complete, a long catalogue might be drawn of subjects belonging to the domain and competency of the State, but also undeniably affecting the government of the Church; such as, by way of example, marriage, burial, education, prison discipline, blasphemy, poor-relief, incorporation, mortmain, religious endowments, vows of celibacy and obedience. In Europe the circle is far wider, the points of contact and of interlacing almost innumerable. But on all matters, respecting which any Pope may think proper to declare that they concern either faith, or morals, or the government or discipline of the Church, he claims, with the approval of a Council undoubtedly Ecumenical in the Roman sense, the absolute obedience, at the peril of salvation, of every member of his communion. . . .

. . . It is well to remember, that this claim in respect of all things affecting the discipline and government of the Church, as well as faith and conduct, is lodged in open day by and in the reign of a Pontiff, who has condemned free speech, free writing, a free press, toleration of nonconformity, liberty of conscience, the study of civil and philosophical matters in independence of the ecclesiastical authority, marriage unless sacramentally contracted, and the definitions by the State of the civil rights (*jura*) of the Church; who has demanded for the Church, therefore, the title to define its own civil rights, together with a divine right to civil immunities, and a right to use physical force; and who has also proudly asserted that the Popes of the Middle Ages with their councils did not invade the rights of princes: as for example, Gregory VII., of the Emperor Henry IV.; Innocent III., of Raymond of Toulouse; Paul III., in deposing Henry VIII.; or Pius V., in performing the like paternal office for Elizabeth.

I submit, then, . . . that England is entitled to ask, and to know, in what way the obedience required by the Pope and the Council of the Vatican is to be reconciled with the integrity of civil allegiance? . . .

. . . It cannot be denied that the Bishops, who govern in things spiritual more than five millions (or nearly one-sixth) of the inhabitants of the United Kingdom, have in some cases promoted, in all cases accepted, these claims. It has been a favourite purpose of my life not to conjure up, but to conjure down, public alarms. I am not now going to pretend that either foreign foe or domestic treason can, at the bidding of the Court of Rome, disturb these peaceful shores. But though such fears may be visionary, it is more visionary still to suppose for one moment that the claims of Gregory VII., of Innocent III., and of Boniface VIII., have been disinterred, in the nineteenth century, like hideous mummies picked out of Egyptian sarcophagi, in the interests of archæology, or without a definite and practical aim. As rational beings, we must rest assured that only with a very clearly conceived and foregone purpose have these astonishing reassertions been paraded before the world. . . . It must be for some political object, of a very tangible kind, that the risks of so daring a raid upon the civil sphere have been deliberately run. . . .

For there cannot be the smallest doubt that the temporal power of the Popedom comes within the true meaning of the words used at the Vatican to describe the subjects on which the Pope is authorised to claim, under awful sanctions, the obedience of the 'faithful.' . . . No impartial person can deny that the question of the temporal power very evidently concerns the discipline and government of the Church – concerns it, and most mischievously as I should venture to think; but in the opinion, up to a late date, of many Roman Catholics, not only most beneficially, but even essentially. . . . Archbishop Manning, who is the head of the Papal Church of England, and whose ecclesiastical tone is supposed to be in the closest accordance with that of his headquarters, has not thought it too much to say that the civil order of all Christendom is the offspring of the Temporal Power, and has the Temporal Power for its keystone; that on the destruction of the Temporal Power 'the laws of nations would at once fall in ruins;' that (our old friend) the deposing Power 'taught subjects obedience and princes clemency.' Nay, this high authority has proceeded further; and has elevated the Temporal Power to the rank of necessary doctrine. . . .

. . . The more recent utterances of the oracle have not descended from the high level of those already cited. They have, indeed, the recommendation of a comment, not without fair claims to authority, on the recent declarations of the Pope and the Council; and of one which goes to prove how far I am from having exaggerated or strained in the foregoing pages the meaning of those declarations. Especially does this hold good on the one point, the most vital of the whole – the title to define the border line of the two provinces, which the Archbishop not unfairly takes to be the true criterion of supremacy, as between rival powers like the Church and the State.

If, then, the civil power be not competent to decide the limits of the spiritual power, and if the spiritual power can define, with a divine certainty, its own limits, it is evidently supreme. Or, in other words, the spiritual power knows, with divine certainty, the limits of its own jurisdiction: and it knows therefore the limits and the competence of the civil power. It is thereby, in matters of religion and conscience, supreme. I do not see how this can be denied without denying Christianity. And if this be so, this is the doctrine of the Bull *Unam Sanctam*, and of the Syllabus, and of the Vatican Council. It is, in fact, Ultramontanism, for this term means neither less nor more. The Church, therefore, is separate and supreme.

Let us then ascertain somewhat further, what is the meaning of supreme. Any power which is independent, *and can alone fix the limits of its own jurisdiction, and can thereby fix the limits of all other jurisdictions, is,* ipso facto, *supreme.* But the Church of Jesus Christ, within the sphere of revelation, of faith and morals, is all this, or is nothing, or worse than nothing, an imposture and an usurpation – that is, it is Christ or Antichrist. ('Cæsarism and Ultramontanism.' By Archbishop Manning, 1874, pp. 35–6. The italics are not in the original.)

But the whole pamphlet should be read by those who desire to know the true sense of the Papal declarations and Vatican decrees, as they are understood by the most favoured ecclesiastics; understood, I am bound to own, so far as I can see, in their natural, legitimate, and inevitable sense. Such readers will be assisted by the treatise in seeing clearly, and in admitting frankly that, whatever demands may hereafter, and in whatever circumstances, be made upon us, we shall be unable to advance with any fairness the plea that it has been done without due notice.

There are millions upon millions of the Protestants of this country, who would agree with Archbishop Manning, if he were simply telling us that Divine truth is not to be sought from the lips of the State, nor to be sacrificed at its command. But those millions would tell him, in return, that the State, as the power which is alone responsible for the external order of the world, can alone conclusively and finally be competent to determine what is to take place in the sphere of that external order. . . .

2.3.4   H. E. MANNING TO THE EDITOR OF *THE TIMES* ON
MR GLADSTONE AND THE VATICAN DECREES, 1874

Sir, – The gravity of the subject on which I address you, affecting as it must every Catholic in the British Empire, will, I hope, obtain from the courtesy that you have always shown to me the publication of this letter.

This morning I received a copy of a pamphlet entitled 'The Vatican Decrees in their bearing on Civil Allegiance.' I find in it a direct appeal to myself, both for the office I hold and for the writings I have published. I gladly acknowledge the duty that lies upon me for both those reasons. I am bound by the office I bear not to suffer a day to pass without repelling from the Catholics of this country the lightest imputation upon their loyalty; and, for my teaching, I am ready to show that the principles I have ever taught are beyond impeachment upon that score.

It is true, indeed, that, in page 57 of the pamphlet, Mr. Gladstone expresses his belief 'that many of his Roman Catholic friends and fellow-countrymen' are, 'to say the least of it, as good citizens as himself.' But as the whole pamphlet is an elaborate argument to prove that the teaching of the Vatican Council renders it impossible for them to be so, I cannot accept this graceful acknowledgment, which implies that they are good citizens because they are at variance with the Catholic Church.

I should be wanting in duty to the Catholics of this country and to myself if I did not give a prompt contradiction to this statement, and if I did not with equal promptness affirm that the loyalty of our civil allegiance is not in spite of the teaching of the Catholic Church, but because of it.

The sum of the argument in the pamphlet just published to the world is this:— That by the Vatican Decrees such a change has been made in the relations of Catholics to the civil power of States that it is no longer possible for them to render the same undivided civil allegiance as it was possible for Catholics to render before the promulgation of those Decrees.

In answer to this, it is for the present sufficient to affirm:—

1. That the Vatican Decrees have in no jot or tittle changed either the obligations or the conditions of civil allegiance.

2. That the civil allegiance of Catholics is as undivided as that of all Christians and of all men who recognize a divine or natural moral law.

3. That the civil allegiance of no man is unlimited, and therefore the civil allegiance of all men who believe in God, or are governed by consciences is in that sense divided.

In this sense, and in no other, can it be said with truth that the civil allegiance of Catholics is divided. The civil allegiance of every Christian man in England is limited by conscience and the law of God, and the civil allegiance of Catholics is limited neither less nor more.

The public peace of the British Empire has been consolidated in the last half-century by the elimination of religious conflicts and inequalities from our laws. The Empire of Germany might have been equally peaceful and stable if its statesmen had not been tempted in an evil hour to rake up the old fires of religious disunion. The hand of one man more than any other threw this torch of discord into the German Empire. The history of Germany will record the name of Doctor Ignatius Von Döllinger as the author of this national evil. I lament not only to read the name, but to trace the arguments of Dr. Von Döllinger in the pamphlet before me. May God preserve these kingdoms from the public and private calamities which are visibly impending over Germany. The author of the pamphlet, in his first line, assures us that his 'purpose is not polemical, but pacific.' I am sorry that so good an intention should have so widely erred in the selection of the means.

But my purpose is neither to criticize nor to controvert. My desire and my duty as an Englishman, as a Catholic, and as a pastor is to claim for my flock and for myself a civil allegiance as pure, as true, and as loyal as is rendered by the distinguished author of the pamphlet or by any subject of the British Empire.

I remain, Sir, your faithful servant

HENRY EDWARD, Archbishop of Westminster.

November 7.

2.4 THE STRUGGLE FOR IRELAND

The Roman Catholic Church was not unique in making temporal claims. Ireland, where alone within the United Kingdom it held the popular ascendancy, was dominated by a minority Church that pledged allegiance to Canterbury and the Crown. A classic justification of English responsibility for the temporal and spiritual welfare of Ireland appeared in the prolix paternalism of W. E. Gladstone's (2.3.3) early work, *The State in its Relations with the Church* (**2.4.1**). So impressed, however, did Gladstone become with the injustice he had acknowledged there that, with a view towards strengthening the Church in the face of resurgent Irish nationalism, he presided in 1868–69 over its disestablishment. But while the Anglican communion experienced mixed fortunes in Ireland, English evangelicals and Scots-Irish Presbyterians overran the country, trying to convert the people to Reformed Protestant ways. James Begg (1808–1883), a Scottish Free Church minister, exemplified the union of Protestant spiritual and political strategies in his 'text-book of missions for the conversion of Romanists', *A Handbook of Popery* (**2.4.2**). By contrast, and in marked distinction also to Gladstone's paternalism, Archbishop Manning (2.1.1, 2.3.4) emphasized the poverty, the populism, and the apolitical character of the united Roman Catholic Church in England and Ireland (**2.4.3**). Manning's understanding and sympathy for the Irish were almost unique, not only among English Catholics, but among English churchmen at large. Yet it was evident at the time that the Irish Catholic Church, at least, presented a different aspect to some of its politically active members. The Archbishop of Dublin, Paul Cullen (1803–1878), urged his clergy in October 1865 to save their parishioners from entering into nationalist conspiracies and to exercise their own faith (in a manner reminiscent of Begg) through the ballot box and the press (**2.4.4**). In practice, obedience to this directive brought politics into the confessional and police onto the streets. John Devoy (1842–1928), a fervent nationalist who became a noted American journalist, had vivid recollections of the alliance of Church – the Roman Catholic Church – and Crown, which the Fenians found unbeatable (**2.4.5**).

2.4.1   W. E. GLADSTONE ON THE STATE IN ITS RELATIONS TO THE CHURCH, 1838

. . . Upon us of this day has fallen (and we shrink not from it, but welcome it as a high and glorious though an arduous duty) the defence of the Reformed Catholic Church in Ireland, as the religious establishment of the country. The Protestant legislature of the empire maintain in the possession of the church property of Ireland the ministers of a creed professed by one-ninth of its population, regarded with partial favour by scarcely another ninth, and disowned by the remaining seven. And not only does this anomaly meet us full in view, but we have also to consider and digest the fact, that the maintenance of this church for near three centuries in Ireland has been contemporaneous with a system of partial and abusive government, varying in degree of culpability, but rarely until of later years, when we have been forced to look at the subject and to feel it, to be exempted, common fairness, from the reproach of gross inattention (to say the least) to the interests of a noble but neglected people.

But however formidable, at first sight, these admissions, which I have no desire to narrow or qualify, may appear, they . . . do not change the nature of truth, and her capability and destiny to benefit mankind. They do no relieve government of its responsibility, if they show that that responsibility was once unfelt and unsatisfied. They place the legislature of this country in the condition, as it were, of one called to do penance for past offences; but duty remains unaltered and imperative, and abates nothing of her demands on our services. It is undoubtedly competent, in a constitutional view, to the government of this country to continue the present disposition of church-property in Ireland. It appears not too much to assume that our imperial legislature has been qualified to take, and has taken in point of fact, a sounder view of religious truth than the majority of the people of Ireland, in their destitute and uninstructed state. We believe, accordingly, that that which we place before them is, whether they know it or not, calculated to be beneficial to them; and that if they know it not now, they will know it when it is presented to them fairly. Shall we, then, purchase their applause at the expense of their substantial, nay, their spiritual interests?

It does indeed so happen, that there are also powerful motives on the other side concurring with that which has been here represented as paramount. In the first instance, we are not called upon to establish a creed, but only to maintain an existing legal settlement, where our constitutional right is undoubted. In the second, political considerations tend strongly to recommend that maintenance. A common form of faith binds the Irish Protestants to ourselves, while they, upon the other hand, are fast linked to Ireland; and thus they supply the most natural bond of connection between the countries. But if England, by overthrowing their church, should weaken their moral position, they would be no longer able, perhaps no longer willing, to counteract the desires of the majority, tending, under the direction of their leaders (however, by a wise policy, revocable from that fatal course), to what is termed national independence. Pride and fear on the one hand are, therefore, bearing up against more immediate apprehension and difficulty on the other. And with some men these may be the fundamental considerations; but it may be doubted whether such men will not flinch in some stage of the contest, should its aspect at any moment become unfavourable.

What if the truth be this; that among many acts of oppression, many of folly, others again of benevolence and justice, partial or not followed out of their consequences, we have done one, especially among these last, which was in itself thoroughly wise and good, had it been viewed as introductory, and not as final? Who can doubt, that in the position occupied by Elizabeth and her government, it was right on their part to carry into Ireland the restoration of the Christian faith (just as they had carried it through England) with the additional advantage of the almost unanimous acquiescence or concurrence of the bishops, and for this purpose to employ the appointed means of religious ministration to the people? But when the initiatory means had been thus adopted, the whole residue of the labour was relinquished. Those wise and salutary measures which brought the people of England from rebelling in favour of the Roman Catholic church and her superstitions, to their present mood of steady attachment to a purified belief, were not extended to Ireland. The names of Bedell and of Boulter are bright upon the desolate retrospect; but the attempt has not been made until within a period comparatively recent, (thank God it has commenced,) to ascertain what results will follow from the general proclamation of scriptural religion throughout Ireland.

Upon us, therefore, has devolved the duty of supplying, under more critical circumstances, the want of all those measures which might have been taken at an earlier period, and we have still the power of truth to befriend us, greater than any that can oppose. Is this faith of our national church deeply rooted alike in our convictions and in our affections? If so, is it one merely separated by some slight shade from the Roman church, not simply such as she is in theory, but such as she is in the aggravations of her practice, and of her practice, above all, in Ireland? If the difference be broad and clear, if it be represented everywhere in character and conduct among that people, do we shrink from asserting on their behalf the truth which they have a right to know, nay a desire to know, but which, by the interposition of an unnatural and an illegitimate authority, they are prevented from knowing?

Public men feel the duty of securing to the subject the advantages of intellectual cultivation. It has been proposed in this country to render such education compulsory, as is actually done in some others. The expediency of such a measure has been doubted, but those who claim to represent the spirit of the age have hardly questioned the right. Is then the benefit of spiritual truth more ambiguous or less extensive than that of intellectual culture, and can those who are bold enough to propose enforcing the reception of the one, be timid enough to shrink from avowing and approving the offer of the other? We have not yet arrived at the general assertion of such monstrous propositions. And it is a question of spiritual truth in Ireland, arrayed against a church which has hidden the light that is in her amidst the darkness of her false traditions, and which adds to the evils of false doctrine those of schism. Yet we speak of a general principle, not merely of the striking and obvious case which has been cited for the sake of illustration.

Because, therefore, the government stands with us in a paternal relation to the people, and is bound in all things to consider not merely their existing tastes, but the capabilities and ways of their improvement; because it has both an intrinsic competency and external means to amend and assist their choice; because to be in accordance with God's word and will it must have a religion, and because in accordance with its conscience that religion must be the truth as held by it under the most solemn and accumulated responsibilities; because this is the only sanctifying and preserving principle of society, as well as to the individual that particular benefit, without which all others are worse than valueless; we must disregard the din of political contention, and the pressure of worldly and momentary motives, and in behalf of our regard to man, as well as of our allegiance to God, maintain among ourselves, where happily it still exists, the union between the church and the state. . . .

2.4.2   J. BEGG ON THE CONVERSION OF ROMANISTS, 1852

. . . Let us briefly state the points, in promoting which an urgent effort on the part of all true Protestants is loudly called for.

I. A spirit of Christian union should be warmly cherished amongst true Protestants. We do not mean that doctrines reckoned essential should be abandoned. But, since our divisions have been largely the cause of the progress of Rome, let us seek to unite in spirit, and in action, in so far as possible, and let our great aim be to rival each other in promoting the cause of God – the salvation of souls – and in opposing the progress of idolatry and superstition. . . . Let us seek,

II. The thorough instruction of the people of Britain in regard to the true nature of the Papal system. There is profound ignorance abroad on this subject amidst much talk and stir, so that, with many people, a smooth Jesuit has all the field to himself. Ministers of the gospel are deeply criminal who do not instruct themselves, and instruct their people, in the true nature and results of Popery – (see 1 Tim.iv.6); and parents and guardians are criminal who suffer their children to remain unwarned, or to go unnecessarily into the way of temptation.

An effort ought to be made, also, to turn the great agency of the press more decidedly in a Protestant direction, and especially to check the loose and ignorant style of writing upon Popery, which still prevails in many of our journals. This can be effectually done by refusing to take such papers; and, on the other hand, by earnestly countenancing and extending the circulation of those that are sound and intelligent. The press follows public opinion as often as it leads it.

III. We must labour to secure the withdrawment of all public support from the Popish system, either at home, or in the colonies, and especially the overthrow of the College of Maynooth, as an impious mockery of God, and a great focus of evil. This object can only be effectually secured by sending true Protestants to Parliament, instead of the nominal pretenders of recent times. But especially,

IV. Missions to Papists must be established in all the leading towns of Britain, and in every district of Ireland. This, after all, will be found to be the most effectual agency, although other duties are not to be neglected.

Two classes of duties especially are manifestly incumbent upon us. We are bound to use all competent means to rouse the Government to a sense of the danger with which all the best interests of the nation are threatened, and to seek to strengthen the hands of such as are disposed to act with propriety, by the return of sound-hearted representatives to Parliament. But, besides duties incumbent upon us as citizens, we have another class still more binding upon us as Christians, viz., to use all scriptural means to expose and arrest the progress of this gigantic evil, and actually rescue, in a spirit of love, its enslaved victims.

To illustrate the vast importance of this, we need scarcely speak of the value of precious souls or the urgent commands of the Redeemer. The zeal and carnal wisdom of Rome may well rebuke our supineness. Although most eager to secure the support of governments, she never forgets the importance of swelling the number of her adherents. She knows that governments will in the end generally reflect the image of the nation; therefore she 'compasses sea and land to make one proselyte.' The highest are not beyond her insatiable ambition. The poorest are not beneath her devouring anxiety. Every new success only inspires her with fresh ardour, whilst she at the same time watches with unceasing jealousy the slightest symptoms of revolt amongst her own adherents, and in those countries where she reigns, brings the whole engines of persecution to put so-called heretics down with unsparing rigour. Why should the love of Christ and of souls be less efficacious on true Christians for good, than the power of superstition is upon its votaries for evil? Why is the zeal and first love of the Reformation cooled? Why is there so little done and given by Protestants to perpetuate privileges which cost our fathers so much toil and blood? . . . On the one hand we have certainly the worst of causes in Popery; but then there is energy, system, sacrifice, and untiring devotedness in promoting it. On the other hand, we have the best of causes, the very cause of God, in Protestantism; but there is no system, little unity, the most paltry sacrifices, when the magnitude of the object is considered, and a constant, and apparently irresistible tendency to go to sleep, until aroused again by a new alarm, – 'The Philistines be upon thee, Samson.'

But besides this, Popery has evidently a great advantage at present in carrying forward her aggressions by the very nature of her system. She establishes hosts of agents in every direction. Unlike Protestant ministers working single-handed, and overborne generally in large cities by innumerable engagements, Popery appoints two, three, and sometimes four priests to a single chapel, and those priests who require no study to repeat the weekly pantomime of which their service consists, have their whole time devoted to the great work of watching their own adherents, and breaking in upon the straggling and unguarded front of weak and divided Protestantism.

The only way of meeting all this effectually, is by some such separate agency as we have now in certain districts of Ireland, . . . only strengthened, enlarged, and extended to every town and district in the kingdom. We must have some men doing nothing else than dealing with Popery. It has been found by actual experiment, that nothing is so effectual in rescuing men from the grasp of the Man of Sin, as the living truth of God brought to bear on the understanding and conscience, at meetings for the express purpose, and in such a way as directly to confront the lying delusions of Antichrist. The Word of God is still a fire and a hammer to break this rock in pieces; and the meetings which are held from week to week, and from Sabbath to Sabbath, in London, Edinburgh, Dublin, and Connaught, have demonstrated, beyond all controversy, not only that we have at our hand a divinely-appointed method of enlightening slumbering idolators, but, by the blessing of the Divine Spirit, of rescuing Papists from the snare of the Roman fowler.

The principles peculiar to this new mode of agency are chiefly two:— 1st, The Irish language is used wherever it is found necessary. Many of the poor Irish understand no other, and they are all deeply in love with their mother tongue. 'Satan never spoke Irish,' is one of their proverbs, of which Rome has taken large advantage, but of the importance of which, till lately, Protestants seemed deeply insensible. It so happens that Gaelic and Irish are nearly alike, and that whilst the native Irish are the most staunch Papists in the kingdom, the Highlanders are amongst the most fervent Protestants. The key of Popish Ireland, therefore, is to a great extent in our hands. . . . If God wrought a miracle of old for the purpose that every man might hear 'in his own tongue the wonderful works of God,' it seems strange that British Protestants have not sooner made a systematic effort upon this principle for the spiritual regeneration of Ireland. Of course, the same object is gained still more successfully by the employment of the native Irish, and especially of native Irish priests, when converted to the faith of the gospel. 2d, But the second principle of novelty consists in not only teaching the Word of God, but directing that Word controversially against the errors of Rome, and inviting free conversational discussion on the part of the adherents of Popery. It is evident that this was to a great extent the method of our Lord's own preaching. . . . This was also the method of the Reformers; and it is high time that it were generally revived, since there is no more effectual way of training men in a knowledge of the truths of God. The great strength of Rome lies in stifling the human intellect, and especially in suppressing the Bible. The recent scenes of 'Bible-burning' in Ireland, are an emphatic declaration of what Rome chiefly dreads. And it is found, that when Papists have been induced to read that Word, and to think for themselves, the spell that bound them is fairly broken. Hence the great value of discussion, and the utility even of those placards, small tracts, and woodcuts which have been copiously distributed in Ireland and in Great Britain with such undoubted effect. If Protestants would only follow up these efforts, which have already issued in the conversion of thousands of

Romanists, with becoming zeal and liberality, we might expect to see glorious results, and Britain might be more and more the illuminated fortress of truth and freedom in the approaching struggle. If the Christians of this country could only understand one another, and act together, – if true Protestants were placed in the van of this great battle in Parliament, – if, instead of paltry and peddling debates, we could get the whole country educated, – if the old system of scriptural catechising were everywhere resumed by the ministers and by the parents in every family, – if all this were accompanied by willing contributions for important Protestant objects, and by an humble trust in the omnipotence of God, – we should have no doubt of immediate, as we have none of ultimate victory. But if we are to act otherwise, we may rest assured that the triumph of Popery in Britain is a mere question of time. 'Deliverance will arise from another quarter,' and Babylon shall without doubt ultimately fall; but God may resolve, in the meantime, to be avenged on a cowardly and degenerate race, unworthy of those noble ancestors who shed their blood like water, to secure for them an unfettered press, a free pulpit, and an open Bible, by letting them feel the full weight of evil of which they refuse to be warned. . . .

2.4.3   H. E. MANNING ON THE CHURCH IN ENGLAND AND IRELAND, 1867

. . . The Catholic Church in England comes *sine sacculo et sine perâ*, in absolute poverty. The robberies of the Reformation have given us at least this advantage in the face of English public opinion. The Church has no worldly interest to serve. To a missionary Church, poverty is a sign of apostleship. Its priests and its bishop live on the free and willing offerings of their flocks. They have not only the independence which poverty alone can give, the freedom from suspicion of avarice and interest, but they have the generous sympathy and self-denying charity of the faithful, perpetually thoughtful and active to minister all they need. In no country under the sun is the labourer counted 'worthy of his hire' more joyfully and nobly than in England and Ireland at this day. The Catholic Church, therefore, preaches to the people of England with Apostolic freedom of speech. 'We seek not yours but you.' We are 'burdensome' to no man; and no jealousy, or envy, or ostentation of riches, tarnishes its light. Even the spoiler has no temptation to rob: 'Cantabit vacuus coram latrone viator.' The Church in England goes to and fro without fear, having nothing worth taking.

For this cause also, it is eminently in England, as the Church of God must always be in all hands, the Church of the poor. It is not the Church of the Crown, certainly. It is not the Church of the aristocracy. It is not the

Church of the landlords in Ireland or in England. It is the Church of the people, springing from them, mingling with them, watching over them. In the reign of Mary it was royal and aristocratic, and multitudes were provoked and blinded to resist it. In James the Second's time, it was the Church of the Crown and of the Court, and of too many interested, venal, and worldly politicians. The people, already poisoned by a century of Protestantism, rose against it in terror, as against a French despotism and a Spanish Inquisition. In these days it is the Church of the poor. What has the people of Ireland had to protect them or to confide in for three hundred years but its Church and its pastors? The Catholics of England are the poor of Ireland and the poor of England mingling together in poverty, labour, mutual kindness, and marriages which unite both races in the unity of Faith. In past times, since the Reformation, the Catholic Church has been an exotic in England – an air-plant suspended over the soil, without root in the earth. It is now deep in the clay, like the tap root of our old forest tree, which pierces downwards, and spreads on every side with an expanding and multiplying grasp. The million Catholics of England are interwoven with the whole population, and form a solid and sensible bulk in our cities and towns, and are more firmly rooted where these are largest, as in London, Liverpool, Manchester, and Glasgow.

Moreover, the Catholic Church re-enters England wholly free from all political action or interest. It is not bound up with any royal house, or disputed succession, or class legislation, or aristocratic privilege, or monopoly of power or wealth. It has no politics but the maintenance of legitimate authority and the widest popular beneficence. All it asks is to be let alone in the exercise of its spiritual mission. It does not petition for help or favour; but only free air and unfettered limbs. It does not invoke Royal Supremacies, Orders in Council, or Acts of Parliament to spread the Council of Trent, or to silence the Thirty-nine Articles. It has no point of contact, and therefore none of collision, with the political world. It is, moreover, visibly and evidently weak in the sphere of politics. The most timid and superstitious alarmist need have no fear of its political action. . . .

2.4.4 P. CULLEN TO THE CLERGY OF DUBLIN ON FENIANISM, 1865

As to what is called Fenianism, you are aware that, looking on it as a compound of folly and wickedness, wearing the mask of patriotism to make dupes of the unwary, and as the work of a few fanatics or knaves, wicked enough to jeopardize others in order to promote their own sordid views, I have repeatedly raised my voice against it, since it first became known at the time of M'Manus's funeral four years ago, and that I cautioned young men against promising or swearing obedience to strangers with whom they were altogether unacquainted, putting themselves at the mercy of plotting spies and treacherous informers, and risking their lives and liberty, and endangering the lives of others, in attempting to carry out projects, hopeless in themselves, which, doing no good to any class, might involve the country in ruin and bloodshed. Would to God that more attention had been paid to such friendly admonitions. If they had been listened to, we would not now have to regret that so many young men are suffering the hardships of prison, and their families overwhelmed with affliction, whilst their seducers are far away from danger, laughing at the simplicity of their dupes and enjoying the wages of iniquity. But even if no advice had been given – if you, Reverend Brethren, in your affection for your flocks, had not cautioned them against Fenianism, should not those who were called on to join it have raised the following questions: Who are its leaders? What public service have they rendered to their country? What claim have they to demand our confidence? Would they sacrifice others to promote their own sordid views? Are they men of religion? Are they men remarkable for their sobriety, their good conduct, and attention to their own affairs? Have they been successful in business? Are they men to whom we would lend money or trust the management of our property? Were they to succeed, would they be good rulers and good magistrates? Would they better the condition of the country? or rather, as needy and desperate adventurers are always disposed to do, would they not introduce despotism and a system of confiscation, and the spoliation of all property, public and private? In the case of the leaders of the Fenians, if these questions had been seriously considered, no men of sense would have joined their ranks. . . . I again beg of you, Reverend Brethren, to act as you have done for the past, making every effort to save your flocks from the contamination of all secret societies. Remind them, from time to time, that good works are not afraid of the light of day, but that crimes seek to conceal themselves in the darkness of night. Remind them, also, that the Catholic Church condemns all secret societies dangerous to the State or the Church, whether bound by oath or not. All who join in such societies are excommunicated, and cannot be absolved as long as they continue connected with them. . . . Fenianism, however, though powerless to obtain what it proposed, had great influence in bringing about mischief: it succeeded in inducing its dupes to engage in breaches of the law, to disturb the minds of others, and to bring public vengeance on themselves. . . . It is our duty as ministers of the Gospel of Jesus Christ, which inculcates humility and obedience, to encourage a love of peace, to inculcate patience and forbearance in the time of trials and sufferings, and to prevent the spread of secret societies, and to check every thing revolutionary. . . . But are we, then, never to seek for the redress of grievances? . . . Certainly not. Nothing is more comfortable to reason and religion than to expose our sufferings to those in power and to call on them for relief. Among us it is most desirable that this should be done by selecting good members of Parliament, able and willing to state our case and defend our rights in the legislative assembly of the nation. We can also call on the press to expose our wants; we can petition and complain until we make ourselves heard. . . . Following this course we shall be acting in conformity with the dictates of our religion, a matter of paramount importance in whatever we undertake. The teaching of the Scripture is quite clear: Let every one, says St. Paul, be subject to higher powers, for there is no power but from God, and those that are, are ordained of God. Therefore he that resisteth the power, resisteth the ordinance of God; and they that resist, purchase to themselves damnation. Whilst the Scripture lays down this doctrine, it is not only foolish, but it is wicked and sinful, and anti-Christian, to give up peaceable means of redress, and to fly to violence, insubordination and revolution. . . . As the gigantic system of penal laws fell to pieces before the powerful and peaceful agitation of O'Connell, so will all other grievances disappear, if public opinion be properly appealed to. . . . But let us recollect that any conspiracies, any recourse to violence or arms, would only rivet our chains and make things worse than they are. . . . The dissipated, the drunkard, those who engage in and encourage secret plots and conspiracies, may think they are patriots, but they are the worst enemies of the country. Uphappily, we have patriots of this kind; patriots, who by dissipating their property and by extravagance, qualify themselves to be a burden in the workhouse on their parish; patriots, who spend their time in idleness or in smoking and drinking, who make it their business to interrupt and censure whatever is undertaken by others whilst they themselves never move a hand to serve their country. I need scarcely add that we have also other patriots who are loud in their promises and professions, but who, acting on selfish motives, are always ready to sell and revile their country where their own interests can be promoted by doing so.

2.4.5   J. DEVOY ON NATIONALISM AND THE CHURCH

The hardest test the Fenians had to face was the hostility of the authorities of the Catholic Church. It was based ostensibly on the oath, but there was overwhelming evidence that Cardinal Cullen, who was mainly responsible for it, was opposed to the Independence of Ireland – the object of the organization. He would have opposed the movement, even if the oath were dropped. He had bitterly opposed the Tenant League in the early 'Fifties, although it only sought reform of the Land Laws by peaceful methods, and was mild compared with the Land League of later days which was supported by Archbishop Croke of Cashel and several other Bishops. His father, Garret Cullen, was a Kildare farmer, who had been a United Irishman and a leader of Rebels in the Insurrection of 1798. My grandfather walked twenty miles each way to attend his funeral and men thronged from all parts of the country to pay their last tribute of respect to the dead Rebel. But the future Cardinal was sent to Rome when a boy and was thirty-five years out of Ireland. He was in Rome in 1848, when he developed a horror of Revolutionists and never could get over the idea that the Fenians were allied with the Carbonari. There was no basis whatever for the theory, but he assumed that there was and acted on the assumption that it was an undeniable fact. The Fenians had no connection whatever with any movement outside of Ireland except the Fenian Brotherhood in America, which was composed entirely of Irishmen and had only one object, the Independence of Ireland.

Dr. Cullen based his assumption of an alliance with the Carbonari on the fact that James Stephens while a refugee in Paris had fought at the barricades in the Red resistance to Louis Napoleon's *Coup d'etat* in 1851, and claimed that he was an enrolled member of the Communist Party. Even if he were, he never tried to convert the Fenians to Communism, and his chief lieutenants. O'Leary, Luby and Kickham, were most conservative men. But the Cardinal stuck to his theory to the last and waged unrelenting war on the organization.

The oath was wholly unnecessary and did not prevent men from turning informer, while it kept many good Nationalists from joining the organization. In America there was no oath, only a pledge of honor, but Bishop Duggan of Chicago denounced the organization as strongly as Cardinal Cullen did in Ireland. A committee waited on the Bishop and asked him what they could do to make the organization harmonize with the Church and he answered: 'Give up your object.' The committee replied: 'But our object is the Independence of Ireland,' and his answer was: 'I have said you must give it up.' That ended the interview. He had given accurate expression to Cardinal Cullen's attitude towards Fenianism.

The members were refused absolution when they went to confession unless they promised to give up the organization, and many thousands of them refused. The form of the question asked by the priest was: 'Did you take the Fenian oath?' It never was: 'Are you a member of the Fenian organization?' Many men availed themselves of this to evade trouble. . . .

Archbishop MacHale of Tuam – 'the Lion of the Fold of Judah' – and Bishop Keane of Cloyne refused to allow their priests to carry out this plan, and when a Papal Rescript condemning the organization was issued it was not promulgated in either Diocese. This encouraged the members in their resistance, and largely counteracted the effect of the Cardinal's hostility. Skibbereen is in the Diocese of Ross, where Bishop O'Hea was a bitter enemy of the organization, but the men had only to cross a small stream to get into the Diocese of Cloyne, and they went by the score at Christmas and Easter and got absolution from a Cloyne priest. In Dublin at that time the Jesuits did not enforce the rule and men from the other parishes had only to go to Gardiner Street Church to get the sacraments denied them in their own.

But in ninety per cent. of the cases it was a flat denial of the right of the priest to ask the question and to bring politics into the confessional. The Fenians were accused of being anti-clerical, but it was the Clericals who were anti-Fenian. And, there can be no doubt that the constant controversies and the continued altar denunciations were fast developing an anti-clerical feeling and several Fenians were temporarily estranged from the Church. The ominous cry of 'No priests in politics' was heard everywhere. Had the fight continued there can hardly be any doubt that it would have resulted eventually in an anti-clerical movement in Ireland. But the fight was begun by the Church authorities on charges that had no foundation and was forced on the Fenians. Some of the altar denunciations were very unjust in their statements and were invariably followed by increased police activities. One priest in Belfast accused Luby, of whom he knew nothing, and who was a most devoted husband, of living with the wife of another man, and the Carbonari myth was constantly flung at us. Several priests were members of the organization, but they were mostly young curates, whose brothers or other near relatives belonged to it. The Parish Priests were almost unanimous in their opposition to us, even in cases where they had been in the Young Ireland Movement.

The most notable instance of this was Bishop Moriarty of Kerry who said 'Hell is not hot enough nor eternity long enough to punish the Fenians'. Gavan Duffy said that he was all right in 1848 and the Bishop himself defined his attitude in a public speech thus: 'When I speak to you from the pulpit or in a Pastoral I speak as your Bishop, but here on this platform I'm plain David Moriarty', – which caused one enthusiast in the audience to shout: 'You're our Bishop if you were boilt.'

There were some comic features in the controversy, as there are in everything in Ireland. In Cork, a Blackpool boy – where they said 'dis' and 'dat' – went to confession and when the priest asked him if he had taken the Fenian oath he said: 'I did, but what has dat to do wid me confession?' The priest answered: ''Tis an illegal society,' and 'de boy from the Pool' replied: 'Yerra, what does I care about deir illaigal? I tinks more o' me sowl.'

His theology was better than the priest's. It was illegal at one time in Ireland to go to Mass, and if Lord John Russell's Ecclesiastical Titles Bill were in force it would be illegal for a Bishop to attach the cross to his signature to a Pastoral. . . .

A public controversy on the subject was carried on in the *Irish People,* in which the hostile priests were called 'felon-setters' and some of the letters pointed out that they were inciting the police to increased activity. That was undoubtedly true. My own Parish Priest, Father Hughes of Naas, only denounced the organization once, and the Peelers, who were all Catholics except Head Constable Hogg and Sergeant Johnson, knew all of us and stared at us while he informed them that an illegal society existed in the parish. That night they followed our men everywhere they went. He based his denunciation on a letter of Cardinal Barnabo (which was not official, but was published) in which the statement was made that the Pope had condemned Fenianism. I wrote a letter to the *Irish People* in which I stressed the activities of the Peelers on that Sunday evening and said that the Pope was misinformed by the English Catholic clique in Rome, and added that an Irish shoemaker was a better judge of Irish politics than his Holiness. The letter appeared in the suppressed number, but the country edition had been sent off before the seizure and I sent copies of the paper to Father Hughes and Sub-Inspector Irwin.

Next morning Father Hughes called on me at 8 o'clock, a few minutes before the mail car brought the Dublin papers containing the report of the *Irish People*'s suppression. I had not signed the letter, but Father Hughes told me he knew that it was I who wrote it, because I was the only man in the town capable of doing so. I admitted I was the writer and defended my action. He said he did not come to argue with me and I said: 'But you are arguing, Father Hughes, and I insist on my right to answer you.' He was particularly worked up over my statement about the Irish shoemaker, which I defended. I had concluded the letter with this statement – a sort of olive branch: 'Altar denunciations have failed elsewhere and it is to be hoped that Father Hughes, who has hitherto refrained from denouncing the movement, will not again make the altar an instrument of political controversy.' This seemed to please him and he said: 'I have up till now kept my parish free from this trouble and you will hear no more of it,' but he added, pointing to four tall poplar trees in the garden in front of the house: 'But those unfortunate men will hang as high as those trees – and they deserve it.' With that he took his departure. He was a dyed-in-the-wool West Briton, whose father was a gombeen man in Carlow, who left him £20,000, which he invested in the Government Funds, and he was the landlord of the premises on which I worked. He did not like being attacked in print and his statement was a surrender.

In a few minutes the mail cars drove in and the *Freeman* contained the report of the seizure of the *Irish People*. I am convinced that if Father Hughes had read it he would not have made the promise. But he kept it.

When I was arrested his servant girl told her sister, who was the wife of one of the draymen where I worked, that he clasped his hands and turning his eyes up to Heaven said: 'Thank God, a firebrand is removed from amongst us.' . . .

That incident illustrates the conditions existing in Ireland at the time. My personal experience later gives a further illustration:

Father Cody, the Chaplain of Mountjoy Prison, was a very zealous priest and a very likable man, but by no means bright – a great contrast to Father Potter, who replaced him during his vacations. His sermons were mere instructions on the catechism and when making his rounds of the cells he always carried a handful of devotional books, which had no attraction for the ordinary convicts – 'The Poor Man's Catechism', 'Think Well On It', St. Alphonsus Liguori's Works, or 'Hell Open to Sinners' – never anything cheerful or interesting. He could not argue at all. He and I were on the best of terms, but we never discussed Irish politics.

One day he said to me: 'Why don't you go to confession?' and I answered: 'Sure, there would be no use because you'd ask me a question that I don't admit your right to ask.'

He turned his face away, prodded the door with his big key and said: 'Oh, I've nothing to do with your politics; I've nothing to do with your politics.' I took this as a promise that he would not ask me if I had taken the Fenian oath, and we arranged a day on which I would go to confession to him.

When I had finished my long story – it was five years old – for I knew there was no use in going to Father Hughes and he never said a word to me about confession, though I met him almost every day in the reading room of the Catholic Institute – Father Cody asked me: 'Did you take the Fenian oath?'

I answered: 'I thought you promised not to ask me that question.'

'Oh, I have to ask it,' he said, 'it's the rule of the Diocese.'

I reminded him that he belonged to one of the orders and was not subject to the jurisdiction of Archbishop Cullen. He told me he was and we proceeded to argue the question, if I may call what he said arguments. I refused to submit and we fixed another day for him to come again. This was repeated five times and on the fifth day I stood up and said: 'Father Cody, I won't argue politics on my knees any more.' . . .

When we got to Millbank we found Father Zanetti, a Jesuit, whose father was Italian and his mother English, as Chaplain. . . . I went to confession and told Father Zanetti . . . I had made an attempt to escape and had hurt a warder in the struggle for possession of his keys, for which I was very sorry, as he was a harmless poor fellow who later told me he made allowance for my state of mind and had no hard feelings against me. When I had finished my tale of sin Father Zanetti said to me: 'You used violence in attempting to escape.' I told him I was a prisoner of war, held by a Government which had no right whatever in Ireland, and that I was justified in using any means in trying to escape.

Then followed a long argument, in which Father Zanetti quibbled a lot. I reminded him that the warders carried heavy oak clubs and that the Civil Guard, who carried carbines, had orders to shoot a prisoner if they could not prevent his escape in any other way and that this justified me in using violence.

'Ah,' said Father Zanetti, 'if he had his carbine levelled and was about to shoot, you would be justified in knocking it out of his hand or striking him.' 'Then it would be too late,' I replied, and added: 'Do you mean to tell me that God Almighty would split hairs as to whether I struck the man with a carbine a second before or a second after he had levelled it at me?'

The argument went on in this way for a long time, and at length Father Zanetti said: 'I am an officer of the prison and it is my duty to see the rules enforced.'

Then I stood up and said: 'Father Zanetti, I came to you as a priest of the Catholic Church. I don't make any confessions to an officer of an English prison.' That was the end of the confession and it was a very long time before I went to confession again. . . .

In describing Fenianism to Sir Horace Plunkett at a dinner in the house of Justice Martin J. Keogh in New Rochelle some years ago, I said: 'We'd have beaten the Bishops only for the English Government, and we'd have beaten the English Government but for the Bishops, but a combination of the two was too much for us.' That was really what the Fenians had to face. . . .

3

NONCONFORMITY AND NEOLOGY

3.1 THE PRINCIPLES OF DISSENT: ENGLAND AND SCOTLAND

OUTSIDE the established Anglican churches, those who practised Christianity according to their conscience were known as Non-conformists or Dissenters. Since the Act of Uniformity in 1662 they had lived and worshipped under potentially crippling disabilities, but the Victorian age brought emancipation. The monopoly of the Establishment was gradually broken down; competitive individualism and free trade became the norm in religious and social life alike. It was at the beginning of this process, as Parliament prepared to consider the emotive question of Church rates, that John Angell James (1785–1859), the Congregational minister of Carr's Lane Chapel in Birmingham, reminded his flock of the two chief principles of Nonconformity: the sole and sufficient authority of the Scriptures and the right and duty of the individual to interpret them (**3.1.1**). Thirty years later, his successor R. W. Dale (1829–1895) explained, in a lecture commemorating the bicentenary of the Act of Uniformity, that the Act had not only failed to eradicate Dissent; it had also proved powerless to stifle the outbreak of nonconformity among the Anglican clergy. Using Oxford as a case study, he pointed out that 'the Evangelicals dissent from the theology of the liturgy; the Tractarians from the theology of the Articles; the Essayists [and Reviewers] from the theology of both' (**3.1.2**). Such considerations led many Nonconformists to conclude that a separation from the Establishment was inevitable, and they hoped that the party in question would be their nearest descendants, the Evangelicals. In 1843 a separation for the sake of spiritual and ecclesiastical freedom had indeed taken place, but within the established Church of Scotland. A detailed narrative of this hopeful precedent, based on first hand accounts, was drawn up in 1884, and the dramatic extract below contains as an insertion the full text of the solemn 'Protest' made in the General Assembly on 18 May 1843 by the Revd David Welsh (1793–1845), who then led the exodus of some 450 evangelical ministers to form the Scottish Free Church (**3.1.3**).

3.1.1   J. A. JAMES ON THE PRINCIPLES OF DISSENT, 1834

. . . Never since the dark and awful day which the Protestants of this country, in imitation of the Papists in France, made for ever memorable by the cruelties of persecution, and on which they laid the foundation of Nonconformity in the expulsion of two thousand holy ministers from the Church of England, has there been so much thought and said about the principles of Dissent, as there is at the present time. The subject has become one of universal interest to the nation, and must soon become one of grave deliberation to the legislature; and, like every other cause, it will *increase* in interest as it approaches the hour of decision. The conflict of opinion is commenced; and where, how, and when it will terminate, is known only to Him who seeth the end from the beginning. The strife of pens, on the arena of controversy, will soon be followed by the strife of tongues, in the seat of legislation. The claims of Dissenters for justice, and of Churchmen for the preservation of their monopoly, will be urged, discussed, and adjusted, during the next session of Parliament. Nor will the minor points alone be brought into discussion, there is a searching spirit of enquiry abroad, which will go to the very root of the matter, and advance at once to the question, 'Are Religious Establishments accordant with the word of God, creditable to the character of religion, or the best means of supplying instruction to the people?' At such time no pious or even patriotic man should feel that he can be neutral; a judgment must be formed, a side taken, and every *legitimate* weapon appropriated and employed. Especially should every Dissenter make himself thoroughly acquainted with the merits, arguments, and bearings of the question in dispute.

On these accounts then, I have determined to address you at the present season on the principles of Nonconformity . . . The whole fabric of Dissent rests on the two following propositions:

1. *The Holy Scriptures are the sole authority and sufficient rule in matters of religion, whether relating to doctrine, duty, or church government.* THE BIBLE, AND THE BIBLE ALONE, IS THE RELIGION OF DISSENTERS. We own no other standard, we allow of no other, and resist all attempts to impose any other upon us. No plea of antiquity, of civil or ecclesiastical authority, of numbers, of expediency, of taste, or of the importance of uniformity, has the smallest weight with us, since neither the writings of fathers, nor the decree of councils, nor the acts of senates, nor the concurrent opinions of divines, much less if possible, the bulls of popes, or the edicts of kings, can, individually or unitedly, frame one single article of faith, or decree one religious ceremony, which on *their* authority, is binding upon the conscience of the most illiterate man in existence. To set up any other authority over conscience than the Word of God, is treason against the

throne of Christ, and they who submit to it are accomplices in the conspiracy.

2. The second proposition on which Nonconformity rests, is, *that it is every man's indefeasible right, and incumbent duty, to form and to follow his own opinion of the meaning of the word of God.* He may consult the works of the living or the dead; he may listen with deference to the arguments of others, who have greater abilities, and better means of acquiring knowledge, than himself; but his ultimate reason for receiving any and every opinion, must be, not thus saith the church, but thus saith the Bible; not thus have my forefathers worshipped God, but thus am I directed by God himself to worship him. We must try creeds, catechisms, articles, and forms of government, by the Bible, and form our own conclusion of their accordance with that unerring standard. – I say not we *may* do it, but we *must;* it is not merely a privilege to be enjoyed, but a duty to be performed. The *people* as well as their teachers, are commanded to 'search the scriptures; to prove all things, and to hold fast that which is good.' Our understanding is given to us for this purpose, and as we must stand or fall for eternity by our religious opinions and practice, we ought not to *believe* by proxy, since we cannot be *saved* by proxy. As no man, nor body of men, has the right, nor can have it, to set up any other standard of religious opinion than the Bible, so neither can they have any right to impose upon us their interpretation of *this*; for if they had, it would in fact be setting up another authority. The doctrines you believe, the duties you perform, the ceremonies you observe, the form of church government you adopt, must all be drawn pure from the Bible, and drawn thence by yourself; aided, it may be, by the wisdom, but not compelled by the authority of others. The denomination in the religious world with which you connect yourself, and the minister to whom you entrust the oversight of your soul's affairs, are to be chosen by yourselves. No man has either a moral or legal right to claim to be your religious instructor without your own consent. In all matters which we have to learn, docility is our first duty, and freedom of thought is the next; and if the most unbounded exercise of this freedom from human authority be once resigned, we are liable to become the slaves of those whose attempts at usurpation are the most subtle, however widely they may have departed from the word of God. Our reverence for the Scripture cannot be too profound, nor our submission to its authority too unresisting; nor on the other hand can we be too jealous and determined in our resistance of every other yoke. I call upon you, therefore, my dear friends, to make yourselves intimately acquainted with the Word of God. Search the Bible, and determine to follow it as your guide wherever it may lead you. Do your uttermost to raise the cry, 'to the Bible,' till it becomes the universal demand, 'to the Bible, to the Bible.' I would not say, 'down with creeds, catechisms, and articles,' but I will say, 'up with the Bible.'

The creed, the church, the articles, that cannot stand the most searching scrutiny of this, is based on falsehood, and amidst the floods and tempests that are rising around it will be swept away, and perish from the earth; and those only will remain, and *they will* remain, that are founded, not upon the quicksand of human opinion, but upon the rock of Holy Scripture.

In the view of Protestant Dissenters, a church of Christ is a spiritual, voluntary, and independent community, distinct in its nature from all secular associations of men, separated from them by the peculiarity of its object and its laws, and neither subject to their direction, nor amenable to their authority. It is a kingdom *in* this world, but not *of* this world. . . .

3.1.2   R. W. DALE ON NONCONFORMITY IN 1862

. . . It may . . . be suggested that Dissent exists because the laws which persecuted it have been long repealed, and that the Act of 1662 has, at any rate, secured Uniformity within the Church itself. I reply that in speaking of Nonconformity in 1862 it is impossible to be oblivious of the present divisions of opinion among the clergy of the Establishment. It is true that they all subscribe the same articles of faith; they recite the same ancient creeds; they confess sin, and offer worship in the words of the same venerable Liturgy; they all wear the prescribed vestments, and administer the sacred rites according to the same rubrics; but it is notorious that, beneath this external show of unity, there are the broadest differences between the theological teaching of many of them and the authoritative documents they have been compelled to approve. From time to time there are controversies as fierce between different parties in the Church, and mutual recriminations as bitter, as though they belonged to religious communities in open hostility to each other. They are all Conformists at the altar, at the font, at the grave's mouth, and in the reading-desk; but multitudes of them become Nonconformists as soon as they write theological treatises, or stand up in the pulpit.

Strangely enough, the great divisions existing in the English Church in our own day, have all had their origin in that University which we are accustomed to think of as the very stronghold and bulwark of good old-fashioned Church-of-Englandism. Most of us, I suppose, have felt, when passing through Oxford, that in the neighbourhood of the stately colleges which line the streets of that glorious city, it must require great courage to resist the authority of antiquity, and to exercise freedom of religious thought. In the magnificent quadrangle of Christ Church, under the shadow of the graceful tower of Magdalen, in the peaceful gardens of St. John's, we should never expect any movement to arise that would disturb the quiet of the English Church, or separate her sons into hostile theological schools.

And yet it was at Oxford that, about one hundred and thirty years ago, John Wesley and George Whitfield began to be alarmed by the discovery that irreligion, unbelief, and the grossest immorality prevailed in all classes of society, and that the clergy were doing very little to prevent the nation sinking fast into atheism and vice. Inspired with a divine fervour, they became the apostles of a new Reformation. As the result of their work, there are now not only great Nonconforming communities, which refer their origin or their renewed strength to those men, their associates and their successors, but there is a large section of the clergy whose spirit and theological opinions must be traced to the same source. It is not necessary that before this audience I should attempt to estimate the obligations of the Church and of the nation to the diligence and earnestness of the Evangelical clergy. They have saved the Establishment from destruction; they have delivered thousands of families from the curse of a formal and heartless ministry; they have taken a noble part in the education of the children of the poor; they have stimulated and directed the zeal of thousands of Christian men and women to the evangelisation of the heathen, and the recovery of great masses of our own population from squalid poverty and gross vice. But the doctrines commonly supposed to be preached by the 'Evangelical' clergy cannot be harmonised with several of the services which the Act of Uniformity obliges them to approve and employ. Tried by the theology of the Articles, the Evangelical clergy are Conformists, as many of us might be; tried by the theology of the services for Baptism, for the Visitation of the Sick, and the Burial of the Dead, they are Nonconformists as really as though they sat at a Kirk session, or preached in an Independent meeting-house.

Thirty years ago, in that same University of Oxford, there arose another party, strong in the learning, the genius, the courage, and the saintly character of their leaders. They had keen, eager, metaphysical disputants among them; they had men rich in ecclesiastical learning; they had poets; they had preachers, who in many of the highest qualities of pulpit eloquence were unsurpassed – I had almost said unapproached – by any of their contemporaries. These men were troubled by the internal confusions and the external dangers of the Church. During the earlier years of this century, the power of Dissent increased with amazing rapidity. The progress of Evangelical opinions in the Church gave point to the attacks of Nonconformists on the unevangelical character of certain parts of the Prayer Book. The discussion of the imperfections of our political system was accomplished with incessant attacks upon ecclesiastical abuses; and at last the success of the protracted struggles for the reform of the House of Commons provoked a universal restlessness and agitation, which seemed to threaten the security of several of our ancient institutions; the Church Establishment especially appeared to be in peril. The imposition of church-rates was resisted. The history of the tithe system was investigated. The justice and expediency of the connection between Church and State was challenged. It was just the time for a new religious party to appear in the Church itself; just the time for a few young scholars and theologians, who had studied with affectionate veneration the writings of the Fathers and of the great Episcopalian divines, to attempt to restore the ancient glories of Episcopacy; and especially to re-awaken, in a turbulent and revolutionary age, the calmer and deeper religious life, the submission to authority, the reverence for antiquity, which characterised the Church of earlier times. The attempt was made with a vigour, a zeal, and an ability which it is hardly possible to overrate; and an immense number of the younger clergy began to preach the doctrines taught in the 'Tracts for the Times.' They had been thrilled and awed by the sermons of Dr. Newman in St. Mary's; they had felt the fascination of the new regions of theological literature which began to be popular at Oxford; their hearts were touched by the piety of the 'Christian Year;' and in every corner of England there began to appear a race of ministers asserting the lofty prerogatives of the Christian priesthood, and teaching that the sacraments of the Church were the only trustworthy channels of Divine grace. They appealed to the authority of the Liturgy; and it was impossible to deny that it justified many of their most prominent distinctive principles. They had learned, however, from their leaders, not only to accept the sacramental teaching of certain offices in the Prayer Book, but to deny the Calvinistic and Evangelical teaching of the Articles. They occupied a position exactly the opposite of that which was assumed by their brethren whose life and thought had been the growth of the revival of the eighteenth century. The Evangelical clergy accepted the doctrinal Articles in their natural sense, and put a meaning of their own on certain parts of the Liturgy: the Tractarian clergy accepted the Liturgy in its natural sense, but put a meaning of their own on the Articles. Tried by the Liturgy, the Tractarians are good Churchmen, and the Evangelicals Nonconformists; but the Evangelicals are good Churchmen, and the Tractarians Nonconformists when tried by the doctrinal Articles.

Later still, in that same University, another party has been rapidly forming, and the whole country has been ringing with the controversy provoked by their first important manifesto. About the exact theological system of this new school it is hard to speak, so undefined are its first principles, so unscientific its methods of inquiry, so vague its announced results; but whatever the positive belief may be of some of the writers of the 'Essays and Reviews,' it is tolerably certain that that belief harmonises neither with the Articles they have signed, the creeds they recite, the daily prayers they offer, or the occasional services they are bound to use. The Evangelicals dissent from the theology of the Liturgy; the Tractarians from the theology of the Articles; the Essayists from the theology of both; and it remains to be seen whether the Act of Uniformity, which has permitted the first two parties to divide the great majority of the clergy between them, is strong enough to prevent the growth and temporary triumph of the third. Never, surely, was a great political and ecclesiastical measure so powerless as this. Leave out of view the moderate Anglicans, represented by the Bishop of Oxford, and the High Church Evangelicals who are daily gathering strength, and in this, the two hundredth year of the operation of the Act which was to reduce all England to uniformity of religious opinion and practice, you will find it difficult to discover, not those who dissent from the teaching of the Prayer Book, but those who completely and thoroughly accept it. . . .

3.1.3   THE DISRUPTION IN THE CHURCH OF SCOTLAND, 1843

At last the decisive day arrived – the 18th of May. Business in Edinburgh was for the most part suspended, and all along the streets there was general excitement, as if men felt themselves in presence of some great event. Already, at break of day, an eager crowd besieged the doors of St. Andrew's Church, where the Assembly was to meet; and no sooner were they opened than every inch of space available for the public was densely crowded. There had been numerous arrivals from all parts of Scotland, and even from abroad. Dr. Stewart, – then of Erskine, – for example, who had been ordered for his health to the south of Europe, tells how he arrived just in time to take part in the proceedings: 'I had to leave my family in London, and hurried down by mail-coach and rail to Edinburgh, to be present at the Disruption – arriving from Constantinople by uninterrupted travelling at four o'clock on the morning of that eventful day.'

The opening scene was at Holyrood, where, as usual, the Lord High Commissioner held his levee, while 'the yearly gleam of royalty was flickering about the old grim turrets.' Never had the reception-rooms of the Palace been more densely crowded, for those who were about to abandon the Establishment sought all the more to testify their abiding loyalty.

'Being a member for the last time,' says Mr. Lewis, of Dundee, 'of the General Assembly of the Established Church in May, 1843, I was in Edinburgh on the appointed day, and attended the levee of Her Majesty's Commissioner, the Marquis of Bute, anxious to show our loyalty to Cæsar when about to give to Christ the things that belong to Christ. While crowding the ante-room, and waiting the opening of the door, the portrait of William III., oddly enough, gave way, and seemed about to fall, some one, as we tried to prop it up, exclaiming, "There goes the Revolution Settlement!" an incident which, a hundred years earlier, had been interpreted as one of evil omen and warning; but, like other omens, it came too late to be of much use.'

At the close of the levee, shortly after noon, the Commissioner entered his carriage; the procession, with its military escort, moved round by the Calton Hill, up the North Bridge, and on to the High Church, where sermon was preached by Dr. Welsh, the retiring Moderator, from the words: 'Let every man be fully persuaded in his own mind.'

'The discourse,' says Dr. James Hamilton, 'was a production which, for wise and weighty casuistry, for keen analysis of motives, and fine discrimination of truth, and for felicity of historic illustrations, would have been a treat to such a congregation at a less eventful season. With the solemn consciousness that in the full persuasion of their own minds, they had decided in another hour to take a step in which character, and worldly comfort, and ministerial usefulness were all involved, each sentence came with a sanction which such sermons seldom carry.'

Service being over, men hurried along the streets and through the gathering crowds to St. Andrew's Church. Outside, the spacious street was an impressive spectacle, with its masses of eager spectators, while inside the Church the dense crowd, after long hours of suspense, were intently waiting for the issue.

'I was one of the first,' says Dr. M'Lauchlan, 'who made his way from the High Church, where Dr. Welsh preached, to St. Andrew's Church, where the Assembly met. When I entered, the seats on the Evangelical side were almost all empty. On the Moderate side they were quite full, with Dr. Cook in front – the ministers from that side not having been at the sermon. I sat beside Dr. John Smyth, of Glasgow. The galleries were packed full, and soon the whole house was crowded. When silence followed the rush of members, as we waited for the Moderator and Commissioner, I turned to Dr. Smyth. His eyes were full of tears, and he remarked, "This is too much." '

It was about half-past two o'clock, or rather later, when Dr. Welsh was seen to enter and take the chair. Soon after there was heard the measured tramp of the soldiery outside, and the swell of martial music, with the sounds of the Queen's Anthem, announcing the approach of the Commissioner, and almost immediately he appeared and took the Throne, the whole assembly rising to receive him. When Dr. Welsh presented himself to the house all the hesitancy which often marked his speaking had left him. 'He was firm and collected,' writes his friend, Mr. Dunlop, 'very pale, but full of dignity, as one about to do a great deed – and of elevation, from the consciousness that he was doing it for the cause of Christ.' In solemn and fitting words the opening prayer was offered, and then a stillness as of death fell over the great assembly. Men held their breath – 'every heart vibrated with a strange awe.'

Again Dr. Welsh rose. 'Fathers and Brethren,' he said, and his voice sounded clear to the furthest limits of the great audience, 'according to the usual form of procedure, this is the time for making up the roll, but in consequence of certain proceedings affecting our rights and privileges – proceedings which have been sanctioned by Her Majesty's Government, and by the Legislature of the country; and more especially in respect that there has been an infringement on the liberties of our Constitution, so that we could not now constitute this Court without a violation of the terms of the Union between Church and State in this land, as now authoritatively declared – I must protest against our proceeding further. The reasons that have led me to come to this conclusion are fully set forth in the document which I hold in my hand, and which, with permission of the House, I shall now proceed to read.'

Then followed the memorable Protest, in which . . . it was declared: . . .

We, the undersigned Ministers and Elders, chosen as Commissioners to the General Assembly of the Church of Scotland, indicted to meet this day, but precluded from holding the said assembly by reason of the circumstances hereinafter set forth, in consequence of which a Free Assembly of the Church of Scotland, in accordance with the laws and constitution of the said Church, cannot at this time be holden, –

Considering that the Legislature, by their rejection of the Claim of Right adopted by the last General Assembly of the said Church, and their refusal to give redress and protection against the jurisdiction assumed, and the coercion of late repeatedly attempted to be exercised over the courts of the Church in matters spiritual by the Civil Courts, have recognised and fixed the conditions of the Church Establishment, as henceforward to subsist in Scotland, to be such as these have been pronounced and declared by the said Civil Courts in their several recent decisions, in regard to matters spiritual and ecclesiastical, whereby it has been held *inter alia*, –

1st, That the courts of the Church by law established, and members thereof, are liable to be coerced by the Civil Courts in the exercise of their spiritual functions; and in particular, in the admission to the office of the holy ministry, and the constitution of the pastoral relation, and that they are subject to be compelled to intrude ministers on reclaiming congregations in opposition to the fundamental principles of the Church, and their views of the Word of God, and to the liberties of Christ's people.

2d, That the said Civil Courts have power to interfere with and interdict the preaching of the gospel and administration of ordinances as authorised and enjoined by the Church Courts of the Establishment.

3d, That the said Civil Courts have power to suspend spiritual censures pronounced by the Church Courts of the Establishment against ministers and probationers of the church, and to interdict their execution as to spiritual effects, functions, and privileges.

4th, That the said Civil Courts have power to reduce and set aside the sentences of the Church Courts of the Establishment, deposing ministers from the office of the holy ministry, and depriving probationers of their licence to preach the gospel, with reference to the spiritual status, functions, and privileges, of such ministers and probationers, – restoring them to the spiritual office and status of which the Church Courts had deprived them.

5th, That the said Civil Courts have power to determine on the right to sit as members of the supreme and other judicatories of the Church by law established, and to issue interdicts against sitting and voting therein, irrespective of the judgment and determination of the said judicatories.

6th, That the said Civil Courts have power to supersede the majority of a Church Court of the Establishment, in regard to the exercise of its spiritual functions as a Church Court, and to authorise the minority to exercise the said functions, in opposition to the court itself, and to the superior judicatories of the Establishment.

7th, That the said Civil Courts have power to stay processes of discipline pending before courts of the Church by law established, and to interdict such courts from proceeding therein.

8th, That no pastor of a congregation can be admitted into the Church Courts of the Establishment, and allowed to rule, as well as to teach, agreeably to the institution of the office by the Head of the Church, nor to sit in any of the judicatories of the Church, inferior or supreme, – and that no additional provision can be made for the exercise of spiritual discipline among the members of the Church, though not affecting any patrimonial interests, and no alteration introduced in the state of pastoral superintendence and spiritual discipline in any parish, without the sanction of a Civil Court.

All which jurisdiction and power on the part of the said Civil Courts severally above specified, whatever proceeding may have given occasion to its exercise, is, in our opinion, in itself, inconsistent with Christian liberty, and with the authority which the Head of the Church hath conferred on the Church alone.

And farther considering, that a General Assembly, composed, in accordance with the laws and fundamental principles of the Church, in part of commissioners themselves admitted without the sanction of the Civil Court, or chosen by Presbyteries composed in part of members not having that sanction, cannot be constituted as an Assembly of the Establishment without disregarding the law and the legal conditions of the same as now fixed and declared;

And farther considering, that such commissioners as aforesaid would, as members of an Assembly of the Establishment, be liable to be interdicted from exercising their functions, and to be subjected to civil coercion at the instance of any individual having interest who might apply to the Civil Courts for that purpose;

And considering farther, that civil coercion has already been in divers instances applied for and used, whereby certain commissioners returned to the Assembly this day appointed to have been holden, have been interdicted from claiming their seats, and from sitting and voting therein; and certain Presbyteries have been, by interdicts directed against their members, prevented from freely choosing commissioners to the said Assembly, whereby the freedom of such Assembly, and the liberty of election thereto, has been forcibly obstructed and taken away;

And farther considering, that, in these circumstances, a free Assembly of the Church of Scotland, by law established, cannot at this time be holden, and that an Assembly, in accordance with the fundamental principles of the Church, cannot be constituted in connection with the State without violating the conditions which must now, since the rejection by the Legislature of the Church's Claim of Right, be held to be the conditions of the Establishment;

And considering that, while heretofore, as members of Church judicatories ratified by law and recognised by the constitution of the kingdom, we held ourselves entitled and bound to exercise and maintain the jurisdiction vested in these judicatories with the sanction of the constitution, notwithstanding the decrees as to matters spiritual and ecclesiastical of the civil courts, because we could not see that the State had required submission thereto as a condition of the Establishment, but, on the contrary, were satisfied that the State, by the acts of the Parliament of Scotland, for ever and unalterably secured to this nation by the Treaty of Union, had repudiated any power in the Civil Courts to pronounce such decrees, we are now constrained to acknowledge it to be the mind and will of the State, as recently declared, that such submission should and does form a condition of the Establishment, and of the possession of the benefits thereof; and that as we cannot, without committing what we believe to be sin – in opposition to God's law – in disregard of the honour and authority of Christ's crown, and in violation of our own solemn vows, comply with this condition, we cannot in conscience continue connected with, and retain the benefits of an Establishment to which such condition is attached.

We, therefore, the Ministers and Elders foresaid, on this, the first occasion since the rejection by the Legislature of the Church's Claim of Right, when the commissioners chosen from throughout the bounds of the Church to the General Assembly appointed to have been this day holden, are convened together, DO PROTEST, that the conditions foresaid, while we deem them contrary to and subversive of the settlement of church government effected at the Revolution, and solemnly guaranteed by the Act of Security and Treaty of Union, are also at variance with God's word, in opposition to the doctrines and fundamental principles of the Church of Scotland, inconsistent with the freedom essential to the right constitution of a Church of Christ, and incompatible with the government which He, as the Head of his Church, hath therein appointed distinct from the civil magistrate.

And we further PROTEST, that any Assembly constituted in submission to the conditions now declared to be law, and under the civil coercion which has been brought to bear on the election of commissioners to the Assembly this day appointed to have been holden, and on the commissioners chosen thereto, is not and shall not be deemed a lawful and free Assembly of the Church of Scotland, according to the original and fundamental principles thereof; and that the Claim, Declaration, and Protest, of the General Assembly which convened at Edinburgh in May 1842, as the Act of a free and lawful Assembly of the said Church, shall be holden as setting forth the true constitution of the said Church, and that the said Claim, along with the laws of the Church now subsisting, shall in nowise be affected by whatsoever acts and proceedings of any Assembly constituted under the conditions now declared to be the law, and in submission to the coercion now imposed on the Establishment.

And, finally, while firmly asserting the right and duty of the civil magistrate to maintain and support an establishment of religion in accordance with God's word, and reserving to ourselves and our successors to strive by all lawful means, as opportunity shall in God's good providence be offered, to secure the performance of this duty agreeably to the Scriptures, and in implement of the statutes of the kingdom of Scotland, and the obligations of the Treaty of Union as understood by us and our ancestors, but acknowledging that we do not hold ourselves at liberty to retain the benefits of the Establishment, while we cannot comply with the conditions now to be deemed thereto attached – we PROTEST, that in the circumstances in which we are placed, it is and shall be lawful for us, and such other commissioners chosen to the Assembly appointed to have been this day holden, as may concur with us, to withdraw to a separate place of meeting, for the purpose of taking steps for ourselves and all who adhere to us – maintaining with us the Confession of Faith and standards of the Church of Scotland, as heretofore understood – for separating in an orderly way from the Establishment; and thereupon adopting such measures as may be competent to us, in humble dependence on God's grace and the aid of the Holy Spirit, for the advancement of His glory, the extension of the gospel of our Lord and Saviour, and the administration of the affairs of Christ's house, according to His holy word; and we do now, for the purpose foresaid, withdraw accordingly, humbly and solemnly acknowledging the hand of the Lord in the things which have come upon us, because of our manifold sins, and the sins of this Church and nation; but, at the same time, with an assured conviction, that we are not responsible for any consequences that may follow from this our enforced separation from an Establishment which we loved and prized – through interference with conscience, the dishonour done to Christ's crown, and the rejection of his sole and supreme authority as King in His Church.

With these closing words, the Moderator laid the Protest on the table – lifted his hat – turned to the Commissioner, who had risen – and bowed respectfully to the representative of Royalty, an act which seemed to many as if the true old Church of Scotland were then and there bidding farewell to the State which had turned a deaf ear to her appeals. Leaving the chair,

Dr. Welsh moved toward the door, and Dr. Chalmers, who all the time had been close at his side, was seen eagerly following, along with Dr. Gordon, Dr. M'Farlan, Dr. Macdonald, and the other occupants of the bench in front.

At the sight of the movement, a loud cheer – but only for a moment – burst from the gallery. At once it was hushed, for the solemnity and sympathy were too deep for such a mode of expression, and silence again fell over the house, as all were eagerly gazing at the seats to the left of the chair. It was a sight never to be forgotten, as man after man rose, without hurry or confusion, and bench after bench was left empty, and the vacant space grew wider as ministers and elders poured out in long procession.

Outside in the street, the great mass of spectators had long been waiting in anxious anticipation, and when at last the cry rose, 'They come! they come!' and when Dr. Welsh, Dr. Chalmers, and Dr. Gordon appeared in sight, the sensation, as they came forth, went like an electric shock through the vast multitude, and the long, deep shout which rang along the street told that the deed had been done. No arrangement had been made for a procession, for the strong wish of the ministers was to avoid all display. But there was no choice. On either hand the crowd drew back, opening out a lane wide enough to allow of three, or at most four, walking abreast. And so in steady ranks the procession moved on its way, while all around they were met with expressions of the deepest emotion.

The writer of this was not a member of Assembly, but in that part of the House allotted to ministers not members he was in a favourable position, where all that went on could be fully seen. After the movement had been made, he remained for some time, side by side with Dr. Horatius Bonar, to witness the departure of friends, and especially to note the effect on the Moderate party who remained behind. At first, Dr. Cook and his friends were all complacency, but as the full extent of the Disruption began to disclose itself, there came an expression of perplexity, which in not a few instances seemed to deepen into bewilderment and dismay.

On leaving the church and falling into the line of procession it was evident that amidst the crowd the first sensation was over, though tears were seen in many eyes, and other signs of emotion could be observed. But what showed most strikingly the magnitude of the movement was the view from that point in George Street where you look down the long vista toward Tanfield, and where one unbroken column was seen, stretching, amidst numerous spectators, all the way till lost in the distance. . . .

The hall at Tanfield had, from an early hour, been crowded by an audience bound together by common sympathies, and anxiously waiting the result. Long hours had passed, and when a shout from the outside announced the appearance of the procession, the excitement grew intense. At last they entered – not only the well-known champions of the

cause, but rank after rank the ministers and elders came pouring in, till all the allotted space was filled; and when friend after friend was recognised, there came from the audience an irrepressible outburst of feeling which carried all before it, and found expression in acclamations and tears.

The opening prayer of Dr. Welsh was an outpouring of devout and holy feeling, which moved every heart in a way never to be forgotten. In proceeding to elect a Moderator, all eyes turned at once to Dr. Chalmers, and at the mention of his name by Dr. Welsh, the whole Assembly rose and broke forth in enthusiastic applause. When he came in and took the chair a singular incident occurred. A heavy passing cloud had for a time cast a gloom over the Assembly, and when Dr. Chalmers rose to give out the opening Psalm, 'O send thy light forth and thy truth, let them be guides to me,' the cloud suddenly broke, the full sunlight came pouring through the windows, brightening the scene, and 'there were some who thought of Dr. Chalmers' text but six months before, Unto the upright there ariseth light in the darkness.' The opening address which followed was worthy of the occasion, vindicating the position of the Free Church, and defining the place she was to occupy.

Thus, with feelings of indescribable relief and thankfulness, the first sederunt of the Free Assembly was brought to a close. Every single step during the anxious hours of that day had been in perfect keeping with the momentous character of the event. Many a heart looked up in gratitude to God for strength in the hour of trial – the feeling which Dr. Landsborough, with expressive abruptness, wrote down at the time in his brief journal of the Disruption day: 'Remained till six o'clock. Exceeding order. Halleluiah! I shall never see the like till heaven.' . . .

3.2   DISSENTING PROFESSORS: SAMUEL DAVIDSON AND WILLIAM ROBERTSON SMITH

The centrifugal tendency of Nonconformist notions of freedom and individuality was never more apparent than in the failure of the centripetal forces of creed and congregation to contain Nonconformist biblical scholarship. By mid-century churchmen such as Jowett and Stanley at Oxford and Connop Thirlwall at Cambridge had developed a liberal enthusiasm for the German critical schools, but it was a Congregationalist divine, the professor of biblical literature in the Lancashire Independent College near Manchester, Samuel Davidson (1807–1898), who first stuck

---

4   David Welsh, with Thomas Chalmers and Robert Gordon, leading the exodus on 18 May 1843 from the General Assembly in St Andrew's Church, Edinburgh, to form the Free Church of Scotland

his head above the academic parapet. In 1856 he cited German authorities in contributing to a revision of T. H. Horne's standard handbook, *An Introduction to the Critical Study and Knowledge of the Holy Scriptures*. The Pentateuch, he maintained, was not written by Moses; errors and imperfections littered the Old Testament text; inspiration extended only to matters of religion and morals. In response, evangelicals in Church and chapel hounded Davidson mercilessly. After a motion was carried in the College – but only by eighteen votes to sixteen – demanding his resignation, he embarked on a non-sectarian educational career that earned him a civil pension from Gladstone for his services to biblical scholarship. Davidson's ignominious defeat inflamed his colleague Thomas Nicholas (1820–1879), the German-educated professor of biblical literature in the Presbyterian College, Carmarthen. In a fat pamphlet, full of 'facts and documents', Nicholas evoked Nonconformist principles by asserting, over against Romish authoritarianism, the freedom of private interpretation as the means of restoring to the Bible its inherent 'simplicity and grandeur' (**3.2.1**). Similar concerns animated William Robertson Smith (1846–1894) two decades later when he fell foul of the Free Church of Scotland for publishing critical views on the Old Testament in the *Encyclopaedia Britannica*. His case dragged through presbyteries, committees, and the General Assembly for five long years, throwing the Church into turmoil. It produced the classic confrontation between the brilliantly arrogant and impolitic young professor – Robertson Smith was only twenty-four when he began teaching in the Free Church theological college at Aberdeen – and the cagey, compromising ecclesiastical statesman – Robert Rainy (1826–1906) was the principal of New College, Edinburgh, and the Free Church's most influential leader at the time – who valued unity through expediency above the pure pursuit of truth. The concluding scene before the General Assembly in 1881 saw the powerful intervention of the militant Reverend Begg (2.4.2), with whom Rainy had made common cause. Robertson Smith also repeated his demand for due process, without which, he argued, it would have to be concluded that an ostensibly free church had 'assumed to itself a civil power' (**3.2.2**). The case, however, was lost, and Robertson Smith left Aberdeen for Cambridge to edit the *Encyclopaedia Britannica* and to serve as professor of Arabic until his much lamented death at the age of forty-seven.

3.2.1 T. NICHOLAS ON DR DAVIDSON'S REMOVAL, 1860

Dr. Davidson has been removed from his professorial chair: but that being said, all is said. He has borne his evil fortune, if evil it be, with a firmness and equanimity behoving the Christian scholar. His trial occasioned him the 'splendid satisfaction,' to use Professor Roediger's words, of finding in his former students an amount of affection and respect for which possibly he was not quite prepared, and brought to his side many earnest and devoted friends. Though doubtless it went to his soul to see many of his brethren forsake him and display so largely the temper of foes, for what he deemed conscientious conviction and faithfully intended service to the Truth, yet that Truth and its most merciful and faithful Author formed his stay, while in silence and quietness he endured the present, having a view to the wider and more auspicious time that was to come. He is the servant of a cause that is to live – the cause of progress, of an intelligent faith, and of a free and secure Bible. It is the cause that, without deserting one unit of the Christian faith, will preserve for Revelation the service of Science and the loyalty of Genius; and will facilitate the performance by an ever-struggling Christianity of the high resolve of occupying the foremost position among the mighty powers of the coming ages, when many shall run to and fro and knowledge shall be increased. This is the School of Antioch as against Alexandria – the Baconian method against the Alchemists. Its principle is to examine first and then conclude (on questions touching the phenomena of Holy Writ) with an unshaken confidence that the conclusions of a sound induction conducted in dependence upon that Spirit by whom holy men of old were moved to write, will prove in ultimate harmony with the clear dogmatic utterances of the record touching faith and salvation. This then is a cause to live. But the cause antagonistic to it must be a cause to die. It already groweth old and is ready to vanish away. God forbid it should be identified with the cause of Christ or of God's Holy Word. It is the cause at best of a mistaken conservatism, of the bondage of the letter, and of the traditions of men. It is at bottom the cause of ignorance against knowledge, and of superstition against an enlightened faith. Failing to command the suffrages of the learned it seeks to buttress its strength by an affectation of super-eminent piety, and utter its own praise in the appropriate and long-lived formula – 'The temple of the Lord, the temple of the Lord, are WE.' Against this odious modern Pharisaism, fell priestly ruler of thousands of the best of Christians in all lands, it is no profanity here to say, *Delenda sit Carthago!*

Dr. Davidson, long before the uproar, had obtained a name as a Biblical scholar, which he cannot lose. His removal from the College is not his removal from the world of literature. The position he has lost was local and limited, the position he still occupies is wide as the literature of the Christian Church and Writings. His works have obtained entrance to our Universities, are quoted and referred to with respect by our chief writers in England and abroad. Indeed, in so far as real position, service to the Church, and fame hereafter, are concerned, the fact of his having been violently thrust out by a local faction, and under such pretexts, will tell greatly in his favour. Without thinking it, his judges have procured for him the honour of a martyr of sacred science, and for themselves the odium of fanatical foes of an intelligent theology. Right or wrong this will be the issue; while the apparent victim will be armed with greater vitality than ever to do battle for Biblical knowledge. . . .

. . . A work in Biblical literature for our day *must* be a mirror of the state of modern thought: if it assume the 'independent' and the 'original' it will be simply an impertinence. Dr. Davidson has a fitness which few possess of analysing and comparing conflicting opinions, and guiding the student through the maze of theory and error to some intelligible standing place, and by all means let him use the gift God has given. In all science, indeed, this recognition of the state of opinion is of paramount importance. Geology, chemistry, and all experimental and natural sciences are perfected by succeeding authors embodying the demonstrations of predecessors and contemporaries, and carrying on the sum total of ascertained truth to balance it with error and conjecture. Sciences which are in great part deductive, and much of whose evidence must rest on probability, as is the case with Biblical criticism, must pursue a strictly similar course. This science must elaborate its conclusions by slow degrees, and by patient research, and the contributions of no honest and acute enquirer can be slighted, for the key to open an intricate difficulty may be found by this hand or that. The man who will pretend to be an 'original' in such work as this, is by that very pretence convicted as a charlatan, and is not to be listened to; and those who forget or are ignorant of the judicial, eclectic character of the critic's functions, are not in a position to speak on the matter. Dr. Davidson has given evidence sufficient of his power to be original and independent as a thinker when his subject-matter admitted. But the learned man is not the mere adventurous self-reliant thinker, who from his own sanctum and the dreams of his own 'subjectivity' concludes as to what the world is and should be; but he is rather 'the man of Ithaca,' who has travelled over many lands, and seen peoples and manners many, and gives forth the products of a sage and various experience. This is what the Biblical student in England wants, and this he must have, despite the ignorant prejudice found here and there against German and other foreign authors. Chinese conservatism but cramps and impoverishes – the Bible and its literature must have a free field, and hold commerce with the whole world. . . .

With two remarks we close. First: The stir created by Biblical research in our country is a proof that a new era is dawning. What Luther said of the Bible we may say of its literature: 'Ego nisi tumultus istos viderem, verbum Dei in mundo non esse dicerem.' Luther was right; the Bible if made known must be followed by commotions; and the wholesome mode of making it truly and fully known, adopted by the Sciences of Criticism and Hermeneutics, is one that must be followed by commotion. In England, distrust of Biblical Science arises from respect for the Bible. This Science has a work to perform which wears the appearance of irreverence, and pious people are shocked. . . . The necessities of the scholar say, Let it still progress. With steady and careful hand let Science take off from the fair form of this glorious temple, planned and finished by the Divine Architect himself, all the stucco covering and petty decoration and paint obtruded upon it by mistaken men, and let its simplicity and grandeur be seen. The Church may fear you dig under its foundations when you are only clearing off the rubbish; that you are defacing when you are only uncovering tracery and inscription; that you are pulling down the wall, when you are only opening up archway or sculptured monument, walled up by monkish stupidity. Respect the excitement, tolerate the clamour – they are only proofs that the temple is had in reverence; but press on the work of improvement – it shall be loved better still, by wiser men, and by equally good, when seen as it ought to be seen.

Second: The *Spirit* which presides over much of the present ferment is not that of liberty and of a healthy hopeful faith. Its exhibitions call for lamentation. That is but a sickly and feeble piety which cannot tolerate difference of opinion, on things not directly touching salvation. However sound a man may be in theology, if he takes an independent ground on questions of criticism and theory, as Dr. Davidson had done, the whole texture of his *faith* is at once looked upon as vitiated. . . . The reasonable maxim, *in dubiis libertas*, is cast away, and a narrow untrustful uniformity imposed – the dictate of a feeble faith, or of a waning charity, or both.

But the debilitated spiritual habit here indicated is not incident alone to a particular College Committee or a particular sect. The clergy of all denominations are in the major part not penetrated by a robust faith, and a fresh scientific theology. Forms of words exercise a regal sway. There is a dread of all enterprize in thought, – a phenomenon in our day confined to theology alone. The moderation which is the result of true culture is rare to find. People, like clergy, of all sects, cling to their Shibboleths, and strive not to learn the pure speech of heaven which must by and by become universally current, and fuse all kindreds into one people. How much of Rome is everywhere! – exacting, coercing, infallible Rome! How puny is forbearance – how eagle-eyed and wolf-hearted is the heresy-hunter! . . .

Some may object to the formula that Christianity is a life rather than a creed; but none will doubt that he is a sound divine who holds and loves the doctrines taught by Christ and his Apostles, though he differ from us on the nature of inspiration, the extent of the canon, or the date or authorship of a book. He is a true Christian who by a living faith has embraced the Redeemer, and by a holy and humble life adorns his cause and aids its triumph over error and sin, though he intellectually embrace but half the articles in which you may choose to draw up and express

Christianity; while he who surpasses all in symbol and ceremony in tithings of rue and washings of cups, will most probably have his whole religion resolved into books and altars, fasts and feasts. *Pectus est quod theologum facit*, was the motto of the devout and philosophic Neander. 'Hold every item of such a creed – conform to every regulation of such a rubric,' says the man of dead letter and empty form. But the spirit-life pleaded for by the former is the power that must issue in fruit and blessing, while the form pleaded by the latter may be that of a mere dead corpse. Let the plant have only the vital principle, give it free scope, light and air, and it will grow into the proportions of a goodly tree, its very irregularities, the fruit of its liberty, only contributing to its natural beauty; while if you have defective vitality all your regular pruning, supporting, shading, will only issue in a stunted, withering, and more rapidly dying plant.

'Pectus est quod theologum facit' – the heart it is which makes the true theologian; let the deep-meaning idea here involved be once adequately pondered and believed, and we shall have less intolerance and more truth, less suspicion and more love. . . .

3.2.2   THE CASE OF PROF. ROBERTSON SMITH, 1881

TUESDAY, MAY 24

Dr. WILSON, the Clerk, said the Assembly was now prepared to take up the report of the committee transmitted by the Commission at the October meeting, with relative minutes and papers, and relative overtures and memorials.

Principal RAINY, who was received with applause, then rose to move the motion of which he had given notice:—

'The General Assembly having had their attention called by the judgment of the Commission in October, and by overtures from Presbyteries, to certain writings of Professor Smith, and in particular to an article, 'Hebrew Language and Literature,' in the 'Encyclopædia Britannica;'

'And considering that said article was prepared for publication by Professor Smith after he had accepted service of libel on account of previous statements made by him on cognate matters;

'And considering that said article was not before last Assembly when they pronounced judgment on said libel, because it did not appear until after the Assembly had risen, and the Professor, in accepting admonition as to the unguarded and incomplete character of previous utterances, gave no indication of its being in existence;

'And having in view also a letter from Professor Smith to the Free Presbytery of Aberdeen, in which he explains and defends his conduct in relation to that article – Find:

'1. That the construction of last Assembly's judgment in Professor Smith's case, on which, in his letter, he claims that the right was conceded to him to promulgate his views in the manner he has done, is unwarrantable; the Assembly therefore repudiate that construction, and adopt the statement on this subject contained in the report submitted to the Commission in October.

'2. That the article, 'Hebrew Language and Literature,' is fitted to give at least as great offence, and cause as serious anxiety, as that for which he was formerly dealt with.

'3. That it contains statements which are fitted to throw grave doubt on the historical truth and divine inspiration of several books of Scripture.

'4. That both the tone of the article in itself, and the fact that such an article was prepared and published in the circumstances, and after all the previous proceedings in his case, evince on the part of Professor Smith a singular insensibility to his responsibilities as a theological professor, and a singular and culpable lack of sympathy with the reasonable anxieties of the Church as to the bearing of critical speculations on the integrity and authority of Scripture.

'5. That all this has deepened the conviction already entertained by a large section of the Church that Professor Smith, whatever his gifts and attainments, which the Assembly have no disposition to undervalue, ought no longer to be entrusted with the training of students for the ministry.

'Therefore, the General Assembly, having the responsible duty to discharge of overseeing the teaching in the Divinity Halls, while they are sensible of the importance of guarding the due liberty of professors, and encouraging learned and candid research, feel themselves constrained to declare that they no longer consider it safe or advantageous for the Church that Professor Smith should continue to teach in one of her colleges.

'The Assembly resolve to resume this matter on Thursday forenoon, with the view of giving effect to this judgment, and with the view of finally disposing of the remaining elements of the case.'

Principal RAINY said – In addressing myself to the motion, . . . it appears to me that, in the case of a professor, the Church has a direct responsibility by her appointment, by the kind of work directly before the whole Church she entrusts to him, by the responsibility in the public eye for his position and his proceedings; and however true it may be that any question of doctrine, as it arises in a professor, is strictly sifted by libel, if you are to deal with the ministerial character – with the fitness of the man to continue to be an office-bearer or a member of the Church, or to occupy on that ground the position of a professor – while that is true, what

you have here ... is a very complicated state of things. ... I am
convinced that a large measure of the difficulties and entanglements, and
more than that, the pressure on the conscience and the exasperation that
has been connected with this matter, has been connected with it just
through the question being raised in the form of maintaining or not
maintaining a professor as our representative in dealing with students.
The evidence of that lies in the history of the proceedings. ... Then I feel
that this state of things greatly endangers the maintenance of a reasonable
liberty in the Church. I have been asked, What is it you mean? According
to your motion Professor Smith is declared to be no longer entrusted with
the training of the students for the ministry. Do you suppose that will
bring the questions to an end, and suppress the diversities and tendency of
the judgment on important matters in this Church? No, Moderator, I do
not suppose it. I believe there are diversities of judgment, and questions to
be raised that are far from being free from difficulty. I know, too, that
many men, who will vote against my motion to-day, and who perhaps on
certain questions have been led to deal with them with some speciality, are
men as loyal to Christ, and who with the desire of all their hearts do serve
Christ and do Christ's work, as any man in this Church. (Applause.) And I
will say to some of those who will vote for my motion to-day, that in all
subsequent dealings and proceedings you will act according to your
conviction of truth and duty; but unless you take it that men who differ
from you in this Church – there are unsatisfactory men in all churches, we
know it well – but unless you take it that many of those who differ from
you are as loyal and devoted to the faith and service of Christ, as genuine
and as hearty believers who have given themselves to Christ in faith and
love as you are, if you do not entertain and cherish that conviction, you
mistake the position in which God has placed you, you mistake the
problem God has given you to solve. But just because I feel that, all the
more I feel there is danger in the Church, under the influence of a
legitimate feeling, I will call it, that she had no reason to expect, and she
has not a right to be called upon placidly to accept and to continue to
tolerate, shall I say, the course that has been pursued in this case, as
described in the motion, by one in the special position that the responsibilities of a professor [entail?], all the more on that account the Church is in
danger of being driven to deal rashly and in a trenchant manner with . . .
wider and much more important questions. . . . And, on the other hand, I
hold that the Church is not in circumstances to decide to do what we are so
often called upon to do, to look fairly and calmly at these questions on
their merits, and decide our final and conclusive position upon them,
until we get disentangled somehow from this element, which, to my mind,
fatally complicates the whole position. Then, I must say I do hold that
teaching like this, and an attitude like this, if the Church is simply to

tolerate and to take no action, will be inevitably misunderstood, will lead to the Church being misconstrued, will give an impulse in a direction of loose and large views about Scripture which this Church ought not to consent to have connected with her name. . . .

. . . Fathers and brethren, think well what you do. It is a great sacrifice not to Professor Smith merely. It is a great sacrifice to us. If you doubt your power, do not use it. (Hear, hear.) If you doubt whether there is a case for the exercise of your power, do not use it; but if you believe that the case has arisen, has become such a case – a complication threatening grave and serious issues that it is no longer fit that even this professor should be maintained in the office which he occupies – and if you believe this is the right way to care for your souls and to place the Church in the best position, thus deliberately and calmly facing with strength and patience all those questions so plainly in the air, and so inevitably questions that remain to be considered – then, if you think that, you must act, and you must take the responsibility and the unpopularity of your action. (Loud applause.)

Mr. JOHN MUIR, Glasgow (elder), seconded the motion. . . .

Dr. WHYTE, St. George's, Edinburgh, in rising to submit the following motion, of which he gave notice the preceding evening, was received with cheers:— 'That the General Assembly, having regard to the overtures on its table anent the case of Professor W. Robertson Smith, and the volume recently published by him in explanation of his opinions, finds that inasmuch as it is the right of every member and office-bearer of this Church, against whom grave charges are brought, to be dealt with constitutionally, after full investigation, it can adopt no course of procedure which prejudices that right. But in view of the acknowledged gravity of the issues involved, and the importance of jealously maintaining the doctrine of the Church as to the authority and inspiration of the Word of God, resolves to appoint a committee to consider maturely the writings of Professor W. R. Smith, published since last Assembly, with power, if they see cause, to prosecute him by libel before the Presbytery of Aberdeen, and in any case to report to next Assembly.' Dr. Whyte, proceeding, said— . . .

As for the motion I lay on your table it speaks for itself. And I will only add three words in putting it into your hands. I claim your intelligent and just support for it for these reasons:— First, because it makes for peace, in that it confines itself to what is necessary to maintain constitutional liberty without adding anything that can have the effect of foreclosing legitimate action on the part of fathers and brethren who intelligently and conscientiously object to Professor Smith's doctrine. Secondly, because this motion directs special attention to Professor Smith's fullest and clearest utterances, and thus makes it possible for future discussion to be fundamental, final, and complete. Third, Because this motion provides for committing the discussion of this whole matter into the hands of the most learned, most trusted, and wisest men in the Church, in the prayer and hope that, by the Divine blessing, a safe and peaceful issue may be found out of our present perplexity.

In conclusion, sir, I repeat my most solemn belief that the motion it is my honoured privilege to lay on your table this morning opens up to you the only safe, righteous, and lasting settlement of this great question. You cannot arrest the movement of mind in Christendom of which these inculpated writings are an outcome. Had this movement of the theological mind been confined to Professor Smith and a handful of German or Germanised scholars like himself, you might have ignored it or arrested its progress in your Church. But the movement is not of them; they are rather of it. They are its children, and they cannot but be its servants. Fathers and brethren, the world of mind does not stand still. And the theological mind will stand still at its peril. No man who knows, or cares to know, anything of my personal sympathies and intellectual and religious leanings will accuse me of disloyalty to the Calvinistic, Puritan, and Presbyterian polity, or neglect of the noble body of literature we inherit from our fathers. But I find no disparity, no difficulty in carrying much of the best of our past with me in going out to meet and hail the new theological methods. Of all bodies of men on the earth the Church of Christ should be the most catholic-minded, the most hopeful, the most courageous, the most generous, sure that every movement of the human mind is ordered and overruled for her ultimate establishment, extension, and enriching. The Church of Christ of all institutions on the earth should be bold to bear all things, believe all things, hope all things, endure all things. And her divine wisdom is shown in times of trial like this when she has to meet foes as they seem to her, and seek as long and lovingly as may be to reduce them to friends. And bear with me while I say it, whether you, fathers and brethren, have the courage of your faith or no, that remains to be seen – but your son and servant under you has that courage to a fault. (Applause.)

Why, sir, does Professor Smith stand to-day accused before this house? What has his error or fault been? It has been this: He thought he saw the opportunity, and perhaps too eagerly and adventurously seized it, of outflanking your great enemy, the unbelieving, disintegrating, and unremorseful criticism of the great foreign schools. He went out in your service, if not at your behest, and he seeks to return to serve you still. He is fitted by gifts, by learning, by sagacity, by descent, and by personal piety, to serve you as few men in any generation possibly can, and you are sitting here deliberating how you can most speedily cast him over your walls to the scorn and rejoicing of the besieging enemy. Surely, surely, the Free

Church of Scotland will not brand herself as such a hard-hearted, short-sighted, panic-stricken mother to her loyal, if adventurous son. I will continue to hope for better things. And I pray that grace and wisdom may be given to you and to your suspected son, so that to him and to you may yet be fulfilled the prophetic promise, 'That he and his brethren may long live to carry in captives among you, so that strangers shall stand and feed your flocks, and the sons of the alien shall be your plowmen and your vine dressers.' (Cheers.)

Professor M'KENDRICK, Glasgow, in rising to second the motion, said – Moderator, . . . the duty has fallen to my lot, and as it is one in which my warmest sympathies are engaged, I feel that to decline to perform it would be an act of unfaithfulness to the Church, and to what I believe to be the interests of truth and of freedom. . . .

Dr. BEGG– . . . There are two motions before the house – that of Dr. Rainy on the one hand, and that of Dr. Whyte on the other – and the real, the only question before the house is, Which of the two motions ought to meet with the approbation of the Assembly? Now, the difference between the two is undoubtedly in substance this, apart from other considerations, that the one proposes a procedure which is of a summary nature, and the other suggests a procedure of a more protracted nature. I wish to take the full responsibility of supporting the motion of Dr. Rainy; and, for my part, I have always held that there is a complete distinction, I do not say betwixt the abstract status of a professor who must be a minister and the status of a minister, but betwixt the status of a minister and the right of a professor to teach the students of this Church, after the Church herself has become convinced that that teaching is not of a satisfactory kind. (Hear, hear.) . . . Now, the real vital question before the Assembly is, Is there ground and reason . . . for coming to the conclusion to which Dr. Rainy's motion points? I think there is, and I think no one can read the report of the Commission, and the remarkable statements which are there quoted from the recent writings of Professor Smith, without coming to that definite conclusion. For example, 'It may fairly be made a question whether Moses left in writing any other laws than the Commandments on the tables of stone.' I hold that to be a flat contradiction of the language of Christ itself, for, 'He answered and said unto them, What did Moses command you? And they said, Moses suffered to write a bill of divorcement, and to put her away. And Jesus answered and said unto them, For the hardness of your heart he wrote you this precept.' Well, can it be a fair question with any Christian man or minister whether Christ was speaking the truth on that occasion or not? ('Oh, oh.') Can it be a fair question when Christ Himself knew what He said? ('No, no.') Is that the kind of doctrine in which men are to be trained for the ministry of the Free Church? Again, 'This lyric drama (that is, the Song of Solomon) has suffered much

from interpolation, and presumably was not written down till a comparatively late date, and from imperfect recollection, so that its original shape
is very much lost.' As to the question of interpolations, that might be
consistent with inspiration. But can you say that there is inspiration of any
intelligible kind in a thing that has been written from imperfect recollection? It is not mere interpolation, but a document which has been written
from imperfect recollection cannot be an inspired document unless you
are to impute to God Himself imperfect recollection. ('Oh, oh,' and cries
of 'Quite right.') Again, 'The chronicler no longer thoroughly understood
the old Hebrew sources from which he worked, while, for the latest part
of his history, he used a Jewish Aramaic document, part of which he
incorporated in the book of Ezra.' That is to say, that the inspired writer
no longer thoroughly understood the old Hebrew sources from which he
worked. Well, was that an inspired man or not, and is the book so
produced an inspired book or not? The statement in the Confession of
Faith is that it is an inspired book. Are we to allow teaching like that in our
Halls, and if it is spread abroad, is the Church to look on and see teaching
like that on the part of one of our theological professors without interpos-
ing? I say 'No.' (Cheers.) Tell me about the Court of Session! I remember
much about the Court of Session in former times, and well respect it in its
own place. Our young friend knows very little of what we know about the
Court of Session. (Laughter.) They might interpose. I cannot tell whether
they will or not, but rather than the Church should tolerate for a year such
teaching as that I would brave all the courts in Christendom. (Cheers.) I
hold that the Free Church this night should give forth a ringing decision,
to the effect that this is our determination, and that we will not be turned
aside from it on any consideration that may be introduced to the contrary.
Let us be firm, brethren. I am one of the few who went through all the old
struggle, and, thanks be to God, I have some strength left for a new
struggle yet. (Applause.) Let us be firm as we were in the past. Our former
struggles taught us to stand for God and truth! (Applause.) Let us do what
is right, and let us fear no consequences. (Loud applause.) . . .

Professor ROBERTSON SMITH, who was greeted with much cheering, said it appeared to him that Dr. Whyte's motion, to which he was
prepared to acquiesce, did not ask the house to pledge itself that there was
cause for a libel against him. What it did say, as he understood it, was, that
there had emerged in his case certain questions, and that, in the opinion
of at least a part of the Church, his views were inconsistent with the
Standards. That being so, Dr. Whyte and others were of opinion that it
was their duty to indicate in opposition to a motion which appeared
unconstitutional, what was the right and proper way. They had thought it
would be well to recommend to the Assembly that the raising of this case
by means of process should not be left to the responsibility of the first man

who chose to take it up, but that the Church should try to get a full report of the merits of his case; and that, having chosen the wisest men to discuss the matter, then, if the case was to go to libel, these men should be the libellers. The motion had nothing to do with Dr. Whyte's personal opinion whether his views were heretical or not. He put it to the house whether what had been stated by Dr. Begg, and several other people, did not amount to a clear statement that in his views there was heresy, and when they had two parties, one of which believed there was heresy in his views, and the other did not, it was desirable the Church should not go on without deliberating on this matter, and it must leave open the contingency that if these parties did not come to be of one mind by mere deliberation, then the matter should be settled by the ordinary legal methods. It had been impossible for the house, in the course of the discussion, to touch any one point of the merits of important views. . . . But he asked how that was to be reconciled with the motion they were asked to adopt. Dr. Rainy having made no attempt to go into the merits, notwithstanding asked, not in his speech, but in his motion, that they should find his article contained statements which were fitted to throw grave doubts on the historical truth and divine inspiration of several books of Scripture. (Applause.) Now, he ventured to think that to accept such a finding, on the ground of such a debate as they had had, was only possible to one section; and that, he was certain, was not a very large section, although, undoubtedly, it was a section which must be respected in the Church. There was a section of the Church – Dr. Begg was one of their spokesmen – they held a theological position of which he desired to speak with every respect; but it was a perfectly well marked theological position, and it had been proved by vote after vote, in every case, in debates on open questions, not to be the position of the majority of that Church. (Hear, hear.) The brethren of the Highlands, it was not denied, held what they would no doubt call a more faithful and truthful view on a number of dogmatical positions than others did. Without in the least denying, but rather highly appreciating, the value of having in the Church that theological element, it was quite certain that those brethren were willing to treat this whole question as one which had been long ago settled, and to hold that the case admitted of no further argument. He was perfectly certain the majority of the Church were not prepared to take the matter in that way. They would have here voting on this motion two sets of men whose arguments and position were as diametrically opposed to one another as the position of those who supported Dr. Whyte's motion was to that of Dr. Rainy's supporters. (Cries of 'No.') Nay, far more so.

Dr. Begg offered one or two cardinal arguments to show that this case was settled – that no more required to be said about it; and one of them was an appeal to the words of our Lord in citing a part of the Mosaic law.

Now, they knew that Dr. Rainy disavowed, and always had disavowed that. (Laughter, and loud applause.) Could any one, he asked, who followed the long and rambling speech of Dr. Rainy, say there would, in the words of the principal himself, be much moral weight in the finding in which the only point of agreement was that he (Professor Smith) should be removed from his Chair, while it did not indicate one particle of agreement between Dr. Begg and Dr. Rainy on the question before them, which Dr. Rainy said would continue to be before them, but which Dr. Begg said must be cut short? (Applause.) The great fault Dr. Rainy found in him was that he had raised a question; and the Principal proceeded to argue, with a logic which he could not appreciate, that, in order that the Church might face that question rightly, they must first remove from the midst of them a man who had ventured to have a decided opinion about it. This was Dr. Rainy's argument. (Laughter.) It was an argument of expediency. He was not concerned to deny that he had assisted in raising the question. The great ground of action was that they were to settle that question in the interests of liberty; but they could not have that liberty until they removed the man who had already made up his mind about it. That was the position they were in. It was a position which could never have emerged upon any judicial process. . . .

It was not, he proceeded, probable that anything he could say would move such a coalition, . . . to prevent the threatened result. But what was dear to him now was that he should not part from his brethren in this Free Church, if part from them that night he must, without doing all that was possible for him, by frank and friendly explanation, to remove trouble. It was impossible to close without one word to express his feeling that they were in the midst of a crisis. They had come to a constitutional crisis. . . . They were now coming on the verge of an entirely new theory of the nature of the Church. One argument of Principal Rainy was that there was a power in reserve in the Church above its ordinary constitution and ordinary law. It seemed that this Church was claiming, not a spiritual power over her professors, but a certain civil power which was not given to her by Act of Parliament, or by her Scriptural constitution. (A voice, "No.") He held it was so; for Dr. Rainy's contention that the visitorial power they had was a power meant, if his argument meant anything, that this Church assumed to itself a civil power. They had now a theory of the power of the Church regulated by no law, and appealing to no Scriptural arguments, for there was not one Scriptural argument in Dr. Rainy's speech, not one that did not come from the region of the commonest expediency – no argument but the argument by which despotism had always been supported, the argument that there must be a power to prevent the State from suffering any ill. There was a Power to preserve the Church from any ill. There was a Power watching over it now in this crisis, and which he and all of them hoped and prayed would not desert the Church, even if on this occasion she might be led wrong. But the Power which watched over the Church was not a power arbitrarily asserted by some body of men without constitution, and on grounds of mere expediency, on grounds of temporary opinion. The Power that was watching over the Church was that Power which enabled them to be patient, temperate, and trustful, to exercise charity and faith towards one another – it was the power of the Lord Jesus Christ, and the power of His Spirit ruling in their hearts.

Principal RAINY, in reply, said – In replying in a few words on this debate, . . . one point of view is this, that there is becoming notorious in the progress of five years a state of affairs summed up in the various heads of this motion, for the cause of which I appeal to your knowledge or recollection. . . . If you have no good grounds for taking up these successive points as points which the progress of your experience has made known to you as true in this case, then I say do not vote for my motion. (Applause.) Now, in the connection I wish also to say that a good deal was made in regard to the two parties that combined. Moderator, that is a matter on which Professor Smith was quite entitled to comment as he did, but I wish to say that while the two parties agreed on the successive heads of this motion, the motion carefully abstains from charging in any part of it anything which has any basis to secure or sanction ground for libel. In regard to the illustrations taken from the course of the debate as to the radical opposition of those who are concerned in support of this motion, I acknowledge that there are diversities of judgment on various points among us. It is very notorious and well known, it is quite true, I believe, that there are various critical views which are regarded with apprehension by some of those who vote for this motion which are not regarded with apprehension by others.

In regard to this matter I might say a great deal, but really I must spare the time of the house. I wish, however, to say this in regard to this critical question. I wish to say with reference to what was said in the early part of the day in regard to critical method, there is, in my opinion, a sound critical method, but in the appreciation of that method there comes the question as to the kind of evidence to be taken and the comparative weight you are to give it as a believer as well as a critic. (Applause.) A great deal was said to-day about settling this critical question – that we should go into a committee to settle these questions. Moderator, you will never settle them to the end of time, and you cannot settle them, and no committee you can appoint can settle them, and no principle you arrive at will settle them. (Applause.) The settlements now in the case must be provisional, they cannot be in their end. And all we are saying is that the Church must be called upon to move, because I grant that as the Church has learned in regard to critical questions in the time past, so must it learn in time to come. (Applause.) She will move as she sees her way, but I do not say she should be dragged headlong. It is essential she should only proceed as she sees her way clear. . . . I feel, Moderator, it is useless to prolong the matter, and I will thus abruptly break off. I leave the whole question to the house with a very deep sense of responsibility. I will only say, if you will allow me, that I wish, with all my heart, that it was Professor Smith putting me out of my chair rather than that I should be putting him out of his. (Loud applause.)

The house was then cleared at half-past eleven for a division. Tellers were appointed, and the members in the galleries came into the body of the hall. . . .

The division was then proceeded with.

Sir HENRY MONCREIFF intimated the result as follows:—

For Dr. Rainy's motion	423
For Dr. Whyte's	245
	——
Majority for Dr. Rainy's	178

The Resolution of the Assembly was as follows:—

'Wherefore [repeating Dr. Rainy's motion] . . . the Assembly resolve to resume this matter on Thursday forenoon, with the view of giving effect to this judgment, and with the view of finally disposing of the remaining elements of the case.'

From which judgment Professor Candlish dissented in his own name, and in the name of all who may adhere to him, for the following Reasons:—

'Because the judgment is founded on a mis-statement as to a matter of fact – viz. that Professor Smith, in his letter to the Presbytery of Aberdeen, claims that the right was conceded to him by last Assembly's judgment to promulgate his views.

'Because vague statements as to the tendency and tone of the writings of a minister of this Church cannot be the basis of definite ecclesiastical action, and, while injurious to him, can effect no real benefit to the Church.

'Because the matters based on in the finding, as causes of offence on Professor Smith's part, were all antecedent to the admonition addressed to him by last Assembly, and there is no recognition of the necessity, in justice to that Assembly, of allowing opportunity for the proper influence of its admonition to Professor Smith.

'Because the declaration, that it is no longer safe or advantageous for the Church that Professor Smith should continue to teach in one of her colleges, can only express the opinion of a majority of this Assembly; and the Assembly is not authorised, in this matter, to speak in the name of the Church.

'Because the declaration must either be entirely inept, or must lead to the summary removal of Professor Smith from his chair, an act which would be a violation of the Scriptural principles of Church discipline, and the form of process hitherto observed in this Church.

'Because the finding is based upon a regard to what seems expedient for the present, and contributes nothing to the settlement of those vital questions regarding the truth of Scripture, which are of lasting importance to the pure and spiritual welfare of the Church.

'Because the finding gives an erroneous interpretation of last Assembly's judgment.' – James S. Candlish, Alexander Whyte, A. Orrock Johnston, John G. M'Kendrick, William Ferguson, Francis Edmonds, Archibald Henderson, Benjamin Bell, elder; A. H. Cowan, Gilbert Beith, W. G. Blackie, Benjamin Bell, minister; Walter Duncan, John W. Laurie, James Clugston, John M. M'Candlish, Thomas Ogilvie, John G. Stewart, George W. Clark, Charles M'Neil, James Fraser, William M. Falconer, James H. Allan, David J. Brackenridge. . . .

THURSDAY, MAY 26

. . . Wherefore, the General Assembly having resumed consideration of the papers transmitted in the case of Professor Smith, with the overtures and memorials, and having in view the judgment pronounced on Tuesday last, hereby appoint and declare that, from the 31st of this month, Professor Smith's tenure of his chair shall cease as regards all right to teach and exercise professorial functions in the College of Aberdeen, and as regards all ecclesiastical rights and powers grounded on his professorial charge. The Assembly appoint the full salary meanwhile to continue, leaving it to future Assemblies, if need be, to regulate that matter, as reason and justice may require. In accordance with this finding the Assembly declare the chair vacant, and direct that the usual steps be taken with a view to the election of a professor at next General Assembly; and, meanwhile, empower the College Committee to make provision for the instruction of the classes during next Session. . . .

Professor BRUCE said – Moderator, I beg to submit the following reasons of dissent:—

Because to appoint and declare that Professor Smith's tenure of his chair shall cease is inconsistent with the terms on which he was appointed to it, inasmuch as no charge has been regularly proved or formulated against his life or doctrine.

Because this act is a violation of the Scriptural principles of discipline, and implies the assumption of a power which is not merely ministerial but lordly and despotic.

Because of the reasons formerly given in against the judgment on Tuesday last which it carries out.

Because, while professedly on that judgment, it goes beyond it by depriving Professor Smith of ecclesiastical rights and powers distinct from the function of teaching.

This document bore the signatures of Professor Bruce, Dr. Whyte, Dr. Marcus Dods, Mr. Benjamin Bell, Professor Salmond, Mr. Henderson, Mr. M'Candlish, and T. W. Laurie. Immediately after its presentation members crowded to the platform to sign it, but it was intimated that that need not be done just then, as the document could be signed at any time. . . .

3.3   THE AFFINITIES OF DISSENT: UNITARIANISM AND BEYOND

Efforts to contain and channel the liberalizing and individuating tendencies of Dissent were made at intervals throughout the Victorian period. One of the grandest schemes, which failed, was begun in 1869 by the eminent and well-connected Unitarian theologian, James Martineau (1805–1900). Appealing to Protestants generally, but especially to liberal Nonconformists, he proposed to establish a Free Christian Union, based on the principle of theological *laissez-faire*, that would 'restore the natural order of religious organization and growth'. Character and conscience, not doctrines, rites, and creeds, would ally 'reformers' of all communions in public testimony to their spiritual quest for the 'Church of the Future' (**3.3.1**). But there were dissenters already beyond the pale of any nominally Christian organization who equally concerned themselves with achieving new forms and manifestations of religious life. John Morley (1838–1923), a refugee from Anglo-Catholic Oxford, had come full-circle and found asylum in the science-based authoritarian cult of Comtean Positivism, which T. H. Huxley unkindly dubbed 'Catholicism minus Christianity'. In his classic essay, *On Compromise*, Morley portrayed the 'humanitarian faith of the future' as an outgrowth of Christian truths, a free doctrinal 'development' in the direction that dissenters had long since taken but which Newman, in his last Anglican publication, *An Essay on the Development of Christian Doctrine* (1845), had scarcely envisaged (**3.3.2**).

3.3.1   J. MARTINEAU ON THE NEW AFFINITIES OF FAITH, 1869

. . . The Reformation did the work of its time, but not of all time: it shifted the authority, without essentially remodelling the inherited theory, of Christianity; and embodied the old scheme of theological thought in its new ecclesiastical constitutions. Nay, in its recoil from shameless laxities, and its jealousy for the Divine holiness, it increased the rigour of the older definitions; it deepened the chasm between man and God, and cast into the abyss every bridge of approach except its own hair-line of transit. Its doctrine of human nature announced a ruin more absolute, and its provision of supernatural grace promised a rescue more precarious and arbitrary, than could permanently accord with the experience and conscience of mankind. Deep as are Augustine's occasional glances into the passionate depths of the soul, scarcely are his reasonings against the possibility of antipodes more out of place in the present age, than his theory of the moral and spiritual universe, which was crystallized in the creeds of the Reformed Churches. It may be doubted whether, if it rested on an unimpeachable authority, it could retain its life in the open air of modern sympathies and relations. But, dependent as it is on the legends of the Creation and the Fall, and on the Pauline reasonings which proceed upon them, it has been weakened, by the progress of Biblical criticism, in its external supports, whilst losing its internal credibility. The result is too notorious to be concealed, and too serious to be let alone. There is an extensive loosening of belief in the 'schemes of salvation,' which Protestant Churches are constructed to administer; an uneasiness in preachers who cannot enforce them without consciously refining them away, and in hearers to whom they bring no real conviction; a mutual understanding to lower the standard of religious veracity, and not ask too much sincerity in profession or in prayer. It is no longer an insult to a clergyman's honour, but rather a compliment to his intelligence, to suspect him of saying one thing and believing another: while the layman, who needs say nothing, uses a right of reticence which no earnest conviction ever claimed. The theology which is supposed to be the sole directing light of human life, and which once tinctured the whole language of human intercourse, takes refuge in ecclesiastical courts and sectarian newspapers, retains a special order of writers to recommend it, and a select number of publishers to distribute it: while the teeming mass of spontaneous literature throws up no trace of it, and freely treats of social, moral, and scientific questions on principles silently at variance with it.

These are symptoms of weakened cohesion and impaired life in a system once compact and vigorous. Side by side with them appear evident marks of new religious sympathies, and the promise of more natural combinations. Theological groups are breaking up not simply by disintegration from within, but by an unexpected play of mutual attractions. Far apart on the great circles of belief lights have appeared which it is impossible to deny are lights of heaven. Is there a man at once intellectual and devout, in any land where the English language is spoken, who does not own spiritual obligations to *both* the Newmans? or who has not on his choicest shelf both the '*Christian Year*' and the '*In Memoriam*'? Is not Mr. Maurice revered as a deliverer by numbers of people, both more and less orthodox than himself? In what cultivated home of English religion has Frederick Robertson not preached his word of power? How little has the repute of 'unsoundness' thinned the mixed multitude which throngs to hear every word of a Stanley or a Jowett? Even Scotland feels the stirrings of the new spirit. It is no longer divided into two encampments, – the children of nature under Burns, – the children of grace under Knox; but, gathering the best minds of the land around such men as Lee, Caird, Tulloch, Macleod, and Wallace, renders its divinity so humane, and its humanity so devout, as to abash the ancient rigour and win over the irreverence it provoked. And this tendency to fusion and readjustment is no mere latitudinarian compromise, the result of indifference or artificial concession, and implying a secret despair of Divine truth. It is a genuine drawing together of soul to soul in defiance of separating lines of definition, – the discovery of a ground of communion deeper than the creeds had shown. It arises not from a contracted but from an enlarged conception of the range and power of sacred truth. Instead of being a mere quiet settlement of quarrels that are past, – the winding-up of an account which it is time to close, – it comes with the surprise of hope, and presses into the future for ampler and more harmonious light.

Persons affected by these influences are ill at ease in their ecclesiastical home, and find their love for it tried by many an uncongenial word or usage. It asks for more concurrence than they can give: and it leaves untouched some affections which long to quit their silence. By the rule of any true assortment, we should say they are misplaced, and are waiting to dispose themselves around new and more natural centres of crystallization. They may very possibly have come to no conscious breach with their inherited orthodoxy, or at least have retained enough of it to save them from any direct transfer of allegiance. But it has ceased to be a religious *essential*, and has descended to the rank of personal *opinion:* towards him who is otherwise minded they cannot keep up the old antipathy: if the piety and charity of a Christian shine through him, they cannot help admitting him to the fellowship of their hearts. When in contact with him they are less sure that his creed is wrong than that his character is right: and crush him as you may in the millwork of your church logic, he will remain alive and whole as a power over their spirits. In every Protestant communion not out of reach of modern culture, and especially in the English and Scotch Churches, and in the Congregational body, this indeterminate state of mind, – clear in spiritual discernment, in suspense on more or fewer definitions of belief, – prevails among vast numbers. They find too much decided for them: they want to be responsible for less doctrine: they would fain take apart for their personal reflection, and reserve among the private rights of their own conscience, many of the topics which their Church has pre-occupied in its corporate constitution or its name. Were everything removed but the simplest conditions of common worship and common work, and were it left to experience to find *how* simple these are, they would welcome the change as a relief from inward bondage, and throw themselves into their religious fellowship with new affection; an affection infinitely higher than that party-spirit which at present is used to override the scruples of conscience and mimic the activities of pity and love. . . .

Among all these persons there is, and there has long been, the movement of a common spirit. They are all averse to both the Sacerdotal and the Atheistical view of the world. They none of them insist on any form of orthodoxy, though it be their own, as essential to the pious union of men or their filial relation to God. The 'unattached,' who find the place of public prayer uncongenial, and have gone 'up into the mountain alone,' are willing to return when the devotion shall speak what they can truly say. The 'broad-churchmen' are ready to widen their communion with the expanding limits of national piety, not excluding the fullest doctrinal theology, but requiring the least. The liberal Nonconformists, weary of sectarian interests, wanting more room for their faith and affections, and finding that companionship in the school of divinity is no guarantee of spiritual sympathy, are longing for a larger fellowship and a freer use of their right of growth. What is the essence of this common spirit pervading such different classes? – Is it intellectual agreement? Is there any sort of creed which these people could club together to propagate? By no means: unless you call it a creed to have a fearless respect for intellectual freedom, and to trust the bonds of piety, righteousness, and love amid large varieties of thought. This trust you may, no doubt, – if you must convert into a dogma everything which the human mind can hold – express in a proposition to be believed. But this is your work at the end, not its way of beginning. Its birth is in the moral and spiritual nature: and those whom it possesses have been carried towards one another, not by deliberate steering to or from the same lines on the logical chart, but by those silent changes in the moral currents beneath, and in the winds of heaven around, which sometimes mysteriously turn the drift of human affairs.

To many of those who feel the impulse of this common spirit, it has appeared that its distinct expression and embodiment could be nothing but a pure good. Without undervaluing the influence of scattered persons of catholic mind, they distrust the religious power which depends upon suppression or reserve, and think the time has come, for those who cannot rest in the present, to mark publicly the direction of their looks towards the Church of the Future. From this conviction has sprung the 'FREE CHRISTIAN UNION,' intended to serve as a rallying-point for reformers who deem the doctrinal requirements of existing sects excessive and super-fluous, and who would be content with any Church inspired, according to the Christian rule, with Love to God and Love to Man. It is not surprising that an organized movement with such an aim should be exposed to criticism from the most opposite sides. . . . We must reproduce the preamble on which the discussion turns.

'Whereas, for ages past, Christians have been taught that correct con-ceptions of Divine things are necessary to acceptance with God, and to religious relations with each other;

'And, in vain pursuit of Orthodoxy, have parted into rival Churches, and lost the bond of common work and love:

'And whereas, with the progressive changes of thought and feeling, uniformity in doctrinal opinion becomes ever more precarious, while moral and spiritual affinities grow and deepen:

'And whereas, the Divine Will is summed up by Jesus Christ Himself in Love to God and Love to Man;

'And the terms of pious union among men should be as broad as those of communion with God:

'This Society, desiring a spiritual fellowship co-extensive with these terms, invites to common action all who deem men responsible, not for the attainment of Divine truth, but only for the serious search of it; and who rely, for the religious improvement of human life, on filial Piety and brotherly Charity, with or without more particular agreement in matters of doctrinal theology. Its object is, by relieving the Christian life from reliance on theological articles or external rites, to save it from conflict with the knowledge and conscience of mankind, and bring it back to the essential conditions of harmony between God and Man.'

This preamble is . . . met by the objection, that, while it denounces sects and disparages doctrine, it proposes to establish a new sect upon a doc-trine of its own. It is, therefore, only a fresh proof that all common religious action must be founded, as the Churches assume, in accordant belief, and involve a creed.

. . . Can it be needful to point out the distinction between 'belief', an inward state of the human mind, and a 'creed,' a 'doctrine,' a 'dogma,' the verbal definition of that state? or to show how illogical is the inference that religious union, because involving belief in common, must be based upon doctrine? All the moral transactions of men with each other – their contracts, their testimony, their resentments – involve also certain beliefs, the assumptions inseparable from our ethical nature. But who would ever propose, as a preliminary to an insurance or a deposit, to know the moral philosophy of the broker or the banker, and be sure of his intuitional or utilitarian orthodoxy? For confidence and co-operation in social relations it is enough that the right affections and character be there: let there be honour, fine temper and veracity, and the united life is secure, however different may be the intellectual reports they give of their own ground. While the philosophers are disputing about the foundation of property, and cannot take even the first step together, all the wealth of the world is under peaceable ownership, and has changed hands a hundred times. While the economists were all in the dark, or all at issue, about the nature of exchange, the hum of a million markets never ceased. No œcumenical council of the wise could even now settle the definitions of Justice and of Right: yet the voice of law has never paused, and the tribunals have never been shut. The religious union of men may be left, just as safely as the moral, to the natural play of spiritual affinities, and the mutual understanding of affection and character; and, for the common life of devout and humane duty, it is quite superfluous to think out its processes and grounds into defined speculative form. The more you keep the pious union waiting for the right theory, the more certain is the theory to go wrong, and the more fantastic become the lines of aberration: for, till the common life has been led, and its inward experiences gained, the very materials are out of reach which thought has to mould into truth. The 'Free Christian Union' simply proposes to restore the natural order of religious organization and growth; to leave the formative power with the sympathetic impulses of Piety and Charity; to be content with the real, though unformulated, common faith in God and the Divine relations of Man which these two forms of love imply; and to let *doctrine, i.e.,* the intellectual statement and definition of particular beliefs, follow, not as a corporate act of the Church, but as a private function of individual minds. This is neither a disparagement of doctrine, nor the announcement of a new one. It certainly alters – if you please, inverts – the relation of doctrine to the combined religious life. But, in doing so – in withdrawing it from the public vote of incompetent assemblies, and delivering it freely over to the domain of personal research – the scheme makes infinitely better provision for its interests and its integrity than by surrendering it to be rent in pieces as the party symbol of the councils and the sects.

As this practical proposal can with no propriety be called a 'new doctrine,' so neither can the 'Union' be correctly called a 'new sect.' A sect is (in religion) an ecclesiastical body formed by schism from previous churches, or in rivalry to them, for the expression of some idea, or the establishment of some usage, unprovided for by them. The 'Free Christian Union,' on the other hand, simply selects from among the ends already contemplated by Christian Churches, the spiritual and catholic elements, and lets them try their binding power apart from other conditions, which often oppress and baffle them. Its supporters do not themselves intend to withdraw, nor do they desire to withdraw others, from their existing ecclesiastical connection, but only to bear witness to what is supremely excellent in it, and help to clear its essence from its accidents. They have provided no place in their scheme for the training or the employment of a clerical order, for any separate institutions, rites, or worship: and the only pulpit which they have proposed to raise was to be served by occasional preachers stepping out for the day from their own denomination, and returning to it again. They believe, no doubt, that in the principle which unites them lies the germ of the future universal church: and if here and there a body of worshippers is already held together by its simple power, they are ready to enter into fellowship with them, and help their work. But this fostering function, this welcome of spontaneous promise, this offer of refuge to those who can save the spirit, apart from the questionable form, belongs to a *society*, not to a *sect*; and is provided for throughout by lay, and not by ecclesiastical, machinery. . . .

3.3.2   J. MORLEY ON RELIGIOUS NONCONFORMITY, 1874

The peculiar character of all the best kinds of dissent from the nominal creed of the time, makes it rather less difficult for us to try to reconcile unflinching honesty with a just and becoming regard for the feelings of those who have claims upon our forebearance, than would have been the case a hundred years ago. 'It is not now with a polite sneer,' as a high ecclesiastical authority lately admitted, 'still less with a rude buffet or coarse words, that Christianity is assailed.' Before churchmen congratulate themselves too warmly on this improvement in the nature of the attack, perhaps they ought to ask themselves how far it is due to the change in the position of the defending party. The truth is that the coarse and realistic criticism of which Voltaire was the consummate master, has done its work. It has driven the defenders of the old faith into the milder and more genial climate of non-natural interpretations, and the historic sense, and a certain elastic relativity of dogma. The old criticism was victorious, but after victory it vanished. One reason of this was that the coarse and realistic forms of belief had either vanished before it, or else they forsook their ancient pretensions and clothed themselves in more modest robes. The consequence of this, and of other causes which might be named, is that the modern attack, while fully as serious and much more radical, has a certain gravity, decorum, and worthiness of form. No one of any sense or knowledge now thinks the Christian religion had its origin in deliberate imposture. The modern freethinker does not attack it; he explains it. And what is more, he explains it by referring its growth to the better, and not to the worse part of human nature. He traces it to men's cravings for a higher morality. He finds its source in their aspirations after nobler expression of that feeling for the incommensurable things, which is in truth under so many varieties of inwoven pattern the common universal web of religious faith.

The result of this way of looking at a creed which a man no longer accepts, is that he is able to speak of it with patience and historic respect. He can openly mark his dissent from it, without exacerbating the orthodox sentiment by galling pleasantries or bitter animadversion upon details. We are now awake to the all-important truth that belief in this or that detail of superstition is the result of an irrational state of mind, and flows logically from superstitious premisses. We see that it is to begin at the wrong end, to assail the deductions as impossible, instead of sedulously building up a state of mind in which their impossibility would become spontaneously visible.

Besides the great change which such a point of view makes in men's way of speaking of a religion, whose dogmas and documents they reject, there is this further consideration leaning in the same direction. The tendency of modern free thought is more and more visibly towards the extraction of the first and more permanent elements of the old faith, to make the purified material of the new. When Dr. Congreve met the famous epigram about Comte's system being Catholicism minus Christianity, by the reply that it is Catholicism plus Science, he gave an ingenious expression to the direction which is almost necessarily taken by all who attempt, in however informal a manner, to construct for themselves some working system of faith, in place of the faith which science and criticism have sapped. In what ultimate form, acceptable to great multitudes of men, these attempts will at last issue, no one can now tell. For we, like the Hebrews of old, shall all have to live and die in faith, 'not having received the promises, but having seen them afar off, and being persuaded of them, and embracing them, and confessing that we are strangers and pilgrims on the earth.' Meanwhile, after the first great glow and passion of the just and necessary revolt of reason against superstition have slowly lost the exciting splendour of the dawn, and become diffused in the colourless space of a rather bleak noonday, the mind gradually collects again some of the ideas of the old religion of the West, and willingly, or even joyfully, suffers itself to be once more breathed upon by something of its spirit. Christianity was the last great religious synthesis. It is the one nearest to us. Nothing is more natural than that those who cannot rest content with intellectual analysis, while awaiting the advent of the Saint Paul of the humanitarian faith of the future, should gather up provisionally such fragmentary illustrations of this new faith as are to be found in the records of the old. Whatever form may be ultimately imposed on our vague religious aspirations by some prophet to come, who shall unite sublime depth of feeling and lofty purity of life with strong intellectual grasp and the gift of a noble eloquence, we may at least be sure of this, that it will stand as closely related to Christianity, as Christianity stood closely related to the old Judaic dispensation. It is commonly assumed that the rejecters of the popular religion stand in face of it, as the Christians stood in face of the pagan belief and pagan rites in the Empire. The analogy is inexact. The modern denier, if he is anything better than that, or entertains hopes of a creed to come, is nearer to the position of the Christianising Jew.* Science, when she has accomplished all her triumphs in her own order, will still have to go back, when the time comes, to assist in the building up of a new creed by which men can live. The builders will have to seek material in the purified and sublimated ideas, of which the confessions and rites of the Christian churches have been the grosser expression. Just as what was once the new dispensation was preached *a Judæis ad Judæos apud Judæos*, so must the new, that is to be, find a Christian teacher and Christian hearers. It can hardly be other than an expansion, a development, a re-adaptation, of all the moral and spiritual truth that lay hidden under the worn-out forms. It must be such a harmonising of the truth with our intellectual conceptions, as shall fit it to be an active guide to conduct. In a world *'where men sit and hear each other groan, where but to think is to be full of sorrow,'* it is hard to imagine a time when we shall be indifferent to that sovereign legend of Pity. We have to incorporate it in some wider gospel of Justice and Progress.

I shall not, I hope, be suspected of any desire to prophesy too smooth things. It is no object of ours to bridge over the gulf between belief in the vulgar theology and disbelief. Nor for a single moment do we pretend that, when all the points of contact between virtuous belief and virtuous disbelief are made the most of that good faith will allow, there will not still

---

*The following words, illustrating the continuity between the Christian and Jewish churches, are not without instruction to those who meditate on the possible continuity between the Christian church and that which is one day to grow into the place of it: – 'Not only do forms and ordinances remain under the Gospel equally as before; but, what was in use before is not so much superseded by the Gospel ordinances as changed into them. What took place under the Law is a pattern, what was commanded is a rule, under the Gospel. The substance remains, the use, the meaning, the circumstances, the benefit is changed; grace is added, life is infused: "the body is of Christ;" but it is in great measure that same body which was in being before He came. The Gospel has not put aside, it has incorporated into itself, the revelation which went before it. It avails itself of the Old Testament, as a great gift to Christian as well as to Jew. It does not dispense with it, but it dispenses it. Persons sometimes urge that there is no code of duty in the New Testament, no ceremonial, no rules for Church polity. Certainly not; they are unnecessary; they are already given in the Old. Why should the Old Testament remain in the Christian church but to be used? *There* we are to look for our forms, our rites, our polity; only illustrated, tempered, spiritualised by the Gospel. The precepts remain, the observance of them is changed.' – Dr. J. H. Newman: *Sermons on Subjects of the Day*, p. 205.

and after all remain a terrible controversy between those who cling passionately to all the consolations, mysteries, personalities, of the orthodox faith, and us who have made up our minds to face the worst, and to shape, as best we can, a life in which the cardinal verities of the common creed shall have no place. The future faith, like the faith of the past, brings not peace but a sword. It is a tale not of concord, but of households divided against themselves. Those who are incessantly striving to make the old bottles hold the new wine, to reconcile the irreconcilable, to bring the Bible and the dogmas of the churches to be good friends with history and criticism, are prompted by the humanest intention. One sympathises with this amiable anxiety to soften shocks, and break the rudeness of a vital transition. In this essay, at any rate, there is no such attempt. We know that it is the son against the father, and the mother-in-law against the daughter-in-law. No softness of speech will disguise the portentous differences between those who admit a supernatural revelation and those who deny it. No charity nor goodwill can narrow the intellectual breach between those who declare that a world without an ever-present Creator with intelligible attributes would be to them empty and void, and those who insist that none of the attributes of a Creator can ever be grasped by the finite intelligence of men. Our object in urging the purpose, semi-conservative, and almost sympathetic quality, which distinguishes the unbelief of to-day from the unbelief of a hundred years ago, is only to show that the most strenuous and upright of plain-speakers is less likely to shock and wound the lawful sensibilities of devout persons, than he would have been so long as unbelief went no further than bitter attack on small details. In short, all save the purely negative and purely destructive school of free-thinkers, are now able to deal with the beliefs from which they dissent, in a way which makes patient and disinterested controversy not wholly impossible . . . .

4

EVANGELICALISM
AND ETHICS

4.1   THE BIBLE, FROM BEGINNING TO END

NO single belief was more characteristic of evangelicals – those in Church and chapel who urged individual conversion and holy living as a right response to the Gospel – than the conviction that the Bible was not only an inspired road-map to heaven, but an inerrant historical guide to God's dealings with humankind. For this evangelicals found themselves almost constantly out of step with the rising intellectual culture of the Victorian age. They produced rank upon rank of doughty controversialists who sallied forth to rescue the Bible from modernity by reconciling it with historical scholarship and scientific facts. Inevitably, their labours embodied rather more ingenuity than learning, and many gifted but misguided individuals ended up in curious blind alleys. Nowhere were the alleys more obscure or the controversialists more ingenious than in the reinterpretation of the beginning and end of history according to the books of Genesis and Revelation. In 1861 Thomas Rawson Birks (1810–1883), an Anglican vicar and later F. D. Maurice's successor as professor of moral philosophy at Cambridge, evinced the extent to which more thoughtful evangelicals could reconcile their idea of a biblical scheme of redemption with the philosophy of historical progress. Marking an interval of about 1,500 years and unveiling the divine plan of six or seven millenia, Genesis, through its unadorned history, and Revelation, through its 'highly poetical visions', disclosed to Birks 'a Divine unity which pervades and animates' the entire Bible (**4.1.1**). Another Anglican clergyman, Joseph Baylee (1808–1883), the founder and principal of St Aidan's Theological College near Liverpool, sought to extract a similar redemptive plan from a harmonious juxtaposition of Genesis and geology. Successive geological ages, punctuated by terraqueous convulsions, revealed to him a pattern of divine moral government that had been carried on through human history and would culminate in the 'last time' (**4.1.2**). Both Baylee and Birks were evidently interested in apocalyptic themes, but it was the Irish preacher and evangelist Henry Grattan Guinness (1835–1910) who excelled all Victorian evangelicals in establishing redemptive history and the millennial prophecy of Revelation on the basis of astronomical calculation. How far prior belief in *The Approaching End of the Age*, to use the title of his most important work, which passed through fourteen editions, affected his elaborate synthesis of numerology, typology, and 'soli-lunar' chronology may be readily surmised (**4.1.3**).

4.1.1   T. R. BIRKS ON THE BIBLE AND MODERN THOUGHT, 1861

The Bible, alike in its histories and prophecies, is flatly opposed to those theories of mankind's gradual and universal progress in moral and religious truth, which have been propounded by unbelieving philosophy, and which sometimes labour, however vainly, to support themselves by an appeal to its own statements. The pictures it sets before us are widely different – a series of rebellions and apostasies, resisted, and partially overcome, by mighty acts of Divine grace; but continually repeated in new forms, till they issue, in the last times, in a solemn and fearful controversy between light and darkness, and in judgment on abounding ungodliness, as well as in rich mercy and grace to those who know God and obey the Gospel of Christ. We are told, in the New Testament, that 'in the last days perilous times shall come,' and that 'evil men and seducers shall wax worse and worse, deceiving and being deceived.' And, however the views of Christians may vary with regard to the future course of Providence, and the final victories of truth – one thing must be plain, to all who read the Scriptures with reverence, that they are nowhere ascribed to a natural law of human progress, but to gracious acts of the Holy Spirit, or direct judgments of Christ, which will overcome and reverse the downward tendency of the human heart, and bind a reluctant and rebellious race, by mercy and judgment, to the footstool of the Most High.

But while the Bible is thus opposed to those spurious theories of progress, which are based on human pride, and contradict the facts of history, it exhibits a progress of a different kind, in the ceaseless unfolding of a scheme of Divine mercy for the redemption and recovery of sinful man. God, in his own nature, is unsearchable: he can be known only as he is revealed. A revelation of moral attributes, since it must consist of the successive acts of God's moral government, must plainly be progressive. Salvation, or the recovery of the soul from the power of sin, is by faith alone. The object of faith is Divine truth. It is by the knowledge of the truth that the souls of men are actually redeemed and renewed. And since the providence of God unfolds itself, from age to age, in new acts of judgment and of mercy, the materials of moral influence are thus increased and multiplied, which the Holy Spirit, the Lord and Giver of life, employs in his gracious work upon the hearts of men, both in their first conversion, and in their later advances in heavenly wisdom. There is thus a double progress, which the Scriptures reveal to us. The first is that of the Divine counsel itself, or the acts of mercy and judgment, which constitute the moral government of the world, and the messages of revelation. This is unintermitted, ceaseless, and unfailing. It admits of no arrest, and no reverse. However dark the moral state of the world may be in special crises of Providence, the stars, even at midnight, move on in their everlasting courses, and prepare the way for a brighter sunrise to follow. The second kind of progress is that of the actual fruits of redemption in each successive age. And this resembles the apparent movements of the planets. There is a general progress, subject to temporary retrocession and decline. Seasons of Divine forbearance, through man's perverseness, lead to spiritual decay. 'Because sentence against an evil work is not executed speedily, the hearts of the sons of men is fully set in them to do evil.' That evil is permitted to reach a certain height, and is then broken to pieces by new acts of judgment, followed by fresh and higher revelations of mercy. And thus, although by a chequered and seemingly irregular course, the work of grace moves on continually, and truth prevails, by a slow but sure advance, from age to age. Even when it seems to decay, and 'the faithful are minished from the children of men' – the time of fear and sorrow is only the season of travail before a joyful birth. Each fresh exhibition of stubbornness and inveteracy of evil illustrates more brightly, in the result, the victorious energy of redeeming love. . . .

The Bible is a history of redemption, but of a redemption still incomplete, and of which the full and open triumph is reserved for days to come. Viewed in the light of this great truth, a singular unity of prophetic hope runs through the whole, and becomes doubly striking, when we compare its earliest and latest messages. No books of the Bible are more contrasted in their general character than Genesis and Revelation. The interval of time which separates them is more than fifteen hundred years. The first is a simple, unadorned history; the second, a series of highly poetical visions. The first is the earliest variety of Hebrew prose; the second, in a language then unborn, embodies the main features of Hebrew poetry. The book of Genesis records common events upon earth; the Apocalypse, to a great extent, is the description of heavenly wonders. One is a preface to the Law, the other a supplement to the Gospel. One was written by the adopted son of Pharaoh's daughter, learned in all the wisdom of Egypt; the other, by an unlearned fisherman of despised Galilee. The first abounds with innumerable details, names of persons, places, and domestic annals of the most minute and various kind; while the other scarcely stoops to set its foot upon earth, but dwells apart as on a mount of transfiguration. When the former was composed, Israel had scarcely begun to be a nation; but when the exile received his visions in Patmos, their national history was closed for ages, and they were already outcasts and wanderers through the earth. All things on earth were changed in this long interval – Egypt, Canaan, and Babylon; only God and his redeeming grace remained unchangeable. Yet the latest book corresponds to the earliest, as the loops and curtains of the tabernacle, or the various parts of the temple, with multiplied harmonies, partly of the most obvious, but in part of the most delicate and unobtrusive kind. Creation has its counterpart in the promise, 'Behold, I make all things new.' The uncreated light which fills the heavenly city; the successive revelation of the beast from the sea, the beast from the earth, and one like to the Son of man; the sabbatic rest of a thousand years, the river from the throne, watering the heavenly Paradise; the great river Euphrates, the gold and precious stones of the New Jerusalem, the tree of life in the Paradise of God; the marriage of the Lamb, the Second Adam, and the clothing in which the Bride is arrayed; the Old Serpent, the deceiver of the nations, the Woman and her mystic Seed, and sore travail; the removal of the curse, and the angel guards at the open gates of the heavenly Paradise; the cry of the martyrs from beneath the altar of burnt offering, and the rainbow around the throne; are all so many distinct allusions, in this closing prophecy, to the earliest chapters of the sacred history. The Old Testament here conspires with the New, and the history of the world's first infancy is seen to be stored with lessons of Divine wisdom, which were to be fully unveiled, after six or seven thousand years, in the final close of the mystery of God.

The Bible, then, amidst the large variety of its contents, which embrace an interval of fifteen centuries in their composition, and seven thousand years in the times to which they refer – in its histories, psalms, proverbs, prophecies, and epistles, earthly facts and heavenly revelations – exhibits, from first to last, the clear signs of a Divine unity which pervades and animates the whole. Its distinct parts are not of separate interpretation. Behind the human authors stood the Divine Spirit, controlling, guiding, and suggesting every part of their different messages. Their words 'came not at any time by the will of man, but holy men of God spake, borne along by the Holy Ghost.' As the Jordan flows underground in part of its course, so this Divine unity may be obscured from hasty observers by the multitude of intervening works of which the whole message is composed, by the variety of historical details, the diversity of manner and style, of age and local circumstance, in the sixty-six books which constitute the Bible. But its sunrise and sunset are equally glorious, and reveal clearly the hidden harmony of the whole revelation. It traces the course of Providence from that creation, in which our earth was prepared for the habitation of men, to the complete accomplishment of that new creation, in which it will be the habitation of righteousness for ever. It begins with the first bridal of Adam and Eve, the parents of all mankind, and closes with the heavenly bridal of the Second Adam, the Lord from heaven and the Church of the Firstborn, in whom the great mystery of that ordinance is fulfilled. It begins with a vision of the earthly Paradise forfeited by sin, and the taste of the forbidden tree of knowledge. It closes with the revelation of a better and heavenly Paradise, where no tree of knowledge is seen, but the tree of life alone, and even its leaves are for the healing of the nations. It begins with the success of the Old Serpent in deceiving Adam and Eve, and ends with the vision of his overthrow by the Seed of the Woman, when he can deceive the nations no more, but sinks under the righteous judgment of God. It begins with man's exclusion from Paradise by the watching cherubim and the flaming sword; and ends with the revelation of the heavenly Jerusalem, whose gates are open continually, while an angel at every gate invites the nations of the saved to bring their honour and glory into the city of God.

The more closely, then, we examine the Bible, the more plainly it will appear to be indeed 'the true sayings of God,' 'the word of God, which liveth and abideth for ever.' In its width, its freedom, and its grandeur, it reflects the largeness of God's universal Providence. Like that Providence, it has its seeming discrepancies, and its real perplexities, much to exercise faith, as well as much by which it is nourished, parts which may appear trivial and superfluous, and depths which repel the frivolous with a sense of impenetrable gloom. Even those who sincerely embrace the Gospel may rest satisfied with a dim and imperfect measure of knowledge, and thus have their faith in it exposed to sore trial, whenever new temptations assail the church of Christ. But in proportion as we search it with humble diligence and earnest prayer, fresh harmonies of Divine truth, new wonders of Divine grace and love, will disclose themselves to our view. One difficulty after another will slowly melt away, and resolve itself into a halo of heavenly beauty. Sixty generations of the church have studied it unceasingly; but this incorruptible manna neither wastes nor corrupts, and they have never exhausted its stores of Divine wisdom. Sixty generations of unbelievers have assailed it on every side with winds of false doctrine, but it has only rooted itself the more firmly in the hearts of Christians, and in the history of the world. And still, after all these ages, there are deep mines of truth in it which have never been explored, harvests of spiritual food still to be reaped by coming generations, and healing medicines for countless evils that are still concealed in the depths of future time. The words of the prophet to Ariel of old will assuredly be fulfilled, soon or late, in all who assail this enduring word of God. 'And the multitude of the nations that fight against her and her munition shall be even as the dream of a night vision. It shall be as when a hungry man dreameth, and behold he eateth, but he waketh, and his soul is empty; or a thirsty man dreameth, and behold he drinketh, but he waketh, and is faint, and his soul hath appetite: so shall all the multitude of the nations be that fight against Zion.' But those who draw near with reverence, and while they meditate, loose their shoes from their feet on this holy ground, will equally find the promise of the Psalmist fulfilled in their own experience: 'They shall be abundantly satisfied with the fatness of thy house, and thou wilt make them drink of the river of thy pleasures: for with thee is the fountain of life, and in thy light we shall see light.' The meteors of false philosophy blaze for a moment, and disappear; but the written word of God is an effluence from the Uncreated Light, and must endure for ever.

4.1.2   J. BAYLEE ON GENESIS AND GEOLOGY, 1857

Three thousand three hundred years have passed away since God delivered to men, by the hand of his servant Moses, an exact account of the creation of the universe, and of the six days' work.

From age to age that divine record has been the admiration of truly scientific and devout minds, and the object of relentless attack from infidels. Ill instructed zeal in its favour has obscured its simple majesty by mistaken comments. . . . Half a century since, these mistaken expositions led many earnest Christians to denounce the conclusions of Geology as contrary to the divine word. A more accurate scientific knowledge, united to a more accurate acquaintance with what the Word of God really says, has long since silenced those objections to Natural Science. A similar result has taken place amongst the better instructed class of scientific men.

MOSES AND HIS MISINTERPRETERS

Simple as is the distinction between an author and his commentators, the two are constantly confounded, by writers who cavil at the Bible, and by a far more respectable class, who have so identified certain interpretations with the Scriptures, that the distinction between them is practically lost. A distinguished Oxford Professor, the Rev. Baden Powell, from whose acute mind and eminently logical powers one might have expected better things, contents himself with a sweeping assertion that it is impossible to reconcile the Hebrew narrative of the cosmogony with the facts of science. An equally distinguished dissenting minister, Dr. Pye Smith, laid down the monstrous theory that Moses was not writing in accordance with science, but only endeavouring to convey to an ill-educated people higher ideas of the greatness and majesty of God.

It would be endless to recapitulate all the theories that have been put forward, from time to time, in order to harmonize the scriptural statements with well ascertained natural phenomena.

One justly exploded theory was, that the six days were six long, perhaps indefinite, periods. With this theory the ascertained facts of Geology are decidedly at variance.

In dealing with the question, what does the Word of God really say? I feel called upon to make my most strenuous protest against confounding the ancient, inspired, and therefore infallible, writers, with modern uninspired, and therefore fallible, commentators.

GEOLOGY, AND HER MISINTERPRETERS

If piety has to complain of misinterpreters of the Word of God, true philosophy has equally to complain of misinterpreters of the Works of God. There is a continual accession of ascertained natural phenomena to the copious stores of human knowledge. These, when classified, harmonized, and organized, are distributed into the various sciences which compose the circle of natural knowledge.

Some sciences are exact and determinate. However they may expand, they never need re-arrangement or correction. Geometry, for example, is admitted on all hands to be an exact science. . . .

There are, again, other sciences, which are still so very little known that they have not yet attained to the rank of an undisputed science. Of these, Geology is one. Within the last fifty years, theory after theory has risen, found favour, and fallen, only to make way for another, which has had in its turn to give way to a new theory; and so this state of things continues to the present moment, and is likely to do for a long time to come.

Were Geologists more modest, this continual succession of exploded, or, at best, greatly modified theories, would redound to their credit, instead of being, as it is now too often, only a painful exhibition of human self-reliance.

How often do we hear sciolists in Geology pronouncing as confidently against the Mosaic cosmogony as if they had attained to exact science in Geology, or had the smallest pretensions to a *scientific* knowledge of the inspired narrative.

The just punishment of such a state of mind is, that vanity induces men to put forward theories and to make assertions, which some future critic makes like the baseless fabric of a vision, leaving not a wreck behind. Yet I am far indeed from decrying imperfect theories. They are the steps of the ladder by which the human mind ascends from a mere accumulation of data to a well-defined and thoroughly demonstrated system. The history of Astronomy is a striking proof of this truth. . . .

So far as the geological question bears upon the Mosaic cosmogony, I think I may reduce the discoveries of Geology to the following statements:

1. Human beings have inhabited this world only within the historic periods, including the Bible records.

2. There is decisive evidence of various violent and very extensive convulsions in the crust of this earth, which produced very great superficial changes.

3. Those convulsions appear to have been produced by the action of subterranean fire, in probable combination with other physical agencies.

4. Each extensive convulsion seems to have been followed by a long period of comparative quiescence, during which great superficial changes occurred.

5. Those undefined and probably very long periods have their records in the fossil remains of animals, plants, and minerals.

6. They have no indications of the arts of civilized life, or of having been under the dominion of intellectual beings who united in their own persons mind and organized matter as men do.

7. Our knowledge of their phenomena does not enable us to give a DEMONSTRABLE theory of any regular gradual progress upwards to the present admirable organization of the earth.

8. Everywhere the upper strata are aqueous and the lowest igneous.

9. The igneous strata are composite in character, and we have no means of ascertaining what had been their previous condition.

10. Each period, ending in a violent convulsion, gives testimony to some moral cause which produced the catastrophe, unless we altogether deny the superintending providence of God.

11. Geology affords abundant evidence that the world was not made by a fortuitous concurrence of atoms, but that it has come from the Creator's hand, who regulates all its changes.

12. Hence we are warranted in inferring a series of moral dispensations in this world, concurrent with its geological periods.

In this point of view Geology is indeed a noble science, and I hope to prove before I have done that Geology and the Bible mutually illustrate each other, the former pointing to the latter and saying, 'Behold the Word of God, which pours a flood of true light upon the phenomena of the Works of God, enabling us to harmonize and organize them, and so obtain from them new views of the great and glorious Author of both.'

THE WORD FOR GOD, AND ITS INFALLIBLE TRUTH. CREATION

How often we hear persons speak of the Mosaic account of the Creation. How few reflect upon the brevity of that account. One short sentence comprises the whole: 'In the beginning God created the heaven and the earth.' This is the whole; and will any man of science deny its infallible truth?

It is want of attention to the distinction between creating and making which has caused so much perplexity and confusion. Moses clearly distinguished the two, in saying, 'All his work which God created and made.' The act of creation was one exertion of Omnipotence at the beginning. Of the condition of the heaven and the earth at the beginning, we have no direct testimony in the Bible. If we may conjecture from the use of the word 'create' and its derivatives, we are warranted in believing that the primary condition of the heaven and the earth was one of great order and beauty. I have been led to this conclusion from an examination of every place where the word occurs in the Hebrew Bible. . . .

THE SIX DAYS' WORK

If it were not so common an error, one could scarcely have supposed that the six days' work should have been called the Creation. The Bible never says that the world was created in six days. Moses' words are: 'In six days the Lord *made* heaven and earth.' He nowhere defines the interval between the original Creation and the six days' work. Should Geology prove that interval to have been countless millions of years, there would be no contradiction to the Mosaic account.

The account of the six days' work is simply a narrative of the last of those changes of which Geology reveals a long series, if we except the comparatively trifling change produced by the Noachic flood. In examining that narrative, the natural philosopher will discover nothing contrary to true Science. It commences with the restoration of light to this earth. I say its restoration; for Moses does not say that light was then for the first time created. He simply tells us that 'God said, Let there be light, and there was light.' . . . Science teaches us that the atmosphere is not necessary to the transmission of light. There is therefore no scientific difficulty in the work of the first day preceding the formation of the atmosphere on the second. In describing the work of the second day, Moses says expressly, 'God *made* the firmament.' Consequently, he was not declaring its creation, but its formation. . . .

The work of the third day was the elevation of the dry land above the waters. Geology affords the most decisive proof of the probability of such an event, even were it not declared in the inspired record; for nothing is more evident than that the greater part of the habitable globe was once covered with water. This was a suitable preparation for the production of the vegetable world.

The work of the fourth day has been more cavilled at than almost any other. How often do we hear the objection that Moses represents the *creation* of the sun, moon, and stars as having taken place on the fourth day. Nothing can be more unfounded. Moses says, 'God made two great lights.' . . . Moses does not say that they never had had that function previously, but that in the restored condition of the earth from that darkness which had been upon the face of the deep, God assigned to the sun and moon the functions of light distributors to the earth.

The fifth day's work was the formation of aquatic animals, and the sixth that of terrestrial ones and man.

In all this, then, we have the natural transition from a state of chaos to the beautiful order and harmony in which we now see the world. . . . We may fearlessly challenge all the natural philosophers in the world to point out a single error in the Mosaic account of the six days' work.

THE CHAOTIC STATE

Moses describes a wonderful state of the earth immediately preceding the six days' work. He says, 'The earth was without form and void, and darkness was upon the face of the deep. And the Spirit of God moved upon the face of the waters.' Geology, so far from contradicting this fact, wonderfully confirms it. The habitable globe bears abundant testimony to the fact that it was once, and for a very long time, covered with water.

The terms by which Moses describes this state of the earth are, 'without form and void.' . . . The words are never used in the Bible for the original condition of anything, but always for a state of degradation and ruin.

Another word employed by Moses is equally remarkable; it is 'the deep.' This word is often poetically employed for the sea; but this is only its metaphorical application. . . . *Thehom*, deep, means literally the agitated, broken-up mass. Could science invent a more accurate name to describe the strata of the earth's crust? Over that deep, or broken-up mass, was the superincumbent weight of waters, compressing it into the condition in which we now behold it.

Farther, Moses tells us that God's care was over the world even during that desolation: 'The Spirit of God moved upon the face of the waters.' What agency was then employed is not revealed to us. It is enough for us to know that there was a divine preparation for the subsequent six days' work. Have we here, then, anything discordant with the facts of Science, or rather, is it not in beautiful harmony with them? Science may well sit at the feet of Revelation, and devoutly bring her accumulated stores to receive, from a higher teacher, order, harmony, and organization. . . .

In the 104th Psalm, we have a beautiful allusion to the manner in which the Lord made the dry land to appear. The Psalm describes the glory of God in nature. In describing the pre-Adamic condition of the earth, David says, 'Thou coveredst it with the deep as with a garment: the waters stood above the mountains.' This was the earth's condition as described by Moses, 'The Spirit of God moved upon the face of the waters.' The Psalm proceeds, 'At thy rebuke they fled: at the voice of thy thunder they hasted away. The mountains ascend, the valleys descend unto the place which thou hast founded for them.' Psalm civ. 6–8. That is, that when God said, Let the waters be gathered into one place, and let the dry land appear, the mountains ascended, the earth's strata upheaved, the elevation of one part being accompanied by the depression of others, the distribution of land and waters which we now see took place. Science comes in here with her corroborative testimony, giving abundant evidence of such upheavals and depressions.

The book of Job furnishes us with another most significant hint, in the Almighty's speech. The dispute amongst Job's friends was upon the moral government of God, whether Job was justly chargeable with hypocrisy and guilt because he was so great a sufferer. After all parties had become silent, the Almighty himself speaks; he appeals to their ignorance, and rebukes their presumption: he convicted them of giving an *ex parte* deci-sion, because they were reasoning from a very small part of human history. They knew nothing of the past – they were as ignorant of the future. The fleeting and temporary present could therefore give but insufficient data upon which to form a judgment.

The Lord appeals to the future when he says. 'Look on every one that is proud, and bring him low; and tread down the wicked in their place. Hide them in the dust together; and bind their faces in secret.' Job xl. 12, 13. In other words, look to the condition of man beyond the grave, before you presume to come to a decision respecting the divine government.

The Lord also appeals to the past: 'Hast thou entered into the springs of the sea? or hast thou walked in the search of the depth?' Job xxxviii. 16. A most significant hint that the divine *moral* government reached back to a period far anterior to Adam, or the six days' work. What are the records which the sea covers? What were the causes why the depth became a broken-up mass?

The same wonderful speech tells us that when the Lord laid the found-ations of the earth, arranging the disposition of land and sea as we now see it, that 'the morning stars sang together, and all the sons of God shouted for joy.' Job xxxviii. 7.

Connecting this with the hint of the disclosures of the moral government of God which the deep could unfold, we see a reason for that angelic joy. The Adamic time was coming, when the mystery of sin would be finished, and the second Adam would destroy the works of the devil.

One other passage will suffice on this part of the subject. St. Paul says, in Rom. xvi. 25–27, 'Now to Him that is of power to stablish you according to my gospel, and the preaching of Jesus Christ, according to the revelation of the mystery which was kept secret since the world began, but now is made manifest, and by the scriptures of the prophets, according to the commandment of the everlasting God, made known to all nations for the obedience of faith; to God only wise, be glory, through Jesus Christ, for ever. Amen.' The expression 'since the world began' is, in Greek, *pro chronōn aiōniōn*, before the eternal times. What a hint we have here of a series, an indescribably long series, of times or dispensations during which there was moral government, but without a clear revelation of the method of redemption. This throws additional light upon the cause of the angelic joy described in Job.

Such a series, doubtless, developed ever-enlarging views of the Divine moral government. Geological successive catastrophæ are their natural chronicles. At length man appeared, and with his fall the promise of the Son of Man, who was to be creature and Creator united – nothing could go higher.

If Geologists can prove a regular ascending gradation, they will only strengthen the scripture testimony that ours are the last times. 'Even now (says St. John) there are many antichrists, whereby we know that it is the last time.' 1 John ii. 18.

The existence of antichrist proves the existence of Christ. Christ is God and man united. Creature could go no higher, therefore the topmost of the ascending scale is reached – it is the last time. Henceforward the only change is to be the same creature, from glory to glory. There is to be an eternity of ages, but not to new beings; 'that in the ages to come he might shew the exceeding riches of His grace in His kindness TOWARD US by Christ Jesus.' Eph. ii. 7. The glory of God is ever hereafter to be revealed to the universe in successive developments of glory in His church: 'Unto Him be glory in the church by Christ Jesus, *throughout all ages*, world without end. Amen.' Eph. iii. 21.

The Bible, and the Bible alone, enables us rightly to read the book of nature. The more we learn of natural truth, the more we see the truth and glory revealed in the Bible. No uninspired mind ever even conjectured such a glorious view of God as the combined and harmonious testimony of Geology and the Bible. Geology teaches us of death and ruin before

Adam. The Bible tells us of a sinner before Adam. 'The devil was a murderer from the beginning.' John viii. 44.

True philosophy combines both testimonies, and thus, in scientifically contemplating the innumerable geological periods, Revelation enables us to read in them the moral government of God, His awful dealings with moral evil, the exhaustlessness of the divine attributes. The same revelation tells us what natural science never could discover, that ruin is not always to be the earth's history; that from this time and onward it is to have an endless succession of ages or dispensations, each one unfolding more and more of the majesty, the glory, the grace, and the love of her Almighty Creator and most blessed Redeemer. To Him, Father, Son, and Spirit, be the glory for ever.

4.1.3   H. GRATTAN GUINNESS ON THE APPROACHING END OF THE AGE, 1878

. . . A marvellous law of harmonious proportion is clearly observable between the chronology of certain *types* of the course of redemption history and that of the actual *events* typified – the reality being to the chronological type, not as a *year* to a day, but as a *soli-lunar cycle* to a day. And what is still more remarkable is that this cycle – a cycle whose epact is exactly one solar year, *measures the most important period in all human history – the earthly lifetime of our Lord Jesus Christ.** . . .

Our Lord's life . . . was composed of the 30 years prior to his baptism, the three years and a half of his ministry, and 40 days after his resurrection, and as it terminated between the feasts of Passover and Pentecost, it must have commenced about the time of the feast of Tabernacles. Now from the day of ascension in A.D. 29, to the first day of the feast of Tabernacles in the 34th preceding year, the interval . . . was 33 solar years 7 lunar months and 7 days, which is the exact measure of the soli-lunar cycle in question.

If it be objected that while the first and last periods of our Lord's life were clearly 30 years and 40 days, yet that the central period of his ministry cannot be proved to have been just three years and a half, we

---

*In every solar year there is an excess of ten days and twenty-one hours, or nearly eleven days, over the lunar year, *i.e.*, over the year as measured by twelve revolutions of the moon, so that when the sun commences his second round, the moon is between ten and eleven days behind hand. In three solar years, the moon has fallen back rather more than a month, in nineteen years it has retrograded seven months, and in 33 years, 7 months and 7 days, it has fallen back *one solar year*. This period is therefore A SOLI-LUNAR CYCLE of a certain order, and seven such periods, or 235 solar years, is a cycle of the same kind, and at the same time a number of complete solar years.

reply that it cannot be proved to have been more or less than that period, and . . . as there are no counter indications, but the reverse, we may safely assume that the Lord's ministry was three years and a half, so nearly as to justify our regarding his earthly life, including its 40 days post resurrection period as in close, if not exact agreement with the 33 years 7 months and 7 days cycle, and to warrant our naming this soli-lunar cycle, 'THE MESSIANIC CYCLE.'

Now the fact that this central and all important period – the lifetime of our Lord – was comprised in such a cycle, naturally suggests the use of that cycle, as *a unit* for the measurement of larger periods. Before we point out the results of regarding it as *one day* of a great *year* of similar cycles, it is needful briefly to recall two points already discussed.

In our study of the law of completion in weeks . . . we showed that a Divine chronologic system exists in Scripture; that it is a system of weeks; that it pervades the law and the prophets, and is traceable in the Gospel and Epistles; that it is especially conspicuous in the Jewish ritual, and in the symbolic prophecies of Daniel and the Apocalypse; and that it comprises weeks, or septiform periods, on a variety of scales, according to the day, or unit of computation, employed.

We considered the week of days, of months, of years, of decades, of weeks of years, of months of years, of years of years, and of millenaries; and we saw good reason to endorse, on new grounds, the ancient view, that in the course of the six first days of the week on this *last* scale, the mystery of God is destined to be finished, and that the seventh millenary of the world's history is to be its sabbath – the millennial reign of Christ on earth.

In considering the week of months . . . we showed further that seven lunar months comprised all the feasts of the Lord, and constituted the sacred portion of the Jewish year, and that these feasts of the Lord, the observances and the chronology of which are set forth at length, and with great exactness in Leviticus xxiii, form a COMPLETE CALENDAR OF DIVINELY ORDAINED TYPICAL CEREMONIES, PREFIGURING THE GLORIOUS HISTORY OF REDEMPTION. The series of feasts thus prophetic of the future, – for the law had 'a shadow of good things to come,' – is introduced by the great law of the sabbatic, or weekly *rest*, a law involving a main principle of all these religious festivals; redemption terminating in the rest of God, and the rest of man in and with his Divine Redeemer. . . .

The antitypical realities which these feasts prefigure centre in the incarnation. The rejection of 'God manifest in the flesh,' and dwelling among men, led to Christ, our Passover, being sacrificed for us. *At that historical point the type and the antitype met*, for the crucifixion, the great act of redemption, was accomplished on an anniversary of the Exodus Passover, and the resurrection itself fell on the very day of the annual wave sheaf, which had for ages prefigured it; while the descent of the Holy Ghost, which baptized the separate disciples into one Church and Body of Christ, took place on the 'day of Pentecost fully come,' so that the birth of the Christian Church, in its corporate character, synchronized with the observance of the ceremonies which had so long foreshadowed it.

Thus three of the most momentous and sacred events in the whole course of history (events than which none of greater importance have ever taken place), the atoning death of the Son of God, his glorious resurrection, and the descent of the Holy Ghost, coincided chronologically with their *prefigurative* ceremonial observances enjoined in Leviticus xxiii.

Thus far the prophecy of the Jewish ritual is, therefore, fulfilled. The remaining three feasts have yet to receive their antitypical accomplishment, but we know from other scriptures that the restoration, repentance, salvation, and blessing of Israel which they foreshadowed, are to take place at the close of the 'Times of the Gentiles.' This is implied in our Lord's own expression, 'Jerusalem shall be trodden down of the Gentiles, *until* the times of the Gentiles be fulfilled;' and in the statement of St. Paul, 'blindness in part is happened to Israel, until the fulness of the Gentiles be come in' (Rom. xi. 25).

Now, the event which terminates the 'Times of the Gentiles' is the coming of Christ and the establishment of his millennial kingdom on earth. But this event does not terminate redemption history. It is only at the close of his millennial reign, when the Son shall have put down all rule and all authority and power, subdued all things to Himself, and destroyed the last enemy, death; and delivered up the kingdom to God, even the Father, it is only *then*, that his peculiar work as Redeemer and Mediator is accomplished.

Redeeming work, therefore, extends, according to Scripture, from the days of Eden to the end of the millennium. Thenceforward the perfect results of the great work remain, but the work itself is accomplished and over. Satan and death and Hades are cast into the lake of fire. There is no more death, neither sorrow, nor crying. The former things are passed away, and the tabernacle of God is for ever with men.

We have then two leading facts; first that the *type* of redemption embodied in the Jewish ritual extended over seven months of the ordinary year; and secondly, that as far as can be ascertained from Scripture the actual *history* or course of redemption extends over seven millenaries. Now the remarkable result of the application of the soli-lunar cycle of 33 years 7 months and 7 days to these periods is, that it brings the week of millenaries into close and special harmony with the week of months. A thousand years contains as many of these soli-lunar cycles as there are days in a month, and consequently *seven millenaries are seven months of such cycles.* The agreement between the chronological type and the great antitype is not, therefore, merely that between a week of months and a week of millenaries, it is far more close and remarkable. THE TYPE BEARS TO THE ANTITYPE THE PERFECT PROPORTION OF A WEEK OF MONTHS ON ONE SCALE TO A WEEK OF MONTHS ON ANOTHER. Either may be regarded as a week of months contained in a year; the former a year of 360 to 365 *days*, the latter a year of 360 to 365 soli-lunar *cycles.*

In the adjoined plate the millenaries measuring the course of human history are divided into Messianic cycles, and may be compared with the months and days of the Levitical calendar sketched in the centre.

A thousand years equal 29¾ Messianic cycles (analogous with the 29¾d. lunar month); *thirty* Messianic cycles (analogous with the 30d. calendar month of the Prophetic Times) equal exactly 1007 solar years and 7 lunations; and 180 Messianic cycles (half 360) equal 6045 solar years, 5 months.

According to the Hebrew chronology, as shown by Mr. Clinton, we have now about reached the termination of the first six thousand years of human history; and history as well as prophecy abundantly confirm the view this fact suggests, that we are now living in the last or closing days of the third great dispensation, and on the verge of another and a better age. *Half a vast year of Messianic cycles, measured from the creation of man, is now expiring;* and as it expires, there dawns upon the world the light which immediately precedes the sun-rising; there arise around us the solemn yet joyful evidences of the nearness of the glorious kingdom of our God. . . .

. . . The conviction of the nearness of the end derived from chronologic prophecy, and from a study of the Divine system of times and seasons, is abundantly confirmed by a multitude of predictions, wholly destitute of the chronologic element. . . . Space obliges us to select only one or two 'signs of the times' of this nature. The angel mentions to the prophet Daniel two very peculiar and definite characteristics of the last days. 'Many shall run to and fro, and knowledge shall be increased.' Now if any well informed and intelligent person were asked, What have been the leading and distinctive characteristic marks of the last half-century, as distinguished from any previous period in the world's history? he would at once reply, 'steam locomotion, and the universality of education and spread of scientific knowledge.' Where one person travelled formerly, ten thousand travel now; universally, incessantly, and in every corner of the earth, the wheels of locomotion are annihilating distance, and facilitating the running to and fro of millions, making the inhabitants of the most distant quarters of the globe almost like next-door neighbours. And never before in the history of mankind has this or anything like it been the case. Similarly, where one person could read and write in the olden time, ten thousand are fairly educated now; and where one secret of nature was

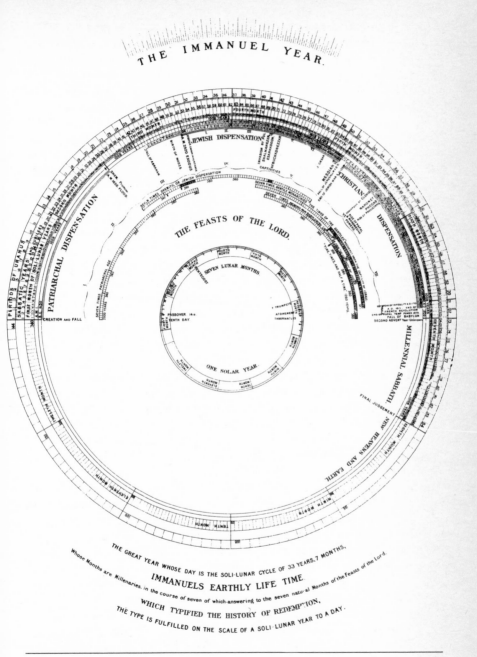

5 The 'approaching end of the age' calculated by Henry Grattan Guinness on the basis of 'soli-lunar chronology' and a historicist reading of the Book of Revelation.

known to the ancients, a thousand are known and turned to practical account by the men of our day. Knowledge is increased as it never was before; indeed, *the school and the locomotive* might be adopted as the devices of the nineteenth century.

Our Lord Himself gave another sign of the closing days of this age. He said, 'This gospel of the kingdom must first be preached among all nations, and *then* shall the end come.'

It may safely be asserted that never since the words were spoken, has the gospel been so widely preached among the nations as it has during the present century. Since the year 1801, when the Church Missionary Society was founded, almost all the Missionary Societies in existence have sprung up, as well as all the Bible Societies. Within the last fifty years, the gospel story has been translated into between two and three hundred additional languages, spoken by six or eight hundred millions of mankind. Colporteurs are distributing it, and preachers expounding it in all lands; and though there are still alas! countless tribes and peoples in the heart of Africa, in the continent of South America, and in the isles of the sea who have never yet heard the gospel message, yet we may say there is no kingdom, no regularly organized civilized 'nation' or community, in which it has not been proclaimed, and in which it has not won some trophies. When it has been preached in *all* nations, then shall the end come.

But perhaps there is no sign of the times more solemnly indicative to the humble student of Scripture, of the approach of the end, than the confident conviction that seems universally to prevail in the professing church, and in the world, that all things continue as they were, *and will so continue*. Not only is there no expectation of impending judgment, there is a bold assumption that no change in the existing order of things is probable, or even possible.

The very idea of a Divine interference in the affairs of this world is scouted as foolish and fanatical; the testimony of history to past interferences of the kind is superciliously explained away, or plainly pronounced to be myth, not real history, and any faith in the testimony of prophecy is regarded as antiquated folly. The reign of eternal law is proclaimed, while a Lawgiver is ignored, the theory of progressive development is advocated, and the evidences of supernatural interruptions in the past, neglected. The state of popular opinion in Christendom at this hour on this point is foretold with marvellous exactness by the Apostle Peter, . . . 'There shall come in the last days scoffers, walking after their own lusts, and saying Where is the promise of his coming? for since the fathers fell asleep, all things continue as they were, since the beginning of the creation.' . . .

This peculiar form of scoffing unbelief foretold as to characterize the

last days, and most conspicuously characterizing these days, has never
before prevailed widely in Christendom. It is an offspring of advanced
scientific knowledge, a result and accompaniment of nineteenth-century
attainments. The ignorance of other ages made men superstitious. Far
from denying the existence of an invisible and immaterial world, far from
questioning the possibility of the supernatural, they were slaves to credulity, and groundless apprehensions, and fell easy victims to the false
miracles and lying wonders of a cunning and covetous priesthood.
Apprehensions of an approaching end of the world, were from time to
time widely prevalent in the dark ages. Bold infidelity, general scepticism
as to all that is supernatural, gross materialism and positive philosophy,
the foolhardy presumption that dares to assert 'all things continue as they
were since the beginning of the creation' and to argue 'and will so continue for ever' – these features are peculiar to the last 150 years, and were
never before so marked as they are *now*.

Were it otherwise, were men willing to heed the testimony of the word
of God, were they observant of the fast thickening signs of the end, were
they generally expecting the final crisis, we might be perfectly certain, *the
end would not be near*. Such is not to be the tone and temper of the last
generation. 'In such an hour *as ye think not* the Son of Man cometh.' Never
was there a day when men were so firmly convinced, that no supernatural
event is to be expected, as they are now. But 'when they shall say, Peace
and safety; then sudden destruction cometh upon them, as travail upon a
woman with child; and they shall not escape.'

That the end of this Christian age, that end so bright with the glow of
coming glory to the true Church, so lurid with the fires of approaching
judgment to apostate Christendom, so big with blessing to Israel, and so
full of hope for the nations of the earth, – is close at hand, seems for those
who accept the testimony of Scripture, beyond all reasonable question.

It is true Israel must first be restored to Palestine; it is true the gospel
must probably first be preached more widely even than it now is; it is true
that 'Babylon' must first fall more completely, as far as we can judge; and it
is true that these things take time. But when we consider the progress that
has been made *in all these directions* during the *last* thirty or forty years – the
elevation in the condition of the land and people of Israel, the removal of
Jewish disabilities, the formation of the Universal Israelite Alliance, the
exploration and survey of Palestine, the decay of the Turkish power; the
increase of missions, the opening up of China, Japan, and interior Africa,
the revival of evangelical truth and effort in the Protestant Church, and
the consequent increase of missionary effort; the separations of Church
and State and the disendowments of national Churches which have taken
place; the spread of infidelity in Christendom, and the increase of open
ungodliness; the overthrow of despotisms and the establishment of

democratic forms of government in their place, – we feel that supposing we are still thirty or forty years distant from the end of the age, all that is predicted may easily come to pass in the interval. Events in our day move rapidly, as if they too were impelled by steam, so that THE APPARENT RATE OF PROGRESS, AND THE APPARENT DISTANCE COINCIDE WELL.

Unless the entire biblical system of sabbatic chronology, have no application at all to the measures of human history as a whole, unless the moral and chronological harmonies which we have traced between the three dispensations be utterly illusive and unreal, unless the divinely instituted typical ritual of Leviticus, have no chronologic agreement with the long course of redemption history, unless there be no meaning in soli-lunar chronology, unless the employment of great astronomic cycles to bound the duration of historic and prophetic periods be a matter of pure accident, unless the singular septiform epacts of these periods be the result of chance, unless in short the whole system which we have traced out in the word and works of God, be utterly groundless and erroneous – then there can be no question that we are living in the very last days of this dispensation . . . .

4.2   BIBLE MORALS: WORK, SEX, FAMILY, GOVERNMENT

Right conduct followed right belief, according to the evangelical ethos, just as surely as moral turpitude arose from theological error. Life was a serious business, the anteroom to eternity; all one's deeds must needs be judged, if not here, then hereafter. The root problem of human conduct, according to the famous Calvinistic Baptist preacher, Charles Haddon Spurgeon (1834–1892), or 'John Ploughman' as he posed in his rustic 'talks' for common people, was 'our evil nature'. Left unchecked, it produced 'idleness' in both the upper and lower classes, which led to physical excess and worse (**4.2.1**). William Guest (1818–1891), a Congregational minister and educator of young women, waxed earnest to young men on the latter theme. By yielding to 'the lower elements of their nature' through sexual indulgence – even privately 'tampering with this perilous fascination' – they destined themselves for social and spiritual ruin (**4.2.2.**). But there was a God-given prophylactic, designed, as Spurgeon put it, to 'nip anything of the sort in the bud'. It was simply the Christian family. Arguing from both nature and revelation, William Garden Blaikie (1820–1899), a Scottish Free Church divine and apologist, glorified the ideal of conjugal love within a web of domestic relationships where father and mother dominate their children in complementary ways to 'get their moral nature rectified' (**4.2.3**). The family was thus not only a 'nursery' for the Church; it also benefited the State, producing upright citizens.

R. W. Dale (3.1.2) the most prominent of public-spirited Dissenting preachers in the latter half of the century, spelt out how such citizens would behave. Tax-paying, office-holding, voting, and military service would all be undertaken as divine obligations, ordained for 'the discipline of human perfection' (**4.2.4**). Here the evangelical emphasis on deliverance from sin through individual conversion assumed a larger dimension, in harmony with the social progressivism of the late Victorian age.

4.2.1   C. H. SPURGEON ON IDLENESS, 1868

A man who wastes his time and his strength in sloth offers himself to be a target for the devil, who is a wonderfully good rifleman, and will riddle the idler with his shots: in other words, idle men tempt the devil to tempt them. He who plays when he should work, has an evil spirit to be his playmate; and he who neither works nor plays is a workshop for Satan. If the devil catch a man idle, he will set him to work, find him tools, and before long pay him wages. Is not this where the drunkenness comes from which fills our towns and villages with misery? Idleness is the key of beggary, and the root of all evil. Fellows have two stomachs for eating and drinking when they have no stomach for work. That little hole just under the nose swallows up in idle hours that money which should put clothes on the children's backs, and bread on the cottage table. We have God's word for it, that 'the drunkard and the glutton shall come to poverty;' and to show the connection between them, it is said in the same verse, 'and drowsiness shall clothe a man with rags.' I know it as well as I know that moss grows on old thatch, that drunken, loose habits grow out of lazy hours. I like leisure when I can get it, but that's quite another thing; that's cheese and the other is chalk: idle folks never know what leisure means; they are always in a hurry and a mess, and by neglecting to work in the proper time, they always have a lot to do. Lolling about hour after hour, with nothing to do, is just making holes in the hedge to let the pigs through, and they will come through, and no mistake, and the rooting they will do nobody knows but those who have to look after the garden. The Lord Jesus tells us himself that when men slept the enemy sowed the tares; and that hits the nail on the head, for it is by the door of sluggishness that evil enters the heart more often, it seems to me, than by any other. Our old minister used to say, 'A sluggard is fine raw material for the devil; he can make anything he likes out of him, from a thief right up to a murderer.' I'm not the only one that condemns the idle, for once when I was going to give our minister a pretty long list of the sins of one of our people that he was asking after, I began with 'he's dreadfully lazy.' 'That's enough,' said the old gentleman; 'all sorts of sins are in that one, that's the sign by which to know a full-fledged sinner.'

My advice to my boys has been, get out of the sluggard's way, or you may catch his disease, and never get rid of it. I am always afraid of their learning the ways of the idle, and am very watchful to nip anything of the sort in the bud; for you know it is best to kill the lion while it is a cub. Sure enough our children have all our evil nature about them, for you can see it growing of itself like weeds in a garden. Who can bring a clean thing out of the unclean? A wild goose never lays a tame egg. Our boys will be off to the green with the ne'er-do-wells unless we make it greener still at home for them, and train them up to hate the company of the slothful. Never let them go to the 'Rose and Crown;' let them learn to earn a crown while they are young, and grow the roses in their father's garden at home. Bring them up bees and they will not be drones.

There is much talk about bad masters and mistresses nowadays, and I dare say that there is a good deal in it, for there's bad of all sorts now as there always was; another time, if I am allowed, I will have a say about that matter; but I am sure there is plenty of room for complaint against some among the working people too, especially upon this matter of slothfulness. You know we are obliged to plough with such cattle as we have found for us; but when I am set to work with some men, I'd as soon drive a team of snails, or go out rabbit hunting with a dead ferret. Why, you might sooner get blood out of a gatepost, or juice out of a cork, than work out of some of them; and yet they are always talking about their rights; I wish they would give an eye to their own wrongs, and not lean on the plough-handles. Lazy lie-a-beds are not working men at all, any more than pigs are bullocks, or thistles apple trees. All are not hunters that wear red coats, and all are not working men who call themselves so. I wonder sometimes that some of our employers keep so many cats who catch no mice. I would as soon drop my halfpence down a well as pay some people for pretending to work, who only fidget you and make your flesh crawl to see them all day creeping over a cabbage leaf. Live and let live, say I, but I don't include sluggards in that license; for they who will not work, neither let them eat.

Here, perhaps, is the proper place to say that some of the higher classes, as they are called, set a shamefully bad example in this respect: our great folks are some of them quite as lazy as they are rich, and often more so; the big dormice sleep as long and as sound as the little ones. Many a parson buys or hires a sermon, so that he may save himself the trouble of thinking. Is not this abominable laziness? They sneer at the Ranters; but there is not a Ranter in the kingdom but what would be ashamed to stand up and read somebody else's sermon as if it were his own. Many of our squires have nothing to do but to part their hair in the middle; and many of the London grandees, ladies and gentleman both alike, as I am told, have no better work than killing time. Now, they say the higher a monkey climbs, the more his tail is seen; and so, the greater these people are, the more their idleness is noticed, and the more they ought to be ashamed of it. I don't say they ought to plough, but I do say that they ought to do something for the state, besides being like the caterpillars on the cabbage, eating up the good things; or like the butterflies, showing themselves off, but making no honey. I cannot be angry with these people somehow, for I pity them when I think of the stupid rules of fashion which they are forced to mind, and the vanity in which they weary out their days. I'd sooner by half bend my back double with hard work than be a jack-a-dandy, with nothing to do but to look in the glass and see in it a fellow who never put a single potato into the nation's pot, but took a good many out. Let me drop on these Surrey hills, worn out like my master's old brown mare, sooner than eat bread and cheese and never earn it; better die an honourable death than live a good-for-nothing life. Better get into my coffin, than be dead and alive, a man whose life is a blank. . . .

4.2.2   W. GUEST ON A YOUNG MAN'S PERILS, 1878

Far be it from me to utter a word that would debar you from the recreations and excitements appropriate to your age. Joy and cheerfulness are your strength and heritage. Monkish austerity and sanctimoniousness are rarely virtues. But our modern life has multiplied, under the name of pleasure, the facilities of vice. The perils that assail young men in great cities are so many, so seductive, and so ruinous to body and soul, as to make an observer tremble. There was once a time, before cities grew so huge, when places of business were homes. The employer admitted young men to the domestic sanctities of his family. They received aid from him in the formation of acquaintances, and had even access to his own circles of recreation. Now, young men in cities can scarcely be said to have a home. Some have not even the privilege of a common room, or a fire in their chamber. They are open, therefore, to every allurement that promises pleasure. Places of business, moreover, are large establishments where the loose moralist can cover vice by self-deceivableness, and where the subtle infidel, the scoffer, and licentious mingle together. Religion is ridiculed, and the clergy spoken of with a sneer. Filthy books are circulated – books of infamy which minister to the vilest tastes, which taint and befoul the imagination with unclean images, and which a man can no more look at without defilement than he can touch molten pitch and be clean.

Wherever a young man turns for worldly amusement he meets danger. Towns swarm with brilliantly lighted saloons, which hold out their meretricious attractions. There is the drama, music, and art. It was ascertained that in two hours one evening six hundred young men entered one music-hall in London. Were these rooms harmless, he would be an enemy to human happiness who objected to them. If they are demoralising and ruinous to the health and character of the inexperienced, he is a friend who points this out. It is little suspected how women with bedizened head-dresses and flaunty robes are folding around them the last shreds of their modesty; how married men hide under white waistcoats polluted hearts; how, while 'grey hairs dance, devils laugh and angels weep;' how bankrupts wear forced smiles; how the victims of disease and death hide their ghastliness by flowers, and light their rapid progress to the grave by flaring gas-light. It is little known how thousands of young men from the religious homes of Scotland and Wales pass into a speedy oblivion after their feet have once crossed the threshold of these rooms in English cities. Alas, what a tale might be told of fathers' hairs whitened, mothers' hearts crushed, sisters' eyes swollen with tears, – over sons once the pride of their homes! . . .

. . . There is a deep and awful mystery in the downward progress of souls, when he who once was the master of sin becomes its slave. Alas, there are scores of men in every neighbourhood who would give all they have to begin life again. A reformed drunkard who moved in good society, once said to me that he would strike off his right hand if the penalty would sweep out of his soul the memories that haunted it. These men never intended to be bad, but step by step they lowered themselves. The lower elements of their nature first were freely indulged, then became importunate, then exacting, then domineering, then uncontroll-able. Dear young man, the pride of a mother, the hope of a father, with an intensity of yearning love I conjure you to pause ere you go into the way of sinners. If your feet have turned aside, retrace, I beseech you, your steps. Your strong 'No' now, may, through God's mercy, turn you from the pit of infamy. But soon weaker will be your will, dimmer your sense of moral beauty, more desperate your passions, till at length you will feel bound, and then find yourself borne over the rapids a lost and helpless wreck.

There are indeed young men who, in an unguarded moment, have gone into scenes of temptation, and have turned away with horror and recoil, like a bird that, having strayed into the poisonous atmosphere of a chemical works, has rushed back quickly to the pure air of heaven. But such cases are the exception. There is a witchery about sin. One night in a music and dancing-saloon may so pollute the imagination as to break down the barriers of years. One throw at a gaming-table, or bet on a race, may so excite the craving for this perilous speculation, that it may be followed by the frenzy and suffering of years of gambling. One indulgence of the lusts of the flesh may so damn a man in his own eyes that in a year he may be utterly foul. Dear young man, nothing deadens the conscience so much as sin; nothing creates a desire for repetition so much as sin; nothing rises in its demands from every concession made to it so much as sin. Among the most striking things in our language is a sentence of Jeremy Taylor on the progress of sin: 'Sin startles a man – that is the first step. Then it becomes pleasing; then it becomes easy; then delightful, then frequent; then habitual, then confirmed; then the man is impenitent, then obstinate; then resolves never to repent, and then is damned.' My young brother, it is in mercy that our heavenly Father sweeps away all the trifling with sin by those strong but loving words – 'Thou shalt *not.*' Our poor self rises; passion raises its tempest of desire; experts in vice solicit; the wrong waits to claim us and hold dominion over us, and our good God who sees the end, says, 'Go not in the way of evil men; avoid it, pass not by it; turn from it, and pass away.' . . .

No, you may not be able to stop when the evil is done. Let me beseech you to take five minutes to consider whither the *beginning* of a wrong companionship leads. The first step may mean an unseen path with an ending of degradation and misery. It *does* mean this in countless cases. I assure you the bitter end I have witnessed in men after an earlier course of wrong-going makes me look on a youth who is stepping on an evil way and choosing an evil companionship with feelings of the keenest anguish. Surely he is only a fool who steps upon a course and will not ask himself what is the probable termination of that course.

But it is not merely the open temptation that is your danger. The impure thought, the harboured imagination, may seem to create a necessity to the indulgence of sin. You have come, it may be, from a pure home. If you allow yourself to hear talk of sin, or allow your spirit to rest on the supposed sweetness of it, you may lower your standard until you readily yield to the miserable way, and you may bind yourself fast in habits of ruin. Let a young man or woman dally with temptation, and they will find plenty of liers-in-wait. It is not, as a rule, the great temptation that ruins; it is imperceptible beginnings. It is these that must be watched and guarded against. The snowflakes are light and fall noiselessly; but let them continue to fall, and soon the highway may be blocked up. It may seem a small thing to go once into a doubtful place, but there may be there an invisible chain with which, by having gone once, you have become irrecoverably bound.

As I am in these addresses to picture life as it is, let facts speak. I feel sure that hundreds of young men would have shunned vice if facts had been told them of its issues. They have few to tell them. It is intensely disagreeable to tell them. But I cannot see young men coming into our great cities without forewarning them of the rocks ahead of them. . . . When I was a minister in Leeds a fine youth came to that town. He was a native of a far-off land. He came to acquire mechanical knowledge prior to becoming the head of a large business house. Wealth and possessions were before him. An attached family circle delighted in him. He was

No. 135. Yield Not to Temptation.

"To him that overcometh will I give to eat of the tree of life."—Rev. ii. 7.

H. R. P.

H. R. PALMER.

1. Yield not to temp-ta-tion, For yielding is sin, Each vic-to-ry will
2. Shun e-vil com-pan-ions, Bad language dis-dain, God's name hold in
3. To him that o'ercom-eth God giv-eth a crown, Through faith we shall

help you Some o-ther to win; Fight man-ful-ly on-ward,
re-verence, Nor take it in vain; Be thoughtful and ear-nest,
con-quer, Though oft-en cast down; He who is our Sa-viour

Dark passions sub-due, Look e-ver to Je-sus, He'll car-ry you through.
Kind-hearted and true, Look e-ver to Je-sus, He'll car-ry you through.
Our strength will re-new, Look e-ver to Je-sus, He'll car-ry you through.

CHORUS.

Ask the Sa-viour to help you, Com-fort, strengthen, and keep you;

He is wil-ling to aid you, He will car-ry you through.

amiable, fascinating, and naturally generous. A group of wild young men determined to allure him to pleasure and sin. He fell into the snare. The billiard-room was visited: it led to the tavern, and then to the brothel. His kind employer remonstrated with him and pointed out the consequences of his courses. It was of no avail. He had consulted the 'secret physician,' or, rather, 'quack.' A severe cold brought to a climax his virulent disorder. His magnificent form was tossed upon a bed of anguish. Loved ones hastened over the sea to seek to save him. It could not be. So loathsome was his chamber that nurses could hardly be secured to attend him, and those most loving him rushed overpowered from his bedside. His pearly teeth all dropped out, and at length, decayed and agonised, he died a dreadful, hopeless death. . . .

But our view of life demands other considerations than those that relate to time and personal dishonour. It is a grand thing to live. A thousand times have I blessed God for this great gift of life. But it is very serious also. Life has its *responsibilities*. Influence, like all things else, is imperishable. Nothing perishes. The leaves of autumn do not perish, they enrich the earth. The fuel of our fires sends curling upwards its light smoke, which bears its properties for other uses. The broken fragments of the mountains through torrent and tempest nourish plants and renovate the earth. So, in like manner, not an act you perform, not a word you speak, can wholly perish. It was probably this that Jesus Christ meant when He spoke of the idle words for which we shall give account at the day of judgment: that is, our words which go from us as light as air may be making others better or worse, and their consequences may look us in the face in the judgment. *Sin is imperishable.* Sin, like the soul, has immortality stamped on it: when once done, *it cannot be undone.* Even a saved man's sins are imperishable in the consequences. . . . There is a thought that often appals me. It is nothing, as it seems, for the seducer to play upon innocence, to instil poison into her sweet affections and her maidenly instincts. He has done, as he thinks, a manly thing, when he has crumpled up the beautiful flower of her chastity, and left it to be fouled in the mire. Ah, hard is the father's shame and the brother's scorn she bears. Cold are the streets that she treads at night, and lonely is the garret where she soon lies down to die. What cares he? Perhaps in a beautiful home he has forgotten her and her child. His turn comes at length to die. If conscience puts in a reminder, he calls the deed an 'indiscretion' of his youth, which signifies little. O man, it *shall* signify. As sure as there is a God in heaven,

---

6 A chorus of advice for young men from Ira Sankey's *Sacred Songs and Solos*, the hymn book most likely to be found in the later Victorian evangelical home.

thou shalt meet again in the great hereafter that deserted one to whom thou didst open the door of ruin. Her own lips shall tell thee how thou didst help to put out in her all that was pure, and to send her into the streets an outcast. It *shall* signify. That child of neglect shall claim thee as its father: an unerring finger shall point it to thee. Before God and holy angels, it shall tell thee of its bare infant feet on snowy street-flags, of night-watchings at omnibus steps, and of the ignorance, and wretchedness, and foul examples, through which its struggling life was passed, and which left it no chance of virtue. From thee it shall demand account of those paternal duties which thou didst incur, and didst never care to discharge. Yes, it shall signify. Oh, there is a solemn irony of Scripture when it saith, 'Rejoice, O young man, in thy youth; and let thine heart cheer thee in the days of thy youth, and walk in the ways of thine heart, and in the sight of thine eyes: *but know thou, that for all these things God will bring thee into judgment. Therefore remove the cause of sorrow from thy heart, and put away evil from thy flesh.*"* . . .

4.2.3   W. G. BLAIKIE ON THE FAMILY, 1888

THE FOUNDATION OF THE FAMILY IN NATURE

It is a striking fact that of all animals, and especially of all domestic animals, man is by far the longest in reaching maturity, or even independence. . . . It is easy to see the end to which this arrangement is subservient. Its natural effects are mainly two. In the first place, opportunity is given for a much longer and closer connection between parents and their offspring. And in the second place, opportunity is given for a much longer and closer connection between the children themselves. Among the inferior animals, the bond of parent and child lasts but a little time, and is soon obliterated; while the bond between brothers and sisters hardly exists at all. The family constitution is reserved for the human race,

---

*There is a sin of which I have hinted. I can do no more. Alas, its terrible temptations, and its awful consequences are becoming frightful. It is not safe to omit notice in an appeal to a young man who may be entering life in a great city. If you could know the little that has come to my knowledge, your very hairs would stand on end. I could tell you of the finest physical constitutions, which, after twelve months' tampering with this perilous fascination, have become pitiable wrecks of disease. I could tell you on medical authority of men now dragging out a useless existence, with reason dethroned, and drivelling in idiotcy. And the punishment once done to the flesh does not depart. Life ends in early death, or is a long suffering of humiliation; yea, worse still, the suffering is perpetuated in the third and fourth generations. Young men starting in life have none to tell them these things, therefore I have forced myself to the hateful task. The displeasure of God against this sin is awful. What would you think of a man who should pluck a flower from a yawning chasm, when there were ninety-nine chances to one that he would fall into the abyss below, and even if extricated, be scarred and begrimed to the end of his days?

and its foundation is laid on an unchangeable basis – the long helplessness of man. It is not an ordinary adaptation that is seen here, but an adaptation in one sphere to a sphere quite different; an adaptation of the physical to the moral, of the material to the spiritual, of the outer world of nature to the inner life of man. . . .

THE IDEAL OF THE FAMILY.

The family is one of nature's combinations, being composed of several constituent parts; and it shows the same properties as are usually found in the other combinations of nature. In such combinations we find two things: first, a natural affinity or attraction of the parts to each other; and second, harmony and repose when the combination is effected, as if some invisible cement had been made use of to bind the whole into one. . . .

. . . In the first place, a natural affinity draws the man and the woman together. There is not only the natural affinity of the sexes, but there is the individual attraction between one man and one woman, the desire to be closely related to each other, which is the true and natural foundation of marriage. It would be a very low view of the marriage relation that would make it flow from instinct alone. Man is surely much more than an animal. . . . The law of affinity that governs all nature's combinations leads us to expect that the foundation of marriage should lie in an affinity or attraction, not of one part of man's nature merely, and not of the lower part of it merely, but of the whole. And when we turn to the Bible we find this view amply confirmed, for it is said, 'Therefore shall a men leave his father and his mother, and shall cleave unto his wife, and they twain shall be one flesh.' There must be some attraction of the higher nature to draw a man from his father and mother, to whom his best affections would naturally induce him to cling. In other words, true marriage has its foundation in the attractive power of love.

And as love is its foundation, so also it is the cement designed to bind the two beings into unity. . . . Love is the moral cement of nature. By its magic power, different temperaments become the complements of each other, opposing tastes find a method of reconciliation, and even contradictory wills, by learning to take and give, to bear and forbear, become like one. Such, we say, is the method by which the combination of elements in a family may come to be marked by that repose and harmony which is found in the ordinary combinations of nature. . . .

. . . Have we not a phrase about 'marriages made in heaven?' What does it mean, but that there is such a degree of natural adaptation and loving affinity between the parties as to show that their union fulfils the design of heaven? In such cases, the conditions of nature's combinations – affinity and harmony – are so apparent, as to leave no doubt that the combination was intended. A very grave old book – the 'First Book of Discipline' of the Reformed Church of Scotland – thus indicates the conditions on which marriage is to be regarded as in accordance with the will of God:— 'the work of God we call when two hearts are so joined, that both require and are content to live together in that holy bond of matrimony.' . . .

There is another important element that enters into the idea of a complete family, and in connection with which, too, provision is made in nature for harmonious combination with the other elements – namely, *children*. It is not difficult to see, either in theory or in practice, that children may very readily become a most discordant element. Every one knows how soon both the will and the passions are developed in them, and how utterly beyond the control, whether of reason, of conscience, or of common sense, these are at first. To bring about the needful and desirable harmony, the parents are furnished with two things, strength and affection. . . . The two must work together, otherwise evil ensues. Strength without affection makes the parents hated; affection without strength gives the children an easy victory over them. Commonly it is to the mother that the larger share of parental love is given, because from hour to hour and from day to day it is she that is most exposed to the children's wayward humours. To the father, again, is given by nature the larger share of strength, because he is responsible for the government of the family, and is usually called to act in those critical moments that determine whether child or parent is to be the true master of the house.

Thus we see how, in the case of families, the great law of nature is exemplified which aims at making all combinations harmonious and efficient. If in the case of any family the combination is discordant, it is because the working out of the plan is abused in the hands of frail human beings. For it is a painful fact in this world's history that nothing so often frustrates the plans of providence as the intervention of man. When divine arrangements fall to be carried into effect by the blind forces of nature, they are carried out with precision and certainty; but when they are dependent on the intervention of man, bungling and defeat are too often the result. Alas, that the lord of creation, the nearest to the Creator in intellectual and moral quality, should so often become a hindrance and even a nuisance, in connection with His plans! Alas that it should so often happen that the more intelligent and independent God's instruments are, the more liable are they to derange and frustrate all!

THE PURPOSE OF THE FAMILY

1. *As regards the fellowship of husband and wife.* It is to be remarked that the reason which is given in the second chapter of Genesis why God made

woman is, that He might furnish the man with a suitable companion; it is not till afterwards that she is named Eve, in token of her motherhood, 'because she was the mother of all living.' Scripture views the relation of the married man and woman, therefore, as having an important end to serve in the divine purpose, even apart from the continuation of the race. They were to be much to one another. The closeness of their union was denoted by the symbol of the rib – they were to become one flesh, and the obligation thus arising for the man to love and cherish his wife was very strong, for 'no man ever yet hated his own flesh, but nourisheth and cherisheth it.' The truth that is brought out in this way in Scripture is obviously in accord with the light of reason too. Man and woman come into this remarkable relation of union in order to promote each other's welfare. . . .

Where the two are one flesh, there must be no contact with other flesh. And here, too, nature provides an abundant reward for those who are faithful to her order. Nothing keeps the fountain of conjugal love so pure and fresh as absolute faithfulness to the marriage bond. The stream of enjoyment flows on calm and pure, and seems to lose nothing with the lapse of years. The heart continues young and fresh in spite of grey hairs and wrinkled faces. On the other hand, the least invasion of license falls like a blight on wedded life, withers natural enjoyment, and ends in aversion if not disgust. . . .

2. *The relation of parents and children.* . . . An essential desideratum for a child is moral training. It may be assumed that if this be neglected, the wilder impulses of his nature will prevail, forces that bring ruin and misery to himself and render him a pest to society. The temper will become ungovernable. Love of play will become too strong for the spirit of industry. Truth will be disregarded, and lies spoken when an object is to be gained thereby. Whatever he desires to have he will seize if he can, no matter what injustice or dishonesty may be committed. All this has to be corrected at the very earliest period of life. The plan of nature commits the chief share of this training to the parents. It is for this end that that twofold force, strength and affection, has been entrusted to them. They must try to get the child's moral nature rectified. Their function is a double one, to teach and to train. They must teach the child what is right and what is wrong, what is wise and what is foolish, and they must urge him to carry their lessons into effect. They must try to fashion his daily habits in accordance with sound principles. They must watch his faults, and constrain him to correct them. They must study his disposition, so as to apply their influence in a suitable way. They must stimulate him to high attainments, trying to get him in love with the divine rules of life, and thus to follow them not with painful reluctance, but with a willing mind. They are to endeavour to send out into the world young men and women

qualified to do their share of the world's work in an efficient manner, and to be helpers, not hindrances, to the order and prosperity of society. In addition to this, a still higher function is committed under Christianity to the father and mother; they are to bring up their children in the nurture and admonition of the Lord, and to try to qualify them alike for the business of this life, and of the life which is to come. . . .

3. We note, . . . next, the relation of *brothers and sisters*. In a well regulated family this is a very important factor. The ideal of the Christian home suggests the thought of Milton's *Comus*, where pure-minded brothers, admiring a dear sister's purity, are concerned lest, alone in the world, she should fall in the way of any of those bloated monsters that would drag even an angel into their filthy sty. Commend us to those homes where brothers and sisters, sharing many a game, and confiding to each other many a secret in their lives, never utter a jest, or word, or allusion, with the slightest taint of indelicacy, and love and honour each other with all the higher affection that none of them has ever been near any of the haunts of pollution. . . .

If, in spite of the holy influence of pure-minded sisters, young men should fall into sensual vice, the pangs of remorse and self-condemnation will be all the sharper, so long as conscience retains aught of its authority, or the heart aught of its appreciation of goodness. In most cases, surely, the influence will be strong in opposition to the power of temptation. Is not a measure of that respect which a brother has for the honour of his sisters due to every woman with whom he comes in contact? Must not every woman be somebody's sister, or at least somebody's daughter? And if the rule to do to others as you would be done by is a righteous rule, how can he be justified in treating any woman in a manner which, if practised towards his sister, would excite his unbounded indignation?

But apart from this painful subject, what a blessed provision we have for the spread of mutual benefit in the contrasted qualities of brothers and sisters attached to each other, and deeply interested in each other's welfare! The sisters interested in the brothers' work and sports, though they do not share them, proud of their successes, always sympathetic in their troubles, and where the Christian spirit reigns, pleading morning and night for their highest good. And the brothers delighting in the affection of their sisters, eager to tell them whatever will interest them, happy in their happiness, and ready to risk all they have when it is necessary for their protection. The glow may pass from their feelings as they get settled in life, with their several duties and interests; but deep in their hearts the root-affection will ever abide, ready to show itself in many a friendly act in times of need, and especially in those dark hours when the heart is bruised with sorrow, and the home darkened by the angel of death. . . .

4. In many families, besides brothers and sisters, there are also *servants*. Where there are such, the moral purpose of the arrangement is not difficult to see. There is a duty to be performed to them, as well as a duty required of them. Respectful consideration and kindly sympathy enter as truly into the duty of employers to their servants as the payment of the stipulated wages. On the other hand, attachment to the family and fidelity to their duty are not less clearly required of the servants. Evidently the purpose of Providence in thus placing servants as members of our wealthier households is to bring together different orders of society, and to establish friendly links between them. If the complaint so often heard be well-founded, that many servants in these days show no manner of interest either in their work or in the family, may the reason not be that many employers in these days show no manner of consideration for their servants or friendly sympathy towards them? And is there not sometimes a darker side in the relation of masters, or of their families, to servants? Can anything be more atrocious, more subversive of God's design, or more fitted to bring down His displeasure, than when advantage is taken of the dependent and defenceless condition of young servants to subvert their principles, and it may be betray them and ruin them? We know that the judgment of God is according to truth against them that do such things. . . .

5. The *friends* and *acquaintances* of a family extend the horizon of interest, affection, and sympathy. They bind society by additional ties. They constitute, too, a public opinion for the family, and especially for the younger members, the influence of which, while in many cases tending to evil, has probably on the whole a greater tendency to good. For the disgrace of evil behaviour is reflected in some degree on this outer circle, as well as on the inner sanctuary of home. On the other hand, good conduct excites the approval of family friends, and success gives them pleasure. Life friendships are often formed; and, in many an instance, life connections closer than friendship, making the bonds still firmer and more enduring. . . .

In conclusion, we may safely affirm that the Christian family, moulded by the rules and actuated by the spirit of the Gospel, has proved the best nursery both for the Church and for the State. The best Christians and the best citizens are those who grow up under its shadow. Instituted in Eden, the family constitution still retains a flavour of paradise, and its joys are still touched with the brightness and purity of those days of innocence. When our Lord came into the world, He sanctified the institution by becoming Himself a woman's son and a member of a human family. The most sublime and inscrutable of all relations, that of the first and second Persons of the God-head to each other, is denoted by words which have their origin in family life. Such an institution surely deserves to be cherished with peculiar care. Its love is the deepest that earth supplies; its joys the purest; and its influence the best, the strongest, and the most abiding.

4.2.4   R. W. DALE ON POLITICAL AND MUNICIPAL DUTY, 1884

. . . As there is no conflict between the Divine Kingdom and the Family, neither is there any conflict between the Divine Kingdom and the State. Christ does not suppress the Family, but purifies and ennobles it. Christ does not suppress the State, but inspires political life with a more generous temper, and directs it to higher ends; He makes loyalty the religious duty of subjects, and under penalty of the Divine displeasure requires rulers to be just.

Unhappily this conception of His work has never yet been firmly grasped by Christendom. In the corrupt ages of the Church, men thought that the Family was not Divine enough for the perfect life; there are many Christian people who are still of the opinion that political activity is inconsistent with saintliness. . . . The Christian theory, as laid down by Christ Himself, and illustrated by the apostles, is, I think, very clear. There are provinces of human life in which the authority of secular governments is sustained by the will of God. Parliaments, town councils, judges, magistrates, have their place in the Divine order. The Christian man is not released from the obligations of citizenship: to him these obligations are strengthened by new sanctions, and for the manner in which he discharges them he will have to give account at the judgment-seat of God.

'Render to Cæsar the things that are Cæsar's.' The precept was suggested by a question about tribute. In its original reference it enforced the duty of paying taxes. Paul describes the levying and collection of taxes as a divinely appointed function of the civil magistrate. This throws quite a new light upon 'Committee of Supply,' upon the Budget, upon the office of Chancellor of the Exchequer, upon Income-tax Commissioners and Custom-house officers, upon the unwelcome documents which we receive from the overseers of the poor and the collectors of rates and taxes. We are to pay 'tribute' because civil rulers are 'ministers of God's service, attending continually upon this very thing.' The tax may be excessive, unfairly levied, unwisely or unjustly spent; if so, the civil rulers are doing their work badly, and will have to account to God for their injustice or their folly. We may try to set them right; in a country with a free constitution, and where private citizens have a large responsibility for the acts of the government, this is a duty. In extreme cases – when, for instance, a tax is levied by an arbitrary exercise of power, and in violation of the recognised rights of the nation, or when a government is so corrupt and tyrannical that the primary objects for which the State exists are not secured – there remains the power, perhaps the duty, of resistance and revolt. But a wise nation will suffer much before it resorts to measures of violence, and good men will be slow to come to the conclusion that the powers which are 'ordained of God' have lost the Divine sanction.

There are some people – honest enough in all their private affairs – who seem to think that a tax or a rate is a claim to be evaded. Paul makes tax-paying a religious duty; 'the demand note' of the collector is backed by the Divine authority, and countersigned by the Divine hand. What happened when Ananias and Sapphira made a false return to the apostles, who were 'ministers of God' representing the Church, we know. It ought to warn us against making false returns to the Income-tax Commissioners, who, according to Paul, and according to the whole Christian conception of secular society, are 'ministers of God' representing the State. The tax may be vexatious, it may be unequal, but while it lasts we ought to return every farthing of our income 'for conscience' sake.'

The same obligation holds in relation to all other public payments. The Custom-house officer is one of the 'ministers of God,' and to evade lawful 'duties' is to evade a Divine claim.

On the other hand, Christian men in Parliament, overseers, members of town councils and of local boards should remember whose servants they are, and should levy taxes and rates justly, and expend them wisely and fairly as the representatives of the authority of God.

But we have not discharged the duty of rendering to Cæsar the things which are Cæsar's when we have paid rates and taxes. In many countries the State requires all men of adult age to serve for a definite number of years in the army; in addition to contributing money to pay for the defence of the country they have to defend it themselves. We have no military conscription in England, but our constitution requires that very large numbers of men should give a considerable portion of their time to certain national and municipal duties; if they refuse to do it the whole system of government breaks down. As long as justice is administered by an unpaid magistracy men must consent to spend dismal hours on the bench. As long as our local affairs are under the control of local authorities elected by the ratepayers men must consent to serve on town councils, to be members of watch committees, markets and fairs committees, finance committees, gas committees, water committees, and the rest; and they must consent to accept the mayoralty. Other men must be willing to serve on school boards, and others to act as overseers and guardians of the poor. Men who discharge these duties pay a voluntary tax levied on personal service. It is a tax which must be paid by some one, and every man has to determine his own share.

As long as we are governed by two Chambers, a member of the House of Lords has no more right to neglect his legislative duties than a police-man to go off his beat before his time, or a bricklayer who is paid for ten hours' work, to work five hours and sleep or smoke the other five. . . . In the House of Commons a man sits by his own consent, and the obligation to discharge the trust he has received from his constituents is too plain to be ignored. . . .

Civil authority – this is the main point I want to assert – is a Divine institution. The man who holds municipal or political office is a 'minister of God.' One man may, therefore, have just as real a Divine vocation to become a town councillor or a Member of Parliament as another to become a missionary to the heathen. In either case it is at a man's peril that he is 'disobedient to the heavenly vision.' The Divine right of kings was a base corruption of a most noble truth; so was the fanatical dream about 'the reign of the saints.' We shall never approach the Christian ideal of civil society, until all who hold municipal, judicial, and political offices, recognise the social and political order of the nation as a Divine institu-tion, and discharge their official duties as ministers of God.

But in this country the responsibilities of government are shared by the people. The great outlines of national legislation and policy are laid down, not in Parliament, not in the Cabinet, but at the polling-booths. It is the electors who make war or maintain peace, who repeal old laws and pass new ones, who interfere, justly or unjustly, between landlords and tenants, masters and servants, parents and children. Those who abstain from voting, determine the national policy as truly as those who vote. . . . It is surely a part of God's service to determine who shall be God's 'ministers,' and for the manner in which we discharge this service we are responsible to God. Not to vote is to act the part of the unfaithful servant who hid his talent in the earth and made no use of it. To vote corruptly is felony; it is to appropriate to our own purposes what we have received as trustees for the town or the nation.

Those who are in the habit of speaking of political life as though it were unfriendly to all the pursuits and interests of the kingdom of Christ, and who therefore decline to discharge their political duties, are strangely inconsistent. If a municipality proposes to open libraries or museums on a Sunday, many excellent Christian people become greatly excited and strain all their influence to prevent what they regard as a desecration of the weekly day of rest; but they do not seem to believe that members of a town council have to get the will of God done on Monday and Tuesday as well as on Sunday, and that Christian ratepayers ought to elect the men who will do it. If a parliamentary oath is to be abolished, these devout persons sign petitions and make speeches against the abolition: for a professed atheist to get into Parliament seems to them a terrible scandal in a Christian country; but many of these same persons regard the actual business of Parliament as so remote from the province of religious duty as to make it a very 'worldly' thing for a Christian man to interest himself in politics; if this is a true account of political life, then all the members of the House of Commons ought to be atheists. I pronounce no judgment in this place on either of these measures. It may be the duty of Christian men to insist that municipalities shall refuse to open libraries, museums, art galleries, on Sunday; it may be their duty to insist that Parliament shall refuse to permit a man known to be an atheist to take the oath. But it is rather odd and not quite intelligible that those who regard politics as the special province of the prince of this world, and who ordinarily shun all contact with political life for fear of losing their spirituality of mind, should now and then become zealous politicians in order to protect the interests of the Christian faith, and to maintain the honour of God. If political forces are so incurably evil, one would suppose that the defence of the kingdom of heaven would be the last purpose for which Christian men would be willing to use them. They pray for kings and magistrates; but if politics are so fatal to Christian fidelity, kings and magistrates are past praying for. They enjoy – apparently without any qualms of con-science – all the advantages of municipal and national institutions; but if municipal and political activity is ruinous to the souls of all who engage in it, Christian men ought to decline the personal advantages which are bought at so fearful a price.

Paul has taught us a nobler and profounder theory of politics. 'The powers that be are ordained of God,' for the maintenance of public order, for the protection of life, of property, and of personal freedom. Civil rulers are 'ministers of God,' and their service is necessary to secure the great ends of civil society, the diffusion of material comfort, the accumu-lation of material wealth, the cultivation of the intellectual life of the race, the transmission from generation to generation of the discoveries of science and the triumphs of art. Apart from civil society some of the noblest and most generous virtues could never be developed. Through the Municipality and the State, as well as through the Family and the Church, the infinite righteousness and goodness and mercy of God have provided for the discipline of human perfection. The true duty of the Christian man is, not to forsake municipal and political life because it is corrupt, but to carry into municipal and political activity the law and the spirit of Christ; to resolve to do his part to secure for his fellow-townsmen and his fellow-countrymen all those blessings which a municipality and a nation, justly, wisely, and efficiently governed, can secure for them; that so 'the powers' which are 'ordained of God' may fulfil the purpose for which He ordained them, and the Divine will be done by civil rulers on earth as it is done by angels and the spirits of the just in heaven.

4.3   A BIBLE PREACHER ANALYSED: JOHN CUMMING

Evangelical teaching on science, history, and morals achieved un-
exampled notoriety in Victorian London through the ministry of a flam-
boyant Scot, the Revd John Cumming (1807–1881). Sunday after Sunday,
from 1832 to 1879, he held forth to congregations numbering up to 1,000
in the National Scottish Church at Crown Court, Covent Garden. Biblical
prophecy was his staple fare – the 'last vial' of the Apocalypse, he predicted, would be poured out from 1848 to 1867 – but this was liberally
garnished with hostility to any deviation from his narrow ecclesiological
and doctrinal line. He opposed the Free Church seceders from the
Church of Scotland. He preached against geologists, Bishop Colenso, and
anyone else who impugned the early history of the Bible. He campaigned
unceasingly against the Church of Rome, and would have taken the fight
into the Vatican Council itself if the Pope, through Archbishop Manning,
had not informed him that his presence was inadmissible. It was in the
wake of this preposterous ploy, and after the Council had adjourned, that
Charles Maurice Davies (1828–1910), a liberal Anglican clergyman and
journalist, reported in the *Daily Telegraph* a Sunday morning's proceedings at Crown Court (**4.3.1**). Davies, a seasoned and relatively detached
observer of religious London, did not conceal his amazement at what he
witnessed, and by all accounts the experience might have been repeated
on almost any Sunday within the previous forty years. Cumming, like
many evangelical preachers, was a master at self-publicity. He issued and
reissued his sermons, lectures, and occasional writings under more than
100 titles. These afford evidence of the continuity in his ministry, and it is
striking that when, in 1855, Marian Evans (1819–1878) – the novelist
George Eliot – analysed eight of the works in the *Westminster Review*, she
pointed up many of the beliefs and attitudes to which Davies would later
call attention. Eliot's anonymous review is at once a passionate indictment
and a triumphal romp. Only one who had struggled to free herself from
the mental and moral straitjacket of evangelicalism could write so inci-
sively. Readers were all but invited to conclude that she and her allies
regarded Cumming as their spiritual inferior. The tone of evangelical
seriousness is unmistakable (**4.3.2**).

4.3.1   C. M. DAVIES ON DR CUMMING IN CROWN COURT

At the convergence of two courts which are opposite the entrance of
Covent Garden and Drury Lane Theatres respectively, stands Crown
Court Chapel, the shrine of Dr Cumming, of Millennial notoriety. Thither I wended my way on a Sunday morning, and, being directed by a
placard to the proper entrance for 'strangers,' found a long *queue*, like that

outside a Parisian theatre, gradually in process of absorption into the building. I defiled along with the rest, and, on entering, saw the well-known features, so familiar in the photographers' shops, of Dr Cumming himself, who had already entered the pulpit or desk – the two are one – arrayed in Geneva gown and bands. Proceedings commenced with an interminable hymn, of I am afraid to guess how many verses, fairly sung, without accompaniment, to a rather monotonous air. Prayer followed; and *what* prayer, think we? Dr Cumming paraphrased – *credite posteri!* – the Lord's Prayer! It was a farrago of the Lord's Prayer, the Litany of the Church of England, and the extemporaneous effusion of Dr Cumming himself. An anthem followed; the 'audience' – it was specially so termed by Dr Cumming – sitting, and then followed a Scriptural exposition.

Now, either my visit to this chapel was most providentially timed, or else Millenarianism forms the staple food of Dr Cumming's flock to an extent of which one dreads to think, for his exposition was based on the veritable 24th of Matthew itself, wherein occur the actual words that had prompted me to visit this particular shrine: 'Of that day and hour' – that is, of judgment – *'knoweth no man;* no, not the angels of heaven; but my Father only.' In the course of a long exposition, Dr Cumming did not say one word about this particular verse. The interpretation of the chapter was the obvious one of dividing it at v. 28, and applying the former portion to the destruction of Jerusalem, the concluding part to the Judgment. The most noticeable feature was the constant intrusion of Greek equivalents for English words, as though Dr Cumming's recent attack upon the Pope in Ecclesiastical Latin had given a classical turn to all his thoughts. For instance, we were informed that 'coming' was *parousia*, and 'kingdom,' *basilea*, and 'witness,' *marturion*, and that 'the world,' *oikoumenē*, gave the name to the Pope's Œcumenical Council. (Dr Cumming probably had not heard of the other etymology, which assigns the name to the French *écume* – 'froth,' – or he might have made 'a hit, a palpable hit.') As a summary, he requested any of his 'audience' to open their morning papers and this chapter side by side, and compare the signs of the *telos tēs oikoumenēs*. A 'paraphrase hymn' from 2 Peter iii. followed, the burden of which was,—

> Yet as the night-wrapped thief, who lurks
>   To seize the expected prize,
> So steals the hour when Christ shall come,
>   And thunder rend the skies.

After a collect and Lord's Prayer began the sermon, and – *toujours perdrix!* – its subject was again selected from Matt. xxiv. 14, and was announced by the preacher himself as 'Good news from the Distant Land.' 'If I were to tell you gold had been found in Scotland,' said Dr C., 'what a rush there would be for the Northern train!' (There is, by the way, a popular idea that the rush is generally the other way, and that return tickets are not taken.) 'I have better news than that; news for all – for the poorest inhabitant of Brewer's Court, or of Drury Court, which beats it hollow, I tell you;' though it was quite certain no denizen of Brewer's Court was there to hear, 'of that which is more satisfying than money or fame' – commodities hardly likely to abound in either of the specified localities. 'We all feel life ebbing away, and' – I am sorry to say Dr Cumming quoted Lord Dundreary – 'that man is a lunatic who does not look forward. The expiration of the Lease of Time is only determined in order to enable us to take possession of the Freehold of Eternity.' From this somewhat incongruous metaphor, Dr Cumming passed to the strongest, because most human, point of his sermon, and eloquently declared his belief that this land to which death conducted us was not really a distant land. 'I do not believe,' he said, 'that at the hour of death there is one moment's suspension of conscious existence. Nay, I even believe that in the so-called insensibility or unconsciousness that often precedes bodily dissolution the dying person is still sensible, still conscious. It is only that the electric wires of the nerves have lost the power of carrying messages from the inhabitants within to those outside. It has become a non-conductor.' The sermon then took a Broad Church tone, but qualified by many narrownesses. This preaching of the Gospel to 'all nations' was now literally fulfilled. Hinduism was beginning to assume the form of a 'detected imposture;' the crescent of Mahometanism was waning; 'the spectral shadow of Rome' was becoming thinner. The Council was the greatest blunder ever committed by an Infallible Pontiff. It disclosed to the world the divisions tearing asunder the body of her who had boasted, 'I sit as Queen.' All these things are in 'our' favour. 'We' are on the winning side; though it was not quite clear to what an extent the 'we' was meant to be inclusive. This kingdom of God, Dr Cumming argued, is not meat and drink, which he explained to mean, not a thing of dalmatics, copes, and incense. It is not Episcopacy nor Presbytery, not sect nor shibboleth, but righteousness, joy, and peace. All men, baptized and unbaptized, sprinkled or immersed – all are sons of God. All are 'born again,' if they only have love for God, and charity to forgive one another's sins. The Pacific of Eternity and the Atlantic of Eternity are now united by Christ, and no sands could ever block up that channel. Above all, this kingdom of God is not Calvinism. Christ will save all who let Him save them.

'Every man and woman here present,' exclaimed Dr Cumming, warming with his theme, 'may be a Christian before yonder dial points to one o'clock,' and it was then pointing to 12.20. 'I like,' he said again, 'to meet with an out-and-out infidel. I can say to such a man, "I respect you, for your doubt is manly." But I have no respect for the man who, believing that God has died for him (*sic*), neglects that fact. Neglect is childish. This Gospel – this "good spell," or glad tidings – is now being preached in every land. We now preach *kērussomen*, this good tidings, good spell, in all the world, *en pasē tē oikoumenē*, for a witness, *eis marturion'*. I here give really an unexaggerated specimen of Dr Cumming's linguistic illustrations. This announcement is made, he argued, by means of the publications of the British and Foreign Bible Society, not necessarily for the conversion of all the nations, but for a witness to them – a witness of the efficacy of the blood that was shed for the remission of their sins, though those sins might be 'as scarlet.' The preacher here apologetically introduced an illustration which he did not feel sure to be 'chemically correct,' and about which I am quite unable to check him. A paper-maker told him that he could utilize all rags for the purposes of his trade – could make them all into white paper with the single exception of 'scarlet' rags. Out of these he could only make pink blotting-paper. 'What a striking illustration! The text in question, you see, does not say, "Though your sins be blue, or purple, or green," but "though they be scarlet, they shall be as white as wool." The impossibility of chemistry is the possibility of Christ.' This good news of the Distant Land it is the mission of the Christian preacher to announce as a herald, not to prove 'like the Scotch divines.' 'There was a certain M.P.,' said Dr Cumming, dropping his voice to the very lowest pitch, as though in recognition of the senatorial dignity, 'who sat here for years. When he came he was an Unitarian. He went away a believer.' Preaching – so I understood the preacher – was to fill up the gaps in revelation, and was better than all 'cathedrals and confessing-boxes.' Do not neglect it. Such was the substance of the peroration. Another paraphrase hymn on Rev. i. 5–9 was then sung – 'Behold, on flying clouds He comes;' an extempore prayer was offered, and benediction was pronounced, and so I passed out into St Giles's, where the string of carriages outside Crown Court seemed little symptomatic of Brewer's Court or Drury Court, the inhabitants whereof, to judge by appearances, had given themselves up to traffic in birds. As I passed through Seven Dials I heard a despairing purchaser pathetically lament that ''en birds' that Sunday morning were 'sellin' at cock prices!'

It will be evident, from the foregoing sketch, that Dr Cumming's hearers are accustomed to 'strong meat.' To such a Millennium as he preached, and which he believed would be realized in this world, possibly none of us would object. It would, indeed, be only what we all pine for, as larger even than that 'common Christianity' which so many talk about, so few realize; it would be a recognition of the universal fatherhood of God – a practice of universal charity to man. But in the course of this one sermon, Dr Cumming cut off from such charity the Hindus, the Mahometans, the Roman Catholics, the wearers of copes and dalmatics, the frequenters of confessing-boxes and cathedrals – nay, in less severe terms, 'the Scotch divines' themselves. Surely, then, the Broad Church principles with which he set out as his major premises become lost when made of individual application in the minor, as body after body of religionists is tried and found wanting. Such was the conclusion to which Dr Cumming's arguments led him – namely, to a very select Millennium, coextensive, it might almost seem, with his own congregation; or else I was guilty of a very false process indeed in my visit to Crown Court.

4.3.2   G. ELIOT ON DR CUMMING'S TEACHING, 1855

Given, a man with moderate intellect, a moral standard not higher than the average, some rhetorical affluence and great glibness of speech, what is the career in which, without the aid of birth or money, he may most easily attain power and reputation in English society? Where is that Goshen of mediocrity in which a smattering of science and learning will pass for profound instruction, where platitudes will be accepted as wisdom, bigoted narrowness as holy zeal, unctuous egoism as God-given piety? Let such a man become an evangelical preacher; he will then find it possible to reconcile small ability with great ambition, superficial know-ledge with the prestige of erudition, a middling morale with a high reputation for sanctity. Let him shun practical extremes and be ultra only in what is purely theoretic: let him be stringent on predestination, but latitudinarian on fasting: unflinching in insisting on the Eternity of pun-ishment, but diffident of curtailing the substantial comforts of Time; ardent and imaginative on the pre-millennial advent of Christ, but cold and cautious towards every other infringement of the *status quo*. Let him fish for souls not with the bait of inconvenient singularity, but with the drag-net of comfortable conformity. Let him be hard and literal in his interpretation only when he wants to hurl texts at the heads of unbelievers and adversaries, but when the letter of the Scriptures presses too closely on the genteel Christianity of the nineteenth century, let him use his spiritualizing alembic and disperse it into impalpable ether. Let him preach less of Christ than of Anti-christ; let him be less definite in showing what sin is than in showing who is the Man of Sin, less expansive on the blessedness of faith than on the accursedness of infidelity. Above all, let him set up as an interpreter of prophecy, and rival Moore's Almanack in the prediction of political events, tickling the interest of hearers who are but moderately spiritual by showing how the Holy Spirit has dictated problems and charades for their benefit, and how, if they are ingenious enough to solve these, they may have their Christian graces nourished by learning precisely to whom they may point as the 'horn that had eyes,' 'the lying prophet,' and the 'unclean spirits.' In this way he will draw men to him by the strong cords of their passions, made reason-proof by being baptized with the name of piety. In this way he may gain a metropolitan pulpit; the avenues to his church will be as crowded as the passages to the opera; he has but to print his prophetic sermons and bind them in lilac and gold, and they will adorn the drawing-room table of all evangelical ladies, who will regard as a sort of pious 'light reading' the demonstration that the prophecy of the locusts whose sting is in their tail, is fulfilled in the fact of the Turkish commander's having taken a horse's tail for his standard, and that the French are the very frogs predicted in the Revelations. . . .

It is because we think this criticism of clerical teaching desirable for the public good, that we devote some pages to Dr. Cumming. He is, as every one knows, a preacher of immense popularity, and of the numerous publications in which he perpetuates his pulpit labours, all circulate widely, and some, according to their title-page, have reached the sixteenth thousand. Now our opinion of these publications is the very opposite of that given by a newspaper eulogist: we do *not* 'believe that the repeated issues of Dr. Cumming's thoughts are having a beneficial effect on society,' but the reverse; and hence, little inclined as we are to dwell on his pages, we think it worth while to do so, for the sake of pointing out in them what we believe to be profoundly mistaken and pernicious. Of Dr. Cumming personally we know absolutely nothing: our acquaintance with him is confined to a perusal of his works, our judgment of him is founded solely on the manner in which he has written himself down on his pages. We know neither how he looks nor how he lives. We are ignorant whether, like St. Paul, he has a bodily presence that is weak and contemptible, or whether his person is as florid and as prone to amplification as his style. For aught we know, he may not only have the gift of prophecy, but may bestow the profits of all his works to feed the poor, and be ready to give his own body to be burned with as much alacrity as he infers the everlasting burning of Roman-catholics and Puseyites. Out of the pulpit he may be a model of justice, truthfulness, and the love that thinketh no evil; but we are obliged to judge of his charity by the spirit we find in his sermons, and shall only be glad to learn that his practice is, in many respects, an amiable *non sequitur* from his teaching.

Dr. Cumming's mind is evidently not of the pietistic order. There is not the slightest leaning towards mysticism in his Christianity – no indication of religious raptures, of delight in God, of spiritual communion with the Father. He is most at home in the forensic view of Justification, and dwells on salvation as a scheme rather than as an experience. He insists on good works as the sign of justifying faith, as labours to be achieved to the glory of God, but he rarely represents them as the spontaneous, necessary outflow of a soul filled with Divine love. He is at home in the external, the polemical, the historical, the circumstantial, and is only episodically devout and practical. The great majority of his published sermons are occupied with argument or philippic against Romanists and unbelievers, with 'vindications' of the Bible, with the political interpretation of prophecy, or the criticism of public events; and the devout aspiration, or the spiritual and practical exhortation, is tacked to them as a sort of fringe in a hurried sentence or two at the end. He revels in the demonstration that the Pope is the Man of Sin; he is copious on the downfall of the Ottoman empire; he appears to glow with satisfaction in turning a story which tends to show how he abashed an 'infidel;' it is a favourite exercise with him to form conjectures of the process by which the earth is to be burned up, and to picture Dr. Chalmers and Mr. Wilberforce being caught up to meet Christ in the air, while Romanists, Puseyites, and infidels are given over to gnashing of teeth. But of really spiritual joys and sorrows, of the life and death of Christ as a manifestation of love that constrains the soul, of sympathy with that yearning over the lost and erring which made Jesus weep over Jerusalem, and prompted the sublime prayer, 'Father, forgive them,' of the gentler fruits of the Spirit, and the peace of God which passeth understanding – of all this, we find little trace in Dr. Cumming's discourses.

His style is in perfect correspondence with this habit of mind. Though diffuse, as that of all preachers must be, it has rapidity of movement, perfect clearness, and some aptness of illustration. He has much of that literary talent which makes a good journalist – the power of beating out an idea over a large space, and of introducing far-fetched à propos. His writings have, indeed, no high merit: they have no originality or force of thought, no striking felicity of presentation, no depth of emotion. Throughout nine volumes we have alighted on no passage which impressed us as worth extracting, and placing among the 'beauties' of evangelical writers, such as Robert Hall, Foster the Essayist, or Isaac Taylor. Everywhere there is commonplace cleverness, nowhere a spark of rare thought, of lofty sentiment, or pathetic tenderness. We feel ourselves in company with a voluble retail talker, whose language is exuberant but not exact, and to whom we should never think of referring for precise information, or for well-digested thought and experience. . . . Indeed, his productions are essentially ephemeral; he is essentially a journalist, who writes sermons instead of leading articles, who, instead of venting diatribes against her Majesty's Ministers, directs his power of invective against Cardinal Wiseman and the Puseyites, – instead of declaiming on public spirit, perorates on the 'glory of God.' We fancy he is called, in the more refined evangelical circles, an 'intellectual preacher;' by the plainer sort of Christians, a 'flowery preacher;' and we are inclined to think that the more spiritually-minded class of believers, who look with greater anxiety for the kingdom of God within them than for the visible advent of Christ in 1864, will be likely to find Dr. Cumming's declamatory flights and historico-prophetical exercitations as little better than 'clouts o' cauld parritch.'

Such is our general impression from his writings after an attentive perusal. There are some particular characteristics which we shall consider more closely, but in doing so we must be understood as altogether declining any doctrinal discussion. . . . It is simply as spectators that we criticize Dr. Cumming's mode of warfare, and we concern ourselves less with what he holds to be Christian truth than with his manner of enforcing that truth, less with the doctrines he teaches than with the moral spirit and tendencies of his teaching.

One of the most striking characteristics of Dr. Cumming's writings is *unscrupulosity of statement*. His motto apparently is, *Christianitatem, quocunque modo, Christianitatem*; and the only system he includes under the term Christianity is Calvinistic Protestantism. Experience has so long shown that the human brain is a congenial nidus for inconsistent beliefs, that we do not pause to inquire how Dr. Cumming, who attributes the conversion of the unbelieving to the Divine Spirit, can think it necessary to co-operate with that Spirit by argumentative white lies. Nor do we for a moment impugn the genuineness of his zeal for Christianity, or the sincerity of his conviction that the doctrines he preaches are necessary to salvation; on the contrary, we regard the flagrant unveracity that we find on his pages as an indirect result of that conviction – as a result, namely, of the intellectual and moral distortion of view which is inevitably produced by assigning to dogmas, based on a very complex structure of evidence, the place and authority of first truths. . . . Now, Dr. Cumming, as we have said, is no enthusiastic pietist: within a certain circle – within the mill of evangelical orthodoxy, his intellect is perpetually at work; but that principle of sophistication which our friends the Methodists derive from the predominance of their pietistic feelings, is involved for him in the doctrine of verbal inspiration; what is for them a state of emotion submerging the intellect, is with him a formula imprisoning the intellect, depriving it of its proper function – the free search for truth – and making it the mere servant-of-all-work to a foregone conclusion. Minds fettered by this doctrine no longer inquire concerning a proposition whether it is attested by sufficient evidence, but whether it accords with Scripture; they do not search for facts, as such, but for facts that will bear out their doctrine. They become accustomed to reject the more direct evidence in favour of the less direct, and where adverse evidence reaches demonstration they must resort to devices and expedients in order to explain away contradiction. It is easy to see that this mental habit blunts not only the perception of truth, but the sense of truthfulness, and that the man whose faith drives him into fallacies, treads close upon the precipice of falsehood. . . .

A grave general accusation must be supported by details. . . . Among Dr. Cumming's numerous books, one of the most notable for unscrupulosity of statement is the 'Manual of Christian Evidences,' written, as he tells us in his Preface, not to give the deepest solutions of the difficulties in question, but to furnish Scripture-Readers, City Missionaries, and Sunday School Teachers, with a 'ready reply' to sceptical arguments. This announcement that *readiness* was the chief quality sought for in the solutions here given, modifies our inference from the other qualities which those solutions present; and it is but fair to presume, that when the Christian disputant is not in a hurry, Dr. Cumming would recommend replies less ready and more veracious. Here is an example of what in another place (Lect. on Daniel, p. 6) he tells his readers is 'change in their pocket . . . a little ready argument which they can employ, and therewith answer a fool according to his folly.' From the nature of this argumentative small coin, we are inclined to think Dr. Cumming understands answering a fool according to his folly to mean, giving him a foolish answer. We quote from the 'Manual of Christian Evidences,' p. 62.

> Some of the gods, which the heathen worshipped were among the greatest monsters that ever walked the earth. Mercury was a thief; and because he was an expert thief, he was enrolled among the gods. Bacchus was a mere sensualist and drunkard; and therefore he was enrolled among the gods. Venus was a dissipated and abandoned courtezan; and therefore she was enrolled among the goddesses. Mars was a savage, that gloried in battle and in blood; and therefore he was deified and enrolled among the gods.

Does Dr. Cumming believe the purport of these sentences? If so, this passage is worth handing down as his theory of the Greek myth – as a specimen of the astounding ignorance which was possible in a metropolitan preacher, A.D. 1854. And if he does not believe them . . . The inference must then be, that he thinks delicate veracity about the ancient Greeks is not a Christian virtue, but only a 'splendid sin' of the unregenerate. . . .

In marshalling the evidences of Christianity, Dr. Cumming directs most of his arguments against opinions that are either totally imaginary, or that belong to the past rather than to the present, while he entirely fails to meet the difficulties actually felt and urged by those who are unable to accept Revelation. There can hardly be a stronger proof of misconception as to the character of free-thinking in the present day, than the recommendation of Leland's 'Short and Easy Method with the Deists' – a method which is unquestionably short and easy for preachers disinclined to reconsider their stereotyped modes of thinking and arguing, but which has quite ceased to realize those epithets in the conversion of Deists. Yet Dr. Cumming not only recommends this book, but takes the trouble himself to write a feebler version of its arguments. For example, on the question of the genuineness and authenticity of the New Testament writings, he says:— 'If, therefore, at a period long subsequent to the death of Christ, a number of men had appeared in the world, drawn up a book which they christened by the name of Holy Scripture, and recorded these things which appear in it as facts when they were only the fancies of their own imagination, surely the *Jews* would have instantly reclaimed that no such events transpired, that no such person as Jesus Christ appeared in their capital, and that *their* crucifixion of Him, and their alleged evil treatment of his apostles, were mere fictions' (Man. of Ev., p. 81). It is scarcely necessary to say that, in such argument as this, Dr. Cumming is beating the air. He is meeting a hypothesis which no one holds, and totally missing the real question. The only type of 'infidel' whose existence Dr. Cumming recognises is that fossil personage who 'calls the Bible a lie and a forgery.' He seems to be ignorant – or he chooses to ignore the fact – that there is a large body of eminently instructed and earnest men who regard the Hebrew and Christian Scriptures as a series of historical documents, to be dealt with according to the rules of historical criticism, and that an equally large number of men, who are not historical critics, find the dogmatic scheme built on the letter of the Scriptures opposed to their profoundest moral convictions. Dr. Cumming's infidel is a man who, because his life is vicious, tries to convince himself that there is no God, and that Christianity is an imposture, but who is all the while secretly conscious that he is opposing the truth, and cannot help 'letting out' admissions 'that the Bible is the Book of God.' . . .

His own faith, apparently, has not been altogether intuitive, . . . for he tells us (Apoc. Sketches, p. 405) that he has himself experienced what it is to have religious doubts. 'I was tainted while at the University by this spirit of scepticism. I thought Christianity might not be true. The very possibility of its being true was the thought I felt I must meet and settle. Conscience could give me no peace till I had settled it. I read, and I have read from that day, for fourteen or fifteen years, till this, and now I am as convinced, upon the clearest evidence, that this book is the book of God as that I now address you.' This experience, however, instead of impressing on him the fact that doubt may be the stamp of a truth-loving mind – that *sunt quibus non credidisse honor est, et fidei futuræ pignus* – seems to have produced precisely the contrary effect. It has not enabled him even to conceive the condition of a mind 'perplext in faith but pure in deeds,' craving light, yearning for a faith that will harmonize and cherish its highest powers and aspirations, but unable to find that faith in dogmatic Christianity. His own doubts apparently were of a different kind.

Nowhere in his pages have we found a humble, candid, sympathetic attempt to meet the difficulties that may be felt by an ingenuous mind. Everywhere he supposes that the doubter is hardened, conceited, consciously shutting his eyes to the light – a fool who is to be answered according to his folly . . . As to the reading which he has prosecuted for fifteen years – *either* it has left him totally ignorant of the relation which his own religious creed bears to the criticism and philosophy of the nineteenth century, *or* he systematically blinks that criticism and that philosophy; and instead of honestly and seriously endeavouring to meet and solve what he knows to be the real difficulties, contents himself with setting up popinjays to shoot at, for the sake of confirming the ignorance and winning the cheap admiration of his evangelical hearers and readers. . . .

The alliance between intellectual and moral perversion is strikingly typified by the way in which he alternates from the unveracious to the absurd, from misrepresentation to contradiction. . . . We find him arguing on one page that the Trinity was too grand a doctrine to have been conceived by man, and was *therefore* Divine; and on another page, that the Incarnation *had* been pre-conceived by man, and is *therefore* to be accepted as Divine. But we are less concerned with the fallacy of his 'ready replies,' than with their falsity; and even of this we can only afford space for a very few specimens. Here is one: 'There is a *thousand times* more proof that the gospel of John was written by him than there is that the *Anabasis* was written by Xenophon, or the Ars Poetica by Horace.' If Dr. Cumming had chosen Plato's Epistles or Anacreon's Poems, instead of the Anabasis or the Ars Poetica, he would have reduced the extent of the falsehood, and would have furnished a ready reply which would have been equally effective with his Sunday-school teachers and their disputants. Hence we conclude this prodigality of misstatement, this exuberance of mendacity, is an effervescene of zeal *in majorem gloriam Dei.* Elsewhere he tells us that 'the idea of the author of the "Vestiges" is, that man is the development of a monkey, that the monkey is the embryo man, so that *if you keep a baboon long enough, it will develope itself into a man.*' How well Dr. Cumming has qualified himself to judge of the ideas in 'that very unphilosophical book,' as he pronounces it, may be inferred from the fact that he implies the author of the 'Vestiges' to have *originated* the nebular hypothesis.

In the volume from which the last extract is taken, even the hardihood of assertion is surpassed by the suicidal character of the argument. It is called 'The Church before the Flood,' and is devoted chiefly to the adjustment of the question between the Bible and Geology. Keeping within the limits we have prescribed to ourselves, we do not enter into the matter of this discussion; we merely pause a little over the volume in order to point out Dr. Cumming's mode of treating the question. He first tells us that 'the Bible has not a single scientific error in it;' that *'its slightest intimations of scientific principles or natural phenomena have in every instance been demonstrated to be exactly and strictly true.'* . . . How does it happen, then, . . . that we find him, some pages further on, engaged in reconciling Genesis with the discoveries of science, by means of imaginative hypotheses and feats of 'interpretation'? Surely, that which has been demonstrated to be exactly and strictly true does not require hypothesis and critical argument, in order to show that it may *possibly* agree with those very discoveries by means of which its exact and strict truth has been demonstrated. And why should Dr. Cumming suppose, as we shall presently find him supposing, that men of science hesitate to accept the Bible, because it appears to contradict their discoveries? By his own statement, that appearance of contradiction does not exist; on the contrary, it has been demonstrated that the Bible precisely agrees with their discoveries. Perhaps, however, in saying of the Bible that its 'slightest intimations of scientific principles or natural phenomena have in every instance been demonstrated to be exactly and strictly true,' Dr. Cumming merely means to imply that theologians have found out a way of explaining the biblical text so that it no longer, in their opinion, appears to be in contradiction with the discoveries of science. One of two things, therefore: either, he uses language without the slightest appreciation of its real meaning; or, the assertions he makes on one page are directly contradicted by the arguments he urges on another.

Dr. Cumming's principles – or, we should rather say, confused notions – of biblical interpretation, as exhibited in this volume, are particularly significant of his mental calibre. He says (Church before the Flood, p. 93): 'Men of science, who are full of scientific investigation and enamoured of scientific discovery, will hesitate before they accept a book which, they think, contradicts the plainest and the most unequivocal disclosures they have made in the bowels of the earth, or among the stars of the sky. To all these we answer, as we have already indicated, there is not the least dissonance between God's written book and the most mature discoveries of geological science. One thing, however, there may be; *there may be a contradiction between the discoveries of geology and our preconceived interpretations of the Bible.* But this is not because the Bible is wrong, but because our interpretation is wrong.' (The italics in all cases are our own.)

Elsewhere he says: 'It seems to me plainly evident that the record of Genesis, when read fairly, and not in the light of our prejudices, – *and mind you, the essence of Popery is to read the Bible in the light of our opinions, instead of viewing our opinions in the light of the Bible, in its plain and obvious sense,* – falls in perfectly with the assertion of geologists.'

On comparing these two passages, we gather that when Dr. Cumming, under stress of geological discovery, assigns to the biblical text a meaning entirely different from that which, on his own showing, was universally ascribed to it for more than three thousand years, he regards himself as 'viewing his opinions in the light of the Bible in its plain and obvious sense'! Now he is reduced to one of two alternatives: either, he must hold that the 'plain and obvious meaning' of the whole Bible differs from age to age, so that the criterion of its meaning lies in the sum of knowledge possessed by each successive age – the Bible being an elastic garment for the growing thought of mankind; or, he must hold that some portions are amenable to this criterion, and others not so. In the former case, he accepts the principle of interpretation adopted by the early German rationalists; in the latter case, he has to show a further criterion by which we can judge what parts of the Bible are elastic and what rigid. If he says that the interpretation of the text is rigid wherever it treats of doctrines necessary to salvation, we answer, that for doctrines to be necessary to salvation they must first be true; and in order to be true, according to his own principle, they must be founded on a correct interpretation of the biblical text. Thus he makes the necessity of doctrines to salvation the criterion of infallible interpretation, and infallible interpretation the criterion of doctrines being necessary to salvation. He is whirled round in a circle, having, by admitting the principle of novelty in interpretation, completely deprived himself of a basis. That he should seize the very moment in which he is most palpably betraying that he has no test of biblical truth beyond his own opinion, as an appropriate occasion for flinging the rather novel reproach against Popery that its essence is to 'read the Bible in the light of our opinions,' would be an almost pathetic self-exposure, if it were not disgusting. Imbecility that is not even meek, ceases to be pitiable and becomes simply odious.

Parenthetic lashes of this kind against Popery are very frequent with Dr. Cumming, and occur even in his more devout passages, where their introduction must surely disturb the spiritual exercises of his hearers. Indeed, Roman-catholics fare worse with him even than infidels. Infidels are the small vermin – the mice to be bagged *en passant*. The main object of his chace – the rats which are to be nailed up as trophies – are the Roman-catholics. Romanism is the master-piece of Satan; but re-assure yourselves! Dr. Cumming has been created. Anti-christ is enthroned in the Vatican; but he is stoutly withstood by the Boanerges of Crown-court. The personality of Satan, as might be expected, is a very prominent tenet in Dr. Cumming's discourses; those who doubt it are, he thinks, 'generally specimens of the victims of Satan as a triumphant seducer;' and it is through the medium of this doctrine that he habitually contemplates Roman-catholics. They are the puppets of which the devil holds the strings. . . . He admits, indeed, that 'there is a fragment of the Church of

Christ in the very bosom of that awful apostasy (Apoc. Sketches, p. 243) and that there are members of the Church of Rome in glory; but this admission is rare and episodical – is a declaration, *pro formâ*, about as influential on the general disposition and habits as an aristocrat's profession of democracy.

This leads us to mention another conspicuous characteristic of Dr. Cumming's teaching – the *absence of genuine charity*. It is true that he makes large profession of tolerance and liberality within a certain circle; he exhorts Christian to unity; he would have Churchmen fraternize with Dissenters, and exhorts these two branches of God's family to defer the settlement of their differences till the millennium. But the love thus taught is the love of the *clan*, which is the correlative of antagonism to the rest of mankind. . . . Precepts of charity uttered with faint breath at the end of a sermon are perfectly futile, when all the force of the lungs has been spent in keeping the hearer's mind fixed on the conception of his fellow-men, not as fellow-sinners and fellow-sufferers, but as agents of hell, as automata through whom Satan plays his game upon earth, – not on objects which call forth their reverence, their love, their hope of good even in the most strayed and perverted, but on a minute identification of human things with such symbols as the scarlet whore, the beast out of the abyss, scorpions whose sting is in their tails, men who have the mark of the beast, and unclean spirits like frogs. You might as well attempt to educate a child's sense of beauty by hanging its nursery with the horrible and grotesque pictures in which the early painters represented the Last Judgment, as expect Christian graces to flourish on that prophetic interpretation which Dr. Cumming offers as the principal nutriment of his flock. Quite apart from the critical basis of that interpretation, quite apart from the degree of truth there may be in Dr. Cumming's prognostications – questions into which we do not choose to enter – his use of prophecy must be *á priori* condemned in the judgment of right-minded persons, by its results as testified in the net moral effect of his sermons. The best minds that accept Christianity as a divinely inspired system, believe that the great end of the Gospel is not merely the saving but the educating of men's souls, the creating within them of holy dispositions, the subduing of egoistical pretensions, and the perpetual enhancing of the desire that the will of God – a will synonymous with goodness and truth – may be done on earth. But what relation to all this has a system of interpretation which keeps the mind of the Christian in the position of a spectator at a gladiatorial show, of which Satan is the wild beast in the shape of the great red dragon, and two-thirds of mankind the victims – the whole provided and got up by God for the edification of the saints? The demonstration that the Second Advent is at hand, if true, can have no really holy, spiritual effect; the highest state of mind inculcated by the Gospel is resignation to the disposal of God's providence – 'Whether we live, we live unto the Lord; whether we die, we die unto the Lord' – not an eagerness to see a temporal manifestation which shall confound the enemies of God and give exaltation to the saints; it is to dwell in Christ by spiritual communion with his nature, not to fix the date when He shall appear in the sky. Dr. Cumming's delight in shadowing forth the downfall of the Man of Sin, in prognosticating the battle of Gog and Magog, and in advertizing the pre-millennial Advent, is simply the transportation of political passions on to a so-called religious platform; it is the anticipation of the triumph of 'our party,' accomplished by our principal men being 'sent for' into the clouds. . . .

The slight degree in which Dr. Cumming's faith is imbued with truly human sympathies, is exhibited in the way he treats the doctrine of Eternal Punishment. *Here* a little of that readiness to strain the letter of the Scriptures which he so often manifests when his object is to prove a point against Romanism, would have been an amiable frailty if it had been applied on the side of mercy. . . . He says 'The Greek words . . . translated "everlasting," signify literally "unto the ages of ages;" . . . that is, ever-lasting, ceaseless existence. Plato uses the word in this sense when he says. "The gods that live for ever." *But I must also admit*, that this word is used several times in a limited extent, – as for instance, "The everlasting hills." Of course, this does not mean that there never will be a time when the hills will cease to stand; the expression here is evidently figurative, but it implies eternity. The hills shall remain as long as the earth lasts, and no hand has power to remove them but that Eternal One which first called them into being; *so the state of the soul* remains the same after death as long as the soul exists, and no one has power to alter it. The same word is often applied to denote the existence of God – "the Eternal God." Can we limit the word when applied to Him? Because occasionally used in a limited sense, we must not infer it is always so. "Everlasting" plainly means in Scripture "without end;" it is only to be explained figuratively when it is evident it cannot be interpreted in any other way.'

We do not discuss whether Dr. Cumming's interpretation accords with the meaning of the New Testament writers: we simply point to the fact that the text becomes elastic for him when he wants freer play for his prejudices, while he makes it an adamantine barrier against the admission that mercy will ultimately triumph, – that God, *i.e.*, Love, will be all in all. He assures us that he does not 'delight to dwell on the misery of the lost:' and we believe him. That misery does not seem to be a question of feeling with him, either one way or the other. He does not merely resign himself to the awful mystery of eternal punishment; he contends for it. Do we object, he asks (Man of Christ. Ev., p. 184), to everlasting happiness? then why object to everlasting misery? – reasoning which is perhaps felt to be cogent by theologians who anticipate the everlasting happiness for themselves, and the everlasting misery for their neighbours. . . .

One more characteristic of Dr. Cumming's writings, and we have done. This is the *perverted moral judgment* that everywhere reigns in them. Not that this perversion is peculiar to Dr. Cumming: it belongs to the dogmatic system which he shares with all evangelical believers. But the abstract tendencies of systems are represented in very different degrees, according to the different characters of those who embrace them: just as the same food tells differently on different constitutions: and there are certain qualities in Dr. Cumming that cause the perversion of which we speak to exhibit itself with peculiar prominence in his teaching. . . . Dr. Cumming invariably assumes that, in fulminating against those who differ from him, he is standing on a moral elevation to which they are compelled reluctantly to look up; that his theory of motives and conduct is in its loftiness and purity a perpetual rebuke to their low and vicious desires and practice. It is time he should be told that the reverse is the fact; that there are men who do not merely cast a superficial glance at his doctrine, and fail to see its beauty or justice, but who, after a close consideration of that doctrine, pronounce it to be subversive of true moral development, and therefore positively noxious. Dr. Cumming is fond of showing up the teaching of Romanism, and accusing it of undermining true morality: it is time he should be told that there is a large body, both of thinkers and practical men, who hold precisely the same opinion of his own teaching – with this difference, that they do not regard it as the inspiration of Satan, but as the natural crop of a human mind where the soil is chiefly made up of egoistic passions and dogmatic beliefs.

Dr. Cumming's theory . . . is that actions are good or evil according as they are prompted or not prompted by an exclusive reference to the 'glory of God.' God, then, in Dr. Cumming's conception, is a being who has no pleasure in the exercise of love and truthfulness and justice, considered as effecting the well-being of his creatures; He has satisfaction in us only in so far as we exhaust our motives and dispositions of all relation to our fellow-beings, and replace sympathy with men by anxiety for the 'glory of God.' . . . A wife is not to devote herself to her husband out of love to him and a sense of the duties implied by a close relation – she is to be a faithful wife for the glory of God; if she feels her natural affections welling up too strongly, she is to repress them; it will not do to act from natural affection – she must think of the glory of God. A man is to guide his affairs with energy and discretion, not from an honest desire to fulfil his responsibilities as a member of society and a father, but – that 'God's praise may be sung.' Dr. Cumming's Christian pays his debts for the glory of God; were it not for the coercion of that supreme motive, it would be evil to pay them. A man is not to be just from a feeling of justice;

he is not to help his fellow-men out of good-will to his fellow-men; he is not to be a tender husband and father out of affection: all these natural muscles and fibres are to be torn away and replaced by a patent steel-spring – anxiety for the 'glory of God' (Occ. Disc. vol. i, pp. 8, 236).

. . . Next to that hatred of the enemies of God which is the principle of persecution, there perhaps has been no perversion more obstructive of true moral development than this substitution of a reference to the glory of God for the direct promptings of the sympathetic feelings. . . . The idea of God is really moral in its influence – it really cherishes all that is best and loveliest in man – only when God is contemplated as sympathizing with the pure elements of human feeling, as possessing infinitely all those attributes which we recognise to be moral in humanity. In this light, the idea of God and the sense of His presence intensify all noble feeling, and encourage all noble effort, on the same principle that human sympathy is found a source of strength: the brave man feels braver when he knows that another stout heart is beating time with his; the devoted woman who is wearing out her years in patient effort to alleviate suffering or save vice from the last stages of degradation, finds aid in the pressure of a friendly hand which tells her that there is one who understands her deeds, and in her place would do the like. The idea of a God who not only sympathizes with all we feel and endure for our fellow-men, but who will pour new life into our too languid love, and give firmness to our vacillating purpose, is an extension and multiplication of the effects produced by human sympathy; and it has been intensified for the better spirits who have been under the influence of orthodox Christianity, by the contemplation of Jesus as 'God manifest in the flesh.' But Dr. Cumming's God is the very opposite of all this: he is a God who instead of sharing and aiding our human sympathies, is directly in collision with them; who instead of strengthening the bond between man and man, by encouraging the sense that they are both alike the objects of His love and care, thrusts himself between them and forbids them to feel for each other except as they have relation to Him. He is a God, who, instead of adding his solar force to swell the tide of those impulses that tend to give humanity a common life in which the good of one is the good of all, commands us to check those impulses, lest they should prevent us from thinking of His glory. It is in vain for Dr. Cumming to say that we are to love man for God's sake: with the conception of God which his teaching presents, the love of man for God's sake involves, as his writings abundantly show, a strong principle of hatred. We can only love one being for the sake of another when there is an habitual delight in associating the idea of those two beings – that is, when the object of our indirect love is a source of joy and honour to the object of our direct love: but, according to Dr. Cumming's theory, the majority of mankind – the majority of his neighbours – are in precisely the opposite relation to

God. His soul has no pleasure in them, they belong more to Satan than to Him, and if they contribute to His glory, it is against their will. Dr. Cumming then can only love *some* men for God's sake; the rest he must in consistency *hate* for God's sake. . . .

Before taking leave of Dr. Cumming, let us express a hope that we have in no case exaggerated the unfavourable character of the inferences to be drawn from his pages. His creed often obliges him to hope the worst of men, and to exert himself in proving that the worst is true; but thus far we are happier than he. We have no theory which requires us to attribute unworthy motives to Dr. Cumming, no opinions, religious or irreligious, which can make it a gratification to us to detect him in delinquencies. On the contrary, the better we are able to think of him as a man, while we are obliged to disapprove him as a theologian, the stronger will be the evidence for our conviction, that the tendency towards good in human nature has a force which no creed can utterly counteract, and which ensures the ultimate triumph of that tendency over all dogmatic perversions.

5

MISSIONS AND
THE MINISTRY

5.1 THE EVANGELICAL APPEAL

VICTORIAN believers had no doubt that salvation was the ultimate aim of Christianity, considered as a system of beliefs and practices. But they differed notoriously as to the beliefs and practices necessary to achieve it. Churchly doctrines and observances were paramount for some, particularly in the established communions. Many others stressed individual conversion through personal faith in Christ. The evangelical appeal for conversion was by far the most common way in which salvation was dispensed to the Victorian world. Its single most influential literary expression was probably *The Anxious Inquirer* by John Angell James (3.1.1), a booklet first published in 1834 and kept constantly in print. In the first chapter James wasted no time in pointing up the dreadful issue at stake: 'Every day brings you nearer to everlasting torments or felicity.' Anxiety about salvation, then, was 'the most reasonable thing in the world' (**5.1.1**). So, too, was a massive effort to rescue the unconverted. Hell-fire put the steam in evangelical missions. At the first general conference of the Evangelical Alliance in 1846, it was proposed to add a ninth article on eternal punishment to the interdenominational 'Basis' of the union after some Americans, represented by the indelicate and pretentious Samuel Cox (1793–1880), who opened the discussion, and Henry Ward Beecher (1813–1887), who closed it, urged that without the article the missionary motive would be blunted and doctrinal inclusiveness might prevail (**5.1.2**). Their hosts acceded to the proposal as a means of achieving inclusiveness among evangelicals.

5.1.1   J. A. JAMES ON ANXIETY ABOUT SALVATION, 1834

Reader, you have lately been awakened, by the mercy of God, to ask, with some degree of anxiety, that momentous question, 'What shall I do to be saved?' No wonder you should be anxious; the wonder is, that you were not concerned about this matter before, that you are not more deeply solicitous now, and that all who possess the word of God do not sympathize with you in this anxiety. Every thing justifies solicitude and condemns indifference. Unconcern about the soul, indifference to salvation, is a most irrational, as well as a most guilty state of mind. The wildest enthusiasm about these matters is less surprising and unreasonable, than absolute carelessness, as will appear from the following considerations.

1. *You are an immortal creature, a being born for eternity, a creature that will never go out of existence.* Millions of ages, as numerous as the sands upon the shore, and the drops of the ocean, and the leaves of all the forests on the globe, will not shorten the duration of your being; eternity, vast eternity, incomprehensible eternity, is before you. Every day brings you nearer to everlasting torments or felicity. You may die any moment; and you are as near to heaven or hell as you are to death. No wonder you are asking, 'What shall I do to be saved?'

2. But the reasonableness of this anxiety appears *if you add to this consideration, that you are sinners.* You have broken God's law; you have rebelled against his authority; you have acted as an enemy to him, and made him your enemy. If you had committed only one single act of transgression, your situation would be alarming. One sin would have subjected you to the sentence of his law, and exposed you to his displeasure; but you have committed sins more in number, and greater in magnitude, than you know, or can conceive of. Your whole life has been one continued sin: you have, so far as God is considered, done nothing but sin. Your transgressions have sent up to heaven a cry for vengeance. You are actually under the curse of the Almighty.

3. *Consider what the loss of the soul includes.* The loss of the soul is the loss of every thing dear to man as an immortal creature: it is the loss of heaven, with all its honours, felicities, and glories; it is the loss of God's favour, which is the life of all rational creatures; it is the loss of every thing that can contribute to our happiness; and it is the loss of hope, the last refuge of the wretched. The loss of the soul includes in it all that is contained in that dreadful word, Hell! – it is the eternal endurance of the wrath of God; it is the lighting down of the curse of the Almighty upon the human spirit; or rather, it is the falling of the human spirit into that curse, as into a lake that burneth with fire and brimstone. How true, as well as solemn, are the words of Christ, 'What shall it profit a man, if he gain the whole world and lose his own soul; or what shall a man give in exchange for his soul?' All the tears that ever have been, or ever will be shed on the face of the earth; all the groans that ever have been, or ever will be uttered; all the anguish that ever has been, or ever will be endured by all the inhabitants of the world, through all the ages of time, do not make up an equal amount of misery to that which is included in the loss of one human soul. Justly therefore do you say, who are exposed to this misery, 'What shall I do to be saved?'

4. This solicitude is reasonable *if you consider that the eternal loss of the soul is not a rare, but a very common occurrence.* It is so tremendous a catastrophe, that if it happened only once in a year, or once in a century, so as to render

it barely possible that it should happen to you, it would be unpardonable carelessness not to feel some solicitude about the matter: how much more, then, when, alas! it is an every day calamity. So far from its being a rare thing for men to go to hell, it is a much rarer thing for them to go to heaven. Our Lord tells us, that the road to destruction is thronged, while the way of life is travelled by few. Hell opens its mouth wide, and swallows up multitudes in perdition. How alarming is the idea, and how probable the fact, that you may be among this number! Some that read these pages will very likely spend their eternity with lost souls; it is therefore your wisdom, as well as your duty, to cherish the anxiety which says, 'What shall I do to be saved?'

5. *Salvation is possible*, for if it were not, it would be useless to be anxious about it. It would be cruel to encourage an anxiety which could never be relieved by the possession of the object which excites it. But your case is not hopeless; you may be saved; you are invited to be saved. Christ has died for your salvation, and God waits to save you; all the opportunities, and advantages, and helps, and encouragements to salvation are round you; the blessing is within your reach; it is brought near to you; and it will be your own fault if you do not possess it. Your solicitude is not therefore directed to an unattainable object.

6. *Salvation has been obtained by multitudes, and why may it not be obtained by you?* Millions in heaven are already saved; myriads more are on the road to salvation. God is still as willing, and Christ is still as able to save you as he was them: why, then, should not you be saved?

7. *And then what a blessing is salvation!* A blessing that includes all the riches of grace, and all the greater riches of glory; deliverance from sin, death, and hell; the possession of pardon, peace, holiness, and heaven; a blessing, in short, immense, infinite, everlasting: which occupied the mind of Deity from eternity, was procured by the Son of God upon the cross, and which will fill eternity with its happiness. Oh, how little, how insignificant, how contemptible, is the highest object of human ambition, to say nothing of the lower matters of men's desires, compared with salvation! Riches, rank, fame, honours, are but as the small dust of the balance, when compared with the 'salvation which is in Christ Jesus with eternal glory.' Who that pretends to the least regard to his own happiness would not say, 'What shall I do to be saved?'

8. *The circumstances in which you are placed for obtaining this blessing, are partly favourable, and partly unfavourable.* The love of God is infinite, the merit of Christ is infinite; the power of the Holy Spirit is infinite: Jehovah is willing and waiting to save you; Christ invites; all things are ready, and the grace of God offered for your conversion. On the other hand, you have a corrupt heart, and are placed in a world where every thing seems to combine to draw off your attention from salvation, and to cause you to

neglect it. Satan is busy to blind your mind; the world, to fill your imagination and heart with other objects, so that even the 'righteous are scarcely saved.' You cannot quit the world, and go into monasteries and convents, but must seek the salvation of your soul amidst the engrossing cares of this busy and troublesome world; where anxiety about the body is so liable to put away anxiety about the soul, and things seen and temporal are likely to withdraw the attention from things that are unseen and eternal. Oh, how difficult it is to pay just enough regard to present things, and yet not too much! How difficult to attend properly to the affairs both of earth and heaven; to be busy for two worlds at once! These circumstances may well excite your solicitude.

Anxiety, then, deep anxiety about salvation, is the most reasonable thing in the world; and we feel almost ready to ask, Can that man have a soul, or know that he has one, who is careless about its eternal happiness? Is he a man or a brute? Is he in the exercise of his reason, or is he a maniac? Ever walking on the edge of the precipice that hangs over the bottomless pit, and not anxious about salvation! Oh, fatal, awful, destructive indifference! Cherish, then, your solicitude. You must be anxious, you ought to be so, you cannot be saved without it; for no man ever was, or ever will be. The salvation of a lost soul is such a stupendous deliverance, such an infinitely momentous concern, that it is impossible, in the very nature of things, it should be bestowed on any one who is not in earnest to obtain it. This is the very end of your existence, the purpose for which God created you. Apart from this, you are an enigma in creation; a mystery in nature. Why has God given you faculties which seem to point to eternity, and desires which go forward to it, if he has not destined you for it? Eternal salvation is the great end of life: get what you will, if you lose this, you have lost the purpose of existence. Could you obtain all the wealth of the globe; could you rise to the possession of universal empire; could you, by the most splendid discoveries in science, or the most useful inventions in art, or the most magnificent achievements in literature, fill the earth with the fame of your exploits, and send down your name with honour to the latest ages of time, still, if you lost the salvation of your soul, you would have lived in vain. Whatever you may gain, life will be a lost adventure, if you do not gain salvation. The condition of the poorest creature that ever yet obtained eternal life through faith in Jesus Christ, although he had but a mere glimmering of intellect, just enough of understanding to apprehend the nature of repentance; although he lived out his days amidst the most squalid poverty and repulsive scenes; although he was unknown even among the poor; and although, when he died, was buried in the pauper's grave, on which no tear was ever shed; is infinitely to be preferred to that of the most successful merchant, the greatest conqueror, the profoundest philosopher, or the sublimest poet, that ever existed, if he lived and died without salvation. The lowest place in heaven is infinitely to be preferred to the highest place on earth. Go on, then, to urge the question, 'What shall I do to be saved?' Let no one turn off your attention from this matter. As long as you covet this, your eye, and heart, and hope, are fixed on the sublimest object in the universe; and when officious, but ignorant friends would persuade you that you are too anxious, point them to the bottomless pit, and ask them if any one can be too anxious to escape its torments? Point them to heaven, and ask them if any one can be too anxious to obtain its glories? Point them to eternity, and ask them if any one can be too anxious to secure immortal life? Point them to the cross of Christ, and ask them if any one can be too anxious to secure the object for which he died?

5.1.2   THE BASIS OF THE EVANGELICAL ALLIANCE, 1846

Rev. EDWARD BICKERSTETH moved:—

> That with a view, however, of furnishing the most satisfactory explanation, and guarding against misconception, in regard to their design, and the means of its attainment, they deemed it expedient explicitly to state as follows:—
>
> That the parties composing the Alliance shall be such persons only as hold and maintain what are usually understood to be Evangelical views, in regard to the matters of doctrine understated, viz.:—
>
> 1. The Divine Inspiration, Authority, and Sufficiency of the Holy Scriptures.
> 2. The Unity of the Godhead, and the Trinity of Persons therein.
> 3. The utter Depravity of human nature in consequence of the Fall.
> 4. The Incarnation of the Son of God, His work of Atonement for sinners of mankind, and His Mediatorial Intercession and Reign.
> 5. The Justification of the sinner by Faith alone.
> 6. The work of the Holy Spirit in the Conversion and Sanctification of the sinner.
> 7. The right and duty of Private Judgement in the interpretation of the Holy Scriptures.
> 8. The Divine institution of the Christian Ministry, and the authority and perpetuity of the ordinances of Baptism and the Lord's Supper.
> 9. The Immortality of the Soul, the Resurrection of the Body, the Judgement of the world by our Lord Jesus Christ, with the

Eternal Blessedness of the righteous, and the Eternal Punishment of the wicked.

My beloved Brethren, it is in weakness, and fear, and much trembling, that I rise to propose to you this important Resolution. . . . I feel, first, the need of it as a means of Union. Without it, our Alliance would be too much like a political crusade against Popery, without any of those Evangelical Principles of light and love, which commend themselves to the Christian mind; and in the form, maintenance, and diffusion of which, we hope to withstand Infidelity and Romanism. There would be no strength in it; for from such an attempted union a large portion of the spiritually minded would at once recoil. I feel, also, that an attempted union, without these principles, would be merely a Confederation, sinking or neglecting the most precious Truths, with nothing to give the devout Christian ground of confidence, or motive for co-operation. What, then, has been the general plan which has guided our minds in compiling this summary of Principles? . . . We thought that it was important to have it general enough to include the great proportion of real Christians; but that it should also be particular enough to exclude those who would impede or weaken us, in regard to our objects and efforts. We can only be thoroughly and completely united and combined, by a large acknowledgment of great Truths in which we agree. . . . With respect to the alterations which have . . . been made by the Aggregate Committee, I was, I confess, at first, not in favour of any alteration, – having some fears, whether we should be able to carry unanimously an additional Article. After having come together, in so large a Conference on the former footing, I felt at first some hesitation in making the addition: but in this I soon found I was short-sighted. I did not look at the largeness of our work – at the wide field which was gradually opening before us. My Scotch Brethren, and my American Brethren, have helped me here. . . . Brethren, from America, shewed to me, and to us all, their peculiar dangers and difficulties from Infidelity in the form of Universalism; and the Calcutta Missionaries also explained the peculiar dangers they had to contend with in India, from the infidelity of the Hindoos; and we had their assurance, that our ninth Article would meet the difficulties of the circumstances in which they were placed. And when our Brethren from Germany had also shown us, how Neologians deny the most awful Truths which we believe, I felt that the Article, No. 9, was most precious and important. It embraces, 'the Immortality of the Soul, the Resurrection of the Body, the Judgement of the World by our Lord Jesus Christ, with the Eternal Blessedness of the righteous, and the Eternal Punishment of the wicked.'. . . . Those who, like myself, were present at the first Meeting in Liverpool, know well, in what doubt, anxiety, and uncertainty we gathered together, as to the possible grounds on which we might unite. They know the deeply interesting discussions which took place then; the earnest prayers which we poured forth; the delightful unanimity with which we came to our summary; and what thanksgivings, with joy of heart, we poured out to our God on that occasion. And I cannot but say, that, at first, we were all startled by the danger which seemed to await the proposal of any addition to the number of those Articles. But the case of our American Brethren has awakened our minds to the great importance of including the ninth Article in the Summary of the Principles of Union. . . . For my part, I dare not withdraw the Truth which has once been so unanimously adopted, lest I should in any way fall under that solemn declaration, 'If any man draw back, my soul shall have no pleasure in him.' Without entering upon the consideration of Amendments which have yet to be proposed, I would only say generally, that it would be extremely difficult to withdraw any of the Articles. Very many have joined, on the ground of these Doctrines being fully agreed in; and I fear we should lose valuable Brethren by the removal of any Article from our summary.

Perhaps I may, for a moment, just advert to one or two of these Articles. Take the 'right and duty of Private Judgement.' I feel that, in these days, when the Papacy has, by a fresh Encyclical Letter, denied the Scriptures to the laity, as injurious to them, – and when Human Traditions are urged, as having an equal claim with the Scriptures to our obedience, – it becomes us to bear witness to the solemn, great, responsible duty of all Christians, to search the Scriptures for themselves, according to the means, and with all the help, which God may have afforded them, and to form for themselves a conscientious judgement of their meaning and application, to guide their principles of faith and their daily conduct. An ever ready objection to this principle is, the multiplied divisions of those who hold it; and the variety of Protestant Denominations, which, in the face of the world, the principle has led Protestants to form. . . . But now, blessed be God! we, the members of different Protestant Churches, holding the same Head, have assembled, from all parts of the World; and, having conferred together with feelings of brotherly love, we have found in the Evangelical Alliance a real unity, far beyond that which can be obtained by the imposition of arbitrary enactments. . . .

I will advert to one more Article, and that part of it which concerns the eternal punishment of the wicked. It is a most awful – a tremendously awful truth; it is one which we cannot bring before our fellow men without the deepest solemnity and awe. We put it in Scripture words; we therefore take the sacred oil, the Word of God, and put it into our own vessels, that we may from thence fill our lamps. Oh dear Brethren, what a motive this gives us to love each other, when we hope that Christ has 'delivered us from the wrath to come'! What a quickening truth it is to make us labour to the utmost to save others! I feel, indeed, that here we have a most heart-stirring and vital, though a most solemnly weighty truth, to the end that, by the terrors of the Law, we may persuade men to embrace the Gospel.

Now let us look at the mighty strength which these principles give us in all our conflicts with our spiritual foes, who are many and mighty. One single Truth – the Unity of the Deity – gave Mahommedanism all its strength, in contending with the fallen and idolatrous Christians of the East. What strength, then, will all these great and glorious Truths give us, in contending with our spiritual enemies! What texts will they afford us at all our Meetings! Oh how I delight in the thought, that these Truths will be expounded, and spread, and commented upon, in Meetings and in Churches, throughout the whole World! and you will have taken the most effectual steps for diffusing the most vital and essential Truths of the Gospel of Christ! What a body of Truth to aid us in our Ministry! I might enlarge upon these topics: but others, I doubt not, will bring the same thoughts before you. We are met in Freemasons' Hall; let us adopt the true principles of freedom – the Truth which makes us free! Let us stand fast in that liberty wherewith Christ has made us free!. . . .

Rev. Dr. S. H. Cox, (of New York.) – I should be more pervaded . . . with a sense of the honour now conferred upon me, if I were not so overwhelmed with a sense of the duty, compared with my meanness in my own sight, and infinitely more in the sight of God. . . . I am persuaded, that we, on this occasion, are to be not only kind, but calm; it is not the heat that enables us to see, but the light only. I would defer with all my soul to my Brethren; and, instead of feeling that temptation which we have often felt, to buckle on the armour, to measure swords with other champions, – I would say, in a higher sense than Burke, 'the age of chivalry is gone;' and let it go, – to Kamtschatka, and then round the orbit of the planet Uranus. A better age has come in; – the age of Christianity, light, and love. We believe, not with frenzy, but with a calm instinctive faith, that our Jesus is King, and that His fifth monarchy is about to spread its rightful jurisdiction over the peopled earth. . . . 'Other foundation can no man lay than that is laid, which is Jesus Christ.' We want the Rock of Ages for our Basis. Your Articles can only in a relative and a most inferior sense be called a Basis. But God, who hath made us able Ministers of the New Testament, will not allow us to be dishonoured by quibbling about words. . . .

. . . I must make a remark upon the Ninth Article, (and I will here too be as brief as I can) because it has been impugned by some honoured and learned Brethren. I assure you all who are here met together, that I believe it is a synopsis, a miniature, of Revelation's glory. If I *could* fall into idolatry, – (for I will not worship anything but what the first and second mandates of the Decalogue authorize) – it would be *here*. I feel such a veneration for it, that I have been kept praising God all night, while I ought to have been sleeping to refresh my nerves for this service; and when I think of its œcumenical display, and its transmission to all the Countries of the Globe, and to all posterity, till the Resurrection trumpet shall awaken the saints to glorify Christ, with their own bodies glorified after the similitude of His own body, – I do feel the ninth proposition to be so complete in all its parts, that I sympathize with my Brethren in their fears, lest the Ark on being touched should be injured. God keep us from injuring it. . . .

. . . I am not to boast of my orthodoxy; but I may say in this Assembly – for there are no ladies in the gallery – that I have often looked on orthodoxy in a Minister of the Gospel as analogous to chastity in a female: it is not to be parted with; and there is no honour in having it; but very much disgrace in not having it. Our whole theology is epitomized in this idea; Christianity, full-orbed, as God gave it, man is required to keep, to love, to perpetuate; and to transmit to coming generations. . . .

. . . By the great grace of God, I think I could act the martyr for that Ninth Article. By the great grace of God, I would rather die than stain its Heavenly glory. Whatever wisdom led those honoured Brethren, who drew up the eight propositions, to bring them to such a close, I cannot tell. It was a strange document, which had no future, with its 'far more exceeding and eternal weight of glory', for a grand appendix. Every one of the eight propositions was true, as far as it went: but it did not go to the grave, – much less rise in triumph beyond it. . . . Christianity here has completely the field of vision; like the Sun that spreads its radiant tide of never ending effluence, inexhaustible; and, of which, a pencil can illumine a hemisphere of this little globe. His sunbeams are brought to the World, unattracted by the World, by their own irradiating effluency, like the grace and truth of God. I see in God's light, and believe with all my soul, the doctrine of the Resurrection of the Dead; without which, I should feel that living was a poor and an absurd business.

But this is solemn as well as glorious. 'When the Son of Man shall come in his glory, and all the holy Angels with Him, then shall He sit upon the throne of His glory. And before Him shall be gathered all nations' – when no other man will ever be born, and no born man ever be born again. 'He shall separate them one from another, as a Shepherd divideth his sheep from the goats.' . . . I ask this question – what is the motive of the great God in telling men of hell? I believe it is nothing but an illustration of this truth – 'God is love.' It is because He does not want men to go there; as Whitefield told his audience once in the outskirts of this city, 'I preach hell, that you may go to heaven;' 'and if there is a heaven,' said a woman, 'I will go there;' 'God help you,' was the answer, 'and so will I.' I believe it is short-sighted misanthropy to hide these truths; I do not mean to say, that we are to recommend men to go to heaven, merely or mainly, by telling them of the pains of hell; but I say *that* motive has its place, *as* every truth has its position, and the whole Revelation of God its finished symmetry. I am before an audience that understand it. I thought, when I rose up, it is out of my power to convince this learned audience; and there is a good reason for it: – they are convinced before I begin. I thought I would not speak to the Amendments – but to the one idea – the five points in the 9th Article – the Immortality of the Soul – the Resurrection of the Body, the Judgement of the World by our Lord Jesus Christ, with the Eternal Blessedness of the righteous, and the Eternal Punishment of the wicked. . . . I conclude by saying, that I hope we shall never be so lost in argument as to forget to steep our thoughts in prayer; and I hope no verbal criticism will rashly disturb the deep foundation of this Basis, until it becomes consolidated before the nations by the immutable strength of God. I believe He will honor it; and those who love it will be with Him, in Christian Union, in the Œcumenical Evangelical Alliance in heaven.

The CHAIRMAN. After the tender appeals of our friend Mr. Bickersteth, and the eloquence you have just heard, – after the manner in which this Resolution has been moved and seconded, I shall not be misapprehended when I say, that I consider it will be both graceful and appropriate, that those who settle this Basis should enter into some detail in supporting the doctrinal view which it contains: but I would venture to suggest to subsequent speakers, that, except upon points which may be raised in discussion, it is not not expedient to dilate upon the grounds on which each Article is supported. . . . I will ask Dr. Byrth, Whether he still intends to move his Amendment?

Rev. Dr. BYRTH rose to move his Amendment. This, in the form in which it was originally given in, was to the effect, that the Basis, in which (as it now stood) one Article had been modified, and another added, – should be restored to its original form. And, after a reference to the difficulties of his position, and fully explaining that his opposition to the Ninth Article did not arise from any doubt whatever in his own mind as to its Scriptural Truth, the Rev. Doctor proceeded to argue for its rejection, on the ground that it was not contained in the original Basis as prepared at Liverpool in October last, and that those Truths only which were absolutely essential to salvation ought to be included in the Basis. . . .

He also took occasion to advert, as an Oxford man, to the reference which had been made to Oxford [by Dr Cox]; and gracefully alluding to the Rev. J. Haldane Stewart, who, like himself, was an Oxford man, he entreated the Meeting not to think all bad that came from Oxford. The errors of Oxford had not affected all her sons. And – though an Oxford man and a clergyman of the Church of England – he peculiarly rejoiced in addressing a Meeting like the present, composed of Laymen as well as

Ministers, who met and consulted together.

Rev. W. Bevan having read the Amendment, – The Chairman said. Before I ask, who will second the Amendment? I should not be worthy of my position as your Chairman, if I did not say one word in reference to an observation that has fallen. *I* am an Oxford man too: and I desire to bear my testimony to the value of the mental discipline, the Classical and Mathematical instruction afforded there. If I am at all able, in this Chair, to distinguish things that differ, and to do my duty as Chairman – I owe it to Oxford.

Rev. J. Haldane Stewart. – Would it not be consistent with the gravity and holiness of our Meeting? would it not be wise, not to use expressions of approbation or disapprobation? – the words of the wise are heard in quietness.

The Chairman. – I must leave that to our friends; it would not become me *to rule* upon it. . . .

Rev. John Howard Hinton rose to second the Amendment. He forcibly and justly maintained that this was a *deliberative Meeting* – fully qualified and authorized to enter into *the whole question* of the Basis, independent of any previous conclusions of the Provisional Committee: and, with reference to the question before them, he argued, that the main design of the Alliance was, to include all godly people; and therefore nothing should be adopted that would exclude a single Believer, however erroneous we might deem his views on some important points. He admitted, however, that it never was the intention to include Roman Catholics, though some of them might be real Christians. He should himself have been strongly in favour of an Experimental Basis; and he maintained, that to testify to Truth was no part of the design of the Alliance, and that the attempt would involve it in difficulties and lead to division.

Rev. T. Binney took much the same view of the design and nature of the Alliance. He had intended to move something to this effect: – 'The idea of an Evangelical Alliance being that of the union of the greatest number of those who hold the Head, however differing in secondary matters, it is of the utmost importance that the Basis of such a confederacy be the simplest possible, consistent with essential Truth, that the Union itself may be the more comprehensive; this Meeting, therefore, anxious to realize this idea, deprecates any addition to the points hitherto held forth as the suggested Doctrinal Basis of the proposed Alliance.' He meant to have moved that, to prevent the addition of the Ninth Article, or any other. . . . The idea of an Alliance to him had always been, that it is something that will bring together those whom Christ has received, however much they might differ from one another. . . . The fewer the Articles included in the Basis, the larger the comprehension would be. He said, . . . I feel pained to say, that there has been a tendency to change the spirit and character of the whole confederacy. I am only giving you *my* impression, and you are very welcome to give me *yours*. Now I framed what I have read, not having any reference to the doctrine of the Ninth Article; and I should like, if I could carry you with me, – I should be satisfied, that this Alliance should consist of those who hold what is generally termed Evangelical Truth; which I think is quite enough.

He further said, that he had hesitated himself about signing the Basis. He had sat many a time in great anxiety of mind before God, hesitating whether he could put his hand to that particular phraseology: and they were going to increase the difficulty with respect to other consciences and tender minds. He thought it of great importance to keep in view what had been suggested by Dr. Byrth: that it did not follow, because persons doubt or deny eternal torments, that therefore they were advocates of universal salvation. With these and some other observations, he supported the Amendment. . . .

Rev. J. BIRT feared that the adoption of the 9th Article would tend to make divisions in families and Churches. He was not aware of any Church, in which the belief of the Eternal Punishment of the wicked was professed: there were other doctrines, the profession and belief of which was required: but he believed there was no Church, which made belief of this doctrine a term of admission to communion. He thought we were making a new criterion of fellowship, a new term of communion, – and he feared the consequences.

Rev. Dr. CUNNINGHAM. – As Mr. Hinton has referred to a statement of mine, I feel I must trouble you for a moment or two. . . . It is quite plain, that the discussion of this question, the omission of the Ninth Article, may lead to a good deal of general discussion as to the character of that Basis: because really the test, by which we ought to be guided in deciding the question, whether another Article shall be added or not, must mainly depend upon the view we take of the object of that Basis. I am persuaded, that a good deal of the difference of opinion that has arisen upon this point, and of the confusion we have got into in discussion, has just been, because we had not in our own minds, or in the formal document which has been brought under our consideration, any very distinct and explicit deliverance as to the real position and real objects of that Basis. This matter has been left somewhat indefinite: I think, upon the whole, rightly and wisely. . . . But I submit, in opposition to Mr. Hinton's view, – that the bearing testimony to Truth, so far as we were united, was one of the objects which, from the commencement of the Alliance, has been contemplated; and which, most assuredly, ought not to be lost sight of. I venture further to say, that an Alliance, such as this, can do something in the way of bearing testimony to great and important Truths; and can do something towards commending them to the hearts and understandings of Christian men, without claiming infallibility, and without pretending to exercise anything like authority over the understandings and consciences of men. . . . The question is, shall one of these great leading points – with respect to which we wish it to be known over all the World that we agree – be, the Resurrection of the Body, a future Judgement, Eternal Rewards, and the Eternal Punishment of the Wicked? I feel the want of a test, whereby to judge of this. That is the reason we have been led to this long discussion. But I have felt, that the Ninth should remain one of those points, with respect to which we wish to bring our testimony to bear on the World; – and, with regard to which, we should hold the views commonly recognised as Evangelical. I think the strong conviction upon this point is, the necessity of another Article. It is true, it is not generally thought much of in this Country. But we are bound to attach due weight to the solemn, deliberate testimony of the American Brethren. If there is to be anything of a statement regarding Truth, – if it is to enter into our consideration, – it is important that it should be given out on that point. Then, with regard to our own Country, as far as the Theological literature of the Country is concerned, we have scarcely anything of the denial of the doctrine of Eternal Rewards and Punishments, except from Unitarians, and men avowedly Infidel. I do not speak of individual instances in a Meeting like this. We must judge from what appears fully and palpably; and I assert, without fear of contradiction, that, as far as concerns the Theological literature of Great Britain, the denial of Eternal Rewards and Punishments has been, with few exceptions, characteristic of a sect whom none of us regard as Evangelical. Therefore the addition of this Article to our Basis, professing the views commonly called Evangelical, is a following out of our general assertion of Evangelical principles, by embodying in our list an Article, in regard to which the views of such as differ from us have been characteristic only of an Un-evangelical or Anti-evangelical sect. . . .

Rev. Dr. Morrison.— . . . I do not, for a single instant, call in question any of those statements made by Mr. Binney, or Mr. Hinton, relative to the personal piety of *some* individuals who may be, as I think, fearfully at variance with Scripture upon the subject of the everlasting destinies of mankind. But this I will say, if you do not adopt a principle similar to that which alters the Articles of your Basis, you will not only include these godly men; but you will open your doors to the admission of every man, and any man, who chooses to hold the doctrine of the Non-eternity of Punishments and Rewards. And I want to know, if you do open your doors so wide as this, how you will conduct yourselves, if thousands in America should come forward, and propose to subscribe every Article of your Creed? How will you act towards them? How will it be possible for you, under your existing Creed, I mean the Provisional Basis, – how will it be competent for you to exclude them from your fellowship? I know that what our friend, Mr. Hinton, has said, looks very well. I wish to say nothing but what will produce kindly feeling, about the Experimental Basis. I do not think, that, clear as my friend's mind is, he would be able to lay down an Experimental Basis which would be satisfactory to himself. Nor do I think that he clearly keeps in view, what is meant by the love of the Brethren. It must be love *in the Truth*, and for the Truth's sake. I fear that the Alliance will commit a *felo de se*, if we do not retain the Article. For if the doctrine of Eternal Punishment, so plainly stated in Scripture, be shut out of the pulpits of Great Britain, farewell to the energy of Evangelical preaching. . . .

Rev. H. GIRDLESTONE suggested an Amendment for the sake of peace: but it was not seconded.

Rev. J. ANGELL JAMES. – I will endeavour to compress what I have to say within as narrow compass as possible. We have arrived at a critical moment in the history of this Alliance, which I am happy to say is already formed; but it depends very much on the decision to which we come on the question before us, whether it shall continue? and, if it continues, whether it shall flourish? . . . Now I will just bring into the discussion, if I may do it without impropriety, some of the transactions which have taken place in the Aggregate Provisional Committee, during its sittings in London. . . . When we came to the discussion of the addition of the Ninth Article, an important and serious question was evidently before us; and those who were present at that Meeting will not easily forget the four anxious hours we spent in considering, whether this Ninth Article should be introduced or rejected? At the commencement of the Meeting many of us, – I myself among them, – were stoutly opposed to the addition of the Ninth Article. We again perceived, that there was no possibility of conciliating the minds of a large section of the Alliance, without that introduction; and we acted on the idea, that it was important, not merely to conciliate friends without, who had not yet come in; but to conciliate and compact the friends within. After four hours' discussion (I believe those who were present will bear me out in the assertion), we came, certainly not to an unanimous decision to introduce that Article: but, if I am correct, in the Aggregate Committee there were not more than four or five hands held up against it. This shows the feeling produced in the Aggregate Committee by the statements of those friends who were anxious for the introduction of the Article: and there appeared to be no likelihood of having a close connexion between our Transatlantic friends and ourselves, if that were rejected. One after another arose, and confessed that the weight of argument adduced was in favour of the Article; and we yielded up our convictions to what they had stated. I think this has some bearing upon the question, in showing what are the views of those who have already had the subject under consideration. Not that I mean to say, that their views are to bind the present Assembly: I still say, I would rather, upon the whole, that the original Basis had not been touched: but since I see, that we hazard, not merely the keeping back of some who have not come in, but the driving out of some who have already joined us, I feel disposed entirely to agree to the introduction of the Article. . . .

The CHAIRMAN. I fall in very much with the sentiments of Mr. James: but it seems to me, that you might come to a conclusion after the next Speaker has spoken.

The Rev. Dr. WARDLAW. – Leaving London, as I soon must, I feel I should have a burden on my conscience, if I did not say a little on this subject. . . . With regard to the Ninth Article, I confess I was one of those who were disposed to be satisfied with the Basis when it originally came forward; and for this reason: I thought it sufficiently distinct; and, therefore, that it would sufficiently answer the purpose designed. But when Dr. Cox from America alluded to the fact, that, in such a Basis, no reference whatever had been made to a Future State, I felt surprise and sorrow; and I could not account for the fact of such an omission, except upon the ground, that we had all considered that point assumed. Yet it did appear a singular thing, that, in the Basis of Christian Truth, there should be no reference whatever to Futurity. I, therefore, am decidedly of opinion, that the Ninth Article should be retained. It is a doctrine I have never been able to view as capable of being disposed of by verbal criticism, – as if it were indefinitely stated. It is one of the most fearful truths of the Bible. It presents the most awful views of the Divine Government we can take. I must own before this assembly, it is a Truth which, of all others, has occasioned the most powerful emotions in my own mind. I have studied the subject, – and alas! with tears and anguish, when I have thought of what is implied in *eternal punishment*. I have trembled, and was almost afraid of thinking upon it. But then it has ever recurred to my mind (and I hope I have not been actuated and influenced, in this emotion, by 'the fear that hath torment') – with regard to my own personal position; I hope in the Son of God: and one consideration which especially binds my soul to Him is this – that He has delivered me from everlasting misery. Again, whenever I have thought on the subject, the question would come back to my mind – Am I to claim for myself greater benevolence than God? And this has led me to the Bible; and there I have found that awful Truth, – written so clearly, and in such a variety of ways, and so universally pervading it, – that I could not resist the conviction without giving up my principles. I have therefore yielded my conviction to God; and rested in the hope, that He will give me strength of principle to acquiesce, with holy joy, in what is to glorify Him for ever; and that the Great Day will be, in this, as in every other respect, the day of the revelation of the righteous judgement of God. I hold this as a most important Article of Truth, fearful as I have felt it. . . .

[It is impossible to describe the solemnity of spirit with which this venerable servant of Christ spoke upon this subject; or the deep impression which it appeared to make upon the whole of the Meeting.]

The Rev. Dr. BEECHER said, that, if this Article had not been introduced and discussed, he could have endured the omission, though with regret, for peace' sake: but, since it had been introduced, it could not now be rejected, without implying, as the public mind would feel, a depreciation of the Doctrine. He admitted that a disbeliever in eternal punishment was within the possibility of God's grace: but the administration of His sovereignty clearly showed, that the instances were few and far between. He pointed out, moreover, the importance of the doctrine in preaching to the unconverted. 'Knowing the terror of the Lord, we persuade men.' What do God's enemies care about sin, – or the commission of sin – when separated from the sanctions of God's government? The disbelief of the doctrine takes away the whole power, by which the Holy Spirit restrains, awakens, convicts, and converts men. He argued, that it should not be the object of this Conference to come together on the lowest possible point of doctrine on which men might be saved: but to include so much of the Evangelical system, that it shall stand up strong in the power of the Holy Ghost: and it could not do so if this doctrine were omitted. In the face of the World it would be sanctioning the doctrine of the non-eternity of punishment. It would give ground for saying that punishment is not eternal. . . .

It had been said by some, that *eternity* was a word so incomprehensible, that nobody could understand it: that children especially could not comprehend it. He, however, undertook to say, there is no word in language which meets the open mind of a child sooner than eternity; it impresses it with a moral power which nothing can obliterate. What is Eternal Punishment? It is suffering that will have no end; that will never, never, never end. God never made a child four years of age, that could not understand what it was;— a duration that should never end: suffering that should never end.

Rev. Dr. BEAUMONT moved that the further discussion of the question be adjourned to the evening sitting.

Rev. JOHN PRESTON seconded the Adjournment.

The CHAIRMAN. – Dr. Byrth being out of the room, I do not see how we can divide on the question.

Rev. Dr. S. H. COX. – We are a deliberative Assembly. I am not going to make a speech: but I am going to intreat our Brethren, that they will give no occasion to any man to retire from the Conference and say, he could not be heard in reply. I am, therefore, for the Adjournment.

The question of Adjournment was then put and carried.

The Rev. Dr. F. A. Cox then engaged in prayer, and the Meeting adjourned till five o'clock in the evening.

5.2 CHURCH AND CHAPEL IN RURAL DISTRICTS

The changing needs of an industrializing society were met unequally by the Victorian churches. Nonconformists generally possessed the organizational flexibility and the ministerial skills required to appeal broadly to an expanding population in town and country alike. The established churches, particularly the Church of England, continued throughout most of the period to represent the staid feudal order that was passing away, a world of closed deferential communities dominated by the Oxbridge-educated priest. The relations between Church and chapel in the countryside were often strained, and some cause for this can be seen in the anonymous *Hints to a Clergyman's Wife*, which achieved a second edition in 1838 (**5.2.1**). Here rank and duty are the predominant themes. The wife, living in subordinate co-operation with her husband, is to become a specialist in the affairs of women. Her object must be to 'make religion a pleasure, not a burden – a privilege, not a task' – providing of course that the religion in question was that of the Church of England. The divisive effects on female parishioners of thus promoting a special relationship with the incumbent may be glimpsed from the narrative by Robert Key, a Primitive Methodist minister, of his evangelizing in the village of Hockering in Norfolk. It was an 'old lady', friendly with the parson, who hindered his early work, while a 'Mrs. Hatley' and her converted husband became the backbone of the local 'society', despite the parson's interference. Key's narrative, together with his account of hostilities in the village of Shipdham, also gives evidence of the coarse irreligiosity of rural life, notwithstanding centuries of Anglican presence, and of the equally crude emotional appeal of Primitive Methodism, which earned it much reproach (**5.2.2**). Religious enthusiasm was not, however, confined to the successors of John Wesley. In 1859 a revival 'broke out' among Calvinists in rural Ulster. William Gibson (1808–1867), a Presbyterian minister and professor of Christian ethics in his denomination's Belfast college, gave a classically credulous but invaluable account of the hothouse atmosphere and wildfire contagion of the revival in his narrative, *The Year of Grace* (**5.2.3**). The 'physical phenomena' he described, now associated with hysterical reactions, bear comparison with events mentioned by Key. Finally, in an address to the Baptist Union in 1879, John Clifford (1836–1923), a prominent liberalizing minister of the denomination, reviewed the continuing plight of Nonconformists – 'Free Churchmen', as they now called themselves – in the face of an entrenched and immensely powerful rural competitor. He called for interdenominational co-operation, but above all for disestablishment (**5.2.4**).

5.2.1 THE DUTIES INCUMBENT UPON A CLERGYMAN'S WIFE, 1832

The sacred obligations which devolve upon the Minister of the Gospel, in the public ministration of the Word, give rise to a variety of lesser duties, in which the co-operation of his wife may be of some importance. The private and retired walks of Christian love and benevolence are more particularly referred to. The distinguishing characteristics of the female are tenderness and compassion. These qualities, when combined with active and persevering diligence, and stimulated by love to her Divine Saviour, will render the services of the Clergyman's wife highly useful to her husband, especially if his charge lie in a country parish. Let it be her first object, on entering so important a situation, to take a calm survey of the station in which Providence has placed her, and to inquire what are those peculiar departments of duty which now more immediately devolve upon her. In some of these she might co-operate with her husband, and labour in conjunction with him. In others she might take a subordinate part. In others she might form independent plans of operation, and exercise her mind in devising those schemes of usefulness for which her sex more peculiarly adapts her.

Under the first class might be included the visitation of the sick, more particularly among the women, at times, and under circumstances, when female attendance is especially needed. The supply of the temporal wants of the sick person naturally devolves upon her; and while administering to their relief, opportunities, from time to time, occur for entering upon the most important of all subjects, and for conferring *spiritual* as well as *temporal* benefit. While seeking to mitigate bodily suffering, let it be her one object and delight to point the sufferers to Him who is the only Refuge – the only Friend and Comforter – the only Hope and Stay in the hour of trial. Their guilt and misery in the ignorance of a Saviour; their constant and entire need of Him; his free and gracious invitations and promises to them; his love in chastening them; the design and the blessed fruits of sanctified affliction; these are the suitable and interesting topics to bring before their minds, with much and earnest prayer for the Divine blessing.

Cottage readings present another opening of usefulness of the same class. The admission to these little assemblies (which, from their simplicity and retirement, form an appropriate work and labour of love for the Minister's wife) should be confined solely to females.

The Sunday school, together with the weekly instruction of the children, where practicable, should likewise be divided between the Clergyman and his partner, the latter superintending the girls, whilst the care of the boys devolves on her husband.

Under the second class might be mentioned the private instruction of the young women of the parish. Their various employments, whether in field labour, manufactories, or at their own homes, together with various local disadvantages, are frequent obstacles to any systematic plan of instruction. As far, however, as may be found practicable, it is of the highest importance to labour in interesting their minds, awakening their consciences, and instructing their hearts. When this primary object is accomplished, confidential intercourse respecting their spiritual difficulties will naturally succeed, and those difficulties will probably be mentioned with far less reserve to the Minister's wife than to the Minister himself. It is obvious that this course of private and familiar communication will materially subserve their more serious and intelligent reception of the truths delivered from the pulpit.

Under the last class would be embraced such *independent* plans of usefulness as her zeal and ingenuity, her love to her God and Saviour, and her desire to promote the spiritual and temporal welfare of her husband's parish might suggest. . . . Let her, for instance, propose rewards and encouragements to cleanliness, diligence, and good order; let her endeavour to find employment for the industrious; let it be her delight to supply comfort to the aged; to give advice and assistance to the young and inquiring; and to open fresh channels of usefulness, from time to time, as circumstances occur. Let it be her constant endeavour to make religion a pleasure, not a burden – a privilege, not a task; and to exhibit the promises of the Gospel in all their freeness, fulness, and suitable application to the wants of sinners. Others may expend their precious hours in the gratification of personal vanity, others may waste

The fleeting moments of too short a life

in the insipid routine of fashionable amusements; – *her* joy will be of a higher nature; *her* delight will be to be found in the poorest cottage, at the bed-side of the sick and dying, and employed in the humblest offices of Christian benevolence and love. With this desire predominant in her heart, the Clergyman's wife will call but a very small portion of her time her own, but, with her husband, will be ever ready to listen to the calls of ignorance and distress. An acquaintance with the individual character and circumstances of his flock is of great importance, in order to avoid that imposition to which female benevolence is so liable, and to adapt her admonitions to their several cases. She will have frequent reason to combine firmness and resolution with her tenderness, and to act upon the deliberate exercise of her judgment rather than yield to the impulse of the present moment.

In order, however, to carry her rules into execution, some arrangement of her time will be necessary. Every moment of the day must have its appropriate employment; every hour must bring with it its own portion of allotted duty. Much watchfulness, consideration, and prayer, will be needed, to preserve her various engagements from interfering with each other, or with her domestic duties; and that she may be ready for all opportunities of devoting herself to the responsibilities of her most interesting charge. To the plans which she has formed, as best calculated to accomplish her purpose, she will, as far as possible, most strictly adhere; stimulated by the influence of Christian motives, and by the advantages which may justly be anticipated from perseverance in a course of regular methodical arrangement. Happy for her, if the exercise of early habits of perseverance, punctuality, application, and industry, and the still more important habits of self-control, self-denial, and self-examination, supply the necessary energy for the present demands upon her. For she who has been early accustomed to keep her intellectual powers in action, and enabled, in some measure, by Divine grace to regulate her inclinations, to set bounds to her desires, to govern her temper, to subdue her natural propensities, to watch against a trifling spirit and a wandering mind, and to consider herself as a responsible creature, will be far better qualified to discharge the obligations of a Clergyman's wife than one who has been unused to restraint and unaccustomed to mental exercise.

Lastly, let the simplicity of her motives mark her every action. Let none be able to say that private or personal feelings influenced any point of her conduct. Let every thing be done as unto the LORD and not unto man.

Need we remark the importance, nay, the indispensable necessity, of *prayer*, in order to preserve an habitual sense of these solemn responsibilities, and to obtain supplies of Divine grace for their conscientious discharge? Nothing must be allowed to break in upon the duties of the closet. The early hour of morning and the retired shades of evening must find her there, humbling herself before her Saviour under a sense of guilt, helplessness, and imperfection, and casting herself upon the covenant of her GOD for renewed and increasing communications of Divine aid to speed her on her way, and to direct and guide her amid the various difficulties which may perpetually arise. 'Ask, and ye shall receive,' must be the motto imprinted on her memory and inscribed on her heart. . . .

5.2.2   R. KEY ON PRIMITIVE METHODISM IN
EASTERN ENGLAND DURING THE 1830s

HOCKERING

Hockering is a village in the county of Norfolk, with a population of about four hundred souls. It is ten miles from the city of Norwich, and five miles from East Dereham. Its inhabitants were in a very low state of mental ignorance – shrouded in darkness, steeped in sin, and covered with pollution. There was not at that time, as far as I could learn, or hear of afterwards, one christian man or woman in the parish. There were two persons who had light – Mrs. Hatley, who had formerly sat under the ministry of the Wesleyans, and W. Copling, who had been a hearer among the Baptists: these were the only two individuals that I could find, or hear of, that had any fear of God before their eyes.

I entered the village late in the summer of the year 1830, and endured one of the most awful conflicts with the enemy of souls that I ever experienced. Prior to the service, I got into a dry ditch covered over with briars and thorns, and for hours wrestled against principalities and powers; the conflict was so horrible, that I was afraid at one time I should lose my reason. I opened my pocket-Bible on Psalm cxxi., and read it; and while reading the last verse, the snare was instantly broken, the powers of darkness were scattered, and hell's legions routed; my soul was, in a moment, filled with light and love.

I at once commenced my work. Seeing a piece of waste land before a respectable house, I knocked at the door, and asked an old lady to allow me the use of it for an hour, on which to preach the people a sermon. The old lady, very abruptly, replied, 'Go away with you; I and the parson are good friends.' I replied that I did not want to break off the friendship existing between her and the parson; I only wanted to stand on the waste piece of land to tell the people about the Saviour. 'Go away with you!' the old lady shouted out, and was about to shut the door in my face. I then told her that I was a servant of Christ, and if she shut the door against me, my Master might shut the door of mercy against her. But the door *was* violently closed, and a little time after I was informed the old lady was a corpse. I make no comment here; I only chronicle the fact.

I went a little further, met a man, and told him I was going to preach. 'Preach, preach!' shouted the fellow, 'if you have got a barrel of beer to give away, I will come.' I took my hymn-book from my pocket, and commenced singing through the street,

Turn to the Lord, and seek salvation, &c.,

with a number of children running after me, which, I must confess, was rather humbling to human pride, (but I was quite willing to be counted a fool for Christ's sake). I then took my stand on a large stone-heap for a pulpit, and the greater part of the inhabitants forming a congregation. A more wild, wicked, rough, uncultivated lot I think it would be difficult to find in the back settlements of America, or the wilds of Africa; but no violence was used, although there was quite enough of noise and clamour.

There lived in the village a man by the name of William Lane, who was not present when the first sermon was preached; but his wife had attended the service, and when she returned home, W. Lane said,

'Well, have you been and heard the parson?'

'Yes,' replied she.

'What did you think of him?'

'I think that he is a very nice man.'

'Ah!' said William Lane, 'but I will keep him out of my bacon-pot.'

This man was a very extraordinary character; he was a terror to the neighbourhood, and a pest to the place. He told me that 'he actually did not know that he had a soul,' although he evidently possessed a mind of the first order.

About a month after the first sermon was preached, he fell into the agonies of a wounded spirit, and while thrashing in the barn, God set his soul at liberty; and as he thrashed, he prayed and shouted aloud the praise of God. He was one of the first that united with us in that place, and a few months afterwards he began to exhort publicly, and became a laborious and successful local preacher. The mind that had been for years buried in the mire of sin, and embedded in the hard rock of unbelief, was so roused to action and exercise by the power of divine grace, that many who heard him were astonished at the intelligent remarks he made – his originality of thought, and the occasional bursts of real soul-moving eloquence, which would roll forth from his lips like streams of fire. It was the opinion of some good judges, that if he had been blessed with a religious training, and properly educated, he would have ranked among the first-class men of his generation. . . .

But, to return to our narrative, a house was soon provided by W. Copling, in which public worship was regularly conducted. . . . A large society was formed, and a great awakening took place. Some were seized with deep conviction in their beds, and others in the fields and barns; others of course mocked, and some became very much afraid: some said that I was a wizard, and carried some charm about with me in my waistcoat pocket, and that I threw it upon the people and bewitched them; and so much did this feeling prevail among a certain class of persons, that I have actually seen some whom I was about to meet, cross over to the other side of the street, to avoid catching the contagion.

One night after preaching, I announced that the class would meet, and invited those who were desirous to get their souls saved, to stay. Mr.

Hatley and Mr. Nelson, were present at the preaching service; they left the house at the close; but after a few minutes, Mr. Hatley said to Mr. Nelson, 'Let us go back and see what they are up to in these class meetings.' He had been a sad reckless character, and he intended to play off a trick upon the preacher. He told his companion that he would make old Key believe that he was a very godly man; and he began to get his fine tale ready, as he said.

They re-entered the house, took a seat, and soon found out what was going on. Mr. Hatley kept trying to get his tale ready. I went on leading the class, leaving these two gents till the last. I went to Mr. Hatley, who was leaning his head upon his hand, with his tale all ready to come out. I laid my hand upon his head, and thundered out. 'How is it with thee!' The moment I touched him the thread of his tale was broken to pieces, and deep distress seized his soul; he fell upon his knees, and began to pray mightily to the Lord to have mercy upon him. After a severe conflict for about half an hour, mercy lifted off his load and made him unspeakably happy. He had never, according to his own statement to me afterwards, had any light, or religious feeling, before that night.

After calling over the names of the members, I said to Mr. Hatley, 'Do you wish to unite with us?' 'Yes,' replied the new-born saint, 'with all my heart, and will give you all the money I have got in my pocket to begin with.' He went home; his wife began to reprove him for being out so late, expecting he had been to one of his old haunts, the public-house. He immediately fell on his knees, and began to praise God aloud for what He had done for his soul. This so deeply affected his wife, that she was stirred up to seek the Lord in good earnest, and found Him to the joy of her soul.

Mr. Hatley was by trade a baker, and like many others, he had foolishly thought that he could not live without Sunday-trading; but as soon as this gracious change took place, he made the trial, closed his shop and oven on the Lord's day, and resolved to follow Christ, whatever might be the consequences.

The parson, hearing what had taken place, paid him a visit, and the following conversation took place between them:—

'Mr. Hatley, I understand you have left off baking on the Sabbath day.'

'Yes, sir; I have.'

'I am very sorry for that; you should bake the people's dinner on the Sunday, then they can come to my church.'

'Yes, sir; but what is to become of the poor baker?'

'Oh! you must look out for that.'

'Yes,' said Mr. Hatley, 'I have looked out for it; and by the grace of God I intend to look out for it; I will bake no more on the Sabbath for any man.' . . .

Mr. Hatley and his wife both became local preachers. He also became the circuit steward, and was elected the station's delegate to the district meetings, and sometimes was appointed a delegate to the conference. He maintained, from the day of his conversion, a spotless character, paid off his old debts, and became very highly respected by all who knew him, especially so by the preachers of the Connexion, whom he sincerely loved, and whom he was always ready to defend and support in maintaining the right. His warm and kindly heart, his gentlemanly appearance, and his noble, manly conduct, secured him friends wherever he went. . . .

The society of Hockering, a few years later, suffered much from emigration. A number of its best members and local preachers went to America. Mr. Hatley and William Lane died in the prime of life. William Guymer, another hard-working and useful local preacher, removed to Lynn. A few years ago, however, a gentleman built a chapel for the Primitive Methodists in the village, and made it secure to the Connexion for ever.

SHIPDHAM

Shipdham is a large village, containing between sixteen and seventeen hundred inhabitants. It lies five miles from East Dereham, and five miles from Watton. Shipdham, Watton, and East Dereham might have been matched against any three places in the kingdom, of similar size, for brutal violence and inveterate hatred of the truth; and of the three places, I think Shipdham was the worst, and maintained a determined opposition the longest.

A gentleman of the place told me, the first time that I visited it, that three parts out of four of its inhabitants never entered the house of God. Open immorality, profaneness, Sabbath, desecration, drunkenness, and deep-rooted enmity to all spiritual things, were the most prominent features of their character. Camping and cricketing on the Sabbath afternoon was their common practice; and from their field sports to the public-house. No one ventured to raise a warning voice to rouse them from their slumber, and to show them their sin and danger.

In the month of June, 1832, I thought I would seize the bear by his beard, in his own den. I went upon the ground where the parties were playing, in the centre of the parish, on the Sunday evening, and took my stand near the school-room, on one side of the ground occupied by the campers, and commenced singing,

Turn to the Lord, and seek salvation, &c.

This soon drew off a large part of the lookers-on, to hear what the babbler would say. I was going on pretty comfortably with the service, when suddenly the ball was sent at my head, with such violence, that it must have fractured my skull, and probably have dashed my brains out, but it passed harmlessly by me, fell upon the tiles of the school-room, and the broken tiles came rattling down behind me. But I kept on with my work, without being in the least dismayed or discouraged; and fixing my eyes upon a fine, strong, robust young man, who appeared very active in the service of Satan, and very prominent among his companions in vice, I thought he would make a good champion for Christ, if we could but get him out of the hands of his old master. On a sudden, I singled him out, and poured forth a flood of red-hot truths upon him in quick succession. The word fastened upon his conscience, tore away the dark shutters from his guilty soul, and held him with a Sampson-like grasp. He could not shake it off, but left his old companions, and came out manfully for Christ and His cause, and became a useful local preacher on the plan.

The rabble, however, nothing daunted, kept up their cruel practices for several years; and even when we had obtained a house to conduct divine worship in, we were constantly annoyed. Sometimes the rabble would besmear the door and windows with a mop dipt in the soil taken from water-closets; at other times rush suddenly into the house during service, and blow the lights out, beating the people about the head, and behaving most indecently. At other times, the preacher would be hooted through the village. Their hearts were like a burning mountain, hot within them, and boiling with rancour and cruelty, heaving and swelling, and pouring forth imprecations, threats, and obscene language.

One Sunday, Mr. W. Hatley, from Hockering, was preaching outside of the house, in the open air, near the window, and the rabble took hold of him, and pushed his head and shoulders through the glass. But in the midst of all this tumult and rage, cruelty and opposition, souls were saved, and a good cause was established, which continues to this day. Several local preachers were raised up, and a number have died in the faith, and passed away to a better country. Some of the poor members suffered much for the cause they had espoused. A poor old Frenchwoman, whose husband had gone the way of all flesh, was shamefully put about and basely treated, because she dared to say that she 'was a thorough Prim-i-tive Methodist.' She would neither bend nor flinch from her profession; was among the first that united with us, and has been a pillar ever since.

A few years ago, a good substantial Connexional chapel was built, under the superintendency of the Rev. J. Scott; and I had the pleasure of taking a part in the opening services. The inhabitants of this place, I am informed, are much improved in their moral habits within these last few years; and the prayer of my heart is, that they may know the day of their visitation, and be led by divine grace to choose the good part that shall not be taken away.

5.2.3   W. GIBSON ON THE ULSTER REVIVAL, 1860

In more than one locality in Ulster, notwithstanding the general deadness, symptoms of awakening began to indicate the approach of a better era. Public attention, however, was soon concentrated on a rural district in County Antrim, which more than any other has been identified with the early history of the movement, and from which, as a common centre, it spread with unprecedented rapidity over the entire north of Ireland.

The place was one which had long enjoyed the benefit of an evangelical ministry. Even in days of darkness and defection Connor had been a favoured district; and under the oversight of a faithful pastorate and vigilant eldership, ever zealous for the purity of communion and the maintenance of a wholesome discipline, the flock were taught alike by precept and example the necessity of separation from the world. . . . Yet, notwithstanding these advantages and opportunities, many had little more than the form of godliness; others, openly careless and indifferent, were unhappily addicted to strong drink and other debasing vices. The merely moral and the sincerely pious mingled together, so far as man could judge, with little to distinguish them from one another; while the victim of intemperance, now and then, and as if to annoy both, appeared among them, to be flouted by the one, and pitied by the other. For years this state of things continued, until after many disheartening delays the long-desired blessing came, and hundreds rose up as from the dead to newness of life.

For a considerable period the winter Sabbath-evening service, which was more especially designed for the outlying population, who had no regular church connexion, and who could not find accommodation in the crowded pews in the previous part of the day, had become unusually large, amounting to many hundreds, even in the darkest nights and the coldest weather; 'and what they heard,' says Mr Moore, 'was very plain, and barren of all attempt at ordinary pulpit refinements. The terrors of the Lord, and the free offers of mercy – heaven or hell – these constituted the almost exclusive theme.' 'It is worthy of notice also,' he adds, 'that the revival of religion, and the reasonableness of expecting such a dispensation, were not unfrequently dwelt on in the stated ministrations of the sanctuary. Extracts were read from the existing memorials of the work of God in Wales, under Daniel Rowlands; in America, under Jonathan Edwards and the Tennents; and in Scotland, under the many eminent ministers who were similarly honoured in other days. The idea of a great revival accordingly took hold of many in the congregation, and many prayers were offered in public and in private that it might be realised in its vitality and power.' 'Depend upon it,' said one of the most intelligent and prayerful men in all the district to his minister some years ago, 'you will yet see good days in Connor.'

It was in the spring of 1855, as I am informed by one who has been brought up in the district, and is now a student for the ministry in the Presbyterian Church, that a movement was commenced in faith and prayer, which was destined, ere long, to spread over the neighbourhood a hallowed influence. At the close of a Sabbath evening at that period, and at one of his Bible-class examinations, Mr Moore was heard addressing a young man present, and affectionately urging upon him the duty of doing 'something more' for God. 'Could you not,' he said, 'gather at least six of your careless neighbours, either parents or children, to your own house, or some other convenient place, on the Sabbath, and spend an hour with them, reading and searching the Word of God?' The young man hesitated for a moment, but promised to try. From that trial, made in faith, originated the Tannybrake Sabbath-school, and in connexion with it, two years subsequently, a prayer-meeting, which yielded some of the first-fruits of the great awakening. . . .

'Among others who were associated in the Sabbath-school prayer-meeting, were the four young men whose names have been much before the public in connexion with the subsequent revival. These four rejoiced together in the glorious work, and took great delight also in each other's society. . . . They resolved to meet at a central place for Christian fellowship, and for this purpose they chose an old school-house in the neighbourhood of Kells, where, in the month of October, about two months subsequent to the commencement of the Sabbath-school prayer-meeting in Tannybrake, those exercises were conducted which have been generally regarded as the origin of the revival. It will be seen, however, . . . that the first stirrings of life were exhibited in connexion with the Sabbath-school prayer-meeting. Three, at least, of the converts were born there, two of whom were scholars, and the third a teacher, while the gracious answers to the prayers offered on their behalf, while labouring under deep conviction, gave a powerful stimulus to prayer itself. From that time the gracious drops began to fall thicker and faster, until the rushing shower descended which has refreshed so many, and left behind verdure and beauty in the heritage of God.'

'For a considerable period,' says Mr Moore himself, 'and before any general interest in religion was manifested by the people, there had been a growing anxiety about salvation. And some cases had here and there occurred of an unwonted character: a sinner, anxious about the state and prospects of his soul, experiencing a sudden, startling visitation of dread, followed by a peace and joy unspeakable – a protracted season of perplexity approaching to despair, succeeded by a view of Christ as a Saviour, full, sweet, restoring. Such instances had been occasionally witnessed, but they were isolated and unnoticed by the generality. About the spring of 1858 a very interesting work began to manifest itself, and to move onwards over a certain district of the congregation. For more than a quarter of a century the 'prayer-meeting' had existed in that locality. . . . Once the meeting in question was so far reduced in numbers that only two came together to call upon the name of the Lord. Still they continued to pray on, and by degrees the little company increased, until it became 'two bands.' . . .

The 'fellowship-meeting' above referred to, was established almost simultaneously with those concerts for prayer. . . . 'The society,' to adopt the words of the Rev. S. J. Moore of Ballymena, 'soon ceased to be a secret one; and slowly one kindred spirit after another was introduced, on the recommendation of some of the original members. For a few months they had to walk by faith. The seed, however, was not long cast upon the waters till the tide ebbed, and the tender blade sprung up.' . . . The first observable instance of conversion occurred in December following. A young man became greatly alarmed. After some time, in answer to earnest prayer by himself and others, he found peace and confidence. Early in January a youth in the Sabbath-school class taught by one of those young men, was brought to the saving knowledge of Christ as his Saviour. Special prayer, about the same period, was frequently offered in the fellowship-meeting in behalf of two persons, who, some three months afterwards, joyfully professed their faith in the Lord Jesus. Faith grew. Hope brightened. 'The power of prayer' began to be known, and felt, and seen. The spring communion came on. Throughout the extensive parish, consisting of some thousand families, it was generally known that, lately, persons had been turned to the Lord among them – some moral, and some wildly immoral. A few had heard of a similar triumph of Divine grace beyond the Atlantic. The services were peculiarly solemn. The Master's presence seemed to be recognised, and His call heard. A great impulse was given to consideration and seriousness, intensifying and extending these general precursors of conviction and revival. The old prayer-meetings began to be thronged, and many new ones established. No difficulty now to find persons to take part in them. The winter was past; the time of the singing of birds had come. Humble, grateful, loving, joyous converts multiplied. The awakening to a sight of sin, the conviction of its sinfulness, the illumination of the soul in the knowledge of a glorious Saviour, and conversion to Him – all this operation, carried on by the life-giving Spirit, was in the Connor district, for more than eighteen months, a calm, quiet, gradual, in some cases a lengthened process, not commencing in, or accompanied by, a 'smiting down' of the body, or any extraordinary physical prostration more than what might be expected to result from great anxiety and deep sorrow.

The awakening thus commenced and spread over a district in which there was a good degree of preparation for its advent. It is a striking fact, that it was not till more than twelve months subsequently, and in the summer of 1859, when the work was spreading generally over Ulster, that some of the other districts of the congregation were blessed with the gracious visitation. Once begun, however, the movement rapidly extended. The great concerns of eternity were realised as they had never been before. People, when they met, talked a new language. Many walked about in deep anxiety about the one thing needful; while others rejoiced in the realised experience of a present peace and a complete salvation. Meetings for Christian converse and prayer began to spread – in a short time the community was altogether changed in its outward aspects, and a pervading seriousness prevailed. . . .

Reserving for the present any discussion respecting the physical phenomena and the explanations of them, it may not be out of place . . . to refer to some of their characteristic features. . . . It may be observed generally, that so far as can be gathered of the great majority of cases, they have been preceded for a longer or shorter period by an agonising sense of sin; sometimes lying dully on the conscience for weeks and months together, sometimes overwhelming as in a moment by its intolerable pressure, and violently demonstrative in its manifestations. The physical prostration itself has taken place under every possible variety of circumstances – at home, abroad, in the church, and in the market-place; in the crowded meeting, and the seclusion of retirement. One is stricken as he plies the shuttle or the loom; another as his eye falls upon some familiar passage, or his ear is arrested by some oft-repeated invitation of the Word; a third while he is engaged in secret meditation or prayer. 'I have known the case of a man,' says the Rev. John Macnaughtan of Belfast, referring to another class of instances, after his visit to Ballymena, 'going home from the market after he had sold his produce, passing along the road-side, and counting his money to see whether it was all right, when he sunk down as if sun-struck, and his money was scattered on the road.'

Of the several stages in the experience of those who have been the subjects of physical prostration, the *first* is characterised by an awful apprehension of impending evil, a fearful looking for a judgment and fiery indignation, accompanied by a crushing pressure on the region of the heart, inducing the loud despairing cry, or the groan of agony. In this state the sufferer is overwhelmed as by the billows of Divine wrath, so that human help is for the time of no avail, and all that man can do is to await the issue, committing it to Him who causeth light to arise in the darkness. Then is the period also of fierce wrestling, real or imagined, with the Evil One, whose personality is apprehended with terrible distinctness, insomuch that the soul is as an arena in which a death struggle is being carried on between the powers of light and darkness.

In the *second* stage, which is generally very sudden in its development, there is a transition from the deep depression before experienced to a calmer state of feeling, and some object earnestly desired and longed for, stands out before the view – the intensity of the mind's gaze being such that no human presence, although many may be intently waiting by, is realised. It is a sort of waking dream, in which the steadfast countenance and upturned eye denote the character of the inward exercise. The labouring chest no longer heaves under its oppressive burden; there is a subsidence of the sob, the groan, the wail of lamentation, and the cold damps are passing off the brow. The arms that tossed about so wildly, are now stretched forth as if to embrace the prized and cherished object, and utterances like these drop from the lips in melting cadence, – 'O blessed Jesus, come! Thou art my hope, my life, my all; wash me in Thy most precious blood; take away this filthy garment, and cover me with Thine own pure righteousness;' or more affecting still, as in the case of that little girl, but eight years old, who exclaimed imploringly, in her native patois, 'O Christ, come to me! and when you come, O dinna lea' me, but aye stay wi' me.' It is in this stage that images flit before the mind with all the vividness of reality, and as if possessed of shape and substance; insomuch that the person, subsequently referring to his experience, will speak *as if* he had seen the dread realities of heaven or hell, although assured on calm reflection that the objects before his vision have only been his own thoughts embodied in that form.

And now a *third* experience ensues. It is that of sensible relief, a lightsome and liberated feeling, of which the chief ingredient is the assurance of forgiveness prompting to the outburst of rapturous praise. The fountains of the soul seem to be opened, and forth flows in unrestrained exuberance the gushing fulness of its joy. The bodily sensations correspond with the inward ecstasy, and even the plainest features glow as with an unearthly beauty. The heavy load, the incubus that weighed down all the spirit's energies, is lifted off, and there is a buoyancy and elasticity proportionate to the depressing burden. The new-born happiness seeks audible expression. The language of the lips is all in unison with the serenity that reigns within. 'Christ and Him crucified' being once apprehended, the grand, the dominant desire is to commend Him to all around. How often, then, are heard such words as those in which a Sabbath-school girl, some thirteen years of age, was addressing her little companions by her bedside, as she lay in much exhaustion after a season of mental agony, while a gleam of spiritual joy played over her pale countenance, – 'O Annie! O Jane, dear, come to Jesus! He'll not put you away. Oh, give Him your heart, give Him *all* your heart, and He'll take away all your sins, and make you as happy as He has made me. Oh that all the sinners about here would come to Him! He has room for them all. He would save them all.'

To the above may be added a *fourth* stage in the prostration – namely, the languor and exhaustion which are the natural reaction from the intense excitement by which the frame has been agitated, and by reason of which not only delicate females, but strong and stalwart men have often been for days unfitted for any manner of work.

Such bodily affections were almost universally associated with the awakening, when, for the first time, it appeared in any neighbourhood; although in many places the work proceeded most satisfactorily without their presence, and they generally subsided as it advanced. From their novelty and publicity they naturally attracted a large share of attention, serving, no doubt, an important purpose, but often stimulating an idle curiosity, and in the case of the uneducated and ill-informed, leading to a confounding of the spiritual process with the physiological characteristics by which it was accompanied. . . .

5.2.4 J. CLIFFORD ON RELIGIOUS LIFE IN RURAL ENGLAND, 1876

It is our privilege to reckon as fellow-workers in the rural districts many brethren not embraced in this Union, who preach the same free Gospel of Christ, maintain the same principles with regard to the sole and exclusive kingship of the Lord Jesus in His Church, inculcate the same doctrine of the government of the Church by Christian people, practise a free ministry of the Word, and look for the increase of the religious life in the rural districts to the same divine sources and by the same divine methods.

In view of the vast and pressing needs of rural England, I wish to ask whether these Free Churches are working in such a manner as to secure the largest possible good; whether there are not circumstances in which we might co-operate with Congregationalists and Methodists in raising the maximum of our general efficiency, and yet retain an unviolated conscience, vigorous *ésprit de corps*, and an unshaken conviction, with the most unfettered liberty to avow it, that the Baptist expression of Church faith and life is the nearest approach to the Divine Ideal we know?

It is notorious that there is a waste of evangelising power, a flagrant surplus of machinery in one spot, and an equally painful lack of it in another. The statistics of the Churches of Derbyshire have been widely published, and are generally known, and from all I can gather about other counties, I fear the Derbyshire returns must be taken as samples of a too general state of things; *e.g.*, a village in Lincolnshire, where Dissent is declining, has a population of a thousand, and there are four places of worship, providing 920 sittings. In the West of England is a village with 336 inhabitants, and the Baptist Chapel will hold 250 and the Independent 150, being 64 in excess of the population. In nine parishes in Derbyshire there is in each an excess of more than a thousand sittings. There are not less than ten Methodist Chapels in the town of Belper and sixteen in Alfreton. Surely such facts as these constitute a strong demand for an attempt at such concerted action as shall avoid, wherever possible, the evils of such misplaced energy.

For these evils are neither few nor small. Other districts suffer for lack of Free Church life. Piety is dwarfed and sickly for want of sympathy and fellowship. Working power is wasted; Christian labourers are in each other's way. Money is not put to its best use. Ministers are soured by inevitable defeat, and starved for want of food. Nonconformity is scandalized. The State-Church points the finger of scorn at the crowding competition in one district, and the barrenness of its neighbours, and says, with a jeer:– 'Chapels, like troubles, never come alone.' And worse than all, religion suffers in its energy and influence, its kindliness and charity, and in its soul-saving power.

More than ever is such concerted action needed now. The Free Churches in the rural districts are passing through a severe trial. The clergy have adopted the principle of extermination. Their policy is the policy of suppression, and wherever they can they will carry it out without stint. On the largest estate in a township in Cheshire, if persons want to take a place, or become servants, they must have a recommendation from the rector. In one part of Norfolk, a powerful family has carried the extinction policy so far, that it has ended in substituting a churchman for every dissenting farmer on the estate, and the consequent emptying of the Independent Chapel: and so on, *ad infinitum.* The Right Hon. John Bright, in a recent speech in the House of Commons, cited, endorsed, and supported the strong assertion of the late President of the Wesleyan Conference, when he said there is no such thing as religious liberty in 2,000 villages of England.

Fashion, too, is setting against us with more force than ever. The *entrée* of society is with the Church people. The road to social position is through the churchyard, and it requires more conscience, more moral courage, than some Dissenters can keep in the same house with increasing wealth and luxury, to restrain them from walking along that road. We ought to reckon with these things, and strain every nerve to maintain men of high Christian character, thorough culture, and fair address in the village pastorate; men who shall watch the movements of designing Ritualistic clergymen; handle cases of persecution as they occur; contend against the clericalism in the schools and in the management of parochial charities; in a word, protect the rights of conscience, and shelter Dissenters from the incessant and worrying persecutions of men whom the State authorises to tyrannize in the most tender and sacred relationships of life. . . .

I am eager to acknowledge, and I do it with all joy, the presence of many noble examples of true godliness and genuine piety in our State Church; of much ardent and self-denying zeal; of earnest purpose and broad sympathies; of consecrated service and pure devotion; but a large induction of facts compels me to say that the influence of the Parliamentary Church upon the village population has in it more of evil than of good.

I scarcely need say the Church has failed to secure and nourish a manly, healthy, and strong spiritual life in the rural parishes. That is admitted and deplored by Canon Ryle, with regard to scores of such parishes, and is proved by incontestable and unbiassed evidence in the Blue Books of 1867 on the employment of children, young persons, and women in Agriculture; evidence which shows most convincingly that the ordinary pictures of Arcadian simplicity and purity painted by the deft fingers of Church defenders belong more to poetry than to fact – to a solitary village here and there, may be, but assuredly not to rural life in its general range and character. Notwithstanding the Establishment has had the exhaustless resources of the State, the magical power of wealth and rank and prestige, the exclusive ownership of the Universities till within a recent date and the sole control of education, yet its failure is grievously conspicuous to the eye of every unbiassed observer, and is painfully felt by many of the villagers themselves.

Would it had only failed! It has done, and is doing, far worse than that. It injures, thwarts, and stultifies the best life of the nation. It is a huge incubus on liberty. It is based, by the confession of a Bishop, on 'religious *in*equality;' and it begets a rancorous and venomed intolerance, a reckless disregard of the rights and feelings of others; destroys the frank cordiality of social life, embitters and poisons relations that ought always to be pleasant and sunny, saps independence, diminishes public spirit, emasculates piety, and fails to regenerate life and ennoble character. Even minds otherwise noble and of a liberal and kindly tone are drawn by the fascination of State ascendency to approve harshness and tyranny as though they were Christian duties, and wear intolerance and wrong as though they were Christian graces; whilst the labouring population becomes more and more averse, first, to the priest and his ways, and, next, to the religion he is supposed to represent.

A gentleman who has visited near upon 400 villages in a Midland county reports that the greater part of the agricultural labourers are alienated from the Church of England. Another correspondent of wide experience and observation says, 'the *animus* of the labourer towards clergymen and the Church is as grave an indictment against the Establishment as is the distrust of all who are subject to him to the Turk.' And history testifies by a hundred facts, of which French revolutions are not the worst, that that nation is in a critical condition whose State-enforced religion excites hostility rather than sympathy, and withers and dwarfs the religious feelings it is meant to inspire and strengthen.

And are these evils diminishing? Diminishing! They wax worse and worse every day. Scores of ritualistic clergymen who are within a pace or two of Rome are wielding their authority as a rod of iron. They take possession of the rural districts as if the whole earth had been put in commission and given over to men who do not 'argue with the laic, but teach him,' who openly practise auricular confession, penance, and absolution, offer prayers for the dead, and sing hymns to the Virgin Mary. The villages are being sown with Roman doctrine, and we know too well that the seeds of priestly caste and Papal error grow into a harvest of enslaved minds, cauterised consciences, corrupted lives, and all the proofs of an immoral religion.

Now, be it distinctly understood, our quarrel is not with the Church, but with the State. We are not requesting the aid of Lord Beaconsfield to suppress Ritualism – we merely demand that this Ritualism shall cease to be armed with the State's authority, supported by the State's gold, and enforced by the State's power; for it is the State which has placed the clergyman in power, put the latch of every door in the parish in his hand, and the conscience of every child in his keeping – invested him with the right to teach, in the name of the nation, the immaculate virtues of the Church and the unpardonable sin of Dissent; and it is as a State-Church that its evil influence is so enormous, and therefore is it that we set forth as one of the foremost religious duties of the Baptist Churches of this Union that of seeking with increasing zeal and determination the total and immediate separation of the State from the Church. . . .

5.3   CHRISTIANIZING THE TOWNS

Late-Victorian Nonconformists were not alone in recognizing the immoderate strength of the Church of England in rural districts. Nor were theirs the only voices demanding change, although the reorganization and redistribution of resources called for by the Revd John Joseph Halcombe (1832–1910) was scarcely in line with Free Church objectives. Disestablishment was precisely what Halcombe feared would be the inevitable result of a persistent failure to provide adequately for the spiritual needs of the towns. To avert this 'catastrophe' he proposed that the work of Church extension should proceed, in conjunction with renewed clerical recruitment, by the subdivision of urban parishes, thereby enabling priest and people to come into closer contact (**5.3.1**). By the 1880s, indeed, Anglican ordinands were being both encouraged and actively prepared to tackle the urban challenge. John Gott (1830–1906), dean of Worcester and formerly vicar of Leeds, lectured divinity students at Cambridge on the qualities needed for the job. He emphasized, first, intellectual cultivation, which would make the church and its priest the 'soul' in the heart of the city (**5.3.2**). Gott's implied elitism was not, however, the only social profile sanctioned by ecclesiastical tradition. In London, the Revd Arthur Henry Stanton (1839–1913) of St Alban's, Holborn, cut a populist image. According to the shrewdly observant Revd Davies (4.3.1), he offered his mixed but decidedly poor congregation a richly sensuous ritualistic religion of the heart. The books he read with the parish mothers were *Nicholas Nickleby* and *Adam Bede* (**5.3.3**). But what undoubted success and notoriety Stanton's ministry enjoyed was as nothing, quantitatively speaking, to the impact of the American revivalists Dwight Lyman Moody (1837–1899) and Ira David Sankey (1840–1908) on their first evangelistic tour of Britain. The mission, which began in 1873 and, unlike subsequent tours, was concentrated mainly in the towns, ended in London with four months of public meetings. Moody's attraction was greatest among the middling and upper classes, who found in the mission a focus for their evangelical energies and a point of union in perilous times. But Moody himself was resolute to reach the masses, and Davies's concluding sketch of the stand-off between the Chicago shoe salesman and the West End great and good again contains a trenchant assessment, as well as a humourous vignette, of Victorian religious life (**5.3.4**).

5.3.1   J. J. HALCOMBE ON CHURCH EXTENSION, 1874

Many causes are commonly assigned for the comparative insecurity of the Established Church at the present time, but we believe that it is mainly to be attributed to the unaccountable manner in which for the last thirty years she has concentrated her efforts on making provision for her country population, a minority which was already fairly provided for, to the neglect of her town population, a majority entirely dependent upon the efforts of the present generation. Let us look to the facts of the case.

According to the census of 1861, the population of the country districts of England, including all towns of 2000 inhabitants and under, was 7,500,000. To minister in these districts we had no fewer than 10,398 incumbents. In our large towns, on the other hand, the population was 13,500,000, and the incumbents only numbered 2431.

But even these figures do not represent the case quite fairly; for whilst the 7,500,000 in the country have more than four times as many clergy as the 15,000,000 in the large towns, they have probably at least ten times the amount of endowments. A large proportion of the town clergy are thus dependent upon pew-rents, and their Sunday ministrations are thereby almost exclusively limited to persons of the upper and middle classes. A large deduction must therefore be made from the total number of town incumbents, before we can arrive at the number who are fairly at work amongst the masses of people forming the bulk of these 15,000,000 souls.

It might be expected that the above disproportionate disposition of our clerical forces would have been, at least to some extent, rectified by the larger number of curates serving in towns. This, however, is not the case, the expenditure of the Pastoral Aid and Additional Curates Societies being to a great extent neutralised by the very competition which their system of working developes. Thus in spite of the aid given by these societies, there were only 2645 curates in our large towns, as compared with 2495 in country places. In other words, the 15,000,000 in our towns had only 150 more curates working among them than the 7,500,000 in the country; whilst the same deduction from the value of their services has to be made in consideration of the fact that a large majority of town curates minister in pew-rented churches.

After making every possible allowance for the wider area over which the country districts generally extend, it is, we submit, impossible to give their due significance to the above figures, and not to allow that the great problem which the Church has to solve, and on the right solution of which her very existence as an Established Church probably depends, is, How are we to deal with these vast masses of our town population? and how may we best rectify the disproportion which exists between the number of the clergy and the amount of endowments available in country as compared with the same in town districts?

Disestablishment can only result from a gradual loosening of the hold which the Church has hitherto had upon the confidence and affection of the majority of the entire population of the country. As long as our parochial system worked in such a manner as to bring the clergy, in every parish in the kingdom, into constant and familiar personal intercourse with the people, there was nothing to fear; but just in proportion as increased numbers of the people are removed from the immediate influence of the clergy, in that proportion the hold which the Church has upon the national mind must be loosened, and the danger of Disestablishment become more imminent. If the population at the great centres of industry is continually increasing, with a rapidity out of all proportion to the increased number of clergy provided to minister amongst them, Disestablishment only becomes a question of time, and the date at which it is likely to take place may be calculated with almost as much certainty as the hour at which the rising tide will attain to a particular height. Circumstances may retard or accelerate the exact date at which the final catastrophe may happen, but happen at length it must and will.

As long as the population increased in country villages it made comparatively little difference to the clergyman in charge whether he had 300 or 600, or even 1200, to deal with. The work might be somewhat more laborious, but the old endowment was just as sufficient, or insufficient, for his support as before. When, however, under a changing condition of national life, the population began to draw off from the parishes to which sufficient endowments were attached in former times, and mass itself in new centres of commercial, manufacturing, and mining industry, the case was very different. For all the good they reaped from the ancient revenues of the Church, these emigrants from their native villages might almost as well have gone to the wilds of Australia or New Zealand. True, the site of every one of these new centres was within the boundary of some ecclesiastical district, but the revenues upon which the new population thus became chargeable were mostly as a single loaf amongst an army.

Thus for all practical purposes of maintaining the old relations between pastor and people, the new districts were totally destitute of provision for their spiritual wants.

From time to time, during the present century, efforts have been made to rectify this state of things, and, as far as church building and the provision of school accommodation is concerned, very substantial evidence of the energy of those who have taken up this work is forthcoming; but it is not so with regard to the means of maintenance for the clergy. In this respect the provision made has borne no sort of relation to the requirements of the case. Even the recent efforts of the Ecclesiastical Commissioners, admirably adapted as they have been, and thoroughly calculated, as far as they have gone, to meet the emergency, have been far too limited to produce any result commensurate with the necessities of the case.

The upshot of all this has been that, as far as two thirds of the population of this country are concerned, the Church of England has ceased, from sheer lack of men, to do in any effectual manner the work entrusted to her; whilst, as a necessary consequence, she is fast losing her hold upon the national mind, and in spite of the supplementary work of various dissenting bodies, the heathenism of our great towns has become as gross in itself and as revolting in its accompaniments as that of any barbarous people with whom we are acquainted. . . .

The creation and endowment of new districts in our large towns is, perhaps, of all others the most important branch of the work of Church extension.

But here we are met by a serious difficulty.

It is generally assumed that it is better to have an incumbent and one or two curates in a parish of 6,000 people, than to divide the district and place [between] either two or three incumbents in charge of the newly created parishes. Much, however, may be said against this assumption.

The chief advantage of the one church serving for the larger district has to be set against many manifest disadvantages. The personal superintendence exercised by the incumbent of a parish exceeding five or six thousand souls is to a great extent only nominal. His time is occupied with work that must be done in the study or on the platform, and he is often compelled to delegate to the assistant clergy who share with him the work of the parish, the greater part of the pastoral visitation of the sick and whole, by which alone that influence can be gained that is so powerful an agent in deepening the religious life and promoting the best interests of the faith. If curates were as seldom transferred from one sphere of labour to another as is the case with incumbents, it would signify but little whether this influence were exercised by the one class or the other. But this is notoriously not the case. In a large staff of curates changes are continually going on, and it takes months or even years for each new comer to attain to the knowledge of the people his predecessor had acquired. This would be to a great extent avoided if the system of mission districts, with permanent curates in charge, were more widely adopted, and if the funds of the Diocesan and National Church Extension Societies were granted more frequently to such districts, with a view to their being developed into independent spheres of work. One pressing difficulty at least would be obviated by this course, as it is notorious that the incumbents of large town parishes have the greatest difficulty in meeting with efficient curates, while for a mission district there is always sufficient competition to allow of a thoroughly competent man being chosen.

The whole subject of the subdivision of parishes is, however, too extensive to be discussed in a paper that is meant rather to draw attention to the weak places in our Church organization than to point out all the remedies that may be suggested for them, and we therefore draw our remarks to a close, earnestly commending the subject we have but imperfectly treated to the thoughtful consideration of all who have the welfare of the Church at heart. There never was a time when there was greater willingness on the part of the laity to respond to any call made upon them for the great work of Church extension; what is wanted is combined action and organized effort from those who, from their position as chief rulers in our ecclesiastical commonwealth, are the natural leaders in the great and blessed work of enlarging the borders of the sanctuary, and whose duty and privilege it is to enlist and direct the armies of the Cross.

5.3.2   J. GOTT ON THE PARISH PRIEST OF THE TOWN, 1887

No one should know better the pulse of our time than he who lives in the heart of it, and has made his cathedral the soul of that heart. Dean Church tells us, 'Never was there a time when the hearts of the people so yearned towards their guides . . . Our obligations seem to be enlarging beyond those of former times . . . Never was there, I believe, a heartier response, not merely to the sympathy and enthusiasm of the young, though that is so remarkable, and with all its risks so inspiring, but from the thoughtful deliberate earnestness of the experienced and mature.' (*Human Life.*)

This is a hasty glance at the speciality of our time. And *it rises to its strength in our towns.*

As it runs through our streets, the stream of life grows into a river. In large towns the good is better than elsewhere for three reasons; it resists more temptation, calling out its whole strength and endurance; it is surrounded with misery, developing its charity and sacrifice; and its environment of means of grace, and the Communion of Saints, is fuller and richer. In large towns the *bad* also is worse, *its* environment too is congenial and very fertile. So on both sides life is more intense.

We increase with a speed that has some awe in it. My own town grows 7000 souls a year. The spiritual meaning of this fact I have no gift to read. It is more than the birth-rate, – two lads are always on the road from the village to the town, the quick, clever, ambitious boy who means to climb, and the fast or vicious boy who seeks the license and the like-minded of a large town; and these two lads add even more force than volume to the river of town life.

Its friction adds greatly to the nerve and excitement of a city; the friction of numbers, of competition, of conflicting interests between master and man, of great wealth and utter poverty, of saintly devotion and loathsome bestiality. Friction is a force that even mechanics have to recognise, how much more the divine science of God in man.

Remember that great towns represent a great impulse that is moving our race. Their present occurrence seems due to a rarely happy time of public institutions, plenty of work well rewarded, and a masterly factory system. This impulse cannot help carrying on the Church, somewhither it will affect it, and be in return affected by it, as the impulses of the tenth, thirteenth, and sixteenth centuries and the Church mutually told upon each other.

And when the Church is the living, lifegiving, soul of our great towns, it will develop a new phase of manifold life, some new spiritual colour and form will bear witness to a new divine energy, some prophecy will be fulfilled, some Christian grace will illumine the world, which at present we know not, or know very slightly. Some new beauty of Holiness, or attribute of God, or gift of the Holy Ghost will renew the Church. How grand and Eucharistal a day is ours or our children's. May our Lord fit us for so noble a task, that He may be glorified, and He alone.

Of all this the parish priest is the personal soul, all this he brings into living touch with God; between all these jarring interests he is the sacred link. What, then, must be the parish priest himself? especially in those towns into which four-fifths of England has gathered itself?

This is the thought I lay before you in these lectures, – the parish priests of the modern town.

And first, *how does he differ from his brother in the country villages?*

(1) In *organization,* – necessary, manifold, penetrating everywhere in the town.

(2) In *high pressure,* which conditions every character and almost every act in a commercial congregation.

(3) In the *intricacies of conscience,* affected by trade, theatres, mass life in factories and shops, and countless forms of Dissent.

(4) In the indifference of a hostile character easily developed into active agencies of *unbelief,* through which a young man has daily to run the gauntlet.

On the other hand, *the country Rector* has his advantages, and contributes to the Church of the land gifts as costly and great, if not more so, than his brother of the city. Surely a holiness is given him, hard to win in the spiritual fuss of town life; and a well-filled leisure is his, out of which he comes forth to conduct Missions and Retreats with reserves of calm strength that are above all price.

But of that I know little. The first day of my Diaconate I was given charge over a district of 8000 souls, and that day was the true sample of my life till to-day. Therefore I can only tell you of those things that have made up my life for nearly thirty years. . . .

In a large tailor's shop in my parish, the workmen employ one of their number, at full tailor's wage, to read the newspapers to them as they sit and sew.

In every quarter of the town and its suburbs free libraries are crowded in meal-time and the winter evenings.

In progressive Clubs the questions of the hour, especially political and religious subjects, are freely discussed.

In the 1000 mechanics' shops, patents ever new quicken and deepen the brain.

In the technical schools that thrive in every town, the brighter lads learn the newest art, English and foreign, and some of the principles that lie underneath it.

In the Yorkshire College the young working men of promise mix their best thoughts with those of Cambridge and Oxford professors.

All these men and their teachers come to Church if they find there someone to teach them real things about a real life. But they test their sermons as they test their cloth or steel, and woe to the dealer in any goods spiritual or material that will not wear. They go to another shop or do without. . . .

It is not learned sermons that they want, they rather suspect all varnished goods. But they think they have a right to expect something intelligent; an article that shows the knowledge and labour of a skilled workman like themselves. Rightly or wrongly, they have an idea that there are a good many quacks about, and ministers who do not take as much pains about their work as a true artisan puts into his.

Have you noticed a characteristic of our chief Home Missioners, i.e. the men who have least room for dogma or Scientific Christianity in their method of preaching? But they are thoughtful students of doctrine. Two of them lately told me they read Wilberforce on the Incarnation together every Advent, and similar books at other seasons of the Church year. A senior wrangler told me he considered another missioner a true theologian, while two others keep Schools of Theology for those who work under them.

You need not stop to think whether your sermon be learned or simple, if it be only real, real help given heartily by one who has both really needed, and found it, for himself; the converted preacher can convert, the penitent can awake penitence; if he has risen from his knees to write, some at least of his hearers will go down on their knees after he has finished his sermon. The preacher who comes fresh from his Lord's Presence will put fresh meaning into familiar truth, and fresh grace into weary lives, and at the end of the Sermon many a heart will bless him as he blesses them.

I am not thinking about *reading up for sermons*, it is as valueless as any reading can be. If you mean to teach our townsmen things they will come again to hear, your mind must not be like a carrier's cart bringing other people's thoughts to market; let your mind be a field in which wiser men's thoughts are sown, to bring forth some thirty, sixty, hundred fold, not at once, but 'in due season.'

The two readings are not different ways of doing the same thing, they do different things, – the reader for immediate use displays his second-hand wares, more or less the worse for their passage through him; but he who reads for God's sake, digests and assimilates his food, and it comes out in the nerve of his nerve, and the mind of his mind. . . .

The only reading for ready use that quickens and deepens one's mind, is the study of a few first-rate books, read straight through for some weekly class of educated people on some consecutive subject that fills a winter; such as the Psalter, or the connection of the Old and New Testament, or the divine Gospel of St. John; for there is a virtue in systematic reading, and a great subject carefully worked through, a divine virtue that hides itself from the man who only goes to his shelves to find straw to hold together his poor unbaked clay.

In times like ours some great subject comes up every other year, – the Athanasian Creed, After death, etc., – read what has been written at different times about it, make a note-book on it, any way digest it.

There is no subject of study so constantly suggested by God Himself, throughout the Bible, as Church history; without it the present is chaos, and the future a blank; and history is so new a study – new lights, new materials, new interlacings, are rising up all around us every year.

Junior Clerical Societies encourage and help our study in every large town now-a-days, and our guild, or young men's class, often suggests a subject of the day that is exercising the public mind, and wants the knowledge and wisdom we alone can earn for it.

Nor does the mischief of this read and run style stop here. If it were only a huckster's way of picking up and puffing off any trifles of the mind that would not sell in the ordinary way of business, it would be unworthy enough; but it spoils the *preacher's* mind as well as that of his *people*. It becomes a substitute for thought; this reader falls quickly into a preacher, who chooses his text, opens his Index Rerum, or his concordances, or row of sermons, or whatever spiritual encyclopaedia he haunts, he dives into his 'Dictionary of the Bible' for facts, and some popular author for fancies, till his own intelligence is starved, losing its energy by want of use, and its growth by unwholesome food, and before he is a Vicar he has ceased to think, and his people follow him. Ah, if you find yourself falling into this way, you had better bring your books together as those men of Ephesus, and burn them before all men, for to you they are no longer a Communion of Saints, but only the handbooks of curious arts, the art of reading without mind, and of preaching without a soul. . . .

5.3.3   C. M. DAVIES ON FATHER STANTON AT ST ALBAN'S, 1873

Father Stanton . . . differs about as widely from the ordinary run of 'High Church' curate as is possible. We are accustomed to think of such as a rather limp individual; – 'tender-eyed' as Leah, and with a falsetto voice perpetually monotoning on G. He is strongly ascetic and severe against 'all the pomps and vanities of this wicked world.' Not so this young 'priest.' As one of the assistants at St Alban's, Holborn, he is, of course, a pronounced and advanced Ritualist. But he is – *credite posteri!* – a member of the Liberation Society! His bugbear is Establishment. 'Mention Church and State to me,' he says, 'and it is like shaking a red cloth before a mad bull.' Some time ago, all the Mrs Grundys of the country were attacking him, and a good many male, or, at all events, clerical Grundys, too, because, when he established the St Alban's Club for working men, he allowed spirits and beer to be sold there, and did not prohibit the use of cards. 'I like my rubber of whist and night-cap; why shouldn't they?' he asked. 'As long as they don't get drunk or gamble, where is the harm in a glass of grog or a game at cards?'

Father Stanton, then, it will be perceived, thinks for himself, and dares to act as he thinks. He does not run in a groove. He presents the apparent anomaly of an excessively High Churchman, strongly seasoned with Democracy.

This peculiarity gives, of course, a tinge to his ministry. He is demonstrative almost to the limits of rant in his preaching, and in other respects has a supreme disregard of little clerical *convenances*. . . .

If one may venture to speak of the *personnel* of one's portrait, there are in Father Stanton's outward man many elements of the pet curate. He is youthful in appearance, with dark, almost olive complexion, and jet black curling hair – not shaven and shorn, after the manner of the ordinary Ritualist; and, softly be it spoken, pretty *dévouées* do like to carry Father Stanton's photo about with them; but Father Stanton is the very reverse of a ladies' man. With all his physical capacities for such a *rôle*, he is infinitely above its littlenesses, and is every inch 'a priest.'

The morning I chose for my expedition to St Alban's was the unpropitious one of the 2nd of February, the Feast of the Purification, when the first snow of 1873 fell, and winter virtually commenced. I had ascertained that Father Stanton was to preach 'at mid-day mass;' and so, though omnibuses had struck and cabs retired into private life, I struggled along against a biting east wind and blinding snow, eventually reaching Brook Street, where St Alban's is situated, when 'Matins,' which immediately precede 'High Mass,' were only about half over. Mr Mackonochie was intoning on a wildly wrong note, and the choir sang a hymn on the Purification to a distresssing Gregorian tone as I entered. There was a fair congregation, far larger than one would have expected from the nature of the weather, which was calculated to act as a decided damper on any æsthetic proclivities one might have had. I scarcely think I should have struggled to St Alban's save for a special purpose.

The altar was vested in white, and there was just a *soupçon* of the smell of incense about the church, but no signs that Candlemas was to be made a high festival of. In fact, Ritualism seems to have dropped out of its philosophy much of the 'Mariolatry' that was suspected in its rudimentary form of Tractarianism. When morning prayers were over, two persons in surplices advanced and censed the altar, leaving their censers, I believe, in a side chapel, so as to keep up the fragrance, for I could see clouds rising a quarter of an hour after the operation was over; but the result was eminently satisfactory. An introit was sung, and then the procession of acolytes, celebrant, epistoler, and gospeler entered the chancel, preceded by a large cross borne aloft. Father Stanton, habited only in surplice, hood, and small white stole, passed to the clergy stalls, while the rest went to the altar. The celebrant had a huge gold cross on the back of his cope, and the acolytes were gorgeous in scarlet cassocks and white surplices. Mr Mackonochie himself occupied the humble position of epistoler. The celebrant intoned the Commandments in so low a voice as to be scarcely audible; but what I do not mean to call offensively the *mise-en-scène* of the 'Mass' was magnificent; and the effect of all the congregation kneeling, when the incarnation was asserted in the Nicene Creed to deep and solemn chords of accompaniment, was solemn in the extreme. The sign of the Cross was devoutly made when 'the Life of the World to come' was mentioned; and so, at the close of the Creed, Father Stanton mounted the pulpit. His hood was fearfully and wonderfully put on; and the effect of his dark fine-cut face against the deep crimson silk was very monastic indeed. But the sermon soon removed all impressions of the kind. He prefaced his discourse with the publication of banns, prayers for the sick, and also 'prayers for the repose of the soul' of one departed. Then he gave out his text, which was from Mal. iii., part of the Scripture appointed for the Epistle of the Festival – 'The Lord whom ye seek shall suddenly come to His Temple.' He dwelt on the peculiar character of the Festival under its double aspect of the Purification of 'our Blessed Lady,' and the Presentation of our Lord in the Temple. It was, he said, like a last look at Christmas, over which was beginning to be cast the dark shadow of the Passion. . . .

In the Temple, how simple was the scene! An old man takes the Child, and a thrill of joy passes through his heart. He had waited for the consolation of Israel. He speaks a few words; and then a woman stricken in years comes in. She utters her prophecy. She recognizes the Lord of lords in the Child. The offering is made, the purification is over, and they leave. Night closes, and the Temple doors are shut. The Lord *had* suddenly come to His Temple. . . .

The great thought of this festival is the superhuman manifestation of God to those who watch for Him. He was not recognized by the scribe who knew the law, by the Sanhedrim, the rulers, the learned, or the mighty. Two old people who had long been waiting were the only ones who knew Him. . . .

Dear friends, he said, this realization of Jesus Christ is far beyond all learning, art, or science. There is given to those who seek it, a light above that of the sun. Christ communicates Himself in His Divine Personality as well as Essence. Religion is unsatisfactory unless we can thus have personal intimacy with Christ. If we have but heard of Him through men and books, He only exerts a secondary power on us. Our conception of Him merely amounts to a moral certainty, as with any other great hero we read of in history. We have seen Him only through the shadow of ideas. We have not taken Him in our arms and gazed on Him with ineffable joy.

There is, you know it well, a special light, transcendent and transluminous. The converted man will say, 'I have read, and heard, and argued laboriously about Christ, but some day there came to me, at the corner of the street, or at my own fireside, or during some sermon, a mystic certainty about Him. The scales dropped from my eyes. I saw my Lord as I had never seen Him before. I felt the power of salvation. I went back again to my books, and, as I read the old pages, a new light flashed upon me. New arguments came which I had never seen before; and Faith got from that mystic light confirmed them. I never can deny this; for to do so would be to deny the secret of my life.'

But, you will still ask, Is it likely *I* shall ever feel like this? I have heard of conscious conversion and intercourse with God, but its seems far above my head. I never felt it, though I have practised religion for years. I cannot put my hand on a particular day of my life, and say, 'On that day I became converted.' How is it I cannot do as others? Do not be distressed. Go on waiting for the consolation of Israel. Do you not see that they in the Temple had been doing so? That old man had been promised that he should see the Lord's Christ. He waited patiently, 'full of the Holy Ghost,' and at last the Lord suddenly came to His Temple. He *did* depart in peace.

So, too, that old woman; she had long fasted and prayed. Day and night, Scripture says, she had waited for the consolation. It had not come, but day after day, and night after night, she still went on – still fasted and prayed. 'In eternity time struck the hour,' and Jesus Christ came. She had not waited in vain; and henceforth she could talk of nothing else to those others who were waiting too. And have you not felt this? You groan and pray to see God: to press Him to your heart and feel Him yours. You want to grasp 'what lies behind all your Prayers, Communions, and Confessions.' You want religion to be a personal affection for Christ, something you can never let go. It shall come to you: when or how I cannot tell; but it shall come. Perhaps it may be at the end of your life, when the shadows of this world pass away, and the morning breaks over the everlasting hills. You shall see the King in His beauty, whom you had tried to follow at such a distance off. Then will you say, 'O God, Thou art my God. Jesus Christ, Thou didst come to earth for me.' And you will be able to add, 'Lord, now lettest thou Thy servant depart in peace; for mine eyes *have seen* Thy salvation!'

A translation of the hymn 'O quam glorifica' followed, and the usual choral communion or 'mass' was proceeded with. During Communion, Keble's exquisite hymn 'Ave Maria' was sung to music, consisting of a tenor solo, with chorus of the words 'Ave Maria' only. Very few persons communicated.

The *cultus* of St Alban's has been too often described to need reiteration here. It was bright with colours, odours, flowers, and music. According to the theory of the Ritualist, these were, of course, no foreign adjuncts supervening on the English system, but simply what the English ritual was and would have been had the Reformation never run riot into Puritanism. When the great bell of the church boomed out among the snow-clouds at the moment of Consecration, a Broad Churchman might not be able to realize the fact in its intensity; but to those who knelt, or rather prostrated themselves there, the Sacramental act *was* a great fact.

When I 'interviewed' Father Stanton in his anything but monastic room in the clergy house, he said, 'The only two points in which we have made concessions are, that we do not light the candles or burn incense during celebration. All else is as before.' The great influence at St Alban's is, he says, in the Confessional; and that influence he attributes to the fact that confessions are made openly in church, not in the vestry with closed doors.

As an instance of the geniality which overlies the whole system at St Alban's, he told me, after describing the numerous guilds, sisterhoods, *crêche*, orphanage, &c., that at the Mothers' Meeting a titled lady once came in and said – 'I suppose, Father Stanton, you read these women a chapter in the Bible while they are at work?' 'Not so,' he said, 'I am at present reading "Nicholas Nickleby," and have just finished "Adam Bede." ' 'Then you begin, at least, with the Collect for the week.' 'As that Collect happened to be "Blessed Lord, who hast caused all Holy Scriptures to be written for our learning," &c., I did not think it quite appropriate to "Nicholas Nickleby," ' he said.

And the congregation who listened to the earnest words of this young preacher are not, be it understood, boys and girls. There were grizzled men, and young men in plenty. The women were in excess that snowy morning, it is true; but the congregation was more evenly balanced than in most London churches, and the poor were decidedly in the ascendant, and fully on a par with the rich. One very aged sister in ecclesiastical dress particularly attracted my attention by the way in which she hung on the words of the preacher and followed the beautiful music. Her face might have been that of a Mater Dolorosa or St Anna. It had a history in itself.

Father Stanton, young as he is, combines, in a very singular degree, the opposite elements of Ritualism and popularity, too often antagonistic, but why? His sermon might have, with few alterations, been preached in a Conventicle. Preached in the ultra-ritualistic Church of St Alban's, Holborn, it was a very exceptional one indeed; and, though not promising, from its subject, to be a distinctive one, proved, perhaps, as fair an example as I could have met with of the apparently incongruous personage – the Democratic Ritualist.

5.3.4 C. M. DAVIES ON 'MOODY-AND-SANKEYISM', 1875

While the American Evangelists were working in the great provincial towns of England and Scotland previously to their London visit, the outer circle, so to say, of the influence they were exerting elsewhere seemed to extend to the metropolis. . . . England had become for them, so to say, another Decapolis, and it was, indeed, an interesting problem whether the vast effects they have produced elsewhere were destined to be reproduced in the metropolis, or whether it should be as of old when Galilee was receptive but Jerusalem remained obdurate. For more than a week previously preparatory services had been held in the Agricultural Hall and other places, while an experiment – which turned out abortive through causes unconnected with the Evangelists or their friends – was made to compass a tabernacle service in Messrs Edgington's mammoth pavilion at the Kensington Oval. On the Sunday before their arrival, too, the burden of many sermons among their more immediate sympathizers was 'How shall we receive them?' But in truth the actual, though not the nominal, preparations for Messrs Moody and Sankey stretched much further back, and long antedated the announcement of their arrival. For a considerable period . . . noontide prayer-meetings . . . had been held in the heart of the City daily – a marvellous parenthesis in the whirl of business – where the hymns of Ira D. Sankey had become familiar in men's mouths. This had been a movement outside the Establishment, but the influence which radiated from these Evangelists as a centre seemed to have crossed the frontier line of the Church of England herself. On all sides there had been what might be claimed to be a 'great spiritual awakening.' The employment of lay agency in the Church had also received an immense impetus of late. It is not only – if at all – that there has been a dearth of clergy, but it has been ascertained that there are depths which can better be sounded by lay than clerical instrumentality, and this fact had certainly paved the way towards that climax, of lay evangelism at which we had now arrived, even if their work elsewhere did not suggest or sanction the idea.

A preliminary prayer-meeting was held at Exeter Hall, and was fairly attended, though neither of the Evangelists was present. Lord Radstock presided, and the Rev. Mr Chapman, chaplain of the Lock Hospital, delivered a suitable address. The number of ministers, clergy, and laymen on the platform was very large, and the singing of Mr Sankey's beautiful hymns was admirably conducted by Miss Bonar and a choir of ladies. Those selected were, first the 100th Psalm, which was given full-voiced and formed a most appropriate commencement; then 'Rejoice in the Lord,' with its refrain, 'Sound His praises, tell the story;' then 'I hear the Saviour say, thy strength, indeed, is small;' and finally, 'Hallelujah, thine the glory, revive us again.' It was in every respect a real revival service. The 'requests for prayers' were numerous and significant.

At the Agricultural Hall, in the evening, the gathering was all that could possibly be desired; every inch of the vast building was filled with a congregation numbering probably 15,000, representing all sections of the population of London. During the hour of waiting some of the best known of Mr Sankey's hymns were sung by an excellent choir, especially the beautiful one, 'Tell me the old, old story.' The pianissimo rendering of some of the passages in this was exceedingly telling, and could be heard distinctly over the whole building; for example, the touching stanza—

> Tell me the story softly,
>   That I may take it in,
> That wonderful redemption,
>   God's remedy for sin.

With admirable punctuality, Mr Moody made his appearance on the platform exactly at half-past seven, by which time the whole of the hall was filled. With some abruptness, and in a decidedly provincial accent, he gave out the verse, 'Praise God, from whom all blessings flow;' adding, 'All sing; let's praise God for what He's going to do.' The congregation responded heartily, every man and woman appearing to join full-voiced in the doxology. Then followed a brief prayer, after which Mr Moody gave out the 100th Psalm, again adding, 'Let all the people sing,' and certainly all the people did. It was a fine sight to see that vast assemblage rise, and a treat to hear their powerful unison. After a brief silent prayer, Mr Moody offered a special supplication for London. It was a great city, he said, but God was a great God. 'Thou God of Pentecost,' he said, 'give us a Pentecostal blessing here in London.' Then followed a solo by Mr Sankey, 'Jesus of Nazareth passeth by,' and for the first time was heard the clear notes of that rich voice ringing through the recesses of that spacious building. One excitable gentlemen caused a little contretemps by proposing a chorus, evidently not wishing that Mr Sankey should have it quite to himself, but Mr Moody was an admirable manager, and easily restrained the interrupter's unseasonable zeal. After 'Rock of Ages' had been sung to the tune of 'Rousseau's Dream,' the climax of the evening was reached. Mr Moody read a passage from 1 Cor. i. 17, with following verses, and commenced his address. God's people, he said, had generally been looked upon as the greatest fools in their respective times. Moses was not the sort of person we should have selected to save three millions of people, and when he asked who he should say had sent him, God 'drew him a blank cheque, and told him to fill it in with the name of Jah whenever necessary. Samson slew his enemies with what? The jawbone of an ass. Be always ready to grab up the first jawbone of an ass you come to, and let the world laugh as much as it likes.' London, he said, was a big city, but there were people enough in that hall then to save London. Amongst other unlikely people whom God had chosen to subserve his ends, he instanced 'The little tent-maker of Tarsus,' and 'The Bedforshire Tinker who wrote the "Pilgrim's Progress." ' His great fear, he said, in coming to London was lest the people should trust in man and forget God. The very teaching of the text was that God was everything and man nothing. There were hundreds of better preachers in London than himself, and yet he specially asked the aid of ministers in the metropolis, because he was not coming to undo their work, but simply to supplement it. He asked the aid of parents, too, and concluded an impressive and captivating address, comprised within most modest limits, by telling a story of a poor mother who had come to him in Liverpool to tell him how she had lost her son, a fine lad of seventeen, whom she believed to be in London. 'Perhaps the lad is before me now,' he said; 'if so, let me tell him his mother loves him still, and so too, like that poor mother, God loves us all.' On this he based a very fervent appeal for unity, and suddenly broke off as if inspired by the occasion, calling on Mr Sankey to sing the appropriate hymn, 'Hold the Fort.'

It was impossible to imagine a more signal success than that which attended this opening meeting. There was nothing sensational in the address, though there were several outbursts of genuine eloquence, agreeably varied with quaint touches of humour that provoked a smile, while they conveyed truths which one felt would go straight home to the hearts of the hearers. The proceedings terminated with the benediction, which was pronounced by the Rev. Dr Allon, of Islington.

I purposely avoided 'following' Messrs Moody and Sankey in their work at the Agricultural Hall in the same way as some correspondents had done, because I wanted to see whether the work really would prove ephemeral, as its detractors predicted, and also because it seemed slightly uninteresting, and not a little unfair withal to report addresses every day, which must in the nature of things involve considerable repetition. I waited with considerable curiosity to see first whether the interest would continue at the North of London, and what probabilities there seemed to be of its being reproduced in other districts, especially at the West End. One day a circular letter was addressed by Mr Moody to the clergy and ministers of the fashionable West End, inviting them to attend a meeting at the Opera House, Haymarket, on a Wednesday morning at ten o'clock, in anticipation of commencing work there the next week. I made a point of being present at that meeting, which consisted of about a hundred and

---

7 Inspired by an incident in the American Civil War, this rousing anthem remained a great favourite in Moody's revivals on both sides of the Atlantic and helped Sankey's *Sacred Songs and Solos* sell millions of copies, making it the evangelists' largest single source of income.

Sacred Songs and Solos.

No. 1. 𝔥𝔬𝔩𝔡 𝔱𝔥𝔢 𝔣𝔬𝔯𝔱 !

"That which ye have hold fast till I come."—Rev. ii. 25.

P. P. B.

P. P. Bliss.

1. Ho, my comrades! see the sig - nal Wav - ing in the sky!
2. See the migh - ty host ad-vanc-ing, Sa - tan lead-ing on:

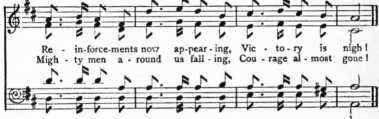

Re - in-force-ments now ap-pear - ing, Vic - to-ry is nigh!
Migh - ty men a - round us fall - ing, Cou - rage al - most gone!

Chorus.

"Hold the fort, for } I am com-ing," Je - sus sig - nals still,
"Hold fort, for }

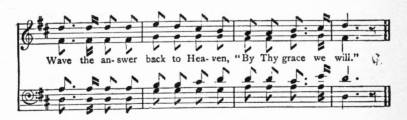

Wave the an- swer back to Hea- ven, "By Thy grace we will."

3. See the glorious banner waving !
   Hear the trumpet blow !
   In our Leader's name we'll triumph
   Over every foe !

4. Fierce and long the battle rages,
   But our help is near :
   Onward comes our great Commander,
   Cheer, my comrades, cheer !

fifty individuals, mostly clerical, but including a few well-known laymen; among others, the Earl of Shaftesbury, Sir Harry Verney, Mr Samuel Morley, M.P., Mr S. Blackwood, &c. As I passed up the familiar staircase, and peeped through the box-doors into the house, I found extensive preparations being made, and everything smelling of fresh-planed deal. The pit was boarded over, and looked like the arena of a large circus, while the stage resembled the seats in an infant school, rising tier above tier. On all sides were heard the sounds of axes and hammers, and with one hasty glance I sped towards the place of conclave. In the chair was the Rev. C. D. Marston, vicar of St Paul's, Brompton, where he succeeded the Rev. Capel Molyneux; and on his right hand was seated Mr Moody in lay attire, and seeming to take little interest in a somewhat warm discussion which was going on around him. He toyed with his umbrella after the manner of a man who had made up his mind and was not to be moved from his purpose, and my subsequent experiences proved that I read his physiognomy aright. The point in debate was this – a large building had been erected at Bow for East London, and the Victoria Theatre was shortly to be secured for the South. The North had already been provided for at the Agricultural Hall, and Mr Moody was so elated with his success there that he could not entertain any proposal to abandon it entirely. In fact he had but one answer (like Wordsworth's little girl) to all questions, and it was 'I wun't.' The original scheme was, it appears, that one month should be given to each London district. That period had now expired at Islington, though the tenure of the hall still continued. Mr Moody averred that the month at the Agricultural Hall ought to be considered one of six weeks, for it had taken him a fortnight to feel the people's pulse, and now his success was most marked. He tested it by the inquiry-room. 'I could not,' he said, 'with a clear conscience, leave 10,000 people at Islington to speak to 3000 at the Opera House.' In reply to those who suggested that a different class would be reached there, he said the poor man's soul was as valuable as the rich man's, and seemed to imply that his own mission was rather to the lower and middle than to the upper classes. To this the Earl of Shaftesbury replied that though it was quite true that the poor man's soul was worth as much as the rich man's, yet Mr Moody must remember that when one of the upper ten thousand was converted his wealth and influence were turned into a right channel, and so he became the means of doing more good. He believed that the simple Gospel preaching of Mr Moody was just what was wanted to win these people, and suggested that he should make the experiment for a week; but Mr Moody played with his umbrella, and looked, though he did not say, 'I wun't.' When, however, Mr Marston leant over to him and suggested that he should leave himself in the hands of the meeting, then he not only looked, but said in an extremely audible stage whisper, 'I wun't leave myself in the hands of no meeting nor no committee.' 'Twas throwing words away,' as Wordsworth said of the immovable little girl above mentioned, and gradually the meeting accommodated itself to this view of things. Mr Morley pleaded, and minister after minister pleaded, that the West should not be neglected. Mr Moody did not think they were being neglected. He thought if he stirred the people up at the morning and afternoon services they would listen to another minister at night. On this the assembly was divided. Some thought that the evening service had better be given up altogether if Mr Moody would not come. Others said that would be a confession of failure. Local ministers urged that there was a vast poor population as well as rich around the Opera House; that Westminister and Chelsea would send their contingents to swell the evening congregations. 'Try it for a week,' again suggested Lord Shaftesbury; 'and if you can't get on with us immovable people, turn to the Gentiles.' But Moody was adamant. He smiled, but his heart was with his Islington Gentiles. A young minister in the back benches timidly said that if Mr Moody could not come Mr Sankey might; but the reply was still, 'No, Sankey wun't.' I never in all my life saw a man so thoroughly impenetrable to all suggestions as this American Evangelist. I have no doubt he owes his success greatly to this, and the meeting evidently thought so too. They accepted what they might fairly have considered discourtesy in another person as a sign that Mr Moody was overruled to do the work in his own way.

Eventually it came to a show of hands. Formal resolutions were framed – (1) That the morning prayer meeting and afternoon Bible class should commence on the following Tuesday, under the personal superintendence of Messrs Moody and Sankey; and (2) that the evening meeting should be held without him, whilst he divided his attention between Bow and Islington. This was to be tried for a week, and it was suggested that the meeting should choose a superintendent for the evenings; but no, again the inflexible Mr Moody must name the man, and he named him in two syllables – 'Black-wood.' About this there was no difficulty. The meeting had in fact already named Mr Stephenson Blackwood, who accepted the office, and all was pleasantly settled.

This nearer view of Mr Moody gave me, as I have said, a very probable clue to his marvellous influence. He was what the Spiritualists call 'positive' to a degree I had never witnessed before. I am quite sure if Mr Moody sat at a *séance* and wished no manifestations to take place, none would. His manner was brusque to a degree that was ludicrous. He always referred to a speaker as 'that man.' 'That man has made my speech for me,' he said of somebody with whom he agreed. 'He's said just what I was a-going to say.' It seemed a marvellous instance of history repeating itself – the herdsman of Tekoa, without man's qualifications, carrying point after point against the Amaziahs, who had all external advantages to command – if mortals ever could command – success.

5.4   THE MISSION TO THE POOR

While the parish organization of the established churches could be adapted to deal with pressing urban needs, the problem of poverty remained generally intractable. The reason was not simply that the urban poor became more numerous in the Victorian age and the churches lacked the qualified personnel to deal with them. Very often the churches themselves also stood in the way of effective outreach. Their wealth and privilege, coupled with a sense of spiritual pride, caused them to regard the poor with a mixture of fear and condescension. And nothing was easier to detect. No amount of parish reforms and mission schemes could finally bridge the class divide, although there were various creative attempts. One 'working clergyman' in London's East End testified to the success of self-help: poor people, led by a suitable missionary curate, had paid for and built up a church for themselves. Revivalist methods had helped extend their work to those who were 'almost heathens', so that within ten years, the clergyman predicted, 'the rant of the political babbler will be in vain' (**5.4.1**). Here the atmosphere of patronage and paternalism is unmistakable, but it was not peculiar to the Church of England. The clergyman's article appeared in the *Wesleyan Methodist Magazine,* which had borrowed it enthusiastically from an Anglican counterpart. Not many years later, though, the established churches evinced a changing attitude. In 1888 Donald Macleod (1831–1916), minister of Park Parish in Glasgow, offered more than prayer and philanthropy in supporting an overture on non-church-going laid before the General Assembly of the Church of Scotland. To him, those in straitened domestic circumstances were not necessarily the 'home heathen'. The Church must create a right public opinion in relation to their needs and throw open its rented pews, thereby bringing one class under the beneficial influence of the other and promoting social stability. The 'mission-hall' with its segregated congregation was no solution at all (**5.4.2**). In London, Samuel Barnett (1844–1913), rector of St Jude's, Whitechapel, would certainly have agreed, although the 'university settlement' movement he inaugurated at Toynbee Hall offered a good deal more than an adjunct to the parochial system that Macleod held dear. In Barnett's work ecclesiastical paternalism became moderately progressive through social and political welfare ministries to 'improve the condition of the people' (**5.4.3**). Yet it may still be wondered whether an Oxbridge college, transplanted as a quasi-colonial 'settlement' into the heart of the ethnic East End, could actually have been regarded by the mass of local inhabitants as 'common ground' on which the classes could meet.

5.4.1 HOME MISSION WORK IN THE EAST OF LONDON, 1875

It used to be thought that it was desirable to build a church *at once* in a spiritually-destitute district. The experience of the Bethnal Green churches suggested a suspicion that there might possibly be a 'more excellent way' of working. Practically it was found at the outset that the Spitalfields weavers and the Bethnal Green shoemakers did not gush out in a burst of irrepressible gratitude for the erection of a church among them, built and subsidized by West End wealth. In fact, like the stalwart men of the Black Country, they were somewhat inclined to "eave 'arf a brick-bat' at their well-intentioned benefactors. The church was reckoned at the value of the proverbial 'gift-horse,' and they were perpetually, in defiance of all established rules of politeness, 'looking it in the mouth.' Was it possible, then, to adopt another plan of action, which might enlist the sympathies of the dwellers in the spiritually-necessitous districts, and make them realise that their new church was not to be regarded as the kindly aggression of West End wealth, but as their own spiritual home, reared by their own exertions, and adorned, at least in some measure, by their own self-denial? Experience had shown that it was no use setting a man down to a good dinner if he had no appetite. Was it possible to create this appetite? The best answer is to write out for you the prescription of the tonic prepared for the districts in question. In other words, I will briefly give you the history of a 'mission:' allowing for varieties of circumstances, the history of one mission may be said to be typical of all.

Five years ago, a new church had been erected in an increasing suburban parish of thirty thousand people. This had been separated from the mother church; but so rapid was the progress of building in the neighbourhood, that the daughter church was compelled to seek help from the Bishop of London's Fund. To build another church at that time was out of the question. What, then, was the mode of action? A site for a possible church in the future was secured, a commodious school-church was erected, and a missionary curate, to whose charge four thousand people were assigned, was appointed. Every Sunday, and at least once in the week, the people were invited to come to the school-church for service. They were encouraged from the first to take an interest in the services, and to regard them as *their own*. Parents whose boys sang in the simple choir, or whose children attended the Sunday-school, formed the nucleus of the first band of worshippers. The first Sunday – it happened also to be New Year's day – was a dreary, bleak day, and at the morning service there were not more than twenty people, and we had ten communicants. Before a year had passed, our communicants numbered ninety-six.

From the very first the object and aim of our work, after presenting to them the great truths of the Gospel, was to teach the people that the work was their own. By their own weekly offerings the frugal expenses of our school-church were maintained; their own sons sang in our choir; many of the elders taught in our Sunday-school. It was one family; and so, when the time came for building the church, the pile, which was rising in their midst, was already for them their own church. We had shared our troubles and joys. In that dark season when the hand of God was upon us in the visitation of sickness, all stood together. The cholera raged among us. Two working men gladly gave up their time to minister to the sufferers. A Committee, consisting exclusively of working men, (for we had no others,) organized and distributed the much-needed relief; and one day the Bishop of London was asked to receive a deputation of working men from the East End of London. What did they want? They wanted a church, and they came to the bishop and asked him to help them. In two years the population had increased to upwards of seven thousand; and on the ground which five years ago was a bare space, there now stands a handsome church, with an old school-church, which will soon be the smallest in a fine group of school-buildings. . . .

One agency, which was very useful, was the *prayer-meeting*. People come to church and listen to a sermon, which impresses them; and, too often, when they return home, the keen edge of the Word is blunted by a return to the ordinary thoughts and cares of life. If possible, therefore, it is a grand thing to 'strike while the iron is hot.' For this purpose a Sunday evening prayer-meeting, held occasionally after evening service, is most useful. A soul-stirring hymn, an extempore prayer, a brief exposition of a verse of Scripture – these things tend to fix and deepen in their hearts the impression which has been made.

Thus also is opened up an opportunity of intercourse with individuals. You have seen that rough fellow in his working-clothes two or three times at church lately. He dropped in shyly at first; and when he found there was no beadle to repel him, he grew bolder. Where in that waste of streets does this man live? Inquiry is made on all hands, but nobody seems to know anything about him. At last one Sunday evening he comes into the prayer-meeting. He is now fairly in the net, and the warm shake of the hand and the word of friendly welcome have paved the way for close dealing with the soul, and earnest pressure upon him of the need of decision. Over this part of the meeting I would desire to draw a veil of reserve, and only say that I have known many who have there 'found peace' with God, and are now consistently walking in the way of God's commandments. . . .

Those with whom we have to deal are too often almost heathens; baptized, indeed, into the name of Christ, but knowing nothing practically of the Gospel. To such the truth must be brought home by simple and unconventional methods, and then deeper teaching can be employed to lead them on in the way of holiness. No doubt the 'respectability' of the National Church has too often had a repellent effect upon the poor and ignorant. The religion of well-cushioned pews was at least not for them. I think it was Dr. Vaughan who said lately that what we want more than anything is to foster 'congregational life.' There is nothing which helps to do this better than the prayer-meeting. People may sit side by side in church Sunday after Sunday, and never know each other; but in the familiar atmosphere of the schoolroom, kindly words are interchanged between those who might otherwise have remained strangers. . . .

It is time, however, to say something about the habits of the people among whom we labour. Dean Stanley has spoken of the 'romance' of East London work. He is right. Those streets, with their dead-level of houses so provokingly like each other, often hide stories that Mudie would find it a fortune to get hold of. You must not, however, imagine that there are no distinctions of class among us. There is the honest working-man, who pays his way, and can look every one in the face, and who, when 'evil days come,' leaves you to find out the distress which his manly heart refuses to reveal. There is a wide chasm between 'the lady who lives in the back kitchen' and 'the lady what has the two-pair back.' There is the woman who has seen better days; and if you happen to ask her where Mrs. So-and-so lives, she replies, with a slight toss of her head, that she really doesn't know, for 'she never makes no acquaintances.' There is the small tradesman who keeps the chandler's shop, and 'the gentleman who goes round with the vegetables,' and 'the good lady who sells the pins and tape.'

There is an innate politeness in the East End mind. They are nature's freeborn ladies and gentlemen. Then what shall we say of the rising generation – the hopeless bundles of 'Ginx's babies' that toddle in our streets, and roll in our gutters? Poor little street Arabs! I suppose now they will be compelled to learn; and I have reluctantly come to the conclusion that there is no hope for them except in compulsory education. When I was in Bethnal Green we had the complaint known as 'famine,' or 'relapsing fever,' widely prevalent among us. All the doctors said that good food was what the children needed, and shook their surgical heads and assured us that 'prevention was better than cure.' Good food, however, was exactly the thing which these poor little ones could not get. I determined to try the experiment of a meat dinner for a halfpenny. We issued fifty tickets at a halfpenny each. The purchaser of the ticket was entitled to a plate of Irish stew and a piece of bread. The dinner cost us a little over a penny, so that the deficiency had to be made up by the contributions of friends. We had these dinners twice a-week, and so popular did our entertainments become, that we fed four hundred children and upwards every week. The meat used was Australian. It was minced very fine, and mixed with a quantity of vegetables. If there were any left over, 'mother' used to send a little dark-eyed urchin with the message, 'Please, mother says, can she buy a basin of soup?'

We got to know and love these shoeless, bonnetless children. A lady of rank sent me some clothing for the more destitute; and one result of our Sunday dinners was that, in addition to our regular Sunday-school, we had to establish a mission-school for some of these little ones. Then we got to know the match-box makers and their wants. I fear if I had met a certain statesman just after he had promulgated his Budget, my language towards him would have been characterised by vigour rather than politeness. Of all the outrageous imposts ever contemplated in a civilized country, the '*ex luce lucellum*' scheme was, in my opinion, the most barbarous and the most heartless.

One of our great difficulties in East London work is the judicious distribution of relief. What is to be done with that gaunt, staring giant whom we encounter each winter? I mean, *Pauperism*. There is much talk about the organization of charitable relief. Indeed, I sometimes fear that we shall soon have all 'organization,' and no 'charity.' Much has undoubtedly been done towards the repression of mendicity; but still, as we prepare each year to face our winter campaign, the vision of this great difficulty comes upon us with increased force. It would be presumption in me to suggest a remedy, when the minds of so many are concentrated on the solution of the problem; and therefore I content myself with mentioning it as one of our greatest difficulties. . . .

You may ask, perhaps, 'What can you do among the people? can you hope even to humanize them?' I answer, 'No!' But the Gospel of Christ can. Men may talk, but my experience in the east of London tells me that we may say with confidence, 'Give us ten years; nay, give us five, and the rant of the political babbler will be in vain.'

5.4.2   D. MACLEOD ON NON-CHURCH-GOING AND HOUSING OF THE POOR IN GLASGOW, 1888

When we touch upon the question of the non-church-going population in Glasgow, we may be struck by the remarkable approximation of the figures given as representing the non-church-goers, and those which represent the people living in one-roomed houses. We assert in this overture that there are 120,000 in Glasgow going to no church; and in that most interesting and touching lecture, 'Life in One Room' [by Dr Russell, the medical officer for the city of Glasgow, which I was permitted to circulate with the Assembly papers], you will find that there are 126,000 of our population living in houses of one room. The coincidence is suggestive. The figures indicate a close connection – as between cause and effect. But even had these figures not been so approximate, we would, upon other grounds, have been compelled to connect the two facts. Undoubtedly life in one room suggests poverty and want of church-clothes, and these must prove quite as great hindrances as religious indifference. The pressure of the struggle for existence, and the hard battle for the necessaries of life – which bring many of our decent working people to the one-roomed house, and compel them to live under the burden of anxieties that often alienate their interest from spiritual things – most undoubtedly influence the habit of church-going. . . .

In asking you to consider for a moment the conditions of life in a one-roomed house, I would caution you against indulging in generalisations which would inflict a cruel wrong on many of our people. We must never put down the people who dwell there, or who go to no church, as necessarily ungodly, coarse, and impure. . . . Nay, far be it from me to apply the term 'home heathen' to those who perhaps never enter our churches. There are thousands, I feel assured, men and women, God-fearing and true, who, through the constraints imposed upon them by those habits of society which expect that every attender at church should be dressed in a particular manner, and also through the evil methods inherent in the system of seat-letting, into which we have permitted almost all our city and parish churches to fall, are compelled against their wills to worship God, as many do worship God, at their firesides. I will go further and assert that, in the sight of God, there is many a life of self-sacrifice and duty lived by poor men and poor women, who have scarcely been taught the Gospel of the Lord Jesus Christ, but which in His eye may be as truly Christian as those of the luxurious and wealthy pietists, who nurse religious sentimentalisms free from the difficulties against which their poorer brethren have to contend. Therefore, I say, we must be very cautious how we apply the term 'home heathen' to those masses who are classified as non-church-going. But, making full allowance for these considerations, assuredly no language can exaggerate the almost tragic picture of life in one room given in the touching lecture to which I have already alluded. Non-church-going! Why, that is the least of it. There is something far more elementary to be considered. It is civilisation itself, with its common proprieties, and its primary duties and privileges, which is being outraged in a fearful number of instances. I ask you to consider these facts: 30 per cent of the houses in Glasgow are houses of one room; 25 per cent, one-fourth of the population, live in one room, with an average of three to each, but embracing thousands in which five, six, and seven inmates are in one room, and hundreds of instances in which there are from eight up to thirteen inhabitants living in one room.

Think of it! Father and mother, grown-up sons and daughters, all compelled to herd together in a single apartment, – nay, in addition to the members of the families, there are one in seven of these single-roomed houses in which there are lodgers (strange men generally) brought in to live amid what ought to be the privacy of domestic life. . . . What a suggestive picture! How shocking and arresting are the facts given by Dr Russell as regards the death-rate among children, belonging to these houses! While 38 per 1000 is the rate of mortality among them, it is only 16 or 17 in larger houses. . . .

. . . I ask you, in the name of common-sense, what can you expect to be the result? Some may say, and they say truly, that these evils are the consequence of intemperance. No doubt it is so frequently. I have myself known a family in which the united earnings came to over £120 a-year living in one room, in which there was not a stick of furniture, and all arising from drink. But if intemperance is often the cause, I assert that it is as often the consequence of these conditions of living. Think of the life of many a working man coming home from his day's hard labour, tired and depressed, to one of these houses. It may be that the wife has a washing, and the atmosphere is full of the steam of the washing-tub and of the clothes hung up to dry, and she, poor soul! is perhaps irritable and tired also; the children, as children always are, noisy and restless; the baby, whom the mother has scarcely time to attend, crying and fretful in the cradle. What can a man in these circumstances do? Do you expect every evening the sweet picture presented of the book taken down to read, and a re-creation in the one-roomed house of 'The Cottar's Saturday Night'? Alas! the room up several stairs in a close in Glasgow is a different affair from the cottage in Ayrshire, amid fresh air and a thousand outside beauties. Where is the man to go for relaxation, or rather for escape from the state of things I have pictured? If he goes to the 'close-mouth' or to the street to smoke his pipe, he is met by the chill air of the foggy frosty night and an atmosphere laden with the smoke and fumes of manufactories. Where is any resource to be found? Need I answer? The only resource he finds is too frequently the public-house. Or, I ask you to imagine the life of the labouring man's wife. She may be, as many of them are, a woman who has been trained to method and system, and who can make the fireside bright for her husband; but how many of these poor mothers, with the very best intentions, have not been so trained? They are overwhelmed with toil – children to clothe, babies to feed, houses to tidy, the washing, cooking, and the thousand little economies that fall upon one who has to manage a little wage, making it meet house-rent, school fees, and a thousand petty expenses, – these, accumulating a burden of care upon what is often a feeble frame and nervous temperament, produce naturally prostration and despair, and a craving for anything which will break up the monotony of ceaseless anxiety, and afford some stimulus and excitement to raise her, even momentarily, above herself. She also is led to the terrible resource of strong drink. Fathers and brethren, you remember the story of Bunyan, who, when he saw the man brought to execution, said – 'There goes John Bunyan but for the grace of God.' Dare we, as we contemplate the trials of our poorer brethren, and the sins of intemperance into which they are so often betrayed, assume the Pharisaic attitude of those who thank God they are not as those who have so fallen in the battle of life? Nay, rather, but for the grace of God and for the circumstances of life in which by His mercy we have been placed, would we be better than they?

I thank God that the Church of Scotland is called on to take up this question of the dwellings of the poor. In these later days we have been taught much by science regarding the influence of 'environment' and of 'the law of heredity.' Let us be thankful for such teaching. Let us wisely reflect upon the close connection between the physical and the moral or spiritual life; but while we accept these lessons, and while we are bound to go to the physical sources out of which the evils we deplore have sprung, we must not forget that we as Christians have a gospel of hope to preach, of which physical science can tell nothing. We have to protest against the necessitarianism which would hand over society to the inexorable fulfilment of the law of heredity and the influence of physical surroundings. We have to declare the possibilities which are involved in every human existence; the possibilities arising from the freedom of the will, with its responsibilities, which God has bestowed upon all men. We have to vindicate the power of spiritual truth and spiritual life, through which we can awake the moral energies that may be lying dormant. We have to carry the Gospel of the good tidings of the Fatherhood of God, and of the redemption that is in the Lord Jesus, to every man, believing that these are the powers whereby the stream of heredity may be turned into a new channel, and man, when he recognises his destiny as made in the image of God, may be brought to create for himself new and better surroundings. But the Church has not been using the full instrumentality committed to her by her great Master. Christ cared for the body as well as for the soul, and it must be ours to embrace within the field of our operations everything which tends to the physical and social as well as spiritual welfare of the people.

But the question arises, What are we to do? Are we to turn the Church into a great house-building society? That assuredly is not its function. What the Church has primarily to do is to create a right public opinion. The Church has to teach the fact that Christianity means more than the saving of a man's soul when he dies; that it has more to do for these so-called 'lapsed masses' than to assault them with armies of district visitors, and shower upon them tracts and good advices, while we are leaving them to swelter in dens, and under conditions where Christian life is so difficult, if not impossible, to realise. If we create a right public opinion, we will soon discover that opinion taking shape in active movement; and I would suggest that it would not be an unworthy act of this General Assembly were it to address a Pastoral Letter to the country, drawing the attention of our people to the evils which have been described, and asking them in the name of Christ and of our common patriotism to take action in the way of remedy. . . .

Another remedy for the evils which are suggested in this overture is the bringing of class into greater contact with class. One of the sad features connected with the growth of our large cities is the wide separation in distance between the houses of the rich and of the poor. This does not exist in so marked a form in London as it does in many of our provincial towns. You will find in London the mews and lanes, where the poor live, in close proximity to the most fashionable squares. It is not so in Glasgow, nor in Edinburgh, nor in many other towns I could name. With us the distance between the West End with its palaces, and the East End with its poverty-stricken streets, may be measured by miles. Our overture, therefore, suggests that something ought to be done to bring the influences which one class of the population can beneficially exercise upon the other into more active operation.

The last remedy embraced in this overture, and on which I would now dwell, is that the Church at large should seek to make the parochial territorial system more efficient. The Presbytery of Glasgow may be described as consisting chiefly of *quoad sacra* parishes, and as I had on a former occasion to state to the General Assembly, so I now repeat it, that these are parish churches only in name, and that they have become this from the system of seat-letting on which they all depend. The effect is such that the churches belong to the seat-holders and not to the parishioners, and the minister belongs to the congregation and not to the parish. I am quite aware that in many instances territorial work of a kind is carried out by the ministers of *quoad sacra* churches; but even with the most earnest labouring in poor localities, these ministers are met by an initial difficulty, for at the church door the poor parishioners who may wish to attend are met by the demand for seat-rents, or else by the necessity of occupying seats that have been allocated to the poor – an alternative which the independent working man of small means is most unwilling to accept. I utterly dislike the separation of classes which is created by a mission-hall for working people, while the church is kept for those who can pay for it. This seems to me a denial of the true character of the Church of Scotland. It is an abnegation of that parochial system on which we have hitherto prided ourselves. . . .

What I propose is, that the General Assembly should inaugurate a movement in favour of Free and Open churches. You might begin by making an experiment, taking one or two of the neediest and most typical districts in some of our great cities. You might select a parish, be it *quoad sacra* or not, to which a district of the kind I have described has been already allocated. You should go to the minister and managers of that church and say – 'We will give you such a grant as will secure you against loss, on condition that you throw this church open to the parishioners, and that the minister shall confine himself to house-to-house work in the parish.' I am aware that this touches again on a delicate point, because the money would be thrown away if you had not the fit kind of minister in such a church who would work efficiently as well as territorially. If he were a lump of wood or a piece of ice, there would be little use in offering to him such a grant. You must have the right kind of man to be minister, as well as the right kind of church and district. I am, however, afraid that such a proposal may be offensive to my friend Dr Story and others, who may suspect us of inaugurating a movement for paying ministers 'by results.' Well, I do not care for such criticism if only the work can be done. You may possibly wound the susceptibilities of 'the profession' in some instances, but that seems a small risk to run compared with the benefits which might accrue to our people.

But . . . everything depends on the motives on which we undertake such a work. If we are entering on this battle against the evils of society for the object merely of getting our churches filled and our church statistics run up; if in going to the people we give them the slightest suspicion that the chief end we have in view is to get them to go 'to our Church,' we will fail, and deservedly fail. But if we go to them in self-forgetfulness; if in our life as well as in our language we say that we do not care what Church they may go to; that we, as a National Church, care chiefly for the good of the nation; that we desire 'not to be ministered unto, but to minister,' – then work done from such motives will never be misunderstood, but will be rich in fruit of the most noble character for our dear country. . . .

Fathers and Brethren, no more important subject can come before you than that which has been so imperfectly touched on by me. No theme should appeal with greater effect to the heart of patriot and Christian. Dr Scott spoke yesterday of the social dangers threatening our country. I do not believe that the opinions to which he referred have touched to any serious extent the working classes in this country. There are many noisy agitators abroad, but I believe that our working men are perfectly sound at heart. Nevertheless, the only security for the stability of our national life lies in the religious life of our people. If any of you wish to be haunted with the nightmare of what a nation can become which has lost faith in God, I would have you read the remarkable article [by Frederick W. H. Myers, in the May number of the 'Nineteenth Century'], which gives a picture of the decadence of faith in France. We have there a revelation of the abyss into which a people can fall which has lost faith in God, a terrible and tragic spectacle of despair, of suicidal mania and hopelessness. Far be it from me to say that France is wholly without faith and religion; but . . . when you remember that what is in France to-day may be over Europe to-morrow, – we are urged as patriots as well as Christians to turn all our strength, and all our best energies and our most earnest prayers, towards the solution of this mighty national problem.

5.4.3 S. A. BARNETT ON THE UNIVERSITIES AND THE POOR, 1884

The poor need more than food: they need the knowledge, the character, the happiness which is the gift of God to this age. . . . Those who have cared for them are not content with the hope offered by 'scientific charity.' They see that the best things might be common, and they cannot stand aside and do nothing. 'The cruellest man living,' it has been said, 'could not sit at his feast unless he sat blindfold,' and those who see must do something. They may be weary of revolutionary schemes, which turn the world upside down to produce after anarchy another unequal division; they may be weary, too, of philanthropic schemes which touch but the edge of the question. They may hear of dynamite, and they may watch the failure of an Education Act, as the prophets watched the failure of teachers without knowledge. They may criticise all that Philanthropists and Governments do, but still they themselves would do something. No theory of progress, no proof that many individuals among the poor have become rich, will satisfy them; they simply face the fact that in the richest country of the world the great mass of their countrymen live without the knowledge, the character, and the fulness of life which is the best gift to this age, and that some thousands either beg for their daily bread or live in anxious misery about a wretched existence. What can they do which revolutions, which missions, and which money have not done?

It is in answer to this question I make the suggestion of this paper. I make it especially as a development of the idea which underlies a College Mission. These Missions, if I understand them rightly, are generally inaugurated by a visit to a college from some well-known clergyman working in the East End of London or in some such working-class quarter. He speaks to the undergraduates of the condition of the poor, and he rouses their sympathy. A committee is appointed, subscriptions are promised, and after some negotiations a young clergyman, a former member of the school or college, is appointed as a Mission curate of a district. He at once sets in motion the usual parochial machinery of district visiting, mothers' meetings, clubs, &c. He invites the assistance of those of his old mates who will help; at regular intervals he makes a report of his progress, and if all goes well he is at last able to tell how the district has become a parish.

The Mission, good as its influence may be, is not, it seems to me, an adequate expression of the idea which moved the promoters. The hope in the College was that all should join in good work, and the Mission is necessarily a Churchman's effort. The desire was, that as University men they should themselves bear the burdens of the poor – and the Mission requires of them little more than an annual guinea subscription. The grand idea which moved the college, the idea which, like a new creative spirit, is brooding over the face of Society, and is making men conscious of their brotherhood, finds no adequate expression in the district church machinery with which, in East London, I am familiar. There is little in that machinery which helps the people to conceive of religion apart from sectarianism, of a Church which is 'the nation bent on righteousness.' There is little, too, in the ordinary parochial mechanism which will carry to the homes of the poor a share of the best gifts now enjoyed in the University. . . .

. . . It is to members of the Universities anxious to unite in a common purpose of bettering the lives of the people, that I make the suggestion that University Settlements will better express their idea. College Missions have done some of the work on which they have been sent, but in their very nature their field is limited. It is in no opposition to these missions, but rather with a view to more fully cover their idea, that I propose the new scheme. The details of the plan may be shortly stated.

The place of settlement must of course first be fixed. It will be in some such poor quarter as that of East London, where a house can be taken in which there shall be both habitable chambers and large reception rooms. A man must be chosen to be the chief of the Settlement; he must receive a salary which, like that of the Mission curate, will be guaranteed by the college, and he must make his home in the house. He must have taken a good degree, be qualified to teach, and be endowed with the enthusiasm of humanity. Such men are not hard to find; men who under a wiser Church government would be clergymen, and serve the people as the nation's ministers; but who, under a Church government which in an age of reform has remained unreformed, are kept outside, and fret in other service. One of these, qualified by training to teach, qualified by character to organise and command, qualified by disposition to make friends with all sorts of men, would gladly accept a position in which he could both earn a livelihood and fulfil his calling. He would be the centre of the University Settlement. Men fresh from college or old University men would come to occupy the chambers. Lecturers in connection with the

University Extension Society would be his fellow-lecturers in the reception rooms. As the head of such a Settlement he would be welcomed by all such classes in his new neighbourhood.

The old Universities exercise a strange charm, and the Oxford or Cambridge man is still held to possess some peculiar knowledge; the fact that three of the most democratic boroughs are represented by University professors has its explanation. 'He speaks beautiful German, but of course those University gentlemen ought to,' was a man's reflection to me after a talk with a Cambridge professor. Those, too, who may be supposed to know what draws in an advertising poster, are always glad to print after the name of a speaker his degree and college. Thus it would be that the head of the Settlement would find himself as closely related to his new surroundings as to his old. The same reputation, which would draw to him fellow-scholars or old pupils, would put him in a position to discover the work and thought going on around him. He would become familiar with the teachers in the elementary and middle-class schools, he would measure the work done by clergy and missionaries, he would be in touch with the details of local politics; and more than all, he would come into sympathy with the hope, the unnamed hope, which is moving in the masses.

The Settlement would be common ground for all classes. In the lecture room the knowledge gathered at the highest sources would, night after night, be freely given. In the conversation rooms the students would exchange ideas and form friendships. At the weekly receptions of all sorts and conditions of men the settlers would mingle freely in the crowd.

The internal arrangements would be simple enough. The Head would undertake the domestic details and fix the price which settlers would pay for board and lodging. He would admit new members and judge if the intentions of those who offered were honest. Some would come for their vacations; others occupied during the daytime would come to live there. University men, barristers, Government clerks, curates, medical students, or business men, each would have opportunity both for solitary and for associated life, and the expense would be various to suit their various means. The one uniting bond would be the common purpose, 'not without action to die fruitless,' but to do something to improve the condition of the people. It would be the duty of the Head to keep alive among his fellows the freshness of their purpose, 'to recall the stragglers, refresh the outworn, praise and reinspire the brave.' He would have, therefore, to judge of the powers of each to fill places to which he could introduce them. To some he would recommend official positions, to some teaching, to some the organisation of relief, to some the visiting of the sick, and thus infuse new life into existing churches, chapels, and institutions. Others he would introduce as members of Co-operative Societies, Friendly Societies, or Political Clubs. He would so arrange that all should occupy positions in which they would become friends of his neighbours, and discover, perhaps as none have yet discovered, how to meet their needs.

To such an institution it is easy to see how development might be immeasurable. A born leader of men surrounded by a group of intelligent and earnest friends, pledged not 'to go round in an eddy of purposeless dust,' and placed face to face with the misery and apathy they know to be wrong, would of necessity discover means beyond our present vision. They would bind themselves by sympathy and service to the lives of the people; they would bring the light and strength of intelligence to bear on their government, and they would give a voice both to their needs and their wrongs. It is easy to imagine what such settlers in a great town might do, but it will be more to the point to consider how they may express the idea which underlies the College Mission, the interest of centres of education in the centres of industry, and the will of University men to improve the condition of the people.

If it be that the Missionary's account of his Mission district fails at last to rouse the interest of his hearers, and if his work seems to be absorbed in the effort to keep going his parochial machinery, amid a host of like machines, the same cannot be the fate of the Settlement.

Some of the settlers will settle themselves for longer periods, and those who are occupied during the daytime will find it as possible to live among the poor as among the rich; but there must also be room for those who can spend only a few weeks or months in the Settlement, so that men may come, as some already have come, to spend part of a vacation in serving the people. This interchange of life between the University and the Settlement will keep up between the two a living tie. Each term will bring, not a set speech about the work of the Mission, but the many chats on the wonders of human life. The condition of the English people will come to be a fact more familiar than that of the Grecian or Roman, and the history of the College Settlement will be better known than that of the boat or the eleven. Thoughts, too, and feelings now too often spent in vain talks at debating societies, will go up to refresh those who are spent by labour, or find an outlet in action. There is no fear that the College Settlement will fail to rouse interest. Its life will be the life of the College. As long as both draw their strength from the common source, from the same body of members, the sympathy of the College will be with the people. Nor is there any fear lest the work of the settlers become stereotyped, as is often the case with the work of Missions and Societies. Each year, each term, would alter the constitution of the Settlement as other settlers brought in other characters and the results of other knowledge, or as their ideas became modified by common work with the various religious and secular organisations of the neighbourhood. The danger, indeed, would not be from uniformity of method or narrowness of aim; rather would it be the endeavour of the Head to limit the diversity which many minds would introduce, and restrain a liberality willing to see good in every form of earnestness. The variety of work which would embrace the most varied effort, and enlist its members in every movement for the common good, would keep about the Settlement the beauty of a perpetual promise.

If we go further and ask how this plan reaches deeper than others which have gone before, the question is not so easily answered, because it is impossible to prophesy that a University Settlement will make the poor rich or give them the necessaries of true life. Inasmuch, though, as poverty – poverty in its large sense including poverty of the knowledge of God and man – is largely due to the division of classes, a University Settlement does provide a remedy which goes deeper than that provided by popular philanthropy. The poor man of modern days has to live in a quarter of the town where he cannot even try to live with those superior to himself. Around him are thousands educated as he has been educated, with taste and with knowledge on a level with his own. The demand for low things has created a supply of low satisfactions. Thus it is that the amusements are unrecreative, the lectures uninstructive, and the religion uninspiring. It is not possible for the inhabitant of the poor quarter to come into casual intercourse with the higher manners of life and thought except at a cost which would constitute a large percentage of his income.

I am afraid that it is long before we can expect the rich and poor again to live as neighbours: for good or evil they have been divided, and other means must, for the present, be found for making common the property of knowledge. One such means is the University Settlement. Men who have the knowledge may become friends of the poor; they may share that knowledge and its fruit as, day by day, they meet in their common rooms for talk or for instruction, for music or for play. The settlers may join in all that is done by other societies, but they, as members of no other society, may share all their best with the poor, and in the highest sense make their property common. They may be the best charity agents, for they will have an experience out of the reach of others, which they will have accumulated through their different agencies. Members of various secular and religious organisations, they may be able to compare notes after the day's work, and offer evidence as to how the poor live which, in days to come, will be invaluable. They may be the best educators, for bringing ever-fresh stores of thought, they will see the weak spots in a routine which daily tires a child because it does so little to teach him, and they will have an opinion on national education better worth considering than the grumbles of those wearied with most things, or the congratulations of officials who judge by examinations. They may be the best Church reformers, for they will make more and more manifest how it is not institutions but righteousness which exalts a nation; how, one after another, all reforms fail because men lie and love self; and how, therefore, the first of all reforms is the reform of the Church, whose mission for the nation is that it create righteousness.

There is, then, for the settler of a University Settlement an ideal worthy of his sacrifice. He looks not to a Church buttressed by party spirit, nor to a community founded on self-helped respectability. He looks rather to a community where the best is most common, where there is no more hunger and misery, because there is no more ignorance and sin – a community in which the poor have all that gives value to wealth, in which beauty, knowledge, and righteousness are nationalised.

5.5   NEW GOSPELS, NEW METHODS

The extension of political and religious liberty, the expansion of the realm of conscience through improved communications, and the rise of faith in science as the means of promoting social and industrial progress brought a commensurate enlargement of the Christian message in Victorian Britain. Salvation was made all-encompassing; the means of grace were multiplied; the methods of ecclesiastical outreach became scientific. Although Anglicans possessed by inheritance a national faith, and at mid-century pioneered a type of 'Christian Socialism', the broadening gospel owed most to Nonconformists. Their enfranchisement and *embourgeoisement* found natural expression in a religion of rising expectations, not only for the individual, but for society as a whole. The city became the focus of their hope; the poor, the unemployed, and the 'fallen' became its objects. In October 1866 George Dawson (1821–1876), a Baptist by heritage and for thirty years the famed preacher of the Church of the Saviour in Birmingham, articulated the 'municipal gospel', as it became known, in his inaugural address at the opening of the town's Free Reference Library. He portrayed a great town as 'a solemn organism through which should flow, and in which should be shaped, all the highest, loftiest and truest ends of man's intellectual and moral nature'. Its library, open to rich and poor alike, was to hold in trust the collective wisdom of the human race and so to serve as the agent of spiritual uplift (**5.5.1**). Dawson's 'holy Communism', the inspiration of so-called municipal socialism, was in advance of the age. But even a quarter-century later, when labour unrest and public disorder had impressed churchmen with the gross inadequacy of material provisions for the urban poor, Cardinal Manning (2.1.1, 2.3.4, 2.4.3), who knew their needs intimately, having helped end the London Dock Strike of 1889, still preached the industrialist Andrew Carnegie's 'gospel of wealth'. Spontaneous philanthropy by rich individuals would serve to 'heal the maladies of society and renew its vital structure' (**5.5.2**). Manning invoked Christ's words in support of this 'constructive socialism', and, like Dawson before him, participated in practical schemes to implement the Gospel's this-worldly demands. But neither of these leaders had the audacity of William Booth (1829–1912), the founder and self-styled 'General' of the Salvation Army, who in 1890 set forth an eclectic panacea for unemployment under the title *In Darkest England and the Way Out*. Here many of the attitudes for which, rightly or not, the Victorian era would become infamous – racism, imperialism, revivalism, individualism, paternalism – jostled together menacingly beneath the Army's regimental banners; and Booth's likening his plan to 'A Great Machine' failed to allay fears that it represented a noxious political threat. That it was not socialism but social engineering he advocated can be seen in his appeal by analogy to scientific laws and industrial processes (**5.5.3**).

5.5.1 G. DAWSON AND THE 'MUNICIPAL GOSPEL', 1866

. . . Mr. Mayor, Gentlemen of the Town Council, Ladies and Gentlemen, there is, probably, no word in the human vocabulary which brings a greater crowd of thoughts to the educated man's mind than that blessed word library. . . . A great library contains the diary of the human race; for it is with the human race as with the individuals of it: our memories go back but a little way, or, if they go back far, they pick up but here a date and there an occurrence half forgotten. But when a man keeps a diary of his life, he can at any time bring the whole of its scenes before him. The memory of the human race is just as short, as fragmentary and as accidental as the memory of the individual; but when the books of mankind are gathered together in a room like this, we can sit down and read the solemn story of man's history, from his birth through all his mutations, and so in learning the history of man we reverence our ancestors, ascertain our own pedigree, and find the secret sources of the life we ourselves are now living. Remember we know well only the great nations whose books we possess; of the others we know nothing or but little. The great Hebrew people – their solemn thoughts and their glorious story lie open to us because we have their books. We know the Greek, we are familiar with the Roman, but as for the nameless tribes which peopled the far deserts of the world, – unchronicled, bookless, libraryless – we have but a name, a date or two, a few myths, some trumpery legends, and that is all. But here in this room are gathered together the great diaries of the human race, the record of its thoughts, its struggles, its doings, and its ways.

The great consulting room of a wise man is a library. When I am in perplexity about life, I have but to come here, and, without fee or reward,

I commune with the wisest souls that God has blest the world with. If I want a discourse on immortality Plato comes to my help. If I want to know the human heart Shakespeare opens all its chambers. Whatever be my perplexity or doubt I know exactly the great man to call to me, and he comes in the kindest way, he listens to my doubts and tells me his convictions. So that a library may be regarded as the solemn chamber in which a man can take counsel with all that have been wise and great and good and glorious amongst the men that have gone before him, – (cheers). . . . Suppose we (as many of us are apt to do) get exceedingly hot in the midst of the various discussions – ecclesiastical, political and social – of our day. Men are very apt to think that the universe is pinned to their little creed, that the world really hangs upon their little conventicles, that their form of faith is the upholding of the Throne of God, and that their little nostrum in politics will be the salvation of the world. I go to one of your meetings and get hot and excited perhaps. I come to believe that if you will carry my bill the millenium will follow; or I think if you carry this other proposal the world will come to an end. When a man has worked himself into this unwise heat a good place for him to go is a great library, and that will quiet him down admirably. . . . Sometimes we give ear to our prophets, our clerical prophets and our lay prophets, foretelling doom, the millennium, or the setting of England's sun in the sea. And we grow quite alarmed until we go into the library and take down book after book and find that this is a very old story after all. I can show you in this room now, how many times the millennium ought to have come. – (a laugh). I can show you how many times the sun of England's prosperity ought to have set in the sea. But the day is as distant (I believe, although I am no prophet,) as the day of doom when that sun shall set. I can show you the eclipse of the universe and the end of all things several times repeated before our day; I can show you the waves of infidelity coming in like a flood a great many times, and the flood happily drying up again just as often. I can show you too that the heats and passions of our times have been before; and when I find that these things have been so oft repeated I cease to feel the sting of fear, and I go out quiet, calm, and tranquil. I have a half mischievous pleasure in my library in putting the great men of old times side by side according to their divergences. I put Calvin close to Arminius and it is wonderful – in a library – how pleasantly they do kiss one another. I put my great Tory next to my Radical and they lie down together as the wolf and the lamb. So when hot, fanatical or furious I simply go home and watch those great men as they lie there in quiet peace, and then I go forward to think of those better days when man's clear knowledge of what is infinite and eternal, separated from that which is but passing away, shall bring us into that blessed place, that deliverance from the foolishnesses and the sins of the flesh which is promised shall be given to all who truly seek it. I go into my library as to a hermitage – and it is one of the best hermitages the world has. What matters the scoff of the fool when you are safely amongst the great men of the past? How little of the din of this stupid world enters into a library, how hushed are the foolish voices of the world's hucksterings, barterings, and bickerings! How little the scorn of high or low, or the mad cries of party spirit can touch the man who in this best hermitage of human life draws around him the quietness of the dead and the solemn sanctities of ancient thought! . . .

But as we cannot dwell upon all the uses and beauties of a library, let us pass on to see that this is a Corporation Library, and in that we see one of the greatest and happiest things about it, for a library, supported as this is, by rates and administered by a Corporation, is the expression of a conviction on your part that a town like this exists for moral and intellectual purposes. It is a proclamation that a great community like this is not to be looked upon as a fortuitous concourse of human atoms, or as a miserable knot of vipers struggling in a pot each aiming to get his head above the other in the fierce struggle of competition. It is a declaration that the Corporation of a great town like this has not done all its duty when it has put in action a set of ingenious contrivances for cleaning and lighting the streets, for breaking stones, for mending ways; and has not fulfilled its highest functions even when it has given the people of the town the best system of drainage – though that is not yet attained. Beyond all these things the Corporation of a borough like this has every function to discharge that is discharged by the master of a household – to minister to men by every office, that of the priest alone excepted. And mark this: I would rather a great book or a great picture fell into the hands of a Corporation than into the hands of an individual – (hear, hear) – for great and noble as has been the spirit of many of our collectors, when a great picture is in the hands of a nobleman however generous, or of a gentleman however large-hearted he may be, he will have his heirs, narrow-minded fools perhaps, or a successor pitifully selfish and small; and this great picture that God never intended to be painted for the delight of but one noble family, or the small collection of little people it gathers around it, may be shut up through the whim of its owner or the caprice of its master, or in self defence against the wanton injury that some fool may have done it. But the moment you put great works into the hands of a Corporate body like this you secure permanence of guardianship in passionless keeping. A Corporation cannot get out of temper, or if it does it recovers itself quickly. A Corporation could not shut up this Library. It is open for ever. It is under the protection of the English law in all its majesty. Its endurance will be the endurance of the English nation. Therefore when a Corporation takes into its keeping a great picture or a great collection of books, that picture and those books are given to the multitude and are put into the best keeping, the keeping of those who have not the power, even if they had the will, to destroy. The time of private ownership has, I hope, nearly come to an end – not that I would put an end to it by law or by any kind of violence; but I hope we shall in the open market bid against the nobility, gentry and private collectors, for it is a vexation when a great picture or a great collection of books is shut up in a private house. . . . What a noble thing it would be if the nobility should take to giving their precious collections to Corporations – (cheers). Bring them here and then they would be open to the multitude; for the spirit of Corporate ownership is necessarily different from the spirit of private possession . . .

Therefore I am glad that this is a Corporation Library. I hope in time to come this Corporation may become as rich in pictures and works of art as it has already become in books, for I believe that one of the highest offices of civilization is to determine how to give access to the masterpieces of art and of literature to the whole people. There is no object higher and nobler than that – to make Raffaelle common, to make Michael Angelo intelligible to the multitude, to lay open to the workman and the peasant what heretofore only rank and riches could possibly command – (cheers). When we speak of this as a Free Library we simply mean that the use is free. We all know that the library must be paid for, and we shall all of us, I believe, rejoice in paying for it. But in opening it we open it for everybody. There are no restrictions in this library. We simply ask a little wholesome cleanliness on the part of the reader's skin, a little fitness on the part of his thumb and finger. We pray him to remember that pages are white, and thumbs sometimes a little black; and that he will, if possible, bring thumb and page into some likeness of colour and fitness for communion. With this little exception, we say to all men, in the solemn spirit of the Gospel, 'Buy here without money and without price.' This is the great genius of the Christian religion, our religion: all things for all men: the highest to kiss the lowest: the manifestation of God in the world in order that the meanest of mankind may be brought to a knowledge of Him. This freedom therefore is the glory of this Library. 'All things for all men' is a holy Communism, a wise Socialism, which leaving property altogether respected, thinks it better to place a great property like this in the hands, as it were, of passionless masters, and so place it at the service of the whole people of the land. . . .

Now Mr. Mayor we probably could not part without some little looking forward to the future. For man's part in immortality is so great that he always looks beyond that day when 'the earthly house of this tabernacle shall be dissolved;' beyond the day when these earthen vessels so gloriously shaped by the Almighty Potter shall have fallen back again into shapeless clay; and he longs, with a pardonable desire, that his name may be remembered, when the place that knew him, knows him no more. That glorious weakness I hope we all of us share – that we would fain haunt some place in this world even when the body is gone; that we desire that our names shall be gratefully spoken of when we have long passed away to join the glorious dead. If this be your passion, there are few things that I would more willingly share with you than the desire that, in days to come, when some student, in a fine rapture of gratitude, as he sits in this room, may for a moment call to mind the names of the men, who by speech and by labour, by the necessary agitation or the continuous work, took part in founding this Library. There are few places I would rather haunt after my death than this room and there are few things I would have my children remember more than this, that this man spoke the discourse at the opening of this glorious Library, the first-fruits of a clear understanding that a great town exists to discharge towards the people of that town the duties that a great nation exists to discharge towards the people of that nation – that a town exists here by the Grace of God, that a great town is a solemn organism through which should flow, and in which should be shaped, all the highest, loftiest and truest ends of man's intellectual and moral nature. I wish then for you, Mr. Mayor, and for myself, that, in years to come, when we are, in some respects forgotten, still now and then, in this room, the curious questions may be asked: Who was Mayor on that famous day? who said grace before that famous banquet? who returned thanks for that gracious meal? who gathered these books together? who was the first man that held that new office of Librarian? I trust his name will be printed whenever the name of this Corporation appears. What his title is to be I don't know – whether it is to be Town Librarian or Corporation Librarian – but I envy him whatever it may be, and I am glad the Corporation has given itself an officer who represents intellect – (cheers) – that it looks upward deliberately and says: We are a Corporation who have undertaken the highest duty that is possible to us: we have made provision for our people – for *all* our people – and we have made a provision of God's greatest and best gifts unto Man – (loud cheers).

5.5.2   H. E. MANNING ON THE 'GOSPEL OF WEALTH', 1890

Mr. Gladstone has told us that this country year by year possesses some six or seven hundred millions of 'irresponsible wealth.' No man is better able than Mr. Gladstone to make such a calculation. If any other man had made this assertion he might have been thought to be a visionary. But the greatest Chancellor of the Exchequer in our day is certainly the best bookkeeper; and when he speaks we may believe. He says truly that if a tithe of this amount, that is, sixty or seventy millions, were given yearly to wise private and public uses, the face of England would be changed. . . .

. . . It may be admitted that it is to the financial and commercial branch of political economy that the immense development of commercial wealth is to be ascribed. But this immense development of commercial wealth has been purchased at the cost of equally immense evils, both physical and moral, and which it is the office of the large and true political economy to heal or to prevent. The over-exertion of any subordinate faculty or function never fails to generate morbid and dangerous states in the general health of the body. There is no doubt that free trade, freedom of contract, free labour, 'buying in the cheapest market and selling in the dearest,' are axioms of commercial prudence. They are hardly worthy of being called a science. Nevertheless this freedom of trade has immensely multiplied all branches of commerce and developed the energies of all our industrial population. But it has created two things: the irresponsible wealth which stagnates, and the starvation wages of the labour market. This cheapest market is the market of the lacklands, penniless and help-less. Free labour means the labour of men who have to choose between food and no food. In four of our western counties wages are so low that men come to London by thousands every year, and being here crowd the dock gates and underbid the permanent workmen who have already reason not to be content with their hire. What happens to one threatens all, and men reasonably and justly unite to stand by each other. Union is self-defence, the first law of nature, and in defending themselves men are defending wives and children who live always upon the brink of want. An accident or a sickness, the caprice or the avarice of an employer, any one of these things – often they come together – and a whole home is hungry for weeks or months. We have these two worlds always and openly face to face, the world of wealth and the world of want: the world of wealth saying in its heart, 'I sit as a queen over all traders and toilers;' and the world of want not knowing what may be on the morrow. Can this secret and stagnant wealth then be irresponsible? Was Dives irresponsible with Laza-rus on his doorstep? We do not read that he refused to help him, or that he sent for police to remove him. He was only unconscious of the neighbour-hood of misery, swathed and surfeited as he was in his own gross indulgence of self.

The 'irresponsibility of wealth' is vividly described in these words: 'Go to now, ye rich men, weep and howl in your miseries which shall come upon you. Your riches are corrupted, and your garments are moth-eaten. Your gold and silver is cankered, and the rust of them shall be for a testimony against you.' This is clearly the capital that pays no taxes, and gives no charity, laid up in secret, and barren of all good to the owner or to his neighbour.

But there are possible worse things than this sterility and stagnation. There are scant hires, and starvation wages, and free contracts enforced by distraint, and rack rents that cannot be paid. The same hand writes again upon the wall: 'Behold the hire of the labourers who have reaped down your fields, which by fraud has been kept back by you, crieth, and the cry of them hath entered into the ears of the Lord of Sabaoth.' And men ask, 'Whom have we defrauded? Were not our contracts free? and if free were they not legal?' But between irresponsible wealth and dependent poverty what freedom can there be? Is it not agree or hunger? The world is lordly and is its own authority; but I make no apologies for appealing from the world to our Divine Master. Whatsoever the world may say or think, His words are, and will ever be, our law. They are too well known to need many quotations; it is enough to repeat one saying: 'Woe unto you rich, for you have received your consolation.' Your consolation is this life, and your irresponsible wealth, which you must leave behind you. . . .

The present condition of our labouring people is one of widespread unrest. They are sore and discontented. The world of capital is alarmed and combining for its defence. The world of labour is uniting to demand a fuller and fairer share in the products of its skill and toil. Every city and town has its unemployed; millions are in poverty; agriculture languishes; land is going out of cultivation; trades are going down; mills and furnaces are working half-time; strikes run through every industry. Is there a blight upon our mountainous wealth? Why is all this?

Where is the remedy? Not in legislation, nor in modern political economy, nor in the present administration of the poor law. Where then can it be found? In the law that created the Christian world: and chiefly in the spontaneous action of individual men, not in 'committees' and 'societies,' but in personal sacrifice, in the charity of humanity and of self-denial.

Two appeals of great weight and force have been made in the last days to the possessors of wealth in America and in England: the one by a man whose public life gives unequalled authority to his words; the other by a private man whose noble fulfilment of the gospel he preaches demands of all men a considerate hearing. Mr. Carnegie tells us plainly, first, that the accumulation of stagnant wealth to be bequeathed to heirs is a vain-glory in the giver, and may be a ruin to the receiver: secondly, that the bequeathing of wealth for charities when the donor is gone out of life is an empty way of making a name for generosity: thirdly, that to distribute all, beyond the reasonable and temperate reserves due to kindred and their welfare, *inter vivos* or now in life, with his own will, judgment, and hand, to works of public and private beneficence and utility, is the highest and noblest use of wealth. This is a gospel, not according to capital, but according to the mind and life of the Founder of the Christian world. It is nothing new. It is no private opinion or exorbitant notion of a morbid prodigality, but the words of soberness and truth. If men so acted they would change the face of the world. It is the Christian Socialism, destructive of the socialism generated by despair in reaction against 'irresponsible wealth,' the true antidote to the selfishness of capital, permeating the commonwealth with an irresistible, healing, constructive influence. Every disciple of Mr. Carnegie will be a master-builder of human society, expelling its gross humours, and renewing the vigorous health of public welfare. Where this constructive socialism prevails the destructive socialism bred of the selfishness of irresponsible capital can never prevail. It is the concentration of land, and money, and power in few hands closed to the public good that generates the despairing extravagance of Socialists and Nihilists. The abnormal conditions of society are thought to be of the essence of society itself: to get rid of the morbid conditions they think that society itself must be destroyed. But wise and just social legislation and generous social actions will heal the maladies of society and renew its vital structure.

The other appeal – which is made by Mr. Gladstone – falls within the power of almost all who are above want. It is simply to set apart a definite minimum of their annual income for the service of God and of their neighbour. The proportion may be fixed by each according to his free will. It may be more or less than a tithe, according to the condition and circumstances of the giver. Whatsoever amount it be, it is alienated from personal use for the benefit of others.

And here will come in the law of liberty, that is, the law of generosity, gratitude, self-denial, freely constraining the will to do not only what natural and Christian sympathy requires of us, but, over-passing these narrower measures, to do all we can – remembering for whom we do it, and for what free sacrifice of Himself we in return deny ourselves. This law, which binds the whole Christian world, binds this country at this day with an especial obligation. It is, with one possible exception, the richest country in the world. It has by steady progression increased in wealth with a profuseness and rapidity unequalled in history; and as it has increased in wealth the proportion given to the service of God and of our neighbour has become less and less. . . . The subscription lists of our manifold charities show us the same names over and over again, and show also the conspicuous absence of a multitude of names representing a fabulous amount of 'irresponsible wealth'; and, finally, an army of humble and unknown names, on whom the great burden, and the greater blessing, of charity is resting. Among such self-denying people there are many who give more than a tithe of all they possess; but no one knows it, and of the wealthy few do likewise.

What Mr. Gladstone invites us to do is to enter freely and gladly upon what may be called a Chivalry of Self-denial. He does not desire to see a society, as a city set upon a hill – but an association knit together by an inward and firm resolve. Each member will judge and fix for himself what proportion of his income he will set apart; but it must be a definite minimum. The names of the members ought to be registered in the hands of some central person; but the proportion fixed for himself by each member would be known to himself alone. There would be no receiver or treasurer, because each member will administer his own income, choosing the objects of his distribution, the measure of his gifts, and the public or private channel through which they shall pass. It may be useful to select and recommend certain works and undertakings, and certain modes of administration; as, for instance, that those who can give large contributions should not fritter them away on many small works, but strike a heavy blow on some greater object; and that those who can only give in small sums should not sink them in great works where they become lost, but give them carefully and kindly in acts of personal and private help.

These two appeals sound in our ears with an imperious note, warning us of a great danger and of the need of energetic action. There is no doubt that the enormous wealth of England and of the United States is a grave peril both in the public and private life of men. As to public life, an American writer in a book lately published says that it is an error to suppose that the American Union is governed by a democracy. It is governed, he says, by a plutocracy, by money and millionaires, by rings and avarice. Neither public life nor judicial integrity is safe where money reigns supreme. We also are threatened by the supremacy of irresponsible wealth. It breeds a cynical and supercilious mind, the worst danger of the governing class. The refined luxury of a rich upper class hardens the heart with impenetrable obduracy. Such hardened men are incapable of governing. They have eyes that cannot see, ears that cannot hear, and hearts that cannot understand the mind and will, the miseries and the sufferings, of the people. A plutocracy here in England would be our ruin. Mr. Carnegie and Mr. Gladstone, like the two witnesses, are prophesying in the midst of the city. What answer they will meet remains to be seen. Nothing can mitigate our social evils but a spontaneous return to the highest counsels of natural and Christian self-sacrifice; in this the people believe, but in nothing else. Neither legislation nor political economy will bring capital and labour to mutual confidence. The administration of the Poor Law is crippled and inadequate. Public opinion is paralysed by doctrinaires. The aristocracy of the poor get food in the workhouse. The million outside are passed by as beyond redemption or help. The sincerity of self-sacrifice wins and changes the hearts of men, and the personal sympathy of men and of women who will go into the midst of those who hunger by day, and shiver by night on the stone benches of the Thames Embankment, is irresistible. This is no new doctrine. It was taught by the life of Him who came to sorrow and to suffer among men. When men see this truth, this Divine Vision of a blissful life of love to God and man, no wealth is irresponsible. All things are a trust, not ours but His, a stewardship with a reckoning near at hand. But fear is the lowest motive of charity: rather it in itself is not charity. Responsible stewardship is not the highest motive. 'So speak ye, and so do, as they that shall be judged by the law of liberty.' That is, 'what can I do? my power measures my duty: and the motive of my duty is love, which has no limit, but the power which God gives to each in poverty or in wealth.'

5.5.3   W. BOOTH ON 'DARKEST ENGLAND AND THE WAY OUT', 1890

WHY 'DARKEST ENGLAND'?

This summer the attention of the civilised world has been arrested by the story which Mr. Stanley has told of 'Darkest Africa' and his journeyings across the heart of the Lost Continent. In all that spirited narrative of heroic endeavour, nothing has so much impressed the imagination, as his description of the immense forest, which offered an almost impenetrable barrier to his advance. The intrepid explorer, in his own phrase, 'marched, tore, ploughed, and cut his way for one hundred and sixty days through this inner womb of the true tropical forest.' The mind of man with difficulty endeavours to realise this immensity of wooded wilderness, covering a territory half as large again as the whole of France, where the rays of the sun never penetrate, where in the dark, dank air, filled with the steam of the heated morass, human beings dwarfed into pygmies and brutalised into cannibals lurk and live and die. . . .

It is a terrible picture, and one that has engraved itself deep on the heart of civilisation. But while brooding over the awful presentation of life as it exists in the vast African forest, it seemed to me only too vivid a picture of many parts of our own land. As there is a darkest Africa is there not also a darkest England? Civilisation, which can breed its own barbarians, does it not also breed its own pygmies? May we not find a parallel at our own doors, and discover within a stone's throw of our cathedrals and palaces similar horrors to those which Stanley has found existing in the great Equatorial forest?

The more the mind dwells upon the subject, the closer the analogy appears. . . . The Equatorial Forest traversed by Stanley resembles that Darkest England of which I have to speak, alike in its vast extent – both stretch, in Stanley's phrase, 'as far as from Plymouth to Peterhead;' its monotonous darkness, its malaria and its gloom, its dwarfish de-humanized inhabitants, the slavery to which they are subjected, their privations and their misery. That which sickens the stoutest heart, and causes many of our bravest and best to fold their hands in despair, is the apparent impossibility of doing more than merely to peck at the outside of the endless tangle of monotonous undergrowth; to let light into it, to make a road clear through it, that shall not be immediately choked up by the ooze of the morass and the luxuriant parasitical growth of the forest. . . . Hard it is, no doubt, to read in Stanley's pages of the slave-traders coldly arranging for the surprise of a village, the capture of the inhabitants, the massacre of those who resist, and the violation of all the women; but the stony streets of London, if they could but speak, would tell of tragedies as awful, of ruin as complete, of ravishments as horrible, as if we were in Central Africa; only the ghastly devastation is covered, corpselike, with the artificialities and hypocrisies of modern civilisation. . . .

Darkest England, like Darkest Africa, reeks with malaria. The foul and fetid breath of our slums is almost as poisonous as that of the African swamp. Fever is almost as chronic there as on the Equator. Every year thousands of children are killed off by what is called defects of our sanitary system. They are in reality starved and poisoned, and all that can be said is that, in many cases, it is better for them that they were taken away from the trouble to come.

Just as in Darkest Africa it is only a part of the evil and misery that comes from the superior race who invade the forest to enslave and massacre its miserable inhabitants, so with us, much of the misery of those whose lot we are considering arises from their own habits. Drunkenness and all manner of uncleanness, moral and physical, abound. Have you ever watched by the bedside of a man in delirium tremens? Multiply the sufferings of that one drunkard by the hundred thousand, and you have some idea of what scenes are being witnessed in all our great cities at this moment. As in Africa streams intersect the forest in every direction, so the gin-shop stands at every corner with its River of the Water of Death flowing seventeen hours out of the twenty-four for the destruction of the people. A population sodden with drink, steeped in vice, eaten up by every social and physical malady, these are the denizens of Darkest England amidst whom my life has been spent, and to whose rescue I would now summon all that is best in the manhood and womanhood of our land. . . .

. . . It may tend, perhaps, to the crystallisation of opinion on this subject if I lay down, with such precision as I can command, what must be the essential elements of any scheme likely to command success.

THE ESSENTIALS TO SUCCESS

The first essential that must be borne in mind as governing every Scheme that may be put forward is that it must change the man when it is his character and conduct which constitute the reasons for his failure in the battle of life. No change in circumstances, no revolution in social conditions, can possibly transform the nature of man. . . . The supreme test of any scheme for benefiting humanity lies in the answer to the question, What does it make of the individual? Does it quicken his conscience, does it soften his heart, does it enlighten his mind, does it, in short, make more of a true man of him, because only by such influences can he be enabled to lead a human life? Among the denizens of Darkest England there are many who have found their way thither by defects of character which would under the most favourable circumstances relegate them to the same position. Hence, unless you can change their character your labour will be lost. . . .

Secondly: *The remedy, to be effectual, must change the circumstances of the individual when they are the cause of his wretched condition, and lie beyond his control.* . . . Favourable circumstances will not change a man's heart or transform his nature, but unpropitious circumstances may render it absolutely impossible for him to escape, no matter how he may desire to extricate himself. The first step with these helpless, sunken creatures is to create the desire to escape, and then provide the means for doing so. In other words, give the man another chance.

Thirdly: *Any remedy worthy of consideration must be on a scale commensurate with the evil with which it proposes to deal.* . . . There must be no more philanthropic tinkering, as if this vast sea of human misery were contained in the limits of a garden pond.

Fourthly: *Not only must the Scheme be large enough, but it must be permanent.* That is to say, it must not be merely a spasmodic effort coping with the misery of to-day; it must be established on a durable footing, so as to go on dealing with the misery of to-morrow and the day after, so long as there is misery left in the world with which to grapple.

Fifthly: *But while it must be permanent,* it must also be *immediately practicable.* Any Scheme, to be of use, must be capable of being brought into instant operation with beneficial results.

Sixthly: *The indirect features of the Scheme must not be such as to produce injury to the persons whom we seek to benefit.* Mere charity, for instance, while relieving the pinch of hunger, demoralises the recipient; and whatever the remedy is that we employ, it must be of such a nature as to do good without doing evil at the same time. It is no use conferring sixpennyworth of benefit on a man if, at the same time, we do him a shilling'sworth of harm.

Seventhly: *While assisting one class of the community, it must not seriously interfere with the interests of another.* In raising one section of the fallen, we must not thereby endanger the safety of those who with difficulty are keeping on their feet.

These are the conditions by which I ask you to test the Scheme I am

about to unfold. They are formidable enough, possibly, to deter many
from even attempting to do anything. They are not of my making. They
are obvious to anyone who looks into the matter. They are the laws which
govern the work of the philanthropic reformer, just as the laws of gravitation, of wind and of weather, govern the operations of the engineer. . . .
If we act in harmony with these laws we shall triumph; but if we ignore
them they will overwhelm us with destruction and cover us with disgrace. . . .

I am under no delusion as to the possibility of inaugurating a millennium by my Scheme; but the triumphs of science deal so much with the
utilisation of waste material, that I do not despair of something effectual
being accomplished in the utilisation of this waste human product. The
refuse which was a drug and a curse to our manufacturers, when treated
under the hands of the chemist, has been the means of supplying us with
dyes rivalling in loveliness and variety the hues of the rainbow. If the
alchemy of science can extract beautiful colours from coal tar, cannot

---

8 A bird's-eye view of General Booth's scheme to solve the problem of the
unemployed. The original key to the chart reads as follows:

> . . . The figures on the pillars represent the appalling extent of the misery and
> ruin existing in Great Britain, as given in Government and other returns.
>
> In the raging Sea, surrounding the Salvation Lighthouse, are to be seen the
> victims of vice and poverty who are sinking to ruin, but whom the officers
> appointed to carry out the Scheme are struggling to save.
>
> On the left, a procession of the rescued may be seen on their way to the
> various Refuges, Workshops, and other Establishments for Industrial Labor in
> the City Colony, many of which are already in existence.
>
> From the City Colony in the centre, another procession can be seen, of those
> who, having proved themselves worthy of further assistance, are on their way
> to the Farm Colony, which, with its Villages, Co-operative Farms, Mills, and
> Factories, is to be created, far away form the neighborhood of the public-
> house.
>
> From the Farm Colony are to be seen Steamers hurrying across the seas,
> crowded with Emigrants of all sorts, proceeding either to the existing Colonies
> of the British and other Empires, or to the Colony-over-Sea, yet to be estab-
> lished; whilst the sturdy baker on the left and the laundress on the right
> suggest, on the one hand, plenty of work, and on the other, abundance of food.
>
> The more the Chart is examined the more will be seen of the great Blessings
> the Scheme is intended to convey, and the horrible destruction hourly going on
> amongst at least three Millions of our fellow-creatures, which we are anxious to
> bring to an end. And the more the Scheme contained in this book is studied and
> assisted, the more will the beautiful prospect held out on the Chart be likely to
> be brought into reality.

Divine alchemy enable us to evolve gladness and brightness out of the agonised hearts and dark, dreary, loveless lives of these doomed myriads? Is it too much to hope that in God's world God's children may be able to do something, if they set to work with a will, to carry out a plan of campaign against these great evils which are the nightmare of our existence? . . .

MY SCHEME

. . . I propose to devote the bulk of this volume to setting forth what can practically be done with one of the most pressing parts of the problem, namely, that relating to those who are out of work, and . . . who are not quartered on the State, but who are living on the verge of despair, and who at any moment, under circumstances of misfortune, might be compelled to demand relief or support in one shape or another. . . .

What is the outward and visible form of the Problem of the Unemployed? Alas! we are all too familiar with it for any lengthy description to be necessary. The social problem presents itself before us whenever a hungry, dirty and ragged man stands at our door asking if we can give him a crust or a job. That is the social question. What are you to do with that man? He has no money in his pocket, all that he can pawn he has pawned long ago, his stomach is as empty as his purse, and the whole of the clothes upon his back, even if sold on the best terms, would not fetch a shilling. There he stands, your brother, with sixpennyworth of rags to cover his nakedness from his fellow men and not sixpennyworth of victuals within his reach. He asks for work, which he will set to even on his empty stomach and in his ragged uniform, if so be that you will give him something for it, but his hands are idle, for no one employs him. What are you to do with that man? . . . To deal with him effectively you must deal with him immediately, you must provide him in some way or other at once with food, and shelter, and warmth. Next you must find him something to do, something that will test the reality of his desire to work. This test must be more or less temporary, and should be of such a nature as to prepare him for making a permanent livelihood. Then, having trained him, you must provide him wherewithal to start life afresh. All these things I propose to do. My Scheme divides itself into three sections, each of which is indispensable for the success of the whole. In this three-fold organisation lies the open secret of the solution of the Social Problem.

The Scheme I have to offer consists in the formation of these people into self-helping and self-sustaining communities, each being a kind of co-operative society, or patriarchal family governed and disciplined on the principles which have already proved so effective in the Salvation Army.

These communities we will call, for want of a better term, Colonies.

There will be—

      (1) The City Colony.
      (2) The Farm Colony.
      (3) The Over-Sea Colony.

THE CITY COLONY

By the City Colony is meant the establishment, in the very centre of the ocean of misery of which we have been speaking, of a number of Institutions to act as Harbours of Refuge for all and any who have been shipwrecked in life, character, or circumstances. These Harbours will gather up the poor destitute creatures, supply their immediate pressing necessities, furnish temporary employment, inspire them with hope for the future, and commence at once a course of regeneration by moral and religious influences.

From these Institutions, which are hereafter described, numbers would, after a short time, be floated off to permanent employment, or sent home to friends happy to receive them on hearing of their reformation. All who remain on our hands would, by varied means, be tested as to their sincerity, industry, and honesty, and as soon as satisfaction was created, be passed on to the Colony of the second class.

THE FARM COLONY

This would consist of a settlement of the Colonists on an estate in the provinces, in the culture of which they would find employment and obtain support. As the race from the Country to the City has been the cause of much of the distress we have to battle with, we propose to find a substantial part of our remedy by transferring these same people back to the country, that is back again to 'the Garden!'

Here the process of reformation of character would be carried forward by the same industrial, moral, and religious methods as have already been commenced in the City, especially including those forms of labour and that knowledge of agriculture which, should the Colonist not obtain employment in this country, will qualify him for pursuing his fortunes under more favourable circumstances in some other land.

From the Farm, as from the City, there can be no question that large numbers, resuscitated in health and character, would be restored to friends up and down the country. Some would find employment in their own callings, others would settle in cottages on a small piece of land that we should provide, or on Co-operative Farms which we intend to promote; while the great bulk, after trial and training, would be passed on to the Foreign Settlement, which would constitute our third class, namely The Over-Sea Colony.

THE OVER-SEA COLONY

All who have given attention to the subject are agreed that in our Colonies in South Africa, Canada, Western Australia and elsewhere, there are millions of acres of useful land to be obtained almost for the asking, capable of supporting our surplus population in health and comfort, were it a thousand times greater than it is. We propose to secure a tract of land in one of these countries, prepare it for settlement, establish in it authority, govern it by equitable laws, assist it in times of necessity, settling it gradually with a prepared people, and so create a home for these destitute multitudes.

The Scheme, in its entirety, may aptly be compared to A Great Machine, foundationed in the lowest slums and purlieus of our great towns and cities, drawing up into its embrace the depraved and destitute of all classes; receiving thieves, harlots, paupers, drunkards, prodigals, all alike, on the simple conditions of their being willing to work and to conform to discipline. Drawing up these poor outcasts, reforming them, and creating in them habits of industry, honesty, and truth; teaching them methods by which alike the bread that perishes and that which endures to Everlasting Life can be won. Forwarding them from the City to the Country, and there continuing the process of regeneration, and then pouring them forth on to the virgin soils that await their coming in other lands, keeping hold of them with a strong government, and yet making them free men and women; and so laying the foundations, perchance, of another Empire to swell to vast proportions in later times. Why not?

6

CLASS AND UNBELIEF

6.1   THE RELIGIOUS CONDITION OF THE MASSES

THE spectre of revolutionary unrest haunted the British churches for much of the Victorian era. It was seen to emanate from false philosophy, personal immorality, and ecclesiastical laxity, which were thought to be essentially connected. It invariably took the form of an artisan, a ruffian, a member of the vast underclass that was numerically dominant. Had not France undergone a violent upheaval from below, fuelled by pervasive paganism? There, but for God's grace, would Britain go – unless true religion and right morals were deliberately inculcated by quickened and vigilant churches. At no time was the peril of mass irreligion impressed on Victorian believers more acutely than in January 1854, when Horace Mann (b.1823) published his analysis of the elaborate statistics of church accommodation and attendance compiled on Sunday 30 March 1851, the day before the general census. Not only, according to these somewhat dubious data, was accommodation in churches lacking for more than half the population able to attend; about half this population – five and a quarter million people – failed to do so. Mann identified them in the main as 'the *labouring* myriads of our country' and sought to account for their non-attendance with a view towards rectifying the problem in the interests of social stability (**6.1.1**). The premise of his analysis, that religious conduct is a better guide to an individual's religious state than mere religious profession, was not, however, uncontroversial. In 1868 Thomas Wright, speaking anonymously for his fellow labourers as 'The Journeyman Engineer', argued in effect that church attendance might equally be taken as an index of personal hypocrisy. Referring specifically to the Church of England, he went much further than Mann – whether more accurately must be judged – in attributing the alienation of the working classes specifically to the Church's confusion of 'the worship of God with that of Mammon'. The greater fault lay with the Church, not the masses, for neglecting true religion (**6.1.2**).

6.1.1   H. MANN ON THE RELIGIOUS CENSUS, 1853

There are two methods of pursuing a statistical inquiry with respect to the religion of a people. You may either ask each individual, directly, what particular form of religion he professes; or, you may collect such information as to the religious *acts* of individuals as will equally, though indirectly, lead to the same result. The former method was adopted, some few years ago, in Ireland, and is generally followed in the continental states when such investigations as the present are pursued. At the recent Census, it was thought advisable to take the latter course; partly because it had a less inquisitorial aspect, – but especially because it was considered that the outward *conduct* of persons furnishes a better guide to their religious state than can be gained by merely vague professions. In proportion, it was thought, as people truly are connected with particular sects or churches, will be their activity in raising buildings in which to worship and their diligence in afterwards frequenting them; but where there is an absence of such practical regard for a religious creed, but little weight can be attached to any purely formal acquiescence. This inquiry, therefore, was confined to obvious *facts* relating to two subjects. – 1. The amount of ACCOMMODATION which the people have provided for religious worship; and 2. The number of persons, as ATTENDANTS, by whom this provision is made use of.

1. – ACCOMMODATION

. . . The summary result of this inquiry with respect to accommodation is, that there are in England and Wales 10,398,013 persons able to be present at one time in buildings for religious worship. Accommodation, therefore, for that number (equal to 58 per cent. of the population) is required. The *actual* accommodation in 34,467 churches, chapels, and out-stations is enough for 10,212,563 persons. But this number, after a deduction, on account of ill-proportioned distribution, is reduced to 8,753,279, a provision equal to the wants of only 49 per cent. of the community. And further, out of these 8,753,279 sittings, a certain considerable number are rendered *unavailable* by being in churches or chapels which are *closed* throughout some portion of the day when services are usually held. There is therefore wanted an additional supply of 1,644,734 sittings, if the population is to have an extent of accommodation which shall be undoubtedly sufficient. These sittings, too, must be provided *where* they are wanted; *i.e.* in the *large town districts* of the country, – more especially in London. To furnish this accommodation would probably require the erection of about 2,000 churches and chapels; which, in towns, would be of larger than the average size. This is assuming that all churches and sects may contribute their proportion to the work, and that the contributions of each may be regarded as by just so much diminishing the efforts necessary to be made by other churches. If, as is probable, this supposition be considered not altogether admissible, there will be required a further addition to those 2,000 structures; the extent of which addition must depend upon the views which may be entertained respecting what particular sects should be entirely disregarded.

Of the total existing number of 10,212,563 sittings, the Church of England contributes 5,317,915, and the other churches, together, 4,894,648. . . .

Whether, by . . . the erection of more churches – the increased employment of the present buildings – and the use of places not expressly dedicated to religious worship; whether by an increase of *accommodation* merely, without other measures, the reluctant people can be gained to practical Christianity, is what will be in some degree decided by inquiring, next, what number of *attendants,* on the Census-Sunday, used the accommodation actually then existing.

2. – ATTENDANCE

. . . The most important fact which this investigation as to attendance brings before us is, unquestionably, the alarming number of the non-attendants. Even in the least unfavourable aspect of the figures . . . and assuming (as no doubt is right) that the 5,288,294 absent every Sunday are not always the same individuals, it must be apparent that a sadly formidable portion of the English people are habitual neglecters of the public ordinances of religion. Nor is it difficult to indicate to what particular class of the community this portion in the main belongs. The middle classes have augmented rather than diminished that devotional sentiment and strictness of attention to religious services by which, for several centuries, they have so eminently been distinguished. With the upper class, too, the subject of religion has obtained of late a marked degree of notice, and a regular church-attendance is now ranked amongst the recognized proprieties of life. It is to satisfy the wants of these two classes that the number of religious structures has of late years so increased. But while the *labouring* myriads of our country have been multiplying with our multiplied material prosperity, it cannot, it is feared, be stated that a corresponding increase has occurred in the attendance of this class in our religious edifices. More especially in cities and large towns it is observable how absolutely insignificant a portion of the congregations is composed of artizans. They fill, perhaps, in youth, our National, British, and Sunday Schools, and there receive the elements of a religious education; but, no sooner do they mingle in the active world of labour than, subjected to the constant action of opposing influences, they soon become as utter strangers to religious ordinances as the people of a heathen country. From whatever cause, in them or in the manner of their treatment by religious bodies, it is sadly certain that this vast, intelligent, and growingly important section of our countrymen is thoroughly estranged from our religious institutions in their present aspect. Probably, indeed, the prevalence of *infidelity* has been exaggerated, if the word be taken in its popular meaning, as implying some degree of intellectual effort and decision; but, no doubt, a great extent of negative, inert indifference prevails, the practical effects of which are much the same. There is a sect, originated recently, adherents to a system called 'Secularism'; the principal tenet being that, as the fact of a future life is (in their view) at all events susceptible of *some* degree of doubt, while the fact and the necessities of a present life are matters of direct sensation, it is therefore prudent to attend exclusively to the concerns of that existence which is certain and immediate – not wasting energies required for present duties by a preparation for remote, and merely possible, contingencies. This is the creed which probably with most exactness indicates the faith which, virtually though not professedly, is entertained by the masses of our working population; by the skilled and unskilled labourer alike – by hosts of minor shopkeepers and Sunday traders – and by miserable denizens of courts and crowded alleys. They are *unconscious Secularists* – engrossed by the demands, the trials, or the pleasures of the passing hour, and ignorant or careless of a future. These are never or but seldom seen in our religious congregations; and the melancholy fact is thus impressed upon our notice that the classes which are most in need of the restraints and consolations of religion are the classes which are most without them. . . .

1. One chief cause of the dislike which the labouring population entertain for religious services is thought to be the maintenance of those distinctions by which they are separated as a class from the class above them. Working men, it is contended, cannot enter our religious structures without having pressed upon their notice some memento of inferiority. The existence of pews and the position of the free seats are, it is said, alone sufficient to deter them from our churches; and religion has thus come to be regarded as a purely middle-class propriety or luxury. It is therefore, by some, proposed to abandon altogether the pew system, and to raise by voluntary contributions the amount now paid as seat rents. The objection and proposal come from churchmen and dissenters too; but from the former much more strenuously than from the latter; and with this addition in their case – that they point out the *offertory,* prescribed by the Rubric, as the specific mode in which the voluntary contributions should be gathered. – To other minds, the prevalence of social distinctions, while equally accepted as a potent cause of the absence of the working classes from religious worship, is suggestive of a different remedy. It is urged that the influence of that broad line of demarcation which on week days separates the workman from his master cannot be effaced on Sundays by the mere removal of a physical barrier. The labouring myriads, it is argued, forming to themselves a world apart, have no desire to mingle,

even though ostensibly on equal terms, with persons of a higher grade. Their tastes and habits are so wholly uncongenial with the views and customs of the higher orders, that they feel an insuperable aversion to an intermixture which would bring them under an intolerable constraint. The same disposition, it is said, which hinders them from mixing in the scenes of recreation which the other classes favour, and induces their selection preferably of such amusements as can be exclusively confined to their own order, will for ever operate to hinder their attendance at religious services, unless such services can be devised as shall become exclusively *their own*. An argument in favour of such measures is supposed to be discovered in the fact that the greatest success amongst these classes is obtained where, as amongst the Methodists, this course is (more perhaps from circumstances than design) pursued. If such a plan were carried out by the Church of England, and by the wealthier Dissenting bodies, it is thought that some considerable advantage would result. It has consequently been proposed to meet so far the prejudices of the working population; and to strive to get them gradually to establish places of worship for themselves. Experiments have been already put in operation with the persons lowest in the social scale; and RAGGED CHURCHES are in several places making a successful start. In several places, too, among Dissenters, special services in halls and lecture rooms are being held, intended wholly for the working class; and the success of these proceedings seems to prove that multitudes will readily frequent such places, where of course there is a total absence of all class distinctions, who would never enter the exclusive-looking chapel.

2. A second cause of the alienation of the poor from religious institutions is supposed to be an insufficient sympathy exhibited by professed Christians for the alleviation of their social burdens – poverty, disease, and ignorance. It is argued that the various philanthropic schemes which are from time to time originated, though certainly the offspring of benevolent minds, are not associated with the Christian church in such a manner as to gain for it the gratitude of those who thus are benefited. This cause, however, of whatever force it may have been as yet, is certainly in process now of mitigation; for the clergy everywhere are foremost in all schemes for raising the condition of the poor, and the ministers and members of the other churches are not backward in the same good labour.

3. A third cause of the ill-success of Christianity among the labouring classes is supposed to be a misconception on their part of the motives by which Christian ministers are actuated in their efforts to extend the influence of the Gospel. From the fact that clergymen and other ministers receive in exchange for their services pecuniary support, the hasty inference is often drawn, that it is wholly by considerations of a secular and

selfish kind that their activity and zeal are prompted. Or, even if no sordid motives are imputed, an impression is not seldom felt that the exhortations and the pleadings of the ministry are matters merely of professional routine – the requisite fulfilment of official duty. It is obvious that these misapprehensions would be dissipated by a more familiar knowledge; but the evil of the case is, that the influence of such misapprehensions is sufficient to prevent that closer intimacy between pastors and their flocks from which alone such better knowledge can arise. The ministers are distrusted – the poor keep stubbornly aloof: how shall access to them be obtained? The employment of LAY-AGENCY has been proposed as the best of many methods by which minds, indifferent or hostile to the regular clergy, can be reached. It is thought by some that that unfortunate suspicion, by the poor, of some concealed and secretly inimical design, by which the regular ministers are often baffled in their missionary enterprises, might be much allayed if those who introduced the message of Christianity were less removed in station and pursuits from those whom it is sought to influence.

4. Another and a potent reason why so many are forgetful of religious obligations is attributable to their *poverty*; or rather, probably, to certain conditions of life which seem to be inseparable from less than moderate incomes. The scenes and associates from which the poor, however well disposed, can never, apparently, escape; the vice and filth which riot in their crowded dwellings, and from which they cannot fly to any less degraded homes; what awfully effective teaching, it is said, do these supply in opposition to the few infrequent lessons which the Christian minister or missionary, after much exertion, may impart! How feeble, it is urged, the chance, according to the course of human probabilities, with which the intermittent voice of Christianity must strive against the fearful never-ceasing eloquence of such surrounding evil! – Better dwellings, therefore, for the labouring classes are suggested as a most essential aid and introduction to the labours of the Christian agent. And, indeed, of secondary influences, few can be esteemed of greater power than this. Perhaps no slight degree of that religious character by which the English middle classes are distinguished is the consequence of their peculiar isolation in distinct and separate houses – thus acquiring almost of necessity, from frequent opportunities of solitude, those habits of reflection which cannot be exercised to the entire exclusion of religious sentiments; but, certainly, however this may be, no doubt can be admitted that a great obstruction to the progress of religion with the working class would be removed if that condition which forbids *all* solitude and *all* reflection were alleviated.

Probably, however, the grand requirement of the case is, after all, a multiplication of the various *agents* by whose zeal religious truth is disseminated. Not chiefly an additional provision of religious *edifices*. The supply of these perhaps, will not much longer, if the present wonderful exertions of the Church of England (aided in but little less degree by other Churches) be sustained, prove very insufficient for the wants of the community. But what is eminently needed is, an agency to bring into the buildings thus provided those who are indifferent or hostile to religious services. The present rate of church-and-chapel-increase brings before our view the prospect, at no distant period, of a state of things in which there will be small deficiency of structures where to worship, but a lamentable lack of worshippers. There is indeed already, even in our present circumstances, too conspicuous a difference between accommodation and attendants. Many districts might be indicated where, although the provision in religious buildings would suffice for barely half of those who might attend, yet scarcely more than half of even this inadequate provision is appropriated. Teeming populations often now surround half empty churches, which would probably remain half empty even if the sittings were all free. The question then is mainly this: By what means are the multitudes thus absent to be brought into the buildings open for their use? Whatever impeding influence may be exerted by the prevalence of class distinctions, the constraints of poverty, or misconceptions of the character and motives of the ministers of religion, it is evident that absence from religious worship is attributable *mainly* to a genuine repugnance to religion itself. And, while this lasts, it is obvious that the stream of Christian liberality, now flowing in the channel of church-building, must produce comparatively small results. New churches and new chapels will arise, and services and sermons will be held and preached within them; but the masses of the population, careless or opposed, will not frequent them. It is not, perhaps, sufficiently remembered that the process by which men in general are to be brought to practical acceptance of Christianity is necessarily *aggressive*. There is no attractiveness, at first, to them in the proceedings which take place within a church or chapel: all is either unintelligible or disagreeable. We can never then, expect that, in response to the mute invitation which is offered by the open door of a religious edifice, the multitudes, all unprepared by previous appeal, will throng to join in what to them would be a mystic worship, and give ear to truths which, though unspeakably beneficent, are also, to such persons, on their first announcement, utterly distasteful. Something more, then, it is argued, must be done. The people who refuse to hear the gospel in the church must have it brought to them in their own haunts. If ministers, by standing every Sunday in the desk or pulpit, fail to attract the multitudes around, they must by some means make their invitations heard beyond the church or chapel walls. The myriads of our labouring population, really as ignorant of Christianity as were the heathen Saxons at

Augustine's landing, are as much in need of missionary enterprise to bring them into practical acquaintance with its doctrines; and until the dingy territories of this alienated nation are invaded by *aggressive* Christian agency, we cannot reasonably look for that more general attendance on religious ordinances which, with many other blessings, would, it is anticipated, certainly succeed an active war of such benevolent hostilities.

Nor, it is urged in further advocacy of these missionary efforts, are the people insusceptible of those impressions which it is the aim of Christian preachers to produce. Although by natural inclination adverse to the entertainment of religious sentiments, and fortified in this repugnance by the habits and associations of their daily life, there still remain within them that vague sense of some tremendous want, and those aspirings after some indefinite advancement, which afford to zealous preachers a firm hold upon the conscience even of the rudest multitude. Their native and acquired disinclination for religious truth is chiefly of a negative, inert description – strong enough to hinder their spontaneous seeking of the passive object of their dis-esteem – too feeble to present effectual resistance to the inroads of aggressive Christianity invading their own doors. . . .

. . . Apart from those exalted and immeasurable interests with which religion is connected in the destinies of all – on which it is the office rather of the Christian preacher to dilate – no inconsiderable portion of the secular prosperity and peace of individuals and states depends on the extent to which a pure religion is professed and practically followed. If we could imagine the effects upon a people's temporal condition of two different modes of treatment – education separate from religion, and religion separate from education – doubtless we should gain a most impressive lesson of the inappreciable value of religion even to a nation's physical advancement. For, whatever the dissuasive influence, from crime and grosser vice, of those refined ideas which in general accompany augmented knowledge, yet undoubtedly it may occur that, under the opposing influence of social misery, increased intelligence may only furnish to the vicious and the criminal increased facilities for evil. But the wider and more penetrating influence exerted by religious principle – controlling conscience rather than refining taste – is seldom felt without conferring, in addition to its higher blessings, those fixed views and habits which can scarcely fail to render individuals prosperous and states secure. Applying to the regulation of their daily conduct towards themselves and towards society the same high sanctions which control them in their loftier relations, Christian men become, almost inevitably, temperate, industrious, and provident, as part of their religious duty; and Christian citizens acquire respect for human laws from having learnt to reverence those which are divine. The history of men and states shows nothing more conspicuously than this – that in proportion as a pure and practical religion is acknowledged and pursued are individuals materially prosperous and nations orderly and free. It is thus that religion 'has the promise of the life that now is, as well as of that which is to come.' . . .

6.1.2   T. WRIGHT ON THE WORKING CLASSES AND THE CHURCH, 1868

The relations, or perhaps I should say the non-relations, between the working classes and religious institutions have of late years attracted a great deal of attention in clerical circles. That the classes in question do not attend places of worship in anything like the same proportion to their numbers as do the upper and middle classes, is admitted upon all hands, thought it is questionable whether this is the case to so great an extent as is generally supposed. The worshippers of some sects – notably the Primitive Methodists – belong almost exclusively to the working classes, while considerable numbers of these same classes are earnest members of the Roman Catholic and other religions. The Established Church seems to find the least favour among those of the working classes who do attend places of worship; and it is probably owing to this circumstance that its ministers have taken a leading part in the recent 'movements' in connection with this matter. . . .

. . . In this case there are faults on both sides, and I trust that I am not unconsciously swayed by class feeling in believing that the greater fault lies with the Church; though it is only just to its representatives to say that they take wrong views upon some of the chief points of difference solely through ignorance of the modes of life and thought prevailing on the other side. Thus their efforts are primarily founded upon the supposition that because the working classes generally do not attend places of worship, they must in a special degree be an irreligious body. That here the premises to a certain extent justify the conclusion I am quite prepared to admit; but then it is only by confounding the spirit of religion with the formal observance of an outward ceremonial that the premises can be made tenable. On this principle even a ritualist would scarcely attempt to support it, and it can only be from want of thought that ministers of religion argue from it in the way they do.

The classes who do habitually attend places of worship frequently do so from other than religious motives. . . . No person with the slightest knowledge of the world – and I take it that even clergymen should have some worldly wisdom – needs to be told that attendance at a place of worship is not necessarily a proof of religious feeling, and yet it is upon the ground of non-attendance that the working classes are stigmatised as irreligious.

If, however, we put aside this evidently unreliable criterion, and judge them by the essentials of Christianity, it will be found that the working classes are not irreligious. Brotherly love abounds among them, and those who have the opportunity of seeing with what kindness and self-sacrifice they assist friends or neighbours in distress know that they have that charity that covereth a multitude of sins. To them, living as they do by manual labour, and following more or less dangerous occupations, the import of the text, that in the midst of life we are in death, is more frequently and pointedly brought home than to any other class; and the lesson is not lost upon them. It often 'gives them pause,' and causes them to think of that hereafter, to fit us for which is the professed aim of all religions. And finally, though, compared with other classes, their lot is often a hard one, they do not take those gloomy views either of this life or that which is to come, which seem to be the sole result of some religious beliefs.

To speak of a wide-spread infidelity among the working classes, or of their being *actively* opposed to religion, or religious institutions, is simply to talk nonsense. Such irreligion as does exist among them applies chiefly to mere ceremonials, is passive, and arises from indifference. Unless Archdeacon Sinclair has an idea that such books as the *Shilling Shakespeare,* or the sixpenny edition of Scott's novels, which circulate largely among the better-educated portion of the working classes, or one or two harmless weekly 'organs' of the clap-trap school of politics, which form the staple reading of the less-educated portion of them – unless the reverend gentleman in question believes these to be infidel works, the ocean of infidel literature which he spoke of as circulating among working men exists only in his imagination.

Here and there among working men there will be found some half-educated shallow-minded man who, from having read a few such books as *The Ruins of Empires* and *The Age of Reason,* has come to the conclusion that to profess infidel beliefs marks him out as a bold and original thinker. But such men are exceptional, and are only laughed at by those among whom they live; and after all their infidelity is of the most harmless character, simply consisting in asking if you really believe that the whale swallowed Jonah, or pointing to the verbal discrepancies shown in the gospels with regard to the inscription placed on the cross at the crucifixion. Among the more thoughtful portion of the working classes there is certainly a considerable amount of that honest doubt in which they believe with the Laureate there lives more faith than in half the creeds. But these doubts are of a doctrinal not an infidel character, and in entertaining them they are not exceptional.

Nor, indeed, are the working classes by any means so exceptional in their general relations with the Church as the representatives of that institution seem to imagine; and in this circumstance lies the germ of their *soreness* against the Church. It is this that turns their passive indifference towards it into active aversion and contempt. The Church speaks to and of the working classes as a specially ungodly section of society, while the real fact is that they are – and this not from choice, but of necessity – only more open than other classes in their non-attendance at public worship, and in what the unco guid consider their desecration of the Sabbath. The Sunday 'outings' of the poor are pointed out and denounced as damnable; while such things as the Sundays at the Zoo and the Sunday dinners at Richmond and Greenwich are left unchidden. . . . Consequently, when in their special addresses to the poor, preachers, with a surprising want of tact, ignore the rich side of the question, those to whom such discourses are directed regard them as insults to themselves, and a proof of hypocrisy upon the part of those by whom they are delivered.

It is chiefly from this reason that sermons to working men upon the Sunday question are non-effective, while as an institution the Church, which by its action in this matter challenges examination and criticism, acts repellently. By its supporters the Church is set forth as an essentially Christian institution, and its doctrines, as embodied in the Prayerbook, are more or less Christian in tone. But thinking working men – those who will have to be the pioneers in any advance of their class – believe that practically the Established Church of England is an institution of the world and the flesh; and when they see advowsons advertised for sale, and hear of pluralists and political parsons, and of men put into family livings to keep them warm for some member of the family, they are inclined to add, and of the devil also. It may be said that working men do not understand the constitution of the Church; and this is true as regards matters of detail, but it only requires the commonest powers of perception to see that the practice of the Church is grossly at variance with its preaching. The surroundings of life make working men look at things in a practical light, and they will never be brought to believe in the real Christianity of a Church which, with ample revenues, displays the disgraceful spectacle of a bishop with thousands a-year preaching a charity sermon for the benefit of poor clergymen, the said poor clergymen being meanwhile, to use a clerical phrase, the real workers in the vineyard. To this it is often replied that, to attract able men to the Church, you must have prizes in the shape of large salaries and high social positions. This working men can readily understand, but only on the ground that even by its supporters the Church is regarded simply as a money-making profession, the same as the law or medicine. But while maintaining the prize line of argument, the advocates of the Church soar far above the merely professional grounds on which alone it can be consistently sustained. They put the Church forward as a purely Christian institution, divine alike in its inception, mission, and the details of its constitution, forgetting meanwhile that such grounds as these are, if followed to their legitimate conclusion, utterly destructive of the prize argument. By a dexterous manipulation, Scripture can be made to support in the letter many things that are in direct antagonism to the spirit of its teachings; but working men have studied their Bibles to little purpose, if the cleverest of text-twisters can give even an appearance of scriptural justification for such a monstrosity – speaking from a purely apostolic point of view – as a modern bishop of the Established Church of England. The Church's greatest weakness is its own want of conformity between its preaching and its practice. That many of the working clergy are Christians in the highest and purest sense, working men are fully aware, and none can esteem such ministers more highly than they do. But the ministers of this class are very often those 'poor clergy' for whose 'relief fund' bishops preach charity sermons, and to which (the fund), if I have been rightly informed, wealthy rectors send their cast-off clothing. So that while these true ministers endear themselves personally to those of the working classes with whom they come in contact, their position imbitters those classes against the Church in its corporate capacity. It may be depended upon that the working classes will never be brought to believe in the purity or earnestness of a Church which leaves many of its best and truest servants to struggle through life on miserably-insufficient incomes, while it passes all kinds of worthless incompetents over their heads to the loaves and fishes at its disposal, simply because the incompetents have political or family influence.

If the prize principle referred to above was honestly carried out, comparatively little could be said against it; but the jobbery, place-hunting, and sinecurism in connection with the patronage of the Church are so notorious, that it is a mere truism to say that the pecuniary prizes in it, though defended on the plea that they are necessary to draw able men into the Church, are not bestowed upon the most able or meritorious of the Church's servants. This is a state of things recognised not only by the opponents of the Church, but by its own truest supporters. . . . Is it a matter for surprise that others, and especially working men, should regard the Church as a modern Temple of Jerusalem – a house of prayer desecrated by buyers and sellers, and money-changers, who must be cast out from its offices ere it can be purified?

Thus it is the Church as an institution is powerless to influence the people; the worldliness and corruption that exist under its wing, and which become hideous hypocrisies when compared with its professed doctrines, act repellently. And while there is nothing in the Church to attract the working classes on purely religious grounds, those social or conventional reasons which are often the sole inducements to other classes for attending church do not exist in their case. If a working man does not attend a place of worship from an active feeling of religion, he need not do so from any reasons of caste. It has not become a habit with him, nor is it in any degree essential to his maintenance of a character for *respectability*, that he should be

A black-leg saint, a spiritual hedger,
Who backs his rigid Sabbath, so to speak,
Against the wicked remnant of the week;

while his wife or daughter can sufficiently display such finery as they can get at market or during a Sunday-afternoon walk.

But while the working classes as a body can only be considered as *not* irreligious by a broad and charitable construction of the spirit of religion, as apart from its set doctrines and formal ceremonials, there are, as I have already incidentally mentioned, many men among them who are actively and truly religious in the ordinary acceptation of the term. For these men the Dissenting sects have the greatest attractions. Their services and ministers are considered simpler and more practical than those of the Church; the ministers are paid with a nearer approach to equality, and have, to a far greater extent than those of the Church, entered their profession from personal predilection, or as they put it, from having 'experienced a call.'

There are also working men who attend places of worship from hypocritical motives – to curry favour with employers or ingratiate themselves with clergymen who have the power of distributing charity. A few attend Dissenting bodies on this ground; but when it comes to such motives as these, Church pays best, and consequently comes in for the largest share of such pauper-souled worshippers.

All this it may be said is merely an attack upon the Church, but it is only incidentally that it is so. In order that the relations between the working classes and the Church may be properly understood, it is necessary to show exactly in what estimation these classes hold the Church, and in the foregoing remarks I have embodied the views generally obtaining among them. Looking at these views, I think it must be admitted that the working-class indifference to the Church is ascribable less to an irreligious feeling than to a contempt for the desecration of the spirit of religion under the guise of a ceremonial systematisation of it. The Church, as it stands, is emphatically not the Church of the people. They believe that on truly Christian grounds it has no claim to reverence or authority, while as a social institution it is not suited to their necessities. So long as the relative position of the working classes, and the habits of life to which it gives rise, remain as they are, it is probable that no Church, however pure, would in the first instance be able to induce them to habitually attend public

worship. But a really apostolic Church – a Church whose servants practised as well as preached the teachings of the great Founder of
Christianity – could do an incalculable amount of good among them,
could lead them to a higher, purer, more actively-religious life, which
would in its turn lead to their becoming sincere observers of the outward
forms as well as of the essentials of religion. But the Established Church is
not of this kind; and ere it can hope to influence the working classes in any
considerable degree it must purify itself – must cease to combine the
worship of God with that of Mammon.

I do not wish to go into the details of the incidental question of the
disestablishment of the Irish Church; but from what I have said it will be
apparent that the working classes would regard the proposed disestablishment (especially if it had been self-sought) as a step in the right
direction – an advance towards internal purification. On the other hand,
their unfavourable opinion of the Church generally can only be deepened
by the spectacle of a bench of bishops grimly fighting against justice and
the spirit of the age; not for any point of faith or doctrine, but for the
retention of State pay originally granted for a tyrannical and bigoted
purpose, and at present chiefly devoted to maintaining sinecurists, and
giving an enforced legal existence to an institution which has no spiritual
life in it. Such a spectacle as this can only strengthen the opinion among
working men that all *really* religious men must look upon the Church as 'a
thing to shudder at,' not support.

6.2 IMMORALITY AND INFIDELITY

Why did Victorian people disbelieve in Christianity? Among the self-
confident, church-going middle classes it remained a commonplace that
the ultimate reason was simply sin. Religious deviance was rooted in moral
deviance; immorality led to infidelity. But the difficulty arose that
unbelievers were often seen to lead exemplary lives. And many of them
appeared to be lovers of truth as well. By 1881, when John Wordsworth
(1843–1911), an Oxford don and later bishop of Salisbury, preached the
first of his Bampton Lectures, such individuals had achieved conspicuous
respectability in British culture as freethinking *littérateurs* and agnostic
scientists. Wordsworth gently contrived to unmask them. Allowing that
'common prejudices' against Christianity may arise from the 'excesses and
errors' of its representatives, he argued that settled unbelief was nevertheless a symptom of 'secret' immorality and intellectual sins such as
indolence, coldness, recklessness, pride, and avarice (**6.2.1**). Although
some contemporaries were inclined to add Wordsworth's arrogant presumption to the list, his concluding remarks on intellectual 'property',

addressed to an acquisitive culture where scientific knowledge had become a new kind of capital, may seem more apposite in retrospect than they did at the time. There was, however, a more forgiving face shown by churchmen who emphasized chiefly the predisposing influence of Christian theology on modern unbelief. Another Oxford don, Aubrey Lackington Moore (1843–1890), historian, theologian, and parish priest, did not hold with Wordsworth that Calvinism merely created prejudice against Christianity, which then became the cloak for moral rebellion. On the contrary, those who rejected Calvinistic Christianity demonstrated a superior morality from the start. 'If . . . I were asked what was the main cause of unbelief in the present day, I should say, not science, not new truths in history and criticism, but a higher tone of morality acting upon an immoral travesty of the gospel of Christ' (**6.2.2**).

6.2.1   J. WORDSWORTH ON THE CAUSES OF UNBELIEF, 1881

. . . Our most merciful Saviour has so definitely linked together the ideas of sin and unbelief, that we must in very justice to those around us explain to them how and why they are so connected. In those hours when, with the shadow of death upon Him, He opened His heart with such loving unreserve to His disciples, Christ prophesied that the first office of the coming Spirit of Truth would be to establish this connection between sin and unbelief: 'When He is come, He will reprove (*or* convict) the world of sin . . . because they believe not on Me' (John xvi. 8, 9). . . .

. . . How is it, we are asked, that such-and-such intelligent and high-minded persons, who profess to give themselves entirely to the search after Truth, whose lives are one continual pursuit of Truth, – how is it that they do not believe in Christ? Can we be right and honest in thinking them sinners? Such men seem to say, 'We would willingly believe if we could; we suffer pain from our unbelief, we feel that it separates us from our friends, and renders our lives less free and powerful, and in many ways diminishes our usefulness and success; but it is the very love of Truth which stops our believing.'

This is a very serious difficulty, and when it is raised in reference to individuals, I do not think we can give a definite answer to it without pretending to an impossible insight into the secrets of other hearts. Nevertheless, a quiet observation of what goes on about us, and especially a study of the undercurrents which influence our own conduct when we are not thinking of public opinion, but acting as inclination moves us, may suggest at least some reasonable explanation of the moral causes of unbelief.

I say the moral causes of unbelief, because I believe these to be the true causes of permanent alienation. I am speaking not of those who really fight with doubt, but of those who acquiesce in unbelief. It is not so much an observation of the uniformity of nature, or a belief in evolution, that makes them first deny miracles, and then deny God. It is the spirit with which they observe this uniformity and this evolution. Christianity has done as much as science, if not more, to enforce the truths that God is a God of order, and that He makes step follow step in delicate progression. But carrying with it a spirit of love and humility, it recognizes in this order and progress a will to which they are subject, and finds nothing strange, nothing disorderly, in the clearer revelation of this will from time to time in events which we call miraculous. To the eye of faith, both nature and miracle are equally natural and equally miraculous, being the expression of the same divine love and power. But this is not the case with those whose moral sense has been injured or darkened by shocks in the conflicts of the world, or by selfishness and fear of the claims of religion, or by narrow limitation of its field of view.

Let us, then, enumerate a few of the ordinary causes which lead men first to doubt, and then to deny, the truth of revelation.

1. In the first place, it is evident that belief is much weakened by prejudice against the excesses and errors, the vices and crimes, committed from time to time in the name of religion. How often do we hear Lucretius quoted, and not always without justice, to emphasise the greatness of the evil to which superstitious zeal has carried even heroic souls! In some cases, e.g., it is notorious that infidelity is a reaction from an over-rigid or erroneous presentation of the truth. A severe Calvinism, or even a hard Anglicanism, has been thrown aside, and with it Christianity itself has seemed to perish*. Sometimes the confusion between sins and legal offences, especially sins of unbelief, which was common to the legislation of many countries, has grown so intolerable to minds in love with freedom, that religion has been identified with a persecuting spirit, and so cast aside as almost absolutely evil. . . . Some of our own old penal laws, though laws of State not specially loved or sanctioned by the Church, have had in their own sphere a most disastrous influence. Sometimes (though happily for England the danger is now rare among ourselves) religion has been shunned as tainted with coarse imposture and brutal superstition; sometimes it has been degraded by the character of its ministers. . . . One detected hypocrite may make a hundred infidels.

The supposed dulness and ignorance of the clergy is another excuse sometimes urged for infidelity. They are reproached for an unscientific

---

*The evidence of Mr J. E. Symes, of Newcastle-on-Tyne, and Mr Stewart D. Headlam, in their speeches on 'Secularism' before the Leicester Church Congress, Sept., 1880, is well worth considering. They emphasise especially the hard views of some Christians on Inspiration, the Atonement, and Future Punishment, as leading the working-classes to reject belief. (*Report*, pp. 353, 650.)

habit of mind, and for bringing everything round to prove a foregone conclusion. There may at times be justice in these aspersions, but a calm review of past centuries will hardly bear out the conclusion that the defenders of Christian truth have been inferior in ability to those who attack it. If, however, the clergy are somewhat slow to embrace new theories, and cling with tenacity to the traditions they have received, is not this far better in them than a rash love of change? If there is one thing you can say with certainty of the books and theories of those whom it is the custom to call 'advanced' thinkers, it is that they will soon be superseded. As long as there is anything to be learnt from the past; as long as truth is laboriously built up by the slow and settled results of experience; as long as history is the mistress of life, and custom and positive law the guardians of morality, so long will the best teachers of religion be those who understand, sympathize with, and reverence the past. . . .

2. I have spoken of some common prejudices which foster unbelief. A second sort of difficulty is not to be passed over, though it is not easy to speak of it without offence. I mean a revolt from the severe claims of religion, and a secret inclination to sin which dwells in many hearts. Such an explanation of unbelief is one from which charity and courtesy alike would shrink, and it often seems obviously inapplicable; but a serious testing of what religion is, and of the very heavy strain which it puts upon the believer, must convince us that this difficulty is no imaginary one.

For experience shews us that no amount of intellect, or high culture, or noble ambition, can save a man from grave moral faults; and that even apparently sincere conviction sometimes breaks down, in cases of men who seem entirely raised above temptation. No one, I believe, can really know his own heart, without knowing also that he is by nature capable of almost any sin, and that there is within him a constant pressure, sometimes gentle, sometimes vehement, tending to make light of the responsibility for sin, and to weaken belief in the justice and love of God. This pressure, if once we yield to it, tends directly to unbelief in revelation; for the morbid conscience longs above all things to slumber, and in the full brightness of revelation it cannot rest. If we are once convinced that God has spoken, all hope of peaceful repose in sin is lost; and therefore he whose heart inclines to sin, instinctively veils himself from the knowledge of revelation, just as the sick man tosses uneasily until the stream of sunlight is curtained from his pillow.

This is the interior state; outside, for a time, there is perhaps no apparent change. The force of sinful inclination appears to have spent itself in producing unbelief. The force of habit still remains to balance it. An equilibrium seems to be produced in the man, and no striking and glaring evil marks the moment of lapse into infidelity. It seems almost as if the state of unbelief were not such a bad one after all, and death may intervene before the strife of powers has been decided within the soul. But often, even to our eyes, there comes a sudden collapse, and the apparent peace which preceded it is found to have been merely a quiet rottenness.

3. I have spoken of such moral failures as all must acknowledge when they occur; and, if one case only of infidelity from such a cause is known to us, surely we have a warning from God, which it were in the highest degree foolish and criminal to disregard. But, besides these so-called 'moral' failures, there are sins attaching to the intellect, which are as essentially and really acts and states of 'immorality' as the grossest outbreaks of vice. . . . Many are the faults which disguise themselves as a love of truth, but perhaps none is more frequent than a selfish intellectual indolence. . . . The intellectual exercise of thinking about God takes the place of the humble attitude of listening to His word, and pouring out the soul in prayer, and worshipping before the altar. The sweet charities and sympathies, the mysterious inspirations which flow from the gatherings of the faithful in the presence of God, the tenderness and confidence of sons, are exchanged for selfish isolation. . . . At last, too often, His very existence as a personal Being comes to be regarded as a speculation, the decision of which has but little interest for the scientific or literary mind, occupied steadily in such matters as are fairly within its grasp and measure.

Very nearly akin to this intellectual indolence is the cool, dispassionate candour on which some sceptics plume themselves, as if it were the best method of attaining religious truth. They seem to forget that revelation comes to them, if it comes at all, from above, not from below, and from a Power in whose presence fear is a duty. If it exist at all, which is the question before them, it is a gift for which they ought to be thankful, not a suppliant upon their charity. They tell us that it is their first duty to preserve their minds from prejudice in favour of revelation; that they are responsible for the legal purity and judicial impartiality of their reason, which is to them the sole arbiter of truth. And so they exclude all hope of finding revelation, lest it should delude them into credulity, and all fear of losing it, lest they should be frightened into superstition. The fact is, that in so jealously guarding the supremacy of reason, they are really wronging what they profess to honour, they unduly limit the field of which it ought to take cognizance, and the position it ought to occupy. . . . Right reason cannot be guardian only of the interests of one faculty or portion of the human soul, but is the director of the whole, and it must take cognizance likewise of the whole evidence offered by human nature. Thus the warm personal love felt by the soul to its Saviour is evidence offered not by the intelligence, but by the heart. The impression of a divine voice speaking in a way which commands obedience in the pages of

Holy Scripture, is evidence again offered, not so much by the intelligence as by the will and the conscience. But reason cannot, dare not, reject a consideration of either. Right reason on the contrary says, If there is a revelation it will touch the heart, it will speak to the conscience in just such a way as the Gospel does; and, so far, I have the evidence I am bound to expect. Unless revelation did produce these effects, it would be irrational to accept it.

If reason, however, restricts itself to merely intellectual evidence, the case of a man like the late John Stuart Mill, according to his own witness, shews how inevitable is the collapse. Other faculties will have their rights somehow or other, or the man will perish. And even in the interests of pure intelligence, who can say that hope and fear, love and joy, are foes to be excluded? Did not hope enable Columbus to find America? Do not affection and inclination, as well as the expectation of success, play a real part in all scientific discovery? Do not feeling and taste give insight into character and argument? Does not experience shew us daily that only he who loves can understand the language of love? Am I then to drive away all my best thoughts, all the quickening impulses of spiritual life, all my fears of losing man's highest good, and even turn against them and hate them as misleading falsities, because they do not happen to be arguments of a peculiar type, reducible to a certain form of syllogism? Am I to call this a reasonable state of mind? No, rather I should be utterly unreasonable if I did so. . . .

This intellectual coldness seems, in fact, to be as sinful as intellectual indolence. Yet some people tacitly make the assumption that the intellect is outside morality; that you have but to follow your own bias and instinct in its sphere, and to disregard the consequences. This is, indeed, a very narrow system of ethics. . . .

There are other sins besides these, to which the intellect is liable, such as recklessness, pride, and avarice, all of which may be disguised as love of truth. Thus there is a mere taste for adventure in the pursuit of know-ledge, which is akin to the common passion for hunting and mountaineer-ing, where the object is not the result obtained, but the lively agitation of spirits which is created by the act itself. The end is in the means, and nothing beyond. This love of adventure lends a certain air of grace and nobility to a man; it makes him brave weariness, physical pain and danger, with a light heart, because he sets them against the power of excitement which fills and masters him, and carries him outside himself. So it is in those who value the seach after truth, more than truth itself. They point, perhaps, to the pains they undergo as a justification of their integrity, and ask us, it may be, to sympathize with them in their failures. But we are tempted to reply, 'You have obtained all that you desired. You do not really care for truth. You do not believe in the power of attaining it. All that you have aimed at was a refined form of intellectual excitement and amusement. In so doing you are doubly guilty, both in cheating yourself of success, which might have been yours if you had sought the truth, not its shadow; and in deluding your neighbours, who have judged you really in earnest, when you were only aiming at a vain and selfish pleasure.'

Again, that the intellect is liable to pride is, of course, notorious; and was, I suppose, a fact as much recognized by the better heathens as by ourselves. In the search after truth, that is to say, the pride of intelligence invests what it obtains with a kind of halo of interests as its own property; just as men, proud in this world, get to respect what lies about them, because of its nearness to the glories that flow from their own persons. The proud man seems to himself a sort of centre of light and dignity, from which an effluence pours forth upon all which he touches, or at least gathers to himself; and this sentiment is hardly less common in the intellectual than in the secular sphere of life. This fault, in another type of character, becomes rather a species of avarice. Truth is looked upon as a kind of property, of which so much may be obtained by diligent and acquisitive habits*, and as a property which lends glory to its possessor, just as acquired capital does honour to the successful merchant. But in either case truth is regarded as valuable, chiefly because of its relation to the man, not because of its objective worth and dignity. And this is the great difference between the selfish and the Christian pursuit of truth. *We* do not look for a mere discovery, an ornament, a treaure, but an objective personality outside us and above us, to which we bow in reverent adoration; a light which is both liberty and law; a power which finds and chooses us, and is not found and chosen by us; a moulding and informing presence, which is none other than the might of Christ our Lord.

In some such way, then, as this we may point out whereabouts may probably be found the answer to the question, 'How can the unbelief of really intelligent men be sinful?' . . .

---

*These topics are treated with great force by Dr Mozley, in his interesting review of *Blanco White's Autobiography;* Essays, vol. ii. cp. especially p. 146: – 'Here is the point. The fact is, that the love of truth, especially in fallen man, is a corrupted affection, just as natural love is. It betrays the selfish element. His mind annexes truth to itself, and not itself to truth. It considers truth as a kind of property; it wants the pride of making it its own; it treats it as an article of mental success; it does not reverence truth as an object, but appropriates it as a thing; it loves it as its own creation, and as the reflection of itself and its labours. The merchant sees himself in his capital, the parent in his child; every one has the image of himself in the shape of some issue from himself; and there is a philosophy which sees such an issue in truth, and makes it, in its sphere, the very embodiment of that of which truth divine is the extinction – the principle of self.'

6.2.2 A. L. MOORE ON THE INFLUENCE OF CALVINISM ON MODERN UNBELIEF, 1890

My object in the present paper is not to assert, or even to prove, the influence which Calvinism has, as a matter of fact, had upon unbelief, but to show the inner inherent connection between the two. . . . The question . . . that I propose to discuss is this – What is there in Calvinistic theology which, however little Calvin meant it, works itself out into a rejection of the Faith of Christ?

That I am not inventing a thesis in order to maintain it may be made clear by reference to facts of which we are all more or less aware. Only I must explain at once that by 'unbelief' I do not necessarily mean 'atheism' or 'agnosticism.' I mean the rejection of that which we all agree to call the Gospel of Jesus Christ; that is to say, the historical fact of the life and death and resurrection of Jesus, the theological truth of the Incarnation and the Divinity of our Lord, and all that under various names flows to us from that central fact of revelation. If Calvinism has encouraged the transition from Christianity to Arianism, or Socinianism, or Unitarianism, or any form of non-Christian theism, my thesis will have been proved, whether or no theism passes on into philosophical pantheism, and from that, as with Strauss, to a practical, if not a speculative, denial of God. By unbelief I simply mean the rejection of what is distinctive of Christian theology.

Two or three facts have forced the question into prominence in my own thought lately.

(i.) First of all, in reading the Reformation History, I find that while antinomianism dogs the heels of Lutheranism, it is Unitarianism which is constantly appearing among the Swiss school. Servetus was the first of a long series, followed rapidly as he was by the two Socinuses, all apparently in good faith starting from orthodox Calvinism, and being eventually repudiated by their co-religionists.

(ii.) This was one fact which made me think. Another was that I once had occasion to investigate the history of a Unitarian chapel. Unitarianism in the place in question was dying or dead. It was kept alive by two adventitious causes: (*a*) A string band, the members of which composed almost the whole of the congregation; and (ß) an endowment. The chapel was supported by a Unitarian minister who drove out every Sunday from a neighbouring town, and left his people from Sunday to Sunday to the parish priest. There was something so anomalous in this state of things, there being obviously no demand for Unitarianism, that for a long time I was puzzled as to its endowment. At last I discovered that it was a *Presbyterian* endowment which had passed into Unitarian hands, and had been recognized as Unitarian by the Dissenting Chapels Act of 1844. On further investigation I found that this was true of a large number of similar endowments – a fact which struck me at the time as strange, but which has since connected itself with other facts.

(iii.) Another fact, which came as a corroboration of what was now a growing suspicion in my mind, viz. that Calvinism was *implicitly* inconsistent with Christianity, was the recent discussion which has taken place place between Mr. Spurgeon and the Baptist Union. We have been told that the sect of the Baptists is honeycombed by unbelief, and Mr. Spurgeon, in order to be true to the Gospel of Christ, feels obliged to separate himself from them. Everybody knows about this controversy as it exists at present, but everybody does not know that it began four years ago in an address by Mr. Spurgeon, which I then cut out of the daily paper, in which he not only stated that the Baptists were 'going over to the Unitarians,' but gave as the reason of it that they were becoming 'too philosophical.' It seemed to me that the two things held together – first, that the Baptists were abandoning Calvinism for Unitarianism; and secondly, that they were 'philosophical' in doing so. To this a few other facts may be added for what they are worth. (*a*) Calvin, the year after he published the 'Institutes,' refused to accept the three Creeds, and was charged with being an Arian. (ß) The Westminster Assembly, in revising the English Articles, omitted that on the Creeds. (γ) The great Puritan poet, Milton, abandoned Christianity for Arianism.

But there is another line of argument which at first looks very different, and which tends in the same way. For various reasons I have lately studied a good deal of infidel literature, from books like Cotter Morison's 'Service of Man,' down to Bradlaugh's 'Freethinker's Text-book,' and the coarser and more blasphemous writings of the *Freethinker,* and atheistical tracts. And I have found not only that in one and all the religion which is caricatured is Calvinism, but that the criticism frequently falls to the ground if we are able to say that Calvinism is not Christianity. In this case it is rather by reaction than by direct logical evolution that Calvinism tends in the direction of unbelief. At a certain stage of its growth the moral consciousness revolts from Calvinism, and either, under stress of the reaction, abandons its faith altogether, or works back to historical and Catholic Christianity. Few things are more pathetic than the attempts of John Stuart Mill to construct a new theology on the basis of the truth that God is love when his nature had revolted from his father's creed. The reaction, though different in degree, is the same in kind when we trace it in the noble protest of men like Maurice and Kingsley and Robertson, with whom the recovery of the central truth of Christianity, that God is love, came as almost a new gospel. I am giving what is only my own opinion, which I entirely submit to the authority of the Church, when I say that those who reject the Catholic eschatology because they have only known it in its Calvinistic dress, certainly cannot be judged as men who wantonly reject truth.

The problem, then, as I put it to myself, was – What is there in Calvinism which leads some men by direct logical result, and others by reaction and revolt, into a rejection of the Gospel of Jesus Christ which Calvin certainly held and intended to set forth?

I am at once met by the difficulty – What is Calvinism? and in which of its many forms has it influenced English thought? . . . It is . . . to the Lambeth Articles, the Hampton Court Conference, and the Westminster Assembly that we must turn for English Calvinism. And it is clearly unfair to assume *à priori* that Calvin is responsible for the later forms of Calvinism.

But though we have no right to assume it *à priori*, I believe there is but little difficulty in proving it as a fact. We often hear it said the Calvinists went far beyond Calvin. My own study of the question leads to a diametrically opposite conclusion. I doubt whether any of Calvin's followers went as far as Calvin himself. The most profoundly immoral and revolting tenets of Calvinism are to be found in the 'Institutes,' and Calvin himself never receded from, but advanced upon the position he originally took up.

There seem to me two ways in which we might attempt to state Calvinistic theology. We might either take its central doctrine, the doctrine of Predestination, by which it is chiefly known, and which most clearly distinguishes it from the Zwinglian type of Swiss theology, or we might attempt to present Calvinism as a whole, reasoned out with logical coherence from its fundamental principle.

I propose to adopt the latter course, both because Calvin himself was a vigorously logical reasoner – and we may feel pretty sure that we are in the main working on his lines – and also because it will help us to understand the interaction of all the parts of a theology or an author. . . .

. . . The conclusion I come to is this—

1. As to *God*. Calvinism sacrifices everything to the conception of Omnipotence, and in so doing makes God immoral and man non-moral.

2. As to *the Fall*. Calvinism enormously exaggerates the depravity of human nature, though in this matter Calvin is less to blame than the later Calvinistic Confessions, and Calvinism in all its forms is, on this point (treated abstractly), nearer to the Catholic view than the Lutherans.

3. As to *predestination*. I believe no Calvinist Confession ever went so far as Calvin's 'Institutes,' because no Confession was so logical and so defiant as Calvin was. But the general conception is common to all, and cuts away the ground from morality in either man or God.

I cannot now hope to touch on Soteriological and Eschatological points. I will only just say – as an apology for leaving my subject in the middle – that we have followed Calvinism to a point from which we may deduce almost *à priori* its views on other matters. The *substitution theory* and its *forensic fictions* followed necessarily from the ignoring of any real moral nature in man on which Divine grace could work. Neither Roman nor Anglican theology would admit that fallen man can recover himself. . . . Yet both would assert that the image of God is marred, not destroyed, and the idea of restoration underlies their view of Christ's redemptive work. Hence the Sacraments become *moral,* not *mechanical* instruments, and the doctrine of irresistible grace is repudiated in defence of the moral nature of man, and a view of freedom without which morality is impossible. My belief is that, if it were worked out, we should find that the Arianism which claims to come out of Calvinism finds its justification mainly in the Calvinistic doctrine of atonement, in which the love of the Son is constantly set over against the justice of the Father, and so the perfect unity of the Godhead is lost, and reason chooses Unitarianism rather than a duality of Gods.

The unbelief which is due to reaction from Calvinistic Christianity will be different in different cases. But the general character is the same. It is the revolt of the moral nature against an immoral religion and immoral views of God.

Difficulties in religion may be intellectual or moral, or, of course, both combined. There is, however, this difference: Intellectual difficulties may conceivably wait, moral difficulties cannot. What I mean is, we are prepared for much in religion which we cannot fully rationalize. A religion which had no mysteries would not be a religion. And then, if the intellectual difficulties lie mainly, as they so often do, in the speculative region, we may still believe that religion is true. But it is otherwise with *moral* difficulties. If religion is seen to be immoral, its reign is over. We cannot have one kind of morality for God and another for man. Conscience, which is the formative principle of religion, is also the great destroyer of a religion seen to be immoral.

Now, the most striking fact in the present day is that unbelief not only claims to be, but so often is, the result of a true protest of the conscience and the moral nature of man. And if Christianity cannot justify itself, and appeal to the highest and truest moral ideas of man, it cannot hope to stand. I for one dare to say it ought not to stand.

If, then, I were asked what was the main cause of unbelief in the present day, I should say, not science, not new truths in history and criticism, but a higher tone of morality acting upon an immoral travesty of the gospel of Christ.

Let me just illustrate that in the case of the three points we have examined – the Calvinistic teaching about God and man, and God's purposes regarding man.

(*a*) The one thing which men take for granted, and assert defiantly in the face of all difficulties, in the sphere of religion, is that, if there is a God, He must be all and more than all that we love and venerate and fain would imitate among men. Now, look at the God of Calvin. He is omnipotent. He has in his omnipotence created beings who can feel both in body and mind, and by an immutable and incomprehensible decree He has designed some for misery, some for blessedness. He willed the Fall, and punishes it with death. Yet He gave to man only free-will and reason enough to be a witness against him. Upon this mass of corruption God puts forth His hand and takes some, but passes by the rest irrespective of their doings. How is it possible, by any reading between the lines, to show that such a Being is either good, or just, or rational? The law of His selection is what, amongst men, we call waywardness and caprice; His mercy is as unjust as His punishments, and His love is imperfect, selective, and limited. . . .

. . . In the present day, this arbitrariness is as great a difficulty as the injustice. For the science of nature has familiarized all of us with the reign of law. Everywhere we see order and meaning. All down the ages we trace the great law of growth. Cataclysms and episodes we no longer look for. We know God's work in nature and in human history as the calm ordering of law, and it is impossible for us to believe that in religion alone He reveals Himself as lawless. But the love and justice of God are no less necessary to us. '*Shall not the Judge of all the earth do right?*' is a question which carries its answer with it. We cannot think of Him in His own nature or in His dealing with us except as being all that we mean by good and just. The celebrated words of J. S. Mill are only profane in form. In spirit they represent the noble protest of a moral nature against the immoral Deity of Calvin.*

(ß) Then there is the Calvinistic view of man, which we have to remind

---

*'Examination of Sir W. Hamilton's Philosophy,' pp. 128, 129. 'If instead of the "glad tidings" that there exists a Being in whom all the highest excellences which the human mind can conceive, exist in a degree inconceivable to us, I am informed that the world is ruled by a being whose attributes are infinite, but what they are we cannot learn, nor what are the principles of his government, except that "the highest human morality which we are capable of conceiving of" does not sanction them; convince me of it, and I will bear my fate as I may. But when I am told that I must believe this, and at the same time call this being by the names which express and affirm the highest human morality, I say in plain terms that I will not. Whatever power such a being may have over me, there is one thing which he shall not do: he shall not compel me to worship him. I will call no being good, who is not what I mean when I apply that epithet to my fellow-creatures; and if such a being can sentence me to hell for not so calling him, to hell I will go.'

ourselves is still being preached from many pulpits – the doctrine of total ruin. Here the special difficulty is that religion is teaching what is disproved before our eyes. Human nature is not what it ought to be if Calvinism were true. It is impossible to say, without destroying the meaning of words, or confusing the moral judgment, that there is not much good in man. Indeed, it has always been the strength of those who have taught religion that they believed that in every heart there was something which goodness might appeal to. Say what we will, it is still true that 'all earthly joys go less to the one joy of doing kindnesses' – that in the most degraded life there is still something of good, some *vestigia Dei,* which may respond to the grace of God. Of all this the Calvinist knows nothing. Man is a corrupt and depraved thing, powerless to do good or to will it, till the grace of God swoops down upon him and recreates him. Till then, he is in no sense a moral being. This is the view which Professor Drummond translated into or disguised in biological terms. He says the unregenerate or unconverted man is spiritually inorganic. He is dead. He doesn't know God. But it is not his fault. He cannot know God. He must wait for a mechanical change, which is somehow to change him into a moral being. I have somewhere in my possession a letter from John Ruskin, written from Italy, some forty or more years ago, in which he rambles off into theological speculations. He had been brought up a rigid Calvinist, well instructed in the Calvinists' three R's, and he had worked away from them, and naively expresses the view as at least a possible one, that the common views of human corruption are a good deal overstated, that perhaps, after all, nature is not wholly bad, that it is only, as he puts it, one of the cogs in the wheel got wrong; the dust of death has got into the delicate machine, and thrown it out of gear. John Ruskin, like J. S. Mill, might have been a loyal member of the Church of Christ if, when he was asking for the bread of Christ, Calvinistic teachers had not given him a stone.

(γ) Of the third point I hardly know how to speak. As a moralist, I can draw no distinction, speculative or practical, between the fatalism of the Stoics, the Predestination doctrine of Calvin, and the Determinism of the modern denier of free-will. Again and again Melanchthon charged Calvinism with Stoic fatalism. Again and again, in modern days, it has been accused of making God the Author of sin. Modern Calvinists repudiate this conclusion, but cling to the premises from which it necessarily follows. To say that man sins as Adam sinned necessarily, but that that necessity is not external, *coactio,* but *sponte sua,* sounds plausible enough till we find that *sponte sua* does not imply any power of choice or any freedom of the will. To say, as Beza does, that God justly decrees what man is unjust in doing, is to confound moral distinctions.

I have dealt with even the part of the subject that I have touched most imperfectly; and I can only hope that my paper, by its obvious incompleteness, may stimulate others to do what I have failed to do. He will have done a real work for the Faith of Christ who clearly distinguishes between that Faith and the immoralities of Calvinism.

6.3 SECULARISM ON TRIAL: HOLYOAKE, FOOTE, BRADLAUGH

Unbelievers were an oppressed majority in the Victorian age, if church attendance be the measure of faith. Britain was a Christian nation not only in name but by law. The state retained the power, formerly vested in the Church, to prosecute and imprison outspoken 'infidels' long after other Dissenters, including Unitarians, had been granted full liberty to practise and propagate their creeds. Although the law was used against unbelievers with decreasing frequency throughout the period, it was applied harshly none the less, sometimes at the behest of religious vigilantes pursuing political vendettas. That this was imprudent and counterproductive many observers had no doubt. The blood of the infidel martyrs became the seed of organized unbelief. In Victorian Britain irreligion was institutionalized on a scale never seen before or since. 'Secularism' was the name under which the movement achieved greatest notoriety, thanks largely to the Christian enemies of George Jacob Holyoake (1817–1906), George William Foote (1850–1915), and Charles Bradlaugh (1833–1891). Holyoake, who began establishing 'secular societies' round the country in 1852, had learned the terror of the Lord as a child from the Revd J. A. James (3.1.1, 5.1.1) and the terror of English law from six months' imprisonment on a conviction for blasphemy in 1842. The transcript of his trial, which freethinkers circulated widely, made clear how a little theological levity, uttered at the wrong moment, could cost a working man dear (**6.3.1**). Another annoyance Secularists had to contend with was lack of redress when wronged. In 1867, for example, an appeal court held in *Cowan* v. *Milbourn* that a defendant in breach of his contract with an unbeliever was entitled to repudiate the agreement once he learned that its performance would involve the promotion of anti-Christian propaganda. This illiberal ruling remained the law until 1883, when it was disapproved by Lord Chief Justice Coleridge (1820–1894) in *Reg.* v. *Ramsay and Foote*. In this case an indictment for blasphemous libel was brought against Foote, editor of *The Freethinker*, and William Ramsay, the manager, for publishing certain statements and a number of 'Comic Bible' cartoons. Lord Coleridge, in summing up, disputed the rule of law upheld in *Cowan* v. *Milbourn*, that 'Christianity is part and parcel of the law of the land'; he made a distinction between indecency and blasphemy; and he made legal history by emphasizing the crucial importance of the manner as opposed to the substance of an alleged blasphemous statement. When the jury could not agree on a verdict, the prosecution was dropped (**6.3.2**). Few doubted, however, that the original aim of the prosecution had been to convict Bradlaugh, president of the National Secular Society, who, it emerged, had severed his connection with the *Freethinker* two years before. Bradlaugh, an avowed atheist, had been elected Liberal MP for Northampton in 1880; he was still trying to swear on the Bible and take his seat in Parliament. A conviction for blasphemy would have blocked his way for good. In 1884 Bradlaugh contrived to admister the oath to himself, for which he ended up in court, facing five charges, each carrying a penalty of £500. Bankruptcy, like blasphemy, was a bar on entry to the Commons. The jury found against him on three counts and Bradlaugh lodged an appeal, which was heard by the Master of the Rolls and two other Lord Justices of Appeal, who held for the Crown (**6.3.3**). But before a further appeal could be heard, a general election took place, Bradlaugh was returned for Northampton with an increased majority, and the Conservative Speaker of the House allowed him to take the oath unopposed. The Attorney General dropped his action, whereupon Bradlaugh introduced a general affirmation bill that became law in 1888.

6.3.1   THE TRIAL OF GEORGE JACOB HOLYOAKE, 1842

On the morning of the 15th of August, 1842 – the Court-house at Gloucester being very crowded – Mr. HOLYOAKE'S name was called, and he took his place at the bar. . . .

The Clerk then proceeded to read the Indictment, as follows:—

> *Gloucester to wit.* – The jurors for our lady the queen, upon their oath, present that GEORGE JACOB HOLYOAKE, late of the parish of Cheltenham, in the county of Gloucester, labourer, being a wicked malicious and evil-disposed person, and disregarding the laws and religion of the realm, and wickedly and profanely devising and intending to bring Almighty God, the holy scriptures, and the Christian religion into disbelief and contempt among the people of this kingdom, on the twenty-fourth day of May, in the fifth year of the reign of our lady the queen, with force and arms, at the parish aforesaid, in the county aforesaid, in the presence and hearing of divers liege subjects of our said lady the queen, maliciously, unlawfully, and wickedly did compose, speak, utter, pronounce, and publish with a loud voice, of and concerning Almighty God, the holy

scriptures, and the Christian religion, these words following, that is to say, 'I (meaning the said George Jacob
Holyoake) do not believe there is such a thing as a god, I
(meaning the said George Jacob Holyoake) would have the
Deity served as they (meaning the government of this
kingdom) serve the subalterns, place him (meaning
Almighty God) on half-pay' – to the high displeasure of
almighty god, to the great scandal and reproach of the
Christian religion, in open violation of the laws of this
kingdom, to the evil example of all others in the like case
offending, and against the peace of our lady the queen her
crown and dignity.

Mr. Holyoake . . . pleaded NOT GUILTY. . . .
. . . The jury was then empannelled, Mr. Holyoake saying he had no
objection to urge which his lordship would allow.
The following is the list of the jury:
Thomas Gardiner, grocer, Cheltenham, Foreman.
James Reeve, farmer, Chedworth.
William Ellis, farmer, Chedworth.
Avery Trotman, farmer, Chedworth.
Simon Vizard, shopkeeper, Oldland.
William Matthews, poulterer, Cheltenham.
Isaac Tombs, farmer, Whitcomb.
William Wilson, maltster, Brimpsfield.
Edwin Brown, farmer, Withington.
Bevan Smith, farmer, Harescomb.
William Smith, miller, Barnwood.
Joseph Shipp, farmer, Yate.
Mr. Holyoake: Can I have a copy of the indictment?
Mr. Justice Erskine: I had one made for you, in consequence of your
application to the court last week.
Mr. Holyoake: Yes, my lord, but I was asked eight shillings and
sixpence for it; and after the numerous exactions I was subjected to at the
sessions, after being brought here by the magistrates, and then not tried, I
did not think myself justified in paying any more.
Mr. Justice Erskine: I ordered a copy to be made for you, but did not
think it necessary that you should have it on any other than the usual
conditions.*
Mr. Holyoake: Can I be allowed to read the indictment against me?

---

*This copy of Indictment occupied *not quite one sheet of paper*, for which *eight shillings and
sixpence* were asked!

Mr. Justice Erskine: Certainly.

The Clerk than handed a copy to Mr. Holyoake. . . .

Mr. Justice Erskine: . . . Now is the time for your defence.

Mr. Holyoake: I am not a little surprised to hear that the case for the prosecution is closed. I have heard nothing, not one word, to prove the charge in the indictment. There has been adduced no evidence to show I have uttered words *maliciously* and *wickedly* blasphemous. I submit to your lordship that there is not sufficient evidence.

Mr. Justice Erskine: That is for the jury to decide.

Mr. Holyoake: I thought, my lord, as the evidence is so manifestly insufficient to prove *malice*, you would have felt bound to direct my acquittal.

Mr. Justice Erskine: It is for the jury to say whether they are satisfied.

DEFENCE

Mr. Holyoake, at a quarter before Twelve o'clock, commenced his defence, as follows:

My Lord and Gentlemen of the Jury: It now becomes my duty to address you, to speak of the nature of the charge preferred against me in this indictment, and of the evidence by which it is attempted to be supported. . . .

. . . It must already be clear enough to you, gentlemen of the jury, that it is not dishonesty in me you are called upon to punish. I am placed here for having acted honestly. Could I have been a hypocrite I should never have stood at this bar. I have morally interfered with no man's opinion; taught no immorality. My only offence is, telling truth. I am unaccustomed to address a jury, and I hope to avoid the charge of presumption or dogmatism, and to influence you favourably in your verdict. I have no wish to offend the prejudices of any man in this court, and have no interest in so doing, when his lordship is armed with the vengeance of the law to punish it. But while I profess respect for your opinions, I must entertain some for my own. There are those here who think religion proper, and that it alone can lead to general happiness – I do not, and I have had the same means of judging. You say your feelings are insulted – your opinions outraged; but mine, however honest, are by you rendered liable to punishment. I ask not equality of privileges in this respect, I seek not the power of punishing those who differ from me, nay, I should disdain its use. Christianity claims what she does not allow, although she says 'All men are brothers.'

This is to me a new position. I am unaccustomed to special pleading, and ignorant of those technicalities of which the gentlemen of the bar are so skilled in the use, and by which they often, in a few minutes, gain as much with the jury as would require from me half-an-hour's close reasoning. It is from no disrespect I did not give my case into the hands of counsel, but because they are unable to enter into my motives. There is a magic circle out of which they will not step – they will argue only what is orthodox – any other course is unprofitable – and you would have had no opportunity of learning my true motives, of comprehending my real feelings, or seeing the true bearings of my case.

I now come to a part of this business which claims your serious attention. . . .

[Here Holyoake spoke continuously for some eight hours, being interrupted only once, by Mr Justice Erskine, about the mid-point.]

I regret I have had to detain you so long. I have to thank your lordship and you, gentlemen of the jury, for the courtesy and attention with which I have been heard. I have now only to sum up the arguments I have adduced.

Gentlemen, If I have occupied you long you will find my apology in the circumstance that your verdict against me will occupy me longer. I could wish that justice to me and your convenience had joined hands. The length of my defence has originated with the charge against me and not with myself. The numerous points touched upon are inherent in my subject, and are not the result of inventions.

As your reflections revert to the ground I have gone over I trust you will remember the peculiar disadvantages under which I labour and the novelty of the position I have been unjustly forced to occupy.

You have seen how the bigotted press of this bigotted district has beset me like tigers; may I hope you will stand between me and the misrepresentation exercised for my destruction. . . .

I trust my being a Socialist will be no fatal consideration in your opinion. That science which has descended to us on the stream of philosophy from the earliest ages, and has been handed forward by the illustrious More; detailed in modern days in the philosophy of Godwin; and so beautifully embodied in the poetry of Goethe, seems rather to deserve careful attention than hasty, unqualified, and vindictive reprehension.

After having been subjected to the rudest insults, treated like a felon, classed with murderers, imprisoned, harrassed for two months, and put to ruinous expenses, may I venture to hope that Christian justice is satisfied, and that I have been punished sufficiently for telling the truth.

I have extricated my moral character from the misrepresentations in which vulgar fanaticism has sought to involve it. Having read to you the testimonials of those who have known me the longest and best, I may say, whatever may be thought of my principles none can censure my motives, no man can impugn my practices. . . .

Of the nature of the charge against me I add no further word. My only crime has been the discharge of my duty, and however I may endure the painful consequences, I shall, I hope, ever deem the cause of them an honor.

For my difference in opinion with you upon the question of Deity, I offer no apology. I have made no contract to think as you do, and I owe no obligation to do it. If I commanded you to abjure your belief, you would instantly spurn such injustice, and if you punish me for not abjuring mine, how will you reconcile it with 'doing as you would wish to be done unto?'

Suppose I had said that which I did not, viz., that there is no God, still I should not deserve the vengeance of the law. If I point to the wrong I see in this Christian country, and ask, is this christianity? you would reply, 'No, what you refer to results from men who live without God in the world.' Then, gentlemen, would you punish me for simply saying that which other men, unpunished, are every day doing?

If I have said religious revenues should be reduced one half, I spoke only the dictates of humanity at this season of national suffering. Surely it is not blasphemous to argue that human misery should be alleviated at the expence of spiritual pride. To send me to gaol for calling on christianity to be benevolent, will be to pronounce it a system at once essentially selfish and legally barbarous. . . .

I ask not equal rights with yourselves. You, as Christians, can imprison, fine, flog, and put to a lingering death all who differ from you. I do not offend your pride by asking to be admitted your equals here. I despise such privileges; I scorn such power; for I hold in contempt its exercise. I claim merely the right to be honest; to speak my convictions; to show a man the right path when I think he takes the wrong one.

It is a melancholy maxim in these courts of law, that the greater the truth the greater the libel; and so it would be with me this day could I demonstrate to you that there is no Deity. The more correct I am the severer would by my punishment, because the law regards the belief in a god to be the foundation of obedience among men. But I trust I have convinced you that my views of this question are strictly in accordance with the highest morality, which you profess to sit here to conserve. That they are compatible with the practice of all our duties to our fellowmen is borne out by eminent authority and long experience. . . . I may add that I should renounce them forthwith did I not believe them to be the soundest foundation of morality. But whether my sentiments are right or wrong the most eminent men, the most exalted philosophers, the wisest of divines, have united in asserting that they can no more be corrected by force than castles can be stormed by logic, and that only wanton cruelty, or perfect ignorance can recommend me to be punished for holding them. . . .

If you view my opinions in a personal point of view, and suppose them destructive of christianity, you must not forget that christianity is said to be founded upon a rock, and that nothing can prevail against it. Hence my conviction will be to proclaim that this is so much vain boasting.

Now permit me to crave your attention to an important point. The church of England declares the blood of the martyrs to have been the seed of the church; which means that persecution, as Lord Brougham has most correctly said, will spread any opinions. All history confirms this conclusion, and the bishops and dignitaries of the church have endorsed it. Hence, upon this high authority it is clear that your verdict against me will infallibly spread my sentiments – the very thing your attention has been invoked to prevent; and you cannot doubt this, unless you set aside the declaration of the church, blazoned in her prayer-books, and attested by her brightest luminaries; and if you doubt their judgment on so plain a point who will believe them, or rely on their decisions in matters of faith?

If the state religion be true, my opinions can never overcome it; and by convicting me you publish your consciousness of error in the cause you are placed there to defend as truth. If God be truth you libel him and his power, and publish the omnipotence of error; and what is here applied to truth belongs chiefly to christianity. She is disgraced by these prosecutions, and her presumptive weakness in reasonable argument proclaimed to the world. . . .

In your churches, as I have read to you, you implore that truth and justice may descend among men, and the supplication is a noble one. Gentlemen, will you pray for truth and justice in your churches and brand it in your courts? And as far as the defence of christianity is concerned it remains with you to say if you will consign to the dungeon the office of the pulpit, and make the truths of the bible to be expounded by gaolers instead of being taught by your ministers.

With you it also remains to determine whether that freedom of thought to which we owe all our national excellence, and which is the fairest privilege man can enjoy shall be restricted on the two most important subjects of human moment, morals and religion.

I might contend with propriety that the answer for which I am indicted was a politico-economical one, and had little relation strictly to morals, and none to religion. But I prefer standing on the ground of honesty, integrity, and truth. Shall it be said that christianity would have left me at liberty had I been a detestable hypocrite, but has dragged me here because I did not stoop to that, but spoke conscientiously? The vulgarity, pollution, and crime congregated in your gaols, little assimilates with my taste, and the rude brutality of its punishments little accords with my delicate constitution. I seek not these things, I assure you, but when they lie in the path of duty I trust I shall ever prefer them to a dereliction from it. But what is the character of a nation that thus fosters impediments in the way of honesty? Is it thus religion exalts us – the heathen were infinitely our superiors.

I turn back to the morality of ancient days, and meditating with delight on their noble sincerity and love of truth, I forget it is my misfortune to live in modern times and among a Christian people. . . .

Gentlemen, christianity also tells me god is love. How will this comport with the verdict that will again consign me to the living tomb I have so recently left? The torture awarded to me falls not on me alone, for then its injustice might more easily be borne; but it falls alike on wife, children, parents, and friends. Homes are desolate, hearths are chilled, and the gloom of the prison mantles everywhere that sympathy exists or that affection and friendship are to be found. In my case too no ground remains to suppose that the sacrifice of me can benefit society, it can only make men tremble at a religion which ought to be love, and converts the honest among them into hypocrites. To suppose the perpetration of such wanton cruelty and wickedness is an acceptable offering to heaven is to convert the almighty into a demon, and to picture him forth with the attributes of a wretch.

But, gentlemen, supposing that it is my sentiments that you are requested to punish; you should first do yourselves the justice to reflect what has been said about them and insinuated in this court; learned divines and sage writers on atheism agree that it is too absurd to need refutation, too barren to satisfy, too monstrous to attract, too fearful to allure, too dumb to speak, and too deathly not to appal its own votaries. It is styled too grave to entertain youth, and too devoid of consolation for the trembling wants of age, too abstract for the comprehension of the ignorant, and too unreasonable to gain the admiration of the intelligent. That it is alarming to the timid, and disquieting to the brave; that it negatives everything, and sets up nothing, and is so purely speculative that it can never have a practical bearing on the business of life. Gentlemen, will you disturb the harmony of these conclusions by a verdict against me, and attack that which never existed, and place upon the grave records of this court a slaying of the self-slain; will you thus draw attention to a subject you perhaps think had better be forgotten, and create a conviction that it must be a greatly important one since you erect it into public notice by directing the thunders of the law at a young and comparatively inexperienced believer in its principle?

Would you test my opinions by my emotions on the bed of death? Let me assure you that if men can expect to die in peace, who can send their fellow men to a gaol because of honest difference of opinion, I have nothing to fear.

I have shown that in the utterance of the words laid to my charge no guilty intention has been proved, even supposing them to be wrong, nor can the circumstances under which they were delivered be considered as the publication of my sentiments; since they occurred in an answer, not in an address – were an explanation not a statement and were publicly solicited not put forward of my own accord. And I have shown that I could not answer otherwise without descending to the meanness of hypocrisy, the cowardice of subterfuge, or the dishonesty of lying, which course reason and honour not only rejects, but christianity itself is said to hold in adherence [abhorrence?].

I now come to the grand point urged against me. I am told I may hold opinions, but must keep them to myself. How coldly insulting and unjust is the declaration. It means I may know and feel what is right, but must never do it. I must see my fellow-men in error, but never put them right. Must live every day below the standard of right my sense of duty and conscience sets up, and all my life long 'prove all things' and never 'hold fast to the good.' While Christian juries are found to sanction so much moral injustice, no wonder christianity is despised.

Upon the illegalities which have characterised the proceedings I have little else I wish to say. The origin of our common law is clearly of this kind and demands your strongest reprehension by a verdict this day of unqualified acquittal. This is not more due in justice to me, than from respect to the judge himself. He and his predecessors have declared that fair discussion is allowable, while the law renders all questioning calumnious and illegal. This is but a mockery of liberty, and keeps the inquirer in everlasting uncertainty, and renders him callous where it is proper he should be respectful.

If the justice of the question is disregarded, policy will teach that the reflections it casts upon christianity should be removed. The common law, as I have shown, is untruthful, insincere, partial, barbarous, redundantly cruel, punishes honesty, encourages hypocrisy, subjugates reason, is part of the hideous inquisition, is unjust, degrades God, brings into contempt that it professes to respect, exhibits contemptible presumption, degrades the most refined religions, and is a libel on human nature. Gentlemen, if by your verdict against me, you sanction this law, what do you sanction for christianity, which is part and parcel of it?

Now gentlemen, my last words are addressed to you, and to your lordship as a man of intelligence and from whom the country expects a decision above the vulgar narrowmindedness of bigotry. A decision in the spirit of the liberal charge to the jury. You have sworn to determine my verdict according to the evidence adduced, and you have summoned the almighty God to bear witness to your solemn intention to abide by your oath. Whatever I may think of this, you acknowledge this sanction as preeminently binding. Now, as no one particle of evidence has been adduced to show that I have committed blasphemy – no law has been read to you defining it, how can you without the most palpable perjury pronounce me guilty? You may be told you are to determine whether I have or have not spoken blasphemy – but gentlemen, your opinion whatever it may be – is it evidence? . . .

. . . But I best prefer appealing to you as honest men, in the spirit of my own reasoning, and thinking; as men with an eye to the improvement of mankind, who would break the unjust shackles that bind them, who would discard prejudice in order to be just, who will not condemn me because I am not rich, and who will listen to humanity rather than to bigotry, and respect truthfulness wherever you may find it. I believe that in every honest heart there is a sense of rectitude that rises superior to creeds, that respects all virtue and protects all truth, that asks for no names and seeks no precedents before resolving to do rightly. That fears no man's frowns, and dares to be just without any man's or custom's permit. That ever generously rises the firm friend of the calumniated and deliverer of the oppressed – to this feeling, gentlemen, only do I appeal, and by its verdict I am willing to abide.

My lord, should the jury be disposed to take a partial and narrow view of the great question at issue in my case, I rely on your lordship's greater experience, more extended knowledge and enlightened views to generously correct such tendency. Your lordship can see beyond the chicanery of the law and the vulgar prejudices of fanaticism. You do know that a great principle is involved in the decision now to be arrived at, affecting the very existence of intellectual progression, individual integrity, and moral virtue, which all government should cherish, and no religion be allowed to oppose. This jury will look to you for the path they are to take, and the verdict which returns me to my home a man or to my cell a slave, rests on your lordship's lips. The thinking portion of this country will estimate your lordship's character by your conduct this day, and posterity will behold the glory or degradation of this nation in the decision to which your lordship, the jury, and this court shall come. . . .

THE CHARGE TO THE JURY

Mr. Justice Erskine: Gentlemen of the jury, although the lengthened address of the defendant has demanded from you so long endurance, in this vitiated atmosphere, I still trust we shall have enough of power left to direct our minds to the parts of this case which are important. The greater part of the time has been wasted on subjects with which you have nothing to do. We are not sitting here as a deliberative assembly to consider whether in respect of such cases as this it is politic or wise to imprison for opinions – whether men ought to be punished for uttering such sentiments – and I shall have nothing to say to you on that point. We have to decide on the law as we find it. . . . I am not going to lay down as law that no man has a right to entertain opinions opposed to the religion of the state, nor to express them. Man is only responsible for his opinions to God, because God can only judge of his motives, and we arrogate his duties if we judge of men's sentiments. If men will entertain sentiments opposed to the religion of the state we require that they shall express them reverently, and philosophers who have discussed this subject all agree that this is right. . . . Men are not permitted to make use of indecent language in reference to God and the Christian religion, without rendering themselves liable to punishment. . . . Sober argument you may answer, but indecent reviling you cannot, and therefore the law steps in and punishes it. . . . What you have to try is that the defendant wickedly and devisedly did intend to bring the Christian religion into contempt among the people, by uttering words of and concerning Almighty God, the holy scriptures, and the Christian religion. The charge is that he uttered these words with the intention of bringing Almighty God, the Christian religion, and the holy scriptures into contempt. You are not called upon to say whether in your judgment the opinions of the defendant are right or wrong – whether it is right or wrong that words like these should be punished, but whether he uttered these words with the intent charged in the indictment. . . . Then the charge is made out, for I tell you that it is an offence at common law. . . . Any man who treats with contempt the Christian religion is guilty of an indictable misdemeanour. You have to consider the language and a passage read to you from a charge of a learned judge. 'It may not be going too far to state that no author or preacher is forbidden stating his opinions sincerely. By maliciously is not meant malice against any particular individual but a mischievous intent. This is the criterion, and it is a fair criterion, if it can be collected from the offensive levity in which the subject is treated, if the matter placed in the indictment contains any such tendency.' If the words had appeared in the course of a written paper you would have entertained no doubt that the person who had uttered these words, had uttered them with levity. The only thing in his favour is that it was not a written answer. The solution given by the defendant is, that although his opinions are unhappily such that he has no belief in a God, he had no intention of bringing religion into contempt. He went on to state that he considered it the duty of the clergymen of the establishment to have reduced their incomes one half. If he had meant this he ought to have made use of other language. You will dismiss from your minds all statements in newspapers, or other statements made out of court, and consider it in reference to the evidence. If you are convinced that he uttered it with levity, for the purpose of treating with contempt the majesty of the Almighty God, he is guilty of the offence. If you think he made use of these words in the heat of argument without any such intent, you will give him the benefit of the doubt. If you are convinced that he did it with that object you must find him guilty, despite of all that has been addressed to you. If you entertain a reasonable doubt of his intention, you will give him the benefit of it.

The jury after a very brief deliberation returned a verdict of GUILTY. . . .

SENTENCE

Mr. Justice Erskine: . . . George Jacob Holyoake, . . . you have been convicted of uttering language, and although you have been adducing long arguments to show the impolicy of these prosecutions, you are convicted of having uttered these words with improper levity. The arm of the law is not stretched out to protect the character of the Almighty; we do not assume to be the protectors of our God, but to protect the people from such indecent language. And if these words had been written for deliberate circulation, I should have passed on you a severer sentence. You uttered them in consequence of a question; I have no evidence that this question was put to draw out these words. Proceeding on the evidence that has been given, trusting that these words have been uttered in the heat of the moment, I shall think it sufficient to sentence you to be *imprisoned in the Common Gaol for Six calendar months.*

Mr. Holyoake: My lord, am I to be classed with thieves and felons?

Mr. Justice Erskine: No. Thieves and felons are sentenced to the Penitentiary – you to the Common Gaol.

The Court adjourned at ten o'clock.

---

9   Early Secularist handbills. In Bradford, local activists took up a challenge and sponsored lectures by Holyoake, with an open discussion, at a price working men could afford. The success of Secularism in the town so worried the Congregational Union as it assembled there two months later that ministers delivered their own lectures 'to the working classes'. One of them, the Reverend Brewin Grant, was sponsored to conduct a general mission to the Secularists, and this led to his great set-debate with Holyoake at London in 1853. The debate first brought Secularism into the public eye and made the word familiar enough to be used without explanation in Horace Mann's census report later that year (6.1.1).

SECULARISM
JUSTIFIED.

In consequence of the requirement made when Mr. HOLY-
OAKE last Lectured in Bradford, by Dr. Ackworth, of Hor-
ton College, that the Principles then attempted to be
enforced should be more formally stated, the Bradford
Branch of the Secular Society have much pleasure in announcing to the Public, that Mr.

G. J. HOLYOAKE
Of London, Editor of "The Reasoner,"
Will deliver other THREE

LECTURES,
IN THE
ODDFELLOWS' HALL,
Thornton Road, Bradford,

On Monday, Tuesday, and Thursday,
The 23rd, 24th, and 26th of August, 1852.

SUBJECTS:

I.--New Development of the principles of Free Inquirers.

II.--Morality shown to be independent of Religion, and
as possible to the Non-Theist as to the Theist.

III.--Eternal Punishments, as taught by Jesus Christ,
shewn to be contradictory to the great precepts on
which his own Moral Character reposes.

As before, opportunity will be afforded to the Ministers of Religion to
question the soundness of any views advanced by Mr. Holyoake.

Admission: Front Seats, 2d.; Back do. 1d.
Doors open at Seven; Chair to be taken at Half past.
*Tickets to be had of Messrs. William Cooke, News Agent, Vicar Lane; J. Mitchell's
Temperance Hotel, Union Street; T. Umpleby, Bookseller, Manchester Road; William
Christian. Tailor, Top of Brick Lane, and at the Doors.* [Parkinson, Printer.

A

PUBLIC DISCUSSION

BETWEEN

MR. G. J. HOLYOAKE,

Editor of the " Reasoner,"

AND THE

Rev. BREWIN GRANT, B.A.,

Editor of the " Bible and the People,"

On SIX THURSDAY EVENINGS, COMMENCING
JAN. 20 & ENDING FEB. 24, 1853,

WILL BE HELD IN THE

COWPER STREET SCHOOL ROOM, CITY ROAD.

SUBJECT—What Advantages would accrue to Mankind generally, and the Working Classes in particular, by the removal of
Christianity and the substitution of Secularism in its place ?

The Topics for each evening are as follows :—

1. The Nature of Secularism.
2. Science the Providence of Man.
3. Morals Independent of New Testament Authority.
4. The Death of Jesus Christ, its Policy and its Example.
5. The Eclecticism of the Apostolical Writings.
6. General Advantages of Secularism.

Doors open at Seven, to commence at half-past Seven.

Admission by Tickets — For the Course, 1s., and 3d. for a
Single Lecture.

To be had at Messrs. Ward & Co.'s, Paternoster Row; and Mr. Watson's,
Queen's Head Passage, Paternoster Row; and at the doors of the School
Room on the Evenings of the Discussion.

6.3.2   LORD CHIEF JUSTICE COLERIDGE ON
REG. V. *RAMSAY AND FOOTE,* 1883

. . . The two defendants are indicted for the publication of blasphemous libels; and the two questions which arise for your consideration are: First, are these publications in themselves blasphemous libels? Secondly, if they are so, is the publication of them traced home to the defendants so that you can find them guilty? I will begin with the last question, though it is reversing the logical order, because it is the shorter and more simple of the two. . . .

The fact of publication by the defendants has hardly been contested. The evidence is all one way; it is uncontradicted, and it is overwhelming. It is proved that the defendant Ramsay sold the papers which contained the libels. It is proved that the articles charged as libellous were inserted by the express direction of the defendant Foote. There is nothing to qualify this proof; the defendants, in fact, do not deny their liability; and though the case is for you, I do not know that I need refrain from saying that, if upon the evidence you have heard, you think both the defendants liable for the publication of these alleged libels, I shall entirely agree with you. . . .

The great point still remains, are these articles within the meaning of the law blasphemous libels? . . . My duty is to explain to you as clearly as I can what is the law upon the subject. My duty, further, is not to answer the speeches of the defendants, (that is no part of the duty of a judge), but to point out to you what in their arguments is in my judgment well-founded, and what is not; and then, when you have listened to me, the question is entirely for you. . . .

Gentlemen, you have heard with truth that these things are, according to the old law, if the dicta of old judges, dicta often not necessary for the decisions, are to be taken as of absolute and unqualified authority – that these things, I say, are undoubtedly blasphemous libels, simply and without more, because they question the truth of Christianity. But, . . . for reasons which I will presently explain, these dicta cannot be taken to be a true statement of the law, as the law is now. It is no longer true, in the sense in which it was true when these dicta were uttered, that Christianity is part of the law of the land. In the times when these dicta were uttered, Jews, Roman Catholics, Nonconformists of all sorts were under heavy disabilities for religion, were regarded as hardly having civil rights. Everything almost, short of the punishment of death, was enacted against them. . . . But now, so far as I know the law, a Jew might be Lord Chancellor, most certainly he might be Master of the Rolls. . . . Therefore, to base the prosecution of a bare denial of the truth of Christianity, *simpliciter* and *per se* on the ground that Christianity is part of the law of the land, in the sense in which it was said to be so by Lord Hale, and Lord Raymond, and Lord

Tenterden, is in my judgment a mistake. It is to forget that law grows; and that though the principles of law remain unchanged, yet (and it is one of the advantages of the common law) their application is to be changed with the changing circumstances of the times. Some persons may call this retrogression, I call it progression of human opinion. Therefore, to take up a book or a paper, to discover merely that in it the truth of Christianity is denied without more, and thereupon to say that now a man may be indicted upon such denial as for a blasphemous libel, is, as I venture to think, absolutely untrue. . . .

Gentlemen, when I last addressed a jury on this subject, I . . . said that, if the law was as contended for, it would be enough to say that anything was part of the law of the land, and that thereupon there could be no discussion and no reform; for that to attack any part of the law, however gravely and respectfully, would be, if not blasphemous yet seditious. Monarchy is part of the law of the land; primogeniture is part of the law of the land; the laws of marriages are part of the law of the land, and so forth. But if the doctrine contended for be true, to republish Algernon Sydney, or Harrington, or Locke, or Milton, would expose a man to a prosecution for a breach of the law of libel. . . . It is clear, therefore, to my mind that the mere denial of the truth of the Christian religion is not enough alone to constitute the offence of blasphemy.

What then is enough? No doubt we must not be guilty of taking the law into our own hands, and converting it from what it really is to what we think it ought to be. I must lay down the law to you as I understand it, and as I read it in books of authority. Now, Mr. Foote, in his very able address to you, spoke with something like contempt of the person he called 'the late Mr. Starkie.' He did not know Mr. Starkie; he did not know how able and how good a man he was. Mr. Starkie died when I was young; but I knew him, and everyone who knew him knew that he was a man not only of remarkable power of mind, but of opinions liberal in the best sense; and if ever the task of lawmaking could be safely left in the hands of any man perhaps it might have been in his. But, what is more material to the present purpose, the statement of the law by Mr. Starkie has again and again been assented to by judges as a correct statement of the existing law. . . . Whether it ought to be or not is not for me to say. I tell you the law as I understand it, leaving you to apply it to the facts of the particular case before you.

There was much force, no doubt, in the way in which Mr. Foote dealt with the passage in his address to you. The vagueness, the uncertainty which he insisted upon are possibly, however, inherent in the subject, and there is perhaps more to be said in favour of Mr. Starkie's view than may appear without reflection. There is a passage in his book taken, I believe, from Michaelis, in which it is pointed out with great truth that in one view the law against blasphemous libel may be for the benefit of the libeller himself, who, if there were no law, might find its absence ill exchanged for the presence of popular vengeance and indignation. . . . It is therefore not so clear to my mind that some sort of blasphemy laws reasonably enforced may not be an advantage, even to those who differ from the popular religion of a country, and who desire to oppose and to deny it. Further, therefore, it must not be taken as so absolutely certain that all these laws against blasphemy are in principle tyrannical. Whether, however, they are so or not, if they exist we must administer them, and the principle upon which we are to administer them is to be found in . . . Starkie.

But I think I ought to go further, and to say that such study as I have been able to make of the cases has not satisfied me that the law ever was laid down differently from the law as laid down by Mr. Starkie. . . . It is perhaps worth observing that this law of blasphemous libel first appears in our books – at least, that cases relating to it are first reported – shortly after the curtailment or abolition of the jurisdiction of the Ecclesiastical Courts in matters temporal. Speaking broadly, before the time of Charles II. these things would have been dealt with as heresy; and the libellers so-called of more recent days would have suffered as heretics in earlier. But I pass to the cases which are reported. . . .

In the case of Taylor (which I cite from Ventris, who was himself a judge, and who gives the best report) Lord Hale had the following words before him; and you must always take a case and an opinion with reference to the subject-matter as to which the case was decided or the opinion given. The words, as Ventris says, were 'blasphemous expressions horrible to hear,' viz., 'that Jesus Christ was a bastard and a whoremaster, that religion was a cheat, and that he feared neither God, the devil, or man.' Those were the words on which Lord Hale had to decide in that case, and what he says is this: 'Such kind of wicked blasphemous words are not only an offence to God and religion, but a crime against the laws [of] State, and Government, and therefore punishable in this court.' That is what Lord Hale held, in one of the earliest cases on the subject. You may find expressions which seem to go further in the reasons which he gives, but before these cases are so glibly cited as they sometimes are, you should look and see what is the subject-matter of the decision. Lord Hale held 'such kind of wicked blasphemous words' to be a blasphemous libel, and if they came before me I too should hold them without hesitation to be a blasphemous libel, though I am no more disposed to hang witches than Lord Hale really was. . . .

There is another case, the last with which I shall trouble you, not indeed exactly in point, but which is sometimes cited in support of the proposition that to attack Christianity is to expose yourself to an indictment for libel. It is the case of *Cowan* v. *Milbourn*, decided in 1867. . . . It was an action in which the owner of some rooms justified a breach of his contract to let them, on the ground that they were to be used for lectures directed against the character of Christ and his teaching, and the defendant's justification was upheld by the court. The late Lord Chief Baron [Kelly] undoubtedly goes the full length of the doctrine contended for, and from his reasons, on the grounds I have already stated, I respectfully dissent. But Lord Bramwell puts his concurrence in the judgment on a totally different ground. . . . So that, if I understand him, his authority cannot be invoked for the proposition that the proposed lectures were necessarily blasphemous libels or the subjects of indictments. I think therefore that anyone who calmly and carefully considers the cases will very much doubt whether the old law is really open to the attacks which have been made upon it. . . .

But whether this is so or not, Parliament at least has altered the law on these subjects; it is no longer the law that none but professors of Christianity can take part or have rights in the State; others have now just as much right in civil matters as any member of the Church of England has. The condition of things is no longer what it was when these great judges pronounced the judgments which I think have been misunderstood, and strained to a meaning they do not warrant. It is a comfort to think that things have been altered. . . .

Such are the rules, as I tell you, by which you are to judge of these libels. But further, you have heard a great deal, powerfully put by Mr. Foote, about the inexpediency of these laws in any view of them, and as to the way in which they are worked. To observe on this is the least pleasant part of my unpleasant duty, and I wish I could avoid it. It might perhaps be enough to say that these are things with which you and I have nothing to do. We have to administer the law as we find it, and if we do not like it we should try to get it altered. In a free country, after full discussion and agitation, a change is always effected if it approves itself to the general sense of the community. Mr. Foote has told you that this movement against him and his friends is to be regarded as persecution; and it is true, as he has said, that . . . irritation, annoyance, punishment which stops short of extermination, very seldom alter men's religious convictions. . . . No doubt, therefore, persecution, unless it is far more thorough-going than anyone in England and in this age would stand, is, speaking generally, of no avail. It is also true, that persecution is a very easy form of virtue. A difficult form of virtue is to try in your own life to obey what you believe to be God's will. It is not easy to do, and if you do it, you make but little noise in the world. But it is easy to turn on some one who differs from you in opinion, and in the guise of zeal for God's honour, to attack a man whose life perhaps may be much more pleasing to God than is your own. When it is done by men full of profession and pretention, who choose that particular form of zeal for God which consists in putting the criminal law in force against some one else, many quiet people come to sympathise, not with the prosecutor but with the defendant. That will be so as human nature goes, and all the more if the prosecutors should by chance be men who enjoy the wit of Voltaire, who are not repelled by the sneer of Gibbon, and who rather relish the irony of Hume. It is still worse if the prosecutor acts not from the strange but often genuine feeling that God wants his help and that he can give it by a prosecution, but from partisan or political motives. Nothing can be more foreign from one's notions of what is high-minded, noble, or religious; and one must visit a man who would so act, not for God's honour, but using God's honour for his own purposes, with the most disdainful disapprobation that the human mind can form.

However, the question here is not with the motives, of which I know nothing, nor with the characters, of which I know if possible less, of those who instituted these proceedings, but with the proceedings themselves, and whether they are legal. The way in which Mr. Foote defends himself is able, and well worthy of your attention; and you must say, after a few words from me, what you think of it. . . . I have two things to say: one in Mr. Foote's favour, and one against him. He wished to have it impressed upon you that he is not, and never has been, a licentious writer in the sense in which Mr. Starkie uses the word licentious. He has not, he says, pandered to the sensual passions of mankind. You will have the documents before you, and you will judge for yourselves. For myself I should say that in this matter he is right. It is a thing in his favour, and he is entitled to have it said. But upon the other point, if the law as I have laid it down to you is correct − and I believe it has always been so − if the decencies of controversy are observed, even the fundamentals of religion may be attacked without a person being guilty of blasphemous libel.

There are many great and grave writers who have attacked the foundations of Christianity. Mr. Mill undoubtedly did so; some great writers now alive have done so too; but no one can read their writings without seeing a difference between them and the incriminated publications, which I am obliged to say is a difference not of degree but of kind. There is a grave, an earnest, a reverent, I am almost tempted to say, a religious tone in the very attacks on Christianity itself, which shows that what is aimed at is not insult to the opinions of the majority of Christians, but a real, quiet, honest pursuit of truth. If the truth at which these writers have arrived is not the truth we have been taught, and which, if we had not been taught it, we might have discovered, yet because these conclusions differ from ours, they are not to be exposed to a criminal indictment. With regard to many of these persons, therefore, I should say they were within the protection of the law as I understand it.

With regard to some of the others, passages from whose writings Mr.

Foote read, I heard them yesterday for the first time, I do not at all question that Mr. Foote read them correctly. I confess, as I heard them, I had, and have, a difficulty in distinguishing them from the alleged libels. They do appear to me to be open to the same charge, on the same grounds, as Mr. Foote's writings. He says many of these things are written in expensive books, published by publishers of known eminence; that they are to be found in the drawing-rooms, studies, libraries, of men of high position. It may be so. If it be, I will make no distinction between Mr. Foote and anyone else; if there are men, however eminent, who use such language as Mr. Foote, and if ever I have to try them, troublesome and disagreeable as it is, if they come before me, they shall, so far as my powers go, have neither more nor less than the justice I am trying to do to Mr. Foote. If they offend against the blasphemy laws they shall find that so long as the laws exist, whatever I may think about their wisdom, there is but one rule in this court for all who come to it. This much Mr. Foote may depend upon.

So far as I can judge, some of the expressions which he read seemed to be strong, shall I say, coarse? – expressions of contempt and hatred for the generally recognised truths of Christianity and for the Hebrew Scriptures which are said to have been inspired by God himself. But Mr. Foote must forgive me for saying that this is no argument whatever in his favour. . . . If he is correct in his citations from these writers, it seems to me that some of them are fairly liable to such a prosecution as his. Suppose they are; that does not show that he is not. What Mr. Foote had to show was not that other people were bad, but that he was good; not that other persons were guilty, but that he was innocent. It is no answer to bring forward these other cases. It is not enough to say these other persons have done these things, if they are not brought before us.

Gentlemen, I not only admit, but I urge upon you, and on everyone who hears me, that whilst laxity in the administration of the law is bad, the most odious laxity of all is discriminating laxity, which lays hold of particular persons and lets other persons equally guilty go scot free. That may be, that is so, but it has nothing to do with this case. The question here is not whether other persons ought to be standing where Mr. Foote and Mr. Ramsay now stand; but what judgment we ought to pass on Mr. Foote and [Mr.] Ramsay, who do stand here. In short and in fine, we have to administer the law whether we like it or no. It is undoubtedly a disagreeable law, or may become so, but I have given you some reasons for

---

10 Almighty God ridiculed – or merely the deity of 'barbarous Hebrews'? The evidence submitted against Foote and Ramsay was taken from issues of *The Freethinker* published between March and June 1882. This cartoon, based on the biblical account of the conquest of Canaan, appeared early in the series.

"COMIC BIBLE" SKETCHES.—XVI.

JEHOVAH ¡THROWING ¡STONES.

" *The Lord cast down great stones from heaven upon them unto Azekah,
and they died.*"—Joshua x., 11.

thinking it not so bad nor so indefensible as Mr. Foote has argued that it is. I think it, on the contrary, a good law that persons should be obliged to respect the feelings and opinions of those amongst whom they live. I assent to the passage from Michaelis, that in a Catholic country we have no right to insult Catholic opinion, nor in a Mohammedan country have we any right to insult Mohammedan opinion. I differ from both, but I am bound as a good citizen to treat with respect opinions with which I do not agree.

Take these publications with you; look at them; if you think they are permissible attacks on the religion of the country you will find the defendants not guilty. Take these cartoons. Mr. Foote says they are not attacks upon, and are not intended for caricatures of, Almighty God. If there be such a being, says Mr. Foote, he can have no feeling for Almighty God but profound reverence and awe, but this he says in his mode of holding up to contempt what he calls a caricature of that ineffable Being as delineated in the Hebrew Scriptures. That is for you to try. Look at them and judge for yourselves whether they do or do not come within the widest limits of the law. If they do, then as with the libels find the defendants not guilty. But if you think that they do not come within the most liberal and largest view that anyone can give of the law as it exists now, then find them guilty. Whatever may be the consequences – you may think the prosecution unwise, you may think the law undesirable, you may think no publications of this sort should ever be made the subject of criminal attack (I do not say you do think so, but you may), it matters not – your duty is to obey the law; not to strain it in favour of the defendants because you do not like the prosecution; not to strain it against them because you do not yourselves agree with the statements they advocate, as you are certain entirely to disapprove of the manner in which they advocate them. Take all these alleged libels into your considerations and say whether you find Mr. Foote or Mr. Ramsay, both or either, guilty or not guilty of this publication. . . .

6.3.3   JUDGMENT ON APPEAL,
THE ATTORNEY GENERAL V. *BRADLAUGH*, 1885

Information in the Queen's Bench Division by the Attorney General to recover penalties of 500*l*. each against C. Bradlaugh for voting as a member of the House of Commons without complying with the provisions of the Parliamentary Oaths Act, 1866. . . .

The fifth count alleged that C. Bradlaugh having been theretofore duly elected to serve as a member of the Commons House of Parliament for the borough of Northampton, and being a person having no belief in a Supreme Being, and being a person upon whose conscience an oath as an oath had no binding force (for all which said matters the said House then had full cognizance and notice by means of the avowal of C. Bradlaugh), did upon the 11th of February, 1884, go through the form of making and subscribing the oath appointed by the Parliamentary Oaths Act, 1866, as amended by the Promissory Oaths Act, 1868, and did thereafter on the 11th of February, 1884, being such member as aforesaid, vote as such member in the said House, and without having made and subscribed any oath, save as aforesaid.

Plea: Not guilty by statute (21 Jac. 1. c. 4, s. 4).

Joinder of issue.

The information was tried at bar in the Queen's Bench Division during the month of June, 1884, before Lord Coleridge, C. J., Grove, J., and Huddleston, B., and a special jury, and the following facts were proved:—

In the spring of 1880 C. Bradlaugh, the defendant, was elected a member of parliament for the borough of Northampton, and on the 3rd of May, 1880, he claimed 'to be allowed to affirm as a person for the time being by law permitted to make a solemn affirmation or declaration instead of taking an oath.' This claim was founded upon the Evidence Amendment Acts, 1869 and 1870. He afterwards expressed his willingness to take the oath usually taken by members of parliament after their election, and it was ultimately referred to a select committee to consider whether the House of Commons had any right to prevent the defendant from taking the oath. During the sitting of the committee the defendant appeared as a witness, and certain questions were put to him as to the effect which the taking of the oath would have upon him, and a letter written by him also was produced before the committee. From his answers to the questions put to the defendant whilst he was before the select committee, and from the contents of his letter, it might be inferred that an oath would have no greater effect upon the defendant's mind than a promise, and that he had no belief in the existence of a Supreme Being although the oath might be binding on his conscience as a solemn promise. Various other proceedings took place with reference to the defendant's claim to take his seat as a member of the House of Commons; but ultimately in February, 1882, he was expelled from the House, and on a new writ being issued for the election of a member for the borough of Northampton, he was again returned. On the 11th February, 1884, whilst the House of Commons was sitting, but without having been called upon by the Speaker, the defendant accompanied by two members of parliament advanced to the centre of the table immediately opposite to the Speaker. As he approached the table, the Speaker rose from his chair and called 'Order, order;' but the defendant, directly he reached the table, proceeded to read from a paper which he had brought with him, and having read the words contained in that paper, he kissed a book which he had brought with him, and which was a copy of the New Testament. He

"KICKED OUT." (?)

signed the paper at the table and left it there together with the certificate of his return. The contents of the paper were as follows: 'I, Charles Bradlaugh, do swear that I will be faithful and bear true allegiance to Her Majesty, Queen Victoria, her heirs and successors, accord[ing] to law; so help me God. (Signed) C. Bradlaugh.' The defendant did not sign the test-roll. Whilst the defendant was doing at the table within the House what is above mentioned, the Speaker sat down and wrote upon a paper, and then rose up and directed the defendant to withdraw, and he accordingly withdrew below the bar. The defendant voted in three divisions of the House of Commons on the 11th of February, 1884. . . .

Lord Coleridge, C.J., in summing-up the case told the jury that whatever might be the form of the oath, the signification was the same, it was the calling upon God to witness, that was, to take notice of what was said, and it was the invoking His vengeance, or the renouncing His favour, if what was said was false, or what was promised was not performed; and further that 'I swear' in an English Act of Parliament meant that 'I invoke the protection or the vengeance of the Supreme Being, according as I perform or break the promise with which such appeal is now made to Him.'

In answer to questions put by Lord Coleridge, C.J., the jury found that . . . upon the 11th of February, 1884, the defendant had no belief in a Supreme Being, and was a person upon whose conscience an oath, as an oath, had no binding force, and that the House of Commons had full cognizance and notice of these matters by reason of the avowal of the defendant. The jury also found that the defendant did not take and subscribe the oath according to the full practice of Parliament, and that the defendant did not take and subscribe the oath as an oath. Upon these findings the Queen's Bench Division, sitting for the trial at bar, ordered a verdict to be entered for the Crown upon the first, fourth, and fifth counts of the information, for separate penalties of £500. . . .

C. Bradlaugh, the defendant in person, . . . stated that his motion in arrest of judgment would be confined to the fifth count. That count disclosed no offence known to the law. By the Parliamentary Oaths Act, 1866, s. 3, every member of the House of Commons was to take the oath set forth in s. 1, for which a shorter form had been substituted by the Promissory Oaths Act, 1868; no distinction existed between going

---

11 Bradlaugh, after delivering his first speech at the bar in the House of Commons on 23 June 1880, was not allowed to affirm or to take the oath. On hearing this, he ignored the Speaker's command to withdraw. He was expelled from the chamber and duly confined to the Clock Tower overnight. *Punch* rightly suggested that this would not be the end of the matter. Bradlaugh's martyrdom had begun.

through as a matter of form what the law required, and actually doing that which the law required; it was admitted on the face of the fifth count that the defendant had gone through the form of making and subscribing the oath necessary to be taken by members of the House of Commons, and no intent to evade the provisions of either the Parliamentary Oaths Act, 1866, or the Promissory Oaths Act, 1868, was alleged; the defendant, therefore, had complied with the law, and the allegations were immaterial that he had no belief in a Supreme Being, and that an oath, as an oath, had no binding force on his conscience.

Sir H. James, A.G., and *Sir H. Giffard, Q.C. (Sir F. Herschell, S.G.,* and *R. S. Wright,* with them), for the Crown, shewed cause against the rule for a new trial or to enter judgment for the defendant, and also against the motion in arrest of judgment. . . .

The argument for the Crown upon the merits of this appeal may be divided into two branches; first, the defendant did not solemnly and publicly make and subscribe the oath within the meaning of the Parliamentary Oaths Act, 1866, even if he had been otherwise competent to take it; and, secondly, the defendant owing to his want of religious belief was incapable of taking any oath. . . .

C. Bradlaugh, the defendant in person, in support of the rule and of the motion in arrest of judgment. First, the defendant stated before the Select Committee of the House of Commons that the oath would be binding upon him: it would therefore be binding upon his conscience, and no evidence could be given that it was not, for his statement must be accepted as conclusive: the Queen's Bench Division ought to have directed the jury that the oath had been duly taken. By 1 & 2 Vict. c. 105, it is declared and enacted that every person shall be bound by an oath administered to him in such form and with such ceremonies as he may declare to be binding; there can be no answer to the argument, that a new class was created by that statute to whom an oath might be administered. As to the mode of administering the oath, it is equally valid whether it is administered to the person taking it by himself or by another person: thus the oath appointed by the Office and Oath Act, 1867 (30 & 31 Vict. c. 75, s. 5) might be administered to the person taking it by himself; it was an oath which might be sworn without reference to religious belief, and did not involve any religious test. . . .

BRETT, M.R. In this case the appeal or appeals is or are against a judgment or judgments of a Divisional Court of the Queen's Bench Division. . . .

A great many questions have been raised in this case. . . . I shall presently have, to the best of my ability, to go through the various points that have been thus taken; but it seems to me that they all can be best solved by coming first to a decision as to what is the meaning of the

Parliamentary Oaths Act, 1866. That Act governs, and will decide, every one of the objections which have been taken on both sides. . . .

. . . We have to consider what does this Act of Parliament mean on the true construction of it, knowing what the state of the law was or had been declared to be at the time when it was passed – what is the meaning of this Act of Parliament when it says that an oath must be taken. Now the jury have found with regard to this point of it:— 'We unanimously agree that the defendant had on the 11th of February, 1884, no belief in a Supreme Being:' that is, no belief in a Supreme Being of any denomination. It would seem to me that that finding alone will of necessity raise this point, but then they go on further in answer to a question:— 'Have the Crown satisfied you that the defendant on the 11th of February was a person upon whose conscience an oath, as an oath, has no binding force,' and the jury said, 'Yes, we are satisfied.' They have found both. It seems to me that the second finding might be properly predicated or found of a person of whom the first could not be found; but that if the first can be properly found, it is really unnecessary to put the second, because it is quite impossible in the case of a person who has no belief in a Supreme Being, that that which he does can be binding on his conscience *as an oath*. What is the law with regard to that? can a person in that frame of mind, according to the law of England, and according to the intention of this Act of Parliament, take an oath? and whatever he does in form, can that which he does in form, be said to be an oath? Now the law has been accepted and acted upon with regard to that point in accordance with and as governed by the decision given in *Omichund* v. *Barker,* ever since that case was decided, and the law has been adopted by every judge who has had to speak of it, really and truly according to the judgment of Willes, C.J., in that case. His has always been taken to be the most prominent and most satisfactory judgment. His judgment is in this form. 'I am of opinion that such infidels as believe in a God, and that He will punish them if they swear falsely, may and ought to be admitted as witnesses in this, though a Christian country.' Observe the care with which he puts is: 'such infidels as believe in a God, and that He will punish them' – he does not say when, where, or how – 'if they swear falsely.' Now we come to the next: 'And on the other hand I am clearly of opinion that such infidels, (if any such there be,) who either do not believe in a God' – that is the first of these findings – 'or if they do, do not think' – this is the alternative, that is, although they do – 'if they do, do not think that he will either reward or punish them in this world or the next, cannot be witnesses in any case nor under any circumstances.' It is not only 'in any case,' but 'nor under any circumstances,' for this plain reason, because an oath cannot possibly be any tie or obligation upon them; of course meaning that as an oath it cannot be any tie or obligation upon them. Therefore there is no necessity that the person taking the oath should believe that he will be liable to be punished in a future state. If there be any belief in a religion according to which it is supposed that a Supreme Being would punish a man in this world for doing wrong, that is enough; but if he does not believe in a God, or if believing in a God he does not think that God will either reward or punish him in this world or the next, in either case according to the law of England as here declared a man cannot be a witness in any case, or under any circumstances. 'He cannot be a witness.' It is true that those words are used, but they are used because the subject matter of inquiry was with regard to a witness. But that same principle, the same law, if there be anything in the reasons given, must apply to the case of any oath, whether the person is a witness or not. The question, whether he was a witness, was logically an accident: the question before the Court was whether the person, although he went through the form of it, could take an oath.

Now, the defendant here has relied more than once upon his saying that an oath was binding upon him – binding upon his conscience. In a most admirable book, Phillipps on Evidence, vol. i., ch. 3, p. 16 [10th ed.], although the reference is not one which I can verify, the author lays this down: 'It is not sufficient that the witness believes himself bound to speak the truth from a regard to character, or to the common interests of society, or from a fear of the punishment which the law inflicts upon persons guilty of perjury.' I should add to that, 'or from what he considered to be in honour binding on himself.' That is not sufficient. The question is, whether he can take an oath. The question is, not whether he is bound in honour; it is whether he is bound by an oath; and that is the decision of Willes, C.J., which has been adopted and recognised in many cases since, particularly in the case of *Miller* v. *Salomons*, where the doctrine was acknowledged to be the right doctrine, and acted upon. The question is, whether the state of mind being such as is described in both the cases, the person can be said to have taken an oath at all. It seems to me clear that by the law of England, he has not taken an oath. He may have taken something which binds him according to his own feelings; but that is not what the Act of Parliament requires. It requires an oath; and he has not taken an oath.

If my view as to this point is right, it puts an end to this case, because if the defendant did not take an oath, the question whether he complied with the other parts of the Parliamentary Oaths Act, 1866, is not material. . . .

COTTON, L.J. This was an appeal from a judgment of the Queen's Bench Division, on an information by the Attorney General to recover some penalties under the Parliamentary Oaths Act, 1866. . . .

I shall take first the argument that there was misdirection, and also the objection to the fifth count. It is really the substantial question in this case.

The Lord Chief Justice laid down, in accordance with what I consider to be the law, what was necessary in order to constitute an oath; and the fifth count does state in terms that the defendant was a person who had no belief in a Supreme Being, and a person upon whose conscience an oath, as an oath, had no binding force. I need not go through the remainder of it, because if that is proved it does shew that he has not complied with the provisions of the Parliamentary Oaths Act, 1866. The 5th section I take alone for the present purpose. That clearly says that if any member of the House of Commons, without having made and subscribed the oath hereby appointed, shall sit during any debate after the Speaker has been chosen, then he is liable to the penalty here sued for. What is meant by 'make oath?' It must mean, make that which is recognised by the law of England as an oath. Parliament undoubtedly is speaking with reference to the well-established law of England and the law of England undoubtedly is this, that if a person is in the unhappy position of not believing in a Supreme Being, or not believing that there is a Supreme Being who will punish for the offence of telling an untruth – it is immaterial whether it is in this or in a future world – then the person who is in that state does not, though he goes through the form of taking the oath, take that which the law of England recognises as an oath. The Master of the Rolls has referred to the case of *Omichund* v. *Barker,* and to the law as there laid down. In that case what the judges had to decide was this, what was the essence of an oath according to the law of England. . . . The judges said it was not necessary to be a Christian, but by the law of England the essence of an oath is that, which is stated in the passage read by the Master of the Rolls. . . . Down to the latest times, what was laid down in *Omichund* v. *Barker* has been recognised, as we recognise it, as correctly stating what the law of England is, as regards taking an oath. . . . But the defendant referred to various other matters, and amongst others he referred to the oath of allegiance; and he said every subject with certain exceptions can take the oath of allegiance. I will only refer to what was said by Martin, B., in the same case of *Miller* v. *Salomons*; he answers it in a word: 'The only oath imposed by the Common Law upon the subjects of this realm is the oath of allegiance, which originated in the old feudal oath of fealty, and this oath all persons capable of taking an oath at all, can lawfully take.' So that the learned judge points out that although there is an oath of allegiance which the common law requires, yet it can be taken only by those persons who can take an oath. Then the defendant refers to certain Acts of Parliament which I think it may be as well to refer to, so as to shew that matters have not been passed over. First, he referred to 1 & 2 Vict. c. 105; but that statute assumes that the oath is taken according to the law of England, and that the person who takes the oath has declared that the form of oath is binding on him. That, therefore, is merely to deal with the form and not with the substance of an oath. The other statute, to which the defendant referred, was 30 & 31 Vict. c. 75. That statute was not intended to alter the character of an oath. The argument was, that the oath under that Act is to be no test of religious belief; therefore that he who has no religious belief at all can do that which the law of England says he cannot do, namely, effectually take what the law will recognise as an oath. That Act was to prevent certain objections being made to believers who did not belong to the Established Church, or who did not come within certain definitions, and it was to prevent any objection being raised to a Roman Catholic, in consequence of his form of religious belief; it was not in any way to alter that, which has been established by the law of England to be essential and necessary in order to make a valid oath. In my opinion, therefore, the direction of the Lord Chief Justice was right. The fifth count does not shew that because the defendant is a person of no religious belief he is punishable by the law of England, but it does shew that what was done by the defendant when he said and wrote down the words of the oath, was not a compliance with the section of the statute; that he became liable to the penalties referred to and imposed by that Act, because he was not capable on the statement of this fifth count, and on the direction of the Lord Chief Justice, of doing that which he purported and attempted in form to do, namely, to take the oath required by the 5th section; and then if that is so, penalties follow, and that is the only question we have to deal with in this action. . . .

LINDLEY, L.J. A great number of questions raised in this case appear to me to be so free from difficulty that I shall not allude to them, especially as they have already been exhaustively dealt with. I shall confine my observations to the few points which present any difficulty. . . .

I come now to what has struck me as the main argument of the defendant. He contended that it was absurd to hold that a man is by law unable to do what the law requires him to do, and that as the defendant was required by the statute to take the oath, an ability to take it must be ascribed to him, and cannot be inquired into. That was really the grand argument which he addressed to us. I agree in the absurdity, but not in the argument deduced from it. If the statute required every person elected to serve in Parliament to take the oath and serve, and if the defendant were criminally prosecuted by indictment or information, or were sued for penalties for not taking the oath and not serving, the absurdity would arise; but the defendant would, it appears to me, be absolved, not by ascribing to him an ability to take the oath which he did not possess, but by holding that as he could not take the oath, he could not be properly elected or prosecuted, and that the statute did not apply to him. He could not be properly elected, nor indicted, nor convicted. . . .

The position of the defendant is somewhat curious, for although the defendant is incapable of sitting and voting by reason of the Parliamentary Oaths Act, 1866, and although he is liable to penalties if he does sit or vote, whether he goes through the form of taking the oath or not (that is the conclusion to which I have arrived), still he is for some purposes a member of parliament, and is entitled to some of the privileges of that position. . . .

The conclusion, therefore, to which I have arrived is this, that if the defendant's arguments were to prevail, and if every member, who uttered the words in the form of the oath required to be taken, were to be held to be capable of taking them as an oath, the oath would be reduced to a meaningless form. For some reason an oath, or, to meet the scruples of some persons, a solemn declaration, is required to be made; and whatever the object may have been, the effect is, as I understand it, to exclude from sitting and voting in Parliament all those persons who, like the defendant, cannot lawfully make a declaration and who cannot take the oath, and to render them liable to penalties if they do sit and vote.

Now it is said that was never contemplated. That is another argument which we have heard. I really do not know whether it was contemplated or was not, but it appears to me that I must hold judicially that the statute has that effect. Whether it was contemplated or not, may be a matter of some speculation. But I am by no means sure, and I certainly am not in a position judicially to hold, that it was not contemplated. This oath was imposed quite within recent years – I mean in its present form – and there seems to have been some reason for requiring it. It is a mistake to suppose – and I think it is as well the mistake should be known – that persons who do not believe in a Supreme Being are in the same position legally as those who do. There are old Acts of Parliament still unrepealed, under which such unbelievers can be cruelly persecuted. Whether that is a state of the law which ought to remain or not, is not for me to express an opinion upon; but having regard to the fact that these Acts of Parliament still remain unrepealed, I do not see my way to hold judicially that this oath was not kept alive by Parliament for the very purpose, amongst others, of keeping such unbelievers out of Parliament. . . . It appears to me, therefore, that the appeal must be dismissed.

Judgment for the Crown.

6.4   IRRELIGION AND FREE RELIGION

The most powerful, if not always the most sympathetic, allies of working-class unbelievers at mid-century, when Secularism became a force in British religious life, were bourgeois radicals and freethinking Dissenters. Shielded by rank and set free in many cases by private wealth to explore the boundaries of legitimate expression, these cultured and literate individuals differed from Secularists more in the manner than in the substance of their unbelief. They congregated, not in pubs and hired rooms, but in the editorial offices of the great periodicals they owned and edited. They published, not penny polemics and shilling harangues, but long, meticulously crafted essays and expensive scholarly books. These, however, were better suited to sway public opinion where it mattered most, in the corridors of power, and undoubtedly did at least as much as Secularists accomplished by their own devices to bring about freedom of religious, or irreligious, expression. William Binns (1827–1901), a Unitarian minister of advanced opinions, writing in the radical *Westminster Review*, exemplified the mixed motives with which the Secularists' middle-class allies operated. By arguing that Secularism was only the obverse side of the unreflective hell-fire biblicism of the 'old theology', against which it had justly reacted, he sought 'to deliver working-class heretics, and to lay the foundation of a new "City of God" ' in a 'free religion' of nature. Unitarian doctrines, he imagined, might hold a special attraction for disillusioned Secularists, even if, as a dying movement, Unitarians themselves were to be incorporated into a larger, liberal church. This, however, did not occur, and the main affinity of Secularism and Unitarianism would appear in retrospect to be their final destiny as effete religious sects.

W. BINNS ON THE RELIGIOUS HERESIES
OF THE WORKING CLASSES, 1862

Every epoch is mere or less heretical. As the earth grows older it grows wiser. It starves on the creeds and systems of earlier times. . . . At present a free religion asks for air and sunlight, and leave to live and grow to whatever stature God may permit. Rising from our emotions, and yearning after the Infinite with all their holy energy, it proposes a treaty of alliance with outside nature, and with each human faculty. It furnishes the instinctive desire, and the spontaneous leaping forth into the darkness in quest of light, but it appoints the intellect guide, and conscience judge; it welcomes browbeaten science to friendship, and history becomes at once a guardian and a prophet, letting no old servants of the race die except by failure of their means of life, and suffering no over-careful gardener of the ancient paradise to root out intruders who offer fragrance and food of a new sort. Its tones vary in clearness and in freedom from sectarian provincialisms, sometimes rising to the rank of a fresh tongue, and sometimes seeming only a difference in accent. But it differs in essence from the old theology, and the courses which at starting appear but the breadth of a line apart, separate more widely as they proceed. The old theology is dogmatic and presumptuous, it plays the priest, assumes infallibility, and hurls random thunderbolts; the new is modest and frank, gives generously to all and takes gratefully from any – it confesses that it does not know all things, and that there is more light in God than has yet been revealed. The heretics are not always consistent, nor have they always the courage to speak out their whole thought. But in the eyes of the orthodox theologians their common sin is belief in progress; the brave are only more impudent, and the timid more deceitful. . . .

. . . The discoverers and writers in literature and science are necessarily heretics almost without being conscious of it, and it would need a daily miracle, in this age when miracles are no more, to prevent their readers catching the infection. The popular theology has only a Sunday existence: human nature and common sense claim the rest of the week. The men of letters who are either servants of, or worshippers in, the orthodox churches are few in number, and minor celebrities at the best. The men of letters *par excellence* belong to the Establishment politically, as they belong to the State, but the Archbishop of Canterbury does not lead their devotions, and they do not bow to the authority of the Hebrew Scriptures. The beginning of the end is indeed approaching. Literature and science are already free, and even in the religious world itself the prospect is more encouraging than we have ever known it before. A spirit of inquiry and progress has worked its way into all the sects; they possess heretics that they know not of, and the former strongholds will soon become untenable.

But there are large classes not ostensibly connected with any denomination, and to whom religion has long since become an unreality. The Church of England claims their allegiance as it claims that of the Dissenters, but its authority is ignored. In the upper ten thousand, when there is no church or chapel attendance, there is still generally a piety of feeling, and a vague artistic sort of faith; pictures and statues preach, nature is a church, and friendship and home affection sing of their divine origin, and help the imagination to construct an ideal heaven. But among the working classes indifferentism and utter belief extensively prevail. Peregrinating bishops produce no effect upon them, and the multiplication of 'steeple-houses' does not multiply congregations. Thoughtful mechanics in railway works and elsewhere follow Secretaries, Directors, and General Managers to listen to an episcopal Saturday afternoon sermon, surrounded by all the implements of their craft, but the preacher is only an ecclesiastical curiosity; in his talk he treats them as if they were ploughboys at their first confirmation; they silently note his assumptions, his fallacies, and his spiritual impertinence as he goes on, and the next day are still less inclined to enter the district church at their doors, and hear a louder-voiced incumbent proclaim the same things diluted. The Census of 1851 took the orthodox public by surprise with the revelations that it made of the numbers regularly absent from public worship. Since then a praise-worthy ambition to improve this state of things has prevailed. But it has pursued mistaken methods, and therefore done little good. The Church of England has fallen back on the schismatic proceedings of John and Charles Wesley; and with a strange blindness to the demands of the age, attempted to evangelize unbelieving artisans with the theology of a century ago, as if the intellect were no more alive among the mechanics of Birmingham and Manchester now, than it was formerly among Cornish miners. Additional churches and chapels in large numbers have been erected by the generosity of the faithful, who have forgotten that it is not new buildings so much as new doctrines that are needed. Revivals, theatre-preachings, midnight meetings for outcasts, and the popularity of Mr. Spurgeon among the elect, have made the matter worse; for the sermonizers have denied development, and required an abnegation of humanity, so that religion has drifted still further away from life and sense.

The Census of 1861 has yielded no religious statistics, but if it had, the shortcomings of orthodoxy would have alarmed itself, for the intelligent members of the working classes, as they have grown in numbers, are proportionably less in the churches in 1861 than they were in 1851. They stand farther off than ever they did. The efforts made have not reached them at all. If they have listened to Mr. Spurgeon's preaching, it has been but as they would listen to the jokes of a circus clown. If they have drawn near to a revival gathering, the whirlwind of excitement, tossing about men and women who already believed, has left them calm, sceptical, and contemptuous. There are artisans in the churches, doubtless, but who are they? With some exceptions they are those to whom theological thinking is utterly strange, and who hold that on theology it is both dangerous and sinful to think. It is a sad confession to make, but it is forced on us by facts – the bulk of the working classes is indifferent, and amongst those who are not indifferent, it is the less thoughtful who believe, and the more thoughtful who deny or doubt. Mission-stations are established exclusively for the poor. And, to a certain extent, the poor attend them, but the intelligent poor only in scanty numbers. The congregations are too much made up of those who watch for the missionary's alms more than they listen to his words. Rightly or wrongly, there is a feeling of dislike to the patronage and condescension that seem implied in the idea of a mission to the poor; so that while the wives often go willingly enough, the more independent husbands stand upon their dignity, and hold aloof. So far as the artisan population is concerned, we believe that the following is a fair classification of those connected with missions and organized congregations, the numbers increasing and the intelligence decreasing in the order here given. 1. Unitarians, Swedenborgians, Quakers; 2. Church of England, Independents, Baptists; 3. Wesleyan Methodists, Wesleyan Association, Primitive Methodists, and smaller sects; 4. Latter-Day Saints, and Roman Catholics. But there are vast multitudes quite unattached; and in the main the representative men of the working classes are among the unattached. We do not say that they openly reject Christianity, but that the current presentations of Christianity neither convince their reason nor win their affections; and they stand in an attitude of uncertainty, willing to affirm if aught worthy of affirmation be offered, yet forced to doubt and strongly tempted to deny.

Unless one mixes with the people freely, reads their literature, hears their speeches, and joins their conversations, it is impossible to conceive how widely spread is this state of mind. The manufacturing towns of the north and the midland counties possess thousands of intelligent men driven alike by logic and by conscience from the religious homes of their youth, seeking fresh ones and finding none. The preachers say 'Come,' and the people reply 'No.' It is important to ask how is this? Is it Christianity that is in fault, or is it the professional expounders thereof? God, and immortality, and the Bible have been so taught as to make scepticism the only refuge for morality to flee to. The working men who never thought were never troubled. They believed what they were told to believe, and with them all was right. Contradictions were trials of faith, and salvation was the reward of credulity. But it was not in the nature of all to take theology for granted. They inquired, and were told that inquiry was infidelity. They doubted, and with a strange perversion of St. Paul were told 'He that doubteth is damned.' And how is it now? Our conviction is, that Secularism is the religion, or the no-religion, of a large minority of thinking artisans. That is to say, they regard this world as the be-all and the end-all, and man as the highest form of existence. There may be other worlds; but as they do not know, they think it presumptuous to affirm them, and a waste of energy to live for them; there may be higher beings than man, but if so they shroud themselves in mystery, leave us unaided in weakness, and break not the eternal silence in reply to our prayers, so that to worship them is to give reality to dreams, and unphilosophically to project from ourselves an imaginary perfection, call it Deity, and strive to grow like it. This is the statement of an extreme position. We have tried to put it as the Secularists themselves would put it, and have purposely chosen to base it on a plea of ignorance rather than on a plea of denial. Secularists are really of three classes – they who wish to believe, but cannot; they who do not wish to believe, know nothing, and will guess nothing; and they who deny. Of these the first are the most hopeful, the second the most numerous, and the third the most difficult. Their common mother is the old theology that is dying, their Redeemer must be the new theology that is to take its place. . . .

There are a few persons who are Secularists naturally. Poetry, aspiration, and reverence are only words to them. They are satisfied to take phenomena as they are, and question not of the causes. Their hopes are bounded by their vision, and belief by experience. This is the only world they see; about the problematic inhabitants of planets and stars they know nothing, and therefore say we will attend to the certain, and not trouble ourselves about the doubtful. Upon such men arguments are wasted. They remain unconvinced in the presence of *à posteriori* and *à priori* logic. To the former they reply, it is more than they can do to look through nature, and that nature's deity beyond, if there at all, is quite invisible; and to the latter, that gratuitous premises involve a gratuitous conclusion. We need not be surprised at this; for all theistical reasonings require a basis of feeling, and of that natural Secularists are destitute. The one all-sufficient answer to the Christian Theist is, 'We cannot feel with you.' To these men, though they are far from being numerous, no special pleading of ours can give faith in immortality and God. Their only chance of conversion to Theism lies in a divine revelation, or the discipline of the hereafter.

But a far larger number become Secularists in the extreme rebound from orthodoxy. Their doubts have a healthy origin, and if properly met by the accredited teachers of the religious world, would be productive of great good. But instead of this, murderous attempts are made to stifle the spirit of inquiry at its very birth, and when these fail, it receives notice to quit the sacred land altogether. No eclecticism is allowed. Once beginning to inquire, the rule is, Believe all or reject all. It is said, 'the woman who deliberates is lost;' and, in another sense, popular theologians affirm the same of those misguided men who hesitate to believe that the spiritual food with which they are fed is the best that can be got. The choice is between it and starvation. The whole Bible and the whole theology, or blank Atheism, are the alternatives often presented: and as the first is impossible, the second is a necessity. The working classes stand on the brink of the theological Rubicon, considering the depth of the stream, and the possible discoveries that may be made in the dreary regions beyond; but still, not wishing to cross, except they are forced, they turn wistful glances to the faiths of youth, and ask to be treated as free men who are willing to believe, but want to know why. It is of no use. The defenders of the Church say the trail of the serpent is over them all, drive them across the river dividing the saved from the damned, as sinners against the Holy Ghost, and make atheists of the men out of whom rational Christians might have been moulded. We are familiar with many instances of this. The inquirer often clings with great tenacity to the belief in God and immortality long after he has abandoned what are popularly known as the distinctive doctrines of evangelical Christianity. Human nature will not let him part with them without a hard struggle; and when at length they go, they go in sorrow and in tears. He does not cast them off, but they are taken from him. He is not permitted to worship God except in the shape of the Athanasian Trinity, or to have any theory of a future state unaccompanied by a nightmare hell. . . .

Even without the too ready help of divines of the 'Eclipse of Faith' School, many minds strongly tend towards Secularism, when they are first liberated from ecclesiastical bondage. For a time they are wild, like a horse which runs away still faster when it has broken loose from the shafts; and we are inclined to think that there may be a wise necessity forcing them to sound, all unaccustomed to the perilous task as they are, the lowest depths of doubt, until, despairing to find satisfaction there, they rise to the surface, and philosophical Christianity, another phase of the ever-growing religion of nature, presents a religious home where the heart has peace, and the intellect freedom. Perhaps none ever know so well what faith in God is as those do who have tried in vain to live without it. The section of which we are now speaking does not primarily ignore the natural cravings of humanity for something holier than our every-day existence reveals. It has faith in goodness and truth, and the fundamental laws of morality. It believes in progress, service, and duty. And, strange to say, still holding fast this faith, it flees to Secularism for refuge, because the proffered religion falls below its own ideal of the useful and the just. The freshly-awakened minds of the working classes try their inherited creeds by the tests which they apply when they are in search of outside truth. They hear from the pulpits of the immoralities of idolatry, the contradictions of the Koran, and the barrenness of philosophy. The Bible is the one divine revelation. Christianity is to be understood as expounded by Wesley's Sermons, Calvin's Institutes, the Larger and Shorter Catechisms of the Church of Scotland, or the Thirty-nine Articles of the Church of England; and there is no other religion which can possibly lead men to heaven. He that believeth Christianity as thus interpreted is saved, he that believeth it not is damned. The incautious pulpit-orators venture to appeal to the reason and moral sense of their congregations, in order to make out cases against the polygamy and war of Mahomet, and the suspicious demon of Socrates. This rash appeal ruins their own cause, for it prompts their hitherto unquestioning disciples to think. Then it turns out that the reason and moral sense invoked to pass judgment on pagan shortcomings, also play sad havoc with home creeds. Mahomet was not alone in his polygamy and war; for the patriarchs had many wives, and meek Moses was a man of plagues, lifting up his hands in prayer to the God of battles even when too weak to fight. It is hard to reconcile Joshua's conquest of Canaan with Christ's Gospel of Peace; and the Trinity of

Brahma, Vishnu, and Siva, three manifestations of the underlying Brahm, seems to be at least equal to that of the pseudo-Athanasius. They would not support human legislators who should propose vicarious punishments; they see no morality in making salvation depend on belief, or justice in holding them responsible for sins committed before they were born, and could not find in their hearts to doom their worst enemies to eternal misery. Therefore they doubt the truth of Christianity. Reason sees contradiction in one doctrine, and the moral sense injustice in another. . . . Their higher natures force upon them the rejection of the popular faith; no middle ground is permitted, and they say – Then we are infidels, atheists, secularists, for surely no religion is better than this religion.

These are experiences terrible and sad, but they are such as many have had to go through. Secularism would only have existed in a few exceptional cases where there was a natural inability to appreciate spiritual realities, if religion had not been irreligiously preached. The good men who are responsible for its wide prevalence at the present time have unwittingly sacrificed to false deities, and Nemesis has now overtaken them. We charitably believe that many of them would be among the first to express regret, and henceforward to trust more generously to the reason and moral sense, whose aid hitherto they have only called in at convenient seasons, were they to hear the working-class confessions of the causes of Secularism, with which we could crowd these pages. We will however limit ourselves to one illustration. Mr. Holyoake is scarcely now one of the working classes, in the sense in which throughout this article we understand the phrase; but we can learn his state of mind when he was one, from his various published writings. . . . His books . . . are the best representatives of the Secularistic School, and are, on the whole, fairly and temperately written. Though of varying ability, and containing much from which the Christian thinker will strongly dissent, the 'Trial of Theism' will repay perusal to those who feel interest in the religious condition of the working classes, and so will 'The Last Trial by Jury for Atheism.'

We know that in various quarters a nobler theology is preached than this which has made men Secularists. Independent, Swedenborgian, Unitarian, and Church of England divines, with different degrees of heresy, eloquence, and force, preach God, Christ, Man, and the Bible in a way that would have kept multitudes of the homeless wanderers within the Christian pale. But these men's sermons, the working classes, when first they cried, 'Lord, I believe, help thou mine unbelief,' did not hear, and their writings they did not read. They know them now perhaps a little, but are in most cases too far gone to be affected by them, for they can no longer stand upon the ground of a common feeling. Even the wish to have a religious faith at all has been crushed out of many hearts. They multiply difficulties with a sad persistency, and, hemmed in by a fatal logic that rejects intuitions and distrusts the affections, they neither see a way of escape, nor hope for one.

Over-Conservatism begets Secularism in religion, and anarchy and red-Republicanism in politics. Disciplined minds can both labour and wait, and be Progressionists and Conservatives at the same time. But this spirit is seldom found in the masses. It is based on a far more thorough culture than they have received: it requires an ability to see the necessary succession of the seasons in the great year of Providence, and a large acquaintance with that revaluation of history which shows how.

Through the ages one increasing purpose runs,
And the thoughts of men are widened by the process of the suns.

The majority of Progressionists and Conservatives, the pioneers of the new theology, and the believers in the full integrity of the old, alike wish Christianity to be universal; and till it is universal its mission remains unfulfilled. And as it is the work of the former to help the latter to depart in peace, so also is it their work to induce to return home those who have been exiled on false pretences.

Negative Secularism doubts or denies God and immortality; positive Secularism dwells exclusively on the duties of this world without reference to any being higher than man, or any state beyond the present; and both forms of Secularism freely criticise the Bible. Their criticisms are too often written in what seems to us a captious and irreverent spirit. That which, rightly or wrongly, so many millions regard as a sacred book ought at least to be protected from sneers. Most people manifest the petty side of human nature sometimes, and Secularists generally manifest it in Biblical criticism. They do not discuss seriously; and their favourite weapons are ridicule and sarcasm. They walk in the footsteps of Paine and Voltaire, but decline to accept their Theism, and are without Paine's talent and Voltaire's genius. They have microscopic eyes for minor faults, chronological errors, contradictions, immoralities, and anthropomorphisms. To them, of these things, the Bible seems full. But they fail to apprehend it as the literary monument of the Hebrew nation, and the history of their religious development. Yet their criticisms are the natural product of the unwarrantable assumptions of the other side. Too much has been asked for, and therefore too much has been denied. . . . The old Theology says: 'The Bible is all divine; from beginning to end it reveals the white light of truth;' and Secularism replies, 'There is nothing divine, and total blackness is there.' There is thus nothing left for Secularism to do but seek imperfections. . . . Noah is only known for his drunkenness, Jacob for his business transactions with Esau, Moses for some curious peculiarities in the Levitical law, and David for his too intimate acquaintance with Bathsheba. This is like describing Washington as an American who owned slaves, and Cromwell as a Huntingdon brewer with warts on his face. . . . Literal interpretation is one of the strongest of Secularist weapons; but it is borrowed from the armoury of Orthodoxy, and they who suffer have no right to complain. Long have they put down free inquiry by the same tyranny of literalism and texts, and it is only a righteous retribution which now commends the poisoned chalice to their own lips. . . .

This alienation of thinking artisans from the Christian faith has not taken place without various attempts to prevent it. But, as we have already seen with respect to the Bible, it is the misfortune of religion, in whatever aspect it is viewed, to suffer nearly as much from its champions as its enemies, if it does not suffer more: for its enemies do at least attack it openly, and avow that their aim is to destroy it, so that we know how to guard against them; but its champions are fatal when they try to protect, and serviceable only when they are silent. We speak here, of course, of those who imagine themselves its champions *par excellence*. But in proportion as they are orthodox they are dangerous; to be useful, they must be heretical. The more learned men of the old theology, however, appear to have made up their minds to battle only with those who keep the Christian name, and leave the Secularists to themselves. Of late years no prominent man has addressed them. They have been abandoned to second and third-rate retailers of the most stereotyped commonplaces. The consequence is, that every day the task of spiritual redemption is becoming more difficult. The artisans grow more thoughtful, the Creeds remain as they were, and their defenders wax more foolish, loud, and angry. Unable, or unwilling, to see how the stream of events steadily flows on, bearing all who fearlessly cast themselves upon it, to wider views and a more human theology, the antiquarians of the religious world stand still, and mutter their incantations in a dead language, with no effect save that of Papal bulls in a Protestant land. The way in which the Rev. Dr. Baylee, Principal of St. Aidan's Theological College, tries to bring the Secular working-classes into the pale of Christianity again is as follows. We copy from his own printed statement. The questions are by Mr. Bradlaugh, and the answers by Dr. Baylee, in a discussion professing to be conducted on Socratic principles, in Liverpool.

'Am I eternal?' 'You are.' 'Was I in existence before I was born?' 'You were.' 'Did I sin before I was born?' 'You did.' 'If I had never been born, should I have been punished for that sin?' 'You would.' And the reverend trainer of sixty future ministers of the Church of England illustrates this by observing that Levi before he was born paid tithes to Melchisedec, and that as we all forget in age what we did in infancy, so we may also forget the sin we committed when we were living in Adam. We are informed that the whole doctrine of original sin is involved in this. It may be so; but we should not require much argument to convince us that the last sin up to that particular time was committed by the Doctor himself when this statement was made. What idea would the twenty thousand people who have read this discussion get of Christianity? . . .

We have now, perhaps, said enough to enable the uninitiated to understand the relation of English Christianity to the sources and aspects of Secularism. Our national Conservatism necessarily makes our religious growth slow. But it is steady and permanent, and a step once made is not retraced. Many of the foremost divines of all sects stand outside the old Creeds, and if they repeat them at all do so in a non-natural sense, while the whole of the higher literature of the age is in the service of Progress. . . .

But while most cultivated men have the ability to be eclectic and the patience to wait, the working classes, not trained to take a grand time view of the order of events, and knowing only that the popular theology first appeals to, and then mocks the reason and moral sense, are driven into Secularism – no world but this, and Atheism – no being higher than ourselves. Hence it is that artisan intelligence nearly always begins by being sceptical, and that the Christianity of the churches is mainly held by those members of the artisan order who have never taken the trouble to ask what it is. In London, in Yorkshire and Lancashire, in the neighbourhoods of Birmingham and Glasgow, the thinking working classes, by tens of thousands, reject Christianity and the Bible, because with the former they are asked to become superstitious, and with the latter to be Bibliolaters, calling science a mistake, contradictions harmony, and immorality divine.

We cannot judge of the extent to which Secularism prevails by the circulation of its periodicals, its organized societies, or the numbers who attend its regular meetings; for these have always been its weak points. Secularism, in its very nature, tends to indifferentism. It has many disciples who have given up the popular theology as intellectually incredible and morally unworthy, and yet do not care to support propagandism. The quiet Secularists are more numerous than the talking ones. . . .

The effective organized strength of Secularism is almost inconceivably insignificant. A reason for this might be found in the very nature of its doctrines. It is hard to band people together to preach a system of negations. . . . Then, too, the heretics of the working classes are victims of many petty persecutions which never affect wealthy inquirers; and that they may be able to earn a living for themselves and feed and clothe their families, they are often driven to nurse doubts in silence and let organized societies languish because they dare not join them. . . . Besides, it must be remembered that Secularists are practically outlaws, and many sessions of Parliament must elapse before bigotry will permit Sir John Trelawny's Bill of Rights to secure them the ordinary privileges of Englishmen. For them the unprejudiced baronet's Oath Bill is a Magna Charta. In the meantime they cannot swear, they are inadmissible as witnesses; their property may be stolen, and they have no redress; they may be murdered, and the murderer escape punishment, except some person other than a Secularist saw the crime perpetrated. Because of these and other facts, Mr. Holyoake says, 'Being outlaws, organization as in churches has never been safe or prudent to attempt.' . . .

Dissatisfied with negations, and prompted by a natural instinct for religion, many former unbelievers have turned their faces eastward again; some, fated to be always in extremes, have swung back to their old positions, unable to do without a faith, and too impulsive to trust themselves with a free one; so that occasionally the Secularist lecturer of one year is the Methodist preacher of another. Swedenborgianism, at once mystical and scientific, has received a few, and would have received more, but for its unfortunate doctrine of the eternally fixed state of the wicked; for seekers after a faith ask why, if they are free to change here, should they be handcuffed for ever hereafter? The humaner sort of Independents, and Broad Churchmen in proportion as they are heretical, have made theology again acceptable to some, while Unitarianism has furnished a home for large numbers. . . . Modern Spiritualism, both in England and America, has won the belief of large numbers who were formerly Secularists. . . . It is, however, clear that many who are driven into unbelief by the old theology cannot contentedly remain there. Whether that in which they have taken refuge be a truth, an imposture, or a delusion, or a mixture of all three, does not matter for our present purpose; they evidently retain religious susceptibilities, and a Christianity in harmony with our whole nature could scarcely appeal to them in vain.

We have . . . alluded to the disciples of a free, rich, and expanding faith. We wish that there were none of them, for they alone can 'administer to the mind diseased' which we have described. We include in that class all Christian thinkers with whom religion is a thing of growth, and Christianity itself one, and the fairest, aspect of a universal fact; and we also include in it all those religious thinkers who though they possess what we deem the spirit of Christianity, decline to assume its name, and possibly dissent from many of its theories.

. . . The theology that is to deliver working-class heretics, and to lay the foundation of a new 'City of God,' must be freer and purer, less Biblical and more natural, less in love with Creeds and Articles, and more with clear language and consistent thought; less given to spend its strength in quickening transient Christian forms, and more devoted to the permanent spirit, than any we are likely to get from Mr. Maurice and his literary coadjutors. . . . The Broad Church can show the working-classes that all theology is not equally bad, and win from them some friendly words; but it can do little more, and comparatively few will accept it as a guide.

The Unitarians have done a great work, but they might have done, and may yet do, a greater. They possess now more earnestness, more trained captains, and a larger numerical force of regimental rank and file, than they have done at any previous period of their history. They have no Trinity, no devil, no everlasting hell, no natural depravity, no vicarious satisfaction. Heretics who may reject their overtures cannot treat them with the moral indignation with which they fairly treat the older theologians. The heart can bring no accusation of cruelty, the conscience of injustice, or the intellect of slavery. Their *theory* of the Bible allows criticism as free as that of Mr. Newman or Mr. Parker. . . . If, then, this sect would exert its full power over the working classes, or be a pioneer of progressive religious thought, its members must be boldly consistent, and care more for truth and growth than for quietness. . . . They have been over-prone to talk about the sacrifices of the old Presbyterians and the battles of Priestley, and to dream that they can win sovereignty by reposing on ancestral laurels. They are a various-minded race of men, who have never yet risen to the level of their duties. Some of them are too old-fashioned to like progress, some too tolerant even for propagandism. . . . If the Unitarians will but be thoroughly faithful to their own free principles, and get rid of what Theodore Parker calls 'a damaged phraseology,' life and usefulness are in store for them; and if as a sect they die, it will be when, becoming the nucleus of a larger church, they will re-light the candle of Latimer and Ridley. England will be illuminated by the fires in which they burn, and death will be their title to universal dominion.

To Broad Churchmen, Unitarians, and those liberal thinkers who in many respects are at one with them, we finally say, though existing creeds may be worn out by time, or so transformed that their founders would not know them, yet, whatever changes come over theology, religion itself is in no danger of perishing. It has passed through many new births, and must pass through many more. . . . Old forms of speech may pass away, old ideals may be left behind, and much that now seems eternal may crumble or be outgrown, but everything which has the right to live will also have the strength to laugh at death. Religion's representative men rise from earthly defeat to spiritual and immortal triumph. Greek Theism was nurtured by the poisoning of Socrates, and the crucifixion of Jesus rooted Christianity in the life of the world. The extreme unbelief of the working classes, and the indifferentism and ill-concealed scorn of many who share their heresies without sharing their rank, will disappear only before a free and catholic faith that waits and works where it does not know, makes Nature paramount over sacred books, hears God in conscience, and watches the workings of His will in the growth of science and the flow of history. Humanity has always yearned after such a faith. It is the Divine spirit which in one shape or another underlies all theologies, and which, with varying success, they aim to interpret. The Bible, the Eddas, and the Koran are records of attempts already made. Each bears witness to a growing thought, leaves behind a past, and in so doing foretells a future. None is perfect, for all are human; none is final, for all are finite. As theologies, the race abandons them in turn, but the common religious instinct out of which they spring, perennially lives and shapes itself afresh into lovelier forms. The Christianity not of the churches, and not merely of the Bible, but as it seems to have existed in Jesus Himself, stands forth as yet the highest and the best, like the *Messiah* in musical art, and like the Himalayas among the mountain-children of nature. And they are its most helpful friends who drop whatever it may possess of the transient, and graft new truths in its permanent spirit, aiming to develop the dialect of a metropolitan province into that absolute religion which is the language of all worlds, being at one with science and civilization, with a free intellect and a manly life, its practice the service of humanity, and its aspiration the love of God.

THE RELIGION OF SCIENCE

7.1 TOWARDS A NEW NATURE

WHILE Victorian Christians solemnly professed that God had created man in His own image, many critics pointed out, with some justification, that in popular theology at least man had merely fashioned God on the model of his own temporal existence. Nature, according to such critics, was a surer basis of knowledge in matters divine than human historical sources; God, if he existed, lurked mysteriously beyond natural phenomena, without anthropic form or feeling. It is, however, perhaps clearer a century later that 'Nature', too, like God, was conceived in the image of its Victorian devotees. The law-bound material and meliorative natural order from which scientists and other critics of popular theology routinely extracted moral precepts was in many ways more than reminiscent of human relationships in a law-abiding materialistic and progressive industrial society. The sources of the new scientific conception of nature were as various as they were complex. At the beginning of the nineteenth century the Revd Thomas Robert Malthus (1766–1834), an Anglican political economist, plunged humanity into nature with his 'principle of population'. Although people generally cannot be exempted, according to Malthus, from the 'physical laws . . . which are observed to prevail in other parts of animate nature', the principle of population, like no other law, 'especially accords' with the 'scriptural view of the state of man on earth' (**7.1.1**). John Stuart Mill (1806–1873), a philosopher and political economist alike, could not have cared less for the scriptural view of man. He drew conviction that society is governed beneficently by natural laws from the French Positivist philosopher Auguste Comte. Progress, or a 'tendency to improvement', was not to be seen as historically inevitable, but as the contingent effect of 'laws of human nature', the chief of which relates to the 'speculative faculties' that determine the 'moral and political state of the community' (**7.1.2**). Thomas Carlyle (1795–1881), formerly intended for the Presbyterian ministry, saturated his speculative faculties in German romantic philosophy, from which he learned a pantheistic reverence for natural law. Like an Old Testament prophet, he proclaimed the essential justice of the 'Universe'; like a Puritan preacher, he called for worship through heroic hard work (**7.1.3**). In Carlyle's literary outpourings religion was finally divorced from theology and attached, in effect, to the teachings of science, which then promised to elucidate the moral order of the world. It remained for a young English Nonconformist named Herbert Spencer (1820–1903) to synthesize the teachings of science in a vision of natural progress that instilled the religion and prescribed the morality by which post-Christian intellectuals might live. Progess was the inevitable result of the Malthusian law of population, according to a famous article by Spencer in the *Westminster Review*. Biology, not intellect alone, secured the destiny of man. The 'greatest perfection' would be brought about by the differential survival of 'the select' of each generation, in whom nature had disciplined the virtues requisite for the control of fertility (**7.1.4**). Here Spencer came within an ace of anticipating Charles Darwin's principle of natural selection, published seven years later.

7.1.1   T. R. MALTHUS ON THE PRINCIPLE OF POPULATION, 1824

. . . If it be found by experience that on land of a certain quality, and making allowance for the ordinary mortality and accidents, sheep will increase on an average, so as to double their numbers every two years, it would be strictly correct to say, that sheep have the natural capacity of increasing in a geometrical progression, of which the common multiple is two, and the term two years; and it might safely be said, that if land of the same quality could be provided with sufficient rapidity, and no sheep were consumed, the rate of increase, would be such, that if we were to begin with the full number which could be supported on an acre of land, the whole earthy part of the globe might be completely covered with sheep in less than 76 years.

If out of this prodigious increase of food, the full support of mankind were deducted, supposing them to increase as fast as they have ever yet increased in any country, the deduction would be comparatively inconsiderable; and the rate of increase would still be enormous, till it was checked, either by the natural want of will on the part of mankind to make efforts for the increase of food, beyond what they could possibly consume, or after a certain period, by their absolute want of power to prepare land of the same quality, so as to allow of the same rate of progress.

Owing to these two causes combined, we see that, notwithstanding this prodigious *power* of increase in vegetables and animals, their actual increase is extremely slow; and it is obvious, that, owing to the latter cause alone, and long before a final stop was put to all further progress, their actual rate of increase must of necessity be very greatly retarded; as it would be impossible for the most enlightened human efforts to make all the soil of the earth equal in fertility to the average quality of land now in use; while the practicable approaches towards it would require so much time as to occasion, at a very early period, a constant and great check upon what their increase would be, if they could exert their natural powers.

Elevated as man is above all other animals by his intellectual faculties, it is not to be supposed that the physical laws to which he is subjected should be essentially different from those which are observed to prevail in other parts of animated nature. He may increase slower than most other animals; but food is equally necessary to his support; and if his natural capacity of increase be greater than can be permanently supplied with food from a limited territory, his increase must be constantly retarded by the difficulty of procuring the means of subsistence.

The main peculiarity which distinguishes man from other animals, in the means of his support, is the power which he possesses of very greatly increasing these means. But this power is obviously limited by the scarcity of land, by the great natural barrenness of a very large part of the surface of the earth, and by the decreasing proportion of produce which must necessarily be obtained from the continual additions of labour and capital applied to land already in cultivation.

It is, however, specifically with this diminishing and limited power of increasing the produce of the soil, that we must compare the natural power of mankind to increase, in order to ascertain whether, in the progress to the full cultivation and peopling of the globe, the natural power of mankind to increase must not, of absolute necessity, be constantly retarded by the difficulty of procuring the means of subsistence, and if so, what are likely to be the effects of such a state of things.

In an endeavour to determine the natural power of mankind to increase, as well as their power of increasing the produce of the soil, we can have no other guide than past experience.

The great check to the increase of plants and animals, we know from experience, is the want of room and nourishment; and this experience would direct us to look for the greatest actual increase of them in those situations where room and nourishment were the most abundant.

On the same principle, we should expect to find the greatest actual increase of population in those situations where, from the abundance of good land, and the manner in which its produce is distributed, the largest portion of the necessaries of life is actually awarded to the mass of the society.

Of the countries with which we are acquainted, the United States of America, formerly the North American Colonies of Great Britain, answer most nearly to this description. . . . Taking, therefore, into consideration the actual rate of increase, which appears from the best documents to have taken place over a very large extent of country in the United States of America, very variously circumstanced as to healthiness and rapidity of progress; . . . and adverting particularly to the great increase of population which has taken place in this country during the last 20 years, under the formidable obstacles to its progress which must press themselves upon the attention of the most careless observer, it must appear, that the assumption of a rate of increase such as would double the population in 25 years, as representing the natural progress of population, when not checked by the difficulty of procuring the means of subsistence, or other peculiar causes of premature mortality, must be very decidedly within the truth.

It may be safely asserted, therefore, that population, when unchecked, increases in a geometrical progression of such a nature as to double itself every twenty-five years.

It would be unquestionably desirable to have the means of comparing the natural rate of the increase of population when unchecked, with the possible rate of the increase of food, in a limited territory, such as that in which man is actually placed; but the latter estimate is much more difficult and uncertain than the former. . . . It must be allowable, if it throws light on the subject, to make a supposition respecting the increase of food in a limited territory, which, without pretending to accuracy, is clearly more favourable to the power of the soil to produce the means of subsistence for an increasing population, than any experience which we have of its qualities will warrant.

If, setting out from a tolerably well peopled country such as England, France, Italy, or Germany, we were to suppose that, by great attention to agriculture, its produce could be permanently increased every twenty-five years by a quantity equal to that which it at present produces, it would be allowing a rate of increase decidedly beyond any probability of realization. The most sanguine cultivators could hardly expect that, in the course of the next two hundred years, each farm in this country on an average would produce eight times as much food as it produces at present, and still less that this rate of increase could continue, so that each farm would produce twenty times as much as at present in 500 years, and forty times as much in 1000 years. Yet this would be an arithmetical progression, and would fall short, beyond all comparison, of the natural increase of population in a geometrical progression, according to which the inhabitants of any country in 500 years, instead of increasing to twenty times, would increase to above a million times their present numbers. . . .

Whatever temporary and partial relief . . . may be derived from emigration by particular countries in the actual state of things, it is quite obvious, that, considering the subject generally and largely, emigration may be fairly said not in any degree to touch the difficulty. And, whether we exclude or include emigration, – whether we refer to particular countries, or to the whole earth, the supposition of a future capacity in the soil to increase the necessaries of life every twenty-five years by a quantity equal to that which is at present produced, must be decidedly beyond the truth.

But, if the natural increase of population, when unchecked by the difficulty of procuring the means of subsistence, or other peculiar causes, be such as to continue doubling its numbers in twenty-five years; and the greatest increase of food, which, for a continuance, could possibly take place on a limited territory like our earth in its present state, be at the most only such as would add every twenty-five years an amount equal to its present produce; it is quite clear that a powerful check on the increase of population must be almost constantly in action. . . . The great question, then, which remains to be considered, is the manner in which this constant and necessary check upon population practically operates. . . .

It is to the laws of nature, . . . and not to the conduct and institutions of man, that we are to attribute the necessity of a strong check on the natural increase of population.

But, though the laws of nature which determine the rate at which population would increase if unchecked, and the very different rate at which the food required to support population could be made to increase in a limited territory, are undoubtedly the causes which render necessary the existence of some great and constant check to population, yet a vast mass of responsibility remains behind on man and the institutions of society.

In the first place, they are certainly responsible for the present scanty population of the earth. There are few large countries, however, advanced in improvement, the population of which might not have been doubled or tripled, and there are many which might be ten, or even a hundred times as populous, and yet all the inhabitants be as well provided for as they are now, if the institutions of society, and the moral habits of the people, had been for some hundred years the most favourable to the increase of capital, and the demand for produce and labour.

Secondly, though man has but a trifling and temporary influence in altering the proportionate amount of the checks to population, or the degree in which they press upon the actual numbers, yet he has a great and most extensive influence on their character and mode of operation.

It is not in superseding the necessity of checks to population, in the progress of mankind to the full peopling of the earth (which may with truth be said to be a physical impossibility), but in directing these checks in such a way as to be the least prejudicial to the virtue and happiness of society, that government and human institutions produce their great effect. Here we know, from constant experience, that they have great power. Yet, even here it must be allowed, that the power of Government is rather indirect than direct, as the object to be attained depends mainly upon such a conduct on the part of individuals, as can seldom be directly enforced by laws, though it may be powerfully influenced by them.

This will appear, if we consider more particularly the nature of those checks which have been classed under the general heads of Preventive and Positive.

It will be found that they are all resolvable into *moral restraint, vice,* and *misery.* And if, from the laws of nature, some check to the increase of population be absolutely inevitable, and human institutions have any influence upon the extent to which each of these checks operates, a heavy responsibility will be incurred, if all that influence, whether direct or indirect, be not exerted to diminish the amount of vice and misery.

Moral restraint, in application to the present subject, may be defined to be, abstinence from marriage, either for a time or permanently, from prudential considerations, with a strictly moral conduct towards the sex in the interval. And this is the only mode of keeping population on a level with the means of subsistence, which is perfectly consistent with virtue and happiness. All other checks, whether of the preventive or the positive kind, though they may greatly vary in degree, resolve themselves into some form of vice or misery.

The remaining checks of the preventive kind, are the sort of intercourse which renders some of the women of large towns unprolific; a general corruption of morals with regard to the sex, which has a similar effect; unnatural passions and improper arts to prevent the consequences of irregular connections. These evidently come under the head of vice.

The positive checks to population include all the causes, which tend in any way prematurely to shorten the duration of human life; such as unwholesome occupations – severe labour and exposure to the seasons – bad and insufficient food and clothing arising from poverty – bad nursing of children – excesses of all kinds – great towns and manufactories – the whole train of common diseases and epidemics – wars, infanticide, plague, and famine. Of these positive checks, those which appear to arise from the laws of nature, may be called exclusively misery; and those which we bring upon ourselves, such as wars, excesses of all kinds, and many others, which it would be in our power to avoid, are of a mixed nature. They are brought upon us by vice, and their consequences are misery.

Some of these checks, in various combinations, and operating with various force, are constantly in action in all the countries with which we are acquainted, and form the immediate causes which keep the population on a level with the means of subsistence. . . .

But if the preventive check to population, that check which can alone supersede great misery and mortality, operates chiefly by a prudential restraint on marriage, it will be obvious, as was before stated, that direct legislation cannot do much. Prudence cannot be enforced by laws, without a great violation of natural liberty, and a great risk of producing more evil than good. But still, the very great influence of a just and enlightened government, and the perfect security of property in creating habits of prudence, cannot for a moment be questioned. . . .

To what extent assistance may be given even by law to the poorer classes of society when in distress, without defeating the great object of the law of property, . . . depends mainly upon the feelings and habits of the labouring classes of society, and can only be determined by experience. If it be generally considered as so discreditable to receive parochial relief, that great exertions are made to avoid it, and few or none marry with a certain prospect of being obliged to have recourse to it, there is no doubt that those who were really in distress might be adequately assisted, with little danger of a constantly increasing proportion of paupers; and in that case a great good would be attained without any proportionate evil to counterbalance it. But if, from the numbers of the dependent poor, the discredit of receiving relief is so diminished as to be practically disregarded, so that many marry with the almost certain prospect of becoming paupers, and the proportion of their numbers to the whole population is in consequence continually increasing; it is certain that the partial good attained must be much more than counterbalanced by the general deterioration in the condition of the great mass of the society, and the prospect of its daily growing worse: so that, though from the inadequate relief which is in many cases granted, the manner in which it is conceded, and other counteracting causes, the operation of poor-laws such as they exist in England might be very different from the effects of a full concession of the right, and a complete fulfilment of the duties resulting from it; yet such a state of things ought to give the most serious alarm to every friend to the happiness of society, and every effort consistent with justice and humanity ought to be made to remedy it. But whatever steps may be taken on this subject, it will be allowed, that with any prospect of legislating for the poor with success, it is necessary to be fully aware of the natural tendency of the labouring classes of society to increase beyond the demand for their labour, or the means of their adequate support, and the effect of this tendency to throw the greatest difficulties in the way of permanently improving their condition.

It would lead far beyond the limits which must be prescribed to this article, to notice all the various objections which have been made by different writers to the principles which have been here explained. Those which contain in them the slightest degree of plausibility have been answered by Mr Malthus in various parts of the late editions of his work, and particularly in the appendix to the fifth edition, to which we refer the reader. We will only, therefore, further notice the objection which has been made by some persons on religious grounds; for, as it is certainly of great importance that the answer which has been given to it should be kept in mind, we cannot refuse a place to a condensed statement of it at the end of this article.

It has been thought that a tendency in mankind to increase, beyond the greatest possible increase of food which could be produced in a limited space, impeaches the goodness of the Deity, and is inconsistent with the letter and spirit of the Scriptures. If this objection were well founded, it would certainly be the most serious one which has been brought forwards; but the answer to it appears to be quite satisfactory, and it may be compressed into a very small compass.

First, It appears that the evils arising from the principle of population are exactly of the same kind as the evils arising from the excessive or irregular gratification of the human passions in general, and may equally be avoided by moral restraint. Consequently there can be no more reason to conclude, from the existence of these evils, that the principle of increase is too strong, than to conclude, from the existence of the vices arising from the human passions, that these passions are all too strong, and require diminution or extinction, instead of regulation and direction.

Secondly, It is almost universally acknowledged, that both the letter and spirit of revelation represent this world as a state of moral discipline and probation. But a state of moral discipline and probation cannot be a state of unmixed happiness, as it necessarily implies difficulties to be overcome, and temptations to be resisted. Now, in the whole range of the laws of nature, not one can be pointed out which so especially accords with this scriptural view of the state of man on earth; as it gives rise to a greater variety of situations and exertions than any other, and marks, in a more general and stronger manner, and nationally, as well as individually, the different effects of virtue and vice, of the proper government of the passions, and the culpable indulgence of them. It follows, then, that the principle of population, instead of being inconsistent with Revelation, must be considered as affording strong additional proofs of its truth.

Lastly, It will be acknowledged, that in a state of probation, those laws seem best to accord with the views of a benevolent Creator, which, while they furnish the difficulties and temptations which form the essence of such a state, are of such a nature as to reward those who overcome them with happiness in this life as well as in the next. But the law of population answers particularly to this description. Each individual has the power of avoiding the evil consequences to himself and society resulting from it, by the practice of a virtue dictated to him by the light of nature, and sanctioned by revealed religion. And, as there can be no question that this virtue tends greatly to improve the condition, and increase the comforts both of the individuals who practise it, and through them of the whole society, the ways of God to man with regard to this great law are completely vindicated.

7.1.2 J. S. MILL ON THE LAWS OF SOCIAL PROGRESS, 1843

. . . It is hardly an exaggeration to say that society has usually, both by practitioners in politics and by philosophical speculators on forms of government, from Plato to Bentham, been deemed to be whatever the men who compose it choose to make it. The only questions which people thought of proposing to themselves were, Would such and such a law or institution be beneficial? and, if so, can legislators or the public be persuaded, or otherwise induced, to adopt it? For hardly any notion was entertained that there were limits to the power of human will over the phenomena of society, or that any social arrangements which would be desirable, could be impracticable from incompatibility with the properties of the subject matter: the only obstacle was supposed to lie in the private interests or prejudices, which hindered men from being willing to see them tried. Students in politics thus attempted to study the pathology and therapeutics of the social body, before they had laid the necessary foundation in its physiology; to cure disease, without understanding the laws of health. And the result was such as it must always be when men even of great ability attempt to deal with the complex questions of a science before its simpler and more elementary propositions have been established. . . .

All phenomena of society are phenomena of human nature, generated by the action of outward circumstances upon masses of human beings: and if, therefore, the phenomena of human thought, feeling, and action, are subject to fixed laws, the phenomena of society cannot but conform to fixed laws, the consequences of the preceding. There is, indeed, no hope that these laws, though our knowledge of them were as certain and as complete as it is in astronomy, would enable us to predict the history of society, like that of the celestial appearances, for thousands of years to come. But . . . an amount of knowledge quite insufficient for prediction, may be most valuable for guidance. The science of society would have attained a very high point of perfection, if it enabled us, in any given condition of social affairs, in the condition for instance of Europe or any European country at the present time, to understand by what causes it had, in any and every particular, been made what it was; whether it was tending to any, and to what, changes; what effects each feature of its existing state was likely to produce in the future; and by what means any of those effects might be prevented, modified, or accelerated, or a different class of effects superinduced. There is nothing chimerical in the hope that general laws, sufficient to enable us to answer these various questions for any country or time with the individual circumstances of which we are well acquainted, do really admit of being ascertained; and moreover, that the other branches of human knowledge, which this undertaking presupposes, are so far advanced that the time is ripe for its accomplishment. Such is the object of the Social Science. . . .

In order to conceive correctly the scope of this general science, and distinguish it from the subordinate departments of sociological specu-lation, it is necessary to fix with precision the ideas attached to the phrase, 'a State of Society.' What is called a state of society, is the simultaneous state of all the greater social facts or phenomena. Such are, the degree of knowledge, and of intellectual and moral culture, existing in the com-munity, and in every class of it; the state of industry, of wealth and its distribution; the habitual occupations of the community; their division into classes, and the relations of those classes to one another; the common beliefs which they entertain on all the subjects most important to man-kind, and the degree of assurance with which those beliefs are held; their tastes, and the character and degree of their æsthetic development; their form of government, and the more important of their laws and customs. The condition of all these things, and of many more which will spon-taneously suggest themselves, constitute the state of society or the state of civilization at any given time.

When states of society, and the causes which produce them, are spoken of as a subject of science, it is implied that there exists a natural correlation among these different elements; that not every variety of combination of these general social facts is possible, but only certain combinations; that, in short, there exist Uniformities of Coexistence between the states of the various social phenomena. And such is the truth: as is indeed a necessary consequence of the influence exercised by every one of those phenomena over every other. It is a fact implied in the *consensus* of the various parts of the social body.

States of society are like different constitutions or different ages in the physical frame; they are conditions not of one or a few organs or func-tions, but of the whole organism. Accordingly, the information which we possess respecting past ages, and respecting the various states of society now existing in different regions of the earth, does, when duly analyzed, exhibit such uniformities. It *is* found that when one of the features of society is in a particular state, a state of all the other features, more or less precisely determinate, always or usually coexists with it.

But the uniformities of coexistence obtaining among phenomena which are effects of causes, must . . . be mere corollaries from the laws of causation by which these phenomena are actually determined. The mutual correlation between the different elements of each state of society, is therefore a derivative law, resulting from the laws which regulate the succession between one state of society and another: for the proximate cause of every state of society is the state of society immediately preceding it. The fundamental problem, therefore, of the social science is to find the laws according to which any state of society produces the state which succeeds it and takes its place. This opens the great and vexed question of the progressiveness of man and society; an idea involved in every just conception of social phenomena as the subject of a science. . . .

The words Progress and Progressiveness, are not here to be understood as synonymous with improvement and tendency to improvement. It is conceivable that the laws of human nature might determine, and even necessitate, a certain series of changes in man and society, which might not in every case, or which might not on the whole, be improvements. It is my belief indeed that the general tendency is, and will continue to be, saving occasional exceptions, one of improvement; a tendency towards a better and happier state. This, however, is not a question of the method of the social science, but an ultimate result of the science itself. For our purpose it is sufficient, that there is a progressive change both in the character of the human race, and in their outward circumstances so far as moulded by themselves: that in each successive age the principal phenomena of society are different from what they were in the age preceding, and still more different from any previous age: the periods which most distinctly mark these successive changes being intervals of one generation, during which a new set of human beings have been educated, have grown up from childhood, and taken possession of society.

The progressiveness of the human race is the foundation on which a method of philosophizing in the social science has been of late years erected. . . . This method, which is now generally adopted by the most advanced thinkers on the Continent, and especially in France, consists in attempting, by a study and analysis of the general facts of history, to discover (what these philosophers term) the law of progress. . . . But while I gladly acknowledge the great services which have been rendered to historical knowledge by this school, I cannot but deem them to be mostly chargeable with a fundamental misconception of the true method of social philosophy. The misconception consists in supposing that the order of succession which we may be able to trace among the different states of society and civilization which history presents to us, even if that order were more rigidly uniform than it has yet been proved to be, could ever amount to a law of nature. It can only be an empirical law. The succession of states of the human mind and of human society cannot have an independent law of its own; it must depend upon the psychological and ethological laws which govern the action of circumstances on men and of men on circumstances. . . . Now, M. Comte alone, among the new historical school, has seen the necessity of thus connecting all our generalizations from history with the laws of human nature; and he alone, therefore, has arrived at any results truly scientific. . . .

The Empirical Laws of Society are of two kinds; some are uniformities of coexistence, some of succession. According as the science is occupied in ascertaining and verifying the former sort of uniformities, or the latter, M. Comte gives it the title of Social Statics, or of Social Dynamics; conformably to the distinction in mechanics between the conditions of equilibrium and those of movement; or in biology, between the laws of organization and those of life. The first branch of the science ascertains the conditions of stability in the social union; the second, the laws of progress. Social Dynamics is the theory of Society considered in a state of progressive movement; while Social Statics is the theory of the *consensus* already spoken of as existing among the different parts of the social organism. . . . While the derivative laws of social statics are ascertained by analyzing different states of society, and comparing them with one another, without regard to the order of their succession; the consideration of the successive order is, on the contrary, predominant in the study of social dynamics, of which the aim is to observe and explain the sequences of social conditions. . . .

In order to obtain better empirical laws, we must not rest satisfied with noting the progressive changes which manifest themselves in the separate elements of society, and in which nothing is indicated but the relation of fragments of the effect to corresponding fragments of the cause. It is necessary to combine the statical view of social phenomena with the dynamical, considering not only the progressive changes of the different elements, but the contemporaneous condition of each; and thus obtain empirically the law of correspondence not only between the simultaneous states, but between the simultaneous changes, of those elements. This law of correspondence it is, which, after being duly verified à *priori*, will become the real scientific derivative law of the development of humanity and human affairs.

In the difficult process of observation and comparison which is here required, it would evidently be a very great assistance if it should happen to be the fact, that some one element in the complex existence of social man is pre-eminent over all others as the prime agent of the social movement. For we could then take the progress of that one element as the central chain, to each successive link of which, the corresponding links of all the other progressions being appended, the succession of the facts would by this alone be presented in a kind of spontaneous order, far more nearly approaching to the real order of their filiation than could be obtained by any other merely empirical process.

Now, the evidence of history and the evidence of human nature combine, by a most striking instance of consilience, to show that there

really is one social element which is thus predominant, and almost paramount, among the agents of the social progression. This is, the state of the
speculative faculties of mankind; including the nature of the speculative
beliefs which by any means they have arrived at, concerning themselves
and the world by which they are surrounded.

It would be a great error, and one very little likely to be committed, to
assert that speculation, intellectual activity, the pursuit of truth, is among
the more powerful propensities of human nature, or fills a large place in
the lives of any, save decidedly exceptional individuals. But notwithstanding the relative weakness of this principle among other sociological
agents, its influence is the main determining cause of the social progress;
all the other dispositions of our nature which contribute to that progress,
being dependent upon it for the means of accomplishing their share of
the work. Thus, (to take the most obvious case first,) the impelling force to
most of the improvements effected in the arts of life, is the desire of
increased material comfort; but as we can only act upon external objects in
proportion to our knowledge of them, the state of knowledge at any time
is the impassable limit of the industrial improvements possible at that
time; and the progress of industry must follow, and depend upon, the
progress of knowledge. The same thing may be shown to be true, though
it is not quite so obvious, of the progress of the fine arts. Further, as the
strongest propensities of human nature (being the purely selfish ones,
and those of a sympathetic character which partake most of the nature of
selfishness) evidently tend in themselves to disunite mankind, not to unite
them, – to make them rivals, not confederates; social existence is only
possible by a disciplining of those more powerful propensities, which
consists in subordinating them to a common system of opinions. The
degree of this subordination is the measure of the completeness of the
social union, and the nature of the common opinions determines its kind.
But in order that mankind should conform their actions to any set of
opinions, these opinions must exist, must be believed by them. And thus,
the state of the speculative faculties, the character of the propositions
assented to by the intellect, essentially determines the moral and political
state of the community, as we have already seen that it determines the
physical.

These conclusions, deduced from the laws of human nature, are in
entire accordance with the general facts of history. Every considerable
change historically known to us in the condition of any portion of mankind, when not brought about by external force, has been preceded by a
change, of proportional extent, in the state of their knowledge, or in their
prevalent beliefs. As between any given state of speculation, and the
correlative state of everything else, it was almost always the former which
first showed itself; though the effects, no doubt, reacted potently upon

the cause. Every considerable advance in material civilization has been preceded by an advance in knowledge; and when any great social change has come to pass, a great change in the opinions and modes of thinking of society had taken place shortly before. Polytheism, Judaism, Christianity, Protestantism, the negative philosophy of modern Europe, and its positive science – each of these has been a primary agent in making society what it was at each successive period, while society was but secondarily instrumental in making *them,* each of them (so far as causes can be assigned for its existence) being mainly an emanation not from the practical life of the period, but from the state of belief and thought during some time previous. The weakness of the speculative propensity has not, therefore, prevented the progress of speculation from governing that of society at large; it has only, and too often, prevented progress altogether, where the intellectual progression has come to an early stand for want of sufficiently favourable circumstances.

From this accumulated evidence, we are justified in concluding, that the order of human progression in all respects will be a corollary deducible from the order of progression in the intellectual convictions of mankind, that is, from the law of the successive transformations of religion and science. The question remains, whether this law can be determined; at first from history as an empirical law, then converted into a scientific theorem by deducing it *à priori* from the principles of human nature. As the progress of knowledge and the changes in the opinions of mankind are very slow, and manifest themselves in a well-defined manner only at long intervals; it cannot be expected that the general order of sequence should be discoverable from the examination of less than a very considerable part of the duration of the social progress. It is necessary to take into consideration the whole of past time, from the first recorded condition of the human race; and it is probable that all the terms of the series already past were indispensable to the operation; that the memorable phenomena of the last generation, and even those of the present, were necessary to manifest the law, and that consequently the Science of History has only become possible in our own time.

The investigation which I have thus endeavoured to characterise, has been systematically attempted, up to the present time, by M. Comte alone. His works are hitherto the only known example of the study of social phenomena on the true principles of the Historical Method. Of that method I do not hesitate to pronounce them a model: what is the value of his conclusions is another question, and on which this is not the place to decide.

I cannot, however, omit to mention one important generalization, which he regards as the fundamental law of the progress of human knowledge. Speculation he conceives to have, on every subject of human inquiry, three successive stages; in the first of which it tends to explain the phenomena by supernatural agencies, in the second by metaphysical abstractions, and in the third or final state confines itself to ascertaining their laws of succession and similitude. This generalization appears to me to have that high degree of scientific evidence, which is derived from the concurrence of the indications of history with the probabilities derived from the constitution of the human mind. Nor could it be easily conceived, from the mere enunciation of such a proposition, what a flood of light it lets in upon the whole course of history; when its consequences are traced, by connecting with each of the three states of human intellect which it distinguishes, and with each successive modification of those three states, the correlative condition of all other social phenomena.

But whatever decision competent judges may pronounce on the results arrived at by any individual inquirer, the method has been found by which an indefinite number of the derivative laws both of social order and of social progress may in time be ascertained. By the aid of these, we may hereafter succeed not only in looking far forward into the future history of the human race, but in determining what artificial means may be used, and to what extent, to accelerate the natural progress in so far as it is beneficial; to compensate for whatever may be its inherent inconveniences or disadvantages; and to guard against the dangers or accidents to which our species is exposed from the necessary incidents of its progression. Such practical instructions, founded on the highest branch of speculative sociology, will form the noblest and most beneficial portion of the Political Art. . . .

7.1.3 T. CARLYLE ON THE RELIGION OF NATURAL LAW, 1843

. . . Hast thou reflected, O serious reader, Advanced-Liberal or other, that the one end, essence, use of all religion past, present and to come, was this only: To keep that same Moral Conscience or Inner Light of ours alive and shining. . . . All religion was here to remind us, better or worse, of what we already know better or worse, of the quite *infinite* difference there is between a Good man and a Bad; to bid us love infinitely the one, abhor and avoid infinitely the other, – strive infinitely to *be* the one, and not to be the other. 'All religion issues in due Practical Hero-worship.' He that has a soul unasphyxied will never want a religion; he that has a soul asphyxied, reduced to a succedaneum for salt, will never find any religion, though you rose from the dead to preach him one.

But indeed, when men and reformers ask for 'a religion,' it is analogous to their asking, 'What would you have us to do?' and such like. They fancy that their religion too shall be a kind of Morrison's Pill, which they have only to swallow once, and all will be well. Resolutely once gulp down your

Religion, your Morrison's Pill, you have it all plain sailing now; you can follow your affairs, your no-affairs, go along money-hunting, pleasure-hunting, dilettanteing, dangling, and miming and chattering like a Dead-Sea Ape: your Morrison will do your business for you. Men's notions are very strange! – Brother, I say there is not, was not, nor will ever be, in the wide circle of Nature, any Pill or Religion of that character. Man cannot afford thee such; for the very gods it is impossible. I advise thee to renounce Morrison; once for all, quit hope of the Universal Pill. For body, for soul, for individual or society, there has not any such article been made. *Non extat*. In Created Nature it is not, was not, will not be. In the void imbroglios of Chaos only, and realms of Bedlam, does some shadow of it hover, to bewilder and bemock the poor inhabitants *there*.

Rituals, Liturgies, Creeds, Hierarchies: all this is not religion; all this, were it dead as Odinism, as Fetishism, does not kill religion at all! It is Stupidity alone, with never so many rituals, that kills religion. Is not this still a World? Spinning Cotton under Arkwright and Adam Smith; founding Cities by the Fountain of Juturna, on the Janiculum Mount; tilling Canaan under Prophet Samuel and Psalmist David, man is ever man; the missionary of Unseen Powers; and great and victorious, while he continues true to his mission; mean, miserable, foiled, and at last annihilated and trodden out of sight and memory, when he proves untrue. Brother, thou art a Man, I think; thou art not a mere building Beaver, or two-legged Cotton-Spider; thou has verily a Soul in thee, asphyxied or otherwise! Sooty Manchester, – it too is built on the infinite Abysses; overspanned by the skyey Firmaments; and there is birth in it, and death in it; – and it is every whit as wonderful, as fearful, unimaginable, as the oldest Salem or Prophetic City. Go or stand, in what time, in what place we will, are there not Immensities, Eternities over us, around us, in us:

> Solemn before us,
> Veiled, the dark Portal,
> Goal of all mortal:—
> Stars silent rest o'er us,
> Graves under us silent!

Between *these* two great Silences, the hum of all our spinning cylinders, Trades-Unions, Anti-Corn-Law Leagues and Carlton Clubs goes on. Stupidity itself ought to pause a little, and consider that. I tell thee, through all thy Ledgers, Supply-and-demand Philosophies, and daily most modern melancholy Business and Cant, there does shine the presence of a Primeval Unspeakable; and thou wert wise to recognise, not with lips only, that same!

The Maker's Laws, whether they are promulgated in Sinai Thunder, to the ear or imagination, or quite otherwise promulgated, are the Laws of

God; transcendent, everlasting, imperatively demanding obedience from all men. This, without any thunder, or with never so much thunder, thou, if there be any soul left in thee, canst know of a truth. The Universe, I say, is made by Law; the great Soul of the World is just and not unjust. Look thou, if thou have eyes or soul left, into this great shoreless Incomprehensible: in the heart of its tumultuous Appearances, Embroilments, and mad Time-vortexes, is there not, silent, eternal, an All-just, an All-beautiful; sole Reality and ultimate controlling Power of the whole? This is not a figure of speech; this is a fact. The fact of Gravitation known to all animals, not surer than this inner Fact, which may be known to all men. He who knows this, it will sink, silent, awful, unspeakable, into his heart. He will say with Faust: 'Who *dare* name HIM?' Most rituals or 'namings' he will fall in with at present, are like to be 'namings' – which shall be nameless! In silence, in the Eternal Temple, let him worship, if there be no fit word. Such knowledge, the crown of his whole spiritual being, the life of his life, let him keep and sacredly walk by. He has a religion. Hourly and daily, for himself and for the whole world, a faithful, unspoken, but not ineffectual prayer rises, 'Thy will be done.' His whole work on Earth is an emblematic spoken or acted prayer, Be the will of God done on Earth, – not the Devil's will, or any of the Devil's servants' wills! He has a religion, this man; an everlasting Loadstar that beams the brighter in the Heavens, the darker here on Earth grows the night around him. Thou, if thou know not this, what are all rituals, liturgies, mythologies, mass-chantings, turnings of the rotatory calabash? They are as nothing; in a good many respects they are as *less*. Divorced from this, getting half-divorced from this, they are a thing to fill one with a kind of horror; with a sacred inexpressible pity and fear. The most tragical thing a human eye can look on. It was said to the Prophet, 'Behold, I will shew thee worse things than these: women weeping to Thammuz.' That was the acme of the Prophet's vision, – then as now.

Rituals, Liturgies, Credos, Sinai Thunder: I know more or less the history of these; the rise, progress, decline and fall of these. Can thunder from all the thirty-two azimuths, repeated daily for centuries of years, make God's Laws more godlike to me? Brother, No. Perhaps I am grown to be a man now; and do not need the thunder and the terror any longer! Perhaps I am above being frightened; perhaps it is not Fear, but Reverence alone, that shall now lead me! – Revelations, Inspirations? Yes: and thy own god-created Soul; dost thou not call that a 'revelation?' Who made THEE? Where didst Thou come from? The Voice of Eternity, if thou be not a blasphemer and poor asphyxied mute, speaks with that tongue of thine! *Thou* art the latest Birth of Nature; it is 'the Inspiration of the Almighty' that giveth *thee* understanding! My brother, my brother!—

Under baleful Atheisms, Mammonisms, Joe-Manton Dilettantisms, with their appropriate Cants and Idolisms, and whatsoever scandalous rubbish obscures and all but extinguishes the soul of man, – religion now is; its Laws, written if not on stone tables, yet on the Azure of Infinitude, in the inner heart of God's Creation, certain as Life, certain as Death! I say the Laws are there, and thou shalt not disobey them. It were better for thee not. Better a hundred deaths than yes. Terrible 'penalties' withal, if thou still need 'penalties,' are there for disobeying. Dost thou observe, O redtape Politician, that fiery infernal Phenomenon, which men name FRENCH REVOLUTION, sailing, unlooked-for, unbidden; through thy inane Protocol Dominion: – far-seen, with splendour not of Heaven? Ten centuries will see it. There were Tanneries at Meudon for human skins. And Hell, very truly Hell, had power over God's upper Earth for a season. The cruelest Portent that has risen into created Space these ten centuries: let us hail it, with awestruck repentant hearts, as the voice once more of a God, though of one in wrath. Blessed be the God's-voice; for *it* is true, and Falsehoods have to cease before it! But for that same preternatural quasi-infernal Portent, one could not know what to make of this wretched world, in these days, at all. The deplorablest quack-ridden, and now hunger-ridden, downtrodden Despicability and *Flebile Ludibrium,* of redtape Protocols, rotatory Calabashes, Poor-Law Bastilles: who is there that could think of *its* being fated to continue?—

Penalties enough, my brother! This penalty inclusive of all: Eternal Death to thy own hapless Self, if thou heed no other. Eternal Death, I say, – with many meanings old and new, of which let this single one suffice us here: The eternal impossibility for thee to *be* aught but a Chimera, and swift-vanishing deceptive Phantasm, in God's Creation; – swift-vanishing, never to reappear: why should *it* reappear! Thou hadst one chance, thou wilt never have another. Everlasting ages will roll on, and no other be given thee. The foolishest articulate-speaking soul now extant, may not he say to himself: 'A whole Eternity I waited to be born; and now I have a whole Eternity waiting to see what I will do when born!' This is not Theology, this is Arithmetic. And thou but half-discernest this; thou but half-believest it? Alas, on the shores of the Dead Sea on Sabbath, there goes on a Tragedy!—

But we will leave this of 'Religion;' of which, to say truth, it is chiefly profitable in these unspeakable days to keep silence. Thou needest no 'New Religion;' nor art thou like to get any. Thou hast already more 'religion' than thou makest use of. This day, thou knowest ten command-ed duties, seest in thy mind ten things which should be done, for one that thou doest! *Do* one of them; this of itself will shew thee ten others which can and shall be done. 'But my future fate?' Yes, thy future fate, indeed? Thy future fate, while thou makest *it* the chief question, seems to me – extremely questionable! I do not think it can be good. Norse Odin, immemorial centuries ago, did not he, though a poor Heathen, in the dawn of Time, teach us that, for the Dastard there was and could be no good fate; no harbour anywhere, save down with Hela, in the pool of Night! Dastards, Knaves, are they that lust for Pleasure, that tremble at Pain. For this world and for the next, Dastards are a class of creatures made to be 'arrested;' they are good for nothing else, can look for nothing else. A greater than Odin has been here. A greater than Odin has taught us – not a greater Dastardism, I hope! My brother, thou must pray for a *soul*; struggle, as with life-and-death energy, to get back thy soul! Know that 'religion' is no Morrison's Pill from without, but a reawakening of thy own Self from within: – and, above all, leave me alone of thy 'religions' and 'new religions' here and elsewhere! I am weary of this sick croaking for a Morrison's-Pill religion; for any and for every such. I want none such; and discern all such to be impossible. The resuscitation of old liturgies fallen dead; much more, the manufacture of new liturgies that will never be alive: how hopeless! Stylitisms, eremite fanaticisms and fakeerisms; spasmodic agonistic posture-makings, and narrow, cramped, morbid, if forever noble wrestlings: all this is not a thing desirable to me. It is a thing the world *has* done once, – when its beard was not grown as now!

And yet there is, at worst, one Liturgy which does remain forever unexceptionable: that of *Praying* (as the old Monks did withal) *by Working*. And indeed the Prayer which accomplished itself in special chapels at stated hours, and went not with a man, rising up from all his Work and Action, at all moments sanctifying the same, – what was it ever good for? 'Work is Worship:' yes, in a highly considerable sense, – which, in the present state of all 'worship,' who is there that can unfold! He that understands it well, understands the Prophecy of the whole Future; the last Evangel, which has included all others. *Its* cathedral the Dome of Immensity, – hast thou seen it? coped with the star-galaxies; paved with the green mosaic of land and ocean; and for altar, verily, the Star-throne of the Eternal! Its litany and psalmody the noble acts, the heroic work and suffering, and true Heart-utterance of all the Valiant of the Sons of Men. Its choir-music the ancient Winds and Oceans, and deep-toned, inarticulate, but most speaking voices of Destiny and History, – supernal ever as of old. Between two great Silences:

> Stars silent rest o'er us,
> Graves under us silent.

Between which two great Silences, do not, as we said, all human Noises, in the naturalest times, most *preter*-naturally march and roll?—...

7.1.4   H. SPENCER ON PROGRESS AND POPULATION, 1852

'In a very recent publication,' says Dr. Whately, 'I have seen mention
made of a person who discovered the falsity of a certain doctrine (which,
by the way, is nevertheless a true one, that of Malthus) *instinctively*. This
kind of instinct, *i.e.*, the habit of forming opinions at the suggestion rather
of feeling than of reason, is very common.' There can be little doubt that
this remark refers to a passage in the preface to Doubleday's 'True Law
of Population,' wherein the writer says:—

> Happening many years ago, in the presence of a late relative, long
> since deceased, remarkable both for the sagacity and extended
> benevolence of his general views on philosophical subjects, to
> draw some of those startling, though not illogical, conclusions
> which seemed to flow from theories then recently broached as to
> this subject, and much in vogue at the time, the reply was this:—
> 'Depend upon it, my dear nephew, that you and I may safely
> decline to yield an implicit assent, though we may not, on the
> instant, be able to refute them, to views from which consequences,
> such as you have drawn, legitimately flow. Though I may not live
> to see it, nor you, a time will come when this mystery will be
> unveiled, and when a perhaps now mysterious, but, beyond
> doubt, a beneficent law will be discovered, regulating this matter,
> in accordance with all the rest that we see of God's moral
> government of the world.'

On comparing these extracts we cannot compliment Dr. Whately,
either upon the fairness of his stricture or the depth of his insight. To
apply the term instinctive to the conclusion thus drawn, indicates a misunderstanding of the mental process leading to it. Not a feeling but a
broad generalisation is the basis on which such a conclusion rests. He who
arrives at it in the manner above implied does so by comparing, in a more
or less conscious way, the alleged truth with other truths, and discovering
that it is not congruous with them. By daily-accumulating experience he
becomes impressed with the inherent tendency of things towards good –
sees going on universally a patient self-rectification. He finds that the *vis
medicatrix naturæ* – or rather the process which we describe by that expression – is not limited to the cure of wounds and diseases, but pervades
creation. From the lowly fungus which, under varying circumstances,
assumes varying forms of organization, up to the tree that grows
obliquely, if it cannot otherwise get to the light – from the highest human
faculty which increases or dwindles according to the demands made on it,
down to the polype that changes its skin into stomach and its stomach into
skin when turned inside out – he everywhere sees at work an essential

beneficence. Equally in the attainment of fitness for a new climate, or skill in a new occupation – in the diminution of a suppressed desire, and in the growing pleasure that attends the performance of a duty – in the gradual evanescence of grief, and in the callousness that follows long-continued privations – he perceives this remedial action. Whether he contemplates the acquirement, by each race, of a liking for the mode of life circumstances dictate – whether he regards the process by which different nations are slowly forced to produce those commodities only, that it is best for the world they should produce – or whether he looks at the repeated re-establishment, amongst a turbulent people, of the form of government best fitted for them – he is alike struck with the self-sufficingness of things. And when, after recognising this throughout the whole organic world, he finds that it extends to the inorganic also – when he reads that though Newton feared for the stability of the solar system, yet Laplace found that all planetary perturbations are self-neutralizing – when he thus sees that perfection exists even where so high an intelligence failed to perceive it – he is still more convinced that in all cases we shall discover harmony and completeness when we know how to look for them. Hence, if any one propounds to him a theory implying in nature an ineradicable defect, he hesitates to receive it. That the human constitution should include some condition which must ever continue to entail either physical or moral pain, is at variance with all that a wide experience teaches him. And finding the alleged fact conflict with universal facts, he concludes that it is probably untrue. He concludes this, not instinctively, but rationally, and his argument corresponds completely with the logical form – as in all other cases I have observed a certain sequence of phenomena, I infer that there will be the same sequence in this case also. Moreover, such a belief is not only a rational, but the truly religious one. Faith in the essential beneficence of things is the highest kind of faith. And considering his position, a little more of this faith would have been by no means unbecoming in the Archbishop of Dublin.

But however right the point of view from which Mr. Doubleday, influenced by his relative, has studied the population question, it does not follow that he has solved it. We are of opinion that he has not done so. There is one fact which seems to us at once fatal to his hypothesis; namely, that is does not fulfil the very condition which it purports to fulfil: it does not disclose a self-adjusting law. . . .

The law which we have . . . traced throughout the animal kingdom, and which must alike determine the different fertilities of different species, and the variations of fertility in the same species [viz., 'the ability to maintain individual life and the ability to multiply vary inversely'], we have now to consider in its application to mankind.

From the fact that the human race is in a state of transition, we may suspect that the existing ratio between its ability to multiply, and its ability to maintain life, is not a constant ratio. From the fact that its fertility is at present in excess of what is needful, we may infer that any change in the ratio will probably be towards a diminution of fertility. And from the fact that, on the whole, civilization increases the ability to maintain life, we may perceive that there is at work some influence by which such diminution is necessitated. Before inquiring for this influence, let us consider what directions an increase of ability to maintain life may take – what scope there is for an increase. In some further development of the co-ordinating system, that is, in some greater co-ordination of actions, the increase must of course consist. But there are several kinds of co-ordination; and it will be well to ask of what kind or kinds increase is most requisite, and therefore most likely. For, doubtless, in conformity with the general law of adaptation, increase will take place only where it is demanded.

Will it be in strength? Probably not. . . .

Will it be in swiftness or agility? Probably not. . . .

Will it be in mechanical skill, that is, in the better co-ordination of complex movements? Most likely in some degree. . . .

Will it be in intelligence? Largely, no doubt. There is ample room for progress in this direction, and ample demand for it. Our lives are universally shortened by our ignorance. . . .

Will it be in morality, that is, in greater power of self-regulation? Largely also; perhaps most largely. Normal conduct, or in other words, conduct conducive to the maintenance of perfect and long-continued life, is usually come short of more from defect of will than of knowledge. To the due co-ordination of those complex actions which constitute human life in its civilized form, there goes not only the prerequisite – recognition of the proper course; but the further prerequisite – a due impulse to pursue that course. And on calling to mind our daily failures to fulfil often-repeated resolutions, we shall perceive that lack of the needful desire, rather than lack of the needful insight, is the chief cause of faulty action. A further endowment of those feelings which civilization is developing in us – sentiments responding to the requirements of the social state – emotive faculties that find their gratifications in the duties devolving on us – must be acquired before the crimes, excesses, diseases, improvidences, dishonesties, and cruelties, that now so greatly diminish the duration of life, can cease.

But whether greater co-ordination of actions take place in any or in all of these directions, and in whatever degree or proportions, it is clear that, if it take place at all, it must be at the expense of fertility. Regarded from the abstract point of view, increased ability to maintain life in this case, as in all others, necessarily involves decreased ability to multiply. Or, regarded in the concrete, that further development of the co-ordinating system, which any advance presupposes, implies further decrease in the production of co-ordinating cells.

That an enlargement of the nervous centres is going on in mankind, is an ascertained fact. Not alone from a general survey of human progress – not alone from the greater power of self-preservation shown by civilized races, are we left to infer such enlargement; it is proved by actual measurement. The mean capacities of the crania in the leading divisions of the species have been found to be—

In the Australian .... 75 cubic inches.
In the African .... 82 cubic inches.
In the Malayan...................................... 86 cubic inches.
In the Englishman .... 96 cubic inches.

showing an increase in the course of the advance from the savage state to our present phase of civilization, amounting to nearly 30 per cent. on the original size. That this increase will be continuous, might be reasonably assumed; and to infer a future decrease of fertility would be tolerably safe, were no further evidence forthcoming. But it may be shown why a greater development of the nervous system *must* take place, and why, consequently, there *must* be a diminution of the present excess of fertility; and further, it may be shown that the sole agency needed to work out this change is – *the excess of fertility itself*.

For, as we all know, this excess of fertility entails a constant pressure of population upon the means of subsistence; and, as long as it exists, must continue to do this. Looking only at the present and the immediate future, it is unquestionably true, that, if unchecked, the rate of increase of people would exceed the rate of increase of food. It is clear that the wants of their redundant numbers constitute the only stimulus mankind have to a greater production of the necessaries of life; for, were not the demand beyond the supply, there would be no motive to increase the supply. . . .

But this inevitable redundancy of numbers – this constant increase of people beyond the means of subsistence – involving as it does an increasing stimulus to better the modes of producing food and other necessaries – involves also an increasing demand for skill, intelligence, and self-control – involves, therefore, a constant exercise of these, that is – involves a gradual growth of them. Every improvement is at once the product of a higher form of humanity, and demands that higher form of humanity to carry it into practice. . . . In all cases, increase of numbers is the efficient cause. Were it not for the competition this entails, more thought would not daily be brought to bear upon the business of life; greater activity of mind would not be called for; and development of mental power would not take place. Difficulty in getting a living is alike the incentive to a higher education of children, and to a more intense and long-continued application in adults. In the mother it induces foresight, economy, and skilful house-keeping; in the father, laborious days and constant self-denial. Nothing but necessity could make men submit to this discipline, and nothing but this discipline could produce a continued progression. The contrast between a Pacific Islander, all whose wants are supplied by Nature, and an Englishman, who, generation after generation, has had to bring to the satisfaction of his wants ever-increasing knowledge and skill, illustrates at once the need for, and the effects of, such discipline. And this being admitted, it cannot be denied that a further continuance of such discipline, possibly under a yet more intense form, must produce a further progress in the same direction – a further enlargement of the nervous centres, and a further decline of fertility.

And here it must be remarked, that the effect of pressure of population, in increasing the ability to maintain life, and decreasing the ability to multiply, is not a uniform effect, but an average one. In this case, as in many others, Nature secures each step in advance by a succession of trials, which are perpetually repeated, and cannot fail to be repeated, until success is achieved. All mankind in turn subject themselves more or less to the discipline described; they either may or may not advance under it; but, in the nature of things, only those who *do* advance under it eventually survive. For, necessarily, families and races whom this increasing difficulty of getting a living which excess of fertility entails, does not stimulate to improvements in production – that is, to greater mental activity – are on the high road to extinction; and must ultimately be supplanted by those whom the pressure does so stimulate. This truth we have recently seen exemplified in Ireland. And here, indeed, without further illustration, it will be seen that premature death, under all its forms, and from all its causes, cannot fail to work in the same direction. For as those prematurely carried off must, in the average of cases, be those in whom the power of self-preservation is the least, it unavoidably follows, that those left behind to continue the race are those in whom the power of self-preservation is the greatest – are the select of their generation. So that, whether the dangers to existence be of the kind produced by excess of fertility, or of any other kind, it is clear, that by the ceaseless exercise of the faculties needed to contend with them, and by the death of all men who fail to contend with them successfully, there is ensured a constant progress towards a higher degree of skill, intelligence, and self-regulation – a better co-ordination of actions – a more complete life.

There now remains but to inquire towards what limit this progress tends. Evidently, so long as the fertility of the race is more than sufficient to balance the diminution by deaths, population must continue to increase: so long as population continues to increase, there must be pressure on the means of subsistence: and so long as there is pressure on the means of subsistence, further mental development must go on, and further diminution of fertility must result. Hence, the change can never cease until the rate of multiplication is just equal to the rate of mortality; that is – can never cease until, on the average, each pair brings to maturity but two children. Probably this involves that each pair will rarely produce more than two offspring; seeing that with the greatly-increased ability to preserve life, which the hypothesis presupposes, the amount of infant and juvenile mortality must become very small. Be this as it may, however, it is manifest that, in the end, pressure of population and its accompanying evils will entirely disappear; and will leave a state of things which will require from each individual no more than a normal and pleasurable activity. That this last inference is a legitimate corollary will become obvious on a little consideration. For, a cessation in the decrease of fertility implies a cessation in the development of the nervous system; and this implies that the nervous system has become fully equal to all that is demanded of it – has not to do more than is natural to it. But that exercise of faculties which does not exceed what is natural constitutes gratification. Consequently, in the end, the obtainment of subsistence will require just that kind and that amount of action needful to perfect health and happiness.

Thus do we see how simple are the means by which the greatest and most complex results are worked out. From the point of view now reached, it becomes plain that the necessary antagonism of individuation and reproduction not only fulfils with precision the *à priori* law of main-tenance of race, from the monad up to man, but ensures the final attainment of the highest form of this maintenance – a form in which the amount of life shall be the greatest possible, and the births and deaths the fewest possible. In the nature of things, the antagonism could not fail to work out the results we see it working out. The gradual diminution and ultimate disappearance of the original excess of fertility could take place only through the process of civilization; and, at the same time, the excess of fertility has itself rendered the process of civilization inevitable. From the beginning, pressure of population has been the proximate cause of progress. It produced the original diffusion of the race. It compelled men to abandon predatory habits and take to agriculture. It led to the clearing of the earth's surface. It forced men into the social state; made social organization inevitable; and has developed the social sentiments. It has stimulated to progressive improvements in production, and to increased skill and intelligence. It is daily pressing us into closer contact and more mutually-dependent relationships. And after having caused, as it ulti-mately must, the due peopling of the globe, and the bringing of all its habitable parts into the highest state of culture – after having brought all processes for the satisfaction of human wants to the greatest perfection – after having, at the same time, developed the intellect into complete competency for its work, and the feelings into complete fitness for social life – after having done all this, we see that the pressure of population, as it gradually finishes its work, must gradually bring itself to an end.

7.2 A NEW REFORMATION

Victorian science, to be free, needed to chart the history of its emancipation. To be both free and religious it had to find its antecedents within the history of ecclesiastical emancipation in Britain. The English and Scottish reformations held promise of new religious liberties; the Puritan reformers, who overthrew Church and Crown, inspired belief in a new moral order. New liberties and a new basis of morality were much in debate throughout the Victorian period, particularly after the papal aggression at mid-century and the defection of prominent churchmen to Rome. A 'new' or 'second' reformation therefore became the clarion call of those who sought religious and moral guidance through the free pursuit of science. In a widely circulated tract, George Combe (1788–1858), an educationist and phrenologist, agreed with his fellow-Scot, Carlyle, that theology and conduct must be brought back into the harmonious relationship they enjoyed among the English and Scottish reformers of the seventeenth century. He foresaw a 'new Christian faith' that would recognize natural laws as the providentially appointed preceptors of humankind (**7.2.1**). Some years later, Thomas Henry Huxley (1825–1895), a young Darwinian zoologist, took up the theme on behalf of 'men of science', who alone were fit, in his view, to be the nation's religious leaders. Already a friend of Combe's and an avid reader of Carlyle, this self-styled 'scientific Calvinist' urged his genteel audience, assembled at the Royal Institution, to cast aside their 'idols' and face the fact that man is a part of the material world, though this might entail 'revolutions of thought and practice as great as those which the sixteenth century witnessed' (**7.2.2**). One such revolution, according to the anthropologist Edward Burnett Tylor (1832–1917) in his ground-breaking work, *Primitive Culture*, would have to take place in theology as it pressed towards a 'new reformation'. The 'ethnographic method' must assist historical scholarship in discerning the permanent, the purely derivative, and the mere surviving elements among Christian doctrines. This would serve to show that 'the science of culture is essentially a reformer's science' (**7.2.3**). Finally, Huxley again, now approaching his seventieth year and embroiled in internecine controversy with the neo-Positivist *littérateur* Frederic Harrison, traced the theological antecedents of his own agnostic naturalism to Reformed Christianity and prophetic Judaism (**7.2.4**). The peroration of his essay, 'An Apologetic Irenicon', is reminiscent of no one so much as Luther, who replied memorably to his inquisitors, 'Here I stand. God help me. I cannot do otherwise.'

7.2.1   G. COMBE ON PRECEPTIVE LAWS AND PROVIDENTIAL ORDER, 1847

The Reformation in the sixteenth century produced a powerful effect on the European mind. The miracles, precepts, and sublime devotional effusions of the Old and New Testaments, excited, with deep intensity, the religious sentiments of the people, introduced ardent discussions on temporal and eternal interests, and, unfortunately, led to furious and desolating wars. Freedom on earth, and salvation in heaven or perdition in hell, were the mighty topics which then engaged public attention.

In the beginning of the seventeenth century, a generation born and educated under these exciting influences, appeared upon the stage. The Reformation was then consummated, but the duty remained of acting it out in deeds. The new generation had read in the Books of the Old Testament of a people whose king was God; whose national councils were guided by omniscience, and whose enterprizes, whether in peace or war, were aided and accomplished by omnipotence employing means altogether apart from the ordinary course of nature. The New Testament presented records of a continued exercise of similar supernatural powers; and the great lesson taught in both seemed, to that generation, to be, that the power of God was exercised as a shield to protect, and an irresistible influence to lead to success and victory in secular affairs, *those who believed aright,* who embraced cordially the doctrines revealed in the sacred volumes, who abjured all self-righteousness and self-reliance, and who threw themselves in perfect confidence and humility on Him as their King, protector, and avenger.

In the first quarter of the seventeenth century, the active members of society in England and Scotland, embraced these views as principles not only of faith but of practice. With that profound earnestness of purpose which is inspired by great ideas, they desired to realize in deeds what they believed in their minds. . . .

In commenting on that period, Thomas Carlyle observes, in his own quaint style, that 'the nobility and gentry of England were then a very strange body of men. The English squire of the seventeenth century clearly appears to have believed in God, not as a figure of speech, but as a very fact, very awful to the heart of the English squire.' He adds, 'We have wandered far away from the ideas which guided us in that century, and, indeed, which had guided us in all preceding centuries; but of which that century was the ultimate manifestation. We have wandered very far, and must endeavour to return and connect ourselves therewith again.'

I ask, How shall we return? This is a grave question, and the answer demands a serious consideration.

The grand characteristic of the Jewish dispensation, on which chiefly these views of the Divine government of the world were founded, was, that it was special and supernatural. In the seventeenth century there was very little of correct scientific knowledge of the elements, agencies, and laws of inorganic and organic nature abroad in society. The Scriptures constituted almost the sole storehouse of deep reflection and profound emotion for the men of that age; and in the absence of scientific know-ledge, they fell naturally into the belief that, as the Scriptures were given for guides to human conduct, the same scheme of Providence, physical and moral, which had prevailed in ancient times, must still continue in force. Their conviction on this point appears to have been profound and sincere, and they attempted to act it out in deeds.

But was there no error of apprehension here? Were they not mistaken in believing that the course of providence was the same in their day as it had been in the times of the Scripture records? A brief consideration of their actions, and the results of them, will perhaps throw light on this topic.

They assumed that the supernatural agencies which had been mani-fested under the Jewish dispensation might still be evoked, and would, in some form or other, be exerted for their guidance and support, if they called for them in a proper spirit. Hence, instead of studying and con-forming to the laws of nature, they resorted to fastings, humiliations, and prayers, as practical means not only of gaining battles and establishing political power, but of obtaining direction in all the serious affairs of life. Their *theology* and their science, so far as they had any science, were in harmony. They did not recognise an established and regular order of nature as a guide to human conduct, but regarded every element of physical nature, and every faculty of the human mind, as under the administration of a special and supernatural providence. They viewed God as specially bending all the powers and processes of human nature and of thought to the direct fulfilment of His will; *and on that will they believed they could operate by religious faith and observances.* In principle, their view of the nature of the divine administration of the world was similar to that entertained by the Greeks, and Romans. Homer's priests and heroes offered supplications to the gods for direct interference in favour of their schemes, and their prayers are represented to have been occasionally granted. Cromwell, and the men of his age, with more true and exalted conceptions of God, still believed in His administering the affairs of men, not by means of a regular order of causes and effects, but by direct exercises of special power.

In this condition of mind I should say that they were inspired by pure and exalted religious emotions, but misled by great errors in theology. There is a wide difference between religion and theology. Religion consists in the devotional emotions which spring up in the mind, on contemplating an object which we have been trained to reverence. 'Theology,' on the other hand, is used to designate the intellectual notions which we form concerning that object. Hence the untutored Indian, the Mahomedan, and the Hindoo, when they sincerely venerate and worship the objects which they have been taught to regard as divine, are *religious*; although their 'theology' may be altogether erroneous. In like manner, the English and Scotch Independents and Presbyterians of the first half of the seventeenth century, were earnestly and profoundly *religious*, although their theological ideas may appear to later generations to have been at variance with nature and truth.

It was, however, under the influence of such views of the course of providence as they entertained, that the existing standards of the Church of England, and the Presbyterian Church of Scotland, were framed; and hence perhaps arose the very meagre recognition of God's providence in the course of nature, as a practical system of instruction for the guidance of human conduct, which characterises them.

After that age, however, the human understanding, by a profounder and more exact study of nature, obtained a different view of the course of providence in the administration of temporal affairs. Science revealed a system in which every object, animate and inanimate, appears to be endowed with peculiar qualities and agencies, which it preserves and exerts with undeviating regularity, as long as its circumstances continue unchanged; and in which each object is adapted, with exquisite wisdom and benevolence, to the others, and all to man. In the words of the Rev. Mr Sedgwick, science unfolded a fixed order of creation, so clear and intelligible that 'we are justified in saying that, in the moral as in the physical world, God seems to govern by general laws.' – 'I am now now,' says he, 'contending for the doctrine of moral necessity; but I do affirm, that the moral government of God is by general laws, and *that it is our bounden duty to study those laws, and, as far as we can, to turn them to account.*'

Here, then, an important revolution has been effected in the views of profound thinkers, in regard to the mode in which Providence administers this world. Science has banished from their minds belief in the exercise, by the Deity, in our [day], of special acts of supernatural power as a means of influencing human affairs, and it has presented a systematic order of nature, which man may study, comprehend, and obey, as a guide to his practical conduct. In point of fact, the new faith has already partially taken the place of the old. Men now act more on the belief that this world's administration is conducted on the principle of an established order of nature, in which objects and agencies are presented to man for his study, are to some extent placed under the control of his will, and wisely calculated to promote his instruction and enjoyment. The creed of the modern man of science is well expressed by Mr Sedgwick in the following words:— 'If there be a superintending Providence, and if His will be manifested by general laws, operating both on the physical and moral world, *then must a violation of these laws be a violation of His will, and be pregnant with inevitable misery.* Nothing can, in the end, be expedient for man, *except it be subordinate to those laws the Author of Nature has thought fit to impress on his moral and physical creation.*' Other clergymen also embrace the same view. The Rev. Thomas Guthrie, in his late admirable pamphlet, 'A Plea for Ragged Schools,' observes, that, 'They commit a grave mistake, who forget that injury as inevitably results from flying in the face of a moral or mental, as of a physical law.'

Notwithstanding, however, this revolution in practical belief, the theology of the British nation has been permitted to retain the forms in which it was moulded in the olden time; and what has been the consequence? The natural order of providence is very meagrely taught by the masters in theology to their followers, as of divine authority, and as regulating this world's affairs. I put the following question in all earnestness. Are the fertility of the soil, the health of the body, and the prosperity of individuals and of nations, – in short, the great interests and duties of mankind, – governed by any regular and comprehensible natural laws, or are they not? If they are not, then is this world a theatre of atheism, it is a world without the practical manifestation of a God. If on the other hand, as I contend, such laws exist, they must be of divine institution, and worthy of all reverence; and I ask, In the standards of what church, from the pulpits of what sect, and in the schools of what denomination of Christians, are these laws taught to either the young or old as of divine authority, and as practical guides for conduct in this world's affairs? If such laws exist, and are not studied, honoured, and obeyed, as God's laws; and if belief in special acts of supernatural administration of the world has died away, are we not actually a nation without a religion in harmony with nature; and, therefore, without a religion adapted to practical purposes?

The answer will probably be made – that this argument is rank infidelity; but, with all deference, I reply that the denial of a regular, intelligible, wisely adapted, and divinely appointed order of nature, as a guide for human conduct in this world, is downright atheism; while the acknowledgment of the existence of such an order, accompanied by the nearly universal neglect of teaching and obeying its requirements, is true, practical, baneful infidelity, disrespectful to God, and injurious to the best interests of man. Let those, therefore, who judge us, take care that they be not judged; and let those who think that they stand, take heed lest they fall. The public mind is opening to such views as I am now unfolding; and they must in future be met by other arguments than cries of irreligion, and appeals to bigotry and passion.

The churches which have at all recognised the order of nature, have attached to it a lower character than truly belongs to it. They have treated science and secular knowledge chiefly as objects of curiosity and sources of gain; and have given to actions intelligently founded on them, the character of prudence. So humble has been their estimate of the importance of science, that they have not systematically called in the influence of the religious sentiments to hallow, elevate, and enforce the teachings of nature. In most of their schools the elucidation of the relations of science to human conduct is omitted altogether, and catechisms of human invention usurp its place.

Society, meantime, including the Calvinistic world itself, proceeds in its secular enterprises on the basis of natural science, so far as it has been able to discover it. If practical men send a ship to sea, they endeavour to render it staunch and strong, and to place in it an expert crew and an able commander, as conditions of safety, dictated by their conviction of the order of nature in flood and storm. If they are sick, they resort to a physician to restore them to health, according to the ordinary laws of organization. If they suffer famine from wet seasons, they drain their lands; and so forth. All these practices and observances are taught and enforced by men of science and the secular press, as measures of practical prudence; but few churches recognise the order of nature on which they are founded, as a becoming subject of religious instruction.

On the contrary, religious professors have too often made war upon science, on scientific teachers, and on the order of nature, from the days of Galileo to the present time; and many of them still adhere, as far as the reason and light of the public mind will permit them, to their old doctrine of an inherent disorder reigning in the natural world. That disorder does prevail is undeniable; but science proclaims that it is to a great extent owing to man's ignorance of his own nature, and of that of the external world, and to his neglect of their relations. Many theologians do not recognise such views, but proceed as if human affairs were, somehow or other, still, in our day, influenced by special manifestations of Divine power. . . .

It is impossible that the public mind can advance in sound and self-consistent practical principles of action in this world's affairs, while . . . conflicting views of science, religion, and the course of God's Providence, are poured forth from the pulpit and the press; and it is equally impossible that the youthful mind can be trained to study, reverence, and obey the course of God's Providence, while it is treated with so little consideration by those who assume to themselves the character of the accredited expositors of the Divine Will.

The questions, then, whether there be an intelligible course of nature revealed to the human understanding, whether it should be taught to the young, and whether the religious sentiments should be trained to venerate and obey it as of Divine institution, are not barren speculations respecting dogmas and doctrines. They touch a highly momentous practical principle. While an impassable gulph stands between the views of God's Providence, on which society in its daily business acts, and the religious faith which it professes to believe, the influence of the latter on social conduct must necessarily be feeble and limited. It is a matter of great importance to have the principles of action and of belief brought into harmony. Nothing can retard the moral and intellectual advancement of the people more thoroughly than having a religion for churches and Sundays, and a widely different code of principles for everyday conduct; and yet this *is*, and *must continue to be*, the case with all the Christian nations, while they fail to recognise the order of providence in nature as a divinely appointed guide to human action.

A second reformation in religion is imperatively called for, and is preparing. The new Christian faith will recognise man and the natural world as constituted by Divine Benevolence and Wisdom, and adapted to each other for man's instruction and benefit. It will communicate to the young a knowledge of that constitution and its adaptations, as the basis of their religious faith and practice in reference to this world; and train them to realize in their own minds and bodies, and in the society to which they belong, *the natural conditions* on which health, prosperity, purity, piety, and peace, depend. Only then will they discover that Christianity is the true fountain, not only of religious faith, but of practical wisdom and of individual and social improvement. Until this discovery shall have been made and acted on, religion will never exert its due influence over human affairs. . . .

7.2.2   T. H. HUXLEY ON MEN OF SCIENCE AND HUMAN ORIGINS, 1860

. . . I have endeavoured to lay before you what, as I fancy, are the turning points of a great controversy; to render obvious the mode in which the vast problem of the origin of species must be dealt with; and so far as purely scientific considerations go, I have nothing more to say. But let me beg you still to listen to a last word respecting the unscientific objections which I constantly hear brought forward on the part of the general public, against such doctrines as those we have been discussing. For this is a matter upon which it is of the utmost importance that men of science and the public should come to an understanding. I have heard it said that it is presumptuous for us to attempt to inquire into such matters as these; that they are problems beyond the reach of the human understanding. Do you remember what was the reply of the old philosopher to those who demonstrated to him so clearly the impossibility of motion? 'Solvitur ambulando,' said he, and got up and walked. And so I doubt not that one of these days either Mr. Darwin's hypothesis, or some other, will get up and walk, and that vigorously; and so save us the trouble of any further discussion of this objection.

Another, and unfortunately a large class of persons take fright at the logical consequences of such a doctrine as that put forth by Mr. Darwin. If all species have arisen in this way, say they – Man himself must have done so; and he and all the animated world must have had a common origin. Most assuredly. No question of it.

But I would ask, does this logical necessity add one single difficulty of importance to those which already confront us on all sides whenever we contemplate our relations to the surrounding universe? I think not. Let man's mistaken vanity, his foolish contempt for the material world, impel him to struggle as he will, he strives in vain to break through the ties which hold him to matter and the lower forms of life.

In the face of the demonstrable facts, that the anatomical difference between man and the highest of the *Quadrumana* is less than the difference between the extreme types of the Quadrumanous order; that, in the course of his development, man passes through stages which correspond to, though they are not identical with, those of all the lower animals; that each of us was once a minute and unintelligent particle of yolk-like substance; that our highest faculties are dependent for their exercise upon the presence of a few cubic inches, more or less, of a certain gas in one's blood; in the face of these tremendous and mysterious facts, I say, what matters it whether a new link is or is not added to the mighty chain which indissolubly binds us to the rest of the universe? Of what part of the glorious fabric of the world has man a right to be ashamed – that he is so desirous to disconnect himself from it? But I would rather reply to this strange objection by suggesting another line of thought. I would rather point out that perhaps the very noblest use of science as a discipline is, that now and then she brings us face to face with difficulties like these. Laden with our idols, we follow her blithely – till a parting in the roads appears, and she turns, and with a stern face asks us whether we are men enough to cast them aside, and follow her up the steep? Men of science are such by virtue of having answered her with a hearty and unreserved, Yea; by virtue of having made their election to follow science whithersoever she leads, and whatsoever lions be in the path. Their duty is clear enough.

And, in my apprehension, that of the public is not doubtful. I have said that the man of science is the sworn interpreter of nature in the high court of reason. But of what avail is his honest speech if ignorance is the assessor of the judge, and prejudice foreman of the jury? I hardly know of a great physical truth, whose universal reception has not been preceded by an epoch in which most estimable persons have maintained that the phenomena investigated were directly dependent on the Divine Will, and that the attempt to investigate them was not only futile, but blasphemous. And there is a wonderful tenacity of life about this sort of opposition to physical science. Crushed and maimed in every battle, it yet seems never to be slain; and after a hundred defeats it is at this day as rampant, though happily not so mischievous, as in the time of Galileo.

But to those whose life is spent, to use Newton's noble words, in picking up here a pebble and there a pebble on the shores of the great ocean of truth – who watch, day by day, the slow but sure advance of that mighty tide, bearing on its bosom the thousand treasures wherewith man ennobles and beautifies his life – it would be laughable, if it were not so sad, to see the little Canutes of the hour enthroned in solemn state, bidding that great wave to stay, and threatening to check its beneficent progress. The wave rises and they fly; but unlike the brave old Dane, they learn no lesson of humility: the throne is pitched at what seems a safe distance, and the folly is repeated.

Surely it is the duty of the public to discourage everything of this kind, to discredit these foolish meddlers who think they do the Almighty a service by preventing a thorough study of his works.

The Origin of Species is not the first, and it will not be the last of the great questions born of science, which will demand settlement from this generation. The general mind is seething strangely, and to those who watch the signs of the times, it seems plain that this nineteenth century will see revolutions of thought and practice as great as those which the sixteenth witnessed. Through what trials and sore contests the civilized world will have to pass in the course of this new reformation, who can tell?

But I verily believe that come what will, the part which England may play in the battle is a grand and a noble one. She may prove to the world that for one people, at any rate, despotism and demagoguy are not the necessary alternatives of government; that freedom and order are not incompatible; that reverence is the handmaid of knowledge; that free discussion is the life of truth, and of true unity in a nation.

Will England play this part? That depends upon how you, the public, deal with science. Cherish her, venerate her, follow her methods faithfully and implicitly in their application to all branches of human thought; and the future of this people will be greater than the past. . . .

7.2.3   E. B. TYLOR ON ETHNOGRAPHIC METHOD
IN THEOLOGY, 1871

. . . That the world sorely needs new evidence and method in theology, the state of religion in our own land bears witness. Take English Protestantism as a central district of opinion, draw an ideal line through its centre, and English thought is seen to be divided as by a polarizing force extending to the utmost limits of repulsion. On one side of the dividing line stand such as keep firm hold on the results of the 16th century reformation, or seek yet more original canons from the first Christian ages; on the other side stand those who, refusing to be bound by the doctrinal judgments of past centuries, but introducing modern science and modern criticism as new factors in theological opinion, are eagerly pressing toward a new reformation. Outside these narrower limits, extremer partizans occupy more distant ground on either side. On the one hand the Anglican blends gradually into the Roman scheme, a system so interesting to the ethnologist for its maintenance of rites more naturally belonging to barbaric culture; a system so hateful to the man of science for its suppression of knowledge, and for that usurpation of intellectual authority by a sacerdotal caste which has at last reached its climax, now that an aged bishop can judge, by infallible inspiration, the results of researches whose evidence and methods are alike beyond his knowledge and his mental grasp. On the other hand, intellect, here trampled under foot of dogma, takes full revenge elsewhere, even within the domain of religion, in those theological districts where reason takes more and more the command over hereditary belief, like a mayor of the palace superseding a nominal king. In yet farther ranges of opinion, religious authority is simply deposed and banished, and the throne of absolute reason is set up without a rival even in name; in secularism the feeling and imagination which in the religious world are bound to theological belief, have to attach themselves to a positive natural philosophy, and to a positive morality which shall of its own force control the acts of men. Such, then, is the boundless divergence of opinion among educated citizens of an enlightened country, in an age scarcely approached by any former age in the possession of actual knowledge and the strenuous pursuit of truth as the guiding principle of life. Of the causes which have brought to pass so perplexed a condition of public thought, in so momentous a matter as theology, there is one, and that a weighty one, which demands mention here. It is the partial and one-sided application of the historical method of enquiry into theological doctrines, and the utter neglect of the ethnographical method which carries back the historical into remoter and more primitive regions of thought. Looking at each doctrine by itself and for itself, as in the abstract true or untrue, theologians close their eyes to the instances which history is ever holding up before them, that one phase of a religious belief is the outcome of another, that in all times religion has included within its limits a system of philosophy, expressing its more or less transcendental conceptions in doctrines which form in any age their fittest representatives, but which doctrines are liable to modification in the general course of intellectual change, whether the ancient formulas still hold their authority with altered meaning, or are themselves reformed or replaced. Christendom furnishes evidence to establish this principle, if for example we will but candidly compare the educated opinion of Rome in the 5th with that of London in the 19th century, on such subjects as the nature and functions of soul, spirit, deity, and judge by the comparison in what important respects the philosophy of religion has come to differ even among men who represent in different ages the same great principles of faith. The general study of the ethnography of religion, through all its immensity of range, seems to countenance the theory of evolution in its highest and widest sense. . . . The essential part of the ethnographic method in theology lies in admitting as relevant the compared evidence of religion in all stages of culture. The action of such evidence on theology proper is in this wise, that a vast proportion of doctrines and rites known among mankind are not to be judged as direct products of the particular religious systems which give them sanction, for they are in fact more or less modified results adopted from previous systems. The theologian, as he comes to deal with each element of belief and worship, ought to ascertain its place in the general scheme of religion. Should the doctrine or rite in question appear to have been transmitted from an earlier to a later stage of religious thought, then it should be tested, like any other point of culture, as to its place in development. The question has to be raised, to which of these three categories it belongs:— is it a product of the earlier theology, yet sound enough to maintain a rightful place in the later; – is it derived from a cruder original, yet so modified as to become a proper representative of more advanced views? – is it a survival from a lower stage of thought, imposing on the credit of the higher by virtue not of inherent truth but of ancestral belief? These are queries the very asking of which starts trains of thought which candid minds should be encouraged to pursue, leading as they do toward the attainment of such measure of truth as the intellectual condition of our age fits us to assimilate. In the scientific study of religion, which now shows signs of becoming for many a year an engrossing subject of the world's thought, the decision must not rest with a council in which the theologian, the metaphysician, the biologist, the physicist, exclusively take part. The historian and the ethnographer must be called upon to show the hereditary standing of each opinion and practice, and their enquiry must go back as far as antiquity or savagery can show a vestige, for there seems no human thought so primitive as to have lost its bearing on our own thought, nor so ancient as to have broken its connexion with our own life.

It is our happiness to live in one of those eventful periods of intellectual and moral history, when the oft-closed gates of discovery and reform stand open at their widest. How long these good days may last, we cannot tell. It may be that the increasing power and range of the scientific method, with its stringency of argument and constant check of fact, may start the world on a more steady and continuous course of progress than it has moved on heretofore. But if history is to repeat itself according to precedent, we must look forward to stiffer duller ages of traditionalists and commentators, when the great thinkers of our time will be appealed to as authorities by men who slavishly accept their tenets, yet cannot or dare not follow their methods through better evidence to higher ends. In either case, it is for those among us whose minds are set on the advancement of civilization, to make the most of present opportunities, that even when in future years progress is arrested, it may be arrested at the higher level. To the promoters of what is sound and reformers of what is faulty in modern culture, ethnography has double help to give. To impress men's minds with a doctrine of development, will lead them in all honour to their ancestors to continue the progressive work of past ages, to continue it the more vigorously because light has increased in the world, and where barbaric hordes groped blindly, cultured men can often move onward with clear view. It is a harsher, and at times even painful, office of ethnography to expose the remains of crude old culture which have passed into harmful superstition, and to mark these out for destruction. Yet this work, if less genial, is not less urgently needful for the good of mankind. Thus, active at once in aiding progress and in removing hinderance, the science of culture is essentially a reformer's science.

7.2.4   T. H. HUXLEY ON THE THEOLOGY OF AN AGNOSTIC, 1892

... Cuvier's aphorism, ... that 'one should clear the ground before beginning to build,' not only, as I think, commends itself to common sense, but it exactly suggests the positive, no less than the negative, side of a purpose I have had in view for the last thirty years. It is Goethe's maxim about 'Thätige Skepsis' in another shape; and it will be observed that it enjoins the clearing of the ground, not in a spirit of wanton mischief, not for destruction's sake, but with the distinct purpose of fitting the site for those constructive operations which must be the ultimate object of every rational man. Neither one lifetime, nor two, nor half a dozen, will suffice to clear away the astonishing tangle of inherited mythology; of carefully maintained ignorance, that hugs itself under the name of reverence; of discreditable prejudice; no less than of creditable affection for old ideals, and of rational alarm lest the wheat should be torn up by the roots along with the tares. There is endless backwoodsman's work yet to be done. If 'those also serve who only stand and wait,' still more do those who sweep and cleanse; and if any man elect to give his strength to the weeder's and scavenger's occupation, I remain of the opinion that his service should be counted acceptable, and that no one has a right to ask more of him than faithful performance of the duties he has undertaken. I venture to count it an improbable suggestion that any such person – a man, let us say, who has well-nigh reached his threescore years and ten and has graduated in all the faculties of human relationships; who has taken his share in all the deep joys and deeper anxieties which cling about them; who has felt the burden of young lives entrusted to his care, and has stood alone with his dead before the abyss of the eternal – has never had a thought beyond negative criticism. It seems to me incredible that such an one can have done his day's work, always with a light heart, with no sense of responsibility, no terror of that which may appear when the factitious veil of Isis – the thick web of fiction man has woven round nature – is stripped off.

I am aware that the world which calls itself 'religious' commonly assumes that it has a monopoly of serious thought; I think it is to be regretted that such presumption should not be confined to it.

But this is not the only flavour of the pulpit which is perceptible in Mr. Harrison's comments. . . . My positivist antagonist ranges himself beside his clerical analogues, puts the same questions, and insinuates, if he does not distinctly profess, the same ability to answer them.

> . . . Has Mr. Huxley himself any mental bias, *pro* or *con*, with reference, let us say, to Creation, Providence, Immortality, and Future Punishment – and, if any, what? . . .

I reply . . . as follows:— . . . I have no doubt whatever that I am burdened with various kinds of 'mental bias,' of some of which I am conscious, while for the knowledge of another and more dangerous set I must look to those useful persons, candid friends. But I am of opinion that it is of the essence of scientific method to check and, if possible, to suppress each and every bias touching the subject of an inquiry; and that no good purpose can be served by making a, probably, very imperfect catalogue of my own temptations to error.

With respect to 'Creation,' I fancy the question has been answered by me with sufficient directness to satisfy even the requirements of my catechist, over and over again. I should have thought it impossible for any one who has done me the honour to cast even a superficial glance through my writings to consider it needful to ask such a question. So far back as 1860 I wrote:—

The doctrine of special creation owes its existence very largely to the supposed necessity for making science accord with the Hebrew cosmogony;

and that the hypothesis of special creation is, in my judgment, a 'mere specious mask for our ignorance.' Not content with negation, I said:—

Harmonious order governing eternally continuous progress – the web and woof of matter and force interweaving by slow degrees, without a broken thread, that veil which lies between us and the infinite – that universe which alone we know or can know; such is the picture which science draws of the world.

It is thirty-two years since these passages were written; twenty-two since they appeared under my name in *Lay Sermons*. Every reader of Goethe will know that the second is little more than a paraphrase of the well-known utterance of the 'Zeitgeist' in *Faust*, which surely is something more than a mere negation of the clumsy anthropomorphism of special creation.

Follows a query about 'Providence,' my answer to which must depend upon what my questioner means by that substantive, whether alone, or qualified by the adjective 'moral.'

If the doctrine of a Providence is to be taken as the expression, in a way 'to be understanded of the people,' of the total exclusion of chance from a place even in the most insignificant corner of Nature; if it means the strong conviction that the cosmic process is rational; and the faith that, throughout all duration, unbroken order has reigned in the universe – I not only accept it, but I am disposed to think it the most important of all truths. As it is of more consequence for a citizen to know the law than to be personally acquainted with the features of those who will surely carry it into effect, so this very positive doctrine of Providence, in the sense defined, seems to me far more important than all the theorems of speculative theology. If, further, the doctrine is held to imply that, in some indefinitely remote past æon, the cosmic process was set going by some entity possessed of intelligence and foresight, similar to our own in kind, however superior in degree; if, consequently, it is held that every event, not merely in our planetary speck, but in untold millions of other worlds, was foreknown before these worlds were, scientific thought, so far as I know anything about it, has nothing to say against that hypothesis. It is in fact an anthropomorphic rendering of the doctrine of evolution.

It may be so, but the evidence accessible to us is, to my mind, wholly insufficient to warrant either a positive or a negative conclusion. To avoid misunderstanding, it seems proper to add that this conception of a not merely general, but universal and all-pervading 'Providence' appears to me to be wholly incompatible with the notion of 'special Providences,' which is all that the mass of men really care about. . . .

I am asked for a distinct and positive assurance as to a moral providence. I envy the light heart with which my interrogator seems to put questions which bristle with difficulties to any one who desires to have a clear conception of their scope. 'Providence,' in the sense of the rational order of the universe (or, if the phrase be preferred, the cause of that order), is undoubtedly as responsible for the phenomena of human existence as for any others. So far as mankind has acquired the conviction that the observance of certain rules of conduct is essential to the maintenance of social existence, it may be proper to say that 'Providence,' operating through men, has generated morality. Within the limits of a fraction of a fraction of the living world, therefore, there is a 'moral' providence. Through this small plot of an infinitesimal fragment of the universe there runs a 'stream of tendency towards righteousness.' But outside the very rudimentary germ of a garden of Eden, thus watered, I am unable to discover any 'moral' purpose; or anything but a stream of tendency towards the consummation of the cosmic process, chiefly by means of the struggle for existence, which is no more righteous or unrighteous than the operation of any other mechanism.

I hear much of the 'ethics of evolution.' I apprehend that, in the broadest sense of the term 'evolution,' there neither is, nor can be, any such thing. The notion that the doctrine of evolution can furnish a foundation for morals seems to me to be an illusion, which has arisen from the unfortunate ambiguity of the term 'fittest' in the formula, 'survival of the fittest.' We commonly use 'fittest' in a good sense with an understood connotation of 'best;' and 'best' we are apt to take in its ethical sense. But the 'fittest' which survives in the struggle for existence may be, and often is, the ethically worst.

So far as I am able to interpret the evidence which bears upon the evolution of man as it now stands, there was a stage in that process when, if I may speak figuratively, the 'Welt-geist' repented him that he had made mankind no better than the brutes, and resolved upon a largely new departure. Up to that time, the struggle for existence had dominated the way of life of the human, as of the other, higher brutes; since that time, men have been impelled, with gentle but steady pressure, to help one another, instead of treading one another mercilessly under foot; to restrain their lusts, instead of seeking, with all their strength and cunning, to gratify them; to sacrifice themselves for the sake of the ordered commonwealth, through which alone the ethical ideal of manhood can be attained, instead of exploiting social existence for their individual ends. Since that time, as the price of the high distinction of his changed destiny, man has lost the happy singleness of aim of the brute; and, from cradle to grave, that which he would not he does, because the cosmic process carries him away; and that which he would he does not, because the ethical stream of tendency is still but a rill.

It is the secret of the superiority of the best theological teachers to the majority of their opponents, that they substantially recognise these realities of things, however strange the forms in which they clothe their conceptions. The doctrines of predestination; of original sin; of the innate depravity of man and the evil fate of the greater part of the race; of the primacy of Satan in this world; of the essential vileness of matter; of a malevolent Demiurgus subordinate to a benevolent Almighty, who has only lately revealed himself, faulty as they are, appear to me to be vastly nearer the truth than the 'liberal' popular illusions that babies are all born good and that the example of a corrupt society is responsible for their failure to remain so; that it is given to everybody to reach the ethical ideal if he will only try; that all partial evil is universal good; and other optimistic figments, such as that which represents 'Providence' under the guise of a paternal philanthropist, and bids us believe that everything will come right (according to our notions) at last. . . .

As to 'Immortality' again. It would be presumption on my part to consider my querist bound to know anything of my writing beyond the book which he has selected for criticism; but I may mention that, about a dozen years ago, I published a little work concerning David Hume, in which he will find all I have to say on that topic. I do not think I need return to 'subjective' immortality; but it may be well to add that I am a very strong believer in the punishment of certain kinds of actions, not only in the present, but in all the future a man can have, be it long or short. Therefore in hell; for I suppose that all men with a clear sense of right and wrong (and I am not sure that any others deserve such punishment) have now and then 'descended into hell' and stopped there, quite long enough to know what infinite punishment means. And if a genuine, not merely subjective, immortality awaits us, I conceive that, without some such change as that depicted in the fifteenth chapter of the second [*sic*] Epistle to the Corinthians, immortality must be eternal misery. The fate of Swift's Struldbrugs seems to me not more horrible than that of a mind imprisoned for ever within the *flammantia mœnia* of inextinguishable memories.

Further, it may be well to remember that the highest level of moral aspiration recorded in history, was reached by a few ancient Jews, Micah, Isaiah, and the rest, who took no count whatever of what might, or might not, happen to them after death. It is not obvious to me why the same point should not, by-and-by, be reached by the Gentiles. . . .

To missionaries of the Neo-Positivist, as to those of other professed solutions of insoluble mysteries, whose souls are bound up in the success of their sectarian propaganda, no doubt, it must be very disheartening if the 'world,' for whose assent and approbation they sue, stops its ears and turns its back upon them. But what does it signify to any one who does not happen to be a missionary of any sect, philosophical or religious; and who, if he were, would have no sermon to preach except from the text with which Descartes, to go no further back, furnished us two centuries since? I am very sorry if people will not listen to those who rehearse before them the best lessons they have been able to learn; but that is their business, not mine. Belief in majorities is not rooted in my breast; and, if all the world were against me, the fact might warn me to revise and criticise my opinions, but would not, in itself, supply a ghost of a reason for forsaking them. For myself, I say deliberately: It is better to have a millstone tied round the neck and be thrown into the sea, than to share the enterprises of those to whom the world has turned, and will turn, because they minister to its weaknesses and cover up the awful realities which it shudders to look at.

7.3 NATURAL ALLIES

The Victorian 'conflict of religion and science' is best interpreted, not as a ding-dong battle between theologians on the one hand, and scientists on the other, but as a demarcation dispute. This occurred, at one level, between the advocates of revealed and natural theology, and at another, among those who were prepared to see religion established on the authority of natural knowledge alone. To the first level of controversy belong the well-known oppositions of Genesis to geology and evolution. At the second level belong the less colourful, perhaps, but certainly the more interesting, subtle, and portentous debates that occurred within the Victorian intelligentsia and only at length became culturally divisive. Law or God, chance or design, reason or experience – differences about such questions among freethinking Dissenters, liberal Anglicans, and professionalizing scientists, could be largely contained for the sake of wider political interests and in the hope that eventually a common faith would emerge for the guidance of national life. When in 1844 the anonymous author of *Vestiges of the Natural History of Creation* – the Scottish publisher Robert Chambers, it turned out – first mooted for a popular audience that this faith might be grounded in a law of organic development, Francis Newman (1805–1897), the polymathic brother of John Henry, embraced the notion and moved rapidly to disabuse fellow-Unitarians that anything but theological good need come of it (**7.3.1**). In 1846 he carried this conviction to University College, London, where he joined other 'intellectuals', as they were then first called, who found a platform for their beliefs in the new series of the *Westminster Review*, which was inaugurated under the editorship of John Chapman (1822–1894) and George Eliot (4.3.2) in 1852. Besides Newman, Chapman, and Eliot, the contributors in the first year included G. Combe (7.2.1), J. Martineau (3.3.1), J. S. Mill (7.1.2), and H. Spencer (7.1.4). In 1854 T. H. Huxley (7.2.2., 7.2.4) assumed responsibility with John Tyndall for the scientific section of the journal. Some indication of the beliefs that united these 'most able and independent minds' can be obtained from the 'Prospectus' drafted by Eliot and circulated with the first issue (**7.3.2**). Ten years later, a broad front among liberal churchmen and liberal scientists was still in evidence when a committee of the latter, with John Lubbock (1834–1913) and William Spottiswoode (1825–1883) as its secretaries, drew up a memorial in support of the authors of *Essays and Reviews*, which was to have been sent to the first of their number, Frederick Temple. The eminent signatories intended this as a counterblast to a letter that had appeared in *The Times* on 16 February 1861, signed by the Archbishop of Canterbury and twenty-five English bishops, endorsing a memorial received by the archbishop from a rural deanery in Dorset. The memorial did not refer to the offending publication, but it is evident from the texts reproduced below that the bishops used it, and were seen to have used it, as an occasion for issuing their own condemnation of the essayists – even if, as was later claimed, the word 'their' in the third paragraph was a misprint for 'these' (**7.3.3**). The scientists' memorial was apparently withdrawn, as Lubbock and others no doubt thought better of adding their voices to the hue and cry of petitioners against *Essay and Reviews* who besieged Convocation that year. In 1868, however, the Reverend Frederic William Farrar (1831–1903), preacher, philologist, and public schoolmaster, broke silence resoundingly in the *Contemporary Review* on the issue of clerical attacks on science. Using history in the manner later made infamous by the polemical works of John William Draper and Andrew Dickson White, Farrar led up to the not unflattering assertion that 'Science is itself one of the noblest forms of Theology' (**7.3.4**). Had he not been supported successfully a few years before by Charles Darwin, among others, for a Fellowship of the Royal Society? But, a decade later, the mood had begun to change. Richard Holt Hutton (1826–1897), formerly a Unitarian and now the Broad Church editor of the *Spectator*, writing with an unequalled grasp of contemporary religious and scientific thought, argued that the failure of a renewed theistic faith to emerge among advanced intellectuals was itself the result of a divine providence acting, ironically, to encourage the exhaustive pursuit of natural knowledge. For by seeking God in vain through sense-experience, 'the physicists . . . are suffering for us, as well as for themselves'. Their arduous quests are 'the best auguries we could have that it is not in physical science that man can ever find his salvation' (**7.3.5**).

7.3.1 F. W. NEWMAN ON *VESTIGES OF THE NATURAL HISTORY OF CREATION*, 1845

. . . Theism is not so easily disturbed, as men of little faith fancy. It has its roots far too deeply fixed in the heart of man, its branches far too broadly overshadow his whole social life, to be harmed by sciences which trace out Cause and Effect. These teach the intellect, no doubt, to think differently of the *mode* in which God has constructed his universe; but they cannot forbid the heart and conscience to recognise God in it. We admire the Universe for what we see and find it to be, quite independently of the question, *how* it came to be what it is. We no longer believe that the very voice of Deity gave twenty-nine commands to move, to the twenty-nine planets and satellites which revolve round our sun; but it would be preposterous to pretend that this has lessened our confidence or lowered our conceptions as to the Divine existence, power and wisdom. At the bottom of those modern alarms, is the same narrow view which made an old Athenian apprehend atheism, from the discovery that lightning was produced, not by the direct manipulation of Jupiter, but by the concurrence of two clouds. More elevated ideas of the Deity have been gained, the more it has been discerned in each separate department of nature that He acts by law, not by muscular force and special interference; and we need not doubt that the same result will follow from every development of sound science in the same direction. . . .

A very bold and at first sight startling attempt, not only to extend the province of Law, in regard to the origination of animal and vegetable life, but even to develop the order and method followed by the Creator, is contained in the able, interesting, and modest-sized volume, entitled, Vestiges of the Natural History of Creation. It opens with a concise summary of the now established Astronomical Cosmogony of Sir W. Herschel and La Place; tracing this earth from its state of vapour, down to the time when a solid crust, comparatively cool, first formed on its surface. At this point, Geology takes up the history, which Astronomy had begun: and in a series of comprehensive chapters, the Author gives a rapid sketch of the very important results, at which the untiring assiduity and versatile accomplishments of great Geologists still in the vigour of life have arrived. It is not our purpose to criticize these chapters in detail. If the Author have advanced any questionable facts, or fallen into any partial errors, yet, we apprehend, it is impossible that he should have gone wrong in any of the greater results on which his whole argument turns. The magnificent conclusions in which all Geologists agree, are these:— that the crust of this earth has gone through a long series of changes in the course of countless thousands of years: that organic life has been successively introduced upon it, according as it became fitted for its reception: that the animals

and plants of lower organization were first introduced: that among vertebrated animals, fishes came first, then reptiles, next birds; afterwards
marsupial beasts; then true mammalia; and finally Man. – Here a most
novel fact comes out, destined to work a grat revolution in human opinion.
*Creation was not confined to the beginning of the world, but even on this earth has
been a slow, and, as it were, a continuous operation.* Previously, there seemed to
be an immense chasm between the origination of species and that of
individuals. Geology has now shown that no such chasm exists: that
Creation cannot be regarded as exceptional and an interference, (if at
least the originating of species be 'creation,') and that we may reason
concerning it from the analogies of our known world, seeing that it has
gone on for ages after that world was in all fundamental respects what it
still is. It was impossible to contemplate the series of geological phenomena, without being struck with a belief, which (as far as we know) was
first clearly stated in print by Sir John Herschel:— 'that the Creator had
given existence to the species of animated beings *according to some law.*'
Before Geology had started on its brilliant career, such an opinion might
have seemed premature: yet there was already accumulating proof of the
same truth from Physiology and Comparative Anatomy. On comparing
vertebrated animals at first sight most unlike, – as a man and an elephant;
a bat, an ostrich, and a horse, – the relation between the bony structure of
all proved to be far more similar than could have been expected in works,
each of which had been executed separately by a special operation. The
conclusion was strengthened exceedingly by a comparison of the internal
parts of animals, and by the continually growing knowledge of the organization of their lower orders. To Geoffrey St. Hilaire, we understand, the
merit belongs to having burst the trammels which confined his predecessors, and of having opened a larger view of animated nature than the
illustrious Cuvier had ventured to take. Undaunted by the stigma of
Atheism which has rested on St. Hilaire, the intrepid Baden Powell, in his
excellent volume upon the Connexion of Natural and Divine Truth, has
calmly reviewed the whole controversy; and has in no ambiguous terms
showed his conviction, that the old-fashioned idea of Creation must in
certain important particulars be remodelled.

Reasons against its soundness show themselves, in fact, on the surface
of Natural History, forbidding us to believe that organic life was originally, any more than at present and in detail, produced by a *special* act of the
Creator, as above explained. First, it is well known that many animals have
useless parts. Such are the nipples of the human male; the fifth claw in
dogs; the callosities in the legs of horses; the bony projections on the ribs
of the ostrich, which serve an important purpose in other birds, but in the
ostrich are too short to be of use. Now, as it is impossible to impute
imperfection to the divine contriver, and as those superfluities *would*

imply imperfection, if each species were made by a separate act of power, the conclusion is hard to avoid, that they were *not* so made; but that these apparent imperfections are (as in the moral world) a necessary consequence of some general law, or agency, which has operated unbidden as to details. Next; particular animals are known to exist, a *separate origination* of which would be most difficult to reconcile with Supreme Benevolence. Who can conceive a hideous worm, created for the express purpose of gnawing the human bowels, and incapable of living elsewhere? – of a fly, the instinct of which teaches it to lay its eggs in the brains of the sheep, to the exquisite torture of the innocent animal? If the foul creatures which eat up diseased bodies while still alive, attacked only the direst transgressors; if we could flatter ourselves that none but a Sulla or a Herod could fall victim to these loathsome diseases; we might get some shuddering comfort in the thought of righteous retribution. But when it is most manifest that we are exposed to these visitations, in common with the lower animals, solely because we are flesh and blood like them; it becomes all but impossible to believe that the Creator had a moral object in creating, and did create by a separate act, every one of these torturing scourges. But besides these special arguments tendered by the details of Natural History, the mere catalogue of the numbers of plants, insects, and other animals, has great weight. As the Copernican system won belief by the contrast of its sublime simplicity to the inextricable complexity into which that of Ptolemy had grown; so, when we read of the hundred thousand species of plants and animals by which this globe is peopled, the eye accustomed to the analogies of the Divine procedure, discerns that all these creatures must have come forth by the operation of law.

As long as it was believed that all animated nature stood in an inseparable relation, both of time and space, to Man, the difficulties of the common hypothesis were more or less concealed. But when so large a number of species is known to be far beyond the reach of man, whether for good or evil, it becomes increasingly difficult to attribute a moral end, as the reason why each one separately was brought into existence. Nor is it at all easy to acquiesce in the idea, that the gigantic Saurians, or mammalia of an extinct race, or the microscopic creatures whose remains lie by millions in an inch of rock, were created that their dead bodies might be of use to man. For countless ages together this globe was an *un*-moral scene of life. Such a state of things is evidently, in itself, imperfect; and is not easily understood, except as a part of that which was to come.

In this stage the Author before us takes up the question; and appeals to the immensity of the universe to confirm the argument that creation (of species) must have proceeded by law. Where there is light, we may infer by analogy that there are eyes; where there is an atmosphere, that there is breath. We know not how to conceive of any moral and worthy object for a special interference, (which must, in fact, be so constantly going on as to make it a sort of daily operation,) to create first a shell-fish in one planet, then a zoophyte in another. If Divine Wisdom sees it fit to cause these creatures to exist, we seem to be imputing a defect of power or wisdom, in imagining a special act for each case; when all that we can discern of the Divine procedure in His best known works, and all the highest exhibitions of intellect in man, would suggest some simpler method. If we cannot doubt organic life to pervade all the globes to which the stars are suns, we must believe it to be produced by Law, as much as the worlds in which it acts. If Law has in it the mechanical element, this is the very point which makes it more appropriate for the production of irrational creatures in a non-ethical world. Nor can any such reasonings be justly taxed with presumption. For we are driven of necessity to select one of two hypotheses: that the Creator originated living species either *by* or *without* special and direct action; and it is very gratuitous to pretend that the latter hypothesis implies haughtier knowledge in the person who adopts it, than the former.

But the present Author goes beyond all this. He not only is convinced that this world has been filled with living beings by law, but that its earlier species were introductory to those which now exist, in a higher sense than that curiously marbled rocks are made of their remains. He believes that the less perfect species preceded the more perfect, partly, no doubt, because the globe was not yet fitted for the latter, but more especially because the former were destined to become parents of the latter. In short, he holds that each species of animals has, in length of time, and in consequence of the changes of vital stimuli, been produced in the way of common generation out of a species immediately below it. As for the primitive species of all, he ventures to conjecture that they gained existence by the action of electric and other forces on pre-existing forms of matter.

We wish here to insist, that however deep the scientific interests attaching to the questions thus boldly mooted, Theism is not concerned with their decision. If it must, at any rate, be conceded that animal species have come forth by a uniform law, and not by special volitions of the Creative energy; if we are not to look for the 'primitive impulse' in this, but in an earlier, stage; if it is no less true that Man, as a species, than that every individual man, came into existence by Second Causes; it cannot be of primary importance with Theology, *what* those Second Causes were. Nor yet ought a belief in creation by law to give any shock to devout sentiment. For if none of us the less regards a Heavenly Father to be his true Creator, because of having had an earthly father, why should the same pious feeling be impaired, by learning that the first man, equally with ourselves, was produced by instrumental and secondary causation? . . .

It may . . . be asked, whether the chasm between Man and other animals is not too great to be bridged over: . . . whether we may not adopt an intermediate view:— viz. if forced to admit that brutes in general have been developed out of lower species, and out of some very few and simple beginnings, may we not still adhere to the belief that *Man* was created by a peculiar and final act of Divine power? – The Author forestalls the idea, by denying that the chasm is so great as we imagine. As to the mere *form* of man, even if the diversity of the human frame from that of the ape be painted in its most vivid colours, it is clear that no 'chasm' can be made out. The disparity of one dog from another is as striking as that of a savage from some of the ape kind. Mr. Owen's researches have proved that the youthful ape is far more like to a child, than the adult to a man; and in the embryo state the similarity is very close. The whole weight of these facts goes to show the reverse of a chasm; viz. *that there has been diverging development out of a common root.*

Nor does it appear at all safe to introduce an ethical argument into physics, – that most seducing *ignis fatuus* of all earlier philosophy. All our experience should warn us against this. An Alfred, or an Isaiah, is ushered into the world under circumstances as humbling as any cat or dog. Physical laws, one and all, take their course ruthlessly against the noblest of our species; and why should we imagine the Divine Creator to have excepted the *origin* of a man from the general system under which all animals and men are believed to exist?

In short, whatever the pre-eminence of the mind of man, the analogies of his body to those of animals form an insuperable objection to the compromise above suggested; insomuch that we seem justified in confidently asserting, that if ever it shall be established that our present species of animals sprang from less perfect kinds, a belief that Man has his bodily origin from the same means will instantly follow. Minds, however, will probably then be found, to teach that at a certain point of time a human soul was infused and *superadded* to the animal form. In regard to the human mind, our Author, while fully conscious of its superior dignity, insists that the state of infancy fills up all chasm between it and the inferior animals, whose moral and intellectual powers we are apt moreover inadequately to value. In the dog we may see nearly all the human passions, and many of our virtues: love and hatred, jealousy and suspicion, pride and shame, sorrow and joy, hope and fear, self-approbation and remorse, emulation and envy, generosity, bravery, self-devotion, faithfulness, gratitude. We do not see in him the higher developments of human intellect: but intellect is hardly in itself the most divine thing in man, essential as it is to all the superior forms of virtue. All scornful refusal to believe that our race may have had its origin from lower animals, our Author justly treats as alike indicative of a wrong unkindliness towards them, and absurd in those who remember the dust whence they are sprung.

Were we acquainted for the first time with the circumstances attending the production of an individual of our race, we might equally think them degrading, and be eager to deny them and exclude them from the admitted truths of nature. Knowing the fact familiarly and beyond contradiction, a healthy and natural mind finds no difficulty in regarding it complacently.— P. 234.

While we see great force in much that the Author urges on this topic, we wish that he did not assume the appearance of underrating the mental gap which separates brute from man. We do not say that the gap is of such a nature as to affect the soundness of his conclusion; yet (in spite of his remark concerning human infancy) we think that it does exist. The power of education and *progress* in the highest of the brutes, soon reaches its limit; but we have every reason to believe that the very lowest human tribe might, in a few generations of cultivation, produce individuals who should compete in talents and genius, with a majority of the most favoured nations. Perhaps this may be hereafter accounted for. Even in the action of those forces which proceed by infinitesimal increase, critical stages occur at which the results are abrupt, and continuity is lost. As science advances with accelerated pace in its later stage, so may it be with the progress of the animal mind; and the human brain, once formed, may of necessity have so outrun in its after-improvement any simultaneous advance of other animals, as to have made the gap wide and startling which was at first insensible. . . .

Most cordially do we believe with our Author, that men of genius, great gifts of God as they are to every country, are sure to come according to fixed laws; so that human progress is matter of certainty. Because we see great things done by eminent persons, we are apt to think that the same would not have been done without those very individuals; but a wider view teaches the contrary. If Newton had never lived, Physical Astronomy might have been retarded by half a century, yet it would have run its own course as certainly. If Cæsar or Alexander had not been born, yet Rome would have become a military despotism, and Persia would have been overrun by Greece. Great men are thrown away upon an age not ripe for them, or on a degenerate people. Roger Bacon and Arnold of Brescia, – Marcus Aurelius and Hannibal, could effect nothing permanent, because they had no kindred spirits in the mass. It may matter greatly to the happiness of one or another state whether a Solon or an Alfred lives through his whole course; but viewing the human race on a large scale, there can be no doubt that God has provided for its welfare in the periodical rise of great geniuses, some of whom will strike their roots into fortunate soil. To expect any *rapid* improvement in mankind, would probably involve nothing but disappointment. Not only do the records of Geology show the extremely late rise of the human species; but its exceedingly slow progress is almost equally manifest in History.

Perhaps no series of events is so painfully instructive on this point, as those of the first thousand years which followed the promulgation of Christianity. Instead of a glorious extension of goodness, truth, and prosperity, a second paganism and rude savageness overspread those parts of Europe concerning which the most brilliant anticipations might have been formed. – Yet when we survey mankind after long intervals; when we contrast modern with ancient savages, as well as modern with ancient cultivation, – the reality of human progress becomes indisputable. In this slow but sure advance, we see marks of the same divine providence, which is evidenced in the periods of Geology and Astronomy. To the Eternal a millennium is as the twinkling of an eye; and while of all other things He may seem to be economic, *Time* is lavishly employed in His greatest works. Whether the animated beings upon this globe, or rather their more glorious after-race, are hereafter to attain such an elevation as our Author reverently augurs, we hardly dare to opine; but that the future will increasingly manifest God's wisdom and power, and the infinite resources of His tranquil expectation, must be most devoutly and unhesitatingly believed.

7.3.2   G. ELIOT ON THE *WESTMINSTER REVIEW*, 1852

The newly-appointed Editors will endeavour to confirm and extend the influence of the Review as an instrument for the development and guidance of earnest thought on Politics, Social Philosophy, Religion, and General Literature; and to this end they will seek to render it the organ of the most able and independent minds of the day.

The fundamental principle of the work will be the recognition of the Law of Progress. In conformity with this principle, and with the consequent conviction that attempts at reform – though modified by the experience of the past and the conditions of the present – should be directed and animated by an advancing ideal, the Editors will maintain a steady comparison of the actual with the possible, as the most powerful stimulus to improvement. Nevertheless, in the deliberate advocacy of organic changes, it will not be forgotten, that the institutions of man, no less than the products of nature, are strong and durable in proportion as they are the results of a gradual development, and that the most salutary and permanent reforms are those, which, while embodying the wisdom of the time, yet sustain such a relation to the moral and intellectual condition of the people, as to ensure their support.

In contradistinction to the practical infidelity and essentially destructive policy which would ignore the existence of wide-spread doubts in relation to established creeds and systems, and would stifle all inquiry dangerous to prescriptive claims, the Review will exhibit that untemporizing expression of opinion, and that fearlessness of investigation and criticism which are the results of a consistent faith in the ultimate prevalence of truth. Convinced that the same fundamental truths are apprehended under a variety of forms, and that, therefore, opposing systems may in the end prove complements of each other, the Editors will endeavour to institute such a radical and comprehensive treatment of those controverted questions which are practically momentous, as may aid in the conciliation of divergent views. In furtherance of this object, they have determined to render available a limited portion of the work, under the head of 'Independent Contributions,' – for the reception of articles ably setting forth opinions which, though not discrepant with the general spirit of the Review, may be at variance with the particular ideas or measures it will advocate. The primary object of this department is to facilitate the expression of opinion by men of high mental power and culture, who, while they are zealous friends of freedom and progress, yet differ widely on special points of great practical concern, both from the Editors and from each other.

The Review will give especial attention to that wide range of topics which may be included under the term Social Philosophy. It will endeavour to form a dispassionate estimate of the diverse theories on these subjects, to give a definite and intelligible form to the chaotic mass of thought now prevalent concerning them, and to ascertain both in what degree the popular efforts after a more perfect social state are countenanced by the teachings of politico-economical science, and how far they may be sustained and promoted by the actual character and culture of the people.

In the department of Politics careful consideration will be given to all the most vital questions, without regard to the distinctions of party; the only standard of consistency to which the Editors will adhere being the real, and not the accidental relations of measures – their bearing, not on a ministry or a class, but on the public good. The work being designed as an exponent of growing thought, the Editors cannot fully indicate the course they will pursue, but their political tendencies may be inferred from their intention that the Review shall support the following Reforms:

A progressive Extension of the Suffrage, in proportion as the people become fitted for using it, with a view to its ultimate universality, as the only equitable system of representation.

Such an adjustment of the Central Government and the local

liberties of the people as, while allowing full scope for the popular energies, will secure the effective execution of measures dictated by the highest intelligence of the nation.

The extension to all our Colonies of a Local Constitutional Government, adapted to their specific wants and capabilities, with the establishment of such relations between them and the mother country as shall best insure their permanent connection, and accord to them that influence in the Imperial Legislature to which they have a rightful claim, and which would tend to the consolidation and stability of the empire.

Free Trade in every department of Commerce.

A radical Reform in the Administration of Justice, especially in the Court of Chancery, including the simplification and expediting of all legal processes.

A thorough revisal of the Ecclesiastical Revenues, with a view to their national and equitable use in promoting the intellectual and spiritual advancement of the people.

National Education, under the combined management of locally-appointed officers and of Commissioners deriving their authority from Parliament; together with such a modification and extension of our University and Public School systems as may render them available irrespective of the distinctions of sect.

In the treatment of Religious Questions the Review will unite a spirit of reverential sympathy for the cherished associations of pure and elevated minds with an uncompromising pursuit of truth. The elements of ecclesiastical authority and of dogma will be fearlessly examined, and the results of the most advanced Biblical criticism will be discussed without reservation, under the conviction that religion has its foundation in man's nature, and will only discard an old form to assume and vitalize one more expressive of its essence. While, however, the Editors will not shrink from the expression of what they believe to be sound negative views, they will bear in mind the pre-eminent importance of a constructive religious philosophy, as connected with the development and activity of the moral nature, and of those poetic and emotional elements, out of which proceed our noblest aspirations and the essential beauty of life.

In the department of General Literature the criticism will be animated by desire to elevate the standard of the public taste, in relation both to artistic perfection and moral purity; larger space will be afforded for articles intrinsically valuable by the omission of those minor and miscellaneous notices which are necessarily forestalled by newspapers and magazines, and equivalent information will be given in a series of Historical and Critical Sketches of Contemporary Literature, comprehending a notice of the most remarkable books, both English and Foreign, that may appear during each successive quarter.

The Review will in future be published by JOHN CHAPMAN, 142, Strand, to whose care all communications for the Editors must be addressed.

7.3.3   SCIENTISTS VERSUS BISHOPS ON *ESSAYS AND REVIEWS*, 1861

[TO THE ARCHBISHOP OF CANTERBURY FROM THE REV. H. B. WILLIAMS ET AL.]

. . . We wish to make known to your Grace and to all the Bishops the alarm we feel at some late indications of the spread of rationalistic and semi-infidel doctrines among the beneficed clergy of the realm. We allude especially to the denial of the atoning efficacy of the Death and Passion of our Blessed Saviour Jesus Christ, both God and Man, for us men and for our salvation, and to the denial also of a Divine Inspiration, peculiar to themselves alone, of the Canonical Scriptures of the Old and New Testament.

We would earnestly beseech your Grace and your lordships, as faithful stewards over the house of God, to discourage by all means in your power the spread of speculations which would rob our countrymen, more especially the poor and unlearned, of their only sure stay and comfort for time and for eternity. And to this end we would more especially and most earnestly beseech you, in your ordinations, to 'lay hands suddenly on no man' till you have convinced yourselves (as far as human precaution can secure it) that each Deacon, who, in reply to the question, 'Do you unfeign-edly believe all the Canonical Scriptures of the Old and New Testament?' answers 'I do believe them,' *speaks the truth* as in the sight of God.

[TO THE REV. H. B. WILLIAMS ET AL. FROM THE ARCHBISHOP OF CANTERBURY]

LAMBETH, FEB. 12 [1861]

REV. SIR, – I have taken the opportunity of meeting many of my Episcopal brethren in London to lay your address before them.

They unanimously agree with me in expressing the pain it has given them that any clergyman of our Church should have published such opinions as those concerning which you have addressed us.

We cannot understand how their [these?] opinions can be held consis-tently with an honest subscription to the formularies of our Church, with many of the fundamental doctrines of which they appear to us essentially at variance.

Whether the language in which these views are expressed is such as to make the publication an act which could be visited in the ecclesiastical courts, or to justify the synodical condemnation of the book which contains them is still under our gravest consideration. But our main hope is our reliance on the blessing of God in the continued and increasing earnestness with which we trust that we and the clergy of our several dioceses may be enabled to teach and preach that good deposit of sound doctrine which our Church has received in its fulness, and which we pray that she may, through God's grace, ever set forth as the uncorrupted Gospel of our Lord Jesus Christ. – I remain, rev. Sir, your faithful servant,

J. B. CANTUAR [Sumner]

I am authorised to append the following names:—

C. J. [*sic* T.] EBOR [Longley]
A. C. LONDON [Tait]
H. M. DUNELM [Villiers]
C. R. WINTON [Sumner]
H. EXETER [Phillpotts]
C. [*sic* G.] PETERBOROUGH [Davys]
C. ST. DAVIDS [Thirlwall]
A. T. [*sic* E.] CHICHESTER [Gilbert]
J. LICHFIELD [Lonsdale]
S. OXON [Wilberforce]
T. ELY [Turton]
T. V. ST. ASAPH [Short]
J. P. MANCHESTER [Lee]

R. D. HEREFORD [Hampden]
J. CHESTER [Graham]
A. LLANDAFF [Olivant]
R. J. BATH AND WELLS [Eden]
J. LINCOLN [Jackson]
C. GLOUCESTER & BRISTOL [Baring]
W. SARUM [Hamilton]
R. RIPON [Bickersteth]
J. T. NORWICH [Pelham]
J. C. BANGOR [Campbell]
J. ROCHESTER [Wigram]
S. CARLISLE [Waldegrave]

TO THE REV. DR. TEMPLE

We the undersigned* have read with surprise and regret a letter in which the Archbishop of Canterbury and the other English Bishops have severely censured the Volume of Articles entitled *Essays and Reviews.*

Without committing ourselves to the conclusions arrived at in the various Essays, we wish to express our sense of the value which is to be attached to enquiries conducted in a spirit so earnest and reverential, and our belief that such enquiries must tend to elicit truth, and to foster a spirit of sound religion.

---

*[Those who signed, or were willing to sign, the memorial in February and March 1861 have been identified from H. G. Hutchinson, *Life of Sir John Lubbock*, vol. 1 (London: Macmillan and Co., 1914), pp. 57–58 and from letters in the Avebury Papers, British Library Department of Manuscripts, Add. 49639.ff.27–54. A dagger (†) denotes those who agreed with the spirit of the memorial but may not have signed it. There were at least four refusals to sign, from John Couch Adams, John Herschel, Charles Kingsley, and Thomas Vernon Wollaston.]

Feeling as we do that the discoveries in science, and the general progress of thought, have necessitated some modification of the views generally held on theological matters, we welcome these attempts to establish religious teaching on a firmer and broader foundation.

While admitting that each writer in the Essays and Reviews is responsible only for the opinions expressed by himself, we address to you, as author of the first article, this expression of our sympathy and our thanks.

[†George Biddell Airy (1801–1892), FRS, Astronomer-Royal; Plumian Professor of Astronomy, Cambridge
Charles Spence Bate (1819–1889), FRS (1861), zoologist
George Bentham (1800–1884), FLS, botanist
George Busk (1807–1886), FRS; President of the Royal College of Surgeons
†William Benjamin Carpenter (1813–1885), FRS; Fullerian Professor of Physiology, Royal Institution
Charles Darwin (1809–1882), FRS, naturalist
Thomas Graham (1805–1869), FRS, chemist; Master of the Mint
Leonard Horner (1785–1864), FRS; President of the Geological Society
John Lubbock (1834–1913), FRS, naturalist and banker
Charles Lyell (1797–1875), FRS, geologist
William Spottiswoode (1825–1883), FRS, mathematician]

7.3.4   F. W. FARRAR ON THE ATTITUDE OF THE CLERGY TOWARDS SCIENCE, 1868

. . . The views of the most numerous clergy will always, by virtue of their influence, be the views of the most numerous laymen. Looked up to in thousands of parishes as the natural leaders of opinion – possessed of an authority which gives to their utterances an almost oracular dignity – this great society is the most powerful that could be imagined to disseminate each fact, which opens before the minds of men a new 'window into the infinite,' and each discovery which sheds a fresh ray of revelation upon the power of God. It has always, in past times, been a heavy disaster and a prelude to yet more perilous catastrophes, when the clergy have opposed the declarations of science till opposition has become no longer possible, and then have defended and admitted them on grounds wholly different from those by which they were established. That such *has* been the case in past ages, and that, in spite of an immense improvement, the spirit of those ages in this respect has not wholly died away, may, I think, be demonstrated by overwhelming evidence. . . .

. . . In this very age, in this very generation, we have seen exhibitions of theological intolerance as disgraceful in spirit as those of the Inquisition.

We have seen learned and honest men denounced, deposed, excommunicated, reduced to poverty, and treated like social pariahs. From pulpit and platform, as in the days of Priestley, we have seen men of science held up in theological discourses to the hatred of an unreasoning mob. We have seen discovery after discovery treated at first as an insult to verbal inspiration, though afterwards it was unhesitatingly accepted. We still unhappily live in an age of persecutions, prosecutions, deprivations, excommunications, ejections for mere differences of theoretical opinion on matters of Biblical exegesis. And one consequence is that on almost all subjects there is perhaps less of defined and independent thought in England than in any country of the world. Charges of neology, charges of rationalism, charges of scepticism, charges of heresy, in pulpits, and pamphlets, and religious periodicals are everlastingly ringing in our ears. The air is echoing with the texts which are hurled about at opposing theories. We still go on presumptuously deifying our own interpretations, imposing 'the senses of men upon the words of God; the special senses of men upon the general words of God; and laying them upon men's consciences together under the equal penalty of death and damnation.'

For what, very briefly, have been the main new sciences of this generation which can by any possibility intersect the orbit of theology? They are of course geology, ethnology, pre-historic archæology, physiology in some of its branches, and the science of language. Is it possible for any one familiar with the contemporary literature of this century, to deny that every one of those has been ushered in with a burst of clerical opposition? If any one does deny it, I ask him, in the name of common candour, to read the published sermons and pamphlets and newspaper articles of every school, of which he may see thousands at the British Museum. A friend of mine, before whom they come officially, writes to me that 'the mass of theological literature coming before me *abounds* in proofs of the suspicion and antipathy with which scientific inquiries are regarded by great masses of the clergy.' Geology occupies in this generation an analogous position to that once occupied by astronomy; it has revealed to us infinite time peopled by myriads of existences, as astronomy revealed infinite space peopled by myriads of worlds. And how was it received? With excited oratory, with savage denunciation. Dean Buckland and Professor Sedgwick were clergymen, but how were they treated? You cannot deny – for the proofs are patent to every one – that they, and that all the early geologists, were met with a storm of invective. 'What was God doing before the first of the six days of creation?' asks the clerical and university author of 'Popular Geology Subversive of Divine Religion,' and he answers the question to his own satisfaction. 'He was decreeing from everlasting a hell for all infidel inquirers.' Now writers of this class in all sorts of 'Mosaical and scriptural geologies,' as they call them, did exactly what I have heard done in modern papers, *i.e.*, they assumed and asserted that their *own* false theory was the religious, and the other was the irreligious. 'They have,' said Professor Sedgwick, 'overlooked the aim and end of revelation, tortured the book of life out of its proper meaning,' and committed 'the folly and the sin of dogmatising,' and 'pretending to teach mankind in subjects on which they themselves were uninstructed.' If we turn to archæology, we find M. Boucher de Perthes attributing to theological prepossessions his inability for many years to obtain any hearing for his interesting discoveries. In the science of language we still find clergymen inculcating from the pulpit on scriptural grounds the ridiculous and exploded hypothesis that all languages are derived from the Hebrew; and we find the belief in its natural origin distinctly characterized as 'a materialistic and atheistic hypothesis.'

In the records of ethnology we find the gentle and illustrious Dr. Morton worried to death by the attacks of a clerical opponent; and we find a man so learned and eminent as Dr. Pusey, conscious as he is of past experience, laying down at the Norwich Congress as *matters of faith* – matters which the Bible has decided, and which no science can overthrow – propositions rejected by such an immense number of scientific men as these two, that mankind originated in a single pair, and that only eight people were saved with Noah in the Ark. Respecting the opinions themselves I need give no opinion, but respecting the utter unwisdom of staking the whole credit of religion on the support of such hypotheses, after the proved and utter fallibility of our scriptural interpretations in so many other matters, I say that it is most perilous; I say that it demonstrates how little as a body we have yet learnt the very *simple* truth that SCIENCE CAN BE REFUTED BY SCIENCE ONLY, and how little right we have to smile at the fulminations of the Vatican, while our own methods and proceedings are in spirit so much the same. Let us take, by way of example, the celebrated Darwinian hypothesis. From one very small point of view – the ethnological – I have, in the Transactions of the Ethnological Society, myself ventured to state some reasons why I think it is not demonstrable, and that there are powerful arguments on the other side. But no man can deny that it is a most brilliant and fruitful hypothesis; that it has exercised a splendid influence over modern science; that it explains many remarkable facts and series of facts hitherto deemed inexplicable; that it was supported with a genius, a patience, a calmness, and a dignity which made its author a very needful and a very noble example to its assailants; and that the name of Charles Darwin, though it is the reverse of acceptable to the majority of the clergy, stands, perhaps, the very highest in the enthusiastic love, and honour, and reverence of scientific men. Yet how was the hypothesis received? We know how it was received at Oxford; we know that the pulpits, not of England only, but of Europe, rang with denunciation of it as subversive of all Scripture, of all morality, and of the dignity of man; and I have myself heard it thundered forth before an enormous meeting by an excited and most influential clergyman, that if there had been any development it was not from the ape to the man, but retrogressive from the man to the ape in the persons of those who supported such a view! Very recently indeed there has been a stand made against these deplorable and dangerous methods of arguments. Two clergymen, at least, at the Wolverhampton Congress had the courage and good sense to admit – as even Archbishop Sumner admitted long ago – that there are and must be irreconcilable discrepancies between science and the mere letter of Scripture; one of them, without being silenced, actually ventured, without anger or discourtesy, to express some limited approval of the hated name of the Bishop of Natal. But what then happened? The most distinguished leader, the most popular favourite of the whole body got up, and carrying with him, as he himself asserts, the sympathies of the vast majority, declared, amid loud cheers – 'that in the name of all humble believers he repudiated the claims of science to have an equal right with God's Bible to lay the foundation of truth – that those who receive the Bible *do not investigate truth: they receive it.* He really could not part from the meeting without delivering his humble protest against the equal claim of science to our reverence, as if we had all *to look for* the truth, as if we had not already received it.' Now, as far as this language had any meaning – and for its meaning you must read the speeches which it was intended to repudiate – I say that it asserts the right of theologians to be the judges of scientific conclusions, and that it might have been delivered equally well in the Sorbonne – before the board of theologians who sat upon Columbus – or at the conclave of cardinals that humbled Galileo. And this speech was received with loud cheers, and is asserted to have represented, beyond all question, the sense of the meeting.

Now much more remains to be said, which would all tend, I think, to prove the position from which I started, that the relations of the clergy to science – which I most gladly and thankfully admit have improved of late, and are gradually improving – are not yet satisfactory. But I will conclude by laying down three positions, which I fear will be rejected by many of my brethren, but with respect to which I am ready to appeal to every scientific man of note in England, whether peace and union between science and theology is even possible without their frank admission. It has been said that the leading clergy are eager – are painfully anxious for peace on the matter, at any price. Will they agree with me in accepting the conditions on which alone a peace is possible?

1. And first, I say, we must give up our schemes of reconciliation, of squaring our Biblical interpretations into modern scientific moulds, of making the words of the Bible bear all kinds of non-natural senses, and

mean what they never have meant, and never by any possibility could have meant. I declare unhesitatingly that such Biblicising science as that found in Gaussen's 'Theopneustia,' and hosts of modern pamphlets, tends as powerfully to alienate men of science from the Bible, as it tends to revolt the consciences of many of the clergy themselves. The Protestant endeavour 'to bend Scripture to fact' is hardly less futile than was that of the Romanist 'to bend fact to Scripture.' To interpolate any number of thousands of years between two consecutive verses, and imply that the writer may have intended it; to twist the plainest and most prosaic statements into vision, allegory, poetry, metaphor, or anything in the world in one place, yet indignantly to refuse all right to do so in another; to say, when the Bible uses every conceivable variety of phrase to imply universality, that these are only Hebraic metonymies for something partial; to interpret, as in a recent book on language, the story of Babel to imply the gradual growth of three families of language; to argue that when man is said to be made of the dust of the earth, 'dust of the earth' was intended to mean oxygen, hydrogen, and carbon; to take a chance allusion in Solomon as a direct prophecy of the theory of the winds; and to make a chance expression in Job a proleptic allusion to the rotation of the solar system round the star Alcyone; – all this is a style of argumentation which, although it may be loudly applauded at party gatherings, can never be accepted as satisfactory by many plain and conscientious minds. To me, at any rate, it looks like 'lying for God,' while all the while we are fighting against him; and I echo the gratitude of Professor Maurice, when he says that 'it is a blessing that the faith of scientific men in the Bible has not wholly perished, when they see how small *our* faith is, and by what *tricks* we are sustaining it. Thank God that scientific men are Christians still, though they have been listening so long to our defences of Christianity.' But supposing we admit these schemes of reconciliation, – supposing that we regard them as not only tenable, but ingenious and delightful, what is the consequence? what do they inevitably prove? Why, if true, they *could* only prove *this:* that the words of Scripture are so elastic, so Procrustean, that they are capable of meanings so diametrically different from all that they were supposed to mean by all to whom for millenniums they have been addressed, that unless we arrogate to ourselves, for the first time in history, an infallible prescience in their interpretation, it must be to the last degree idle to adduce them at all, either for or against any scientific discovery. Since theology – after violently using the words of Scripture, time after time, in opposition to the reception of new truths – has *always* been obliged in the end to admit her exegesis to have been hopelessly erroneous, these reconciliation schemes, if true, would only show the utter incompetency of theology for the certain or final interpretation of Scripture, and make her resign her professorial chairs in favour of those who so often, so imperatively, and in matters of such enormous interest and importance, have refuted her when she was in the wrong, and supplied her with the only possible means of setting herself right.

2. Then, secondly, I say that we must deliberately abandon that disastrous doctrine of Scriptural infallibility in scientific matters – that degrading idolatry of the dead letter – that doctrine of 'verbal inspiration,' as it is called, which leads, as Bunsen says, to fetichism in worship, to untruth in philosophy, and to unreality in religious thought. It is a doctrine in no sense required by a single document of the Church of England. It is a doctrine wholly alien to the spirit, and wholly unsupported by the claims of the Scriptural writers themselves. It is a doctrine which may be refuted by the plainest and most cogent arguments, alike literary, moral, and historical. It is a doctrine which has been pregnant with deep disasters; it has been the barrier to science, the bane of ethics, and the curse of theology. If it be the worst error of the Roman system that it thrusts priests, and churches, and saints between the soul and God, it has been the error of many Protestant sects that they have placed the utterances of a book between man and his Heavenly Father, with whom, as the book itself teaches us, we all live, or ought to live, in direct, immediate, living, personal communion. It substitutes formal dogmas for the progressive, incessant, permanent revelation of the Creator in all his works, and in all his ways, to the spirit of every individual man. By the fruits of this doctrine you shall know it. The sacred book is the most precious boon which God ever gave to man; but to this perversion and misuse of it we owe every error of judgment and cruelty of action of which we have spoken this evening. To it we owe the defence of slavery. To it we owe the fight for 'passive obedience.' To it we owe the degrading doctrine of 'the right divine of kings to govern wrong.' To it we owe that crime, which has been preached as a duty, the murder or persecution of our opponents for their theological opinions. To it we owe the burning of witches. To it we owe the theory of polygamy. There is hardly a tyranny of kings or priests – hardly an error in sociology or science – which has not appealed to it, or relied on it. They were Divine lips that told us that *the letter killeth*. From it have flowed forth, as from a fountain, the turbid streams of falsehood in science, and injustice in conduct – the disturbed consciences of the many, and the terror-stricken faith of the few. If this truth is to be generally held by the clergy, if it is to be made part and parcel of our theology, if it be thought that any youthful and perhaps ignorant clergyman may refute the most veteran man of science, – who perhaps, after all, knows his Bible far better, – by quoting against him the literal meaning of some Scripture text, then there must long continue to be an opposition between the clergy and science, even if there does not come, sooner or later, an

overwhelming catastrophe to our national religion. And if there be a conflict between the clergy and science, can anyone read history and doubt which will win? After centuries of conflict the Church, when she has thus mistaken her mission, cannot claim a single victory. Every burning, every imprisonment, every persecution, every calumny, every falsely-attached stigma of infidelity, every text impressed into the service of error, every attempt to kindle in the supposed cause of religion the blind excitement of the half-educated mob, has only rebounded with tenfold force upon those that have used them – not demolishing the antagonistic discovery, but only giving it fresh vigour and fresh impetuosity after it has overwhelmed the barrier of a momentary resistance.

3. Then, thirdly and lastly, I say, that we *must* take humbler ground. In this age, sacerdotalism, priestcraft, theological assumption, are a danger-ous anachronism. Men of science deprecate our opposition, but they will certainly dislike our patronage. They claim with us an honourable friendship, a mutual confidence. A knowledge of divine things is, thank God, very far indeed from being an exclusive patrimony of the clergy. Scientific men, for the most part, have shown themselves quite as well acquainted with anything which can be called theology – ay, even with technical theology – as nine-tenths of the clergy themselves. Science is *constantly* performing great services to true religion, but it is only in a very limited and rhetorical sense that the sciences can now be called the handmaids of theology. A speaker at a recent Church Congress said, 'that though they may fly from her, and lose themselves for a time in the dark wilderness of atheistic speculation, they must in the end return to their mistress and submit themselves to her hand.' If this means that the clergy are to legislate for the men of science in their own sphere, it is not true; and if it only means that truth must always redound to the knowledge and glory of God, it is at least expressed in a confused and declamatory manner, which is, alas! but too common among us. Again and again I say that, if theology be only a true interpretation of the revelations of God, then *Science is itself one of the noblest forms of Theology*. It has deepened indefinitely our sense of the mysteries around us; it is the reading of that world which even Plato called 'God's epistle to man;' and which Cam-panella said was 'God's primary autograph;' and which Galileo described as 'a great book ever lying open before our eyes, but which cannot be understood until we first know the language and learn the characters in which it is written.' Once more I must say that God, by the discoveries of science, has revealed to us more fresh truth respecting His own glory than all theology has declared for us since the last of the apostles. The infini-tude of space which He inhabits, – the infinitude of time in which He works, – the majestic onward flow of His mighty laws, 'in the uninterrup-ted rhythm of cause and effect,' – the long reign of physical dissolution

over untold myriads of vanished organisms, – the infinite physical insig-
nificance of the little planet we inhabit in the illimitable cosmos of suns
and systems, – the fact that in that little orb we occupy but a thin pellicle of
air over a thin film of earth, being but 'the last holders of a precarious lease
in an ancient tenement,' – all these truths about God and about ourselves,
which at once dilate the strong conception of the Divine with so kindling a
majesty, and dwarf the pride of the human with so crushing a dominion, –
have been revealed to us, not by Fathers, not by schoolmen, not by
commentators on the Old or New Testament, but by the hopeful, patient,
resolute students of the works of God's hands. These men it is who have
unclenched from the granite hand of Nature her magnificent secrets.
These men, in their search for truth, have, with sheer labour, 'climbed by
these sunbeams to the Father of lights.' And are we the clergy to deny such
lessons of God's works? Are we to put out the eyes of these men? Are we to
bid *them*, who have been so long our teachers, to sit, forsooth, at our feet,
and listen while, by the light of our imperfect and often-blundering
exegesis, we lay down the law to them on their own subjects, and order
them to shape their conclusions thus or thus? Are we to tell them that,
because of our very limited views of interpretation, this or that casual
allusion of Isaiah or of Genesis is to be a final refutation of all their
theories, – is to be as the 'flammantia mœnia mundi,' which they cannot
and dare not overleap? Are *we*, of all people in the world, to bid them
abandon that noble, dauntless, burning love of truth which gives shape to
the purposes, and hopefulness to the struggles of an earnest though
perplexed generation? Or rather shall we not – in obedience to that
pointed finger of heaven which we see in all history – lay aside, at once and
for ever in all matters of science, our old assumptious style of 'Non Ego,
sed Dominus,' – bound, as it was, 'by the thunder and denunciation of
curses and anathemas,' – and adopt in lieu of it the infinitely humbler,
truer, and grander tone of the great Apostle of the Gentiles, – 'secundum
consilium meum,' – and 'Ego, non Dominus?' . . .

7.3.5   R. H. HUTTON ON THE VARIOUS CAUSES OF SCEPTICISM, 1878

. . . So far as we can see, the theory that the spiritual and moral law of
action and reaction will account for all dominant errors, is an exaggeration of the function of a valuable, though limited principle. Doubtless,
asceticism and monasticism lead to reactions in which the fibre of human
character is dangerously relaxed; doubtless, mysticism encourages the
growth of rationalism, and rationalism in its turn some kind of regression
to idealism and mysticism. Still, these complementary phases of faith are
not sufficient, or nearly sufficient, to account for all we see; nor could they

be so, unless man were indeed alone in the world, and the Hegelianism which explains all his convictions as partly the growth of, and partly the recoil against, previous convictions, were true. What it leaves out of account is the free, reciprocal action – not necessarily determined by any considerations of this sort, – of God on man, and if we may say so without irreverence, since this is clearly the teaching of Christ, – of man on God. Luther never forgot this most important of all the explanations of the growth or decay of the religious life. 'We say to our Lord God,' he said, 'that if he will have his Church, he must keep it, for we cannot keep it; and if we could, we should be the proudest asses under heaven.' And Luther implied, of course, that it might please God to humble the Church, to make it feel his presence less at one time, as well as more at another; to give it, for his good purposes, times of aridity, conventionality, and artificiality, as well as times of rich and flowing faith. And if it be true, as Christ teaches, that man may take the initiative with God, as well as God with man, – that times of trust are times of grace, that knocking leads to opening, – that when man throws himself on God, God pours a new tide of spiritual life into man, then, surely, one of the explanations of a want of faith in the invisible is a previous want of appeal to the invisible, – a self-occupation in thoughts and things which turn us away from the invisible, a life of absorption in the superficial phenomena of existence, a generation of outward interests and outward service. This is an explanation almost opposite to that of the law of action and reaction. That law would suggest that to an age of too much outwardness and coldness, an age of pietism or mysticism would inevitably succeed. Yet such is by no means the universal experience of men. On the contrary, the age in which it was said that 'the word of the Lord was precious in those days, – there was no open vision,' immediately preceded the age in which the Jews demanded a king, because their faith in that succession of divine judges by which they had been distinguished from the neighbouring peoples, had in great measure disappeared. The times distinguished by the apparent silence of Heaven frequently lead to periods which are relatively periods of secularism in human history, not to periods of true and deep religious life. And the recent access of Atheism seems to be even more due to an apparent dryness of the spiritual life of man (which may be quite as much due to the will of Heaven as to the will of man) than to any reaction from former superstitions. As Luther would have said, God has not thought fit to keep his Church as he once kept it. God may have willed that, for a time, it would be better for man to try to the full, what he could, and what he could not do, without conscious trust in himself. He may have willed, – as he certainly appears to have willed during many generations even of the life of the people who were specially trained to reveal his mind to the world, – to withhold that stream of spiritual inspiration which is perhaps the only thing corresponding, in the religious life, to what the physicists call 'verification' in the world of positive phenomena. We hear on all sides the complaint of the Agnostics that it is not their fault if they do not believe in God, – that they will believe at once, if his existence can be verified to them, – that, as Professor Huxley puts it, 'no drowning sailor ever clutched a hen-coop more tenaciously' than they would clutch a belief in God which could be verified. If they do not exactly cry aloud, they yet seem to cry under their breath, with the prophet, 'Oh, that thou wouldest rend the heavens, that thou wouldest come down, that the mountains might flow down at thy presence!' – in other words, that if only something physical might 'verify' the divine presence for them, they would be only too happy to accept it. And yet in almost the same breath they declare, – and declare most reasonably, – that nothing physical could prove it, that happen what might, they could only interpret any physical event as a new aspect of nature, that nature is so large and so elastic, that no room is left in it for anything physical to rank as supernatural. Well, it is obvious that such a state of mind as this is one which could be changed by the direct touch of the divine spirit, and by that only, – by an event of the soul, not an event of the body, — by the power which convinces the conscience, not by any power which only enlarges the experience of the senses.

But it does not follow that because no such event happens, – because the only verification of which the case admits, does not take place, – the Agnostic has either, on the one hand, the least right to suppose himself entitled to assume the negative view to be true; or on the other hand, may fairly be regarded by those who do recognise as final evidence, the influence of God over their soul, as morally inferior to themselves. Neither of these conclusions is true. The Agnostic is not right, for his negative experience, however frequently repeated, cannot outweigh a single clear experience of a positive kind. But none the less, he must not, on account of this negative experience, be treated as morally inferior to one who has verified the existence of a divine will over him and in him; – for if it has become, as doubtless it has, for the advantage of mankind that hundreds of generations should have felt the need of high social and moral laws, before ever social and moral laws were established and obeyed, and that hundreds of generations more felt the need of a clear recognition of constant physical laws, before physical laws were discovered and turned to account, why should it not also be for the advantage of man that certain classes, even in the modern times of larger knowledge and higher aims, should be taught to feel acutely the need of a divine light for the true interpretation even of those physical principles of order, which they are so strenuous in asserting and enforcing in their apparent divorce from any spiritual principle? We may say roughly, – a very great thinker indeed did say, – that during the middle-ages thinking men were chiefly occupied in sounding their own minds, to see how much light the careful exploring of those minds might shed on the external order of things; and that a knowledge of the insufficiency of the study of mind to explain the laws of matter, was the first step to that true study of the laws of matter which followed. And we believe that the eminent Agnostics of the present day may be said to be discharging the similar function, of exaggerating indefinitely the influence of material laws in things moral and spiritual, – in order eventually to show their well-marked limits; – that they are trying (and failing) to prove that material laws are the true keys to the knowledge of mental and moral life, just as the middle-ages tried and failed to show that moral and spiritual laws were the true keys to the knowledge of material life. And it would be just as foolish to suppose the modern physicists inferior to those who do not fall into their error, only because they are not equally fascinated by their truths, as it would have been to denounce the Schoolmen as morally inferior to the first heralds of the new science, only for trying to deduce principles of astronomy out of the *a priori* and abstract conceptions of the human mind. The truth is, that in every great stage of human progress there is, and must be, an undue appreciation of the step just made. In some sense, it may be said that Providence is the real cause of that undue appreciation. It is, of course, the divine guidance which determines the main lines of direction and intensity for human thought; and if the Creator withdraws himself at times from the vision of men, or of some men, it is no doubt for the benefit of all men that he does so. To speak of those who do not themselves see God as 'living without God in the world,' is itself atheism. You might as well suppose that before the atmosphere was recognised as having weight and substance, men who did not know the difference between it and a vacuum, lived without the air they breathed. God is not less behind the consciousness of men who have no glimpse of him through their consciousness, than he is within the heart of those who worship him; and the only real rejection of God is the resistance to his word, whether it be felt as his word, or only as a mysterious claim on the human will which it is impossible adequately to define. We hold that, in a sense, God is himself, in all probability, no unfrequent cause of the blindness of men to his presence. He retires behind the veil of sense, when he wishes us to explore the boundaries of sense, and to become fully aware of a life beyond. The physicists in every school are doing this great work for us now. They are explaining, defining, mapping all the currents of physical influence, and from time to time crying out, like Professor Huxley, for 'the hen-coop' of which, like shipwrecked sailors, they see no sign; like Professor Tyndall, for the elevating idealism which is conspicuous by its absence in all their investigations; like Professor Clifford, for something to replace the theism of Kingsley and Martineau. To suppose that the men who are doing this great work, – who are mapping for us the quicksand and sunken rocks of physical scepticism, – are necessarily deserted by God, because they do not see him, is to be more truly atheist than any physicist. There is a scepticism which is of God's making, in order that we may see how many of the highest springs of human life are founded in trust, – how everything else fails, even in the highest minds, to produce order, peace, and calm. The physicists of to-day are suffering for us, as well as for themselves. It is their failure to find light, which will show where the light is not, and also where it is. As Mr. Mallock well says, in the best paper he has yet written – that in the *Nineteenth Century*, on 'Faith and Verification,' – the pitiful cries of modern physicists, as they raise their hands to what they deem a spiritual vacuum, are about the best auguries we could have that it is not in physical science that man can ever find his salvation.

7.4 NATURAL RELIGION: CONVERSION, DEVOTION, MISSION

With or without a recognizable God, the new science-based religion of Nature found expression in ways already familiar from conventional Christian practice. Moral seriousness, ceremonial observance, and evangelistic zeal were evident in adherents of both the old faith and the new, and these resemblances may be explained by the simple fact that the religious ethos was endemic. A change of heart did not necessarily accompany a change of creed, except perhaps in some cases where the individual became a militant atheist. Frederic Harrison (1831–1923) was an Oxford High Churchman who converted to the systematic and authoritarian Positivism of Auguste Comte and remained its foremost English defender throughout a distinguished career as a lawyer and man of letters. His spiritual autobiography, published in 1907, explained how the transition was made and under what influences. Harrison quoted a diary of 1861 as evidence that *Essays and Reviews* and the brilliant analysis of the volume he published in the *Westminster Review* marked his final *bouleversement*. He had come to see that the logical result of intellectual double-dealing among Broad Churchmen must be a new naturalistic religion (**7.4.1**). T. H. Huxley (7.2.2, 7.2.4), who was much taken with Harrison's review at the time, always acknowledged strong clerical affinities in himself, despite his public reputation as a devil incarnate. In 1870, the year his first collection of essays appeared with the title *Lay Sermons*, he delivered an address in London under the auspices of the Sunday Lecture Society. In attendance was the ever-observant Revd Davies (4.3.1 etc.), who aptly sensed the significance of the occasion. Here was an eminent scientist pronouncing on the fraught subject of the origins and affinities of human nature: the 'supremacy' of tall, fair nomadic northerners to the dark people of the south, and the racial unity of Teuton, Celt, and Saxon, which to Davies carried a clear political message. He found but an 'ill-defined frontier line' between the lecture and liberal religious sermons (**7.4.2**). No attempt, however, was made by Huxley to evangelize his audience or to inspire zeal among the faithful. That he could do so is amply attested, but in general the missionary enterprise was left, as it was among the churches, to men of a more practical bent. In 1882, for example, John Robert Seeley (1834–1895), professor of modern history at Cambridge, published a book entitled *Natural Religion* to show that religious faith need not depend on supernaturalism and that the Christian faith in particular is purified by science. Natural religion he viewed as the spirit of 'the great ruling civilisation of the world'. Its doctrines of science, progress, and liberty must be carried to 'outlying people' for the sake of 'equilibrium', as they are admitted into the 'modern City of God' (**7.4.3**). Still more sanguine was the vision of a remoter future in *The Martyrdom of Man* by William Winwood Reade (1838–1875), an intrepid young traveller and autodidact. His passionate evocation of universal history, full of excitement and foreboding, effectively secularized the message of the cross and made humanity its own dying and rising redeemer. Science, according to Reade, is the engine of human progress; God remains eternally elusive, a numinous Unknown. This 'gospel for heretics', as it has been called, culminated in a passage, reproduced in part below, which contains perhaps the most eloquent peroration in agnostic literature (**7.4.4**).

7.4.1   F. HARRISON ON THE MAKING OF A POSITIVIST, 1850–61

At the age of eighteen I went to Oxford as a scholar of Wadham, which was then the eminently Protestant College, the Warden, Dr. Symons, being one of the leaders of the ultra-evangelical party, with a wife from a Quaker family. . . . There was a small group of pronounced Puseyites, amongst whom I was counted. . . . Of the students about two-thirds at least had come from Anglican parsonages, . . . and about two-thirds were destined for Holy Orders. Nearly all the tutors were priests. . . . We were compelled to attend the Chapel service every day and twice on Sunday; and to hear the University sermon, of which we had to bring up abstracts and summaries.

Here were all the elements of theological inquiry and debate. The College contained men of all shades of belief within the Anglican pale and one or two avowed sceptics who knew more divinity and had greater dialectic ability than the rest of us. We often spent most of Sunday, until the early hours of Monday morning, discussing the Sermon of the day, combating each other's 'heresies' and 'superstitions,' or in ridiculing the Warden's stale sophisms about the 'argument from design.'

No method could be devised more certain to breed a confused chaos of religious thought than University sermons. . . . Every Master of Arts in orders had his turn, and he naturally took the occasion to expound his cherished dogma. Sunday after Sunday, year after year, the official pulpit rang with some different point of view, from the extreme Ritualist to the ultra Calvinist. The select preachers and the Bampton Lecturers often broached a more philosophic scheme of thought. The thoughtful student who is obliged to summarise these diatribes, has every phase of theological thought forced upon his attention. The creed – 'necessary if we are to be saved' – of one Sunday becomes the heresy of the next. Priests who had all but 'gone over with Newman' followed priests who had driven him forth with Protestant anathemas. One set of these sermons has been incorporated into the argument of Herbert Spencer's Agnosticism. . . . I have seen the benches of the undergraduates in the gallery quivering with the emotion caused by some perfervid Catholic exhortation. I have seen the same benches shake with irrepressible delight at some brilliant logical dilemma. How can the minds of keen young students retain their calm or any fixity of thought, when week by week they are swept by 'every wind of doctrine' – winds that blow in turn from each quarter of the theological compass, which they 'box' with incessant revolutions. . . .

Very slowly, gradually, and peaceably, under this continual ebb and flow of theological discussions, my school taste for ritualism and my calm acceptance of orthodox doctrine melted away into a sense of suspended judgment and anxious thirst for wider knowledge. I now began to read the *Westminster Review*, between 1850 and 1860 at the acme of its brilliancy and influence. John Henry Newman led me on to his brother Francis, whose beautiful nature and subtle intelligence I now began to value. His *Phases of Faith, The Soul, The Hebrew Monarchy*, deeply impressed me. I was not prepared either to accept all this heterodoxy, nor yet to reject it; and I patiently waited till an answer could be found. I read Theodore Parker's American *Discourses*; and, if I was not converted to 'Universal Salvation,' certainly he and Maurice and Francis Newman relieved my youthful mind of any fear of an eternity of Hell. . . . The *Westminster Review* with articles on Strauss' *Life of Jesus*, Renan and Bauer on the Scriptures, Humboldt's *Cosmos*, and constant Essays by Herbert Spencer, W. Call, W. R. Greg, Mill, the two Lewes and Francis Newman, opened to us the whole of the critical study of the Scriptures and the Creeds as far as it had gone down to the appearance of Spencer's *Synthetic Philosophy* and C. Darwin's *Origin of Species*.

I was at Oxford altogether as student and resident fellow and tutor, some six years, and during the whole of that time my opinions on the crucial problems of religion and philosophy had been gradually and quietly widening and forming. The criticisms on the inspiration of Scripture and the credibility of the Creeds made by W. R. Greg, F. Newman, Strauss and his translator George Eliot, had by this time completely shaken my hold on the conventional orthodoxy. But I moved on very cautiously by slow steps. . . . When I came up to London to study law I was fond of hearing the Choir at Lincoln's Inn and F. D. Maurice preach. His sermons demolished what remains of orthodoxy I had. With much force and real pathos, he would enlarge on the weak side, especially on the moral blots, of the Scripture record or of the Church Creed. Having completely gained our assent, he would wind up with some conventional and effusive peroration, which came to this – that preposterous as was the doctrine and immoral the ordinance from a purely human point of view, we ought to accept it as a sublime sort of *auto da fé*; we ought to hug our fetters, and revel in our darkness as faithful Christians within the pale of the true Church. How many of us recoiled from this abject *Credo quia impossibile – quia inhumanum* – which seemed to be the final word of this truly devout, high-minded, and generous priest! . . .

By the time I had reached full manhood I had entirely assimilated Mill's *Logic*, Herbert Spencer's earlier *Essays*, Lewes' *History of Philosophy*, and I was a convinced disciple of the Philosophy of Experience as against all forms of the Intuitional schools. In a College essay, as an undergraduate, I had boldly declared that the future of modern thought could rest only on some type of the Positive Philosophy. I now read Comte in Harriet Martineau's translation, in the intelligent summary of Littré, and in the perfunctory sketch of G. H. Lewes. I carefully studied and was profoundly impressed by Comte's view of general history and by his original scheme of a new science of society. I entirely accepted both, but did not apply them to religion or the organisation of society. Of all that I knew nothing; and in fact it was at that date neither completed nor published.

I now sought and obtained an interview with Auguste Comte in Paris, who gave me one of his mornings whilst the third volume of his Polity was in the press. He received me with a simple dignity which at once charmed me; inquired of my knowledge and what more I wished to learn of his system; and then answered each point with perfect freedom and brilliancy of exposition. I told him that I had been bred up a believer in God, and so remained; that I was impressed by his scheme of philosophy and especially by the evolution of history so far as I knew it in the previous work (the *Philosophie*). He said that many of his followers, especially women, clung to the theological beliefs in which they had been brought up; that he made no attempt to dispel these, as all his teaching was *positive* and not *negative*; that as my education at Oxford had left the physical sciences aside, I was not in a fit state of intellectual preparation to decide for myself these ultimate problems.

I felt the truth of this, and I resolved to remedy the defects of an academic education by devoting myself to gain some knowledge of natural science, at least enough to understand the logic and dominant results of the four great physical sciences, especially of biology. . . . When I came back to London, at the age of twenty-four, I set myself steadily to study the elements of physical science; I succeeded in mastering the elementary text-books of Astronomy, Geology, Physics, and Biology; using the manuals of Sir W. Grove, of Herschel, Lyell, and Tyndall. I attended lectures of Richard Owen, Thomas Huxley, John Tyndall, and Edward Liveing. The latter gave me private lectures on the brain of man and the principal senses, with preparations, skeletons, and the like. I read the main biological works of Owen, Huxley, C. Darwin, A. R. Wallace, and of Todd, Bowman, Rymer Jones; and I studied the admirable French manuals of Gall, Béclard, Broussais, Blainville, and Bichat. At the same time I studied the anatomical collections in the British Museum, and in the College of Surgeons, and dipped into those large encyclopædias of practice – Dr. Reynolds' *System of Medicine*, and T. Holmes's *System of Surgery*, which I always have kept at hand on my library shelves. I did my best to master the whole of Comte's *Positive Philosophy* and Herbert Spencer's *Synthetic Philosophy* to which I was one of the original suscribers, reading each volume as it came out. . . .

I thus became saturated with the sense of invariable law and the relative nature of Man, his planetary abode, and the limits of his possible knowledge. My nearest friends were Doctors of Medicine and Professors of History, all steadily converging to the Positive System which co-ordinates the physical and the moral sciences under a complex interdependent set of synthetic laws. At the house of Richard Congreve I made the acquaintance of George Eliot and of George Henry Lewes. At the house of John Chapman, Editor of the *Westminster Review*, I made the acquaintance of Francis Newman, Herbert Spencer, R. W. Mackay and other writers in the *Review*. In the seven years that had passed since I took my degree, I had become rooted in a conviction of the universal reign of Law, of the possibility of a real Social science, and in Comte's Scheme of historical evolution. To this now was added a general knowledge of Comte's *Positive Polity*, completed in 1855, and a thorough study of the *Origin of Species* and Herbert Spencer's *Synthetic Philosophy*.

How did this scientific and philosophical preparation react upon my religious belief? I shrank from making any clear sweep of theological doctrines and quietly held on to the general lines of what is oddly called Natural Religion. The sceptical attack on Scripture and Creed has never much interested me. Indeed the moral and intellectual tone of what is commonly called Infidelity was always alien to me; and that of positive Atheism was intensely repulsive. I steadily observed Comte's profound epigram: – 'The Atheist is the most irrational of all the Metaphysicians' – *i.e.* he gives to an insoluble problem the solution for which there is the least to be said. I did not read Tom Paine, Voltaire, or Bradlaugh, nor had I any dealing with the 'Iconoclast' and Free-Thought movement. It was inconsistent and illogical to hold firmly the positivist scheme of philosophy and of sociology, and yet formally to hold a vague and arid Theism. . . .

At the same time, though the German and French criticism of the Bible was familiar to me it did not seem to me of decisive importance. I read the Bible and judged it for myself. . . . No person, no book, no theory, was at all needed to teach me that what we call the Bible was the very miscellaneous literature of an extraordinary, but half-humanised people. Nor did I want sermons or tracts in divinity to show me that the entire scheme of Salvation as propounded in orthodox form was a mere Vision, like Dante's *Inferno* or Bunyan's *Pilgrim's Progress*. . . . I now enjoyed as sublime poetry what had before been supernatural revelation or formal ordinance. The long historical sequence of moral and religious evolution from Adam to John at Patmos, mythical as it was, seemed to me an invaluable record of human evolution. The whole scheme of Man's Fall through sin, his reconcilement to his Maker by the love and sacrifice of a divine Saviour, Man's ultimate Redemption and entering into Celestial Bliss – all this became to me a magnificent Allegory – rich with moral and devotional teaching to the human soul, but regarded as objective *fact*, as a worthy ideal of human regeneration, no more to be believed in as *true*, no more to be admired as a *moral standard*, than Plato's *ideas*, or any other beautiful but fantastic hypothesis to be read in these exquisite Dialogues. . . .

If I have ever felt any hesitation about so large a change in belief, any qualm of conscience in placing so vast a body of sacred things on a firmer and rational basis, this would have been checked in me by watching the fabric of dishonest 'adaptation,' fantastic defence, and spurious equivocations, continually raised by official champions of orthodoxy. I felt deeply the moral evil of all this wriggling and prevaricating. It seemed to me as if Milton's Satan was at the ear of Eve whispering to forge illusions, phantasms, and dreams. Full of this indignation I wrote for the *Westminster Review* my criticism of *Essays and Reviews* which I called *Neo-Christianity*. . . . No one was more surprised than I was at the hubbub which ensued in the Clerical world, nor more disgusted at the intolerance with which Mr. Jowett and his friends were assailed. A young lawyer who had never published a line did not suppose that a review of his in a free-thought organ was at all likely to cause a panic in the Church of England. He did

not think the *Westminster Review* could ever disturb, or even enter, orthodox circles, and he had the sense to see that all he had done was to put a
match to an explosive train of thought, which had been long and
laboriously prepared by far wiser and abler men. . . .

. . . It so happens that in a chest of private papers I came upon an old
locked Diary which I wrote for my own eye nearly half a century ago. In it
I had written down as truly as I could what were my own thoughts, beliefs,
and hopes, just after the publication of 'Neo-Christianity,' and during the
excitement of the attack on *Essays and Reviews*. This statement, or confession, it may be called, was dated 1st January 1861. I was then aged
twenty-nine, a barrister beginning practice in Lincoln's Inn. The responsibility of suddenly finding myself in the midst of a fierce theological
struggle, had made me resolve to meditate seriously on my own belief and
aims in life. . . . It was a season with me of some despondency and
disappointment. I hardly looked, and hardly hoped, to have a long life –
indeed the first page of the locked Diary was inscribed *'pereuntis peritura.'*
It was indeed a kind of *testamentum in procinctu*. But as it is a perfectly
authentic account of a youthful mind undergoing a deep upheaval, with
many scruples I copy it out as it stands in the old Diary.

A CONFESSION OF FAITH   (Diary — *January* 1861.)

I believe that before all things needful, beyond all else is true
religion. This only can give wisdom, happiness, and goodness to
men, and a nobler life to mankind. Nothing but this can sustain,
guide, and satisfy all lives, control all characters, and unite all
men. True Religion alone must rule in every heart, brain, and
will, over every people of the whole earth; inspire every thought,
hallow every emotion, and be the guide of every act.

Thus the soul of each and the souls of all may be knit in one
accord, and every faculty of every being, and every being of every
race, may come to join in one; and all may rest in one common
faith, each live in the great life, work for the common end, and
offer homage to one great Power, above all, in all, and for all.
Surely they who know and feel this and live thereby do well, and
follow right and truth, though their knowledge be uncertain of
what they worship and obey – whether they adore by name Osiris,
Vishnu, Jove or Thor, Virgin, Humanity, or God.

What is this true religion? We know not. As yet, it is not. Yet
nearer, perhaps, than we think. Much is now clear. Much is
coming into light. Dimly we may now see a faith guiding all hearts
and lives in one.

When I contemplate the great harmony which stretches

through man and nature, and that vast whole which lives, moves and grows together by equal laws, in natural concord, sympathy, and help, I cannot but recognise one guiding Hand, and acknowledge one great Author. All-powerful? I know not. All-wise? I cannot tell. All-good? I dare not say. Yet surely this vast frame does testify to a Power very awful. Its symmetry points to a Mind truly sublime. And the perpetual goodness, tenderness, and beauty of all breathing things are witness to a Goodness truly adorable.

Can it ever be that men shall cease to ask – How came this wonder? Whose this wisdom? Whence this Goodness?

I think not. Yet, when they do ask, what must be the answer?

Can it ever be that every thought, emotion, and effort of man can unite in one save as he acknowledges, adores, and serves one who is the centre of all things, both man, and brute, and earth, the source of all we honour in man, of all we love in the things around us, through whom there flows the universal goodness which makes a mother's love and the tenderness of the parent bird – which inspires the joy of all living things and clothes the visible world in loveliness and grace?

Therefore, I believe that God is: who made, loves, and protects man and all things.

How then shall we know him? – do His will? – serve Him? Has he left us without help, without light, without promise? Inspiration – Revelation – Gospel – there is plainly none. The diviner's rod is past. The oracles are dumb. The tables of stone are broken. The ancient legends are cast aside. So too are old fictions of innate knowledge, of conscious Truth – of Natural Theology. Scripture and Miracles alike are past. Man must be his own Gospel. He must reveal truth to himself – by himself. He must found, or frame, his own Religion – or must have none.

And is he powerless for this? Is he left helpless? Has he not the strength to live, and the mind to learn how best to live?

Truly, if by patient thought and earnest effort, man can build up for himself the law of his life – learn to know his highest happiness – his best training, his truest duty, then he is thereby fulfilling the law of Him who placed him here; then he is revealing to himself the will of his Creator, and is most truly serving Him with that only service which man can know or perform.

It is this – or nothing. If, when man knows all he can know of man and of nature, he knows not God; if, when he works out his duty in his life, he does not serve him; if, the submission of his whole soul to that highest law and Power which he can certainly see and know, is not worship – then are such things not for men.

This at least the thoughtful spirit will desire and will do – come what may. Thus will he live in confidence and peace, not swaying in perplexity, nor wasting in despair – much less turning again to broken idols.

What may his law of life be? Has man yet reached this goal of human existence? Has he proved the real grounds of truth? As I think – yes. Auguste Comte, as I believe, has truly raised this to be the foundation of all life and thought. He has given order to the sum of all knowledge – wide enough for all minds – deep enough for all hearts – practical enough for all action. In this now long since I rest, in this I live. Through this only do I hope, and work, and trust. This is my real – my sole – my abiding religion.

Much therein I do not see. Much is dark, unmeaning, strange. Yet there is enough abundantly clear and firm, wherein to have faith – whereby to live. . . .

7.4.2   C. M. DAVIES ON
PROFESSOR HUXLEY'S SUNDAY LECTURE, 1870

When first I commenced these unorthodox effusions . . . I mentioned, in passing, my visit to St George's Hall on a Sunday afternoon to hear Dr Carpenter lecture on 'The Deep Sea.' The fact of my having received a circular from the 'Sunday Lecture Society,' containing a statement of their past operations and projected work, showed me, not only that the work whose commencement I then chronicled was still going on, but that it was progressing with every sign of success, and endorsed with the names of approvers so eminent as scarcely to allow of its being passed over silently in a series of papers professing to represent the current phases of religious life in London.

Besides the world-known name of Professor Huxley, the lecturer for the day, I found such names as Dr Spencer Cobbold, Professor Blackie, and Erasmus Wilson among the others; while, as though to remove any doubts as to the 'propriety' of devoting a Sunday to science instead of religion, specially so-called – for may not the two be made synonymous? –

---

12   The Sunday Lecture Society was organized in November 1869 by William Henry Domville, proponent of 'a new Westminster Confession of Faith for the laity of the 19th century'. Among the Society's vice presidents were Huxley, Herbert Spencer, William Spottiswoode, John Tyndall, and Charles Darwin. Huxley also presided over the organizational meeting, although he declined to serve as president in 1884 while holding the same office at the Royal Society.

THE SUNDAY LECTURE SOCIETY.

To provide for the delivery on Sundays in the Metropolis, and to encourage the delivery elsewhere, of Lectures on Science,—physical, intellectual and moral,—History, Literature, and Art; ESPECIALLY IN THEIR BEARING UPON THE IMPROVEMENT AND SOCIAL WELL-BEING OF MANKIND.

The Ninth Lecture of the present series will be delivered

AT

St. George's Hall, Langham Place,

ON

SUNDAY AFTERNOON, MARCH 13th, 1870,

At Half-past Four o'clock precisely,

BY

PROFESSOR HUXLEY,

LL D., F.R.S.,

On "The Forefathers of the English People on the Mainland of Europe and Asia."

The Society's following Lecture will be :—

10th—March 20. **A. H. GREEN**, Esq., **M.A. Cambridge**, **F.G.S.** (of Her Majesty's Geological Survey), on "The connexion between the Scenery and Geological Structure of a Country."

Payment at the Door, Threepence, Sixpence and One Shilling.

8 - 7.3.70— 250.

I descried two 'reverend' titles among the lecturers. The Rev. Allen D. Graham, M.A., Oxon. (designated in 'Crockford for 1868' as Curate of St Paul's, Covent Garden), was to enlighten the Sunday audience on 'Witchcraft, and the Lessons we learn from it'; while the Rev. Professor Lewis Campbell, M.A., Oxon. (described as formerly Tutor of Queen's College, Oxford, and Vicar of Milford, Hants, now Professor of Greek in the University of St Andrew's), was also announced, though without his subject being named. Need I say that these reverend titles removed any lingering scruples, and that I resolved to make Professor Huxley my preacher for the day? In sober earnest, this Sunday Lecture Society had become now a *fait accompli*, and demanded notice. . . .

. . . The circular of the society said – and I believe truly – 'The committee have spent, since the month of December, upwards of £70 merely in advertising in the newspapers. No fewer than 6000 circulars, containing the list of persons approving the objects of the society, and 16,000 of the handbills announcing the present series of lectures, have been printed and distributed. Yet, notwithstanding this, the committee believe that the society's lectures are but little known of (*sic*) by residents in London, or even in the immediate vicinity of St George's Hall.' Repeating my original warning, then, that my mission is simply to describe, not to criticize or pronounce for or against, I give the records of this Sunday's experience. . . .

The subject chosen by Professor Huxley was, 'The Forefathers of the English People on the Mainland of Europe and Asia.' He commenced by calling the attention of his audience to the two types of *physique* noticeable at the present day in Britain – the one tall, fair, and light-haired, the other short and dark, with curling black hair. Passing over the gradations obtained by intermixture, he found that these two types were existent in the earliest accounts of Britain – those, namely, of Cæsar, Tacitus, and Strabo – which descriptions stood in much the same relation to the Romans as Captain Cook's account of Tahiti to us. Cæsar tells us of the fair-haired inhabitants of Kent; Tacitus mentions the dark Silures of South Wales. In a linguistic point of view the peoples were one; for English were non-existent, and there were only the two types of Celtic – the Cymric and Gaelic.

The two races then were one, and the problem is, whence came these two races with one language? Geography gives a suggestion. The east coast of England is separated by a brief space of sea from Scandinavia, Denmark, North Germany, and the north of France. In the same way the south and south-east of England are separated by a still smaller space from France. Now, we may check the obvious inference deducible herefrom by noticing the distribution of races on the Continent. It would be possible, Professor Huxley observed, to draw an oblique line from the mouth of the Seine to the mouth of the Rhone, and divide the tall, fair people north of that line from the short dark people south of it. This fact is confirmed by the statistics of stature drawn up for purposes of the conscription. Such a line might, in fact, extend from the North of Ireland to the Himalayas, and still to the north would be the tall fair people, and to the south, the short dark. Such a difference was not traceable to climate, because still further north you come again upon dark people, to wit, the Laps, a Mongolian race quite distinct from the dark people of the south.

The combined Continent may, then, be divided into three zones or belts: 1, the dark Laps; 2, the fair Celts; 3, the dark Celts. The distinction comes to be, then, between the Xantho-chroi, or tall and fair, and the Melano-chroi, or dark. The inference, therefore, was, that these two divisions of Celts came from the Continent to our island. The invasion of the Saxons, Jutes, Danes, and Northmen, changed the language of Britain, *but added no new physical element.* Therefore, argued the Professor, we must not talk any more of Celts and Saxons, for all are one. 'I never lose an opportunity of rooting up that false idea that the Celts and Saxons are different races.' If Professor Huxley could only get Pat to recognize this, he might do more to root out Fenianism than the suspension of Habeas Corpus or any amount of Church and Land Tenure Bills!

Professor Huxley went on to prove the identity of the Gauls and Germans in the earliest historical times. Both were a fair-haired race, of tall stature and powerful frame. He compared their habits, going into some amusing details – for instance, these Celts were eminently a trouser-wearing race. Gaul was divided into Braccata and Togata – the former Celtic, the latter Roman. The Highland costume of the present day, therefore, was eminently unnational. It was Roman, not Celtic. The Germans, too, were the earliest known possessors of soap; proving again – as in their adoption of trousers – their superiority over the Romans. Possibly, however, the soap was used rather as an ornament than for purposes of cleanliness, to redden the hair – a process still adopted in the Fiji Islands. The hypothesis finally advanced was that the tall fair people north of the line above mentioned, breaking through the natural barriers of the Alps, Carpathians, and Hercynian forest in Europe, as through the Himalayas in India, dispossessed and virtually exterminated the dark people to the south, driving them into mountain districts, as the Britons were afterwards driven by successive invaders into Cornwall and Wales.

The dark people are the remains of the southern mountaineers, sometimes, as in the case of the Basque people, proving their separate origin by linguistic peculiarities, whilst the resemblances of Sanscrit, Latin, Greek, and modern European languages attest the supremacy of the nomadic inhabitants of the northern plains, across which, Professor Huxley observed, 'you might drive a cart for four or five thousand miles from

Holland to China without encountering any elevation worth speaking of.' So, then, the upshot is, we are all one people, and, as was quaintly said, 'it is wicked to talk about Anglo-Saxons.' Teuton and Celt are distinctions without a difference from this time forth and for evermore.

The audience was a very large and intelligent one, comprising many eminent scientific men, quite a fair quota of ladies, a sprinkling of the rising generation, and altogether a collection of heads that would have delighted a phrenologist or physiognomist. Surely there is another old prejudice that must be rooted up by such a gathering as this. Whatever else we may be called, the English people must no longer be set down as a race of unmitigated Sabbatarians.

It is against this, and this only, that the Sunday Lecture Society desire to protest. They are not a Church, like the body that gathers in the same hall later in the day, and calls itself 'The Church of Progress.' They carefully avoid all theological subjects; but they hold that 'History, Literature, and Art, especially in their bearing upon the improvement and social well-being of mankind,' are proper subjects for Sunday study. It would be difficult to assail such a position – very difficult to say where the practical sermon merges into the lecture.

Then, again, the persons who attended the Sunday lecture, one could see at a glance, were not the people who go to church or are likely to do so until the calibre of the clergy and the style of sermons are widely different from the present. Mr Conway's congregation, as well as Mr Conway himself, and several leading Unitarians, were present; but those who are familiar with Unitarian sermons, or with Mr Conway's discourses, will be aware there is but an ill-defined frontier line between them and a lecture by Professor Huxley. It will probably take some time to familiarize the present generation with Sunday lectures. There will be need of caution lest while we avoid one extreme we run into another. We do not want the Continental Sunday in London. In fact, despite all their small scorn of our Sabbatarianism, our Continental neighbours are to a large extent adopting and appreciating our English 'Lord's Day.' But there is a wide difference between opening theatres and music-halls on Sunday, and opening museums or giving lectures on science and kindred subjects. Probably all, except very extreme religionists, will agree that, next to going to church, attending such a lecture as the one I have sketched above is a legitimate mode of spending Sunday; indeed, we may yet see the day when even those who go to church in the morning, and perchance the evening too, may still find time in the afternoon for such an interesting disquisition as the one I listened to on the subject of our forefathers in the olden time.

7.4.3   J. R. SEELEY ON THE RELIGIOUS MISSION OF
A SCIENTIFIC CIVILIZATION, 1882

. . . Religion in its public aspect now appears to be identical with civilisation. . . . When Western civilisation is confronted with the races outside it or the classes that have sunk below it, what does it feel irresistibly impelled to teach? Science, that is definiteness of conception, accuracy of observation and computation, intellectual conscientiousness and patience, and closely connected with these, the active spirit which rejects fatalism and believes that man's condition can be bettered by his efforts. What else? Humanity, not limited by tribe or nation, and including all principles affecting man's dealings with his kind, respect for women, respect for individual liberty, respect for misfortune. Again what else? Delight and confidence in nature, opposed alike to the superstitious dread of idolatry and to the joylessness of monasticism or puritanism.

This, then, is our civilisation; and what is the religion that inspires it? That scientific spirit of observation and method is the worship of God, whose ways are not as our ways, but whose law is eternal, and in the knowledge of whom alone is solid wellbeing. That spirit of active humanity is Christianity, and it is supplemented by several other forms of the worship of Man which have grown up round it. Lastly, that enjoyment of the visible world is a fragment saved from the wreck of Paganism. It is the worship of the forms of Nature derived from Greece, first widely diffused at the *Renaissance,* and welcomed since and spread still more widely by artist natures from age to age.

We have remarked that a civilisation or religion which to those who live in the midst of it is imperceptible as an atmosphere becomes distinctly visible in contrast with the outer world. Greeks felt their Hellenism in contact with barbarism and Jews their election in contact with the Gentiles. When the contrast becomes intense a condition of unstable equilibrium is created; the religion becomes aggressive or missionary, and one of those great spiritual movements takes place which mark at long intervals the progress of humanity, such as the conversion of all nations to Judaism, to Romanism, to Hellenism. Now there never was a time when the equilibrium was so unstable as it is now between the great ruling civilisation of the world, which is no longer the narrow civilisation of some single city or tribe, but the great common tradition of a brotherhood of great nations, and the outlying peoples. Whereas in past times the better civilisation had to protect itself from destruction and became missionary in self-defence, now it is rather tempted to be apathetic from too triumphant superiority. It weighs the question whether barbarism should not rather be exterminated than converted, and while it does so the question answers itself, for the nations are baptized with gin and the chaff of humanity is burnt up with unquenchable fire-water.

Thus the modern religion finds a vast work ready for its hands, a work which will compel it to give itself some organisation. The children of modern civilisation are called to follow in the footsteps of Paul, of Gregory, of Boniface, of Xavier, Eliot, and Livingstone; but they must carry not merely Christianity in its narrow clerical sense but their whole mass of spiritual treasures to those who want them. Let us carry the true view of the Universe, the true astronomy, the true chemistry, and the true physiology to polytheists still lapped in mythological dreams; let us carry progress and free-will to fatalist nations and to nations cramped by the fetters of primitive custom; let us carry the doctrine of a rational liberty into the heart of Oriental despotisms; in doing all this — not indeed suddenly or fanatically, not yet pharisaically, as if we ourselves had nothing to learn — we shall admit the outlying world into the great civilised community, into the modern City of God. . . .

7.4.4   W. W. READE ON THE RELIGIOUS CONQUESTS OF SCIENCE, 1872

. . . America is the happiest country in the world. There is not a man in the vast land which lies between the oceans, who, however humble his occupation may be, does not hope to make a fortune before he dies. The whole nation is possessed with the spirit which may be observed in Fleet Street and Cheapside; the boys sharp-eyed and curious, the men hastening eagerly along, even the women walking as if they had an object in view. There are in America no dull-eyed heavy-footed labourers, who slouch to and fro from their cottage to their work, from their work to the beer-house, without a higher hope in life than a sixpence from the squire when they open a gate. There are no girls of the milliner class who prefer being the mistresses of gentlemen to marrying men of their own station with a Cockney accent and red hands. The upper classes in America have not that exquisite refinement which exists in the highest circles of society in Europe. But if we take the whole people through and through, we find them the most civilised nation on the earth. They preserve in a degree hitherto without example the dignity of human nature unimpaired. Their nobleness of character results from prosperity; and their prosperity is due to the nature of their land. Those who are unable to earn a living in the east, have only to move towards the west. This then is the reason that the English race in America is more happy, more enlightened, and more thriving, than it is in the mother-land. Politically speaking, the emigrant gains nothing; he is as free in England as he is in America; but he leaves a land where labour is depreciated, and goes to a land where labour is in demand. That England may become as prosperous as America, it must be placed under American conditions; that is to say, food must be cheap, labour must be dear, emigration must be easy. It is not by universal suffrage, it is not by any act of parliament that these conditions can be created. It is Science alone which can Americanize England; it is Science alone which can ameliorate the condition of the human race.

When Man first wandered in the dark forest, he was Nature's serf; he offered tribute and prayer to the winds, and the lightning, and the rain, to the cave-lion, which seized his burrow for its lair, to the mammoth, which devoured his scanty crops. But as time passed on, he ventured to rebel; he made stone his servant; he discovered fire and vegetable poison; he domesticated iron; he slew the wild beasts or subdued them; he made them feed him and give him clothes. He became a chief surrounded by his slaves; the fire lay beside him with dull red eye and yellow tongue waiting his instructions to prepare his dinner, or to make him poison, or to go with him to the war, and fly on the houses of the enemy, hissing, roaring, and consuming all. The trees of the forest were his flock, he slaughtered them at his convenience; the earth brought forth at his command. He struck iron upon wood or stone and hewed out the fancies of his brain; he plucked shells, and flowers, and the bright red berries, and twined them in his hair; he cut the pebble to a sparkling gem, he made the dull clay a transparent stone. The river which once he had worshipped as a god, or which he had vainly attacked with sword and spear, he now conquered to his will. He made the winds grind his corn and carry him across the waters; he made the stars serve him as a guide. He obtained from salt and wood and sulphur a destroying force. He drew from fire, and water, the awful power which produces the volcano, and made it do the work of human hands. He made the sun paint his portraits, and gave the lightning a situation in the post-office.

Thus Man has taken into his service, and modified to his use, the animals, the plants, the earths and the stones, the waters and the winds, and the more complex forces of heat, electricity, sunlight, magnetism, with chemical powers of many kinds. By means of his inventions and discoveries, by means of the arts and trades, and by means of the industry resulting from them, he has raised himself from the condition of a serf to the condition of a lord. His triumph, indeed, is incomplete; his kingdom is not yet come. The Prince of Darkness is still triumphant in many regions of the world; epidemics still rage, death is yet victorious. But the God of light, the Spirit of Knowledge, the Divine Intellect is gradually spreading over the planet and upwards to the skies. The beautiful legend will yet come true; Ormuzd will vanquish Ahriman; Satan will be overcome; Virtue will descend from heaven, surrounded by her angels, and reign over the hearts of men. Earth, which is now a purgatory, will be made a paradise, not by idle prayers and supplications, but by the efforts of man himself, and by means of mental achievements analogous to those which have raised him to his present state. Those inventions and discoveries which have made him, by the grace of God, king of the animals, lord of the elements, and sovereign of steam and electricity, were all of them founded on experiment and observation. We can conquer nature only by obeying her laws, and in order to obey her laws we must first learn what they are. When we have ascertained, by means of Science, the method of nature's operations, we shall be able to take her place and to perform them for ourselves. When we understand the laws which regulate the complex phenomena of life, we shall be able to predict the future as we are already able to predict comets and eclipses and the planetary movements.

Three inventions which perhaps may be long delayed, but which possibly are near at hand, will give to this overcrowded island the prosperous conditions of the United States. The first is the discovery of a motive force which will take the place of steam, with its cumbrous fuel of oil or coal; secondly, the invention of aerial locomotion which will transport labour at a trifling cost of money and of time to any part of the planet, and which, by annihilating distance, will speedily extinguish national distinctions; and thirdly, the manufacture of flesh and flour from the elements by a chemical process in the laboratory, similar to that which is now performed within the bodies of the animals and plants. Food will then be manufactured in unlimited quantities at a trifling expense; and our enlightened posterity will look back upon us who eat oxen and sheep just as we look back upon cannibals. Hunger and starvation will then be unknown, and the best part of the human life will no longer be wasted in the tedious process of cultivating the fields. Population will mightily increase, and the earth will be a garden. Governments will be conducted with the quietude and regularity of club committees. The interest which is now felt in politics will be transferred to science; the latest news from the laboratory of the chemist, or the observatory of the astronomer, or the experimenting room of the biologist will be eagerly discussed. Poetry and the fine arts will take that place in the heart which religion now holds. Luxuries will be cheapened and made common to all; none will be rich, and none poor. Not only will Man subdue the forces of evil that are without; he will also subdue those that are within. He will repress the base instincts and propensities which he has inherited from the animals below; he will obey the laws that are written on his heart; he will worship the divinity within him. As our conscience forbids us to commit actions which the conscience of the savage allows, so the moral sense of our successors will stigmatize as crimes those offences against the intellect which are sanctioned by ourselves. Idleness and stupidity will be regarded with abhorrence. Women will become the companions of men, and the tutors of their children. The whole world will be united by the same sentiment which united the primeval clan, and which made its members think, feel, and act as one. Men will look upon this star as their fatherland; its progress will be their ambition; the gratitude of others their reward. These bodies which now we wear, belong to the lower animals; our minds have already outgrown them; already we look upon them with contempt. A time will come when Science will transform them by means which we cannot conjecture, and which, even if explained to us, we could not now understand, just as the savage cannot understand electricity, magnetism, steam. Disease will be extirpated; the causes of decay will be removed; immortality will be invented. And then, the earth being small, mankind will migrate into space, and will cross the airless Saharas which separate planet from planet, and sun from sun. The earth will become a Holy Land which will be visited by pilgrims from all the quarters of the universe. Finally, men will master the forces of nature; they will become themselves architects of systems, manufacturers of worlds. Man then will be perfect; he will then be a creator; he will therefore be what the vulgar worship as a god. But even then, he will in reality be no nearer than he is at present to the First Cause, the Inscrutable Mystery, the GOD. . . .

. . . We teach that there is a God, but not a God of the anthropoid variety, not a God who is gratified by compliments in prose and verse, and whose attributes can be catalogued by theologians. God is so great that he cannot be defined by us. God is so great that he does not deign to have personal relations with us human atoms that are called men. Those who desire to worship their Creator must worship him through mankind. Such it is plain is the scheme of Nature. We are placed under secondary laws, and these we must obey. To develop to the utmost of our genius and our love, that is the only true religion. To do that which deserves to be written, to write that which deserves to be read, to tend the sick, to comfort the sorrowful, to animate the weary, to keep the temple of the body pure, to cherish the divinity within us, to be faithful to the intellect, to educate those powers which have been entrusted to our charge and to employ them in the service of humanity, that is all that we can do. Then our elements shall be dispersed and all is at an end. All is at an end for the unit, all is at an end for the atom, all is at an end for the speck of flesh and blood with the little spark of instinct which it calls its mind, but all is not at an end for the actual Man, the true Being, the glorious One. We teach that the soul is immortal; we teach that there is a future life; we teach that there is a Heaven in the ages far away; but not for us single corpuscles, not for us dots of animated jelly, but for the One of whom we are the elements, and who, though we perish, never dies, but grows from period to period and by the united efforts of single molecules called men, or of those cell-groups called nations is raised towards the Divine power which he will finally attain. Our religion therefore is Virtue, our Hope is placed in the happiness of our posterity; our Faith is the Perfectibility of Man. A day will come when the European God of the nineteenth century will be classed with the gods of Olympus and the Nile; when surplices and sacramental plate will be exhibited in museums; when nurses will relate to children the legends of the Christian mythology as they now tell them fairy tales. A day will come when the current belief in property after death (for is not existence property, and the dearest property of all?) will be accounted a strange and selfish idea, just as we smile at the savage chief who believes that his gentility will be continued in the world beneath the ground, and that he will there be attended by his concubines and slaves. A day will come when mankind will be as the Family of the Forest, which lived faithfully within itself according to the golden rule in order that it might not die. But Love not Fear will unite the human race. The world will become a heavenly Commune to which men will bring the inmost treasures of their hearts, in which they will reserve for themselves not even a hope, not even the shadow of a joy, but will give up all for all mankind. With one faith, with one desire they will labour together in the Sacred Cause – the extinction of disease, the extinction of sin, the perfection of genius, the perfection of love, the invention of immortality, the exploration of the infinite, the conquest of creation.

You blessed ones who shall inherit that future age of which we can only dream; you pure and radiant beings who shall succeed us on the earth; when you turn back your eyes on us poor savages, grubbing in the ground for our daily bread, eating flesh and blood, dwelling in vile bodies which degrade us every day to a level with the beasts, tortured by pains, and by animal propensities, buried in gloomy superstitions, ignorant of Nature which yet holds us in her bonds; when you read of us in books, when you think of what we are, and compare us with yourselves, remember that it is to us you owe the foundation of your happiness and grandeur, to us who now in our libraries and laboratories and star-towers and dissecting-rooms and workshops are preparing the materials of the human growth. . . . The supreme and mysterious Power by whom the universe has been created, and by whom it has been appointed to run its course under fixed and invariable law; that awful One to whom it is profanity to pray, of whom it is idle and irreverent to argue and debate, of whom we should never presume to think save with humility and awe; that Unknown God has ordained that mankind should be elevated by misfortune, and that happiness should grow out of misery and pain. I give to universal history a strange but true title – *The Martyrdom of Man*. In each generation the human race has been tortured that their children might profit by their woes. Our own prosperity is founded on the agonies of the past. Is it therefore unjust that we also should suffer for the benefit of those who are to come? Famine, pestilence, and war are no longer essential for the advancement of the human race. But a season of mental anguish is at hand, and through this we must pass in order that our posterity may rise. The soul must be sacrificed; the hope in immortality must die. A sweet and charming illusion must be taken from the human race, as youth and beauty vanish never to return.

8

BEYOND CHRISTENDOM

8.1 RELIGIOUS HISTORY AS APOLOGETICS

THE attitude of Victorian Christians to other religions and their adherents was an unstable mixture of curiosity, missionary zeal, and defensiveness. Generally defensiveness got the upper hand, even when the other interests remained strong. The reason was quite simple. False faiths and infidel enthusiasms had held sway over the great mass of humankind since the dawn of recorded history. Christianity, on a global and historical scale, was a minority creed. Where was the divine purpose in concealing the true light from most of the people most of the time, then, for their unbelief, consigning them eternally to outer darkness? Was Christianity not a religion like the rest, concocted by human imagination, only rather less successful than some in securing devotees? In answering such questions Victorian believers developed various apologetic strategies. Three of these appeared in books by the Scottish Free Church philosopher James McCosh (1811–1894), the Broad Church theologian F. D. Maurice (1.2.3), and the liberal Anglican anthropologist John Lubbock (7.3.3). In *The Method of the Divine Government, Physical and Moral*, which passed through twelve editions, McCosh explained religious history, by physical analogy, as the product of attractive and repulsive 'principles' inherent within sinful human nature (**8.1.1.**). Maurice, in his Boyle Lectures, *The Religions of the World*, granted no such power to mere human corruption. Islam, Hinduism, Buddhism, and even modern infidelity, were to him divinely appointed 'witnesses', both for the Gospel and against Christian error and indifference (**8.1.2**). In Lubbock's *The Origin of Civilization and the Primitive Condition of Man*, however, neither God nor man explained religious history. Evolution was now in charge. History revealed a natural progress of 'more correct ideas and nobler creeds', linked to the growth of science. 'True religion is, without Science, impossible', Lubbock declared. The corollary that science did not lead to atheism was obviously the apologetic pay-off. Whereas religious evolution was indicated by a reduction in the number of deities to approximately one, further progress in the same direction was not to be expected. On the contrary, Lubbock made 'atheism' the lowest stage of religious development (**8.1.3**).

8.1.1   J. McCOSH ON THE RELIGIOUS HISTORY
OF MANKIND, 1850

Our ordinary philosophic historians have utterly failed in their attempts to explain the world's history so far as it relates to religion or superstition, because they have not taken into account those principles in man's nature which now draw him towards a supernatural power, and again drive him away from it. . . .

These two, the attracting and repelling principle, do not, as might be supposed, nullify or destroy each other, but produce motion and powerful action like the attractions and repulsions of electricity. According as the one or other prevails, according as there is excess or defect, there is motion towards God, or motion away from God – there is belief, or there is scepticism. Some of the most extraordinary events in the history of individuals, of families, and of nations, are to be explained by these agencies. They have been the real moving power in the production of events in which ordinary observers have discovered other and more obvious and superficial causes, just as electricity is now acknowledged to be the cause of changes in physical phenomena, which were before referred to more palpable agents, such as heat and light. The sudden changes in men's religious opinions, and the religious movements which form so curious and melancholy a chapter in the world's history, can be understood only by the help of these deeper principles, just as the changes in the weather, the currents of the atmosphere, and the gathering and scattering of the clouds, can be explained only by the attractions and repulsions of polar forces. These deeper principles of our nature are capable of producing results of the most appalling magnitude. The winds of feeling, the waves of passion, and the fires of lust, the old and recognised elements, do not produce greater effects upon each other, and upon the more earthly ingredients in man's nature, than does the more latent principle that derives its force from the repelling and attractive power of conscience. No human arithmetic can estimate the velocity with which this current, positive or negative, will rush in to fill the vacuum which may have been produced in the heart of an individual man, when the worldly hopes which filled it have been torn away, or in the heart of a nation when it is without a creed, or when its creed has become obsolete, and is felt to be indefensible. The lurid lightning does not produce a more rapid effect in the physical world, nor does the accompanying thunder raise a deeper feeling of awe, than the religious impulse has done at some periods, and the hatred of religion has done at other periods in the history of the world.

It is thus that we are to account for the powerful impulse which religion, or the hatred of religion, has given to the minds of individual men and of nations. Hence the frenzy – hence the bigotry of infidelity. Hence, too, the frenzy – hence the bigotry of superstition. Hence we find men now mad upon their idols, and now mad against them – now honouring, and forthwith beating them. . . .

Such phenomena as these, whether connected with superstition or infidelity, have baffled all ordinary historical philosophers, or philosophic historians, to account for them. After we have read all that they can say about human madness and human passion – about pride, vanity, and malice – we feel as if they had merely explained some of the accompaniments of these great movements, and shown why the stream took a particular direction, but without at all exploring the stream itself, which leaps up from one of the profoundest depths of the human heart, and needs from the other powers and propensities only a channel to flow in.

The more popular of the false religions which have spread themselves over the world – the superstitions of the East, of ancient Greece and Rome, of Mohammed, and of the corrupt Christian Church – have all given the most ample scope to these impulses in our nature, and to some of the worst passions in the human heart besides. What a strange compound, yet banded firmly together, of licentiousness and yet of rigidity, of loose morality and of unbending ritual! No system of superstition will be extensively adopted unless it provides for these opposing wants of our nature, unless it give open or secret license to wildness, and allow room or find employment for remorse. The two peculiar features of man's existing condition are evil passions and an evil conscience. No superstition can become popular which does not provide or admit something to meet the craving demands of both. Hence the grossness of Paganism, with its horrid and cruel sacrifices: hence the licentiousness and the tortures practised around the same Indian temple. . . . Hence the love of war, with the stringent formularies that distinguished Mohammedanism in the days of its youth and vigour. The apostate Christian Church seems to unite in itself all the elements found separately in every other supersitition, and to be Catholic and all-embracing, not in its truths, but in its errors. . . . In the bosom of that Church there have been embraced at the same instant unbridled scepticism and profligacy, grasping ambition and the most profound deceit, with the asceticism of the anchorite, and the blind faith of the devotee. These things may seem inconsistent, and so they are; but their inconsistency is to be found in human nature, the character of which they exhibit, as the unwholesome food which the diseased stomach demands points out the nature and craving power of the malady with which it is afflicted.

When a religion waxes old in a country – when the circumstances which at first favoured its formation or introduction have changed – when in an age of reason it is tried and found unreasonable – when in an age of learning it is discovered to be the product of the grossest ignorance – when in an age of levity it is felt to be too stern, – then the infidel spirit takes courage, and with a zeal in which there is a strange mixture of scowling revenge and light-hearted wantonness, of deep-set hatred and laughing levity, it proceeds to level all existing temples and altars, and erects no others in their room. . . .

When Popery was waning in France, in the days of Louis XIV., when the lives of the clergy brought reproach on religion, and its superstitions could not stand the sifting light of modern science – then infidelity, long lurking, as it ever lurks, in the midst of superstition, found vent in those sneers which are always the appropriate and true expression of scepticism, expressive at once of its wantonness and deep malignity. In the present day, the superstitions of India, in which theology and cosmogony are so closely interwined that they must stand or fall together, are being undermined among the higher classes by the advancement of European science. One look through the telescope dispels all the illusions of the Brahminical faith, and blots out of existence as many myriads of gods as it brings into view myriads of stars reflecting the glory of the one living and true God. The result is a widening scepticism among the Hindoos of the higher castes.

But no nation can be long without a religion. There are times in every man's history when he feels that he needs to be strengthened by faith in a higher power; and mankind generally will never consent systematically to cut the last tie that connects them with heaven. The attracting principle *must* operate; and being a universally active and powerful principle, it insists on a creed and religious worship as its appropriate expression.

Human sagacity cannot predict what building may be raised on the ruins of ancient superstitions, among the half-civilized nations of the East; but it can certainly foretell, proceeding on the known principles of the human mind, that when infidelity has advanced a little farther with its work of devastation, nature, which abhors a vacuum, will demand something positive to fill up the void. If scriptural truth does not pre-occupy the ground, it may be feared that the superstition which grew so vigorously on the debris of fallen empires in the middle ages of Europe, and which has been transplanted into the rich but wild soil of South America, and of not a few of the British colonies, may yet find its seeds taking congenial root in the heaving plains on which the superstitions of India and China are soon to decay. . . .

8.1.2   F. D. MAURICE ON THE RELIGIONS OF THE WORLD AND THEIR RELATIONS TO CHRISTIANITY, 1847

. . . The aspect of Christianity in the first ages . . . is that of a youthful, growing, victorious doctrine; its roots laid in the depths; its branches spreading over the earth, and reaching to heaven. But then came Mahometanism, utterly exterminating that Persian doctrine with which the Christian teachers had so unsuccesfully fought; bringing Egypt, [a] great part of Asia, and a section of Europe, under its yoke. . . . This faith . . . had conquered much from the Gospel, and had scarcely, through twelve centuries, yielded to any permanent impression from it. The latter assertion is almost as true of Hindooism, in spite of the establishment of a Christian empire in the East. Buddhism still holds a third of the globe in almost undisturbed possession. Now a person comparing these two sets of facts will be very likely to say, 'Supposing your answers to the philosophical objectors, who maintain that Christianity is a decaying, nearly obsolete, creed be ever so relevant and strong, yet what are they when weighed against this startling confirmation of their statements? Must not that faith have had a fitness for other ages, an unfitness for ours, which during six centuries accomplished so much, which now seems to be accomplishing almost nothing; which could then encounter the wisdom and power of those nations that we still recognize as having been the wisest and mightiest in the world, which now fails in a conflict with the ignorant and incoherent worshippers of Buddha. And if you escape by pleading that the human professors of this doctrine are less sincere and energetic than they were, what is this but saying that it depends on human energy; that it is, in fact, a human system, strong whilst those who hold it are strong — sure to wither when their zeal withers?' Such an objection as this cannot be evaded, In considering it, I shall be led to examine . . . different steps, . . . beginning with the question, How did Christianity address itself to the systems with which, in its infancy, it came into collision?

I am forced to use the word *Christianity*, for many purposes it is a convenient one. But I must remind you, that it was not a word which was familiar to the Apostles, or to those who succeeded them in the first ages. We are not told that they went forth preaching Christianity. The writer of the Acts of the Apostles says that they preached the 'Kingdom of God,' or 'the Gospel of God,' or 'Christ,' or 'the Gospel of Christ.' To expound these words fully, would be to expound the New Testament. But this meaning lies upon the surface of them: the Apostles came witnessing of a Lord and King; the Lord and King of men. The proclamation of the Crucified Man, as the Son of God, was their Gospel, or good tidings. In that character men were invited to receive Him. . . .

A redemption of man, a redemption of all that had been lost or disorderly in creation, was equally assumed in the preaching to Greeks, Romans, and Goths:— It was set forth as an accomplished fact; as laying the only right and reasonable ground-work for human life; as that of which the Church, by its very existence, bore testimony. And it was signified in the word *Redemption*, that the partakers of it were not brought into some novel or unnatural state, but into that for which they were created, that which was implied in their human constitution.

If this was the nature of Christian preaching and its success, we may understand where it was likely to encounter the greatest obstructions. The Persians believed in two rulers of the world, one good, one evil. . . . The two powers were regarded as having each a right over man, his flesh and his external circumstances being especially the property of the dark Spirit. What mighty evidences there seemed to be in favour of this hypothesis! How all history, from its beginning onwards, seemed to vouch for it! What obstinacy in the old forms of evil; what new floods of it were continually pouring in as from a perennial source! In the third or fourth centuries, when the Roman empire was tottering to its fall, under the weight of its own wickedness, the proofs of Ahriman's sovereignty were surely not less than they had been before. Had the Gospel of Christ permanently altered this state of things? . . .

We have good evidence that no question was so profoundly agitating to men's minds in the first ages as this. The Magians . . . succeeded in re-establishing their old doctrine, and with it the old Persian empire. But the belief in rival powers of good and evil, to the latter of which the origin of all visible things might be ascribed, spread far beyond its limits. It incorporated itself with all the religious and philosophical views of the age; it penetrated deeply into the Church of Christ, was the great characteristic of its most prevalent heresy, and mingled, in different forms and measures, with every other. Of all tests of the reality of Christian humility and faith, the greatest seems to have been the power of practically meeting this temptation, of resisting the conclusion that a perfectly good being could not be the author and ruler of the universe; that man could not really be a holy and redeemed creature; that the material world, at all events, must be given up as an evil thing. . . .

But soon a voice was heard, speaking these words in the ears of both Persians and Christians: 'This earth is the possession of the One Lord, the God of Abraham; He claimed it as His when He called out Abraham, and promised that he and his seed should possess a portion of it. The earth is still His. Those who say he has an equal or rival are liars.' This was Mahomet's language. His sword was ready to make it good. The Magian faith, the Persian empire, fell to pieces before it. Of all the Mahometan enterprizes this was the most startling, and that by which its other triumphs may be best understood. We complain of Mahometanism for its hard outward character; for the materialism of its acts and its rewards. But see how well suited it was on this very ground to meet precisely that evil tendency to which men's minds had yielded. The denial of God's dominion over the actual world; the notion, that though He might have a reign somewhere else, it was not here; this unbelief was destroying all ordinary morality, all simple trust in a Father, was introducing atheism, or else devil-worship, among those who pretended to worship the Holy God, and utterly to renounce his enemies. No mere spiritualism, if it had been ever so fine and true, could have broken this spell. Palpable proofs were wanted that the kingdoms of this very earth were subject to an Unseen and Absolute Sovereign. And the Mahometan conquests, though so mighty a testimony against Christians, were not a testimony against the Gospel, but for it; a testimony to one necessary, forgotten portion of it; a proof that, if the Church of Christ forgets its own proper position, God can raise up the strangest instruments to do his work. . . .

If men could . . . forget that the outward world was redeemed to be a part of God's kingdom, and if their inward life suffered terribly from this forgetfulness, it became manifest in the course of ages that they could quite as easily lose sight of that which was specially and emphatically the Christian doctrine while they seemed to admit and prize its material results. Since the active energies of men's minds have been awakened, since we have felt that it is our vocation to subdue the earth, to trade, colonize and conquer, this has become the characteristic temptation of all Christian nations, perhaps I may say, especially the characteristic one of our own; for it lies close to some of our highest virtues, to our business-like habits, our love of action, our impatience of what does not look real and practical.

Englishmen in the last century seem for the most part to have persuaded themselves that man is not a mysterious being; that the Gospel does not address him as such; that its main use is to check disorders which the law cannot entirely redress, to make servants respectful to their masters, to keep the humble classes from interfering with the privileges of their superiors; that the kingdom of heaven is a place where certain rewards are bestowed hereafter for decency of conduct here. Those who refused to act upon these maxims, and earnestly devoted themselves to a spiritual life, fancied, not unnaturally, that the desires of which they were conscious did not properly belong to human beings; that all men ought to have them, but that in fact scarcely any had them; that the unseen world is for the select few, not for mankind.

But to Englishmen in the eighteenth century, the continent of India revealed itself with its treasures and its wonders. Its material treasures might help to strengthen the worldly appetite which went in search of them; but its wonders, well considered, might surely have supplied the counteraction, might have proved that men everywhere need a kingdom of heaven as well as a kingdom on earth. The Hindoo lives in a world of thought. He is certain that divine knowledge, the knowledge of Brahm, is the highest end of life. He cannot be satisfied till he is united with the

Divinity. The divine man, he says, must be a twice-born man, must be raised out of his natural condition, must not lose himself in communion with outward things. Indications of this faith are forced upon the observation of every Englishman in India; he may explain them as he will but he cannot deny them. Do they not say to him just perhaps when the associations of his childhood are about to be cast off altogether – 'What you used to hear from your nurse and your mother may after all mean something. You were told that you were a twice-born man, a member of Christ, a Child of God, an inheritor of the kingdom of heaven. May there not be treasures nearer to you than these Indian treasures, treasures which are yours by the clearest title, and yet which you have never reduced into possession? If you could impart them to these subjects of ours, might you not do that for them which the best legislation cannot do? Will you not at least ask whether the Hindoo is wrong in thinking that man is made for something else than to buy and sell, to eat, drink, and die; and whether if he is right, there is any escape from his restless self-torture, except in the calm faith that it is our Father's good pleasure to give us that kingdom which the idolater would at the price of any anguish wring from the objects of his worship?'

Here then is a voice coming from the most opposite quarter to that whence the other was brought to us – a voice of the most different kind. Yet it comes as a witness not against but for that which we have been taught to believe, a witness not for but against our indifference to it. So that these two voices compared together, may, I think, help to answer the question we have been examining, whether Christianity be not dependent for its evidence and its success upon the faith of those who promulgate it. There cannot be a truer assertion than that this is the criterion of a human system; there cannot be a more undoubted prophecy than that the Gospel, if it be a human system, must perish, as all systems are perishing. On the other hand, if it were anything more than this, we should expect that the weakness, heartlessness, cowardice, baseness of its advocates would themselves be in some way converted into demonstrations of its truth; that when men were holding their peace respecting it, the stones would cry out. Have we not found this to be the fact? You say that Islamism has not fallen before the Cross. No, but Islamism has become one of God's witnesses for the Cross when those who protended to bear it had really changed it for another standard. You say that Hindooism stands undisturbed by the presence of a triumphant Christian nation. Yes, for Hindooism has been wanted to teach this nation what it is very nearly forgetting itself, very nearly forcing others to forget, that Christianity is not a dream or a lie. . . .

. . . To look out upon the world, and see a valley covered with the dry bones of different systems, to hear them clashing together as if they might be joined to each other, and then to be told, 'It is all in vain; there is no voice which can bid the breath enter into these bones; perhaps it might have come from Christians, but it does not; they too occupy part of this valley; they have become dry bones, very dry indeed; clashing always, never uniting'—such an announcement as this, however softened by thoughts of the past or the future, must be a very mournful one. But that third great religion of the world comes to turn the current of these thoughts, to check this despondency. We are but ill provided with a theory, say the Buddhists; we have tried many, and little fruit has come of them. But this we are assured of: you Christians may not have heard it, but there is a quickening, life-giving Spirit, which is meant for humanity; which all may possess together; which alone can bring a universe out of chaos, unity out of division. Wonderful testimony to be borne from the ends of the earth, from such a medley of strange people, so different in their thoughts, so incoherent in their utterances! Is not the report of it like the sound of that rushing mighty wind, which was heard on the day of Pentecost, not indeed itself the promised Power, but the type and herald of it? Does it not say that we too might have cloven tongues to declare, in different tones and measures, according to the different thoughts, habits, and apprehensions of men, the same wonderful works of God, and that these tongues might be of fire if only the living inspiration were confessed and obeyed by us? Does it not bid us remember that with this Spirit of peace and love and a sound mind we have been sealed; that the Name of the Father, and the Son, and the Holy Ghost, which was to be the blessing, the permanent blessing, of Pentecost, has been bestowed upon us; that we hold this Spirit, not as the Buddhists dream, by our own right, – to be therefore the witness of our independence, flowing from no source whence it may be replenished – but as the very bond of our dependence and childhood, as the Spirit of adoption, whereby we are to cry, Abba, Father; as the power whereby we can ask and receive a new life day by day. If so, there is cause enough for humiliation in all of us, for despair in none. The broken limbs of the world may yet be united, if the broken limbs of the Church be united first. But are these the limbs of a great system, or of a living body? . . . If the Scripture language is true, if the Church is a body constituted in a Head, the Buddhist proclamation carries with it the reproof and consolation which we require. There is a Power which can bring us not into some imaginary condition of excellence, but precisely into our true condition: which can remove the individual interests, selfish feelings, national antipathies, narrow apprehensions that all our efforts to produce unity have only evoked and strengthened; which can bring down our high notions and conceits of what we are and what we do; which can enable us to be God's servants and to do His work in the world He has redeemed. Having confessed our rebellion against this Spirit, and sought the renewal of it in us and in the whole Church, we shall no longer say, as we have been tempted to say, 'The power of evil is supreme over the universe; only there has been a special deliverance vouchsafed to us;' we shall, from our hearts, abjure such blasphemous Manicheism; we shall say boldly to all people among whom we go, 'The devil is not your master, he has no right to your worship: the God, in whom is light and no darkness at all, has claimed you and the whole creation for his own. His marvellous light is as much for you as for us. We only enjoy it upon the condition of renouncing all exclusive claim to it, upon the condition of bidding you enter into it.'

Buddhism, then, like Hindooism and Mahometanism, has its lesson for us. We are debtors to all these in a double sense. Nor, I think, is it otherwise with . . . modern infidels. . . . Our obligations to them are not slight if they have been sent to break down a low grovelling notion we had formed of our own position and work; if they have been employed to convince us that human systems must indeed perish, one and all, that what survives must be something of a much higher derivation, of a more permanent character. We owe them the deepest gratitude if they have led us to ask ourselves whether there is any faith, and what kind of faith it is, which must belong, not to races or nations, but to mankind; still more, if they have forced us to the conclusion, that the real test, whether there be such a faith, and whether it has been made known to us, must be action, not argument; that if it exist, it must shew that it exists; that if it have power, it must put forth its power. So, in this nineteenth century, the opponents of Christianity will return to the maxim which the wisest of them announced in the first: 'If this be of men, it will come to nought; if it be of God, we cannot overthrow it.' . . .

8.1.3 J. LUBBOCK ON THE EVOLUTION OF RELIGION, 1870

The religion of savages, though of peculiar interest, is in many respects perhaps the most difficult part of my whole subject. I shall endeavour to avoid, as far as possible, anything which might justly give pain to any of my readers. Many ideas, however, which have been, or are, prevalent on religious matters, are so utterly opposed to our own that it is impossible to discuss the subject without mentioning some things which are very repugnant to our feelings. Yet, while savages show us a melancholy spectacle of gross superstitions and ferocious forms of worship, the religious mind cannot but feel a peculiar satisfaction in tracing up the gradual evolution of more correct ideas and of nobler creeds.

As a general rule savages do not set themselves to think out such questions, but adopt the ideas which suggest themselves most naturally; so that, as I shall attempt to show, races in a similar state of mental development, however distinct their origin may be, and however distant the regions they inhabit, have very similar religious conceptions. Most of those who have endeavoured to account for the various superstitions of savage races have done so by crediting them with a much more elaborate system of ideas than they in reality possess. . . . Explanations, however, such as these are radically wrong.

I have felt doubtful whether this chapter should not be entitled 'the superstitions' rather than 'the religion' of savages; but have preferred the latter partly because many of the superstitious ideas pass gradually into nobler conceptions, and partly from a reluctance to condemn any honest belief, however absurd and imperfect it may be. It must, however, be admitted that religion, as understood by the lower savage races, differs essentially from ours; nay, it is not only different, but even opposite. Thus, it is an affair of this world, not of the next. Their deities are evil, not good; they may be forced into compliance with the wishes of man; they generally require bloody, and often rejoice in human, sacrifices; they are mortal, not immortal; a part, not the authors, of nature; they are to be approached by dances rather than by prayers; and often approve what we call vice, rather than what we esteem as virtue.

In fact, the so-called religion of the lower races bears somewhat the same relation to religion in its higher forms that astrology does to astronomy, or alchemy to chemistry. Astronomy is derived from astrology, yet their spirit is in entire opposition; and we shall find the same difference between the religions of backward and of advanced races. We regard the Deity as good; they look upon him as evil; we submit ourselves to him; they endeavour to obtain the control of him; we feel the necessity of accounting for the blessings by which we are surrounded; they think the blessings come of themselves, and attribute all evil to the interference of malignant beings.

These characteristics are not exceptional and rare. On the contrary, . . . though the religions of the lower races have received different names, they agree in their general characteristics, and are but phases of one sequence, having the same origin, and passing through similar, if not identical, stages. This will explain the great similarities which occur in the most distinct and distant races, which have puzzled many ethnologists, and in some cases led them to utterly untenable theories. . . .

Although, however, we find the most remarkable coincidences between the religions of distinct races, one of the peculiar difficulties in the study of religion arises from the fact that, while each nation has generally but one language, we may almost say that in religious matters, *quot homines tot sententiæ*; no two men having exactly the same views, however much they may wish to agree.

Many travellers have pointed out this difficulty. . . . Many also of those to whom we are indebted for information on the subject, fully expecting to find among savages ideas like our own, obscured only by errors and superstition, have put leading questions, and thus got misleading answers. We constantly hear, for instance, of a Devil; but, in fact, no spiritual being in the mythology of any savage races possesses the characteristics of Satan. Again, it is often very difficult to determine in what sense an object is worshipped. A mountain, or a river, for instance, may be held sacred either as an actual Deity or merely as his abode; and in the same way a statue may be actually worshipped as a god, or merely reverenced as representing the Divinity.

To a great extent, moreover, these difficulties arise from the fact that when man, either by natural progress or the influence of a more advanced race, rises to the conception of a higher religion, he still retains his old beliefs, which long linger on, side by side with, and yet in utter opposition to, the higher creed. The new and more powerful Spirit is an addition to the old Pantheon, and diminishes the importance of the older deities; gradually the worship of the latter sinks in the social scale, and becomes confined to the ignorant and the young. Thus, a belief in witchcraft still flourishes among our agricultural labourers and the lowest classes in our great cities; and the deities of our ancestors survive in the nursery tales of our children. We must therefore expect to find in each race traces – nay, more than traces – of lower religions. Even if this were not the case, we should still be met by the difficulty that there are few really sharp lines in religious systems. It might be supposed that a belief in the immortality of the soul, or in the efficacy of sacrifices, would give us good lines of division; but it is not so: these, and many other ideas, rise gradually, and even often appear at first in a form very different from that which they ultimately assume.

Hitherto it has been usual to classify religions according to the nature of the object worshipped: Fetichism, for instance, being the worship of inanimate objects, Sabæism that of the heavenly bodies. The true test, however, seems to me to be the estimate in which the Deity is held. The first great stages in religious thought may, I think, be regarded as—

Atheism; understanding by this term not a denial of the existence of a Deity, but an absence of any definite ideas on the subject.

Fetichism; the stage in which man supposes he can force the deities to comply with his desires.

Nature-worship or *Totemism*; in which natural objects, trees, lakes, stones, animals, &c., are worshipped.

Shamanism; in which the superior deities are far more powerful than man, and of a different nature. Their place of abode also is far away, and accessible only to Shamans.

Idolatry, or *Anthropomorphism*; in which the gods take still more completely the nature of men, being, however, more powerful. They are still amenable to persuasion; they are a part of nature, and not creators. They are represented by images or idols.

In the next stage the Diety is regarded as the author, not merely a part of nature. He becomes for the first time a really supernatural being.

The last stage . . . is that in which morality is associated with religion. . . .

The lower savages regard their deities as scarcely more powerful than themselves; they are evil, not good; they are to be propitiated by sacrifices, not by prayer; they are not creators; they are neither omniscient nor all-powerful; they neither reward the good nor punish the evil; far from conferring immortality on man, they are not even in all cases immortal themselves.

Where the material elements of civilisation developed themselves without any corresponding increase of knowledge, as, for instance, in Mexico and Peru, a more correct idea of Divine power, without any corresponding enlightenment as to the Divine nature, led to a religion of terror, which finally became a terrible scourge of humanity.

Gradually, however, an increased acquaintance with the laws of nature enlarged the mind of man. He first supposed that the Deity fashioned the earth, raising it out of the water, and preparing it as a dwelling-place for man, and subsequently realised the idea that land and water were alike created by Divine power. After regarding spirits as altogether evil, he rose to a belief in good as well as in evil deities, and, gradually subordinating the latter to the former, worshipped the good spirits alone as gods, the evil sinking to the level of demons. From believing only in ghosts, he came gradually to the recognition of the soul: at length uniting this belief with that in a beneficent and just Being, he connected Morality with Religion; a step the importance of which it is scarcely possible to over-estimate.

Thus we see that as men rise in civilisation, their religion rises with them. The Australians dimly imagine a being, spiteful, malevolent, but weak, and dangerous only in the dark. The Negro's deity is more powerful, but not less hateful – invisible, indeed, but subject to pain, mortal like himself, and liable to be made the slave of man by enchantment. The deities of the South Sea Islanders are, some good, some evil; but, on the whole, more is to be feared from the latter than to be hoped from the former. They fashioned the land, but are not truly creators, for earth and water existed before them. They do not punish the evil, nor reward the good. They watch over the affairs of men; but if, on the one hand, witchcraft has no power over them, neither, on the other, can prayer influence them – they require to share the crops or the booty of their worshippers.

It appears, then, that every increase in science – that is, in positive and ascertained knowledge – brings with it an elevation of religion. Nor is this progress confined to the lower races. Even within the last century, science has purified the religion of Western Europe by rooting out the dark belief in witchcraft, which led to thousands of executions, and hung like a black pall over the Christianity of the middle ages.

The immense service which Science has thus rendered to the cause of Religion and of Humanity, has not hitherto received the recognition which it deserves. Science is still regarded by many excellent, but narrow-minded, persons as hostile to religious truth, while in fact she is only opposed to religious error. No doubt her influence has always been exercised in opposition to those who present contradictory assertions under the excuse of mystery, as well as to all but the highest conceptions of Divine power. The time, however, is approaching when it will be generally perceived that, so far from Science being opposed to Religion, true Religion is, without Science, impossible; and if we consider the various aspects of Christianity as understood by different nations, we can hardly fail to see that the dignity, and therefore the truth, of their religious beliefs, is in direct relation to their knowledge of Science and of the great physical laws by which our universe is governed.

8.2 JUDAISM IN ENGLAND AND ITS FOES

Exotic faiths from round the world, wherever the Union Jack was planted, posed a mighty challenge to Victorians who believed that Christianity would one day be accepted universally as the only true religion. But at home there was also a mighty challenge, in their very midst; and it is a testimony both to the insularity of this religion and to the imperial vision of the churches that it was so neglected. Judaism, originally a national faith, had been transplanted into Britain over several centuries from the Diaspora on the Continent. With few notable exceptions (the Rothschild family being one), the immigrants had perpetuated their traditions in closed communities, outside the mainstream of British culture. But in the Victorian era modernization and assimilation set in. One of the first signs of this was a religious split. In 1836 some of the members of the Spanish and Portuguese congregation in London addressed their elders with a memorandum, urging revision of the liturgy, the use of an organ in public worship, and changes in the observance of holy days. After these suggestions were rejected, the members gave notice of their secession from the Spanish and Portuguese synagogue to found the first Reform Synagogue in Britain, the 'West London Synagogue of British Jews'. Although their intention was 'to arrest, and prevent *secession* from Judaism', the traditionalist element were appalled. When the new congregation published its revised forms of prayer, the

Chief Rabbi and other authorities issued a formal condemnation that, even in English translation, manages to convey the intensity and florid style of the Hebrew original (**8.2.1**). It is remarkable that thirty years later, when the Revd Davies attended in turn the worship of an East End Orthodox congregation and the service of the West London Synagogue in Portman Square, he should have commented on just the sort of differences that had led to the original split (**8.2.2**). Judaism was not, however, completely ignored by the Christian Establishment, even though its peculiar challenge as an ancient national faith may have been underestimated. Jews, as non-Christian citizens of a Christian state, remained subject to a single civil disability: they could not be seated in Parliament. Whig attempts to amend the parliamentary oath, which contained the words 'on the true faith of a Christian', were defeated time and again in the House of Lords. The Tory arguments were well represented by Lord Chelmsford (1794–1878), the Lord Chancellor, and his Conservative opponent, the aged Lord Lyndhurst (1772–1863), himself three times Lord Chancellor, on the last such attempt before passage of the Jews Relief Act in 1858. Interestingly, no bishop participated in the debate until the Marquess of Londonderry goaded an Irish prelate into declaring against the proposal on the usual anti-semitic religious grounds (**8.2.3**). For the most 'progressive' view of Judaism in the contemporary Church one must look to Baden Powell (1796–1860), professor of geometry at Oxford, Fellow of the Royal Society, contributor to *Essays and Reviews*. The Old Testament and its religion must be entirely abandoned, Powell argued in *Christianity without Judaism*. The Jewish faith is 'less advanced' than Christianity, which is 'far higher, . . . more spiritual' (**8.2.4**). This was the voice of liberalism versus Sabbatarianism, of geology versus Genesis, of modernity against the past.

8.2.1   THE FOUNDING OF THE REFORM SYNAGOGUE, 1841

TO THE GENTLEMEN ELDERS OF THE SPANISH AND PORTUGUESE SYNAGOGUE

7th Elul, 5601, 24th August, 1841.

Gentlemen:— Having so often expressed our sentiments both to your respected body, and to the meetings of the Yahidim, on the important subject of the improvements, which, in our opinion, were so much required in our form of public worship, as well as on some other points, and having on so many occasions ascertained your total disinclination to attend to our suggestions, or even to consider our views, we cannot entertain the idea, that our present communication will excite any surprise in your minds. In fact, we intimated at the meeting of Yahidim, in 5599, (on the proposition being made for the abrogation of Law, No. 1, of the Yahidim), that our object was to establish a new synagogue, on the principles we had so long advocated, and that we adopted this as the best, if not the only course for satisfying our own conscientious scruples, and for avoiding the repetition of discussions tending to excite and foster ill feelings.

In conformity with these views, and with this avowal, we have, in concert with gentlemen of other congregations, adopted the measures requisite to fulfil our intentions, and having made considerable progress, we thought it right before actually opening the intended place of worship, to lay before you, a written statement of the principles on which it is to be conducted. We take this course, not only out of respect to the congregation of which we are members, but also for the purpose of removing any misapprehension that might otherwise have been entertained respecting our views. In order to preserve proper decorum during the performance of Divine Worship, it is essential that the whole congregation should assemble before the commencement of prayer, and remain until its conclusion. To secure the observance of this regulation, and at the same time to obtain a full attendance of members, as well as of their wives and children, we have determined that the service shall commence at a more convenient hour, viz., on Sabbaths and Holidays, at half-past nine, in summer, and at ten in winter; also, that the service shall be limited to a moderate length, for otherwise the mind will, in most instances, be unable to maintain, during the entire period, that solemn and devout attention without which, prayer is unavailing. Hence the service, including the reading of the portions of scripture and a religious discourse, will, on no occasion, except on the day of atonement, exceed in duration two hours and-a-half. To bring the service within this limit and yet to afford time for its distinct and solemn performance, it became necessary to abridge the existing forms of prayer, whilst it also afforded the opportunity of removing those portions which are not strictly of a devotional character. A careful revision on this plan of the daily and Sabbath Prayer-book, has been already completed, and considerable progress has been made with the Festival prayers. We confidently anticipate that little objection can be raised to these revised forms of service, since they consist, almost without exception, of portions of the existing Prayer-book, together, with passages of scripture. An impartial consideration will convince you that by omitting the less impressive and restraining and blending the more beautiful portions of the Portuguese and German Liturgies, an improved ritual has been formed. The effect of solemn song, in inspired devotional feeling is generally admitted, we have, therefore, determined that the service shall be assisted by a choir.

To familiarize the rising generation, with a knowledge of the great principles of our holy faith – to teach them their duty as Israelites, and as men, must be considered one of the primary objects of public worship. To accomplish these important purposes, religious discourses delivered in the English language, will form part of the morning service on every Sabbath and Holiday. Offerings may be requisite for the maintenance of the synagogue, but as they do not form an integral part of the service, it is considered desirable that they should interfere as little as possible with the devotional character of the place, and that they should not, by occasioning interruptions to the reading of the law, mar its effect. We have, therefore, decided on discontinuing the custom of calling up, as it has long ceased to maintain its original objects, viz., that of enabling individuals to read portions of the law. At present, however, it merely affords the opportunity of making offerings, since those called up do not themselves read the law, but only hear it read in common with the rest of the congregation. We have appointed the three great festivals for the offering of the congregation, which with the voluntary offerings on other occasions, will be made on the return of the law to the Ark; they are to be unaccompanied with personal compliments, and limited to two essential objects; the relief of the poor, and the support of the establishment. It is not the intention of the body, of which we form part, to recognize as sacred, days which are evidently not ordained as such in scripture, and they have consequently appointed the service for holy convocations, to be read on those days only thus designated.

We have already stated, that to effect our object, we have associated ourselves with gentlemen of other congregations, thus rendering it requisite to decide, whether the Hebrew should be pronounced after the manner of the Portuguese, or Germans, and under the conviction that the former is the more correct, we have adopted it.

One of the benefits anticipated by us from the establishment, we are forming is, that the junction of members of different congregations to which we have already adverted, will lead to the abolition of the useless distinction now existing in relation to those who are termed Portuguese and German Jews, but who, in fact, are neither Portuguese nor Germans but natives, and in many instances descendants of natives of the British Empire, and we have, accordingly, given the intended place of worship, the designation of 'West London Synagogue of British Jews.'

Such are the views we have endeavoured to carry into effect, and we earnestly assure you, they have not been suggested by any desire of schism, or separation, (as seems to be implied in some Resolutions passed at a late Meeting of Yahidim), but through a sincere conviction that substantial improvements in the public worship are essential to the weal of our sacred religion, and that they will be the means of handing down to our children, and to our children's children; our holy faith in all its purity and integrity. Indeed, we are firmly convinced, that their tendency will be to arrest, and prevent *secession from Judaism – an overwhelming* evil, which has at various times so widely spread among many of the most respectable families of our communities. Most fervently do we cherish the hope that the effect of these improvements will be to inspire a deeper interest, and a stronger feeling towards our holy religion, and that their influence on the minds of the youth of either sex, will be calculated to restrain them from traversing in their faith, or contemplating for a moment the fearful step of forsaking their religion, so that henceforth no 'Israelite born,' may cease to exclaim, 'Hear, O! Israel, the Lord our God, the Lord is one!'

In thus establishing a new Synagogue, on the principles hitherto not recognized or approved by your body, we may possibly encounter a considerable difference of opinion, and a strong prejudice against our proceedings; but having been actuated solely by a conscientious sense of duty, we venture to hope that on further consideration, our intentions and our motives will be duly appreciated, and that those kindly feelings, which ought to exist between every community of Jews will be maintained in all force between the respective congregations which you represent, and the small body whose views we have herein endeavoured to explain.

Before concluding, we are anxious to impress on your minds that we are most desirous of continuing to make, through you, a contribution towards the relief of the poor, and to devote some of our time and attention to the superintendence of these excellent institutions connected with the 'Parent Synagogue.'

Influenced as we are by a sense of duty to offer our assistance in these works of charity towards our poorer brethren, we should derive no small gratification if, in thus co-operating with you to satisfy the claims of humanity, we should find that we are thereby establishing a bond and symbol of connexion with the old congregation, and assuring you that its welfare will never be a subject of indifference with us, we shall but express the words which we utter so frequently in our daily orisons;— 'May He who maketh peace in his high heavens, in his mercy grant peace unto us and to all Israel. Amen.'

TO ALL WHO BEAR THE NAME OF ISRAEL. FROM THE CHIEF RABBI, AND THE BETH-DIN OF THE SEVERAL CONGREGATIONS OF GREAT BRITAIN.

[24 October 1841]

Our brethren, the children of Israel, who pursue justice, and seek the Lord!

Incline your ears to the words of righteousness; hearken that your souls may live!

It is known throughout the dispersions of Israel, that the prayers and blessings which we address to the Creator of the world (blessed be His holy name), have been arranged and appointed, by our sages of the great convocation, among whom were some of our Prophets, and that these forms have been adhered to by the whole house of Israel, from generation to generation, for more than 2,000 years.

But now behold, we have seen innovations newly springing up, and a new book of prayer, called 'Forms of Prayer, used in the West London Synagogue of British Jews, edited by D. W. Marks, printed by J. Wertheimer and Co., A.M. 5601,' in which it is evident to the eyes of all, that the manner and order of our prayers and blessings have been curtailed and altered, and otherwise arranged, not in accordance with the oral law by which we have so long been guided in the performance of the precepts of the Lord, and of which it is acknowledged, that 'whoso rejecteth the authority of the oral law, opposeth thereby the holy law handed down to us on Mount Sinai, by Moses the servant of the Lord;' and without which it is also admitted, that we should have no knowledge of the written law.

Seeing this evil, we have risen and strengthened ourselves for the service of God, in order to remove and set aside the stumbling block from the path of our brethren the sons of Israel, and hereby we admonish every person professing the faith of Israel, and having the fear of God in his heart, that he do not use, or in any manner recognize the said book of prayer, because it is not in accordance with our holy law, and whoever shall use it for the purpose of prayer will be accounted sinful; for the wisest of men hath said, 'That he who turneth away his ear from hearing the law, even his prayer shall be an abomination;' but he who regardeth his soul will avoid the iniquitous course thereby attempted, and pursue the righteous faith so long trodden by our ancestors. And we supplicate the Lord God of our fathers, to incline and unite our hearts that we may all serve him with one accord, and that he may bring peace and brotherly love among us, and that the Redeemer may speedily come to Zion. These are the words of truth and justice!

(Signed)

S. HIRSCHELL, Chief Rabbi.	J. LEVY.
DAVID MELDOLA.	A. LEVY.
A. HALIVA.	A. L. BARNETT.

8.2.2 SYNAGOGUE SERVICES, 1870

... Probably many persons are as little aware as I was myself up to a certain period, of the immense difference existing between the Reformed and Orthodox Jews. As the Jewish is eminently a national faith, this difference does not, of course, extend to essentials; but, in point of discipline and ritual, the distinction may be not inaptly described as almost identical with that existing between the Protestant and Catholic bodies in Christianity. The Reformers do not acknowledge the force of many of the traditional laws, which are observed by the Orthodox Jews, and at the Berkeley Street Synagogue there is an organ accompaniment to the service, and the prayers are considerably abridged.

Determined then to go to head-quarters for my information, I . . . attended a Friday evening service at the Great Synagogue, Duke's Place, Aldgate. As, according to Jewish mode of reckoning, Sabbath comes in at sunset on Friday, this would, of course, represent the first Sabbath service, and it is technically termed the 'Service of the Reception of the Sabbath.' The hour varies with the time of year. On the fine autumn evening when I paced the little side street running out of the great metropolitan thoroughfare, with its quaint old-fashioned Jewish book-shops, the hour of service was half-past five. I got there half an hour before that time, and found the spacious building already lighted up, with large chandeliers suspended from the ceiling, and literally fulfilling their name, since no gas is used in the Great Synagogue. Eighteen dozen candles are used when the chandeliers are all lighted, and the effect must be grand in the extreme. It was imposing enough on the occasion of my visit, when the edifice was only partially illuminated. It is with the greatest diffidence I always enter a place of worship, with the manners and customs of which I am unfamiliar. When I go to a Roman Catholic Chapel I am constantly divided in opinion as to whether I shall openly avow my Protestantism by going to my seat straightway, or enter under false pretences with a genuflection. Most peculiarly did I feel this 'foreign' sensation when I entered the Great Synagogue. Above all did my Christian courtesy seem to protest against the retention of my hat, but an obliging verger soon put me at my ease, gave me a prayer-book, with the Hebrew and English service, and handed me literally to the 'chief seat in the synagogue,' for I found, almost to my dismay, that I was representing Baron Rothschild.

In the centre of the building on the basement was a large railed platform for the Reader, Wardens, and Choir, whilst at the end of the building was the 'Ark,' or veiled receptacle for the Law. Spacious galleries ran round the building, in which, behind a *grille*, were the places for the female congregation. Before the ark, and around the central platform, were huge tapers burning, just as one sees in a Roman Catholic place of worship. Indeed there were many points in which the ceremonial reminded me of the ritual of Catholicism. For instance, on entering the Synagogue most of the worshippers bowed towards the 'Ark,' just as the Roman Catholic makes obeisance towards the High Altar, and, at the conclusion of the service, the Chief Rabbi laid his hands on children, and blessed them, as a Roman prelate might do. Dr Adler, who is a venerable-looking man, entered in due time, clad in a sort of academic gown, with a purple collar and cap of the same colour, and took his place in a small pew

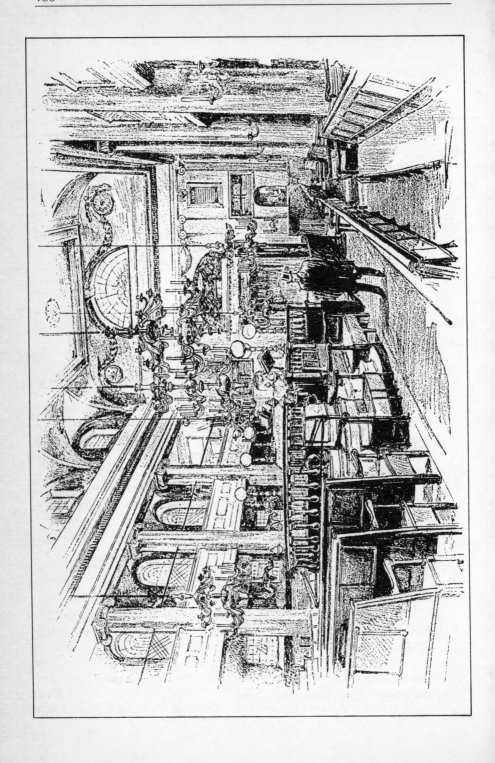

on one side of the recess containing the Ark. In this pew he remained during the entire service, and most of the time with his back to the congregation, appearing to be absorbed in private prayer. The Reader took his place on the platform facing the Ark, and the Choir was ranged behind him, and presently the service began with a musical intonation on his part, to which the choir responded in a plaintive air, so ornate as almost to have a secular sound. It reminded me forcibly of that most pathetic Welsh melody, 'Ar hyd y nos;' I say this with no sort of disrespect. I was amazed at the musical beauty of the service. The Reader's part was most florid, and would have frightened a Minor Canon into fits, whilst the choral portions continually reminded me of well-known airs, but throughout there seemed to run an undercurrent of plaintiveness – almost of sadness – as though it were really being sung by captive Jews beside the waters of Babylon. I do not know whether this character is studiously given to the singing, or is really a spontaneous unstudied effect of the Jews' position as a dispersed people. It was singularly beautiful, and impressed me profoundly.

If I must speak plainly, however, I cannot say that the service appeared to me to produce any perceptible effect on the congregation. There seemed that almost *distrait* appearance which one so often notices in Catholic as contrasted with Protestant worshippers. This results, of course, in these cases from the different genius of the service. In one case the priest to a great extent does something to which the congregation only express assent by their presence: in the other they themselves worship, with the minister only for their mouthpiece. I own I expected to find the latter characteristic more largely permeate Jewish devotion, but I seemed to be disappointed. There was the constant dropping in of fresh members of the congregation, all through the service. Some were evidently praying heart and soul, but – so at least it seemed to me – praying *by themselves*, and apart from the public service. Two young men behind me engaged in light conversation so loud as almost to annoy me, but prayed volubly and loudly at certain portions of the service. The effect of these exceedingly rapid prayers of the congregation was curious in the extreme. Some quite sang their prayers, others murmured them in a low *bourdon* kind of voice, but all with the greatest rapidity. I soon lost myself in the intricate mazes of the prayer-book, and could not, until the very end, get over a kind of dissipated feeling at keeping my hat on; but the musical beauty of the service lingered with me. The parting hymn, or 'Yigdal' (corresponding

---

13 The Great Synagogue, Duke's Place, Aldgate, built in 1722, headquarters of the largest section of Jews in England, the German Orthodox party (Ashkenazim), and presided over by the Chief Rabbi, Dr N. M. Adler.

to the Christian Doxology), was really one of the sweetest compositions I ever heard. The Reader's portion was as difficult as the recitative of an opera, only more melodious, and quite different from the monotonous Gregorian music to which corresponding portions of the service are sung in a Roman Catholic Church. The prayer for the Queen and Royal Family, which is used at every synagogue-service, sounded incongruous enough, since the names were inserted in the vernacular, whilst the body of the prayer was of course, like the rest of the service, in Hebrew. . . .

. . . The West London Synagogue of British Jews represents the more advanced school of thought among the Hebrew community; and, though their differences from the 'orthodox' touch no essentials, they are still sufficient to cause a withdrawal of countenance on the part of the Chief Rabbi, and therefore constitute the West London Synagogue *quasi* Dissenters. After tabernacling first in a room in Burton Street, and next in a small synagogue in Margaret Street, the West London British Jews opened a handsome synagogue in Upper Berkeley Street, Portman Square. As this advanced or 'reformed' body is to a great extent composed of the higher or more educated classes, whose tendency is 'most to congregate' towards the west, the corresponding change of locality has become a necessity. The building, which is an exceedingly handsome one of Byzantine character, was designed by Messrs Davis and Emmanuel, of Finsbury Circus, and has been erected by Messrs Myers, of Lambeth, at a cost of £20,000. It is capable of containing 1000 persons – that is, 500 males on the ground floor, and an equal number of females in the gallery. The organ, by Messrs Gray and Davison, is placed at the east end of the building behind the tabernacle.

The religious ceremony, which attracted a large congregation, commenced with the carrying in procession of the 'scrolls of the law,' and their deposition in the ark. This was performed by Revs. Professor Marks, A. Löwy, and several influential Jewish laymen. During this portion of the proceedings some versicles were chanted, and, at its conclusion, an appropriate Hebrew prayer was read by Rev. Mr Löwy, the assistant minister. Then an eloquent sermon was preached by the chief minister, the Rev. Professor Marks. He selected as his text 1st Chronicles xx. 28: 'And David said unto Solomon his son, "Be strong and of good courage, and do it; fear

---

14   The West London Synagogue in Upper Berkeley Street, Portman Square, to which the Reform congregation removed on 22 September 1870 under the leadership of the Revd D. W. Marks, professor of Hebrew in the University of London.

not, nor be dismayed; for the Lord, even my God, will be with thee; he will not fail thee nor forsake thee until thou hast finished all the work for the service of the house of the Lord." ' This was read first in Hebrew, and then translated into English words differing scarcely at all from the Authorized Version. This, the preacher observed, was a spiritual watchword, in which the Divine aid was promised to every good work. On this the starting-point of their new period of congregational history, he would deviate somewhat from ordinary pulpit utterances, and aim rather at delivering a public address than a homily. 'It was now,' he said, 'thirty years since the congregation, whose third synagogue he consecrated to-day, had started into being. Never, in an equal time, had so much been done for the Jews of Britain. In those three decades the Jews had gained great advantages. The prejudices of centuries had been conquered, and the barriers of exclusion had come down, one after another, before the advance of civilization. Every disqualification had been removed, and there was absolutely no distinction between the Jew and his Christian brother. So had it been with our inner communal life. Education had made rapid strides. There were no longer religious tests at the universities; and our youths had shown themselves well able to maintain their ground among their compeers. So, too, with schools for the poor. There were few among the Jews who now lacked the common franchise of education.' Passing to spiritual matters, it was impossible, the Professor remarked, to call up without pain the recollection of what the synagogue was thirty years ago. The sacred office was performed more as a stereotyped task than as the spontaneous effusion of pious hearts. The ritual was burdened with pages of the private works of pious rabbis, and with polemical and metaphysical discussions quite alien from the spirit of prayer. Pulpit teaching there was absolutely none. Such was the Anglo-Jewish Synagogue in the year 1841, when a few thinking Israelites formed a small congregation in Burton Street, with a view of improving certain outward forms, for which improvements they had in vain petitioned the ecclesiastical authorities. They were met in turn by stolid apathy, by honoured prejudices, and by heated opposition from those who reverenced mere antiquity. It was the common fate, he said, of all who heeded conscience and duty more than authority. 'So we went on our quiet way, and this synagogue shows our progress. In this we seem to see the literal fulfilment of our text. We have failed, it is true, to find conciliation in the acts of the clerical body; but our lay brethren of other synagogues have lost all angry feelings. Amongst educated laymen we see a nascent feeling that the spirit of Judaism is large enough to embrace in its loving grasp all who cling to the eternal prin-ciples of Moses and the Prophets, without rigid uniformity as to mere formulas. You Israelites,' the Rev. Professor said, in a powerful apostro-phe, 'who would appropriate the genius of the age, must bend to the inexorable fact that the communal tie will be proved, not by narrowness, but by breadth; not in unbending uniformity of ritual, but by the great and immutable truths of Sinai.' All synagogues, he said, had awakened. They were no longer merely houses of prayer, but also of pulpit instruction. How far this fact was due to the influence of Burton Street, he did not pause to inquire. The fact was matter of history. Services had been abridged or subdivided. Choral music had been introduced. The pulpit formed a prominent feature in every synagogue. Contrasting synagogue life of to-day with the date of Burton Street, he thanked God that he had lived to see the triumph of the West London Synagogue. 'Yet,' he remarked in a different strain, 'a cloud descends, as I speak, to mantle my joy. The forms of many are absent from our midst. We see around us the offerings of filial piety to their memory, and, though separated bodily, we are yet one with them in spirit. Finally,' he concluded, 'I consecrate this synagogue to the love, knowledge, and reverence of the One only God and Father of all men, and to the doctrines revealed by Moses. I consecrate it to the same ritual that has obtained amongst us since we became a congregation, believing that, while the principles of Judaism are immutable, its forms are capable of infinite adaptation, even as I believe that wherever God is worshipped in spirit – be it in synagogue, church, chapel, or mosque – there he is present. I consecrate it to the spirit of love that recognizes in every human being a child of God, a brother, and a sister, and to those humane principles which the Scripture says shall prevail when the promised Messiah appears, and when "the earth shall be filled with the knowledge of the Lord as the waters cover the sea." '

After the sermon Professor Marks offered a short prayer, and the ceremony concluded with the ordinary office for the day.

8.2.3 THE LORDS DEBATE ON THE ADMISSION OF JEWS TO PARLIAMENT, 1858

The LORD CHANCELLOR said: My Lords, . . . I need scarcely assure your Lordships that I am influenced by no personal feeling – that I am actuated by no prejudice upon this question. I feel only an earnest desire to support a principle which I believe to be necessary to maintain in order to secure the welfare and even the character of this country. . . . The foundation generally laid, my Lords, for the right of admission of the Jews to the Legislature is, that in every free State the citizens are all entitled to a perfect equality of civil rights. I think that there is a fallacy lurking under that argument, arising out of an ambiguity of the term. If, by the term 'civil rights,' be meant what is ordinarily understood by it – namely, the right of enjoying property, of personal security; or, in short, of everything which can be comprehended in the words 'civil and religious freedom,' within the limits of the constitution – then, I say, I entirely agree with the proposition. But if, by the term 'civil rights,' be meant a claim to be admitted to political office or to Parliament, then I take it on myself to deny its accuracy. I contend, my Lords, that no such rights exist indiscriminately for all citizens. The right to political office is one conferred by the State with certain conditions and qualifications and which it thinks proper to impose. . . . I must, my Lords, have read very imperfectly the history of my own country, if I have not found throughout its pages traces of the particular qualification of the profession of Christianity being imposed as a condition, especially for the possession of supreme power, or for a seat in the Legislature. . . . I quite admit the historical account of the original insertion of those important words – 'On the true faith of a Christian' in the oath; I quite admit the whole history of the discovery of that celebrated treatise on equivocation which was revised by the Jesuit Garnett; and that in consequence of the discovery then made, these words were inserted in the oath with the view of rendering it more binding upon the consciences of Roman Catholics. But . . . these important words 'on the true faith of a Christian' were re-inserted in the 13th William III., and this appears to me to be one of the most striking legislative declarations of the intention of Parliament to provide against any person having a seat in the Legislature who could not profess himself to be a Christian. The Legislature bound up with the Protestant succession the acknowledgement of the faith of Christianity. . . . My Lords, it is said that we have already given sentence against our exclusive system; because you have admitted the Jew to the elective franchise, and permitted him to enjoy the office of Mayor, of Sheriff, and of Magistrate; and this has been accounted a powerful and unanswerable argument in favour of their admission to Parliament. But, with great deference to those who use that argument, I cannot concur in its force. Take the case of the elective franchise, and how is it possible to establish any analogy between the case of giving him perhaps the twenty thousandth part of a choice in the election of a Christian representative, and giving him power himself to take a part in making laws for the country. I cannot myself perceive any analogy between the two cases. Then, my Lords, with regard to his exercising the different magisterial offices, I will say that, to the honour of those Jews who have been placed in these positions, they have filled them with the greatest respectability, and with the highest credit to themselves. But whilst acting in these capacities the Jew is under the law; and if he breaks the law he subjects himself to punishment. However, place the Jew, my Lords, amongst the Legislators of the country, and there is no law he has to submit to but the law of his own conscience; otherwise he is irresponsible, though he is part of the governing body of the country, and is to take part in the important function of making laws for a Christian people. . . . My Lords, it is an old and a true maxim, but one which commends itself to the hearts of our people, that Christianity is part of the law of England. Whatever else may be the meaning of the expression, it certainly must be understood to convey this important truth – that Christianity is thoroughly and essentially bound up with our Constitution. Your Lordships will find that it pervades almost every institution of the country. You will find that homage is paid to it by frequent observances, and in no place more strikingly than in the Houses of the Legislature. We begin our deliberations daily, by invoking the blessing of Almighty God upon our labours; and we do so through that Holy Name, by which alone we believe our prayers will be rendered acceptable. We go forth thus consecrated to our duties; and what are those duties? Not merely the control and direction of matters of low worldly policy, of earthly power, or commercial prosperity; but the eternal welfare of the people is committed to our legislative guardianship. The highest – the most important – the most essential of our legislative functions is the cause of religion. . . . The Jew, if he be sincere – if he be what he has always been represented – if we are to take the Jewish people in general, and not selected specimens, – must have the most inveterate hostility to the Christian religion. Then, if I am right in saying that the highest function of a Christian Legislature is the care of the Christian religion and its extension among the people, can you place within it a person who is hostile to the highest principles by which it ought to be governed? These reasons have always pressed upon my mind in the part which I have taken in resisting the admission of even a single Jew to Parliament. . . .

Lord LYNDHURST: . . . The abiding rule which governs us with respect to the administration of oaths is this, – that the oath should be framed in such a way as is most binding on the conscience of the person to whom it is tendered. Accordingly, we propose by this Bill to strike out of the oath the words 'on the true faith of a Christian' when the oath is to be administered to a person of the Jewish persuasion. But my noble and learned Friend says, that if you strike out those words you admit members of the Jewish religion to seats as representatives in Parliament. I ask, why should they not be so admitted? Are they not our fellow-subjects and the native subjects of this realm, and entitled to the same privileges as are enjoyed by other native subjects? On what foundation can their exclusion be maintained? Is there any specific Act of Parliament depriving them of their right to sit in Parliament? . . . Will any person pretend to say that there is any such Act? . . . My noble and learned Friend has said, that the present is not a question of religious toleration or religious liberty, but a question of power and privilege, and that the Legislature, therefore, is entitled to deal with it. The Legislature, I admit, can do what it thinks proper in conferring power and privilege; but my noble and learned Friend has taken a very narrow and insufficient view of religious liberty. Religious liberty I hold to be this – that every man with respect to office, power, or emolument should be put on a footing of perfect equality with his neighbour, without regard to his religious opinions, unless those opinions are such as to disqualify him for the proper performance of the duties of his office. Is there any other principle upon which in this enlightened age religious liberty can be founded? It is true that you do not fine men or imprison them on account of their religious opinions; but if you deny them the fair emoluments of office and fair objects of ambition, you inflict upon them an injury greater than fine, and, in many instances, greater even than imprisonment. You violate the very principle of religious freedom, and establish a rule which would justify persecution. Where are you to stop? Men may possess certain religious opinions – are they harmless? If so, why do you punish them? Why should not those men be on an equality with their fellow subjects?

But my noble and learned Friend goes to another argument, that you would 'unchristianize' the Legislature by introducing a few Jews into it – an old and favourite argument of those who oppose Bills of this description. When that argument was first used in this House it met with an entire and complete refutation from a most reverend Prelate, then a Member of this House – Archbishop Whately. How did he answer it? He asked, 'Is England A Christian country? You answer in the affirmative; but, though a Christian country, it does not consist exclusively of Christians: it is composed of Christians and a small number of Jews; but still you call it a Christian country. What is the constitution of Parliament? It represents the country. If it is to represent the country fairly, how can you for a moment contend that, if there were a small number of Jews in Parliament, therefore the Legislature would be unchristian?' To that no answer has ever been given. Allow me to go a little further. Are your courts of justice, are your municipal corporations Christian? But you have Jews in your corporations – you admit Jews to your tribunals; and who denies that your municipal corporations are Christian although Jews are members of them; nor that your tribunals are Christian though Jews sit there? How, then, is it possible that the introduction of a few Jews can unchristianize the Legislature? . . . Has the least inconvenience or the slightest disadvantage resulted from the admission of the Jews to the Legislature of foreign countries? If it has not, are you not called upon, on every principle of religious liberty to extend the same privilege to them in this country? . . . It is said that the Jews cannot be trusted to legislate when religion is in question. . . . But, my Lords, has any practical inconvenience of this kind resulted from the admission of Roman Catholics into the Legislature? No one will pretend that there has been any such result. Do the Jews proselytize? No; on the contrary, they are opposed to proselytism. Is there any reasonable ground for supposing that if they were admitted into Parliament they would interfere with our Church? Not in the slightest degree. Do they look up to a foreign Power as their head? In no respect whatever can this be said of them. So far from being enemies of the Church you allow them to present to benefices, which you do not permit Roman Catholics to do, and in no instance has any complaint ever been made as to the exercise of their patronage. . . . My Lords, most earnestly, most sincerely, and most zealously do I hope that your Lordships will so decide that this may be the last time that I shall have the opportunity of addressing you on this subject. . . .

The Marquess of LONDONDERRY said, it was remarkable that of all those right rev. Prelates to whom their Lordships were wont to look for lessons of improvement, instruction, and guidance, not one of them had addressed a word to their Lordships about the morality or the immorality, the propriety or the impropriety, of admitting Jews to Parliament. Let it not be said that this measure would unchristianize the Legislature, or that their prayers would become a farce if a Jew were admitted to the House, with some Member of the right rev. Bench rising to give his opinion on the question. For his part he would not allow his religion to be guided by statesmanship, neither would he receive lessons on this subject from any Peer till he had heard from those who ought to instruct him and this House what was their opinion on the matter. For his own part . . . he was sure that the Jews had been, and that they would be again, God's chosen people. Their Lordships might do as they would – they would act according to their own judgment – it was sufficient for him to have the honour of standing up and recording his protest against this attempt to exclude the Jew from his political privileges.

The Bishop of CASHEL: My Lords, I rise to answer the appeal which has just been addressed to this Bench by the noble Lord. I wish to say that, in voting against the clause for admitting the Jews, I am actuated by no unkind feeling towards them. I love them, and have perhaps a greater regard for them than many of those who vote for their admission to seats in the Legislature. I feel, I hope, towards them in the same spirit as the Apostle, who said they were enemies for the Gospel's sake, but beloved for their father's sake. They are the children of Abraham, but they are degenerate children who walk not in the steps of their father. It was said by our Lord himself that Abraham 'rejoiced to see his day, and he saw it and was glad;' but the degenerate children of Abraham, in the day of the Saviour's humiliation, cried out, 'Crucify him, crucify him!' and the Jews of the present day show themselves the true children of their fallen fathers, by blaspheming that holy name and speaking evil of Him whom Christians love. I cannot, therefore, agree that they ought to be admitted to the Houses of Parliament. We have the authority of the beloved Apostle of the Lord, – 'If there come any unto you, and bring not this doctrine, receive him not into your house, neither bid him God speed.' There is another reason why I cannot do so. It was declared from the earliest times, as the distinguishing character of the Jews, – 'The people shall dwell alone, and they shall not be reckoned among the nations.' They well stand among the nations of the earth as a separate people. I agree with the noble Lord that the Jews will again become the people of God; but that will not be till they, being converted to the faith of Christ, are brought to say, – 'Blessed is He that cometh in the name of the Lord.' . . . There is yet another reason for not consenting to that clause which shall admit them into Parliament. I believe that a good Jew would not come into this House. I believe so because, on that memorable occasion when their fathers cried out, 'Crucify him, crucify him,' it is written that they went not into the Roman Judgment Hall lest they should be defiled, but that they might eat the passover; but Pilate went out unto them. So I believe that a good, honest, conscientious Jew would not enter into your Lordships' House or the other House of Parliament. I have no doubt that the mere money-changing, money-brokering Jew would come in; but, to admit such, I am not willing to be a party to withdrawing the profession of the Christian faith. It is a remarkable fact that not a single petition has come from the Jews themselves, asking for admission to seats in Parliament. As the noble Marquess has called upon the right reverend Bench for an opinion on this question, I have thought it my duty to say these few words, and I thank the House for the patience with which it has heard me. . . .

8.2.4   B. POWELL ON CHRISTIANITY WITHOUT JUDAISM, 1857

The view given us of the Divine dispensations in the Bible is, from first to last, that of *progressive adaptation* to the wants and capacities of different ages and nations:– a limited and restricted, imperfect and temporary dispensation to one people; the rest left to a more free but unaided condition of natural light; both neglecting, abusing, and corrupting the means they had: and, finally, a new and more perfect way of salvation laid open to both and to all in the Gospel.

Thus, to recur to the Old Testament is to go back to a less advanced state of things – to retrograde, instead of 'going on towards perfection.' If we follow a religion of nature, or of vague sentiment, we may, no doubt, take up the Bible, and select, at pleasure, such texts here or there as we may choose to wrest to our purpose. But this is a perversion of its obvious design.

If the express declarations of the New Testament are to be taken as the announcement of the pure doctrines of Christianity, its tenor is manifest:— 'God spoke in times past, in sundry portions, and under different forms, to the fathers' – in His earlier dispensations; but 'in these last days' – in this final dispensation – 'unto us, by His Son.' It may be true that of old 'God spake these words,' but not, therefore, TO US. Our concern is not with what was of old, or at *first*, but with what has been revealed in these *last* days. The Old Testament is to us nothing, except as applied in the New; like the moon, in itself dark, it shines to us only by the reflected light of the Gospel. *Temporary* dispensations have passed away. With *national* and *local* dispensations, even if they were not temporary, we have no concern. We Gentiles are 'not under the Law,' not because its obligation has been *abolished*, but because, to us, it *never existed*. The New Testament does not bring us under the Old. If we were not 'under grace,' we should only be under 'nature,' not under the Law. The Gospel, as addressed to the Gentiles, is essentially new and independent of any previous dispensations. Meats and days, ordinances and sabbaths, if primeval, have ceased – if Judaical, are national.

We may trace, in the ordinances of the Law, the types of the Gospel; in its shadows, the realities of Christianity. In this sense, it is very true that the Old Testament is 'not contrary to the New' [Art. vii]. But because they are not at variance, they are not, therefore, identical; they may be in *harmony*, but they are not in *unison*.

To attempt to introduce Old Testament observances into Christianity under the plea of utility and policy, is to disparage Divine authority. Expediency is not to be set up against truth; the sole rule of a consistent Christian, in such matters, must be the Gospel, in its full and final disclosure in the apostolic writings. To adopt any other rule, is to pretend to know more of the will of God than is revealed.

Christianity at once recognises an universal moral law, exalts and enlarges it, and sets it on a firmer basis. Distinctions of days have no connexion with morality. The Sabbath is inseparable from the six days' creation, and with it ceases to be applicable. The whole tenor of the Old Law was a formal and positive service, with stated times and ordinances; that of the New is a perpetual consecration of daily life. The Law sanctified *rest*; the Gospel sanctifies *work*. Under the Gospel dispensation no one day can be more holy than another. Its service is a perpetual one, 'in spirit and in truth;' its worship, 'prayer without ceasing.'

Christianity is not the religion of Moses, nor of Abraham, nor of Adam, but something far higher, more advanced, more spiritual. The old dispensations lowered heavenly things to human weakness; the new seeks to raise human weakness to heavenly things. To mix it with extraneous additions, even from those older dispensations, is to pervert its very nature and object, which is to supersede and crown them all, – to impair its efficacy by engrafting on it an unevangelic formalism most alien from its spirit, – to lay it open to the attacks of the objector, and give the strongest handle to scepticism. And to instil such principles in education in these times, is but to lay the train for a fearful reaction. On the contrary, it ought to be the more peculiar endeavour of every sincere and enlightened advocate of the Gospel to vindicate its spiritual and rational character, and the purity and simplicity of its practical principles, – at once the source of its power, the ground of its stability and perpetuity, and the main plea of its internal evidence: and when intimately combined, as those practical principles must essentially be, with its sublime spiritual doctrines – received as matters, not of knowledge, but of faith, and in the comprehensive spirit of charity, – the perception and acknowledgment of Christian truth will increase with the progress of human enlightenment, till, 'going on to perfection,' it attain that promised condition, when the 'veil upon the hearts' of men, 'in the reading of the Old Testament,' 'shall be taken away,' – and 'all with open face beholding, as in a glass, the glory of the Lord, shall be changed into the same image, from glory to glory, as by the Spirit of the Lord.'

8.3   A SCIENCE OF RELIGION: FRIEDRICH MAX MÜLLER

No one did more to acquaint the Victorian age with non-Christian religions, or with *religion* as a mode of human cognition and experience, than the German expatriate linguist and orientalist Friedrich Max Müller (1823–1900). Brought to England in 1846 under the patronage of the Prussian ambassador Baron von Bunsen, Max Müller settled in Oxford, translated the *Rigveda*, and from 1879 until his death edited and published *The Sacred Books of the East*, which was completed afterwards in fifty volumes. He became professor of comparative philology at Oxford in 1868 and achieved a formidable reputation outside the university through two series of Royal Institution lectures on the 'science of language' (1861, 1863), his Hibbert Lectures on the 'origin and growth of religion' (1878), and four series of Gifford Lectures (1888, 1890, 1891, 1892) on the phenomena of religious history. In a single year, 1873, Max Müller published a pair of lectures epitomising how his 'science of religion' understood Christianity in its relations with the religions of the world. The first lecture, delivered at the Royal Institution, portrayed religious history as the *'Divine education of the human race'*, in which the 'growth' of the knowledge of God, from childlike simplicity to adult-like perfection, has been ever characterized by a dialectical movement between the spiritual and material senses of religious language. Here certain resemblances to the views of McCosh (8.1.1), Maurice (8.1.2), and Lubbock (8.1.3) must not be allowed to obscure Max Müller's deep-seated and unswerving dependence on German idealistic philosophy. Indeed, his notion that the 'inevitable excrescences' of a religion were merely corruptions of the 'highest ideal' present in 'the mind of its founder' brought him into conflict during the latter part of his career with evolutionary anthropologists, who regarded the excrescences as primitive or surviving religious forms (**8.3.1**). The second lecture in which Max Müller epitomised the bearings of his 'science of religion' was delivered in Westminster Abbey. Dean Stanley, who invited him, had obtained beforehand an opinion from Lord Chief Justice Coleridge on the legality of the evening address, but still a storm of protest ensued. Critics berated a layman for desecrating the sacred precincts with Broad Church sympathy for heathen faiths. Yet the most striking thing about the address appears in retrospect to be Max Müller's supreme confidence that the Gospel, as he understood it, would 'conquer all other religions'. Christianity was to be propagated as a faith that need 'hardly find utterance'. The higher synthesis in the conflict of world religions was to be based on a silent reform of the one. Whether this reformed faith would still have claim to be called Christianity, or whether, as Max Müller suggested, it would be a 'new religion', remained a crucial ambiguity (**8.3.2**). It was, indeed, the main point at issue between the Broad Churchmen and their critics.

8.3.1   ON THE GROWTH OF RELIGION, 1873

. . . No judge, if he had before him the worst of criminals, would treat him as most historians and theologians have treated the religions of the world. Every act in the lives of their founders which shows that they were but men, is eagerly seized and judged without mercy; every doctrine that is not carefully guarded is interpreted in the worst sense that it will bear; every act of worship that differs from our own way of serving God is held up to ridicule and contempt. And this is not done by accident, but with a set purpose, nay, with something of that artificial sense of duty which stimulates the counsel for the defence to see nothing but an angel in his own client, and anything but an angel in the plaintiff on the other side. The result has been – as it could not be otherwise – a complete miscarriage of justice, an utter misapprehension of the real character and purpose of the ancient religions of mankind; and, as a necessary consequence, a failure in discovering the peculiar features which really distinguish Christianity from all the religions of the world, and secure to its founder his own peculiar place in the history of the world, far away from Vasish*tha*, Zoroaster, and Buddha, from Moses and Mohammed, from Confucius and Lao-tse. By unduly depreciating all other religions, we have placed our own in a position which its founder never intended for it; we have torn it away from the sacred context of the history of the world; we have ignored, or wilfully narrowed, the sundry times and divers manners in which, in times past, God spake unto the fathers by the prophets; and instead of recognising Christianity as coming in the fulness of time, and as the fulfilment of the hopes and desires of the whole world, we have brought ourselves to look upon its advent as the only broken link in that unbroken chain which is rightly called the Divine government of the world.

Nay, worse than this: there are people who, from mere ignorance of the ancient religions of mankind, have adopted a doctrine more unchristian than any that could be found in the pages of the religious books of antiquity, viz. that all the nations of the earth, before the rise of Christianity, were mere outcasts, forsaken and forgotten of their Father in heaven, without a knowledge of God, without a hope of salvation. If a comparative study of the religions of the world produced but this one result, that it drove this godless heresy out of every Christian heart, and made us see again in the whole history of the world the eternal wisdom and love of God towards all His creatures, it would have done a good work. . . .

. . . If we believe that there is a God, and that He created heaven and earth, and that He ruleth the world by His unceasing providence, we cannot believe that millions of human beings, all created like ourselves in the image of God, were, in their time of ignorance, so utterly abandoned that their whole religion was falsehood, their whole worship a farce, their whole life a mockery. An honest and independent study of the religions of the world will teach us that it was not so – will teach us the same lesson which it taught St. Augustine, that there is no religion which does not contain some grains of truth. Nay, it will teach us more; it will enable us to see in the history of the ancient religions, more clearly than anywhere else, the *Divine education of the human race*.

I know this is a view which has been much objected to, but I hold it as strongly as ever. If we must not read in the history of the whole human race the daily lessons of a Divine teacher and guide, if there is no purpose, no increasing purpose in the succession of the religions of the world, then we might as well shut up the godless book of history altogether, and look upon men as no better than the grass which is to-day in the field and to-morrow is cast into the oven. Man would then be indeed of less value than the sparrows, for none of them is forgotten before God.

But those who imagine that, in order to make sure of their own salvation, they must have a great gulf fixed between themselves and all the other nations of the world – between their own religion and the religions of Zoroaster, Buddha, or Confucius – can hardly be aware how strongly the interpretation of the history of the religions of the world, as an education of the human race, can be supported by authorities before which they themselves would probably bow in silence. We need not appeal to an English bishop to prove the soundness, or to a German philosopher to prove the truth, of this view. If we wanted authorities we could appeal to Popes, to the Fathers of the Church, to the Apostles themselves, for they have all upheld the same view with no wavering or uncertain voice. . . .

But . . . we need not appeal to any authorities, if we will but read the records of the ancient religions of the world with an open heart and in a charitable spirit – in a spirit that thinketh no evil, but rejoices in the truth wherever it can be found. . . .

I wish I could read you the extracts I have collected from the sacred books of the ancient world, grains of truth more precious to me than grains of gold; prayers so simple and so true that we could all join in them if we once accustomed ourselves to the strange sounds of Sanskrit or Chinese. . . .

I wish we could explore together in this spirit the ancient religions of mankind, for I feel convinced that the more we know of them, the more we shall see that there is not one which is entirely false; nay, that in one sense every religion was a true religion, being the only religion which was possible at the time, which was compatible with the language, the thoughts, and the sentiments of each generation, which was appropriate to the age of the world. I know full well the objections that will be made to this. Was the worship of Moloch, it will be said, a true religion when they burnt their sons and their daughters in the fire to their gods? Was the worship of Mylitta, or is the worship of Kâlî a true religion, when within the sanctuary of their temples they committed abominations that must be nameless? Was the teaching of Buddha a true religion, when men were asked to believe that the highest reward of virtue and meditation consisted in a complete annihilation of the soul?

Such arguments may tell in party warfare, though even there they have provoked fearful retaliation. Can that be a true religion, it has been answered, which consigned men of holy innocence to the flames, because they held that the Son was like unto the Father, but not the same as the Father, or because they would not worship the Virgin and the Saints? Can that be a true religion which screened the same nameless crimes behind the sacred walls of monasteries? Can that be a true religion which taught the eternity of punishment without any hope of pardon or salvation for the sinner, however penitent?

People who judge of religions in that spirit will never understand their real purport, will never reach their sacred springs. These are the excrescences, the inevitable excrescences of all religions. We might as well judge of the health of a people from its hospitals, or of its morality from its prisons. If we want to judge of a religion, we must try to study it as much as possible in the mind of its founder; and when that is impossible, as it is but too often, try to find it in the lonely chamber and the sick-room, rather than in the colleges of augurs and the councils of priests.

If we do this, and if we bear in mind that religion must accommodate itself to the intellectual capacities of those whom it is to influence, we shall be surprised to find much of true religion where we only expected degrading superstition or an absurd worship of idols.

The intention of religion, wherever we meet it, is always holy. However imperfect, however childish a religion may be, it always places the human soul in the presence of God; and however imperfect and however childish the conception of God may be, it always represents the highest ideal of perfection which the human soul, for the time being, can reach and grasp. Religion therefore places the human soul in the presence of its highest ideal, it lifts it above the level of ordinary goodness, and produces at least a yearning after a higher and better life – a life in the light of God.

The expression that is given to these early manifestations of religious sentiment is no doubt frequently childish: it may be irreverent or even repulsive. But has not every father to learn the lesson of a charitable interpretation in watching the first stammerings of religion in his children? Why, then, should people find it so difficult to learn the same lesson in the ancient history of the world, and to judge in the same spirit the religious utterances of the childhood of the human race? . . .

Ancient language is a difficult instrument to handle, particularly for religious purposes. It is impossible to express abstract ideas except by metaphor, and it is not too much to say that the whole dictionary of ancient religion is made up of metaphors. With us these metaphors are all forgotten. We speak of spirit without thinking of breath, of heaven without thinking of the sky, of pardon without thinking of a release, of revelation without thinking of a veil. But in ancient language every one of these words, nay, every word that does not refer to sensuous objects, is still in a chrysalis stage: half material and half spiritual, and rising and falling in its character according to the varying capacities of speakers and hearers. Here is a constant source of misunderstandings, many of which have maintained their place in the religion and in the mythology of the ancient world. There are two distinct tendencies to be observed in the growth of ancient religion. There is, on the one side, the struggle of the mind against the material character of language, a constant attempt to strip words of their coarse covering, and fit them, by main force, for the purposes of abstract thought. But there is, on the other side, a constant relapse from the spiritual into the material, and, strange to say, a predilection for the material sense instead of the spiritual. This action and reaction has been going on in the language of religion from the earliest times, and it is at work even now. . . .

I call this variety of acceptation, this misunderstanding, which is inevitable in ancient and also in modern religion, the *dialectic growth and decay*, or, if you like, the *dialectic life of religion*, and we shall see again and again, how important it is in enabling us to form a right estimate of religious language and thought. The dialectic shades in the language of religion are almost infinite; they explain the decay, but they also account for the life of religion. You may remember that Jacob Grimm, in one of his poetical moods, explained the origin of High and Low German, of Sanskrit and Prakrit, of Doric and Ionic, by looking upon the high dialects as originally the language of men, upon the low dialects as originally the language of women and children. We can observe, I believe, the same parallel streams in the language of religion. There is a high and there is a low dialect; there is a broad and there is a narrow dialect; there are dialects for men and dialects for children, for clergy and laity, for the noisy streets and for the still and lonely chamber. And as the child on growing up to manhood has to unlearn the language of the nursery, its religion, too, has to be translated from a feminine into a more masculine dialect. This does not take place without a struggle, and it is this constantly recurring struggle, this inextinguishable desire to recover itself, which keeps religion from utter stagnation. From first to last religion is oscillating between these two opposite poles, and it is only if the attraction of one of the two poles becomes too strong, that the healthy movement ceases, and stagnation and decay set in. If religion cannot accommodate itself on the one side to the capacity of children, or if on the other side it fails to satisfy the requirements of men, it has lost its vitality, and it becomes either mere superstition or mere philosophy.

If I have succeeded in expressing myself clearly, I think you will understand in what sense it may be said that there is truth in all religions, even in the lowest. . . . The world has its childhood, and when it was a child it spoke as a child, it understood as a child, it thought as a child; and . . . in that it spoke as a child its language was true, in that it believed as a child its religion was true. The fault rests with us, if we insist on taking the language of children for the language of men, if we attempt to translate literally ancient into modern language, oriental into occidental speech, poetry into prose. . . .

The *parler enfantin* in religion is not extinct; it never will be. Not only have some of the ancient childish religions been kept alive, as, for instance, the religion of India, which is to my mind like a half-fossilised megatherion walking about in the broad daylight of the nineteenth century; but in our own religion and in the language of the New Testament, there are many things which disclose their true meaning to those only who know what language is made of, who have not only ears to hear, but a heart to understand the real meaning of parables.

What I maintain, then, is this, that as we put the most charitable interpretation on the utterances of children, we ought to put the same charitable interpretation on the apparent absurdities, the follies, the errors, nay, even the horrors of ancient religion. . . .

If we have once learnt to be charitable and reasonable in the interpretation of the sacred books of other religions, we shall more easily learn to be charitable and reasonable in the interpretation of our own. We shall no longer try to force a literal sense on words which, if interpreted literally, must lose their true and original purport, we shall no longer interpret the Law and the Prophets as if they had been written in the English of our own century, but read them in a truly historical spirit, prepared for many difficulties, undismayed by any contradictions, which, so far from disproving the authenticity, become to the historian of ancient language and ancient thought the strongest confirmatory evidence of the age, the genuineness, and the real truth of ancient sacred books. Let us but treat our own sacred books with neither more nor less mercy than the sacred books of any other nations, and they will soon regain that position and influence which they once possessed, but which the artificial and unhistorical theories of the last three centuries have well-nigh destroyed.

8.3.2   ON CHRISTIAN MISSIONS, 1873

. . . The three religions which are alive, and between which the decisive battle for the dominion of the world will have to be fought, are the three missionary religions, *Buddhism, Mohammedanism, and Christianity.* Though religious statistics are perhaps the most uncertain of all, yet it is well to have a general conception of the forces of our enemies; and it is well to know that, though the number of Christians is double the number of Mohammedans, the Buddhist religion still occupies the first place in the religious census of mankind. . . .

Between these three powers, then, the religious battle of the future, the Holy War of mankind, will have to be fought, and is being fought at the present moment, though apparently with little effect. To convert a Mohammedan is difficult; to convert a Buddhist, more difficult still; to convert a Christian, let us hope, well nigh impossible.

What then, it may be asked, is the use of missionaries? Why should we spend millions on foreign missions, when there are children in our cities who are allowed to grow up in ignorance? Why should we deprive ourselves of some of the noblest, boldest, most ardent and devoted spirits and send them into the wilderness, while so many labourers are wanted in the vineyard at home?

It is right to ask these questions; and we ought not to blame those political economists who tell us that every convert costs us 200*l*., and that at the present rate of progress it would take more than 200,000 years to evangelise the world. There is nothing at all startling in these figures. Every child born in Europe is as much a heathen as the child of a Melanesian cannibal; and it costs us more than 200*l.* to turn a child into a Christian man. The other calculation is totally erroneous; for an intellectual harvest must not be calculated by adding simply grain to grain, but by counting each grain as a living seed, that will bring forth fruit a hundred and a thousand fold.

If we want to know what work there is for the missionary to do, what results we may expect from it, we must distinguish between two kinds of work: the one is *parental*, the other *controversial*. Among uncivilised races the work of the missionary is the work of a parent; whether his pupils are young in years or old, he has to treat them with a parent's love, to teach them with a parent's authority; he has to win them, not to argue with them. I know this kind of missionary work is often despised; it is called mere religious kidnapping; and it is said that missionary success obtained by such means proves nothing for the truth of Christianity; that the child handed over to a Mohammedan would grow up a Mohammedan, as much as a child taken by a Christian missionary becomes a Christian. All this is true; missionary success obtained by such means proves nothing for the truth of our Creeds: but it proves, what is far more important, it proves Christian love. . . .

The case is different with the controversial missionary, who has to attack the faith of men brought up in other religions, in religions which contain much truth, though mixed up with much error. Here the difficulties are immense, the results very discouraging. Nor need we wonder at this. We know, each of us, but too well, how little argument avails in theological discussion; how often it produces the very opposite result of what we expected; confirming rather than shaking opinions no less erroneous, no less indefensible, than many articles of the Mohammedan or Buddhist faith.

And even when argument proves successful, when it forces a verdict from an unwilling judge, how often has the result been disappointing; because in tearing up the rotten stem on which the tree rested, its tenderest fibres have been injured, its roots unsettled, its life destroyed.

We have little ground to expect that these controversial weapons will carry the day in the struggle between the three great religions of the world.

But there is a third kind of missionary activity, which has produced the most important results, and through which alone, I believe, the final victory will be gained. Whenever two religions are brought into contact, when members of each live together in peace, abstaining from all direct attempts at conversion, whether by force or by argument, though conscious all the time of the fact that they and their religion are on their trial, that they are being watched, that they are responsible for all they say and do – the effect has always been the greatest blessing to both. It calls out all the best elements in each, and at the same time keeps under all that is felt to be of doubtful value, of uncertain truth. Whenever this has happened in the history of the world, it has generally led either to the reform of both systems, or to the foundation of a new religion.

When after the conquest of India the violent measures for the conversion of the Hindus to Mohammedanism had ceased, and Mohammedans and Brahmans lived together in the enjoyment of perfect equality, the result was a purified Mohammedanism, and a purified Brahmanism. . . .

The same effect which Mohammedanism produced on Hinduism is now being produced in a much higher degree on the religious mind of India by the mere presence of Christianity. That silent influence began to tell many years ago, even at a time when no missionaries were allowed within the territory of the old East India Company. Its first representative was Ram Mohun Roy, born just one hundred years ago, in 1772, who died at Bristol in 1833, the founder of the Brahma-Samāj. A man so highly cultivated and so highly religious as he was, could not but feel humiliated at the spectacle which the popular religion of his country presented to his English friends. He drew their attention to the fact that there was a purer religion to be found in the old sacred writings of his people, the *Vedas*. He went so far as to claim for the Vedas a divine origin, and to attempt the foundation of a reformed faith on their authority. In this attempt he failed. . . .

. . . The successor of Ram Mohun Roy, the present head of the Brahma-Samāj, the wise and excellent Debendranāth Tagore, was for a time even more decided in holding to the Vedas as the sole foundation of the new faith. But this could not last. As soon as the true character of the Vedas, which but few people in India can understand, became known, partly through the efforts of native, partly of European scholars, the Indian reformers relinquished the claim of divine inspiration in favour of their Vedas, and were satisfied with a selection of passages from the works of the ancient sages of India, to express and embody the creed which the members of the Brahma-Samāj hold in common.

The work which these religious reformers have been doing in India is excellent, and those only who know what it is, in religious matters, to break with the past, to forsake the established custom of a nation, to oppose the rush of public opinion, to brave adverse criticism, to submit to social persecution, can form any idea of what those men have suffered, in bearing witness to the truth that was within them.

They could not reckon on any sympathy on the part of Christian Missionaries; nor did their work attract much attention in Europe till very lately, when a schism broke out in the Brahma-Samāj between the old conservative party and a new party, led by Keshub Chunder Sen. The former, though willing to surrender all that was clearly idolatrous in the ancient religion and customs of India, wished to retain all that might safely be retained: it did not wish to see the religion of India denationalised. The other party, inspired and led by Keshub Chunder Sen, went further in their zeal for religious purity. All that smacked of the old leaven was to be surrendered; not only caste, but even that sacred cord – the religious riband which makes and marks the Brahman, which is to remind him at every moment of his life, and whatever work he may be engaged in, of his God, of his ancestors, and of his children – even that was to be abandoned; and instead of founding their creed exclusively on the utterances of the ancient sages of their own country, all that was best in the sacred books of the whole world, was selected and formed into a new sacred Code.

The schism between these two parties is deeply to be deplored; but it is a sign of life. It augurs success rather than failure for the future. It is the same schism which St. Paul had to heal in the Church of Corinth, and he healed it with the words, so often misunderstood, 'Knowledge puffeth up, but charity edifieth.'

In the eyes of our missionaries this religious reform in India has not found much favour: nor need we wonder at this. Their object is to transplant, if possible, Christianity in its full integrity from England to India, as we might wish to transplant a full-grown tree. They do not deny the moral worth, the noble aspirations, the self-sacrificing zeal of these native reformers; but they fear that all this will but increase their dangerous influence, and retard the progress of Christianity, by drawing some of the best minds of India, that might have been gained over to our religion, into a different current. . . .

If we think of the future of India, and of the influence which that country has always exercised on the East, the movement of religious reform which is now going on, appears to my mind the most momentous in this momentous century. If our missionaries feel constrained to repudiate it as their own work, history will be more just to them than they themselves. And if not as the work of Christian missionaries, it will be recognised hereafter as the work of those missionary Christians who have lived in India, as examples of a true Christian life, who have approached the natives in a truly missionary spirit, in the spirit of truth and in the spirit of love; whose bright presence has thawed the ice, and brought out beneath it the old soil, ready to blossom into new life. These Indian puritans are not against us; for all the highest purposes of life they are with us, and we, I trust, with them. What would the early Christians have said to men, outside the pale of Christianity, who spoke of Christ and his doctrine as some of these Indian reformers? Would they have said to them, 'Unless you speak our language and think our thoughts, unless you respect our Creed and sign our Articles, we can have nothing in common with you.' . . .

. . . When we stand before a common enemy, we soon forget our own small feuds. But why? Often, I fear, from motives of prudence only and selfishness. Can we not, then, if we stand in spirit before a common friend – can we not, before the face of God, forget our small feuds, for very shame? If missionaries admit to their fold converts who can hardly understand the equivocal abstractions of our Creeds and formulas, is it necessary to exclude those who understand them but too well to submit the wings of their free spirit to such galling chains? When we try to think of the majesty of God, what are all those formulas but the stammerings of children, which only a loving father can interpret and understand! The fundamentals of our religion are not in these poor Creeds; true Christianity lives, not in our belief, but in our love – *in our love of God, and in our love of man, founded on our love of God.*

That is the whole Law and the Prophets, that is the religion to be preached to the whole world, that is the Gospel which will conquer all other religions – even Buddhism and Mohammedanism – which will win the hearts of all men. . . .

Let missionaries preach the Gospel again as it was preached when it began the conquest of the Roman Empire and the Gothic nations; when it had to struggle with powers and principalities, with time-honoured religions and triumphant philosophies, with pride of civilisation and savagery of life – and yet came out victorious. At that time conversion was not a question to be settled by the acceptance or rejection of certain formulas or articles; a simple prayer was often enough: 'God be merciful to me a sinner.'

There is one kind of faith that revels in words, there is another that can hardly find utterance: the former is like riches that come to us by inheritance; the latter is like the daily bread, which each of us has to win in the sweat of his brow. We cannot expect the former from new converts; we ought not to expect it or to exact it, for fear that it might lead to hypocrisy or superstition. The mere believing of miracles, the mere repeating of formulas requires no effort in converts, brought up to believe in the Purā*n*as of the Brahmans or the Buddhist *G*ātakas. They find it much easier to accept a legend than to love God, to repeat a creed than to forgive their enemies. In this respect they are exactly like ourselves. Let missionaries remember that the Christian faith at home is no longer what it was, and that it is impossible to have one creed to preach abroad, another to preach at home. Much that was formerly considered as essential is now neglected; much that was formerly neglected is now considered as essential. I think of the laity more than of the clergy: but what would the clergy be without the laity? There are many of our best men, men of the greatest power and influence in literature, science, art, politics, aye even in the Church itself, who are no longer Christian in the old sense of the word. Some imagine they have ceased to be Christians altogether, because they feel that they cannot believe as much as others profess to believe. We cannot afford to lose these men, nor shall we lose them if we learn to be satisfied with what satisfied Christ and the Apostles, with what satisfies many a hard-working missionary. If Christianity is to retain its hold on Europe and America, if it is to conquer in the Holy War of the future, it must throw off its heavy armour, the helmet of brass and the coat of mail, and face the world like David, with his staff, his stones and his sling. We want less of creeds, but more of trust; less of ceremony, but more of work; less of solemnity, but more of genial honesty; less of doctrine, but more of love. There is a faith, as small as a grain of mustard-seed, but that grain alone can move mountains, and more than that, it can move hearts. Whatever the world may say of us, of us of little faith, let us remember that there was one who accepted the offering of the poor widow. She threw in but two mites, but that was all she had, even all her living.

8.4   RELIGION IN EVOLUTION

Unlike Max Müller and most of the other great and good Victorians who wrote on religion, Benjamin Kidd (1858–1916) was neither an academic nor a clergyman. He began his career as a second-division civil servant and spare-time amateur naturalist; he ended it as an internationally renowned sociologist. What transformed his life was a single book, *Social Evolution*, written under the patronage of the chief mandarin at Inland Revenue and purporting nothing less than 'a biological basis for our social science'. It sold 75,000 copies in English and was translated into at least ten languages. It captured the mood of *fin de siècle* socialists and imperialists who feared for the future of advanced societies under conditions of international competition. Kidd believed that the morality of socialism stood to reason, but that reason, if given free rein in society, would bring progress to an end and lead to national degeneration by relieving the Darwinian struggle for existence. By the same token, reform-minded individualists who thought it rational to struggle ethically against nature ignored the fact that on Darwinian premises there could be no rational sanction for individual ethical conduct. A truly progressive social morality was, according to Kidd, to be found only in the 'ultra-rational' sanctions of religion. Religion, by encouraging altruism, subordinated individual conduct to the needs of the group and held society together by fostering conditions under which all could be admitted to competitive struggle through 'equality of opportunity'. From this rational justification of the social function of the irrational, then, two corollaries followed: first, the populist corollary that the unreflective, non-intellectual or irrational mass of people were more likely to believe and act in ways conducive to evolutionary progress than the elite whose excess of well-meaning reason would bring progress to a halt; and second, the anti-hereditarian corollary that the fittest in the struggle for existence would not necessarily be the strongest or the brightest, but those whose religious culture of altruism enabled their group to function most compactly and efficiently. Although these arguments may sound ominous to late twentieth-century ears, their force and novelty in the Victorian world should not be underestimated. Kidd did not pronounce on the truth of ultra-rationality in religion, which he equated with belief in the supernatural, but he was widely understood to have lent it support by showing it to be 'natural and inevitable' at every stage in evolution. In Kidd's analysis, moreover, supernatural religion had an inexorable social function, and this served as encouragement for some to grant it a leading role – how dysfunctionally may now be judged – in the propagation of national culture and the pursuit of imperial conflict.

B. KIDD ON THE FUNCTION OF RELIGIOUS BELIEFS IN THE EVOLUTION OF SOCIETY, 1894

. . . If we are ever to lay broadly and firmly the foundations of a science of human society, . . . there is one point above others at which attention must be concentrated. The distinguishing feature of human history is the social development the race is undergoing. But the characteristic and exceptional feature of this development is the relationship of the individual to society. . . . Fundamental organic conditions of life render the progress of the race possible only under conditions which have never had, and which have not now, any sanction from the reason of a great proportion of the individuals who submit to them. The interests of the individual and those of the social organism, in the evolution which is proceeding, are not either identical or capable of being reconciled, as has been necessarily assumed in all those systems of ethics which have sought to establish a rational sanction for individual conduct. The two are fundamentally and inherently irreconcilable, and a large proportion of the existing individuals at any time have . . . no personal interest whatever in this progress of the race, or in the social development we are undergoing. Strange to say, however, man's reason, which has apparently given him power to suspend the onerous conditions to which he is subject, has never produced their suspension. His development has continued with unabated pace throughout history, and it is in full progress under our eyes.

. . . What has then become of human reason? It would appear that the answer has, in effect, been given. The central feature of human history, the meaning of which neither science nor philosophy has hitherto fully recognized, is, apparently, the struggle which man, throughout the whole period of his social development, has carried on to effect the subordination of his own reason. The motive power in this struggle has undoubtedly been supplied by his religious beliefs. The conclusion towards which we seem to be carried is, therefore, that the function of these beliefs in human evolution must be to provide a *super-rational* sanction for that large class of conduct in the individual, necessary to the maintenance of the development which is proceeding, but for which there can never be, in the nature of things, any *rational* sanction.

. . . Evolutionary science is likely in our day to justify, as against the teaching of past schools of thought, one of the deepest and most characteristic of social instincts, viz., that which has consistently held the theories of that large group of philosophical writers who have aimed at establishing a rational sanction for individual conduct in society – a school which may be said to have culminated in England in 'utilitarianism' – as being on the whole (to quote the words of Mr. Lecky) 'profoundly immoral.' It would appear that science must in the end also justify another instinct equally general, and also in direct opposition to a widely prevalent intellectual conception which is characteristic of our time.

From the beginning of the nineteenth century, and more particularly since Comte published his *Philosophie Positive*, an increasingly large number of minds in France, Germany, and England (not necessarily, or even chiefly, those adhering to Comte's general views) have questioned the essentiality of the supernatural element in religious beliefs. In England a large literature has gradually arisen on the subject; and the vogue of books like *Natural Religion*, attributed to Professor J. R. Seeley, and others in which the subject has been approached from different standpoints, has testified to the interest which this view has excited. A large and growing intellectual party in our midst hold, in fact, the belief that the religion of the future must be one from which the super-rational element is eliminated.

Now, if we have been right so far, it would appear that one of the first results of the application of the methods and conclusions of biological science to human society must be to render it clear that the advocates of these views, like the adherents of that larger school of thought which has sought to find a rational basis for individual conduct in society, are in pursuit of something which can never exist. There can never be, it would appear, such a thing as a rational religion. The essential element in all religious beliefs must apparently be the *ultra*-rational sanction which they provide for social conduct. When the fundamental nature of the problem involved in our social evolution is understood, it must become clear that

that general instinct which may be distinguished in the minds of men around us is in the main correct, and that:—

No form of belief is capable of functioning as a religion in the evolution of society which does not provide an ultra-rational sanction for social conduct in the individual.

In other words:—

A rational religion is a scientific impossibility, representing from the nature of the case an inherent contradiction of terms.

The significance of this conclusion will become evident as we proceed. It opens up a new and almost unexplored territory. We come, it would appear, in sight of the explanation why science, if social systems are organic growths, has hitherto failed to enunciate the laws of their development, and has accordingly left us almost entirely in the dark as to the nature of the developmental forces and tendencies at work beneath the varied and complex political and social phenomena of our time. The social system which constitutes an organic growth, endowed with a definite principle of life, and unfolding itself in obedience to laws which may be made the subject of exact study, is something quite different from that we have hitherto had vaguely in mind. It is not the political organisation of which we form part; it is not the race to which we belong; it is not even the whole human family in process of evolution. The organic growth, it would appear, must be the social system or type of civilisation founded on a form of religious belief. This is the organism which is the seat of a definite principle of life. Throughout its existence there is maintained within it a conflict of two opposing forces; the disintegrating principle represented by the rational self-assertiveness of the individual units; the integrating principle represented by a religious belief providing a sanction for social conduct which is always of necessity ultra-rational, and the function of which is to secure in the stress of evolution the continual subordination of the interests of the individual units to the larger interests of the longer-lived social organism to which they belong. It is, it would appear, primarily through these social systems that natural selection must reach and act upon the race. It is from the ethical systems upon which they are founded that the resulting types of civilisation receive those specific characteristics which, in the struggle for existence, influence in a preponderating degree the peoples affected by them. It is in these ethical systems, founded on super-rational sanctions, and in the developments which they undergo, that we have the seat of a vast series of vital phenomena unfolding themselves under the control of definite laws which may be made the subject of study. . . .

But . . . let us see if the conclusion to which we have been led respecting the nature of the element common to all religious beliefs can be justified when it is confronted with actual facts. Are we thus, it may be asked, able to unearth from beneath the enormous overgrowth of discussion and controversy to which this subject has given rise, the essential element in all religions, and to lay down a simple, but clear and concise principle upon which science may in future proceed in dealing with the religious phenomena of mankind?

It is evident, from what has been said, that our definition of a religion, in the sense in which alone science is concerned with religion as a social phenomenon, must run somewhat as follows:—

A religion is a form of belief, providing an ultra-rational sanction for that large class of conduct in the individual where his interests and the interests of the social organism are antagonistic, and by which the former are rendered subordinate to the latter in the general interests of the evolution which the race is undergoing.

We have here the principle at the base of all religions. Any religion is, of course, more than this to its adherents; for it must necessarily maintain itself by what is often a vast system of beliefs and ordinances requiring acts and observances which only indirectly contribute to the end in question, by assisting to uphold the principles of the religion. It is these which tend to confuse the minds of many observers. With them we are not here concerned; they more properly fall under the head of theology.

Let us see, therefore, if this element of a super-rational sanction for conduct has been the characteristic feature of all religions, from those which have influenced men in a state of low social development up to those which now play so large a part in the life of highly-civilised peoples; whether, despite recent theories to the contrary, there is to be discerned no tendency in those beliefs which are obviously still influencing large numbers of persons to eliminate it.

Beginning with man at the lowest stage at which his habits have been made a subject of study, we are met by a curious and conflicting mass of evidence respecting his religious beliefs. The writers and observers whose opinions have been recorded are innumerable; but they may be said to be divided into two camps on a fundamental point under discussion. In no stage of his development, in no society, and in no condition of society, is man found without religion of some sort, say one side. Whole societies of men and entire nations have existed without anything which can be described as a religion, say the other side. In one of the Gifford Lectures, Mr. Max-Müller well describes the confusion existing among those who have undertaken to inform us on the subject. . . . Underlying all this, there is, evidently, a state of chaos as regards general principles. Different writers and observers, when they speak of the religion of lower races of men, do not refer to the same thing; they have themselves often no clear conception of what they mean by the expression. They do not know, in short, what to look for as the essential element in a religion.

Now, there is one universal and noteworthy feature of the life of primitive man which a comparative study of his habits has revealed. 'No savage,' says Sir John Lubbock, 'is free. All over the world his daily life is regulated by a complicated and apparently most inconvenient set of customs as forcible as laws.' We are now beginning to understand that it is these customs of savage man, strange and extraordinary as they appear to us, that in great measure take the place of the legal and moral codes which serve to hold society together and contribute to its further development in our advanced civilisations. The whole tendency of recent anthropological science is to establish the conclusion that these habits and customs, 'as forcible as laws,' either have or had, directly or indirectly, a utilitarian function to perform in the societies in which they exist. Mr. Herbert Spencer and others have already traced in many cases the important influence in the evolution of early society of those customs, habits, and ceremonies of savage man which at first sight often appear so meaningless and foolish to us; and though this department of science is still young, there is no doubt as to the direction in which current research therein is leading us.

But if, on the one hand, we find primitive man thus everywhere under the sway of customs which we are to regard as none other than the equivalent of the legal and moral codes of higher societies; and if, on the other hand, we find these customs everywhere as forcible as laws, how, it may be asked, are those unwritten laws of savage society enforced? The answer comes prompt and without qualification. They are everywhere enforced in one and the same way. Observance of them is invariably secured by the fear of consequences from an agent which is always supernatural. This agent may, and does, assume a variety of forms, but one characteristic it never loses. It is always supernatural. We have here the explanation of the conflict of opinions regarding the religions of primitive man. Some writers assume that he is without religion because he is without a belief in a Diety. Others because his Deities are all evil. But, if we are right so far, it is not necessarily a belief in a Deity, or in Deities which are not evil, that we must look for as constituting the essential element in the religions of primitive men. The one essential and invariable feature must be a supernatural sanction of some kind for acts and observances which have a social significance. This sanction we appear always to have. We are never without the supernatural in some form. The essential fact which underlies all the prolonged and complicated controversy which has been waged over this subject was once put, with perhaps more force than reverence, by Professor Huxley into a single sentence. 'There are savages without God in any proper sense of the word, but there are none without ghosts,' said he; and the generalisation, however it may have been intended, expresses in effective form the one fundamental truth in the discussion with which science is concerned. It is the supernatural agents, the deities, spirits, ghosts, with which primitive man peoples the air, water, rocks, trees, his dwellings and his implements, which everywhere provide the ultimate sanction used to enforce conduct which has a social significance of the kind in question. Whatever qualities these agents may be supposed to possess or to lack, one attribute they always have; they are invariably supernatural.

When we leave savage man, and rise a step higher to those societies which have made some progress towards civilisation, we find the prevailing religions still everywhere possessing the same distinctive features; they are always associated with social conduct, and they continue to be invariably founded on a belief in the supernatural, . . . using this term in the sense of ultra-rational. The conception of the supernatural has become a higher one than that which prevailed amongst primitive men, and the development in this direction may be distinguished actually in progress, but the belief in this sanction survives in all its force. The religions of ancient Greece and Rome at the period of their highest influence drew their strength everywhere from the belief in the supernatural, and it has to be observed that their decay dated from, and progressed *pari passu* with, the decay of this belief. . . .

If we turn again to Mohammedanism and Buddhism, forms of belief influencing large numbers of men at the present day outside our own civilisation, we still find these essential features. The same sanction for conduct is always present. The essence of Buddhist morality Mr. Max-Müller states to be a belief in *Karma*, that is, of work done in this or a former life which must go on producing effects. . . . We have only to look for a moment to see that we have in this the same ultra-rational sanction for conduct. There is and can be no proof of such a theory; on the contrary, it assumes a cause operating in a manner altogether beyond the tests of reason and experience.

We may survey the whole field of man's religions in societies both anterior to, and contemporaneous with our modern civilisation, and we shall find that all religious beliefs possess these characteristic features. There is no exception. Everywhere these beliefs are associated with conduct, having a social significance; and everywhere the ultimate sanction which they provide for the conduct which they prescribe is a super-rational one.

Coming at last to the advanced societies of the present day, we are met by a condition of things of great interest. . . . The observer remarks at the outset that there exist now, as at other times in the world's history, forms of belief intended to regulate conduct in which a super-rational sanction has no place. But, with no want of respect for the persons who hold these views, he finds himself compelled to immediately place such beliefs on one side. None of them, he notes, has *proved* itself to be a religion; none of them can so far claim to have influenced and moved large masses of men in the manner of a religion. He can find no exception to this rule. If he desired to accept any one of them as a religion he notes that he would be constrained to do so merely on the *ipse dixit* of the small group of persons who chose so to describe it.

When we turn, however, to these forms of belief which are unquestionably influencing men in the manner of a religion, we have to mark that they have one pronounced and universal characteristic. The sanction they offer for the conduct they prescribe is unmistakably a super-rational one. We may regard the whole expanse of our modern civilisation and we shall have to note that there is no exception to this rule. Nay, more, we shall have to acknowledge, if we keep our minds free from confusion, that there is no tendency whatever to eliminate the super-rational element from religions. Individuals may lose faith, may withold belief, and may found parties of their own; but among the religions themselves we shall find no evidence of any kind of movement or law of development in this direction. On the contrary, however these beliefs may differ from each other, or from the religions of the past, they have the one feature in common that they all assert uncompromisingly that the rules of conduct which they enjoy have an ultra-rational sanction, and that right and wrong are right and wrong by divine or supernatural enactment outside of, and independent of, any other cause whatever.

This is true of every form of religion that we see influencing men in the world around us, from Buddhism to the Roman Catholic Church and the Salvation Army. The supernatural element in religion, laments Mr. Herbert Spencer, 'survives in great strength down to our own day. Religious creeds, established and dissenting, all embody the belief that right and wrong are right and wrong simply in virtue of divine enactment.' This is so: but not apparently because of some meaningless instinct in man. It is so in virtue of a fundamental law of our social evolution. It is not that men perversely reject the light set before them by that school of ethics which has found its highest expression in Mr. Herbert Spencer's theories. It is simply that the deep-seated instincts of society have a truer scientific basis than our current science.

Finally, if our inquiry so far has led us to correct conclusions, we have the clue to a large class of facts which has attracted the notice of many observers, but which has hitherto been without scientific explanation. We see now why it is that, as Mr. Lecky asserts, 'all religions which have governed mankind have done so . . . by speaking, as common religious language describes it, to the heart,' and not to the intellect; or, as an advocate of Christianity has recently put it – A religion makes its way not by argument, or by the rational sanctions which it offers, 'but by an appeal to those fundamental spiritual instincts of men to which it supremely corresponds.' We see also why, despite the apparent tendency to the disintegration of religious belief among the intellectual classes at the present day, those who seek to compromise matters by getting rid of that feature which is the essential element in all religions make no important headway; and why, as a prominent member of one of the churches has recently remarked, the undogmatic sects reap the scantiest harvest, while the dogmatic churches still take the multitude. We are led to perceive how inherently hopeless and misdirected is the effort of those who try to do what Camus and Grégoire attempted to make the authors of the French Revolution do – reorganise Christianity without believing in Christ. A form of belief from which the ultra-rational element has been eliminated is, it would appear, no longer capable of exercising the function of a religion.

Professor Huxley, some time ago, in a severe criticism of the 'Religion of Humanity' advocated by the followers of Comte, asserted, in accents which always come naturally to the individual when he looks at the drama of human life from his own standpoint, that he would as soon worship 'a wilderness of apes' as the Positivist's rationalised conception of humanity. But the comparison with which he concluded, in which he referred to the considerable progress made by Mormonism as contrasted with Positivism, has its explanation when viewed in the light of the foregoing conclusions. Mormonism may be a monstrous form of belief, and one which is undoubtedly destined to be worsted in conflict with the forms of Christianity prevailing round it; yet it is seen that we cannot deny to it the characteristics of a religion. Although, on the other hand, the 'Religion of Humanity' advocated by Comte may be, and is, a most exemplary set of principles, we perceive it to be without those characteristics. It is not, apparently, a religion at all. It is, like other forms of belief which do not provide a super-rational sanction for conduct, but which call themselves religions, incapable, from the nature of the conditions, of exercising the functions of a religion in the evolution of society.

In the religious beliefs of mankind we have not simply a class of phenomena peculiar to the childhood of the race. We have therein the characteristic feature of our social evolution. These beliefs constitute, in short, the natural and inevitable complement of our reason; and so far from being threatened with eventual dissolution they are apparently destined to continue to grow with the growth and to develop with the development of society, while always preserving intact and unchangeable the one essential feature they all have in common in the ultra-rational sanction they provide for conduct. And lastly, as we understand how an ultra-rational sanction for the sacrifice of the interests of the individual to those of the social organism has been a feature common to all religions we see, also, why the conception of sacrifice has occupied such a central place in nearly all beliefs, and why the tendency of religion has ever been to surround this principle with the most impressive and stupendous of sanctions. . . .

SOURCES

1 THE CHURCH AND ITS CREEDS

1.1 THE HIGH CHURCH: A COUNTER-REFORM AT OXFORD

1.1.1 R. H. Froude, 'Remarks on State Interference in Matters Spiritual', in *Remains of the Late Reverend Richard Hurrel Froude, M.A., Fellow of Oriel College, Oxford*, pt. 2, vol. 1 (London: J. G. & F. Rivington, 1839), pp. 185, 187–96.

1.1.2 [J. H. Newman], 'Thoughts on the Ministerial Commission respectfully addressed to the Clergy', *Tracts for the Times*, no. 1 (London: printed for J. G. & F. Rivington, 1833), pp. 1–2, 4.

1.1.3 J. H. N[ewman], 'Remarks on Certain Passages in the Thirty-Nine Articles', *Tracts for the Times*, no. 90, 1841; 3d ed. (London: printed for J. G. & F. Rivington, 1841), pp. 80–83.

1.2 BAPTISM AND ETERNAL DAMNATION

1.2.1 *Gorham* v *Bishop of Exeter: The Judgment of the Judicial Committee of Privy Council, delivered March 8, 1850, reversing the decision of Sir H. J. Fust*, 1850; 2d ed. (London: [Seeleys], 1850), pp. 5, 9–11, 18–20.

1.2.2 Roundell Palmer to Lady Brodie, [1850], in Roundell Palmer, Earl of Selborne, *Memorials: Part I. Family and Personal, 1766–1865*, vol. 2 (London: Macmillan and Co., 1896), pp. 68–69.

1.2.3 F. D. Maurice, 'Concluding Essay: Eternal Life and Eternal Death', in idem, *Theological Essays*, 1853; 4th ed. (London: Macmillan and Co., 1881), pp. 377–80, 394–406.

1.3 THE BROAD CHURCH: A REFORMED BIBLE

1.3.1 B. Jowett, 'On the Interpretation of Scripture', in F. Temple et al., *Essays and Reviews*, 1860; 4th ed. (London: Longman, Green, Longman, and Roberts, 1861), pp. 373–85, 387–89.

1.3.2 J. W. Colenso, *The Pentateuch and Book of Joshua Critically Examined*, 1862ff.; People's ed. (London: Longman, Green, Longman, Roberts & Green, 1865), pp. 5–6, 59–66.

1.3.3 A. P. Stanley, 'Theology of the Nineteenth Century', *Fraser's Magazine*, 71 (Feb. 1865), 252–57.

1.4 THE 'REVOLUTION OF 1869'

1.4.1 G. A. Denison, *The Church of England in 1869; Review of the Position: A Lecture delivered to the Leeds Church Institute, October 12, 1869* (London: Rivingtons, 1869), pp. iii–vii, 2–3, 10–13.

1.4.2 F. Temple to Canon [F. S.] Cook, 16 Oct. 1869, and to Archdeacon [Philip] Freeman, [undated], in E. G. Sandford, ed., *Memories of Archbishop Temple by Seven Friends*, vol. 1 (London: Macmillan and Co., 1906), pp. 285–87.

1.5 TESTS AND THE TESTAMENTS: OXFORD REVISITED

1.5.1 'University Tests Bill . . .', *Hansard Parliamentary Debates* (Lords), 3d ser., 206 (8 May 1871), 338–47, 376–78.

1.5.2 C. Gore, 'Preface to the Tenth Edition', in idem, ed., *Lux Mundi: A Series of Studies in the Religion of the Incarnation*, 1889; 10th ed., 1890 (London: John Murray, 1904), pp. xvii–xviii, xxiv–xxx.

1.6 A PARTING VIEW: LESLIE STEPHEN

L. Stephen, 'The Broad Church', *Fraser's Magazine*, n.s., 1 (Mar. 1870), 313–25.

2 GENDER, POLITICS, AND ROME

2.1 CONVERSION AND MASCULINITY

2.1.1 H. E. [Manning], *England and Christendom* (London: Longmans, Green, and Co., 1867), pp. xxxiii–xxxv.

2.1.2 F. St. George Mivart, 'Early Memories of St. George Mivart', *Dublin Review*, 174 (Jan.–Mar. 1924), 10, 12–26.

2.1.3 C. Kingsley, *David: Four Sermons preached before the University of Cambridge* (Cambridge: Macmillan and Co., 1865), pp. 5–10, 70–73 (adapted).

2.2 MARY AND WOMANKIND

2.2.1 F. W. Faber, *The Foot of the Cross; or, The Sorrows of Mary*, 1858 (London: Burns, Oates & Washbourne, [1886]), pp. 41–45, 47–48, 50–56, 59–67.

2.2.2 C. M. Yonge, *Womankind*, 1876; 4th ed. (London: Walter Smith, 1881), pp. 1–2, 4–8.

2.2.3   T. Hancock, 'The Hymn of the Social Revolution' (1886), in idem, *The Pulpit and the Press, and Other Sermons, most of which were preached at S. Nicholas Cole Abbey* (London: S. C. Brown, Langham & Co., 1904), pp. 22–27.

2.3   THE POPE: A THREAT TO ENGLAND?

2.3.1   F. W. Faber, *Devotion to the Pope* (London: Thomas Richardson and Son, 1860), pp. 15–23.

2.3.2   'First Dogmatic Constitution on the Church of Christ', in Philip Schaff, *The Creeds of Christendom, with a History and Critical Notes*, 1877; new ed., vol. 2 (New York: Harper & Bros., 1919), pp. 262–71.

2.3.3   W. E. Gladstone, *The Vatican Decrees in their Bearing on Civil Allegiance: A Political Expostulation* (London: John Murray, 1874), pp. 34–43, 45–46, 48, 51–55.

2.3.4   H. E. [Manning], 'Mr. Gladstone and the Vatican Decrees' (letter to the editor), *The Times*, 9 Nov. 1874, p. 9, col. 6.

2.4   THE STRUGGLE FOR IRELAND

2.4.1   W. E. Gladstone, *The State in its Relations with the Church*, 1838; 2d ed. (London: John Murray, 1839), pp. 79–83.

2.4.2   J. Begg, *A Handbook of Popery; or, Text-book of Missions for the Conversion of Romanists: Being Papal Rome tested by Scripture, History, and its Recent Workings, . . . with an Appendix of Documents* (Edinburgh: Johnstone and Hunter, 1852), pp. 319–26.

2.4.3   H. E. [Manning], *England and Christendom* (London: Longmans, Green, and Co., 1867), pp. xcvi–xcix.

2.4.4   Archbishop [Paul] Cullen to the clergy of Dublin, Oct. 1865, in *Ireland and the Holy See: A Retrospect, 1866 v. 1883; Illegal and Seditious Movements in Ireland contrasted with the Principles of the Catholic Church as shown in the Writings of Cardinal Cullen* (Rome: printed at the Propaganda-Press, 1883), pp. 15–18.

2.4.5   John Devoy, *Recollections of an Irish Rebel: The Fenian Movement, its Origin and Progress; Methods of Work in Ireland and in the British Army; Why it failed to achieve its Main Object, but exercised Great Influence on Ireland's Future; Personalities of the Organization; The Clan-na-Gael and the Rising of Easter Week, 1916: A Personal Narrative* (New York: Charles P. Young, 1929), pp. 118–25, 127.

3 NONCONFORMITY AND NEOLOGY

3.1 THE PRINCIPLES OF DISSENT: ENGLAND AND SCOTLAND

3.1.1   J. A. James, *The Principles of Dissent, and the Duties of Dissenters: A Pastor's Address to his People*, 1834; 3d ed. (London: Hamilton, Adams, and Co., 1861), pp. 5–8.

3.1.2   R. W. Dale, *Nonconformity in 1662 and 1862: A Lecture delivered in Willis's Rooms, St. James's, May 6th, 1862, for the Central United Bartholomew Committee* (London: W. Kent & Co., [1862]), pp. 61–65.

3.1.3   T. Brown, *Annals of the Disruption, with Extracts from the Narratives of Ministers who left the Scottish Establishment in 1843*, new ed. (Edinburgh: MacNiven & Wallace, 1892), pp. 83–93, 95–96; *Proceedings of the General Assembly of the Free Church of Scotland, held in Edinburgh, May 1843* (Edinburgh: John Greig & Son, 1853), pp. 12–15.

3.2 DISSENTING PROFESSORS: SAMUEL DAVIDSON AND WILLIAM ROBERTSON SMITH

3.2.1   T. Nicholas, *Dr. Davidson's Removal from the Professorship of Biblical Literature in the Lancashire Independent College, Manchester, on account of Alleged Error in Doctrine: A Statement of Facts, with Documents, together with Remarks and Criticisms* (London: Williams & Norgate, 1860), pp. 126–33, 135.

3.2.2   *Proceedings and Debates of the General Assembly of the Free Church of Scotland, held at Edinburgh, May 1881* (Edinburgh: printed by Ballantyne, Hanson & Co., 1881), pp. 77, 81–83, 85, 89–90, 119–21, 124–26, 129–34, 189–90.

3.3 THE AFFINITIES OF DISSENT: UNITARIANISM AND BEYOND

3.3.1   J. Martineau, *The New Affinities of Faith: A Plea for Free Christian Union* (London: Williams & Norgate, 1869), pp. 7–11, 15–23.

3.3.2   J. Morley, *On Compromise*, 1874; 2d ed. rev. (London: Chapman and Hall, 1877), pp. 121–28.

4 EVANGELICALISM AND ETHICS

4.1 THE BIBLE, FROM BEGINNING TO END

4.1.1   T. R. Birks, *The Bible and Modern Thought* (London: Religious Tract

Society, [1861]), pp. 406–408, 413–17.

4.1.2 J. Baylee, *Genesis and Geology: The Holy Word of God defended from its Assailants* (Liverpool: Adam Holden, 1857), pp. v–vi, 7–20.

4.1.3 H. Grattan Guinness, *The Approaching End of the Age in the Light of History, Prophecy, and Science*, 1878; 10th ed. (London: Hodder and Stoughton, 1886), pp. 449–51, 454–60, 482–86.

4.2 BIBLE MORALS: WORK, SEX, FAMILY, GOVERNMENT

4.2.1 C. H. Spurgeon, 'To the Idle', in idem, *John Ploughman's Talk; or, Plain Advice for Plain People*, 1868 (London: Passmore & Alabaster, [1915]), pp. 9–13.

4.2.2 W. Guest, *A Young Man's Safeguard in the Perils of the Age* (London: Hodder and Stoughton, 1878), pp. 13–22, 24–27.

4.2.3 W. G. Blaikie, *The Family: Its Scriptural Ideal and Its Modern Assailants* (London: Religious Tract Society, [1888]), pp. 3, 5–16, 18–21, 28–34, 60–61.

4.2.4 R. W. Dale, 'Political and Municipal Duty', in idem, *The Laws of Christ for Common Life* (London: Hodder and Stoughton, [1884]), pp. 187–88, 193–98, 201–204.

4.3 A BIBLE PREACHER ANALYSED: JOHN CUMMING

4.3.1 C. M. Davies, 'Dr. Cumming in Crown Court', in idem, *Unorthodox London; or, Phases of Religious Life in the Metropolis*, 1873–75; 2d ed. rev. (London: Tinsley Bros., 1876), pp. 120–24.

4.3.2 [G. Eliot], 'Evangelical Teaching: Dr. Cumming', *Westminster Review*, n.s., 8 (Oct. 1855), 436–46, 448, 450–57, 459–62.

5 MISSIONS AND THE MINISTRY

5.1 THE EVANGELICAL APPEAL

5.1.1 J. A. James, 'Deep Solicitude about Salvation Reasonable and Necessary', in idem, *The Anxious Inquirer after Salvation Directed and Encouraged*, 1834 (London: Religious Tract Society, [1850?]), pp. 1–7.

5.1.2 *Evangelical Alliance: Report of the Proceedings of the Conference held at Freemasons' Hall, London, from August 19th to September 2nd inclusive, 1846* (London: Partridge & Oakey, 1847), pp. 77–83, 86–87, 89–91, 93–96, 99–110.

5.2   CHURCH AND CHAPEL IN RURAL DISTRICTS

5.2.1   Anon., *Hints to a Clergyman's Wife; or, Female Parochial Duties Practically Illustrated*, 1832; 2d ed. (London: Samuel Holdsworth, 1838), pp. 1–9.

5.2.2   R. Key, *The Gospel among the Masses; or, A Selection of Remarkable Scenes, Incidents and Facts, connected with the Missionary Village Work and Experience . . .*, [1866?]; 2d ed. (London: R. Davies, 1872), pp. 33–36, 38–42, 44, 72–75.

5.2.3   W. Gibson, *The Year of Grace: A History of the Ulster Revival of 1859* (Edinburgh: Andrew Elliot, 1860), pp. 18–24, 50–53.

5.2.4   J. Clifford, *Religious Life in the Rural Districts of England: Paper read at the Baptist Union, held at Birmingham, October 2–5, 1876* (London: Yates & Alexander, 1876), pp. 13–20.

5.3   CHRISTIANIZING THE TOWNS

5.3.1   J. J. Halcombe, 'Church Extension', in idem, ed., *The Church and Her Curates: A Series of Essays on the Need for More Clergy and the Best Means of Supporting Them* (London: W. Wells Gardner, 1874), pp. 2–5, 15–16.

5.3.2   J. Gott, *The Parish Priest of the Town: Lectures delivered in the Divinity School, Cambridge,* 1887; 2d ed. rev. (London: Society for Promoting Christian Knowledge, 1889), pp. 6–9, 11–16.

5.3.3   C. M. Davies, 'Father Stanton at St. Alban's' (1873), in idem, *Orthodox London; or, Phases of Religious Life in the Church of England,* 1874–75; 2d ed. rev. (London: Tinsley Bros., 1876), pp. 16–20, 22–24.

5.3.4.   C. M. Davies, 'Moody-and-Sankeyism' (1875), in idem, *Unorthodox London; or, Phases of Religious Life in the Metropolis,* 1873–75; 2d ed. rev. (London: Tinsley Bros., 1876), pp. 267, 271–78.

5.4   THE MISSION TO THE POOR

5.4.1   Anon., 'Home-Mission Work in the East of London', *Wesleyan Methodist Magazine*, 5th ser., 21 (Jan. 1875), 85–89.

5.4.2   D. Macleod, *Non-church-going and Housing of the Poor: Speech delivered in the General Assembly, 30 May 1888, . . . in support of Overture on Non-church-going by Presbytery of Glasgow* (Edinburgh: William Blackwood and Sons, 1888), pp. 8–18.

5.4.3   S. A. Barnett, 'The Universities and the Poor', *Nineteenth Century*, 15 (Feb. 1884), 255–61.

5.5   NEW GOSPELS, NEW METHODS

5.5.1   G. Dawson, *Opening of the Free Reference Library, October 26, 1866: Inaugural Address* (Birmingham: E. C. Osborne, [1866]), pp. 9–17, 23–24.

5.5.2   H. E. [Manning], 'Irresponsible Wealth', *Nineteenth Century*, 28 (Dec. 1890), 876, 879–85.

5.5.3   [W.] Booth, *In Darkest England and the Way Out* (London: Salvation Army, [1890]), pp. 9, 11–15, 84–93.

6   CLASS AND UNBELIEF

6.1   THE RELIGIOUS CONDITION OF THE MASSES

6.1.1   H. Mann, *Census of Great Britain, 1851: Religious Worship, England and Wales. Report and Tables. Presented to Both Houses of Parliament by Command of Her Majesty* (London: printed by George E. Eyre and William Spottiswoode for Her Majesty's Stationery Office, 1853), pp. cxix, cxlviii, cl–cli, clviii–clxii, clxvii–clxviii.

6.1.2   [T. Wright] The Journeyman Engineer, 'The Working Classes and the Church', in idem, *The Great Unwashed* (London: Tinsley Bros., 1868), pp. 79–96.

6.2   IMMORALITY AND INFIDELITY

6.2.1   J. Wordsworth, *The One Religion: Truth, Holiness, and Peace desired by the Nations, and revealed by Jesus Christ: Eight Lectures delivered before the University of Oxford in the year 1881 on the Foundation of John Bampton . . .* (Oxford: Parker & Co., 1881), pp. 6–14, 16–24.

6.2.2   A. L. Moore, 'The Influence of Calvinism on Modern Unbelief', in idem, *Lectures and Papers on the History of the Reformation in England and on the Continent* (London: Kegan Paul, Trench, Trübner & Co., 1890), pp. 501–506, 514–18.

6.3   SECULARISM ON TRIAL: HOLYOAKE, FOOTE, BRADLAUGH

6.3.1   *The Trial of George Jacob Holyoake, on an Indictment for Blasphemy, before Mr. Justice Erskine, and a Common Jury, at Gloucester, August the 15th, 1842; from Notes specially taken by Mr. Hunt; the Authorities cited in the Defence being quoted at Full Length* (London: printed and published for the 'Anti-Persecution Union' by Thomas Paterson, 1842), pp. 1–3, 5, 9,

59–68.

6.3.2 'Reg v. Foote', *Law Times Report*, n.s., 48 (7 July 1883), 734–40.

6.3.3 'The Attorney General v. Bradlaugh' (28 Jan. 1885), *The Law Reports: Queen's Bench Division*, vol. 14 (London, 1885), pp. 668–72, 678, 681–84, 696–98, 706–10, 714, 717–20.

6.4 IRRELIGION AND FREE RELIGION

[W. Binns], 'The Religious Heresies of the Working Classes', *Westminster Review*, n.s., 21 (Jan. 1862), 60–61, 65–68, 70–73, 75–79, 81–82, 84–86, 88–97.

7 THE RELIGION OF SCIENCE

7.1 TOWARDS A NEW NATURE

7.1.1 [T. R. Malthus], 'Population', *Supplement to the Fourth, Fifth, and Sixth Editions of the Encyclopaedia Britannica . . .*, vol. 6 (Edinburgh: printed for Archibald Constable and Co., 1824), pp. 307–308, 313–14, 316–17, 331–32.

7.1.2 J. S. Mill, *A System of Logic, Ratiocinative and Inductive: Being a Connected View of the Principles of Evidence, and the Methods of Scientific Investigation*, 1843; vol. 2 (London: John W. Parker, 1846), pp. 538–42, 591–97, 600, 610, 612–17.

7.1.3 T. Carlyle, 'Morrison Again', in idem, *Past and Present* (London: Chapman and Hall, 1843), pp. 305–13.

7.1.4 [H. Spencer], 'A Theory of Population deduced from the General Law of Animal Fertility', *Westminster Review*, n.s., 1 (April 1852), 468–70, 496–501.

7.2 A NEW REFORMATION

7.2.1 G. Combe, *On the Relation between Religion and Science* (Edinburgh: Maclachlan, Stewart, & Co., 1847), pp. 1–8, 12–13.

7.2.2 T. H. Huxley, 'On Species and Races, and their Origin' (1860), in M. Foster and E. R. Lankester, eds., *The Scientific Memoirs of Thomas Henry Huxley*, vol. 2 (London: Macmillan and Co., 1899), pp. 391–94.

7.2.3 E. B. Tylor, *Primitive Culture: Researches into the Development of Mythology, Philosophy, Religion, Language, Art, and Custom*, 1871; 2d ed., vol. 2 (London: John Murray, 1873), pp. 449–53.

7.2.4 T. H. Huxley, 'An Apologetic Irenicon', *Fortnightly Review*, n.s., 52 (1 Nov. 1892), 565–71.

7.3   NATURAL ALLIES

7.3.1   F. W. Newman, 'Art. III. – "Vestiges of the Natural History of Creation". London: John Churchill, Princes-st., Soho. 1844', *Prospective Review*, 1 (1845), pp. 60–66, 70–72, 81–82.

7.3.2   [G. Eliot], 'Prospectus of the "Westminster and Foreign Quarterly Review", under the direction of new editors', *Westminster Review*, n.s., 1 (1852), [iii–vi].

7.3.3   Rev. H. B. Williams with the clergy of the first division of the rural deanery of Dorchester, to J. B. Sumner, Archbishop of Canterbury, [before 12 Feb. 1861], *Guardian*, 16 (20 Feb. 1861), 166; J. B. Cantuar [Sumner] to Rev. W. Fremantle, 12 Feb. 1861, *The Times*, 16 Feb. 1861, p. 10, col. 4, and in R. T. Davidson and W. Benham, *Life of Archibald Campbell Tait . . .*, vol. 1 (London: Macmillan and Co., 1891), pp. 282–83; 'To the Rev. Dr. Temple', [after 16 Feb. 1861], Imperial College of Science and Technology, Huxley Papers, 22.63, and British Library Department of Manuscripts, Avebury Papers, Add. 49639.f.29.

7.3.4   F. W. Farrar, 'The Attitude of the Clergy towards Science', *Contemporary Review*, 9 (Dec. 1868), 600–601, 612–19.

7.3.5   [R. H. Hutton], 'The Various Causes of Scepticism', *Spectator*, 51 (19 Oct. 1878), 1299–300.

7.4   NATURAL RELIGION:
CONVERSION, DEVOTION, MISSION

7.4.1   F. Harrison, 'Apologia pro Fide Mea: Introductory' (1907), in idem, *The Creed of a Layman: Apologia pro Fide Mea* (London: Macmillan and Co., 1907), pp. 13–25, 27, 30, 38–42.

7.4.2   C. M. Davies, 'A Sunday Lecture by Professor Huxley' (1870), in idem, *Unorthodox London; or, Phases of Religious Life in the Metropolis*, 1873–75; 2d ed. rev. (London: Tinsley Bros., 1876), pp. 29–34.

7.4.3   [J. R. Seeley] The Author of 'Ecce Homo', *Natural Religion*, 1882; 3d ed. (London: Macmillan and Co., 1891), pp. 193–95.

7.4.4   W. Reade, *The Martyrdom of Man*, 1872; 26th ed. (London: Kegan Paul, Trench, Trubner & Co., n.d.), pp. 510–15, 536–39, 543–44.

8   BEYOND CHRISTENDOM

8.1   RELIGIOUS HISTORY AS APOLOGETICS

8.1.1   J. McCosh, 'The Religious History of Mankind', in idem, *The*

Method of the Divine Government, Physical and Moral, 1850; 12th ed. (London: Macmillan and Co., 1882), pp. 48–52.

8.1.2 F. D. Maurice, *The Religions of the World and their Relations to Christianity considered in Eight Lectures . . .,* 1847; 3d ed. rev. (Cambridge: Macmillan & Co., 1852), pp. 219–21, 226–28, 231–32, 237–40, 242–46.

8.1.3 J. Lubbock, *The Origin of Civilization and the Primitive Condition of Man: Mental and Social Condition of Savages,* 1870; 4th ed. enl. (London: Longmans, Green, and Co., 1889), pp. 205–10, 391–93.

8.2 JUDAISM IN ENGLAND AND ITS FOES

8.2.1 The seceding members to the Gentlemen Elders of the Spanish and Portuguese Synagogue, 24 Aug. 1841, and The Chief Rabbi and the Beth-Din to the Jewish public, 24 Oct. 1841, in M. Margoliouth, *The History of the Jews in Great Britain,* vol. 3 (London: Richard Bentley, 1851), pp. 78–88.

8.2.2 C. M. Davies, 'Synagogue Service' and 'Judaism – the West London Synagogue' (1870), in idem, *Unorthodox London; or, Phases of Religious Life in the Metropolis,* 1873–75; 2d ed. rev. (London: Tinsley Bros., 1876), pp. 188–95.

8.2.3 'Oaths Bill . . .', *Hansard Parliamentary Debates* (Lords), 3d ser., 149 (27 April 1858), 1758–65, 1767–68, 1771–79, 1792–94.

8.2.4 B. Powell, *Christianity without Judaism: A Second Series of Essays, including the Substance of Sermons delivered in London and Other Places* (London: Longman, Brown, Green, Longmans, and Roberts, 1857), pp. 215–20.

8.3 A SCIENCE OF RELIGION: FRIEDRICH MAX MÜLLER

8.3.1 F. Max Müller, *Introduction to the Science of Religion: Four Lectures delivered at the Royal Institution . . .* (London: Longmans, Green and Co., 1873), pp. 221–23, 225–27, 229–31, 261–64, 267–68, 274–75, 278–82.

8.3.2 F. Max Müller, *On Missions: A Lecture delivered in Westminster Abbey on December 3, 1873 . . .* (London: Longmans, Green, and Co., 1873), pp. 38–53.

8.4 RELIGION IN EVOLUTION

B. Kidd, 'The Function of Religious Beliefs in the Evolution of Society', in idem, *Social Evolution* (London: Macmillan and Co., 1894), pp. 98–104, 106–108, 110–16.

GENERAL INDEX

INDEX OF NAMES, LITERARY REFERENCES AND SOURCES